A HISTORY OF ITALIAN LITERATURE

A History of Italian Literature

By ERNEST HATCH WILKINS

Revised by Thomas G. Bergin

Harvard University Press
Cambridge, Massachusetts
London, England

10 9 8 7 6 5
Library of Congress Catalog Card Number 74-80444
ISBN 0-674-39701-0
Printed in the United States of America

Foreword

FOR THE last twenty years Professor Wilkins' *History* has been an indispensable aid to the study of Italian letters in English-speaking countries. The informed serenity of its assessments has made it a dependable guide for the general reader seeking to familiarize himself with the major currents and the pattern of development in what is, in many ways, the most original and influential of European literatures. The factual information, accurate and authoritative, that the work contains has made it invaluable as a reference work as well. During its two decades of circulation, time has neither invalidated the authenticity of the facts nor questioned the justice of its critical appraisals. Professor Wilkins' book has been neither outdated nor superseded.

It remains true, however, that nearly a generation has passed since the material for the first edition was compiled. And the last two decades, more fertile than many in the past, have yielded rich harvests not only in contributions of contemporary Italian writers of all categories but also in increased interest among English-speaking scholars and critics. Since the publication of the first edition the centennial celebrations for Dante, Petrarch, Michelangelo, Machiavelli, and other Italian writers have had world-wide resonance, serving both to illustrate the aforementioned growth of interest in the literature of the peninsula and to stimulate that interest. The result has been an abundant flow of translations, commentaries, and interpretations.

In view of such developments it has seemed advisable, in bringing out a new edition of the *History*, to add to the body of the work a chapter on the literature of the Italian Republic, which had barely come into being at the time of publication of the first edition, and likewise to enlarge the bibliography, by adding significant items chosen from the numerous translations and studies which have appeared in English during the interval. A map of Italy and a chronological chart have also been supplied in this edition.

In dealing with the literary activity of the years of the Republic I have endeavored to follow the criteria set by Professor Wilkins and, to the best of my ability, his approach to the subject. I should like to express my thanks to Frances Frenaye and Guido Lopez, who very kindly read my chapter in typescript and made many useful suggestions for its improvement.

Thomas G. Bergin

Madison, Connecticut
June 1974

Preface

THIS BOOK has been written in the hope that it may prove to be of interest to many readers, whether or not they have any knowledge of the Italian language or any previous interest in the literature of Italy. Most of the many illustrative quotations are given in English translation only, and passages or words quoted in Italian are accompanied by English translations, except in cases in which the meaning is so obvious that translation seems unnecessary. The amount of space allotted to the several authors and subjects is determined by what is thought to be the degree of their natural interest for American and English readers; hosts of minor authors are disregarded; special attention is given to literary relations between Italy and the English-speaking countries; and relevant background material is provided. A selective list of English books that are translations of Italian works or deal with Italian literature will be found in the Appendix.

Since literary composition in Italian became general and noteworthy only in the thirteenth century, the history of Italian literature is regarded in this book as beginning with that century. Italian authors have of course written usually in Italian, but some have written at times in languages other than Italian: often in Latin, fairly often in Italian dialects, sometimes in French, sometimes in English, and occasionally in still other languages. Any attempt to separate literature written in Italian from literature written in other languages by the same men or by their companion writers would be unjustifiably artificial. In this book, accordingly, Italian literature is regarded as comprising all literary composition by Italian writers from the thirteenth century on, whether in Italian or in other languages. On the other hand, Italian literature is not regarded as comprising the Italian writings of non-Italians — the Italian sonnets of Milton, for example — except in the cases of two or three men who, though not of Italian birth, came to Italy while they were still young, and became virtually Italians.

For reasons indicated in Chapter 1, Italian literature is regarded as comprising not only written literature in the ordinary sense but also folk literature and the literature of the minstrels and their successors.

Each writer is treated as a single entity, even if he wrote in several genres.

Readers interested in following the development of particular genres will find guiding references in the Index.

The distinction of several successive groups of writers is made not upon any extraneous basis (such as the conventional division by centuries), but solely upon the basis of the facts of literary history itself: a List of Literary Periods will be found in the Appendix.

The terms "Middle Ages" and "medieval" are used to designate a period beginning with the collapse of the Roman Empire and continuing through the fourteenth century, and the term "Renaissance" is used to designate an overlapping period beginning late in the thirteenth century and continuing into the early seventeenth century.

The translations, unless otherwise noted, are my own.

I am exceedingly grateful to Edward Williamson for abundant and invaluable help, most generously given; to L. F. Solano, H. A. Mathes, Philip Koch, and Sergio Pacifici for help at special points; to the Directors and to members of the staffs of the Harvard University Library and of the Harvard University Press; to the Cornell University Press for permission to quote from the translation of *The New Science* of Vico by T. G. Bergin and M. H. Fisch (1948); to the T. Y. Crowell Company for permission to quote from my translation of essays by Papini (1922); and to the *Encyclopaedia Britannica* for permission to quote from Croce's article on Aesthetics.

E. H. W.

Newton Centre, Massachusetts
February 26, 1954

Contents

	Introduction	1
1	Early Folk Literature and Minstrelsy	9
2	St. Francis of Assisi	13
3	Frederick the Second and his Circle	17
4	Poetry of the Latter Half of the Thirteenth Century	23
5	Prose of the Latter Half of the Thirteenth Century	36
6	Dante in Florence	41
7	Dante in Exile	50
8	The *Divine Comedy*	59
9	Contemporaries of Dante	73
10	Petrarch	80
11	Boccaccio	101
12	Contemporaries of Petrarch and Boccaccio	113
13	Writers of the Late Fourteenth Century	117
14	The Militant Humanists	123
15	Contemporaries of the Militant Humanists	131
16	Lorenzo de' Medici	136
17	Florentine Humanists	148
18	Luigi Pulci and Other Florentine Writers	158
19	Neapolitan, Ferrarese, and Other Writers	167
20	Bembo	177

21 Ariosto 185
22 Michelangelo and Other Poets 196
23 Machiavelli and Guicciardini 208
24 Castiglione and Other Prose Writers 226
25 Comedy and Tragedy 237
26 Poetry of the Mid-Sixteenth Century 244
27 Prose of the Mid-Sixteenth Century 251
28 The Pastoral Play and the *Commedia dell' Arte* 263
29 Torquato Tasso 268
30 Giordano Bruno 282
31 The Drama in the Late Sixteenth Century 289
32 Marino and Other Poets 292
33 Campanella 299
34 Galileo and Other Prose Writers 307
35 Early Opera 314
36 A Stagnant Interval 319
37 Metastasio and Other Arcadians 324
38 Vico 334
39 Goldoni and Carlo Gozzi 342
40 Parini and Other Writers 355
41 Alfieri 365
42 Foscolo and Other Writers 376
43 Manzoni 388
44 Leopardi 399
45 Contemporaries of Manzoni and Leopardi 411
46 Mazzini 420
47 Contemporaries of Mazzini 429
48 Carducci and Other Poets 436
49 De Sanctis, Verga, and Other Writers 448

50 Pascoli and Other Poets 460
51 Fogazzaro and Other Writers 470
52 Writers of the Twentieth Century 478
53 The Literature of the Republic 496
APPENDIX
A List of Additional Writers 527
A List of English Translations and Books in English Dealing with Italian Literature 529
A Chronological Chart 549
INDEX 561

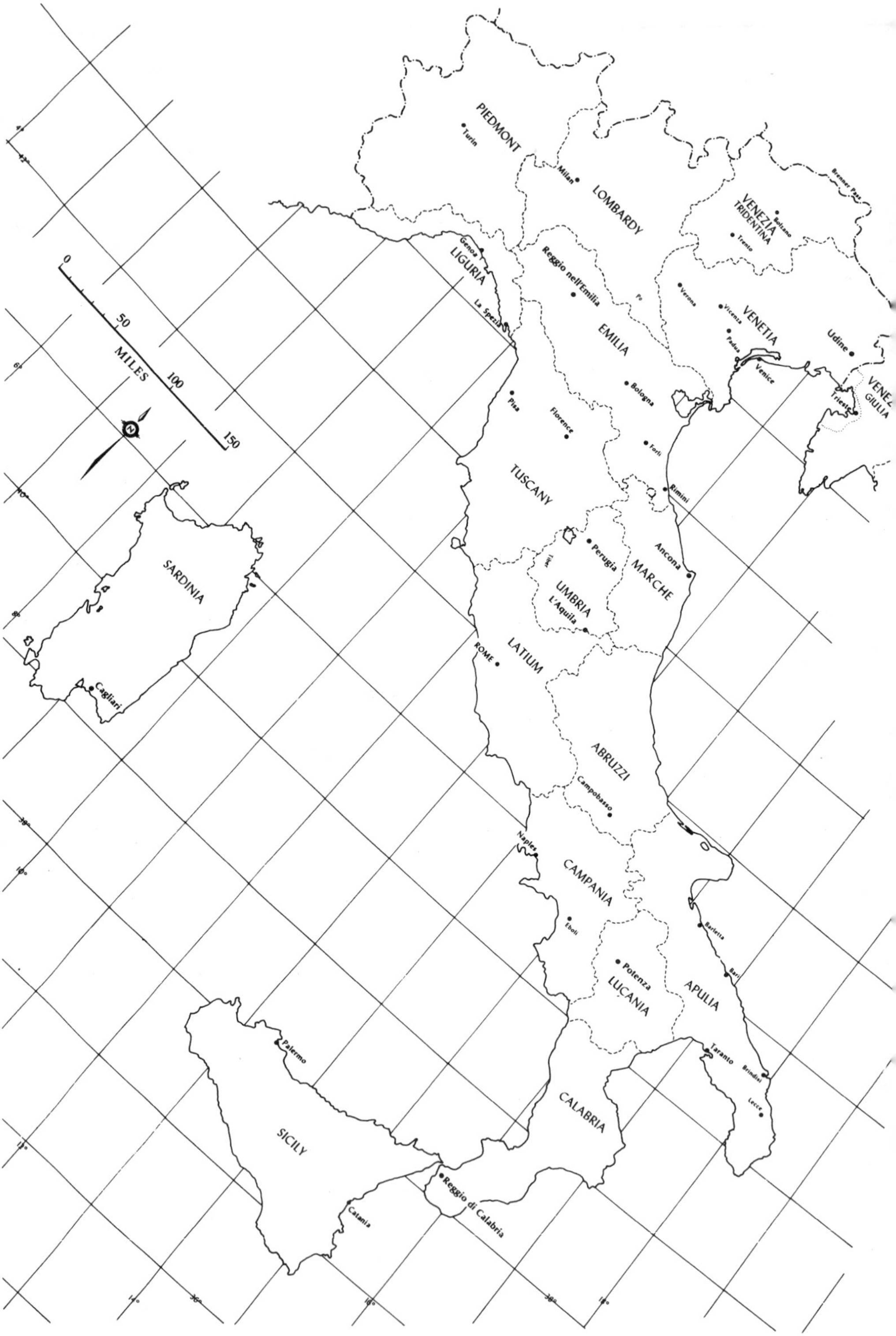

0
50
100
150
MILES
N
PIEDMONT
Turin
Milan
LOMBARDY
VENEZIA TRIDENTINA
Bolzano
Trento
Brenner Pass
Genoa
LIGURIA
La Spezia
Reggio nell'Emilia
Po
EMILIA
Verona
Vicenza
Padua
VENETIA
Venice
Udine
Trieste
VENEZIA GIULIA
Bologna
Pisa
Florence
Forlì
TUSCANY
Rimini
Perugia
Ancona
MARCHE
UMBRIA
L'Aquila
SARDINIA
Cagliari
ROME
LATIUM
ABRUZZI
Campobasso
Naples
CAMPANIA
Eboli
Barletta
Bari
Potenza
LUCANIA
APULIA
Taranto
Brindisi
Lecce
Palermo
SICILY
CALABRIA
Reggio di Calabria
Catania

INTRODUCTION

The Backgrounds of Italian Literature

THE GENERAL BACKGROUND

IN THE YEAR 1200 Italy consisted, politically, of three main divisions: Northern Italy; the States of the Church; and Southern Italy and Sicily. The Holy Roman Empire claimed sovereignty over most of Northern Italy: Venice, however, was already an independent state, and several other large cities were on the verge of independence. The Church, which claimed a universal sovereignty in spiritual matters, claimed temporal sovereignty over an irregular belt of territory, including Rome, that stretched across the middle of the peninsula. The Church claimed sovereignty over Southern Italy also; but Southern Italy was in point of fact under imperial control, as was Sicily. The great island, conquered by the Arabs in the ninth century and by Norman warriors in the eleventh, had only recently been added to the Empire, as a result of the marriage of Henry VI with the Norman heiress. Palermo was at this time the most cosmopolitan and the most brilliant city in Italy.

In the Christian-Islamic conflict, which had been continuous since the seventh century, the initiative had passed to Christendom. Jerusalem had been won in the first crusade; but the second and third crusades had been less successful, and the Holy City was again in Arab hands.

Economic life was basically agricultural; but industry, trade, and money-lending were developing in the cities. Inter-city trade was increasing; and the great coastal cities were trading vigorously with the East, fighting each other, meanwhile, on the sea.

Religion played a very large part in life. God and Satan were very personal; angels hovered; devils lurked; saints mediated; miracles were expected; Hell, Purgatory, and Heaven were near at hand — and the Church held the keys. The immense organization of the Church overspread all Italy. Faithful ministry and high-minded administration were by no means wanting; but corruption and superstition were rife. The leading monastic order was that of the Benedictines, whose first and chief monastery was at Monte Cassino. The Carthusian and Cistercian orders also had monasteries in Italy. Great and long enduring religious excitement had been aroused late in the twelfth century by the Calabrian Abbot Joachim, a Cistercian monk, who prophesied that as the Age of the Father, reflected in the Old Testament, had been followed by the Age of the Son, reflected in the New Testament, so that Age would shortly be followed by the Age of the Holy Ghost — an Age in which the reign of violence, injustice, and all manner of evil would be replaced by a reign of peace and love and holiness. This Age, Joachim prophesied, would begin in the year 1260.

Schools served a very small proportion of the people. The Church maintained schools for the training of the clergy, and schools for laymen as well. Private teachers, sometimes under Church or city license, maintained small schools of their own. In Bologna, a school of law which had been thriving since the late eleventh century had in 1158 received its charter as a university: it was destined to serve not only as a very great educational institution, but, for Italy, as a focal point where educated youths from all parts of the country met and shared each other's literary interests.

Italian and other translators, using either Greek texts or Arabic versions, had begun the renewal of knowledge of the Greek philosophers. In the Middle Ages, the only generally known writings of those philosophers were the *Timaeus* of Plato and two of the logical treatises of Aristotle; but Plato's *Meno* and *Phaedo* and the rest of the logical treatises had been translated in the course of the twelfth century, and the *Metaphysics* and some of the scientific treatises of Aristotle were translated about 1200.

Thanks to twelfth-century translations of Ptolemy, the Universe, in educated thought at least, had become Ptolemaic: the round earth stood at the center, and all other heavenly bodies revolved around it. Much geographical information had been gathered at the Sicilian court. Nature lore was in the main a tissue of fables. A far-famed school of medicine at Salerno profited by the use of Arabic medical knowledge and of recent translations of Galen and Hippocrates; but medicine in general was an ineffective compound of tradition, superstition, and guesswork.

The only significant architectural activity was in the construction of religious buildings — churches, *campanili*, baptisteries, cloisters. Five architectural styles were in use: the Tuscan Romanesque, the Lombard Romanesque, the Gothic, the Byzantine, and the Sicilian. The Gothic, a logical French derivative from the Lombard Romanesque, was making its first appearances in Italy. The single great current Italian example of the Byzantine style, St. Mark's in Venice, was in process of reconstruction. The Sicilian style was eclectic, borrowing elements from Islamic architecture as well as from various European styles.

Sculpture was mainly a matter of church decoration — bas-reliefs on the façade and elaborately carved capitals within. Southern Italy had developed a special liking for bronze cathedral doors. The first sets had been brought from Constantinople in the eleventh century; but Southern Italian sculptors, soon afterward, had begun the making of their own bronze doors, in which the panels bore figures or scenes in bas-relief. Rome and Pisa were the centers of a rather slight pictorial activity. Painting was exclusively religious, and consisted chiefly in the fresco decoration of interior church walls and in the production of large crucifixes. Mosaic was still in use, to some extent, for the interior decoration of churches and baptisteries.

Church music had progressed slowly from the austere unisonal Gregorian chants to a somewhat greater melodic freedom, the development of rhythmic measure, and the acceptance of a second voice part. Secular music, always rhythmic, flourished as folk song and in the voices and the hands of minstrels.

Minstrels were the chief providers of entertainment. In the halls of well-to-do patrons or before eager gatherings of humble folk in villages or in little city squares, they plied their varied trade — juggling, tumbling, clowning, dancing and leading dances, playing their harps or viols, jesting, pantomiming, monologuing, singing and reciting, and taking whatever compensation they could get, in cash or in kind.

THE LINGUISTIC BACKGROUND

Every spoken language changes, constantly but very slowly, in many ways, chiefly in pronunciation, inflection, syntax, and vocabulary. Its rate of change is somewhat accelerated when education is relatively slight and rare, and is somewhat retarded when education is substantial and widespread. If two adjacent regions have at a given moment the same spoken language, the changes that take place in that language will be the same in both regions as long, but only as long, as their interrelations remain manifold and constant. If their interrelations slacken, the spoken language of one region will come to differ more and more from that of the other region.

In ancient times, after the establishment of Roman power throughout Italy, Latin, the spoken language of Rome, gradually displaced the languages that had previously been spoken by the various Italic peoples, though the persistence of some pre-Roman linguistic habits caused certain minor regional variations in speech. For several centuries the spoken Latin of Italy, while itself constantly but slowly changing, remained fairly uniform, except for the minor regional variations just mentioned. But after the disintegration of the Roman Empire the several regions lapsed into a relative (though by no means an absolute) separateness — favored by the divisive features of the peninsula — in which the people of any one region had relatively little concern with the peoples of other regions. Under these conditions the spoken languages of the several regions became more and more different from each other; and that differentiation has continued even to the present day. The several differentiated regional languages, each a continuant of the original spoken Latin, are called dialects.

The form of spoken Latin that we call Italian developed in the thirteenth and fourteenth centuries, when a marked increase in the interrelations of different regions led naturally to the development of a kind of common speech for the use of those who were involved in such interrelations. The Italian language is not identical with any single dialect; but it was based on the Tuscan dialect, and resembles it closely. The reasons why this dialect rather than any other became the basis for a common Italian speech were partly geographic, partly commercial, and partly literary: the literary reasons will appear in Chapter 4. Since the days of its first development the Italian language has itself undergone some change; but the rate of that change has been very slow.

When a people achieves a written language, that language at first corresponds rather closely to the language then spoken; but from that time on, while the spoken language proceeds inevitably to change, the written language, fortified by the conventions of education, resists change, and may indeed remain essentially unchanged for a very long time.

Thus the written Latin of ancient Rome, which reflected rather closely the spoken Latin of a very early period, has remained essentially unchanged even to the present day. For many centuries those Italians who had occasion to write used, or tried to use, the traditional written Latin. Their conservatism in this respect, as the centuries passed, was reënforced by their pride in a language that recalled to them the days when Rome was empress of the world. During the Middle Ages their frequent lack of adequate education resulted in many imperfections in the Latin they wrote.

Inadvertent use, within Latin documents, of words and forms influenced by or taken from the spoken language begins as early as the sixth century of our era. The first prose sentences deliberately written in the spoken language are records of oral evidence embodied in legal documents of the late tenth century.

By the twelfth century the difference between the current spoken language and the traditional written Latin had become painfully great; and by this time, also, writers in Northern and Southern France had begun to make literary use of their current spoken languages. In the course of the twelfth century a very few Italians made some use of their own dialects for literary purposes. Such use became more abundant in the early years of the thirteenth century; and use of the newly developing common Italian speech for literary purposes began before the middle of that century. Use of the dialects for literary purposes continued sporadically through the thirteenth century; diminished greatly in the fourteenth and fifteenth centuries; and has increased somewhat in more recent centuries, though it remains a minor phase of literary activity. Throughout the thirteenth century and the two following centuries the traditional written Latin continued to be, in the thought of most Italian writers, the primary written language of Italy: but in those same centuries literature in Italian, produced side by side with literature in Latin, was proving superbly its own vital powers. By the middle of the sixteenth century Italian had won its place as the primary written language of Italy; and since that time the use of Latin has been secondary and more and more exceptional.

THE LITERARY BACKGROUND

When the writing of Italian literature began there were four literatures of which Italian writers had, or might have had, some knowledge: the Classic Latin, the Early Christian and Medieval Latin, the Provençal, and the French.

While the Latin classics had been held in general esteem in Italy during the early Christian centuries, they fell into relative disesteem thereafter, though Italian familiarity with them never died out entirely. Virgil, Ovid, Statius, and Lucan were, in the Middle Ages, the best known of the poets, and Cicero and Seneca the best known of the prose writers. Passages from many poets were preserved in medieval anthologies, and much material from the Latin historians was preserved in medieval epitomes. Allegorical interpretation of Virgil and of other classic poets was in vogue.

Medieval Latin literature, with its prefatory Early Christian Latin literature, is vast in extent and European in the range of its authorship. It includes hymns, dramatic sequences and tropes, didactic poems (often satiric or allegorical), narrative poems, imaginary debates in verse (as between the rose and the violet), secular lyrics (amatory or jocose), religious and philosophical and other treatises, sermons, letters, histories, lives of saints, fables, fictional narratives (especially collections of short stories), and compendia of different kinds.

Its two greatest writers, St. Augustine and Boethius, are among the earliest. St. Augustine dominates the philosophical and theological thinking of the Middle Ages as a whole. Building upon the Christian scriptures, the Christian tradition, and the authority of the Christian Church, he enriches his philosophy in particular by drawing extensively on Platonism and Neoplatonism, which he accepts gladly insofar as they are not in conflict with essential Christian doctrines. His work is indeed the main medium in which the

Platonic spirit lives on through the Middle Ages. In the *City of God* he surveys with an unprecedented and a magnificent sweep of vision the origins, the development, and the destiny of mankind. His *Confessions*, the first such intimate record of inner experience, have always been widely read. The *Consolation of Philosophy* of Boethius, a noble work written during an unjust imprisonment, rests upon the imagination that Philosophy, in the guise of a beneficent lady, appears to the prisoner, converses with him at length, and does in truth console him. The prose of the *Consolation* is interspersed with several poems.

Among the finest hymns of the Middle Ages are those of St. Ambrose, St. Gregory the Great, and St. Bernard. The *Dies irae*, of uncertain authorship, dates probably from the twelfth century. The liturgical drama was flourishing, in that century, in Italian as well as in Transalpine churches. In the less learned and more popular types of verse, notably in many hymns and in the jolly twelfth-century songs of the Goliards, the Classic Latin quantitative forms gradually gave place to rhythms based on natural verbal stress, and rhyme came into common use.

Letter writing became, especially in Italy, a highly specialized activity. A proper letter had five divisions: *salutatio*, *captatio benivolentiae*, *narratio*, *petitio*, and *conclusio*; and its phrasing followed certain quasi-rhythmic patterns known collectively as the *cursus*.

Among the most influential of the fictional narratives were versions of the Oriental *History of the Seven Sages*, and the *Historia regum Britanniae* of Geoffrey of Monmouth, the main source of the vernacular Arthurian cycle.

* * *

In France, as in Italy, the spoken language, in the early Christian centuries, was spoken Latin, which through the Middle Ages progressed on its normal path of gradual change. There was a general political and social division between the north and the south of France, and there was a marked differentiation in the spoken languages of the two regions. Both these languages — French and Provençal — were used for literary purposes long before the spoken language of Italy was so used.

In Provence the troubadour lyric must have come into being before 1100. The first preserved poems are of the early twelfth century, and the fullest flowering came in the second half of that century. Though of secondary beauty and interest in itself, the troubadour lyric is the fountainhead from which the main streams of the later European lyric are derived, for it set the fashion for the courtly lyric of northern France, for that of Spain, for the German Minnesong, and, both directly and indirectly, for the courtly lyric of Italy. It calls, therefore, for some particular attention.

The troubadour lyric was produced for the feudal courts of Southern France. It was intended to be sung; and the troubadours themselves composed both words and music. The troubadours were minstrels of a high order, honored and well rewarded in the courts they frequented. Some of their poems dealt with love, and some with current political circumstances. The love of which, typically, the troubadours sang — they and their heirs in poetry, even their distant heirs for many generations — was what they called *fin' amors*, "fine love," by which they meant, essentially, love of the heart and the mind. Usually, though not necessarily, their poetry was addressed to married women. Such love, so addressed, was within the conventions: its development was not unnatural in view of the fact that marriage, on the courtly level, was a matter not of personal choice but of parental command, and it was particularly natural in the Provençal setting, in which the lady was in most cases socially superior to the poet. The typical political poem, called a *sirventés*, was an actual political weapon, composed as a matter of feudal service, and often very spirited.

The poetic form mainly used for both types was the *canso*, a poem of several stanzas, usually five or six or seven. Each succeeding stanza follows the metrical pattern of the first in respect to the length of the corresponding lines and the rhyme scheme. In many cases the series of regular stanzas is followed by a shorter stanza, called a *tornada*, in which the poet may speed the poem on its way, or add a final sentiment or a final thrust. In a variety of the *canso* known as the *tenso* alternate stanzas are composed by different poets, who propose and defend opposing points of view; and in some other poems a single author maintains an imaginary debate, alternate stanzas being assigned to himself and to some other person.

Among the most famous troubadours of the twelfth century were Arnaut Daniel, Bernart de Ventadorn, Bertran de Born, and Jaufre Rudel. Arnaut Daniel devised a special type of the *canso* known as the *sestina*, which consists of six stanzas and a *tornada*, each stanza consisting of six lines whose terminal words do not rhyme, but are repeated, in changing terminal positions, from stanza to stanza. A less famous man, the Monk of Montaudon, developed a minor genre which was destined to prove fortunate, a genre comprising the *enueg* and the *plazer* (these words mean "annoyance" and "pleasure"). The *enueg*, in which the stanzas begin typically with some variant of the verbal phrase *m'enueja*, is an amusing listing of things and experiences that annoy the poet; and the *plazer*, with the recurring phrase *mi platz*, is its happy counterpart.

In the latter part of the century several troubadours came into Northern Italy, where they frequented the feudal courts. One of these visiting troubadours, Raimbaut de Vaqueiras, wrote two poems that are partly in the dialect of Genoa. There exist also two *tensos* of this period, wholly in Provençal, in each of which one of the speakers is a troubadour and the other an Italian feudal lord. It may be that the stanzas ascribed to these Italian noblemen were actually composed by them; but it is more probable that each of the *tensos* was written in its entirety by the troubadour concerned.

* * *

In Northern France the spoken language was used for literary purposes as early as the end of the ninth century; but the first significant literary manifestation of the French spirit is in the epic *chansons de geste*. These were written in verse of a simple type, and were intended to be sung by minstrels. The finest of them all, the *Chanson de Roland*, dates, in its extant form, from the late eleventh century or the early twelfth. The *Roland* and many other *chansons de geste* deal with the crucial Christian-Saracen conflict. Somewhat similar in character, but more romantic, were verse narratives dealing with heroes and heroines of the ancient world. The most influential of the romances of this type was the *Roman de Troie* of Benoît de Sainte-More. The Arthurian stories — stories of the Arthurian court, of Tristan and Isolde, and of the Quest of the Grail — were told and retold in verse. Shorter verse narratives, called *lais*, were also popular.

* * *

Late in the twelfth century the activity of the Minnesingers began in Germany. They were the German equivalents of the Provençal troubadours, from whom they derived, to a considerable extent, both the form and the content of their poems — though they made innovations in form and were often independent and personal in thought and phrase. At least four minnesingers were at various times with Henry VI while he was in Italy. Arabic poetry, brilliant during the centuries of the Arab dominion in Sicily, enjoyed court favor there even after the Norman conquest. The musical and formal character of the Minnesong and of the Arabic lyric must have been known to many who did not understand the words.

* * *

From the eleventh and twelfth centuries there have survived, in various Italian dialects, half a dozen tiny bits of verse, one short poem, and a collection of brief sermons; and there are two or three longer poems that may have been written just before 1200. These primitive compositions, interesting though they are for their firstness, belong rather to the pre-history than to the history of Italian literature. Not until the thirteenth century did the use of the spoken language for literary purposes become at all general, or yield results of any really literary value: the thirteenth century, therefore, may fairly be regarded as the first century of Italian literature.

CHAPTER 1

Early Folk Literature and Minstrelsy

ITALIAN LITERATURE exists on three cultural levels: it includes folk literature, the literature of the popular entertainers, and literature in the ordinary sense. Folk literature consists mainly of folk songs and folk tales; the literature of the popular entertainers — the minstrels and their successors — comprises songs and narratives in verse or prose designed to attract either sophisticated or unsophisticated audiences; and literature "in the ordinary sense" comprises compositions of many types written by men or women of some education with a view to the interest and the pleasure of other men or women of some education. These three levels are by no means sharply set off from each other: there is indeed much interplay between them, an interplay in which the popular entertainers have been the most active agents.

* * *

The "folk" consists of the peasantry and the humbler city dwellers. Their own literature, stored in their memories and brought forth freely for their own enjoyment, is always in the dialect of the region concerned. It includes both verse and prose, or rather both *song* and prose: for nearly all of the verse exists only as song, the words and the music being inseparable in folk consciousness. The song itself is of two types, lyric and narrative.

The most frequent and most distinctive type of the folk lyric is a single-stanza octave, with eleven-syllable lines, which is commonly called the *strambotto*, or, in its Tuscan varieties, the *rispetto*.* Of the early history of the *strambotto* we have no certain knowledge; but there is some basis for the

* The word *strambotto* and the word *rispetto* as a poetic term have no English equivalents.

opinion that it existed in Sicily early in the thirteenth century, and in Tuscany before the end of the century.* In its Sicilian form the stanza consists of eight lines, rhyming alternately, as in this example:

> Darrieri a ssa finescia ogni matina
> La rínnina vi veni a rrisbiggiari;
> Aspetta a bbui la rrosa damaschina,
> Aspetta a bbui lu giggiu ppi sparari.
> Nun còddanu li stiddi a la matina,
> Si 'un vi vièninu prima a salutari:
> Cu' è ca viri a bbui, rrusedda fina,
> L' armuzza si la senti spiccicari.†

In the earliest Tuscan variety of the *strambotto* the seventh line introduces a new rhyme, which is repeated in the eighth, the last two lines thus constituting a rhymed couplet.

Most *strambotti* are love songs; but some are songs of grief or of wrath, some are satirical or lightly humorous, some are occupational, and some are religious. The singing of *strambotti* is done by men and women alike in many of the scenes and phases of peasant life: in the fields, in mountain pastures, at the threshing floor, in vineyards, in groves where olives or nuts are being gathered. Women sing as they sit spinning by the door or do their washing at the brook; smiths and cobblers sing at their tasks.

Besides the *strambotti* the folk stock includes lyric songs of many other kinds: *ballate* (dance songs), serenades, Epiphany songs, May songs, dirges, religious songs, lullabies, children's songs, and ephemeral songs of various sorts. The typical *ballata* consists of a two-line refrain and several stanzas. The leader of the dance first sings the refrain, which is then sung by the dancers in chorus; the leader then sings a stanza; the dancers then sing the refrain; the leader then sings a second stanza; the dancers repeat the refrain — and so on.

The narrative songs vary in form and in length. They are often dramatic in structure, the persons of the story speaking for themselves. Some are religious and some secular. The religious narratives, which tell the Gospel stories and the legends of many saints, are more numerous, longer, and more specifically Italian: such songs are often sung on pilgrimages or at religious festivals. The secular narratives are in the main romantic, and most of them are tragic: their themes appear, in some cases, in the ballads of other European countries.

* This is a minority opinion. The currently prevailing opinion is that the *strambotto* originated in Tuscany in the fourteenth century.

† "Outside that window every morning the swallow comes to waken you; the damask rose waits for you, the lily waits for you before it opens. The stars do not set in the morning till first they have come to greet you: whoever beholds you, little rose so fine, feels his heart riven."

The songs, whether lyric or narrative, are usually sung by a single voice. At times, when the melody is such as to make it possible, a second voice may join in, paralleling the first; and in certain types of song, as in the *ballate*, there is singing by several voices. When the singers are at work they sing without instrumental accompaniment; when they are at leisure there may be an accompaniment by guitar or accordion or other instrument. The melodies are often of great beauty.

Folk song is to a considerable extent the creation of the folk itself. Many *strambotti* have come into being through peasant improvisation, especially in Sicily and Tuscany. The minstrels and their successors as popular entertainers have constituted a second source for folk song, notably in the case of the romantic narrative songs. Some of the songs they have brought to the folk have been compositions of their own, and some have been the work of more literate writers.

Both lyric and narrative songs may spread from place to place, with such alterations as differences in dialect or in memory or in local fancy may require or suggest. Many songs thus appear, with little change in substance, in different parts of Italy. The passage of a song from one community to another may occur whenever persons of the two communities are brought together, as for instance on pilgrimages, at festivals, in migrations of workers, by intermarriage, or even in military service. The minstrels and their successors have played their part also in the diffusion of songs from one Italian region to another.

As the Italian folk has its own songs, so also it has its own stories. Handed down in oral tradition from generation to generation, they are told over and over again with verbal fidelity, in the long evenings, by the open door or by the hearth. These stories are of many kinds. The majority are those in which the main persons are benevolent or malevolent supernatural creatures possessing magic power. Other stories are essentially tales of romantic human adventure; in others the leading figures of Gospel and legend are made, without irreverence, the protagonists in amusing experiences; many are tales of peasant cleverness or of peasant stupidity; some are ghost stories, some nursery stories, and some hardly more than anecdotes. Whatever their content, they are rich in their revelation of folk hopes and fears, joys and sorrows, and ways of life.

Some stories, especially those in which Christ and St. Peter and their companions walk familiarly the peasant earth, appear to be peculiar to Italy; but the stories of other types are common, in the main, to the European folk in general. Thus the Italian peasants have their versions of Beauty and the Beast, of Bluebeard, of Cinderella, and of Puss in Boots; and many of their stories, also widely spread in Europe, come ultimately from the great Oriental collections. Most of the stories that are not peculiarly Italian were presumably brought to Italy, largely from France, by the same minstrels to whom some of the material and some of the diffusion of folk song has been due.

The Italian folk has also its didactic literature, in the form of proverbs, often pointed by rhyme and rhythm and touched with humor and with realism. Most proverbs are common, in substance, to many lands. Even without a previous knowledge of Italian one might readily guess the English equivalent of such as these:

> Chi tace consente.
> Non è tutto oro quel che riluce.
> Non v' è rosa senza spine.
> Roma non fu fatta in un giorno.

There is also a minor folk literature of amusement which includes, in particular, a stock of riddles — some in verse — and a stock of witty sayings.

* * *

The varied activities of the minstrels and their successors have always included singing and recitation. In the earliest times their singing was presumably limited to simple lyrics and brief narrative songs: later on they sang also longer narrative poems. Similarly, the scope of their recitation, beginning presumably with brief jests and anecdotes, came to include stories of some length. Monologues involving the impersonation of one or more characters were certainly in vogue at an early date; and at times two minstrels working together put on amusing dialogues.

The service of the minstrels and their successors has been primarily to the folk, to whom, in addition to immediate entertainment, they have given songs and stories as cherished and enduring gifts. Often, however, they have attracted educated interest as well; and they have participated to some extent in the making of literature "in the ordinary sense."

CHAPTER 2

St. Francis of Assisi

DURING THE PAPACY of Innocent III (1198 – 1216) the Church attained its highest pinnacle of temporal power. Innocent extinguished the Albigensian heresy in Provence by means of a crusade to which, as to the crusades against the Eastern infidels, he had summoned the princes of Europe; and he sealed his work with the holding of the great Lateran Council of 1215, attended by prelates and ambassadors from all over Christendom.

Two new monastic orders developed at this time: the Franciscan, of which some account will be given presently, and the Dominican. These orders differed from the older ones in that Franciscans and Dominicans were not held aloof from the world, but mingled in it, preaching, and begging their bread.

The Fourth Crusade, in 1204, was diverted, by Venetian influence, to Constantinople, and resulted in the capture of that city and the substitution of westerners for Greeks as rulers of the Eastern Empire. The first phase of the Fifth Crusade, an attack on Egypt in 1218 – 1221, was unsuccessful. The University of Padua, destined to be a worthy companion of the University of Bologna, was founded in 1222. The beautiful cloister of St. Paul's Outside the Walls at Rome was begun at this time.

In Provence the activity of the troubadours continued, but their great days were past: the destruction wrought by the Albigensian crusade put an end to the society in which their art had flourished. Many of them crossed the Alps, finding hospitality in Northern Italy, especially at the young and brilliant court of the Este family, whose castle rose on a height between Padua and Ferrara. The work of the troubadours was well known, also, at the University of Bologna. The troubadours themselves did not frequent the city — *studentes mali pagatores*, it was said.

* * *

Francesco Bernardone, born in 1182, lived in his early youth the carefree life of a prosperous merchant's son; but after the turn of the century experiences of warfare, captivity, and serious illness led him into a state of distressed perplexity. In 1207, in the presence of the Bishop of Assisi, he renounced all that he had received from his father and all ties with his father — an event referred to later as the wedding of Francis with the Lady Poverty. For the next two years he lived in deliberate destitution, toiling with his own hands to restore a little crumbling church and two crumbling chapels. One day, at Mass, he heard a priest read these words from the Gospel of Matthew:

> And going, preach, saying: The kingdom of heaven is at hand. Heal the sick, raise the dead, cleanse the lepers, cast out devils. Freely have you received: freely give. Do not possess gold, nor silver, nor money in your purses, Nor scrip for your journey, nor two coats, nor shoes, nor a staff. For the workman is worthy of his meat.

These words became forthwith the program of his life, and his enthusiasm soon brought him his first companions. With them he went to Rome; had audience with the great pope; sought approval for his plan of promoting a fraternal life of religious devotion, of freedom from possessions, and of service to the infinitely needy; and received a somewhat hesitant encouragement. The Order was formally recognized by the Lateran Council, and thereafter grew swiftly. In a world of violence, Francis and his companions preached peacefulness; in a world of arrogance they preached humility; in a world of greed they preached the unimportance of all possessions; in a world of selfishness and hatred they preached selflessness and an invincible love. Francis did his best to keep his growing Order imbued with its original ideals. In 1219, undertaking the first modern missionary journey, he preached in Egypt before the Sultan al-Malik al-Kamil — without results, save in personal good will. He died in 1226, and was canonized in 1228. Lives and legends, some of them of much beauty, multiplied for a century; and a great church, destined to become a shrine of art as well as of piety, rose soon in Assisi above his rude stone tomb.

He was a simple, pure, and radiant spirit, delighting in every element of the life of nature, and in every element of the life of man insofar as he deemed it to be not evil. His love for his fellow men was eager and inexhaustible, and his disregard of self was absolute. His love of God was of mystic intensity. His intelligence and his knowledge — which included some acquaintance with the French language and with the Arthurian stories — were wholly at the service of his ministry. He was gifted with imagination, with the poetic instinct, and with a quiet humor. He called himself and his companions *giullari di Dio*, "minstrels of God."

In the history of Italian literature St. Francis has significance not only because of his great general influence on Italian life and because of his special influence on later Italian writers, but because he is himself the author of the first noble composition in an Italian dialect: a psalm, not formally titled, which is called sometimes *Laudes creaturarum* — "The Praises of God's Creatures" — and sometimes the Canticle of the Sun. It is written in free verse, the lines being linked by assonance. It begins:

Altissimo, onnipotente, bon Signore,
tue so le laude, la gloria e l'onore et onne benedizione.

Its first nine stanzas and its concluding stanza may be rendered thus:

Most high, omnipotent, good Lord,
Thine are the praises, the glory, and the honor and all blessing.
To Thee alone, Most High, are they due,
And no man is worthy to name Thy name.
Praised be Thou, my Lord, with all Thy creatures,
Especially our Sir Brother Sun,
Who maketh day, and Thou givest light through him.
And he is beautiful and radiant with great splendor:
Of Thee, Most High, he beareth significance.
Praised be Thou, my Lord, for Sister Moon and the stars:
In heaven Thou hast formed them, bright and precious and beautiful.
Praised be Thou, my Lord, for Brother Wind
And for air and cloud and clear sky and all weather
Whereby Thou givest Thy creatures sustenance.
Praised be Thou, my Lord, for Sister Water,
Who is very useful and humble and precious and chaste.
Praised be Thou, my Lord, for Brother Fire,
Through whom Thou givest light at night:
And he is beautiful and joyous and robust and strong.
Praised be Thou, my Lord, for Sister our Mother Earth,
Who doth sustain and govern us
And bringeth forth divers fruits with colored flowers and herbage. . .
Praise and bless my Lord
And give thanks and serve Him with great humility.

Between the ninth stanza and the concluding stanza there intervene two stanzas in praise of those who pardon for love of God, and two stanzas in praise of Sister Death. These four stanzas may have been in the poem as it was first composed; but according to a very early tradition they were written by St. Francis on two later occasions.

The other writings of St. Francis are in Latin. Among those of greatest interest are the psalmodic Praises of God, the Salutation of the Virtues, the mystic Prayer to Obtain Divine Love, and the Letter to Brother Leo.

* * *

During these same early years a few North Italians were writing in their own dialects, or in Provençal, or (in one instance) in German. Of those who wrote in their own dialects the most noteworthy are two Lombards — Uguccione da Lodi, whose didactic verse, lightened by an occasional gleam of realism, was apparently intended to be a vehicle for Waldensian doctrine, and Gerardo Patecchio, who wrote, among other things, an entertaining poem known as *Le noie*, "Annoyances," which continues in Italy the genre devised by the Monk of Montaudon. Tommasino di Cerclaria, a cleric serving in far Northeastern Italy, wrote for his German neighbors an immense poem on conduct, called *Der Wälsche Gast*, "The Italian Guest." Its fifteen thousand lines treat topics of many sorts, from table manners to the virtues of steadfastness and moderation.

CHAPTER 3

Frederick the Second and His Circle

THE CENTRAL FIGURE of the second quarter of the century is the Emperor Frederick II, who was also, in all probability, among the poets. He was certainly a patron of poets: it was at his court that the composition of Italian poetry first became a conscious literary enterprise shared by members of a considerable group of writers.

Frederick, born in 1194, grew up in Palermo, where he was well educated, some of his teachers being Arabs. Before he came of age, he plunged into the political struggle, going first to Germany, where in six strenuous years he succeeded in establishing his authority. Thereafter he spent most of his restless life in Italy. Palermo was his capital, but he was seldom there; his favorite region was the Southern Italian mainland. In 1228 he undertook a crusade (counted as the second phase of the Fifth Crusade); but instead of fighting he scandalized the papal world by making a treaty with Sultan al-Malik al-Kamil (before whom St. Francis had preached), by the terms of which Jerusalem was surrendered to him. Throughout his years of empire Frederick was in constant conflict with the cities of Northern Italy: it was in the course of this conflict that the terms "Ghibelline" and "Guelf" came into common use in Italy, the term "Ghibelline" being applied to those who supported the emperor, "Guelf" to those who opposed him. He was in frequent conflict, also, with successive popes: repeated excommunications were followed by repeated apparent reconciliations. In 1245 the Pope declared him deposed, and from that time his power waned rapidly. He died in 1250.

He was a man of keen and active intelligence, with a limitless curiosity as to all sorts of matters, from birds and beasts and the physical life of man to mathematical theory and the eternal questions of philosophy and theology. He knew Italian, Latin, German, French, Greek, and Arabic. He was of extraordinary versatility: an organizer of government, a legislator, a commander, interested in agriculture, an expert and enthusiastic hunter, the designer of part of one of his castles, a writer, and a generous patron of scholars, poets, and men versed in various arts and sciences. He founded and fostered the University of Naples. A contemporary chronicler called him *Stupor mundi* — "the wonder of the world." The one written work that is surely his is an elaborate Latin treatise on falconry, notable for its minute and accurate observation, and for the several hundred extraordinarily careful illustrations contained in a manuscript prepared presumably under his direction.

The first group of Italian poets consisted of some thirty men, nearly all of whom were associated directly or indirectly with the court of Frederick II. They may well be called "the Frederician poets." * About a third of the group were Sicilians; half a dozen were from Southern Italy; and half a dozen were Tuscans. Several of them had had legal training, presumably at the University of Bologna. They were acquainted with the Provençal lyric and the North French lyric, and with the form, at least, of the German Minnesong.† Two Frederician poems, both by Sicilian poets, are in the Sicilian dialect: no others are preserved in their original form. Probably all the poets who were actually Sicilians wrote in the Sicilian dialect, modifying it more or less for literary use. Just how the non-Sicilian members of the group wrote, we do not know.

There are extant about 125 Frederician poems: about 85 are *canzoni*, and most of the rest are sonnets. The Fredericians' chief title to fame is metrical: their *canzone* set the pattern for the main Italian lyric form; and some one of them invented the sonnet.

The *canzone* is an adaptation of the Provençal *canso*: for certain variations from the Provençal practice it seems probable that the Fredericians found models in the Minnesong. The Frederician stanza is on the average a little longer than the Transalpine stanzas; and the Frederician *canzoni* show a marked effort, on the part of their authors, to attain metrical originality.

The Frederician sonnet consists of fourteen eleven-syllable lines. Its rhyme-structure divides it into two parts, an octave and a sestet. The rhyme-scheme for the octave is always ABABABAB; the sestet rhymes CDECDE in about twenty cases and CDCDCD in about ten cases.‡ Most of the Frederician

* They are traditionally called "the Sicilian poets," but the adjective "Sicilian" lacks adequate justification, especially since the court was seldom in Sicily.

† Frederick II was well acquainted with Walther von der Vogelweide; other Minnesingers were associated with the court of Frederick in Germany and in Italy; three poets, at least, of the Italian group visited Germany; and it is probable that a considerable number of German minstrels frequented the court of Frederick.

‡ There is no agreement as to the source — if any — of the sonnet. The identity of the octave with the Sicilian form of the *strambotto* is too striking to be overlooked — but there is no documentary evidence of the existence of the *strambotto* in the Fred-

sonnets are by Giacomo da Lentino, and some of the others are by younger men: there is then some inherent probability that the invention of the sonnet is due to Giacomo. There is of course no certainty as to which of the Frederician sonnets is the earliest; but such slight evidence as there is points to one of Giacomo's beginning

Molti amadori la lor malatia
portano in core che 'm vista nom pare —

Many lovers bear their distress in their hearts, so that it does not visibly appear.

In content the Frederician poems are largely derived from Provençal models, and most of them are conventional and rather dull: the love they voice is, naturally, *fino amore*. A few of the sonnets were written in correspondence. In one case a writer propounds a problem for two others to answer; in another case a debate by two men runs through a series of five sonnets. Such prolonged debate constitutes a *tenzone* — the equivalent of the Provençal *tenso*.

Three or four poems are attributed to the Emperor, but only one of them — an elaborate and dignified, but uninspired, *canzone* beginning *De la mia disianza*, "Of my desire," — is probably by him. Two of Frederick's sons, Frederick of Antioch and Enzo, were certainly among the poets.

The most interesting member of the group aside from the Emperor was the imperial chancellor, Pier della Vigna, for many years the intimate and very influential counsellor of the Emperor, whose final and apparently unjustified loss of confidence in him led to Piero's imprisonment and suicide. There are extant three *canzoni* of his, and one sonnet. He wrote much more extensively in Latin. His official letters, couched in a style of some grandiosity and considerable obscurity, were very famous in their day. Among his unofficial letters are a love letter consisting of a long series of prose sentences each of which is followed by a quoted line of Latin verse, and a letter, addressed to the Empress, on the relative merits of the rose and the violet.*

The two best poets among the Fredericians were Giacomino Pugliese and Rinaldo d'Aquino. Giacomino wrote a deeply felt *canzone* on the death of his lady, beginning

Morte, perché m' hai fatto sí gran guerra —

Death, why hast thou made such war upon me —

---

erician period. The sestet rhyme-scheme CDECDE may possibly reflect an Arabic model. It is often asserted that the sonnet is a detached *canzone* stanza: but there does not exist among the Frederician *canzoni* any stanza that is at all similar to the sonnet.

* There is extant an anonymous prose letter addressed to Piero on the true nature of nobility — the first of several thirteenth-century treatments of this theme. The conclusion reached is that uprightness is to be preferred to nobility of birth.

a poem echoed even in Dante. Rinaldo, in the name of a woman whose lover was just starting for the Holy Land, wrote a poem which, in its simplicity, expresses perhaps more poignantly than anything else then written the distress that must have been wrought by the separations caused by the crusades:

> Never can I find comfort or joy: the ships are in the harbor, and are setting sail. He who is best of all is going beyond the seas; and I, alas, what shall I do in my grief? . . .
>
> When he took the cross, certainly I did not think of this — he who loved me so, I who loved him so! . . .
>
> The ships are setting sail: may they go in a good hour, and my love with them, and all those that go upon them. Father, Creator, guide them to a safe harbor, for they go in service of Thy Holy Cross.

The liveliest Italian poem of this period was not written by any one of Frederick's poets, and deals not with courtiers but with folk of a lowly social level. Presumably the work of a Sicilian minstrel called Cielo d'Alcamo, it is a gay and spirited dialogue between a lover and a woman who, in the opening lines, is called

> Rosa fresca aulentisima
> c' apari inver la state —
>
> Fresh and most fragrant rose, blooming in summertime.

Probably it was intended to be performed by a pair of minstrels.

* * *

Meanwhile, in certain portions of Northern Italy, Provençal remained the chosen language for use in the writing of lyric verse. The center of this activity was Genoa, where several men engaged in such writing as an avocation. The best poet among them — and a better poet than any Frederician — was Lanfranco Cigala, who wrote love lyrics of a delicate beauty, and some political and religious verse.

The best known of all Italian writers in Provençal verse is Sordello of Mantua, who became a troubadour and went about with his songs from court to court in the good old fashion, his wanderings taking him to Provence, Spain, and Portugal. Most of his verse is undistinguished; but he wrote one *sirventés* that made a great immediate impression, led Dante to choose him for a brief but highly honorable bit of guidance in the *Purgatorio*, and still vibrates with a vital scorn. It is a lament for the death of his patron Blacatz, in which he makes use of the medieval motif of the eaten heart:

> I would mourn for Lord Blacatz . . . All worthiness is perished in his death. So fatal is the loss that I have no hope it can ever be repaired, unless in this way, that the heart be taken from his body, and that the princes who have no heart eat of it: then shall they be of great heart.

> First let the Emperor eat of it, for he has great need of it, if he wishes to conquer the men of Milan, who have conquered him . . .

He then reviews, with stinging satire, the plights of the kings of France, England, Castille, and Aragon, and of the Counts of Toulouse and of Provence.*

* * *

The first composition in Italian prose that has any literary pretension is a tiny collection of fifteen sentence-length formulae, grouped under the title *Gemma purpurea*, to be used in writing letters. The author is Guido Faba, who taught rhetoric at the University of Bologna. He had already written a Latin treatise, *Summa dictaminis*, on the art of letter writing; and his Italian formulae are condensations of more extensive Latin models appearing in this work. His prose has a deliberately rhythmic quality. His language is an Italianized Bolognese.

A little later, perhaps about 1242, there appeared a work entitled *Parlamenta et epistole*, probably by the same author, which contains nearly a hundred Italian models, accompanied by Latin versions, for entire letters, public addresses, or other writings. Among them is this petition, headed *De filio ad patrem pro pecunia*:

> I have come to the garden of philosophy, a garden fair, delightful, and glorious, and I have desired to pluck flowers of divers colors, so that I might make a wreath of marvelous beauty which should shine upon my head, and in our own city should give forth a gracious fragrance to our friends and kinsmen. But the keeper of the garden has forbidden me, unless I should tender him pleasant and honorable gifts. Wherefore, inasmuch as I have nothing to spend, if your liberality desires that I attain to such great honor, kindly send me money forthwith, so that I may remain in the garden into which I have entered, and gather precious fruit.

* * *

Among the Italians who at this time were writing in Latin prose the most prominent was Albertano da Brescia, a North Italian jurist. The best known of his three moral treatises is his *Liber consolationis*, which has the form of a dialogue between a certain Melibeus and his wife Prudentia, who, in a time of misfortune, consoles her husband and counsels him to forgive those who have injured him. This work proved to be very popular, and was translated

* Browning, struck by the figure of Sordello in the *Purgatorio*, made him the hero of a long poem: but the characteristics of Browning's Sordello are not those of Dante's Sordello, and the narrative bears only a slight trace of what is known of the actual Sordello.

into several languages. Chaucer, who knew it in a French version, derived from it his Tale of Melibeus.

* * *

Not long after the death of St. Francis the great church at Assisi was begun. It consists really of two churches, a Lower Church, dark and crypt-like, and a superimposed simple Gothic Upper Church, which is as full of light as the Lower Church is of mystery. At about the same time, also, the mosaic decoration of the choir niche and the dome of the Florentine Baptistery was begun. This was the century's most elaborate enterprise in mosaic decoration; and it was destined, by virtue rather of its position than of its artistic qualities, to have great influence. To the boy Dante its representations of scenes and persons of Heaven and of Hell were to give unforgettable visual impressions of the Other World.

CHAPTER 4

Poetry of the Latter Half of the Thirteenth Century

THE SECOND HALF of the thirteenth century was marked by violent local warfare, by political upheavals, by extreme religious excitement, by a sudden flowering of activity in architecture, sculpture, and painting, and by a sudden and great expansion of literary production in Italian. It was marked also by the emergence of Tuscany, and especially Florence, into cultural primacy.

With the death of Frederick II the power of the medieval empire came virtually to its end, and the fragmentation of Italy began. Frederick's son Manfred held out for a time in Southern Italy; but the pope offered the kingdom of Naples and Sicily to Charles of Anjou, who won his realm in 1266, at the battle of Benevento, in which Manfred met crushing defeat and tragic death. In 1282 Sicily, in a movement known as the Sicilian Vespers, revolted against the French rule, and called in Peter of Aragon to be its king.

In Northern Italy the collapse of the empire opened the way for the seizure of control in several cities by powerful families. Milan fell to the Visconti; Verona to the Della Scala; Rimini to the Malatesta; and Ravenna to the Polenta. The Este continued to control Ferrara. Genoa and Venice remained as "republics" — they were in reality merchant oligarchies.

The Tuscan cities were rent with internal factional strife — the old names of Ghibelline and Guelf persisting, but with more local meanings than in the days of Frederick — and were often fighting against each other. The bitterest rivalry was that between Florence and Siena, and the most famous battle was that of Montaperti, in 1260, in which the Florentine forces were crushed by Siena and the then exiled Ghibellines of Florence. For a moment the fate of Florence hung in the balance. The proposal that the city should be razed was defeated by Farinata degli Uberti, leader of the Ghibellines. Florentine recovery and development were, however, extraordinarily rapid. The prosperity of the city was increased by the vast broadening of the business of its enterprising merchant companies. The Bardi and the Peruzzi furnished funds to princes and to prelates both in and out of Italy, and served as collecting agents for the papacy. Shortly before the end of the century a bitter feud broke out between two groups (both mainly Guelf) of great Florentine families, groups that came to be known as the Whites and the Blacks respectively. In June 1300, several of the leaders of both groups were banished.

The last and strongest pope of the period was Boniface VIII. He grievously misused his power; but he reorganized and greatly enlarged the Papal library, and he founded the University of Rome. He proclaimed the year 1300 as the first Holy Year: tens of thousands of pilgrims from all parts of Christendom thronged to the Holy City. The order of the Augustinian Hermits, destined to contribute largely to the cause of learning as well as to the cause of religion, was consolidated in 1256.

The Sixth and Seventh Crusades proved ineffective. In 1261 Greek control of the Eastern Empire was reëstablished.

In 1258 a great wave of religious excitement arose in Umbria, whence it swept over Italy — an excitement due in part to the unforgotten prophecy of the Abbot Joachim that a New Age would begin in 1260. Hordes of men and women and children gathered in city squares or marched in long processions, scourging themselves, and crying out in penitence and prayer. This movement, commonly referred to as that of the Flagellants, infused new life into the existing local church-sponsored lay confraternities, and led to an increase in the number of such organizations. In their meetings the members engaged in penance, in prayer, and in other devotional exercises, including singing.

The period was one of philosophic as well as religious excitement, though the center of philosophic excitement was not in Italy, but in France, where scholasticism, invigorated by newly acquired and newly absorbed knowledge of Aristotle, was at its height. The eternal conflict between the Platonic and the Aristotelian views of life — the former considering man as the divinely ensouled center of all creation, the latter considering nature as a whole, and man as a part thereof — was becoming specifically a conflict between Averroistic Aristotelianism on the one hand and Augustinianism on the other. Some of the implications of Aristotelianism were not without danger for Christian doctrine, and certain expressions of Aristotelianism were condemned by the Church. Yet the general greatness of Aristotle was beyond all doubt; and St. Thomas Aquinas, the greatest of medieval theologians, now undertook the task of capturing Aristotle for Christianity, retaining and developing everything in Aristotle that was not definitely counter to Christian doctrine, but holding firmly to that doctrine whenever the conflict seemed beyond solution. The vast resulting system of thought is set forth in the greatest of the voluminous works of St. Thomas, the *Summa Theologiae*. The exposition follows relentlessly the accepted logical procedures: no attempt is made to achieve a literary style. In the same years the Platonic-Augustinian position was defended and developed by St. Bonaventure, whose writings, since they are of literary quality, will be referred to in a later chapter.

In May 1291, the brothers Ugolino and Vadino Vivaldi, of Genoa, undertook to sail westward across the Atlantic, hoping thus to reach India. Their two ships were last sighted from the Moroccan coast.

Meanwhile, Florence was entering an era of extraordinary architectural activity. The first city palace, the Bargello, was begun about the middle of the century; the church of Santo Spirito in 1269; Santa Maria Novella in 1278; and San Marco, Santa Croce, the Cathedral, and the second city palace, now called the Palazzo Vecchio, all between 1290 and 1300. For churches the prevailing style was the weak Italian version of the French Gothic. Elsewhere in Tuscany, Pisa was completing its cathedral group by the addition of the Camposanto.

Pisa was the adopted home of the first truly great Italian sculptor, Nicola Pisano. His best known works are the large pulpits in the Pisan Baptistery and in the Cathedral of Siena, both adorned with extensive series of bas-reliefs, impressive in their native vigor and in a dignity gained through study of classic sculpture. The leading painters, all of them men who combined respect for the austere Byzantine tradition with an attempt to move beyond its limitations, were, in Florence, Cimabue; in Siena, Duccio; and in Rome, Cavallini. Cimabue brought into the old forms a new religious fervor; Duccio a new grace; and Cavallini a new classic dignity. The main pictorial enterprise of this half century was the fresco decoration of the Upper Church of St. Francis of Assisi.

* * *

In this period most of the influential writers who chose to write in any form of the spoken language of Italy were Tuscan, and the Tuscan dialect, somewhat Italianized (that is, somewhat modified by the influence of non-Tuscan dialects and of Latin) came to be generally recognized, except in Piedmont, Liguria, Lombardy, and Venetia, as the normal vernacular language for literary use. Before the end of the following century the unquestioned literary supremacy of Dante, Petrarch, and Boccaccio completed the establishment of Italianized Tuscan as the common Italian language of all Italy.

From this point on it is to be assumed that the language of the vernacular verse and prose to be considered is fairly to be called Italian, except in cases in which some statement to the contrary is made.

* * *

The three leading lyric poets of this half century were Guittone d'Arezzo, Guido Guinizelli, and Guido Cavalcanti. Guittone was the first prolific Italian poet — about 300 poems of his are extant — and he was the first significant Italian poet whose home was in Tuscany. He was born in or near Arezzo, about 1225. In his youth he wrote many love poems, some of them *canzoni*, the rest sonnets. In content these poems imitate the verse of the Provençal troubadours, from which they borrow attitudes, experiences, metaphors, and phrases. They are heavy, verbose, and essentially plebeian; one is aware, however, of a mind at work, thinking seriously, and with signs of a moralizing tendency, about the themes that are being treated. In many *canzoni* Guittone makes use of the terminal *tornada* of the Provençals (commonly called *commiato* or *congedo* in Italian: both words mean "leave-taking"), which the Frederician poets had disregarded. In his terminal stanzas he sometimes turns to the poem itself, telling it whither to go; sometimes addresses his lady; and sometimes names a friend to whom the poem is to be sent. He did a great deal of metrical experimentation. Two of his sonnets have for the octave the rhyme-scheme ABBAABBA, which was destined to replace in general favor the simple original ABABABAB. He was the first poet to make written use of the *ballata*, existent previously as a folk form.

He was intensely Guelf: the defeat of the Florentine Guelfs at Montaperti stirred him deeply, and roused him to the writing of the first Italian political *canzone* — an Italian *sirventés* — beginning

Ahi lasso! or è stagion di doler tanto —
Alas! now it is time to grieve so much —

a poem that towers above the rest of Guittone's verse.

In or about 1260, in the course of the prevalent religious excitement, Guittone was converted; and not long afterward he joined the order of the Knights of the Blessed Virgin Mary. He remained a busy member of that order for the rest of his life, which lasted until 1293 or a little later. His conversion, far from putting an end to his poetic activity, gave it a new stimulation, directing it into moral and religious channels that were really more congenial to him. The *canzoni* and sonnets of his later years are almost as numerous as his earlier love poems; and they are superior by reason of their driving moral and religious earnestness. The most notable of his *canzoni* is one in which he discusses the nature of nobility: his verdict is that it is the heart, and not ancestral blood, that constitutes true nobility. Two of the poems are *plazers*, the old Provençal genre lending itself well to moralizing use.

In addition to his lyrics Guittone wrote some thirty-five letters, in most of which he sends moral or religious exhortation to his correspondents. A few of these letters are in verse, in forms approximating that of the *canzone*; the others are in an irregularly rhythmic prose. Two are of much more interest than the rest: one a letter sent to the city of Florence soon after the battle of Montaperti, perhaps with a copy of Guittone's *canzone* on that battle, the other a letter which starts out almost as if it were to be a love letter, but soon takes a religious turn. Since it is quite possible that this particular letter, because of its union of the idea of feminine charm and the idea of religious service, had a determining influence on other and greater poets, it is here quoted in a much condensed translation:

> Most charming Lady:
>
> Almighty God has endowed you with such a marvelous perfection of all excellence that you seem to be rather an angelic than a terrestrial being. We were indeed not worthy that so precious and marvelous a person should dwell on earth. But I believe that it pleased Him to set you among us in order that you might be as it were a mirror, wherein we all might learn to shun vice and to attain virtue, and because you are the desire and the delight and the satisfaction of all who see you and hear you speak. Wherefore you are beholden to Him to serve and love Him with all your heart and with pure and perfect faith, so that the nobility of your spirit, the greatness of your heart, your beauty, and your charm may lead you not to forget Him, but rather to find all your pleasure in serving Him, so that in the court of Paradise you may be as marvelously great as you are among us here.

Guido Guinizelli was a Bolognese jurist. In 1274 he was banished from Bologna with other Ghibellines; he died two years later. As poet, he was in the first instance a faithful follower of Guittone — to whom he once sent a *canzone* and a sonnet, calling Guittone, in the sonnet, *caro padre meo*, and asking him to correct the imperfections of the *canzone*.

The extant verse that is surely by Guinizelli comprises about twenty poems — *canzoni* and sonnets. The earlier poems are uninterestingly Guittonian: but the rest are very different, and of a far higher order of poetry. The most beautiful and the most memorable of them all is a *canzone*, beginning

Al cor gentil ripara sempre amore,

which has as its main theme the idea that love dwells inherently and exclusively in the noble heart. The first two stanzas read thus, in Rossetti's translation:

Within the gentle heart Love shelters him,
  As birds within the green shade of the grove.
Before the gentle heart, in Nature's scheme,
  Love was not, nor the gentle heart ere Love.
    For with the sun, at once,
So sprang the light immediately; nor was
    Its birth before the sun's:
And Love hath his effect in gentleness
    Of very self; even as
Within the middle fire the heat's excess.

The fire of Love comes to the gentle heart
  Like as its virtue to a precious stone;
To which no star its influence can impart
  Till it is made a pure thing by the sun;
    For when the sun hath smit
From out its essence that which there was vile,
    The star endoweth it.
And so the heart created by God's breath
    Pure, true, and clean from guile,
A woman, like a star, enamoureth.*

In the third stanza the inherence of love in the noble heart is likened to the shining of the flame at the top of the candle, and to the presence of the diamond in iron ore. In the fourth stanza Guinizelli enters the long debate as to the nature of nobility, and asserts that true nobility is a matter not of inheritance but of inner excellence. The fifth stanza introduces the idea that the lady should bestow upon her faithful lover the essence of her own nobility; and for this the poet finds an audacious simile: the lady's shining bestowal is likened to God's shining bestowal of himself upon the obedient angelic hosts. The last stanza is a dramatic scene in heaven. The poet, standing at the judgment seat, is challenged by God for using a divine relationship in a mere simile of earthly love:

My lady, God shall ask, "What dared'st thou?"
  (When my soul stands with all her acts review'd);
"Thou passed'st Heaven, into My sight, as now,
  To make Me of vain love similitude.
    To Me doth praise belong,
  And to the Queen of all the realm of grace
    Who endeth fraud and wrong."
Then may I plead: "As though from Thee he came,
    Love wore an angel's face:
Lord, if I loved her, count it not my shame."

* "Gentle" and "gentleness," as Rossetti here uses these words, have the meanings "noble" and "nobility." The verse translations in the rest of this chapter are also by Rossetti.

No other one of the poems of Guinizelli reaches the exaltation of this *canzone*, but there are a few sonnets, such as this one, that attend it not unworthily:

Yea, let me praise my lady whom I love,
  Likening her unto the lily and rose:
  Brighter than morning star her visage glows;
She is beneath even as her Saint above.
She is as the air in summer which God wove
  Of purple and vermilion glorious;
  As gold and jewels richer than man knows.
Love's self, being love for her, must holier prove.
Ever as she walks she hath a sober grace,
  Making bold men abash'd and good men glad;
    If she delight thee not, thy heart must err.
No man dare look on her his thoughts being base:
  Nay, let me say even more than I have said;—
    No man could think base thoughts who look'd on her.

Guinizelli may or may not have derived from Guittone the idea that the qualities of beauty and of angelic service are combined in his lady; but in any case he fused those ideas in a vital poetic union that was destined to have a profound influence on Dante, who, in his turn, called Guinizelli *il padre mio*.

Among the other sonnets of Guinizelli there are two of very different character: one is a violent imprecation, intended to be humorous, against a troublemaking old woman; and one, just touched with humor and with realism, tells of a bright-eyed Lucia with a parti-colored hood upon her head.

As Dante called Guinizelli *il padre mio*, so he called Guido Cavalcanti his "first friend"—though Guido, born probably between 1250 and 1255, was considerably the older of the two. The Cavalcanti were one of the great Guelf families of Florence. Guido, a man of lofty intellect and strong emotions, exceedingly proud and scornful, was deeply versed in philosophy, yet ready to take his violent share in personal or factional feuds. He came nearest, probably, to peace of mind in his hours of philosophic study, from which he gained mastery of the difficult and elaborate psychological theories of the time. He had the reputation of being an unbeliever. In 1292, whatever his motives, he started on what was ostensibly a pilgrimage to Santiago de Compostela, but he did not go beyond Toulouse. Toward the end of the century he became active as a leader of the Whites; and in June 1300, he was among the factional leaders who were banished. He became ill in exile, and was presently allowed to return to Florence, where he died in August.

Cavalcanti's poems—sonnets, several *ballate*, and two *canzoni*—are about fifty in number. The most immediately delightful of them all are three sonnets and three *ballate* which are poems of glowing praise, reminiscent of the similar poems of Guinizelli. But the religious quality of Guinizelli's love is not present here, and the idea of the interdependence of love and inherent nobility is not stressed. Yet these poems, in their greater human simplicity, are as vibrant and as beautiful as the sonnets of Guinizelli. One of them begins:

> Who is she coming, whom all gaze upon,
> Who makes the air all tremulous with light?

But these joyous poems are by no means characteristic of Cavalcanti.

The most elaborate of his poems is an exceedingly difficult *canzone* on the nature of love, beginning

> Donna me prega, per ch' io voglio dire —
> A lady entreats me, wherefore I am ready to speak —

a *canzone* famous for centuries, and the object of several commentaries. In Cavalcanti's thought, love is a human psychological phenomenon, amenable to scientific analysis and exposition. Such exposition he undertakes in this *canzone*; and, in spite of the intricate character of his doctrine, he succeeds in setting it forth, highly condensed, in a poem which is at the same time a metrical *tour de force*, and not untouched with beauty. The love with which he is concerned is of course "fine" love. He maintains that love may exist continuously in the mind as the cherishing of an ideal image of feminine beauty; that it becomes intensely active emotionally when a man cherishing such an image beholds, and is beheld by, a woman who seems to him to be the counterpart of the ideal image in his mind; that he then seeks responsiveness, being in a deathlike distress until it is attained, or if it is withdrawn; and that the active phase of love ends whenever — typically as a result of tensions inherent in the experience itself — the ideal and the real images cease to coincide in the lover's mind.

This concept of love pervades most of Cavalcanti's other lyrics, giving to many of them a somber, even a tragic quality: the words *morte* and *morire* — indicating not physical death but the quenching of vitality in the distress of love — recur constantly. Yet the sadness is compatible with great beauty.

Many of his poems are given a dramatic character by the introduction of sentences supposed to be uttered in direct discourse by various persons, real or imaginary: his lady, other ladies, friends, onlookers, love, his heart, his mind, thoughts, sighs, voices, images, the poem itself. And a great many of his poems are peopled with *spiriti* — fanciful personifications of psychological faculties or of special psychological phenomena. It was presumably in his philosophical studies that he first found such *spiriti*, and the idea appealed to him so much that he gave it his own extensive personal developments, sometimes subtle, sometimes whimsical. He could even find amusement in his own use of the idea: one of his sonnets has at least one *spirito* in every line.

Most of Cavalcanti's poems were written for a lady named Giovanna, to whom he gave, in poetry, the name of Primavera, "Springtime." A few of his later poems were written for a certain Mandetta of Toulouse, who had reminded him of his own lady: these too are deeply felt, and in essence sad, but they are of a gentler and calmer sadness. Several of his sonnets were written in correspondence: they vary from one addressed to Dante in friendly anxiety to others that are in some sense humorous. One of his most beautiful *ballate* is modeled very skillfully upon the French *pastourelle*. The last of all his poems, and the most moving, is a *ballata* written in exile, as he felt the shadow of death closing upon him. After his death his *ballata*, his soul, and his voice are to go, together, to his lady:

> Because I think not ever to return,
>   Ballad, to Tuscany,—
>   Go therefore thou for me
>   Straight to my lady's face,
>   Who, of her noble grace,
>   Shall show thee courtesy. . .
>
> Ah! ballad, unto thy dear offices
>   I do commend my soul, thus trembling;
> That thou may'st lead it, for pure piteousness,
>   Even to that lady's presence whom I sing.
>   Ah! ballad, say thou to her, sorrowing,
>   Whereso thou meet her then:—
>   "This thy poor handmaiden
>   Is come, nor will be gone,
>   Being parted now from one
>   Who served Love painfully."
>
> Thou also, thou bewilder'd voice and weak,
>   That goest forth in tears from my grieved heart,
> Shalt, with my soul and with this ballad, speak
>   Of my dead mind, when thou dost hence depart,
>   Unto that lady (piteous as thou art!)
>   Who is so calm and bright,
>   It shall be deep delight
>   To feel her presence there.
>   And thou, Soul, worship her
>   Still in her purity.

Cavalcanti was influential, as older companion and as exemplar, upon several younger Florentine poets; but he did not pass on to any one of them his own peculiar darkling torch.

Meanwhile, scores of lesser poets, most of them Tuscan or Bolognese, were writing love lyrics, or, in a few cases, lyrics of other types. By and large they followed Guittone's lead, with more or less individual variation. One of these poets, Rustico di Filippo, is notable not so much for his love lyrics, though they are not without a personal note, as for his humorous sonnets.* The word "humorous," as applied to these and to many later groups of sonnets, is to be understood as covering poems of many different varieties. Some are merely amusing, some are satiric, some are caricatures, some are violent personal attacks, some are indecent, some are nonsense verse, some are roughly realistic, and some are bits of everyday familiar life, rendered smilingly, but even, at times, with compassion. Rustico has instances of several of these varieties: the best of all his poems is a sonnet of familiar compassion.

A minor figure, interesting because she is the first woman known to have written in Italian verse and because she is quite possibly the addressee of the letter by Guittone quoted above, is a Florentine woman known only as *La Compiuta Donzella*, "the accomplished damsel." She is the author of three graceful sonnets.

* * *

The first Italian writer who may fairly be called a man of letters was the Florentine Brunetto Latini, born about 1220. A notary by profession, and a Guelf, he served his city well in many important offices. In 1260 he was sent as envoy to Alfonso the Wise of Castile, to seek his aid against Manfred and the Ghibellines. The outcome of the battle of Montaperti made it impossible for him to return to Florence, and he went to France, where he stayed until 1266, when, after the battle of Benevento, the Guelfs had again the upper hand. For the three remaining decades of his life he played in Florence the part of an elder statesman, influential culturally as well as politically, and held always in high honor and gratitude.

His two main works were both written in France. The first, the *Tresors*, is a large and learned — if at times naïve — encyclopedia, written in French prose. The first of its three parts treats of the history of the world and of Italy in particular, and of astronomy, geography, and natural history; the second treats of the virtues and the vices; and the third treats of rhetoric and politics. Brunetto wrote in French, he says, for two reasons: because he was in France, and because the French language *est plus delitable et plus commune a tous langages*. The *Tresors* had an immediate and extraordinary fortune in Italy: before the end of the century it received three translations or adaptations in prose, and two in verse.

The second, known as the *Tesoretto*, the "Little Treasure," is an unfinished didactic poem, encyclopedic and allegorical, ostensibly relating experiences of the poet. His imagined journeyings take him through a wood to a mountain, a valley, a meadow, and a plain, and thence to Montpellier and to Mount Olympus. Among the allegorical *personae* are Nature, Prudence, Temperance, Fortitude, Justice, Courtesy, Liberality, Loyalty, Pleasure, Fear, Desire,

* These are the first Italian humorous sonnets, unless the last two sonnets mentioned among the poems of Guinizelli were earlier: the dates are uncertain.

Love, and Hope. The *Tesoretto* is devoid of poetic feeling, but it has a triple historical interest: it is the first Italian poem of its kind; it is the first Italian work to show the influence of the French *Roman de la rose*; and it had some influence upon the *Divine Comedy*.

* * *

The movement of the Flagellants, as has been said, infused new life into the lay confraternities, one of whose main activities was singing. Their songs were called *laude*; and their *laude* were now cast in the form of the *ballata*, a form that lent itself well to confraternity singing. Some of the *laude* are hortatory, extolling virtue, renunciation, and voluntary suffering, or reproving sinfulness; some are hymns; and some are narrative, telling the stories of Christ or of the saints.

The *lauda* in its *ballata* form had in it the germ of a dramatic development. This development was fostered by the tendency toward responsive participation which is natural in religious groups; by the fact that in many of the narrative *laude* various persons were supposed to be speaking; and by the example of the liturgical drama. More and more of the later *laude* were of a dramatic character. At first, presumably, even after assignment of the several parts, those parts were sung rather than spoken; and the use of properties, costumes, and stage settings, whenever it began, must at first have been rudimentary.

The most powerful poetic voice of the religious movement of the half century was that of the Umbrian Jacopone da Todi, born in 1230. He too, like so many other early Italian writers, was a jurist: he too, like Guittone, underwent conversion and joined a religious order — in this case the Franciscan order.* He became an outspoken champion of the strict observance of Franciscan discipline, and an outspoken enemy of all ecclesiastical laxity and corruption. His convictions led him to attack Boniface VIII in violent poetic invectives; and in 1297 Boniface excommunicated him and had him imprisoned. Six years later he was released from prison and from excommunication by Boniface's successor. He died in 1306.

Nearly all of Jacopone's ninety-odd poems are in the *lauda* form: many of them are of considerable length. They are hard reading, partly because of difficulties in the thought, partly because of extensive and apparently deliberate use of dialectal forms, and partly because the phrasing is highly laconic. More than half of his poems are devoted to moral or religious exhortation or exposition: these reveal a thoughtful mind, and an active imagination that finds its materials in the base as well as in the sublime. In many of them two

* The moving legendary story of the circumstances of his conversion is partially retold in Matthew Arnold's sonnet beginning

That son of Italy who tried to blow,
Ere Dante came, the trump of sacred song.

or more persons speak in direct discourse, often in regular dialogue, stanza by stanza — as in dialogues between the body and the soul, between two friends (one errant, one reforming), between God and a sinner, between the poet and a dead nun, between two old men (one rich, one poor), between a dead man and his heedless heirs, between a living man and a man in his grave (this is the best known and the most macabre of the poems of this group). In other poems Jacopone turns with lamentation and with stinging satire upon ecclesiastical corruption, and upon Boniface VIII in particular. In still other poems Jacopone pours forth the emotions of his own soul as he reports the joy of mystic union with the divine love, or contemplates that love as made manifest in the sacrifice of the Cross.

The most famous of all his poems is a dramatic narrative of the Crucifixion, beginning

Donna del paradiso,
lo tuo figliolo è preso,
Iesú cristo beato —
Lady of Paradise, thy son is taken, Jesus Christ the blest.

The narrative is cast entirely in direct discourse, distributed among several speakers. It is as if Jacopone had himself stood on Golgotha, had shared with deepest sympathy in every emotion, and had heard, and now was rendering, every word, spoken or unspoken, and every outcry. John speaks, and Mary; the hostile people shout; Christ from the cross speaks lovingly to his mother, and she to her son; and the poem culminates in Mary's almost unbearably poignant lamentation.

Of this poem the *Stabat mater*, long attributed to Jacopone, but in reality of unknown authorship, is the stately Latin companion. One of the chief treasures of all hymnology, it has been borne familiarly down the centuries in the musical settings of Josquin des Prés, Palestrina, Alessandro Scarlatti, Pergolesi, Haydn, Rossini, Schubert, Verdi, Dvořák, and still other composers.

Among the other *laude* of the period there are a few, long attributed to Jacopone, that are now thought to have been written by some poet or poets belonging to the heretical sect of the *Spirito di Libertà*.* Two of these *laude*,

Amor de caritate, perché m'hai sí ferito —
Love of love, why hast thou so wounded me? —

and

Sopr' onne lengua, Amore, bontà senza figura —
Love beyond all speech, goodness transcending form —

are among the most extraordinary rhapsodies in all the literature of Christian mysticism. There are stanzas in which the poet seems not so much to be

* The heresy of this sect consisted in maintaining that through the mystic experience the soul did not merely achieve an ineffable harmony with God, but itself became and remained divine, and as such was above good and evil.

attempting to report his ecstasy after its occurrence as to be letting it record itself, moment by moment, as it occurs.

* * *

Meanwhile, in Genoa and elsewhere in Northern Italy, the writing of lyrics in Provençal continued, and came to its conclusion. In Lombardy and Venetia several men were writing verse in their respective dialects. The ablest of these poets was Bonvesin da Riva, of Milan. His most ambitious poem, known as the *Libro delle tre scritture*, tells, in its first part (the "black" writing), of human life and of the twelve punishments of Hell; in its second part (the "red" writing), of the Passion of Christ; and in its third part (the "golden" writing), of the death of one who dies in the faith, and of the twelve joys of Paradise.

* * *

Amid the general surge of intellectual activity evident in the later decades of the thirteenth century a few men undertook the study of the Latin classics with a new eagerness, a new insight, and a new thoroughness, finding in them, in general, the presentment of a civilization far greater than their own, and, in particular, models for the writing of new works that might in form and style renew the classic literary tradition. Turning deliberately away from composition in Italian, they wrote in Latin both their scholarly treatises and their more or less original works in verse or prose. The combination of enthusiastic and scholarly study of the classics with current production in the Latin language and in classicizing form and style, manifest first in these men, constitutes the long-enduring phenomenon which, in literary history, is commonly called humanism. The early humanists varied considerably in the degree of their detachment from the characteristics of medieval scholarship and literature; and they and their successors varied considerably in their individual scholarly interests and in the nature of their writings.

The first center of humanistic activity was Padua; and the man who, more than any other, deserves to be regarded as the first Italian humanist was a Paduan judge, Lovato Lovati (1241–1309). His extant writings, all in Latin, show a newly intelligent and a newly appreciative acquaintance with the then familiar classic authors. He had and he conveyed to the younger members of his group special enthusiasms for Livy and for Seneca. He was highly esteemed, even by Petrarch, as a poet; but his two long poems are lost (except for six lines of one of them). Their themes were medieval and contemporary: one was on Tristan and Isolde, the other on the pestilential strife of Guelfs and Ghibellines. His extant and shorter poems are Horatian and Ovidian in their classic traits.

CHAPTER 5

Prose of the Latter Half of the Thirteenth Century

THE USE OF ITALIAN PROSE for literary purposes, merely incipient before 1250, became voluminous immediately thereafter. Throughout the latter half of the century, however, Italian prose was used more extensively for translation, from the Latin and from the French, than for original writing. Some of the works translated were historical, some didactic, and some fictional — among them the *History of the Seven Sages*, stories of Troy and of Rome, and stories of the Round Table and of Tristan and Isolde.

* * *

The first truly Italian work of fiction is a collection of *novelle* (the word *novella* means "short story"), generally called the *Novellino*. It exists in a shorter form, containing just a hundred *novelle*, and called accordingly *Le cento novelle antiche*, and in a longer form, containing about 150 *novelle*, called *Libro di novelle et di bel parlare gientile*. The shorter form is very probably of this half-century; the longer form contains some later elements. The full title of the shorter form reads:

> This book treats of certain flowers of speech, of fair courtesies, and of fair replies, and of fair and excellent deeds, and gifts, according as they have come, in times past, from many excellent men.

The several *novelle* are in general very short indeed. Some of them are stories of action or experience; some are brief anecdotes; some are accounts of clever sayings, leading often to a release from difficulties. The persons of the *novelle* include Hercules, Narcissus, Hector, Alexander, Aristotle, Diogenes, Socrates, David, Solomon, Christ and his disciples, Cato, Seneca, Trajan, Charlemagne, several Arthurians, Prince Henry of England, Richard Coeur de Lion, Frederick II, Charles of Anjou, Prester John, the Sultan Saladin, knights and ladies, ambassadors, officials, warriors, priests, bishops, nuns, angels, sages, astrologers, magicians, peasants, merchants and townfolk generally, rascals, moneylenders, doctors, professors, students, and minstrels. But whatever the age or the region from which they come, they are all dressed, as it were, in contemporary costumes and customs. Even Narcissus *fu molto buono et bellissimo cavaliere.*

The general spirit of the *novelle* is chivalric, though there is plenty of bourgeois humor, sometimes salacious. The stories are well told: the teller concentrates on the story itself, and carries it to its goal directly, without embellishments, cleverly, and with an unfailing verve. Among the best stories are those of A Verdict Given in Alexandria, Three Necromancers and the Emperor Frederick, The Justice of Trajan, The Three Rings, and The Lady of Shalott.

The *novelle* are derived from many sources, Oriental, Biblical, classic, medieval Latin, and French. Some come from recent but more or less legendary history, or from reminiscence; one, at least, exists as a folk tale.

* * *

Arthurian stories, long familiar in Italy, had been brought there, in the first instance, by minstrels. In the latter half of the thirteenth century manuscripts of French Arthurian prose romances were brought into Italy, and some of these romances, as has already been indicated, were translated into Italian prose. Within this period, also, a few Italians, depending largely on French sources, but showing some measure of personal invention, wrote Arthurian romances of their own.

The first Italian to attempt such writing, as far as we know, was a certain Rustichello of Pisa, whose romance, written presumably about 1275 and entitled *Meliadus*, is not much more than a compilation of material drawn from the French *Palamède* and *Tristan*. Rustichello chose to write not in Italian prose but in French prose — as did a number of other Italians of this same period. In French prose also, as will presently appear, Rustichello wrote his version of the *Travels* of Marco Polo.

Somewhat later, but still before the end of the century, an unknown writer produced the first Arthurian romance to be composed in Italian prose: the *Tristano riccardiano* (so called because the manuscript in which it is preserved is in the Riccardiana library in Florence). The story, excellently told, follows the general lines of the familiar Tristan story; but there are many variations in episode and in detail.

Italian prose was used also, in this half century, for the composition of several local chronicles and a good many didactic treatises.

* * *

In 1271, when Marco Polo was seventeen years old, his father and his uncle, Venetian merchants, took him with them on a journey to the court of Kubilai Khan. Their route led from Asia Minor, through Persia and Afghanistan, over the Pamir plateau and the Gobi desert, through the great reaches of Mongolia, and at last, after nearly four years of travel, to Shangtu, the summer residence of Kubilai, who had made Peking his capital. For seventeen years they remained at his court, where they were highly honored. The young Marco, extraordinarily energetic and observant, was sent on many official missions, and pleased Kubilai with his reports of strange things that he had seen. For three years he served as governor of Yang-chou. In 1292 the three Venetians started homeward, as pilots for a fleet taking a Mongol princess to a royal wedding in Persia. In their two-years' voyage they touched Indochina, many islands — including Java, Sumatra, and Ceylon — and various points on the Indian coast. A third year brought them back to Venice; and there — except, possibly, for a period of brief captivity in Genoa — Marco lived on until 1324 or 1325.

Not long after his return from China, Marco made his marvelous record of the marvels of the East. The chances are that he wrote his story in his own Venetian dialect; but its earliest extant form is a version in French, entitled *Le divisament dou monde*, "The Description of the World," which is the handiwork of Rustichello of Pisa.* In any case, diffusion of the work in various languages began at once, and has never ceased.

The first of its four Books covers the journey to China; the second is devoted to Kubilai and his realm; the third describes Japan, many islands, and part of India; the fourth tells briefly of certain Persian rulers and of the Tartars. The narrative, unpretentious, packed with detail, and constantly interesting, is now regarded as reliable insofar as it reflects Marco's own observations; and the interwoven material of other sorts, evidently fascinating to Marco, is fascinating still. One traverses regions wild or beautiful; sees multitudes of birds and beasts and growing things; visits nomadic tribes and scores of different cities; resides at the highly civilized court of the great Khan; hunts, fights, governs, and is festive and benevolent with him; learns of many strange faiths and strange ways of life; admires horses, falcons,

* There is a commonly accepted story to the effect that Marco was captured by the Genoese in a seafight in 1298; that he was imprisoned in Genoa; that Rustichello was a captive in the same prison; and that Marco dictated his recollections to Rustichello. There is however no adequate basis for this story, which in certain respects is quite improbable.

precious stones, coal ("black stones used for fuel"), bridges, palaces, pavilions, gardens, rugs, silks, weapons, armor, paper money, pleasure craft, and merchant ships; and listens to tales of the Three Wise Men of the East, of Genghis Khan, of the Old Man of the Mountain, of Prester John, of the One-eyed Cobbler, and of the Wrestling Princess. And one is very glad that Marco Polo came safely back to Venice.

* * *

Within this same half century notable works were written in Latin prose by several Italians — among them two Franciscans, a Dominican, and a jurist.

The Umbrian Giovanni Fidanza, destined to be known as St. Bonaventure, entered the Franciscan Order in his youth, and was eventually made General of his Order. As has already been indicated, he was the chief thirteenth-century representative of Augustinianism. He was a mystic by conviction and by experience. His chief work, the *Itinerarium mentis in Deum*, written in 1259 in mountain solitude, is aflame with the certainty that reason is but the divinely given means of enabling the soul to ascend to God and to lose itself in the divine illumination. He wrote also, at the request of his Order, an official life of St. Francis.

The *Cronica* of Salimbene of Parma, finished in 1287, is the most remarkable historical work produced in Europe in the thirteenth century. Salimbene, born in Parma in 1221, entered the Franciscan order in his early youth. The course of his duties sent him all over Italy and into France; and wherever he went he kept his keen eyes and ears open, and his shrewd and amused mind alert. His history covers the period from 1167 to 1287; and its range radiates irregularly from Parma through Italy and, to some extent, into the rest of Europe. While he makes some use of older writings, he relies very largely upon his own active memory: his typical statement of authority is *ut vidi oculis meis*. His book is rambling, crude, trivial, realistic, and full of anecdotes and of frank and incisive appraisals of persons and events. Salimbene's moods vary from sympathy and joviality to indignation and a bedeviled superstitiousness. He inserts, at will, all sorts of things he happens to remember: bits of verse in Italian or Latin or French, little *novelle*, proverbs, pithy sayings. His language and style fit the contents of his book; they too are uneven, unconventional, and vigorous. From no other work can one gain so vivid an insight into the fear-darkened life of the thirteenth century as this *Cronica* affords.

One of the best known and best loved books of the latter part of the century, a book known and loved by many later generations as well, is the *Legenda sanctorum* of Jacopo da Varazze, a Dominican monk who became Archbishop of Genoa. It consists of about two hundred short chapters, each devoted to the life of a saint or to one of the festivals of the church. It is a comforting and a charming book: comforting in its lovingness and in its assumption that life can be of the order of goodness it depicts, and charming in its childish tenderness and happiness. Its readers soon gave it the name *Legenda aurea*, "The Golden Legend."

In 1287 the jurist Guido delle Colonne finished his *Historia destructionis Troiae.* Despite its title, this work is not a history: it is a condensed translation of the *Roman de Troie* of Benoît de Sainte-More. It played a considerable part in making the Troy legend familiar in Italy and elsewhere. In England Chaucer probably made some use of it; Lydgate's *Troy Book* was the best of several early metrical translations; Caxton's prose version (made from a French translation), printed about 1474 under the title *The Recuyell of the Historyes of Troye*, was the first book printed by Caxton and the first book printed in English; and Caxton's version was probably among the sources of Shakespeare's *Troilus and Cressida.*

CHAPTER 6

Dante in Florence

DANTE ALIGHIERI was born in Florence in May 1265, of a Guelf family of good standing. The world he knew as a boy centered in a house on the little square of San Martino, in the midst of the city, almost under the bells of the ancient Abbey. He must have gone eagerly and often to the Arno — flowing perpetually out of unknown mountain distances, on toward Pisa and the sea — and to the Baptistery, then the chief pride of Florence, which gave him, in the glowing mosaics of its vaulting, his first visual impressions of the Other World. His mother died in his early boyhood, his father in 1277. In that same year he was formally betrothed to Gemma Donati: their marriage was probably celebrated some ten years later. In 1289 he took part in two military expeditions, one against Arezzo, in the course of which he fought in the battle of Campaldino, and one against Pisa, in the course of which he witnessed the surrender of Caprona.

His *fino amore* was given to Beatrice Portinari. In his *Vita nova* he states that he was first drawn to her in his ninth year, that he sought her often during his boyhood, and that in his eighteenth year he had an experience, on meeting her, which marked the beginning of his active love. That love continued until her death in 1290, and, transformed, thereafter. There is no reason to question the reality or the depth of his love for her: neither is there any reason to think that she ever responded to it, or understood it.

In his youth and his young manhood Dante was primarily a lyric poet. Some of his earliest poems were written for ladies other than Beatrice: the emotional burden of these poems is slight, but two or three of them are delightful. The earlier poems for Beatrice, while they reflect a more deeply felt experience, hardly foretoken the new poetry that was to come. Three were occasioned by special griefs: in one he appeals from her anger and implies that she has refused to give him her salutation; and in two others he refers to the fact that she, with other ladies, has derided him.

These earliest poems reveal the young Dante as an eager craftsman, gifted with a clear visual imagination and with a considerable power of vigorous phrasing. They show also that he was well acquainted with the poetry of the Fredericians, of Guittone, and of Cavalcanti, and with some Provençal poetry. The influence of Cavalcanti is particularly evident in the poems for Beatrice: dismay and death are present, as are the *spiriti*, and many of the poems are made dramatic through the introduction of direct discourse.

Then, suddenly, comes the *canzone* beginning

> Donne ch' avete intelletto d'amore
> i' vo' con voi de la mia donna dire —
>
> Ladies that have intelligence in love,
> Of mine own lady I would speak with you — *

Dante's first great poetic achievement. His *fino amore* is transformed: self-seeking and worldly hitherto, it has now become selfless and religious. The influence of Cavalcanti, insofar as it had brought with it insistence upon the concepts of dismay and death, has given way to the influence of Guinizelli. The theme, announced in the opening stanza, is the praise of the poet's lady — pure praise, unsullied by any remnant of hope for personal response. The outpouring of praise begins majestically in the second stanza, with a scene in Heaven:

> An Angel, of his blessed knowledge, saith
> To God: "Lord, in the world that Thou hast made,
> A miracle in action is display'd
> By reason of a soul whose splendours fare
> Even hither: and since Heaven requireth
> Nought saving her, for her it prayeth Thee,
> Thy Saints crying aloud continually."
> Yet Pity still defends our earthly share
> In that sweet soul; God answering thus the prayer:
> "My well-beloved, suffer that in peace
> Your hope remain, while so My pleasure is,
> There where one dwells who dreads the loss of her;
> And who in Hell unto the doom'd shall say,
> 'I have looked on that for which God's chosen pray.'"

Dante's thought is already sweeping from Heaven to Hell. The third stanza sets forth the praise of the soul of Beatrice. After its opening phrases it reads:

> For as she goes by
> Into foul hearts a deathly chill is driven
> By Love, that makes ill thought to perish there;
> While any that endure to gaze on her
> Must either be made noble, or else die.
> When one deserving to be raised so high

* This and the other verse translations in this chapter are by Rossetti.

Is found, 'tis then her power attains its proof,
Making his heart strong for his soul's behoof
    With the full strength of meek humility.
Also this virtue owns she, by God's will:
Who speaks with her can never come to ill.

Beatrice, then, has not only the power to ennoble, but also the power — exercised, it is implied, through her greeting — to assure salvation. The fourth stanza praises her beauty:

She hath that paleness of the pearl that's fit
    In a fair woman, so much and not more;
    She is as high as Nature's skill can soar;
        Beauty is tried by her comparison.

The fifth stanza is a *commiato*.

The *canzone* is followed — in the series of poems chosen later by Dante for inclusion in the *Vita nova* — by nine poems, all of very high poetic quality. Three are sonnets of pure praise, quieter companions of the *canzone*, and certainly among the most beautiful sonnets ever written. The first of the three reads thus:

My lady carries love within her eyes;
    All that she looks on is made pleasanter;
    Upon her path men turn to gaze at her;
He whom she greeteth feels his heart to rise,
And droops his troubled visage, full of sighs,
    And of his evil heart is then aware:
    Hate loves, and pride becomes a worshipper.
O women, help to praise her in somewise.
Humbleness, and the hope that hopeth well,
    By speech of hers into the mind are brought,
        And who beholds is blessed oftenwhiles.
        The look she hath when she a little smiles
    Cannot be said, nor holden in the thought;
'Tis such a new and gracious miracle.

The theme of praise, now dominant in Dante's mind and verse, was of course not new in itself: both Guinizelli and Cavalcanti had written sonnets of praise, sonnets by which Dante was undoubtedly influenced. Dante's praise is distinguished chiefly by its clearer selflessness and, at moments, by its higher exaltation.

One of the other sonnets of this group, a simple statement of the nature of fine love, begins thus:

Amore e 'l cor gentil sono una cosa,
    sì come il saggio in suo dittare pone —

Love and the gentle heart are one same thing,
    Even as the wise man in his ditty saith.

The "wise man" is of course Guinizelli, and the "ditty" is the *canzone* beginning *Al cor gentil.* The most elaborate of the nine poems is a very dramatic narrative, in *canzone* form, of a fever-dream premonition of the death of Beatrice.

Her death was followed by a period of intense grief, during which he wrote, inevitably, poems expressive of that grief. Then came an incipient new love, stirred by the sympathy shown him by an unnamed Pitying Lady, and expressed in four sonnets, which reflect different phases of the conflict he felt between this new affection and his loyalty to Beatrice. Loyalty, proving the stronger, led him to the writing of a few final sonnets for Beatrice, and to the composition, probably before the end of 1293, of the *Vita nova*, "The New Life."*

This little book is a collection of thirty-one of the poems written by Dante in previous years — all thirty-one relating directly or indirectly to his love for Beatrice — introduced and connected and interpreted in Italian prose. A typical chapter consists of a central poem, preceded by an account of the circumstances under which it was composed, and followed by a formal analysis. Thus the *Vita nova* in its general appearance resembles the *Consolation of Philosophy*.

The book as a whole tells the story of Dante's love for Beatrice. It is therefore primarily a record of inner experience, covering Dante's early affection, his delight in receiving the salutation, his grief when it was denied him, his unhappiness under derision, his devotion to the pure praise of his lady, his distress after the death of Beatrice, the sympathy of another lady, the resulting conflict of loves, and the triumph of the love of Beatrice. This inner experience, however, rests upon a varied course of outer experience, reported so clearly — though always as subsidiary — that one has the sense of living and moving with Dante in and about his Florence, and of meeting a really very large number of the persons who touched his life. The scenes are many: streets of Florence, with various passers-by, Dante's own room, a church, a riverside, a wedding feast, a funeral, a journey. The persons include not only Dante, Beatrice, and the Pitying Lady, but also a sister of Dante, the father and a brother of Beatrice, Guido Cavalcanti, Guido's lady Giovanna, many other ladies, many other friends, and, constantly present among the visible folk, *Amore*.

Yet the book is much more than a personal record. Dante, indeed, would hardly have written it at all, would certainly not have written just what he wrote, if he had thought of his love for Beatrice as being merely a personal matter, even as being merely an instance of *fino amore* at its very best. There

* The title is in Latin, though the body of the work is in Italian: the practice of giving Latin titles to vernacular works was common in Dante's time. Generally, and rightly enough, the book is given the Italian title *Vita nuova*.

is a remarkable difference between the poems, on the one hand, and the prose of the *Vita nova* on the other, a difference one can hardly appreciate unless one reads the poems in sequence by themselves, without reference to the prose. For the poems, noble as they are in their highest moments, are relatively simple, direct, and self-complete; whereas the prose, equally beautiful, is curiously wrought, symbolic, heightened, excited, mystic. Dante himself, at a later time, called the work *fervida e passionata.* While Beatrice lived, Dante had indeed attributed to her a divinely given quality of beneficence; but this attribution, however deep its sincerity, had been essentially a matter of poetic devotion: Beatrice was supreme in the perfectness of her ministry rather than in its very nature. But after her death, reviewing again and again his cherished memories, and following her, with his vivid imagination, into the luminous Heaven where now she dwelt, he came to think of her ministry as unique in kind: she seemed now to have been attended all her life and in her death by signs and portents, indicating that she had been in very truth a specially commissioned representative of divine goodness on earth. What had once been a fine poetic concept came thus to be enacted into reality. His eyes had been holden: now they were opened, and he could see what he had not seen before. So the whole story is told from this new point of view. Every event has its higher significance. Wondrous coincidences occur within the walls of Florence; visions hover in the Tuscan air.

Beatrice, for instance, was a "nine": she was in her ninth year when she first appeared to him; it was nine years later that he first experienced the virtue of her salutation; the first dream of her that he reports came to him in the first of the last nine hours of the night; her name stood inevitably ninth in a poem (now lost) in which he listed the sixty fairest ladies of Florence; his premonition of her death came to him upon the ninth day of his illness, and she died (if one followed certain Oriental calendars) on the ninth day of a ninth month, and in a year (1290) in which, in her century, the perfect number, ten, was fulfilled for the ninth time. And the number nine is a trinity of trinities.

But Dante, to whom alone the full significance of Beatrice had been revealed, was also a "nine" — though he leaves the clear inference to the reader: he too was in his ninth year when Beatrice first appeared to him; one of his visions came to him in the ninth hour of the day; and most of the experiences of nine-ness recorded in his book were his as well as hers, some of them more his than hers. When he wrote the *Vita nova,* therefore, he thought of himself as having, in some sense, and in relation to Beatrice, a special divine commission. It does not follow, however, that he had, at this time, any clear idea as to the specific content of that commission.

The most memorable chapters of the *Vita nova* are the eleventh, in which Dante tries to tell what the salutation of Beatrice had meant to him, and the very last chapter of all, which, in its brief entirety, is, in Rossetti's translation, as follows:

> After writing this sonnet, it was given unto me to behold a very wonderful vision; wherein I saw things which determined me that I would say nothing further of this most blessed one, until such time as I could discourse more worthily concerning her. And to this end I labor all I can; as she well knows. Wherefore if it be His pleasure through whom is the life of all things, that my life continue with me a few years, it is my hope that I shall yet write concerning her what has not hitherto been written of any woman. After the which, may it seem good unto Him who is the Master of Grace, that my spirit should go hence to behold the glory of its lady; to wit, of that blessed Beatrice who now continually beholds His countenance *qui est per omnia saecula benedictus.*

The hope therein expressed, though held in long abeyance, was to find its fulfillment in the *Divine Comedy*.

The nine or ten years that followed the writing of the *Vita nova* brought to Dante two new experiences: an intensive study of philosophy, and participation in the political life of Florence. His own statement, made in the *Convivio*, with regard to his study of philosophy, is to the effect that he first sought comfort in the *Consolation of Philosophy* of Boethius and in the consolatory portion of Cicero's *De Amicitia*, and that (like Boethius) he came to think of Philosophy as a noble lady. "Then," he says,

> I began to go there where she was truly revealed, that is, to the schools of the religious and to the disputations of students of philosophy; so that in a brief time, perhaps thirty months, I began to feel so much of her sweetness that love of her drove out and destroyed all other thought.

There were two "schools of the religious" in Dante's Florence, one maintained by the Dominicans, the other by the Franciscans. In the Dominican school study centered on St. Thomas Aquinas, Albertus Magnus, and Aristotle as interpreted by St. Thomas; in the Franciscan school study centered on St. Augustine and on St. Bernard and other mystics. Dante probably frequented both schools. What he meant by "the disputations of students of philosophy" we do not know: probably they were occasional discussions by groups of educated men concerned with the problems of philosophy. There is some ground for thinking that in such discussions Dante came to know and to revere Brunetto Latini. In any case, Dante's study was intense — so intense, he tells us, that for a time his eyesight was impaired. His study did not cease with this more or less formal experience, and it was not limited to subjects we should now regard as philosophic. From this time on Dante took all knowledge to be his province, and with unfailing resolution sought to possess himself of all that was potentially his. By the time of his exile he was one of the most widely read of all men then living.

Dante became a member of the Council of the Captain of the People in November 1295, and served to April 1296; and he was a member of the Council of One Hundred from May 1296, to the end of September, and of some one of the Councils in 1297. In May 1300, he was sent as envoy to San Gimignano to discuss affairs of the Guelf League. For the two-month term beginning in mid-June 1300, he was one of the Priors of the city: it fell to him to share in the action banishing the leaders of the Whites and the Blacks — among them his "first friend." From April to September 1301, he was again a member of the Council of One Hundred; and in October he was one of three envoys sent to Rome to negotiate with Boniface VIII. He took an active part in council discussions; his sympathies were with the Whites, but he stayed clear of active partisanship; in matters involving any clash of interests between the people and the great families he upheld the interests of the people; and his judgment was sound with respect to diplomatic and military policies. He was recognized as being one of the very ablest of the political leaders of Florence.

Of Dante's inner life during these years of philosophic and political activity we have no sure record. The single piece of evidence that is almost certainly reliable is a passage in the *Divine Comedy* in which Beatrice reproaches Dante for faithlessness to her memory, with a severity that indicates something more serious than the episode of the Pitying Lady as told in the *Vita nova.*

Most of the thirty or forty poems that are certainly or very probably of these years fall into one or another of three groups. The half-dozen poems of the first group are allegorical. They are ostensibly love poems, but the lady they celebrate is Philosophy. That Dante should have thought of philosophy as a noble lady is only natural: Boethius had personified philosophy as a noble lady, and Dante, like Boethius, had found consolation in philosophy. But whereas the Philosophy of Boethius is matronly and austere, Dante's Philosophy is youthful and love-worthy: it is clear that Dante associated his Philosophy with his Pitying Lady, from whom he had received some measure of consolation. This group of poems centers in two *canzoni*, both of great beauty. One of them resumes and transforms the theme of the conflict of loves that had appeared in the sonnets written for the Pitying Lady and included in the *Vita nova*: but the love that is now to prevail is love for Philosophy. The other is devoted to praise, similar in its quality to the praise once given to Beatrice, and very impressive in its thoughtful phrasing: this *canzone* was set to music by Dante's friend Casella.

The second group consists of two didactic *canzoni.* The first, on nobility, is the final and most comprehensive thirteenth-century discussion of that familiar theme: Dante, like his poetic predecessors, finds nobility to be a personal quality, not an inherited prerogative. The second is on *leggiadria*, by which Dante means courtesy in a very broad sense. Both poems are strictly dialectic in method: they proceed from the refutation of false opinions to the demonstration of true opinions. These two *canzoni* are heirs, in a sense, of the moralizing *canzoni* of Guittone; but Dante's are distinguished by the fine precision of their thought, and each attains, in its final stanza, a certain reflective beauty: one of the final stanzas describes the four ages of the noble life, the other sets forth the proper characteristics of the courteous life. The two poems are notable chiefly because they are the first writings in which Dante manifests a social concern, and because they are marked by the first faint flashes of his satiric indignation — directed, here, against those whose conduct violates his canons of nobility and courtesy. Formally, both *canzoni* show a heightened interest in metrical elaboration.

The third group consists of four poems — two *canzoni* and two *sestine* — which ostensibly express love for a maiden so hardhearted that Dante calls her Pietra, "Stone." They are very different from his poems for Beatrice and for Philosophy: they are without a word of praise — except for beauty — and are devoted entirely to the expression of the suffering caused by the maiden's unrelenting hardness. Some scholars think that these poems reflect a real experience; others, that they are allegorical; others still, that they are merely fictional, and that they were composed as deliberate poetic *tours de force*. It is clear, in any case, that they were written under the direct influence of the poetry of Arnaut Daniel. The first of the two *canzoni* is a very beautiful development of the theme of love in winter — a theme that had been treated by Arnaut. The several stanzas of the poem follow the same pattern: each begins with a perfect rendering of winter sights or sounds or silences, and ends with a brief contrasting statement of the poet's ardency. This *canzone* is notable also because it contains Dante's first display of an expert knowledge of astronomy. The wintry mood continues in the two *sestine* — the first Italian *sestine*. In these two poems, however, the poet's interest seems to be less in thought and imagery — though these are often of much beauty — than in the solution of the exceedingly difficult metrical problems he has set himself, problems especially difficult in the second *sestina*, in which, in a variation peculiar to this one poem, the length of the stanza is doubled. In the second *canzone*, masterly in its craftsmanship, the poet breaks into a strangely violent and vengeful invective against the hardness he cannot soften.

Among the other poems written in these same years are a charming *ballata* and two or three related poems written for an unidentifiable maiden who may or may not be one with Philosophy or with Pietra, and several sonnets written in correspondence, some of them humorous.

In November 1301, the Blacks seized power in Florence; and in January 1302, their systematic reprisals began. On January 27 Dante Alighieri, accused (falsely) of barratry, was ordered to restore the funds he had (not) extorted and to pay a fine of 5000 florins, with the provision that all his property should be confiscated if restoration and payment were not made within three days; was banished from Tuscany for two years; and was disqualified for life from holding public office. To this action Dante made no reply. His property was confiscated; and on March 10 he was banished for life, and condemned to be burned alive if he ever fell into the hands of officers of Florence.

CHAPTER 7

Dante in Exile

THE REMAINING YEARS of Dante's life, years in which he ate the bitter bread and climbed the hard stairways of exile, were lived within the first quarter of the fourteenth century. In the course of that period Italy lost the papacy, and was stirred by a brief imperial apparition. Clement V, a Frenchman elected pope in 1305, removed the papal see to Avignon, where it was to remain, under an unbroken series of French popes, for seventy years: this French detention of the papacy is often called the Babylonian captivity. Henry VII, elected emperor in 1308, entered Italy in 1310, desiring to be crowned in Rome, which had witnessed no imperial ceremony since the days of Frederick II. His coming roused the Italian Ghibellines to unwarranted heights of expectation, and the Italian Guelfs to determined opposition. He was crowned in Rome; but he had nothing but the crown to show for his exertions when, after a series of ineffective sieges, he died, near Siena, in 1313. The ablest of the local despots of this period was Can Grande della Scala, lord of Verona from 1311 to 1329—to whom Dante was to dedicate the *Paradiso*.

The main new contemporary architectural enterprise was the building of the south wing—the wing facing the canal—of the Palace of the Doges in Venice. The main sculptural enterprise was the decoration of the façade of the Cathedral of Orvieto with an extraordinary series of bas-reliefs, representing biblical scenes and figures, and the Last Judgment: the sculptors are unknown. In Tuscany, Giovanni Pisano, son of Nicola, turned from his father's Roman strength to a Gothic emotionalism. Giotto, the first unquestionably great Italian painter, dominated his field, beyond rivalry. Among his greatest series of frescoes are two that depict the life of St. Francis, one in the Upper Church at Assisi, the other in the Bardi Chapel in Santa Croce in Florence. He was the first painter to achieve three-dimensional reality. His persons have sturdy substance and an impressive dignity; and he tells his stories with an honest and effective concentration upon that which is essentially significant.

* * *

The White Guelfs who were expelled from Florence in 1302 formed at once a governing body of their own, in which Dante had some responsibilities. They were bent on returning by force of arms, and for that purpose they gained the alliance of previously exiled Florentine Ghibellines and of various enemies of Florence. Desultory warfare began, but the exiles and their allies were soon hopelessly defeated. Dante, disgusted with the dissensions, the self-seeking, and the stupidity of his companions, broke with them, and thereafter remained aloof from all partisanship.

He never again beheld the towers of Florence. He desired passionately to return; but when amnesty was offered, in 1315, the offer was attended by such humiliating conditions that he refused it indignantly. Of his life in exile he wrote, in the *Convivio*:

> Throughout almost all the regions into which our speech extends I have wandered, all but begging my way, and showing against my will the wounds that Fortune has dealt me — wounds for which the blame is too often imputed to him who has received them. Verily I have been a ship without sail or helm, driven to divers ports and river-mouths and shores by the dry wind of grievous poverty.

His first refuge was in Verona, with the Della Scala, and his second with the Malaspina, lords of the Lunigiana (a region in the Northern Apennines); he lived for a time in Lucca; he visited Verona again; and there are indications that he did in fact traverse Northern Italy from shore to shore.

He was greatly excited by the advent of Henry VII, and in an encyclical of highly wrought eloquence he summoned the princes and peoples of Italy to welcome Henry as a heaven-sent redeemer who would heal all their woes. Dante himself had audience with the Emperor not long after his entrance into Italy. Thereafter, in impassioned letters, he first threatened the Florentine Blacks with imminent imperial vengeance, and later reproached Henry for his delay in inflicting that vengeance. Henry did lay siege to Florence; but he could not take it, and withdrew. His failure and death must have brought to Dante the bitterest of all the many griefs his proud spirit knew in exile.

In or about 1318 he found a final and most honorable refuge in Ravenna, under the appreciative protection of Guido Novello da Polenta. Scholars gathered around him; Giovanni del Virgilio, a Bolognese teacher and classicist, suggested to him that he might receive poetic coronation in Bologna,*

* This idea presumably came into the mind of Giovanni del Virgilio because of the poetic coronation of Mussato which had taken place in Padua in 1315: this coronation will be referred to in Chapter 9.

but he replied that coronation would be welcome only if it could be achieved in his own city; he went once more to Verona, where he delivered a scientific dissertation in Latin, entitled *Questio de aqua et terra*; and he served once as envoy to Venice. He died in Ravenna on September 14, 1321.

Throughout the hardships of his exile Dante, as scholar and as poet, grew from strength to supreme strength.

The earliest of the three *canzoni* that are certainly of this period, beginning

> Tre donne intorno al cor mi son venute,
> e seggonsi di fore:
> ché dentro siede Amore —
>
> Three ladies have come near to my heart, and sit around it: for Love sits within —

is a mature and stately poem, one of the greatest of all Dante's lyrics. It is allegorical: the three ladies represent Justice and two specific derivatives of Justice. In its general aspect the poem deplores the evil state of a world from which Justice and her children have been exiled, and in its personal aspect it finds consolation in an exile shared with such divinities. Its most famous line is

> l' essilio che m' è dato, onor mi tegno —
>
> I hold as an honor the exile that has been conferred upon me —

yet it is at the same time a plea for recall from that exile. The style of the poem is of an intensely refined clarity; the visualization of its persons is memorable; the dialogue between Justice and Love is very dramatic; and the explicitly personal conclusion has both deep pathos and great dignity. Of the other two *canzoni*, one is a love poem of uncertain significance, and the other a didactic poem on the theme of liberality.

The *Convivio*, the "Banquet," the first of the four major works of Dante's exile, and the first great work written in Italian prose, was begun about 1304, and left unfinished about 1307. Like the *canzone Tre donne* it has both a general and a personal aspect: in its personal aspect the *Convivio* also is a plea, a massive plea, that the author, shown now to be capable of producing such a work as this, be recalled to Florence — or, if not so recalled, that he be welcomed and held in honor elsewhere.

The banquet Dante sets before his readers is a feast of knowledge: he spreads his tables with all of the knowledge he has been able to acquire, insofar as he regards it as valuable for those of his fellow men who in respect to learning have been less privileged or less persistent than he. In its general aspect, therefore, the *Convivio* is written for the public benefit. It is quasi-encyclopedic in its intended range; but its topics are limited, in the main, to those that Dante believed to be of social concern; and its structure is quite unlike that of any other encyclopedic work. Each Book — after the first, which is prefatory — consists, or was to consist, of one of Dante's own *canzoni*, followed by a long and elaborate commentary on that *canzone*. This commentary, in most cases, consists, or was to consist, of two parts: a commentary upon the literal meaning of the *canzone*, and a commentary upon its allegorical meaning. There were to have been fourteen Books in all, after the preface. The *canzoni* were the wine of the banquet, the commentaries its bread. Thus the *Convivio*, like the *Vita nova*, consists partly of verse and partly of prose: the *Convivio* is indeed, in a sense, a second *Vita nova*, of which, however, the heroine is not Beatrice, but Philosophy.

In the opening chapter of the prefatory Book, Dante states his purpose, quoting, by way of first premise, Aristotle's magnificent assertion that "all men have by nature the desire to know," and adding thereto, as second premise, his own conviction that *ciascuno uomo a ciascuno uomo naturalmente è amico*, "every man is by nature a friend to every other man": Dante, therefore, must needs share his knowledge. In most of the remaining chapters of Book I Dante justifies himself for writing in Italian rather than in Latin: these chapters constitute the first "defense and illustration" of the Italian language.

The theme of Book II is the general character of Philosophy. The *canzone* with which it opens is the first of the two *canzoni* referred to in the previous chapter as constituting the center of the group of allegorical poems written during Dante's last years in Florence. Among the topics discussed in the commentary are the four possible interpretations of poetry (literal, allegorical, anagogical, and moral); the immortality of the soul; and the ten heavens.

Book III is devoted to the praise of Philosophy. The opening *canzone* is the second of the two allegorical *canzoni* just referred to. Many topics are discussed in the commentary, among them the nature of love; the faculties of life, feeling, and reason; the diffusion of divine goodness; the position of man in the universe; the nature of friendship; the sun as a symbol of God; and the problem of evil. Two kinds of friendship are distinguished: personal friendship, and *la naturale amistade . . . per la quale tutti a tutti semo amici*, "the innate friendship whereby we are all friends to all men."

Book IV, the last to be completed, is a treatise on nobility: the opening *canzone* is, naturally, Dante's didactic *canzone* upon that theme. Of the many fine passages in the commentary, the finest, perhaps, is his discussion of the nature of the imperial authority. When Dante wrote this book he had become convinced that the greatest immediate need of the world was freedom from conflict; that such freedom could be attained only if the world were ruled as one world; and that the Roman Empire of old and its continuant, the Holy Roman Empire of his own day, were divinely ordained for the exercise of such singleness of authority. So now he writes:

> As an individual man for his completeness requires the domestic companionship of the family, so a family for its completeness requires a neighborhood, since otherwise it would suffer many lacks which would hinder the attainment of felicity. And since a neighborhood cannot in all regards be self-sufficient, for the satisfaction of all its wants there must needs be a city. Moreover a city, for the sake of its crafts and for self-defense, must needs have dealings and brotherly relations with neighboring cities, and for this reason the kingdom was instituted. Now inasmuch as the mind of man does not rest content with a limited possession of land, but always, as we perceive by experience, desires the glory of acquiring more, conflicts and wars must needs arise between kingdom and kingdom: which things are the tribulation of cities, and through cities of neighborhoods, and through neighborhoods of families, and through families of individual men; and thus the attainment of felicity is impeded. Wherefore, in order to do away with these wars and their causes, the whole earth, and all that is given to the human race to possess, must be a monarchy, that is, a single princedom, and must have a single prince, who, possessing all things, and having nothing left to covet, may keep the kings confined within the borders of their kingdoms, so that peace may reign among them: in which peace the cities may have rest; in which rest neighborhoods may love each other; in which love families may satisfy all their wants; and when these are satisfied man may attain felicity, which is the end whereunto man was born.

Among the other topics discussed in Book IV are the innate desire of the soul to return to God; the classification of the virtues; the joy of the active life, by which Dante means loyal participation in the life of human society, and the joy of the contemplative life, by which he means the contemplation of the nature of God as manifested in all his works; and the four ages of man.

The *Convivio* as a whole is a very learned work, learned not only in the fields that are more specifically philosophical, but also in all the science of the time, especially in astronomy. Aristotle, who is for Dante "the Philosopher" *par excellence*, is his chief authority; but he draws also on the *Timaeus* of Plato, Euclid, the Neo-Platonic pseudo-Dionysius, Cicero, Seneca, Livy, Orosius, St. Augustine, Boethius, Alfraganus, Averroes, Albertus Magnus, Thomas Aquinas, the Latin poets, and, of course, the Bible. Dante's own thought is keen, imaginative, and tensely sustained. His style varies from scholastic aridity to high eloquence. References to personal experiences and to men and events of Dante's own time enliven the exposition at many points.

Not long after Dante had begun the *Convivio* he began also another and shorter work, the *De vulgari eloquentia*, "On the Vernacular Language." This, like the latter part of the prefatory book of the *Convivio*, is a "defense and illustration" of the Italian language: but it goes into much greater linguistic and stylistic detail; it is addressed not to a general public but to an educated minority; and it is written, accordingly, in Latin.

Like the *Convivio*, the *De vulgari eloquentia* is unfinished. Its intended length is uncertain: only the first book and part of the second were completed. Even in its fractional state, however, it is remarkable for its pioneering in the field of linguistic history and analysis, for the breadth of Dante's survey of the language and the poetry of Western Europe, and for the light it throws on Dante's estimation of earlier and contemporary Italian poetry.

Beginning with a recognition of the difference between the vernacular language and Latin, Dante maintains that the vernacular language is primary and natural, and (being of course mistaken in this respect) that Latin is a secondary and artificial language devised for the common convenience of men who differed from each other in their vernacular languages. He has however an extraordinarily clear recognition of the fundamental facts of continuous linguistic change and of local differentiation:

> No human speech can remain stable, but must continually change, temporally and locally. If those who lived in olden times in a given city should come to life again and speak as once they spoke, their speech would be very different from that of their living descendants. Nor is it surprising that such change should commonly pass unnoticed, for the rate of such change is very slow, whereas the lifetime of any given man is very brief. Similarly, the spoken languages of different regions must vary from each other, if not stabilized by intercommunication.*

Dante asserts the existence of three main linguistic families in Europe — the Eastern, the Northern, and the Western — and the existence of three major branches of the Western group — the Provençal, the French, and the Italian. Each of these three branches has grounds for claiming preëminence: the Provençal because it was the first to be used for lyric poetry; the French for its prose writings, such as the *Arturi regis ambages pulcerrime*, "the most beautiful adventures of King Arthur"; and the Italian for its closeness to Latin and for the sweetness of its lyric poetry. In Italy, Dante distinguishes fourteen main dialects, and asserts that each of them has many local variations. No one of these dialects, he says, is worthy to be used for literary purposes: it was necessary, therefore, that a common Italian language be devised, a language that should be worthy to be called illustrious.

The second Book discusses the use of the illustrious vernacular in poetry. Many Provençal, French, and Italian poems are cited (by their first lines) as examples. Three subjects are said to be suitable for poetic treatment: arms (as used to maintain peace), love, and righteousness. Dante cites Bertran de Born, Arnaut Daniel, and Guiraut de Bornelh as Provençal representatives of these three kinds of poetry; says that no Italian poet has yet won distinction as a poet of arms; and cites his friend Cino da Pistoia as the typical Italian poet of love, and himself as the Italian poet of righteousness. He then enters upon a detailed discussion of the technique of the *canzone*, which he regards as the noblest of vernacular poetic forms.

The writing of the *Divine Comedy*, begun in or about 1307, was to be

* A condensed paraphrase.

Dante's main task for most of the rest of his life; but there came a moment when his convictions as to the necessity for the reëstablishment of the imperial authority, as to the proper relationship between Church and Empire, and as to the basic purposes of human life had become so compelling that he paused to set them forth directly in a powerful Latin treatise which he called, simply, *Monarchia.* These convictions were not new: they had found a first expression in the *Convivio*, but that expression had been only incidental, and the convictions themselves were now much more fully matured and more complete. The specific purpose of the *Monarchia* is to prove that the Emperor is coördinate with the Pope, not subject to him.

This work, fortunately finished, is in three Books. In the first, Dante argues, very effectively, that the existence of a universal empire is necessary for the well-being of mankind. He begins with a fine statement of his urgent belief that the privileged possession of knowledge carries with it the responsibility to use that knowledge for the public good. Among the major points of his argument are these: the purpose of civilization as a whole is to actuate the potentialities of the human mind; such actuation can be attained only when there is universal peace; *genus humanum maxime Deo assimilatur quando maxime est unum*, "the human race is most like unto God when it is most unified"; perfect justice requires the existence of an ultimate judge; any system of government that comes short of universal empire subjects the individual citizen to oppression by self-seeking rulers who are uncontrolled.

The second book develops the thesis that the Roman Empire was divinely ordained: it is assumed that the Holy Roman Empire inherits the ancient ordination. The imperial claim is justified by the nobility of the Roman race; by miracles performed in its favor; by the devotion of Roman citizens to the state; by the efficiency of Roman rule; by the uniqueness of Roman success in achieving empire; and by Roman victories in critical ordeals of battle. Dante was thoroughly and eagerly conversant with Roman history: the whole book, starred with quotations from the Latin poets, glows with his enthusiasm. His chief hero is Cato, "that austere champion of true liberty."

The opening chapters of Book III are devoted to refutation of the arguments of those who assert that the Emperor is subject to the Pope. The closing chapters maintain that the Empire existed before the Church and that the authority of the Empire was recognized by Christ and by St. Paul; that the exercise of temporal authority is not consistent with the spiritual function of the Church; and finally, in the last chapter of all, that God desires mankind to attain, in peace, the blessedness of this life, and that such attainment is possible only under an imperial government of the whole world.

This concluding chapter is, for the understanding of Dante's thought, the most important passage in all his prose writings: for it sets forth with systematic and shining clarity the whole scheme of human life, as Dante saw it. Man, he says, is of a dual nature, in part mortal, in part immortal. There are set before him, therefore, two kinds of blessedness: the blessedness of this life, insofar as he is mortal, and the blessedness of the eternal life, insofar as he is immortal. The blessedness of this life consists in the *operatio proprie virtutis*, by which Dante means the exercise of the highest human faculties. The blessedness of the eternal life consists in the *fruitio divini aspectus*. The experience suggested by these words, and not defined in the *Monarchia*, was by no means, in Dante's thought, anthropomorphic: it is realized, in the last canto of the *Divine Comedy*, as the supreme experience of power, of wisdom, and of love. The temporal blessedness is symbolized by the Earthly Paradise; the eternal blessedness by the Heavenly Paradise. The temporal blessedness is to be attained under the guidance of Philosophy (conceived as embodying all human wisdom) and through the practice of the moral and the intellectual virtues; the eternal blessedness is to be attained under the guidance of Revelation and through the practice of the theological virtues (Faith, Hope, and Love). The nature of the temporal blessedness and the means of attaining it are made known to us by human reason, acting through the philosophers; the nature of the eternal blessedness and the means of attaining it are made known to us by the Holy Spirit, acting through the Prophets, the Sacred Writers, Christ, and his Disciples. The temporal blessedness is to be attained under the government of the Emperor; the eternal blessedness under the government of the Pope. In the *Divine Comedy*, in perfect accordance with this scheme, Virgil, typifying Philosophy, guides Dante to the Earthly Paradise; and Beatrice, typifying Revelation, guides him thence, through the nine heavens, to the Empyrean.

The schematic parity of the two blessednesses, as thus asserted, is unprecedented: St. Thomas treats the blessedness of this life as merely ancillary to the eternal blessedness. Dante, of course, recognized — none more clearly — the far greater importance of the eternal blessedness; and it may well be that the logic that underlies his scheme was primarily political. But his statement is nonetheless, in effect, a proclamation of his conviction that life on earth may be blessed in its own directly God-given right — a conviction that illumines the intensity of Dante's concern for human righteousness and human justice, and places him far in advance of his time, far in advance of many men of later generations.

Some ten years after Dante's death Pope John XXII ordered that the *Monarchia* be burned.

In the course of his years in Ravenna, Dante wrote two Latin eclogues, in reply to similar poems sent to him by Giovanni del Virgilio, and the *Questio de aqua et terra*, to which reference has already been made.

Dante doubtless wrote a good many letters: there are extant about a dozen, in Latin, and largely in the *cursus*, which are certainly or probably by him. The most noteworthy are the three, already referred to, that are related to the expedition of Henry VII; a letter to the Italian cardinals, lamenting bitterly the papal desertion of Rome and the prevalent ecclesiastical avarice, and urging the reëstablishment of the papal see in its own proper holy city; a letter to a Florentine friend, refusing to take advantage of the humiliating amnesty offered in 1315; and a letter to Can Grande della Scala which is of the utmost importance, for it contains Dante's own introductions to the *Divine Comedy* as a whole and to the *Paradise* in particular.

CHAPTER 8

The Divine Comedy

DANTE'S OWN INTRODUCTION to the *Divine Comedy*, written for Can Grande, contains statements on six matters: the subject of the poem, its protagonist, its form, its purpose, its title, and its classification. He prefaces his discussion of the subject with the statement that the poem has two meanings, one literal, the other allegorical. He then says that the subject of the poem in its literal meaning is "the state of spirits after death," and in its allegorical meaning "man, as by good or evil use of his free will he merits just reward or renders himself liable to just punishment." The poem, then, is much more than an objective account of the Other World: the sights and sounds of that world are so presented as to show that its terrible or its glorious experiences are not arbitrarily assigned, but result inevitably, through the operation of an infallible and all-powerful justice, from man's use of his own free will. Moreover, the spirits who exemplify the various eternal fates are, except for the background hordes, not nameless types: they are in general the impressive spirits of individual men and women who had actually lived, and lived with some degree of fame, upon this earth — many of them contemporaries of Dante, or of his immediate forebears.

The protagonist of the poem is the writer himself.

Formally, the poem is divided into three parts, or canticles; each canticle is divided into cantos; and each canto is divided into tercets. The three canticles are of course the *Inferno*, the *Purgatorio*, and the *Paradiso*. The *Inferno* has thirty-four cantos, and the *Purgatorio* and the *Paradiso* thirty-three each: a hundred in all. The metrical scheme, invented for this poem, and so successful that it has been used by hosts of later poets, may be seen in the six opening lines:

Nel mezzo del cammin di nostra vita
mi ritrovai per una selva oscura,
chè la diritta via era smarrita.

Ah quanto a dir qual era è cosa dura
esta selva selvaggia e aspra e forte
che nel pensier rinnova la paura! *

The line is the standard Italian hendecasyllabic line. In each tercet the first and third lines rhyme together, and enclose a line that does not rhyme with them but ends with a new rhyme that is to become the enclosing rhyme of the following tercet. This metrical scheme is called *terza rima.*

The style of the poem, regarded as a phase of the form, is, throughout or at various times, "poetic, fictional, descriptive, digressive, metaphorical, and characterized by the use of definition, analysis, proof, refutation, and examples."

Finis . . . est removere viventes in hac vita de statu miserie et perducere ad statum felicitatis: "the purpose . . . is to rescue those living in this life from a state of woe and to lead them into a state of blessedness." This statement, by far the most important of all the introductory statements, calls for extended comment.

Dante and his age believed that for every human being a finite period of life on earth would be followed by an infinite period of life after death; that if a man at the moment of his death were in harmony with God, his spirit, after a finite period in Purgatory, would thereafter dwell forever in blessedness with God in Heaven; and that if a man at the moment of his death were out of harmony with God, his spirit would thereafter dwell forever in Hell, deprived of the sight of God.

Dante's conception of this matter differed in two vital respects, however, from that of the ordinary man: in the first place, the ordinary man did not grasp the difficult concept of eternity, whereas to Dante that concept was marvelously clear; and in the second place, the ordinary man, while he had an idea that a spirit would be very happy in Heaven or very unhappy in Hell, had no clear concept of such happiness and unhappiness, whereas to Dante this concept also was marvelously clear. The ordinary man's consciousness of the matter might fairly be represented by a diagram in which the lines for eternity would be much longer, but *only* "much longer," than the line for life on earth, and would at the same time be less clear. On the basis of a consciousness so limited, the ordinary man could, and did, take chances: the contrast between life before death and life after death was for him not so sharp as to compel his constant attention, and the moment of death seemed so far away that it was easy for him to neglect the establishment in himself of those religious attitudes and practices which would make it probable that his spirit would be, at death, in harmony with God. Unconsciously, or

* "Halfway through the journey of this life I found myself astray in a dark wood, for the right way had been lost. Ah, how hard a thing it is to tell what it was like, this wood wild and rough and dense, which even as I think of it renews my fear!"

even half-consciously, he might seek or accept some sinful type of happiness in this life even at the risk of great and long-lasting unhappiness after death. But Dante's consciousness of the matter could be suggested, in somewhat similar form, only by a diagram in which life on earth and life in Purgatory are each represented by a dot, symbolizing that which is infinitesimal, followed by lines which should be not only infinite in length, but perfectly clear.

Dante, moreover, knew, and could not fail to know, the difference between his consciousness and that of the ordinary man in respect to these matters. Dante, knowing eternity, knowing the joys of heaven, knowing the torments of Hell, moved in a world of ordinary men who did not know these things, who by their ignorance were in danger of losing intense eternal joy and of incurring intense eternal woe. Dante, therefore, uniquely endowed as he knew himself to be, could do no less than devote himself to the compelling proclamation of this infinitely vital matter. Since he was writing for ordinary men, he chose Italian rather than Latin as linguistic medium. Since he was forever and essentially a poet, he chose poetry as his literary form; and because of the vital importance of what he had to say, he spent himself unsparingly in the effort to make his poem a noble and effective instrument for his proclamation. The *Comedy* is the greatest of all poems, yet it is only secondarily a poem: it is primarily an instrument of salvation.

The title of the poem is *Incipit Comedia Dantis Alagherii florentini natione, non moribus*: "Here begins the Comedy of Dante Alighieri, a Florentine by birth but not by conduct." The title, then, is in Latin, though the poem is in Italian — and it does not contain any word that means "divine." It was not until 1555 that an Italian editor, in his enthusiasm for the poetic supremacy of the work, set the word *divina*, on his title page, before the word *comedia*: the innovation won immediate and lasting favor. The term "comedy," as Dante used it, carried no implication of dramatic form: it meant for him any poetic work which, beginning in unhappiness, ends in happiness. In that sense Dante's poem, which begins with Hell and ends with Paradise, is *the* comedy *par excellence*. The word "comedy" itself was thought by Dante to signify also "a song of the people" — a term applicable to his work because it was written in the vernacular rather than in Latin. The bitter reference to Florence reveals both Dante's passionate concern for his native city and a power of satire which is amply manifest throughout the poem.

The poem is to be classified as an ethical work: that is, as a treatise designed not as a speculative exercise, but as an instrument for the production of an effect — for the production, in this case, of the most vitally important of all possible effects.

While the action of the *Comedia* begins in its very first sentence, the first two cantos of the *Inferno*, taken together, serve mainly as a prologue for the poem as a whole. In the letter to Can Grande, Dante says that a prologue necessarily contains two elements, a statement of contents and an invocation, and that its function is to win the reader's good will, attention, and confidence. The statement of contents for the *Comedia* appears near the end of the first canto, in lines that may be rendered thus (Virgil is speaking to Dante):

> Whence for your good I deem it best that you follow me, and I will be your guide; and I will lead you hence through an eternal place where you shall hear the desperate cries and shall see the woeful spirits of old who all bewail the second death. And then you shall see those who are content in fire, because they hope, in good time, to reach the company of the blessed. And if to that company you shall desire to ascend, there shall be a spirit worthier for such guidance than I am: with her I will leave you when I depart from you.

The invocation appears early in the second canto. The reader's good will is stirred at the outset by sympathy for the plight of the protagonist; attention is captured by the dramatic accounts, one in the first canto and one in the second, of the two simultaneous initial actions, one on earth and one in Heaven; and confidence results from the immediate presentation of the two guides — Virgil, the rescuer, and Beatrice, whose swift descent, on Dante's behalf, to bid Virgil go to Dante's aid is reported in the second canto. The second canto seeks, in particular, to dispel the feeling, which some of Dante's contemporaries would have been very likely to have, that Dante lacked the authority requisite for the protagonist and the writer of such a work. Dante meets the objection by taking it upon his own lips and giving to it the poetic answer that the journey is ordered by Heaven — by Mary, by St. Lucy, and by Beatrice. Nor is that answer entirely fictitious: it is merely a poetic assertion that Dante is divinely commissioned for his task. And Dante believed with an unwavering belief that he was the holder of a unique divine commission.

In Canto III, Virgil and Dante come to the gate of Hell, with its famous dread inscription, beginning *Per me si va nella città dolente*:

> Through me one goes into the woeful city; through me one goes into eternal woe; through me one goes among the lost souls. Justice moved my high maker; the divine power made me, the supreme wisdom, and the primal love. Before me were no things created save things eternal, and I last eternally. All hope abandon, ye who enter here.

Passing through the gate, they traverse, on the same level, a region peopled with the despicable spirits of those who were neither good nor bad, and reach the shore of the Acheron, where they watch Charon, the demonic ferryman, as he transports a load of wailing spirits to their doom. At the beginning of Canto IV, Virgil and Dante find themselves across the river, on the brink of the profound, dark, and stormy abyss of Hell, from which there rises to them "a thunder of infinite lamentation."

Dante imagines Hell as an immense conical cavity, its axis running from a point directly below Jerusalem to the center of the earth. The sides of the cavity are not smooth, but are broken by seven terraces on which, and in the frozen lake that forms the bottom of the abyss, the woeful spirits find eternal lodgment. One of the terraces is divided by a great circular wall into two concentric rings. There are, then, in the entire abyss, nine separate "circles."

The first circle, Limbus, is quite different from those that lie below. The spirits assigned to it were not sinful: if Christians, they lacked baptism; if pagans, they "did not duly worship God." They suffer only in that they cannot attain the Heaven they long for — in that, without hope, they live in desire.

Hell proper, the Hell of punishment, beginning with the second circle, extends to the base of the abyss. It is divided into two parts: the Upper Hell; and the Lower Hell, or "City of Dis." Each part consists of four circles, all on different levels, except that the two middle circles, the fifth and sixth, are on the same level, and separated by a great wall. The sins punished in the Upper Hell are those of incontinence — sins that result from lack of control in yielding to impulses derived from dispositions that in themselves are good rather than evil. Those punished in the Lower Hell are sins of evil disposition. These are of three classes: Heresy, punished in the sixth circle; Violence, punished in the seventh circle, and Fraud, punished in the eighth and ninth circles. Fraud, in turn, is divided into Deceit, which violates merely the general "bond of love that nature makes," and Treachery, which violates also some special human bond, such as that of kinship.

In the Upper Hell the several circles have no concentric subdivisions, nor has the circle of Heresy; but the circle of Violence is divided into three concentric rings, the circle of Deceit — called Malebolge, "the evil pouches" — into ten, and the circle of Treachery into four.

In every circle, and in every ring of each divided circle, Dante beholds hordes of spirits. Typically, though not in all cases, several spirits are named by Virgil, or are recognized by Dante himself; and in almost every region Dante converses with one or more of them. The spirits with whom he does converse are presented in an amazing variety of ways, with an extraordinary vividness not only of outer visualization but also of inner psychological revelation. They tell, in general, of the most significant or the most moving of their experiences on earth, even though, as Francesca da Rimini, prefacing the climax of her own tragic story, says to Dante,

> Nessun maggior dolore
> che ricordarsi del tempo felice
> nella miseria —

There is no greater grief than to remember,
in suffering, one's time of happiness —

and they stand out in a reality that no other dramatist — for in this essential aspect of his work Dante is truly a dramatist — has ever surpassed.

Moreover, by one of the greatest of all his great intuitions, Dante chooses as his representative suffering spirits, in many cases, persons whom he regarded as worthy of esteem and of affection, persons for whom his readers also would naturally have, or would by the poem itself be stimulated to have, a like regard. In many of the conversations little or nothing is said as to the spirit's fatal sin, and much is said that brings out the spirit's nobility. By this procedure Dante lifts the *Inferno* to a poetic level it could not otherwise have attained, avoiding what might otherwise have been a terrible monòtony of unworthiness, providing passages of relief from hellish sights and sounds, and at the same time emphasizing most powerfully the essential doctrine that the eternal fate of the soul depends upon its being or not being in harmony with God at the moment of death. These were noble spirits, yet their nobility could not save them from eternal damnation. Such, to take only the supreme instances, are Paolo and Francesca, Farinata degli Uberti, Piero della Vigna, Brunetto Latini, Ulysses, and Ugolino. Ulysses, speaking from within his tongue of fire, tells thus of his last voyage:

> When I departed from Circe . . . neither fondness for my son, nor piety for my old father, nor the due love which should have made Penelope glad, could overcome within me the ardor which I had to become experienced of the world, and of the vices of men, and of their virtue. But I put forth on the deep, open sea, with one vessel only, and with that little company by which I had not been deserted. . . I and my companions were old and slow when we came to that narrow strait where Hercules set up his bounds, to the end that man should not put out beyond. . . "O brothers," I said, "who through a hundred thousand perils have reached the West, to this so brief vigil of your senses which remains wish not to deny the experience, following the sun, of the world that has no people. Consider your origin; ye were not made to live as brutes, but to pursue virtue and knowledge." . . . And turning our stern to the morning, with our oars we made wings for the mad flight . . . The light beneath the moon had been five times rekindled and as many quenched, since we had entered on the passage of the deep, when there appeared to us a mountain dark in the distance, and it seemed to me so high as I had never seen one. We rejoiced, and soon it turned to lamentation, for from the new land a whirlwind rose and struck the fore part of the vessel. Three times it made her whirl with all the waters, the fourth it made her stern lift up and the prow go down, as pleased Another, till the sea had closed over us.*

The infernal landscape is visualized with the utmost clarity: the livid Acheron; the fuming marsh of Wrath; the fiery battlements of the City of Dis, and the field of burning tombs within; the writhing trees of the grove of

* Norton's translation.

suicides; the iron plain of Malebolge, with its deep corrugations and its jagged transverse ridges; the perforated valley of the Simonists; the barrators' stream of seething pitch; the silent frozen lake of Treachery.

The grim landscape echoes with reality of sound. As the cantos pass we hear — amid the wailing of the damned and the snarling of the demonic guardians — the howling of beasts; the whirlwind's roar; the rushing forest chase; the plunging cataract; the horn of Nimrod; and the unequaled alternation of succeeding cries and silences that space the narrative of Ugolino.

From the central ice Virgil and Dante make their toilsome way up the course of a spirally winding little stream, through the mass of the hemisphere opposite that containing Hell, until at last they come forth — as we are told in the last line of the *Inferno* — *a riveder le stelle*, "to behold the stars again."

By a mighty act of poetic genius Dante created for his Purgatory an immensely high mountain — the mountain beheld by Ulysses — soaring in isolation from the surrounding seas at the antipodes of Jerusalem. Thus his Purgatory leads from earth to heaven; and it presents an utter contrast to his subterranean Hell: here are the peaceful open air and the light of sun and stars, instead of the dark and stormy abyss. Here, too, are songs instead of cries of woe: for the spirits of Purgatory, though they suffer, are nevertheless "content in fire, because they hope, in good time, to reach the company of the blessed." Suffer they must: for though they are beyond sinning they still retain something of the old disposition to sin, and that disposition must be purged away before they are qualified to enter Heaven.

Moreover, by a similar creative act, Dante calls into being, and locates on the lower slopes of his mountain, a region not previously known to poetry or to eschatology: Antepurgatory, wherein the spirits of those who, though in harmony with God at the moment of death, had died under excommunication, or had through negligence postponed repentance until the last moment, must wait for a considerable length of time before they are admitted to Purgatory proper, which occupies the upper slopes of the mountain. This means not only that Dante on his own authority introduces into the procedure of salvation an element that is in accordance with his own acute sense of justice, but also that the first nine cantos of the *Purgatorio* are completely free from any scene of suffering. Had Dante not achieved this imagination, had the second canticle been devoted, from the start, to the report of Purgatorial suffering — bitter enough, though so much slighter than the suffering of Hell — the result would have been monotony and anticlimax. As it is, the reader finds in the opening cantos a welcome and a novel episode of rest and of relief.

The mountain has a third division also, for its level summit is the Earthly Paradise.

It is on the shore of the mountain that Virgil and Dante emerge at the end of their upward journey from the center of the earth. Virgil is still the guide; but Purgatory is new country to him, and he himself, from this time on, needs direction. Such direction is given first by Cato, chosen because of his utter devotion to liberty to be the guardian of the mountain where souls are to be set free. Presently, over the morning sea, come spirits, ferried from the mouth of the Tiber, by a luminous angel, to the place of their liberation:

> and lo! . . . a light along the sea coming so swiftly that no flight equals its motion. . . . Then on each side of it appeared to me a something, I knew not what, white, and beneath, little by little, another came forth from it. My Master still said not a word, until the first white things appeared as wings; then, when he clearly recognized the pilot, he cried out: "Mind, mind thou bend thy knees: Lo! the Angel of God: fold thy hands: henceforth shalt thou see such officials. See how he scorns human instruments, so that he wills not oar, or other sail than his own wings, between such distant shores." . . . Then, as the Bird Divine came more and more toward us, the brighter he appeared; so that my eye endured him not near by, but I bent it down: and he came on to the shore with a little vessel, swift and light . . . At the stern stood the Celestial Pilot, such that he seemed inscribed among the blest; and more than a hundred spirits sat within. "*In exitu Israel de Egypto*" they were all singing together with one voice, with whatso of that psalm is after written. Then he made them the sign of the Holy Cross; whereon they all threw themselves upon the strand; and he went away as he had come.*

As Virgil and Dante move onward and upward they find, here and there, groups of spirits, with some of whom they converse. But there are no such hordes of spirits here as in the Hell, and most of those seen here are of Dante's own time. They tell their stories, some in several tercets, some with an intense compact brevity. Not all these spirits were persons of goodly life. Manfred says of himself: "Horrible were my sins." This is the reverse of the device whereby men of noble life appear among the denizens of Hell, and serves to point again the critical necessity of being in harmony with God at the moment of death.

Within Antepurgatory the Valley of the Princes is an especially lovely place. Here are gathered, peaceably, an emperor, several kings, and a marquis, men whose postponement of repentance was due to their immersion in the cares of state. They are identified by Sordello, serving here as a special guide, who deals with them, from the greatest to the least, in the same pattern in which the living Sordello, in his lament for the death of Blacatz, had dealt with the princes of his own time.

Dante finds the climbing hard; but he is given new strength by Virgil's assurance that he shall see Beatrice, smiling and happy, at the mountain's summit.

* Norton's translation.

Evening comes:

> It was now the hour when the desire of those at sea turns homeward, and their hearts grow tender, on a day when they to their dear friends have said farewell; and when the pilgrim, newly entered on his journey, is pierced with love, if he hears in the distance the sound of bells that seem to mourn the dying day.

In the night Dante is carried far up the side of the mountain, in his sleep, by St. Lucy. He wakes, at daybreak, before the massive gate of Purgatory, guarded by a key-bearing angelic warder, vicar for St. Peter. Entering by the gate into Purgatory proper, the travelers climb at once to the first of the seven Purgatorial terraces — terraces high in the open air, and of less and less radius as one ascends. The seven dispositions that are purged away correspond to the seven deadly sins: the several terraces differ from each other, in respect to the kinds of suffering they bear, as thoroughly as the terraces of Hell had differed from each other. At one moment the whole mountain trembles, as in an earthquake, and at that same moment all the spirits of the whole mountain break together into an exultant cry, *Gloria in excelsis Deo*: for the trembling means that some spirit, its purgation complete at last, is now free to take its upward way. The spirit thus released in this instance is Statius, who, joining Virgil and Dante, serves them as guide until they reach the Earthly Paradise. Among the spirits with whom Dante talks on the terraces are his friend Forese Donati, and two poets to whom Dante gladly pays his debts of gratitude: Guido Guinizelli and Arnaut Daniel.

Philosophic discussions of a high seriousness constitute a new element in the *Purgatorio*. Among them are a discussion of the relation between papacy and empire — a condensed poetic equivalent of the *Monarchia* — and discussions of the difference between temporal and spiritual possessions, of instinctive and elective desires, and of the relation between the body and the soul.

When the pilgrims reach the broad and level summit of the mountain Virgil has come to the end of his range of knowledge and of his task as guide; and in his final words he bids Dante move, from this time on, as his own master:

> Expect no further word or sign from me. For your own will is now made free, upright, and whole: whate'er it bids you, you may rightly do. Wherefore I crown and mitre you as ruler over yourself.

The summit is an Earthly Paradise indeed: a most beautiful forest, musical with bird-song, traversed by the clearest and sweetest of streams. Through the forest there advances slowly a luminous symbolic pageant, its elements representing, in various ways, Christ, the Holy Spirit, the Prophets, the Sacred Writers, and the Virtues — the very ministers of blessedness enumerated in the last chapter of the *Monarchia*. Central in the pageant is a triumphal chariot, empty at first: but in it presently, after the procession has come to a halt, and within a cloud of flowers cast about her by the persons of the pageant, Beatrice appears. She is veiled with a white veil; but Dante's recognition is immediate:

> And my spirit . . . through a hidden virtue that emanated from her, felt the great potency of olden love.

Then the drama turns in a way unforeseen. For Dante, in justice, cannot feign that her first words to him hold greeting: they hold instead a reproof for his faithlessness, a reproof unspeakably bitter to him, though it is moved by a holy love. Only after probing indictment and after his full confession is she ready to grant him welcome. Then she lifts her veil; and restores to him, in the midst of Eden, the salutation she had denied to him so long before.

Virgil has disappeared: Philosophy, symbolized in him, had brought Dante to the attainment of the Temporal Blessedness, symbolized by the Earthly Paradise. Now Beatrice, symbolizing Revelation, and fulfilling thus the divine commission Dante had in his youthful imagining ascribed to her, is to guide him to the Empyrean, wherein the Eternal Blessedness is made manifest.

The *Paradiso* opens with a majestic and boldly assertive statement of its theme:

> The glory of Him who moves everything penetrates through the universe, and is resplendent in one part more and in another less. In the heaven which receives most of His light I have been, and have seen things which he who descends from thereabove neither knows how nor has power to recount; because, drawing near to its own desire, our intellect enters so deep, that the memory cannot follow after. Truly whatever of the Holy Realm I could treasure up in my mind shall now be the theme of my song.*

The account of the contents of the *Paradiso* contained in the last paragraph of the letter to Can Grande is as follows:

> There will be a process of ascent from heaven to heaven; there will be a bringing of tidings as to the spirits of the blessed found in the several heavens; and it will be shown that true blessedness consists in the contemplation of the very source of truth . . . Wherefore, to reveal the glory of the blessedness of these spirits, many things will be asked of them . . . which afford great value and delight. And since when one is come unto the source and origin of life, namely God, there is nothing more to be sought, since He is Alpha and Omega, that is, the beginning and the end . . . the treatise ends in God Himself, *qui est benedictus in secula seculorum.*

As he undertook the designing of the *Paradiso*, Dante had to face two major problems. The spirits of the redeemed are all blest to the fullness of

* Norton's translation. The words "most" and "I have been, and have seen" are to be read as emphatic.

their capacity to receive blessedness: how then could he treat them with group variations comparable to those of the two preceding canticles? All these spirits have their abode in the Empyrean, in the immediate presence of God: how then could they be presented in a gradual series of regions? For these questions, taken in combination, Dante found a magnificent solution. All the spirits are blest to the fullness of their capacity to receive blessedness: but their capacities vary, by predestination, both in quantity and in quality. And while they have their eternal abode in the Empyrean, it is vouchsafed to Dante that they should appear to him, in the several heavens, in groups corresponding to their variations in capacity for blessedness.

Dante's astronomical lore now comes into full play. There are, for him as for Ptolemy, nine spatial revolving heavens, each a spherical shell within the heaven of next greater radius, from the Heaven of the Moon, nearest the Earth, to the outermost *Primum mobile*. Each of the first seven heavens carries one of seven heavenly bodies: the Moon, Mercury, Venus, the Sun, Mars, Jupiter, and Saturn. The eighth heaven carries the constellations; the ninth is clear space.

The visual medium of the *Paradiso* is pure light. As Beatrice and Dante rise from heaven to heaven they enter the permeable and lucent substance of the several planets, and against the glowing background spirits appear as individual lights. Even portraiture is sacrificed: facial lineaments, still faintly seen in the two lowest heavens, are thereafter hidden in radiance. In the handling of his images of light on light Dante displays an extraordinary resourcefulness. The background lighting varies at times in color — it may be ruddy, or silver, or golden — and the individual lights, often in motion, vary in intensity and in dimension. Impressions of sound are often given simultaneously with impressions of light. In the upper planetary heavens the spirits group themselves in patterns of light. In the Sun spirits of the wise gather and move in circles; in Mars soldiers of Christ appear in the semblance of a great cross:

> As the mysterious Milky Way shines in the skies with its lesser and its greater lights, so within the star the radiances grouped themselves in constellation, forming the venerable sign of the cross. And here my memory overwhelms my speech, for that cross flashed forth Christ, so that I can find no worthy expression for it. But he who takes up his own cross and follows Christ will yet forgive me for this silence, when for himself he shall behold Christ gleaming thus. From arm to arm of the great cross, and from head to foot, lights were moving, brightly scintillating as they met together and in their passing, putting me in mind of a beam of sunshine in a dark room on earth, and of the motes that gleam as they move through it. And as a viol or harp, strung in accord of many strings, may render an impression of sweet harmony to one who does not yet make out the melody, thus, from the lights which appeared to me there, a melody was gathered through the cross which filled me with love ere I could understand the words.

In Jupiter spirits of the just appear first in a series of letters and finally in the form of an imperial eagle; in Saturn contemplative spirits move up and down a ladder of golden light. In the Heaven of the Constellations the whole host of the redeemed is assembled in the form of a triumphal procession.

Dante's first conversation in the *Paradiso* is with Piccarda Donati, sister of his friend Forese. Piccarda, reft, in life, from the cloistered peace she had sought, speaks of the peace of Heaven:

> And in His will is our peace: it [His will] is that sea to which there moves all that it creates and that nature molds.

Some of the most memorable of the later conversations are those with the Emperor Justinian, who gives a swift summary of the course of Roman history; with St. Thomas, who in a full canto tells of the life of St. Francis; and with Cacciaguida, Dante's own crusader ancestor, who prophesies his exile.

There are many discussions in the *Paradiso* on various themes, some astronomical, most of them theological. Some, but not all, by any means, have faded, now, into a scholastic dimness. The finest is the superb paean of Canto VII on the Redemption.

Leaving the world of space, Beatrice and Dante enter the Empyrean, the realm of pure spirit, pervaded by supreme light, love, and joy:

> Light of the mind, filled with love; love of the True Good, filled with joy; joy that transcends all sweetness.

Blinded at first by the intensity of the light, and seeing next a lovely foreshadowing of what he is presently to behold, Dante is then enabled to achieve a complete vision of the hosts of Heaven. The spirits of the blessed appear to him as seated in a vast amphitheater, which is likened to a white rose. All are looking upward toward the Source of all light, to which Dante still cannot lift his eyes. Between that Source and the spirits of the blessed, angels, ascending and descending, mediate understanding, peace, and love. Dante, as he gazes, stands in the great circle of light that forms the arena of the amphitheater, the golden center of the rose. Beatrice makes clear to him the general form of the amphitheater; but then, as his ever-questioning mind turns again to her, he finds by his side not Beatrice, but St. Bernard, who, symbolizing Contemplation, is to guide the final upward effort of his eyes. To Beatrice, returned to her own place in the rose, Dante tenders his utter thankfulness: she, far away though she seems, looks at him and smiles — then turns again to the Source of light.

After pointing out to Dante some of the loftiest persons of the amphitheater, St. Bernard offers a prayer to the Virgin, asking her to enable Dante to lift his eyes even to the Eternal Light. Then Dante looks upward to the intensely radiant Point that symbolizes the Divine Presence. But achievement demands more than an upward look; for penetration of the intense descending radiance can be but the gradual gain of resolute will. Steadily he holds to the great endeavor, straining upward and upward, until at last his sight attains the very Point itself, attains a supreme consciousness of power, wisdom, love. Keenly intellectual still, he gazes, wondering at the twofold nature, human and divine, of the God-radiance, until there comes a flash of ultimate revelation in which all wonder is satisfied.

The whole poem, cathedral-like in its inexhaustible variety, is cathedral-like also in its architectonic unity — a unity based in its grand but never rigid symmetry and in the linking progress of the protagonist from the dread forest to the Empyrean. The sense of unity is reënforced in many ways: by anticipatory indications of experiences yet to come; by reminiscences of experiences that have already been narrated; by contrasting parallelisms between passages in successive canticles, as for instance between Charon's ferrying over the Acheron and the Angel's ferrying over the seas to the Mountain of Purgatory; and by summaries, or surveys, of past experiences, or of space traversed. From the Constellation of the Twins Dante surveys heaven and earth alike:

> With my sight I returned through all and each of the several spheres, and saw this globe such that I smiled at its mean semblance. . . . I saw the Moon enkindled without shadow. The aspect of the Sun I here endured, and I saw how Mercury and Venus move around and near him. Then appeared to me the temperateness of Jove, between Saturn and Mars, and then was clear to me the varying which they make in their position. And all the seven were displayed to me — how great they are and how swift they are, and how far apart they are in their abodes. While I was revolving with the eternal Twins, the little threshing-floor we grow so fierce about appeared to me, from its hills to its river-mouths.

Dante possesses in supreme degree the power of finality of phrase — the power, that is, by which the glowing concept so magnetizes, so draws to itself just the true words, and so assembles them within the rhythm, that they ring perfectly in memory. The *Divine Comedy* is full of such lines and groups of lines, a storehouse of quotations that have served for the enrichment of later literature and later life.

The influence of Dante has been very great indeed, especially, of course, in poetry, but also in critical and religious thought, and in the fine arts — as in the drawings of Botticelli and of William Blake — and music; and especially, of course, among his own countrymen, who can hardly escape the memory of his deeply graven lines, but also in other lands. His influence has never led to any significant imitation of the *Divine Comedy* as a whole, but it has led to an extraordinary number of translations, in verse and prose, in many languages, and to the writing of voluminous commentaries and of numberless interpretative books and essays. It has manifested itself most constantly and most fruitfully in the echoing or the adaptation of certain passages; in the development of themes that Dante states with luring brevity; in the re-creation of characters so vital that again and again they claim new birth; in the use of the *terza rima*; and most of all in ways still subtler and more intimate — in the deep stirring of the poetic impulse, and in the ennoblement of the poetic ideal and the poetic art.

Thus, in England, Chaucer's Monk retells the story of Ugolino, and the prayer of St. Bernard reappears as the *Invocacio ad Mariam* of the Second Nun's Tale; Milton makes frequent use of Dantean material both in his prose and in his verse; Gray's *Elegy* stems from the vesper passage in the *Purgatorio*; Shelley, who knew and understood Dante more completely than any other English poet, draws extensively from him, especially in the *Prometheus Unbound*, the *Epipsychidion*, and the *Triumph of Life*; and Tennyson's Ulysses learns from Dante's heroic voyager

> To follow knowledge like a sinking star,
> Beyond the utmost bounds of human thought.

The profound and timeless gratitude of generations on generations of poets and of other readers is most perfectly voiced, perhaps, in the two sonnets prefixed by Longfellow to his translation of the *Divine Comedy*. One of them ends thus:

> Ah! from what agonies of heart and brain,
> What exultations trampling on despair,
> What tenderness, what tears, what hate of wrong,
> What passionate outcry of a soul in pain,
> Uprose this poem of the earth and air,
> This mediaeval miracle of song!

But the *Comedy* is much more than a medieval miracle. The other sonnet, in which the *Comedy* is represented as a cathedral, ends with these still nobler lines:

> So, as I enter here from day to day,
> And leave my burden at this minster gate,
> Kneeling in prayer, and not ashamed to pray,
> The tumult of the time disconsolate
> To inarticulate murmurs dies away,
> While the eternal ages watch and wait.

CHAPTER 9

Contemporaries of Dante

THE POWERFUL LYRIC personalities of Cavalcanti and Dante made a decisive impression upon lesser lyrists, contemporary or junior, of the Florentine area. These lesser men, accordingly, though never reaching heights or profundities, celebrate ladies of angelic beauty and beneficence, seek salutation, cherish inner images, suffer grievously when favor is withheld, people their verses with *spiriti*, present Love, Heart, Soul, and Poem in dramatic converse, and borrow many ideas and many phrases from their masters.

The best known of these men and the closest in friendship to Dante was Cino da Pistoia. He was only secondarily a poet: like so many of his predecessors he was by profession a jurist. He was born between 1265 and 1270, and died in 1336 or 1337. Dante and Petrarch both thought well of him: Dante, in the *De vulgari eloquentia*, designated him as the Italian poet of love. His verse, however, is, in the main, imitative and pallid. His poetic heart beats rather faintly, and with a repetitive plaintiveness. He is at his best in poems of absence; in a few sonnets in which, for the moment, he is free of the conventions; and in a very few other poems that are in some way distinctive — one of them a sonnet on the mountain grave of his lady, Selvaggia. He sent a long consolatory *canzone* to Dante after the death of Beatrice, and composed a *canzone* on the death of Henry VII. His chief poetic service lies in the fact that his verse contains a good many minor motifs which Petrarch was to remember and renew, giving them much more grace and much more life than they had originally possessed.

Somewhat more gifted than Cino are the Florentines Lapo Gianni and Gianni Alfani. Lapo, of whom Dante speaks with praise in the *De vulgari eloquentia*, is the more facile and the more cheerful: his verse is lighthearted even when his heart is formally distressed. Gianni Alfani, writing half of his half-dozen poems from exile, is more personal and more thoughtful, and weaves the texture of his phrasing somewhat more firmly. Both men write chiefly in the *ballata* form.*

* * *

Antipodally different, and endowed with a far larger fund of poetic energy, was the Sienese scapegrace Cecco Angiolieri (c. 1260–c. 1313), the first master (though not the initiator) of Italian humorous and realistic verse. Cecco seeks his excitements among the common venalities; but there is nothing common in the vividness with which he drafts his little dramas of sight and sound, of desire and folly and mischance. One is transported instantly into the plebeian midst of the life of old Siena, and one is led to know with perfect certainty that that life was as real as our own.

Cecco's verse has distressing accents: pennilessness tinges all his experiences with frustration; he attributes that pennilessness to the unrelenting avarice of his parents, and turns upon them with invectives of parricidal hatred; and the sum of all his failures and antipathies vents itself in all-inclusive imprecation:

> If I were fire, I'd burn the world away;
> If I were wind, I'd turn my storms thereon;
> If I were water, I'd soon let it drown;
> If I were God, I'd sink it from the day.†

Yet he obviously enjoyed the brilliance of his own hyperboles, and even the sonnets that voice bitterness or melancholy ring with an exultant consciousness of pungent rhythmic wit. Love is for him "a thorn without a rose."

Folgore da San Gemignano (*fl.* 1305–1316), a genial minstrel, preserved in verse something of the entertainment he was purveying to the gay companies for which he sang. For one such Sienese company he wrote a delightful series of sonnets for the several months: in each sonnet he offers his

* Cavalcanti, Dante, Cino, and the two Florentines just mentioned are traditionally treated — sometimes with the inclusion of other men — as members of a group or "school" whose style is called *il dolce stil nuovo*, "the sweet new style." The phrase comes from a passage in the *Purgatorio* in which Dante is contrasting such poems as his own *Donne ch'avete intelletto d'amore* with the older Frederician and Guittonian poetry. Scholars have tried strenuously to determine just what Dante meant, and just what body of poetry he had in mind; but their conclusions are widely divergent. The truth is that one cannot be sure what Dante meant, or just what poetry he was thinking of. It would seem better, therefore, to drop the conventional categorical terminology, especially since it tends to demote the highly individual and influential Cavalcanti to the status of a mere member of a group, and to minimize somewhat even the distinctiveness of Dante. Cavalcanti and Dante are far above the need of any inclusive appellation: the lesser men may with entire justice and adequacy be classed as "followers of Cavalcanti and of Dante."

† Rossetti's translation.

listeners pleasures appropriate for the month concerned. The first six begin thus:

For January I give you vests of skins,
And mighty fires in hall, and torches lit.

In February I give you gallant sport
Of harts and hinds and great wild boars . . .

In March I give you plenteous fisheries
Of lamprey and of salmon, eel and trout.

I give you meadow-lands in April, fair
With over-growth of beautiful green grass.

I give you horses for your games in May,
And all of them well-train'd unto the course.

In June I give you a close-wooded fell,
With crowns of thicket coil'd about its head.*

He wrote also a similar series of sonnets for the days of the week, and a few less professional poems, among them some vigorous satiric outcries of Guelf distress.

Of the several lengthy didactic poems written in Tuscany in Dante's time the most notable are the anonymous *Intelligenza*, which celebrates a beautiful and majestic lady who symbolizes intelligence; the anonymous *Fiore*, a clever freely modified summary, in a sequence of sonnets, of the *Roman de la rose*; and two poems by the Florentine Francesco da Barberino (1264–1348). One of these is a heavily allegorical work called *Documenta amoris*, "The Teachings of Love." The other, entitled *Del reggimento e costumi di donna*, "On the Conduct and Manners of Women," treats the whole course of feminine life, from girlhood, through marriage, motherhood, and widowhood, to old age; gives special rules for the conduct of lay sisters, nuns, hermits, servants, nurses, slaves, barbers, bakers, fruiterers, weavers, millers, poulterers, beggars, shopkeepers, church attendants, and tavern-keepers; lists some fifty epigrammatic rules of conduct; and discusses such matters as pre-natal care, the preservation of beauty, tribulation and consolation, love problems, conversational challenges and replies, riddles, and prayer.

Among the many shorter didactic poems of the time is a *canzone* on poverty, more sensible than inspired, that is attributed to Giotto.

* * *

Within this period unknown minstrels, some in Venetia and some in Tuscany, were engaged in forms of poetic activity which were to have great influence upon the development of the later Italian epic. Into Venetia they

* Rossetti's translation.

were bringing the Carolingian *chansons de geste*, holding to the French metrical form (assonant stanzas of irregular length), and holding more or less faithfully to the substance of the French stories and to the French language. Their retention of an ostensibly French language was doubtless due largely to a desire to impress listeners with the authenticity of their narratives; but they inevitably Italianized their French enough to make it locally intelligible. Their activity led presently to the composition of new epics, dealing with the traditional French themes, and written in a curious hybrid Franco-Venetian language. The earliest extant specimens of this kind of epic production are a poem entitled *Entrée d' Espagne*, by an anonymous Paduan author, and an anonymous cyclic collection of poems, known now as *La geste francor*. The authors were perhaps minstrels of a superior kind, perhaps amateurs: in any case they wrote with a view to minstrel use of their compositions. In content, they modified and enlarged their French material very freely, and gave to the Italian epic certain features it was destined to retain. Thus Roland is said to be of Italian birth; all traitors are grouped as members of the single house of Maganza; the main narrative is interrupted now and again by romantic episodes of adventure; and love, though not yet a major element, plays a larger part than it does in the French models. In the *Entrée d' Espagne* Charlemagne undertakes to conquer Spain; in the resulting conflict below the Pyrenees eleven of the twelve peers of France are conquered by the giant Ferragu, whom Roland then slays at the end of a terrific but courteous three-day duel; later events lead to a breach between Roland and Charlemagne; Roland makes his way to the Orient, where, among many adventures, he saves a charming princess, Dionés, from an objectionable fiancé, and becomes bailiff of Persia; and finally, bringing with him the young Persian prince Sanson, he returns to Aude and to Charlemagne. The Franco-Venetian writers made use also, though to a much smaller extent, of the French romances in verse.

In Tuscany, meanwhile, the romances in verse were being naturalized by other minstrels, who, dismissing both the French language and the French metrical form, recast their material in Tuscan, and in a metrical form, new to narrative poetry, which was to become the standard form of the later Italian epic. The unit of this new form is an octave composed of eleven-syllable lines, the first six lines rhyming alternately, the last two having a new rhyme of their own: the rhyme-scheme is thus ABABABCC. It is possible that this octave was devised by some minstrel or minstrels; but it seems more probable that the first minstrel or minstrels to make use of it simply took over, for narrative use, the Tuscan form of the *strambotto*.* Their

* See pp. 9–10. This is a minority opinion. The existence of the Tuscan *strambotto* in this period is not documented: but lack of documentation does not prove non-existence in the case of an early folk form.

poems, called *cantari*, are of less than epic length. The two earliest, apparently, of those that are still extant are the *Febusso e Breusso*, derived from the French *Palamède*, and the *Cantare di Florio e Biancifiore*, derived from the French *Floire et Blanchefleur*. The *cantari* proved to be extremely popular: production continued for two hundred years. Some themes are Arthurian, some are Carolingian, some are derived from French *lais*, some are classic, some are religious, and some are taken from folk stories. Adventures and escapes, enchantments and miracles, held the simple listening audiences spellbound.

Both epics and *cantari* were sung, not recited, by the minstrels, who used simple stringed instruments for accompaniment. Poems that were too long to be sung in a single session were sung in a series of sessions.

* * *

Production in prose was at this time voluminous and varied. It included much translation and compilation from the Latin and from the French, and much original writing. The most elaborate of the Italian Arthurian prose romances, the *Tavola ritonda*, appears to be of this period, at least in substance. It is a combination of many Arthurian legends, drawn, freely modified, from the prose *Tristan* and from several other French sources, with the introduction of a good many newly invented episodes.

In the field of history the most notable work of the period was the chronicle of the Florentine merchant Giovanni Villani (c. 1270–1348). In 1300, the Holy Year, he went as a pilgrim to Rome, and there the historical spirit was stirred within him:

> Finding myself on that blessed pilgrimage in the holy city of Rome, beholding the great and ancient things that are therein, reading of the great deeds of the Romans, and considering that our city of Florence, the daughter and creation of Rome, was ascending to greatness while Rome was declining, it seemed fitting to me to bring together in this chronicle all the beginnings of the city of Florence, and then to set forth in detail the doings of the Florentines, and to make brief mention of the notable events of the world: and so in the year 1300, when I came back from Rome, I began this book.*

Villani's *Cronaca* is of vast extent. The first of its twelve Books gathers biblical, classical, and legendary material; the next six Books bring the history of Florence up to the time of his own manhood; the last five record contemporary events, many of which were known to him as eyewitness and participant. As far as he can he tells his story year by year, in the usual fashion of medieval chroniclers. Very fortunately, his interests as merchant and as

* The translation is slightly abbreviated. One is reminded of the experience that led Gibbon to write of *The Decline and Fall of the Roman Empire*.

active citizen — he held many public offices in Florence — led him to deal not only with warfare and factional strife, but also with political, economic, and social conditions and changes. For his own period he is enlightening, and generally trustworthy. His historical interests — largely as a result of his business connections and journeyings — range beyond Italy into Transalpine Europe and into the Orient. He seeks no philosophy of history; but it is noteworthy that he is the first historian to recognize that the barbarian invasions and the decline of the Roman Empire marked the beginning of a new era in Italy.

A much shorter work, the *Cronica delle cose occorrenti ne' tempi suoi* of Dino Compagni (c. 1255–1324), is a concentrated presentation of the causes, the main facts, and the consequences of the division of the Florentine Guelfs into the White and Black factions. Dino writes compactly, vigorously, and with a prevailing moral concern that breaks out now and again in passages of eloquent indictment. He sees and depicts men and events with a revealing clarity. His verdicts are confident and incisive.

* * *

Albertino Mussato (1261–1329), the most striking figure in the Paduan humanistic group, served his city-state loyally and well as a soldier and as ambassador to Pope Boniface and to Henry VII. His most famous work is the *Ecerinis*, the first humanistic Latin tragedy. Its subject is the career of an infamous mid-thirteenth-century tyrant, Ezzelino da Romano, and it is essentially an indictment of tyranny. Like the tragedies of Seneca, on which it was modeled, it proceeds rather by oratory than by action. It made an extraordinary impression in Padua; and its completion was celebrated, on December 3, 1315, in a spectacular civic ceremony. Courts, schools, shops, and offices were closed; Mussato was accompanied to the City Palace by city officials and by the University in a body; and there he was crowned with a wreath in which laurel, ivy, and myrtle were intertwined. In later years he wrote two long Latin histories: the *Historia augusta*, which deals with the life of Henry VII, and in particular with his Italian expedition; and a supplementary work that deals with the history of Italy in the years from 1313 to 1329.

Meanwhile, humanism was making its appearance elsewhere, especially in Bologna, where its chief early representative was Giovanni del Virgilio, who reproached Dante for writing in Italian, and in Tuscany, where its chief early representative was Geri d' Arezzo, whose writings, now almost wholly lost, consisted of letters — he made a collection of his own letters — and of satires. In Florence itself the humanistic spirit was beginning to stir in Dante's day — though the young tradition of writing in Italian was already too strong to be displaced. Dante's own enthusiasm for ancient Rome was as great as that of the humanists, and he was able to reply to Giovanni del Virgilio in Latin eclogues at least as good as those of the Bolognese professor: but humanism played only a minor part in Dante's consecrated thought.

CHAPTER 10

Petrarch

THE CONTINUED PRESENCE of the papal court in Avignon drew many Italians to the French city, and resulted in the development of mutual Franco-Italian cultural relations — the Italian influence increasing (thanks largely to Petrarch) as the decades passed.

The chief secular court in Italy, from about 1310 to 1343, was that of King Robert of Naples, who had literary velleities, and gave some encouragement to humanistic studies. He was also Count of Provence, and the ties between Naples and Provence were therefore close. The Emperor Charles IV came into Italy in the Winter of 1354–1355, to be crowned in Rome. His coming stirred once again the dwindling hopes of those who clung to the concept of the Empire as the basis of Italian peace and greatness; but his stay was brief and ignominious.

The career of Rienzi was the most exciting political phenomenon of the mid-century. His eloquent genius, fed on the lore of ancient Rome, fired him with the ambition to restore the glories of the Republic and the Empire. Leading the Roman people in 1347 in a successful uprising against the nobles, he made himself Tribune of Rome, dramatized his part with impressive classic forms and ceremonies, and presently summoned all the states of Italy to effect a union that should deliver the land from its divided and miserable plight and restore its ancient greatness. But the Empire and the Papacy, very naturally, opposed him; the possession of power bred in him the fatal passions of dictatorship; he lost and then regained dominance; and at last, in 1354, he was struck down on the steps of the Capitoline Palace.

The employment of *condottieri* and mercenary troops was becoming more and more extensive, and more and more deplorable in its consequences. Professional soldiers of fortune, commanding bodies of hired professional troops, were engaged by princes and by cities to do their fighting for them. These bands, having no native loyalty to their employers, were often loath to fight, ineffective, predatory, and treacherous; yet for nearly two hundred years they constituted almost the only type of forces used in the internecine warfare that ravaged many portions of the peninsula.

Florence suffered a severe financial crisis in the years 1339–1345: the Bardi and the Peruzzi, overconfident of their own power, had undertaken to finance the military expenses of both France and England, who were fighting each other. The crash came when King Edward III repudiated his debts. The Bardi and the Peruzzi both failed, and never regained importance in the banking world.

The Black Death swept over all Western Europe in 1348. The mortality, in that frightful year, was almost past belief. Three quarters of the population died in Siena and in Pisa; and the figures were similar for other cities. Boccaccio says that a hundred thousand persons died in Florence in four months. Petrarch says that on going out one found the streets filled with the dead and the dying, and that on return one found one's home a house of death.

Three famous towers now rose in Italy: Giotto's Campanile in Florence, beside the new Cathedral; the slender Mangia, soaring high above the City Palace of Siena; and the rebuilt Campanile of St. Mark's, near the great church in Venice.

For the Florentine Baptistery, which had entrances on the South, North, and East, three sets of monumental bronze doors were desired. The South doors were done in bas-relief, at this time, by Andrea Pisano.

Primacy in painting passed, for the time being, to Siena, and in particular to Simone Martini, who in his altarpieces displayed a fastidious grace and a fine decorative imagination, and in his frescoes delighted to show forth knightly pride, saintly legend, and celestial majesty. He painted not only in Siena, but also in Assisi and in Avignon.

The years from 1340 to the end of the century saw the rise, the full flowering, and the decline of a phase of secular musical composition known as the *Ars nova.* This movement was of French origin, but it developed in ways of its own in Italy. The first significant Italian composers known to us by name and by the preservation of their works wrote in these years. Their favorite forms — each corresponding to a current poetic form — were the madrigal, the *caccia*, and the *ballata*: the madrigal and the *caccia* as poetic forms will be mentioned below.

* * *

Petrarch's father, a Florentine notary and a friend of Dante, incurred, in 1302, the wrath of the Black rulers of Florence. He escaped from the city, and took refuge in Arezzo; and there, in 1304, his son Francesco was born. In 1312 the family — father, mother, Francesco, and a younger son, Gherardo

— moved to Avignon, where the father found employment. Francesco's first schooling was at Carpentras, where he studied with a Tuscan expatriate, Convenevole da Prato, who seems to have made a very deep and stimulating impression upon his pupil. Destined for his father's profession, Petrarch studied next at Montpellier and then at the University of Bologna; but he disliked the law, and gave it up in 1326, when, on his father's death, he returned to Avignon. There, presently, he became associated with members of the great Roman Colonna family; and in or about 1330 he received the tonsure, thus taking his place in the ecclesiastical profession, and entered the service of Cardinal Giovanni Colonna. As the years passed, and with the receipt of a few benefices, he became more and more independent — and after 1347 entirely independent — of this service. In the summer of 1337 he left Avignon for Vaucluse, a lovely valley, some fifteen miles east of Avignon, into which the River Sorgue springs suddenly forth from the base of a high cliff. With all his many later changes of residence, Vaucluse always remained for him, in fact or in anticipation or in memory, the dearest spot on earth. His changes of residence were indeed extraordinarily numerous. Within the twelve years from 1341 to 1353 he lived three times, for a year or more, in Parma, and three times, for a year or more, at Vaucluse. From 1353 on he lived in Italy: first in Milan, then in Padua, then in Venice, then in Padua again, then finally at Arquà, a village a dozen miles southwest of Padua, where he died in 1374.

He had become famous as scholar and as poet even in his youth, and with the increase of his fame princely patrons and cities sought his presence. He was in effect the guest of the Correggio in Parma, of the Visconti in Milan, of the Carrara in Padua, and of the Republic in Venice.

From each of his residences he was frequently absent on excursions, visits, or journeys, long or short, some voluntary, some official. "A pilgrim everywhere," he called himself:

> Nullaque iam tellus, nullus mihi permanet aër,
> Incola ceu nusquam, sic sum peregrinus ubique —
>
> No land, now, no air is constant for me;
> As I am nowhere a dweller, so am I a pilgrim everywhere.

The highest moment of his life was his coronation as poet in Rome, on April 8, 1341, an event which, more than any other single event, stands out as a beacon signifying that one cultural age was soon to pass and another had already begun. He had desired coronation ever since his early youth, and had done his best both to deserve and to obtain it. His desire, due in the first instance, perhaps, to the teaching of Convenevole, was certainly fed upon knowledge of the classic Capitoline contests, and was certainly strengthened by knowledge of the coronation of Mussato. Strangely enough, coronation came to him not in his maturity and after he had given ample proof of his poetic ability, but in his early manhood, and before he had produced any of his major works. He owed his triumph less to what he had already written than to his success in convincing members of the Colonna family and some other influential persons that he was in fact and in prospect a great Latin poet. On his way to Rome he went to Naples, there to be examined with regard to poetic theory and practice by King Robert, who pronounced him worthy to receive the laurel crown; then, with this royal sponsorship, he went on to the Imperial and Holy City. The scene of the coronation was the audience hall in the Senatorial Palace on the Capitoline. No such ceremony had been witnessed in Rome since the Capitoline contests had ended a thousand years before; and the hall was filled with a deeply moved throng. Trumpets sounded; Petrarch delivered an oration upon the nature of poetry; one of the two Roman Senators then in office placed the laurel wreath upon Petrarch's head, gave him a diploma of coronation, and declared him to be a Roman Citizen; the Populus Romanus ratified the proceedings by acclamation; and then the main persons of the scene, and doubtless many others, went together through the city and across the Tiber to St. Peter's, where Petrarch laid his wreath upon the altar.

Petrarch was a man of powerful and active mind, of strong personal desires, of generous enthusiasms, and of violent antipathies.

He was in the highest degree eager for knowledge. He mastered all the classic literature known in his day, storing more of it in his library and in his memory than any other man had ever done since classic times, and rescuing certain works of Cicero that had lain in virtual oblivion in Liége and in Verona; and he mastered as well the writings of St. Augustine and of other Church Fathers. He even undertook the study of Greek, but made no substantial progress: he cherished Greek manuscripts of Plato and of Homer, though he could not read them. His scholarship was persistent, precise, analytical, critical, and reflective. He got all the evidence he could possibly get on the many subjects in which he was interested; he sought exact meanings, and quoted *ipsissima verba;* he analyzed, mentally, the content of whatever he read; he compared variant accounts and opinions, and judged between them carefully and with assurance; and whatever he learned was woven safely into the texture of his thought. His greatest philological achievement was the construction and the transmission of a text of Livy much more complete and much better than any known in the Middle Ages.

He was sensitive to all forms of beauty, especially to beauty of voice and of instrument (he played the lute), and to beauty of word and phrase and rhythm. He loved natural beauty, both the larger beauty of lake and mountain and the more intimate and solitary beauty of Vaucluse and of the woods in which he was wont to wander, by day or by night. He owned a Madonna by Giotto; and Simone Martini painted for him a miniature portrait of Laura, and decorated for him the first page of his great Virgil.

He was imaginative: a sight, a sound, a happening was likely to suggest to him, swiftly, other sights, sounds, happenings, which took on thereby an ever-increasing richness of connotation and of similitude; visions came to him by riverside, in woodland, or in dream; his mind was astir not only with experiences remembered but with experiences conceived as possible; he was conscious of the reality of the life that had been lived long centuries ago, and of the life that posterity was still to live.

With all his busy acquisition, his mind was constantly and urgently creative. He was prolific in his writing, both in Latin and in Italian. He felt as actively as he thought, and he must give expression to what he felt. And because of the attendant qualities of his mind he must write with accuracy; and if he were writing verse he must, after the first outpouring, revise and revise until his lines attained both a faithful recording of his inner experience and a perfect metrical and verbal beauty.

Yet his mind had its limitations. He was not a profound thinker: he was innocent of metaphysics, and he never originated any memorable philosophic idea. In clarity of visualization he could not compare with Dante. Even in his conception of poetry he was handicapped by the medieval insistence on its allegorical significance.

He was a man of strong personal desires. His inner life, as he in his own analytical interpretation understood it, was a perpetual conflict of three desires: his love, his longing for fame, and his hope of salvation. His desire for fame, or for glory — he used the terms interchangeably — was of not less than extraordinary intensity. It was born within him, he says; and it dwelt with him to the end of his life. His longing for glory was self-centered, but it was not narrowly selfish: his self included much more than his physically bounded self, and the self that longed for glory was consciously the self of a vigorous and emergent culture. His love and his desire for glory were not in conflict with each other: they were indeed linked in his mind by the much-proclaimed identity of his lady's name and the name of the laurel. But they were both in conflict with his hope of salvation. If he was to be sure of salvation, was he not unutterably foolish to let himself be distracted by love for one human creature, by concern for a fame that might indeed survive him, but would soon be lost in the long reaches of eternity? Ought he not to abandon the world entirely and become a monk, as his beloved brother had done? This conflict he never solved: his love and his desire for glory might be sinful, but he could not bring himself to give them up. The religion that imposed this conflict upon him was clearly medieval: Dante, with his *beatitudo huius vitae*, was in this respect far more modern.

A fourth desire, never a source of conflict, and always richly satisfied, was his desire for friendship. His circle of friends, continental in its scope, including all sorts and conditions of men from princes of church and state to humble folk, was wider than that of any other man then living, wider, perhaps, than that of any man who had lived before his time. He must have had, for his friends, a very strong personal magnetism, in which his fame, his manifold distinction, the wealth of his conversation, his readiness to share whatever he had, and an unmistakably glowing affectionateness all had their part. Many of his poems are addressed to friends; and it is to the vast range of his friendship that we owe the vast series of his letters.

He was a man of generous enthusiasms: for antiquity, for poetry, for morality, for Italy, and for Rome. His classic learning was fired with enthusiasm not only for the qualities of classic literature, but also for the noble civilization that that literature revealed, a civilization far superior, in Petrarch's thought, to the fragmentary, ravaged, and fear-darkened life of his own time. His enthusiasm for poetry, most clearly and most formally expressed in his Coronation Oration, has as its most precious result the plenitude and the beauty of his own verse. While he was neither a philosopher nor a prophet, he was an enthusiastic moralist. In the ethical area Cicero and Seneca and Augustine were peaceably at one, and doctrinal problems were of slight account. Immorality — though Petrarch's own life was not quite blameless — was an offense to his sense of fineness and of dignity; and he could and did speak out with effective conviction, in verse and in prose, for truth and honor and justice and fidelity.

Italy he loved with a deep and abiding love — for the beauty of its landscape, for the excellences of its cities, for its heroes and its saints, for all its glorious past, and for its undying bequests to later life. One of the briefest of his Latin poems, composed at the crest of the Mont Genèvre Pass on his final return from France to Italy, reads, in a pale translation, thus:

All hail, thou land most holy, dear to God,
Land that art safe for the good, that the proud must fear,
Thou land more bounteous than all other realms,
Than all more fertile, and than all more fair,
Splendidly towering, girt with thy double sea,
Thou single venerable home of arms, of laws,
And of the Muses, rich in treasure and men!
Nature and art together wrought for thee,
And gave thee then as mistress to the world!
All absence past, eagerly I return
With thee to dwell henceforth. My weary life
Thou wilt refresh; and thou wilt grant to me
Enough of earth to shelter me in death.
Thee now from Mount Gebenna's leafy height
Rejoicing I behold, O Italy!
The clouds are left behind. A gentle breeze

Toucheth my brow, as though thy very air
Rose quietly in its flow to welcome me.
My fatherland I see, and greet in joy:
Hail, beauteous homeland, glory of the world!

Rome was the most hallowed place on earth to him. There antiquity had reached its full flowering; there God had willed that His Church should have its capital; there Emperors and Popes had held sway over all the world; and of Rome he himself, son of a Florentine exile, had, in the highest moment of his life, been made a citizen. It is no wonder that he was swept into the upsurgence of Rienzi, or that he suffered bitter disillusion when Rienzi's own fatal faults led to his fall.

Petrarch's main antipathies were for the corruption of the papal court, for France, for the use of mercenary troops, for the medical profession, and for Aristotelianism, especially for Averroistic Aristotelianism. These antipathies, most of which were strongest in his later years, involved him in controversies which showed him sometimes to advantage and sometimes to disadvantage (he did not take criticism or opposition well), and led him to the writing of vigorous invectives, in prose and in verse. His attacks on the corruption of the papal court are contained chiefly in a few stinging poems and in the *Epistolae sine nomine*. His hostility to France was due in large part to the French control of the papacy, and in large part to unfounded and blatant French scorn for Italy. The deplorable results of the employment of mercenary troops he had seen with his own eyes. Doctors, he thought, did more harm than good, and professed a knowledge they did not in fact possess: his hostility to them was enlarged to include the defense of poetry as against unappreciative and disparaging pseudo-science. Aristotelianism in general seemed to Petrarch to be perilously un-Christian; and Aristotelianism as developed by Averroes seemed to him to be nothing less than Satanic, and roused him to extremes of vituperation.

* * *

Most of the writings of Petrarch are in Latin. While he composed and revised and collected his Italian poems *con amore*, it seems never to have occurred to him that they could approach his Latin works in significance. He was in his own eyes a writer in Latin, using what was to him the true literary language of Italy, the language made illustrious by Virgil and Horace and Cicero and Seneca and so many other ancient writers; and it was upon his Latin writings that he based his hope of enduring fame. These writings include short poems, prose letters, an epic, a collection of biographies, orations, an analysis of his own inner life, historical and literary collectanea, eclogues, penitential psalms, moral and religious treatises, invectives, and a guidebook.

His earliest extant composition is a Latin elegy, written in his teens, on the death of his mother. Over the years he wrote a hundred or more short, or relatively short, Latin poems, nearly all of them in unrhymed hexameters. Among them, in addition to those already mentioned, are descriptions of Vaucluse and of his life there, letters urging successive popes to return from Avignon to Rome, an account of his coronation, a lament for King Robert, poems addressed to Virgil and to Horace, and poems on his love for Laura, on the preservation of the ruins of Rome, on one of his dogs, on the irresponsibility of a certain critic, on his house in Parma, and on the prerogatives of Italy. Their poetic quality is high: the best of them are worthy companions to the best of the Italian lyrics. The French critic Henry Cochin says that if they had been written in Italian they would be *une des merveilles de la littérature du monde.* In 1350 and thereafter Petrarch made a collection of these poems, known as the *Epistolae metricae*, including only those that he thought most significant.

Petrarch wrote an immense number of letters — more, perhaps, than anyone had ever written before him. The earliest appear to date from his university days; the latest of all, written a month before his death, ends with the words *Valete amici, valete epistole.* The number of his addressees is great beyond any precedent: a hundred and fifty are known to us by name. They include the Emperor Charles IV and his Empress, King Robert, Charles of Valois, members of the Visconti and of several other ruling families, doges of Genoa and of Venice, the people of Florence and the people of Rome, Rienzi, several chancellors, two popes, several cardinals, many bishops and archbishops, many members of religious orders, courtiers, scholars, teachers, poets, musicians, jurists, warriors, physicians, university friends, a courier, and a minstrel.

The letters vary greatly in character, in subject, and in importance. They include accounts of all sorts of personal experiences and problems; descriptions of Vaucluse and of his other homes; reminiscences; letters of invitation, thanks, excuse, congratulation, consolation, exhortation, reproof, and recommendation; praises of Italy and of certain Italian cities; characterizations; discussions of antiquity, poetry, authorship, style, scholarship, and the collecting of books; discussions of abstract subjects, such as fame, fortune, friendship, humility, and solitude, and of specific subjects, such as astrology, diet, dogs, dreams, earthquakes, gout, minstrels, pestilence, and servants; attacks on the various objects of his antipathies; treatises on education, government, and the military art; comments on the state of the world and on current events; pleas for peace between Genoa and Venice; and arguments for the return of the papacy to Rome. Of exceptional and very interesting character are a letter describing an ascent of Mont Ventoux, a letter to his brother Gherardo on the nature of poetry, a letter to Boccaccio containing a Latin translation of Boccaccio's story of the Patient Griselda; ten letters to Cicero, Seneca, and other ancient writers; and a long but unfinished autobiographical letter to Posterity.

They are, in general, of fine quality. The modern reader may grow weary of their lengthy moralizations, of their masses of classic instances, and of controversies that have long since lost their bitterness; but there is no mistaking their importance, even in their less appealing aspects, and most of them are still very much alive. Petrarch's descriptions of his journeys are vivid and entertaining, even exciting at times; his narrative, enlivened often with direct discourse, is fluent and effective; he draws memorable portraits; all that he has to say of poetry and of scholarship is significant; his treatments of humble themes take one into the homely realities of the life of his time; and his treatments of loftier themes, especially of political themes, are often eloquent. Some of the early letters still show traces of the *cursus;* but, under the influence of Cicero and Seneca, Petrarch rejected the *cursus*, and his rejection led presently to its general abandonment.

He kept copies of most of the letters he wrote; and about 1345 he decided to make a selective collection of them. The actual collection, begun soon thereafter, grew and grew. He planned originally to have it contain all the letters he cared to preserve; but eventually he decided to make two main collections, one of the letters of his youth and middle life, one of the letters of his old age. The first collection, finished soon after 1360, bears the title *Familiarum rerum liber*. The letters of the later collection are called the *Epistolae seniles*. A minor collection of letters dealing chiefly with the corruption of the papal court was made between 1350 and 1360: these are known, from the fact that no names of addressees are given, as the *Epistolae sine nomine*. In each case the making of the collection involved revision, sometimes very drastic revision, of the letters selected for inclusion. Each collection as a whole was, in the intention of Petrarch, a work of art.

The first two major works undertaken by Petrarch were the *De viris illustribus*, a collection of biographies, and the *Africa*, an epic. Both were begun in or about 1338; both were at various times carried toward completion; neither was ever completed. They were the two works on which, for the greater part of his life, Petrarch most definitely based his hope of enduring fame; but his own final attitude toward them seems to have been one of discouragement, and they have not been widely read in later centuries.

Petrarch thought of himself as being an historian as well as a poet. His interest in the past, however, lay rather in men than in events: he was a biographer rather than a general historian. The *De viris illustribus*, as originally planned, was to consist of a series of biographies beginning with that of Romulus and ending with that of Titus. Of these biographies he wrote twenty-four, the last being that of Julius Caesar, which is as long as all the others put together. Late in the course of his work on the collection he decided to enlarge it at the beginning and at the end, by prefixing lives — which he actually wrote — of twelve Biblical and mythological figures, from Adam to Hercules, and by adding lives — which he never wrote — of twelve more Romans, from Flaminius to Trajan. He drew his material largely from Livy, but from many other sources as well. He used his sources carefully, and with signs of truly critical discrimination.

The *Africa* deals with the career of Scipio Africanus. The best known portion of the poem is the episode of the love of Masinissa and Sophonisba — the first modern version of the Sophonisba story. Other notable passages are the dedication to King Robert; the lament of the dying Mago (this lament, on the vanity of human life, was the only part of the *Africa* released in Petrarch's lifetime); and several passages in the latter part of the poem that deal with the nature of poetry.

Petrarch's Coronation Oration is a remarkable composition, not only because of the circumstances of its delivery, but also in itself. Its three main parts discuss respectively the difficulty and ardor of the poetic task, the allegorical character of poetry, and the rewards of the poetic task. Its structure is that of a medieval sermon: but the text with which it opens and the many supporting quotations are drawn from classic sources.

In the years 1342 and 1343 a moral and religious crisis led Petrarch to the writing of the *Secretum*, which embodies a searching, even a relentless, self-analysis. It is cast in the form of a dialogue, the interlocutors being Augustine and Petrarch. Augustine, representing the religious ideal, reproaches Petrarch for his failure to live in accordance with that ideal; Petrarch struggles, unhappily but vigorously, in remonstrance and in self-defense. The two interlocutors represent, of course, two phases of Petrarch's own divided personality. The choice of St. Augustine as the religious challenger was natural: he was, among the Church Fathers, the one whom Petrarch knew best and admired most wholeheartedly; and he was the author of the *Confessions*, which served as precedent for the *Secretum.*

The theme of the first of the three Books is Petrarch's failure to attain spiritual happiness. In the second Book, Augustine examines Petrarch in respect of the Seven Deadly Sins. In some cases Petrarch denies any guilt whatsoever, and in some cases he reports mingled failure and resistance; but in the case of the seventh sin, accidie (slothful melancholy), he admits grave failure:

> The onslaughts of other evils, though frequent, are brief and momentary; but this plague seizes me at times with such tenacity that for whole days and nights it holds me in its grasp and tortures me; and my life then has the semblance not of light and of true life, but of Tartarean night and bitter death.

At the beginning of Book III, Augustine startles Petrarch by saying to him:

> You are bound, right and left, with two adamantine chains, which prevent you from meditating either on death or on life . . . you are like a miser who, held in captivity by chains of gold, would like to be set free, but is unwilling to give up his golden chains.

These chains are Petrarch's love for Laura and his desire for glory. The argument rages: Augustine marshals all the resources of his logic and his authority; Petrarch defends himself valiantly, maintaining as well as he can the nobility of his love and his desire. The debate is indecisive. Augustine does not yield in the least; and Petrarch, though he is shaken, cannot bring himself to renounce either of his chains.

Petrarch's next major project was the composition of a work called *Rerum memorandarum libri*, which was to be a voluminous treatise on the cardinal virtues, each duly analyzed into its component phases. The treatment is by *exempla* — biographical or anecdotal examples — of which, for any given topic, there are, in most cases, three groups: *romana*, *externa* (chiefly Greek), and *moderna*. Petrarch actually wrote, however, only an introductory Book and three Books on Prudence. The portions of the work that have the greatest continuing interest are the *exempla moderna* (among whose personages are Henry VII, King Robert, and Dante) and a series of some fifty chapters which constitute a collection of witty sayings.

Two other treatises, shorter but still substantial, the *De vita solitaria* and the *De otio religioso*, were completed not long afterward. The *De vita solitaria* is concerned mainly with the moral and religious aspects of the life of solitude; but many passages deal with the more general or with the literary satisfactions of such life, or with the contrasting miseries of city life. Such chapters as those on "The Freedom and the Mental Activity of the Solitary Man" and "The Benefits Conferred upon the Solitary Man by Woods and Fields and Streams" may be read with special pleasure.

Petrarch's dearly loved brother Gherardo had become a Carthusian monk at about the time of Petrarch's moral and religious crisis. The completeness of Gherardo's solution of his own inner conflict appealed greatly to Petrarch, though he himself could never achieve renunciation. He wrote to Gherardo often, and went twice to visit him in the monastery of Montrieux, in Provence. It was after one of these visits that Petrarch wrote his treatise "On the Peacefulness of Monastic Life," which extols the advantages of such life with respect to freedom from material cares and with respect to resistance to temptation, and deplores the vanity of human interests.

In the same years in which these two treatises were written Petrarch wrote most of his twelve eclogues, which he gathered in a collection called *Bucolicum carmen*. They are modeled, inevitably, upon the eclogues of Virgil. All of them, under the pastoral veil, present actual persons, circumstances, and events. The several themes are the contrast between Petrarch's own life and that of Gherardo; the death of King Robert; Petrarch's love for Laura; the nature of the poetic task; the rise of Rienzi; the corruption of the papal court (treated in two eclogues); a final farewell to Cardinal Colonna; the Black Death; the laurel (with a review of ancient poets); the death of Laura; and the Anglo-French war of 1356.

Petrarch's antipathy to physicians had led him, in the winter of 1351–52, to send to Pope Clement VI, who was then very ill, a letter attacking physicians in general. One of them replied; to this reply Petrarch in turn replied at length; the physician replied again; and Petrarch wrote a ponderous final reply. A little later he put his two replies together in a work commonly called *Invective contra medicum.* Its main interest lies not in Petrarch's violent attacks, but in his vigorous defense of poetry, which the replying physician had attacked. The lines of Petrarch's defense, however, are medieval:

> The task of the poet is to adorn the truth with beautiful veils, so that it may be hidden from the silly common herd. . . If you can open your eyes you will see that poets are resplendent with glory and fame and immortality, which they confer not only upon themselves but upon others whom they may deem worthy of celebration.

The main new work of the latter part of Petrarch's life, the most voluminous and the most immediately popular of all his works, is the *De remediis utriusque fortunae.* The meaning of the title and the general character of the work are quaintly indicated in the full title of an English translation published in 1579:

> Phisicke against Fortune, aswell prosperous, as aduerse, conteyned in two Bookes. Whereby men are instructed, with lyke indifferencie to remedie theyr affections, aswell in tyme of the bryght shynyng sunne of prosperitie, as also of the foule lowryng stormes of aduersitie. Expedient for all men, but most necessary for such as be subiect to any notable insult of eyther extremitie. Written in Latine by *Frauncis Petrarch,* a most famous Poet and Oratour. And now first Englished by Thomas Twyne.

The form is that of a dialogue. The first Book sets forth the remedies for the dangers inherent in more than a hundred varieties of prosperous fortune: the interlocutors are Joy, Hope, and Reason. Book II sets forth the remedies for more than a hundred varieties of adverse fortune: the interlocutors are Grief, Fear, and Reason. The underlying theme is the mutability of fortune; the mood is essentially Stoic; the purpose is to help men to attain moral dignity. While the work as a whole is tedious, it is rich in human understanding, and contains effective statements of typical human experiences.

The most notable works of the later years are the *Itinerarium breve de Ianua usque ad Ierusalem et Terram Sanctam* and the *De sui ipsius et multorum ignorantia.* The *Itinerarium* is a guidebook prepared for a friend who was planning to go to the Holy Land. The account of the Italian coast from

Genoa to Naples and the detailed account of Naples and its environs rest on Petrarch's firsthand knowledge: the latter part of the little book is compiled from written sources. The information given is not merely geographical, but covers matters of historical, literary, and general interest as well. "You must not fail," Petrarch says, in his account of Naples, "to visit the Royal Chapel, where my fellow-townsman [Giotto], the foremost painter of our age, has left great monuments of his genius and his skill."

While Petrarch was living in Venice, four Venetian devotees of Aristotle ventured to express the opinion that their city's famous guest was "a good man, but ignorant," whereupon his wrath overflowed into the composition of the last and most powerful of his invectives, to which he gave the brilliant title *De sui ipsius et multorum ignorantia*, "On His Own Ignorance and That of Many Others." In it he charges his opponents with stupidity in their unquestioning acceptance of what they took to be authority, and with blindness in their undiscriminating admiration of Aristotle; he takes his stand firmly on the side of the Platonists and the Augustinians; and he reasserts the dignity of man.

* * *

With all his classical predilections, Petrarch was appreciatively aware of the vernacular poetry of his Provençal and Italian predecessors. He counted Cino da Pistoia among his older friends; four of the stanzas of one of Petrarch's early *canzoni* end with lines quoted from Arnaut Daniel, Cavalcanti, Dante, and Cino respectively; the general scheme of one of the early *canzoni* was suggested by that of one of Dante's *canzoni*; the theme of a late sonnet was suggested by a poem by Arnaut; and Dante, Cino, Guittone, Guinizelli, and Cavalcanti, together with Arnaut and several other troubadours, are named with honor in the first of the *Triumphs*. So with all his conviction that Latin was the proper language for high poetic achievement, Petrarch did not disdain to write in Italian also. He must soon have realized that the Italian language gave him a second poetic instrument quite as lovely as the Latin, and better suited for some of the subtler things he wanted to say; and he was soon spending great care in the composition and revision of his Italian verse.

There are extant nearly four hundred Italian lyrics that are certainly by Petrarch, and a few others that are probably his. Most of them are sonnets; but about thirty are *canzoni*, a few are *sestine*, a few are *ballate*, and four are madrigals. Petrarch is the earliest poet whom we know to have written madrigals; but it is not likely that his were the first of all. His madrigals are tiny poems, idyllic in content, consisting of two or three tercets, with or without a concluding line or couplet.

The most frequent theme of Petrarch's Italian lyrics is his love for a lady whom he calls usually "Laura" and once "Laureta." We do not know her surname or identity. His love, truly a *fino amore*, was not of the exalted quality of Guinizelli's love, nor of the dark quality of Cavalcanti's, nor of the beatific quality of Dante's; it was essentially a simple human love, idealized, to be sure, but not idealized beyond the measure of usual poetic idealization. There is no reason to question its sincerity or its strength. It received little or no encouragement. Petrarch's main hopes were that he might be from time to time in Laura's company and that she might at least be kind; and that he might at some time be able to tell her fully the long story of his love. She died in the Black Death: Petrarch's deeply affectionate remembrance continued as long as he lived.

Many of the poems written in her lifetime are poems of praise for her beauty or her excellence; and many derive their accents from special occasions: sights of Laura among other ladies, or in springtime by a riverside; leave-takings, absences, returns, scenes revisited; anniversaries. But the most characteristic poems of all are those in which the theme is the poet's inner experience, in a wide variety of moods and circumstances. Many such poems are poems of self-analysis, centered often upon the perpetual conflict within the poet's heart between joy and sorrow, between hope and hopelessness.

One of his early sonnets, beginning *Solo e pensoso*, tells of solitary wandering:

> Alone and pensive I slowly tread the loneliest fields, ready to flee if my eyes note that human foot has pressed the ground. Thus only do I find defense from full perception, for in my looks, whence gladness has departed, one may read the burning of my heart. So I believe that hills and mountains, now, and woods and rivers know the temper of my life, that from all else is hid. Yet ways so rough and wild I cannot find that Love comes not with me, conversing, he with me and I with him.

Another sonnet, in which the opening phrases of the first two lines really mean "If this be love" and "If it be not love," was translated and expanded by Chaucer as the song of Troilus in the *Troilus and Criseyde*, the first quatrain being rendered thus:

> If no love is, O God! what fele I so?
> And if love is, what thing and which is he?
> If love be good, from whennes comth my woo?
> If it be wikke, a wonder thynketh me,
> Whenne every torment and adversite
> That comth of hym may to me savory thynke;
> For ay thurst I the more that ich it drynke.

One of the stanzas of a *canzone* beginning *Chiare, fresche, et dolci acque*, "Clear, cool, sweet stream," preserves this memory:

From the fair branches there descended — sweet in remembrance — a rain of blossoms upon her, and she sat humbly amid the glory, covered now with the lovely shower. Some fell upon her dress, some on her blond tresses — pearls upon gold, they seemed, that day — some on the ground, some on the stream; some, hovering in the air, seemed to say: "Here reigneth Love."

In one sonnet he writes:

Favors that heaven seldom bestows, a virtue rare and beyond human wont, under blond hair a mind mature, and in a humble woman beauty high and divine, incomparable and wondrous charm, a singing that one hears within one's heart, angelic grace, an ardent spirit . . .

and another sonnet, beginning with the resonant line

Chi vuol veder quantunque pò Natura,

reads thus:

Let him who would see what Nature and Heaven can achieve among us come to behold her who is alone a sun, not only to my eyes, but to the blind world that heeds not virtue; and let him come soon, for Death first steals those who are best, and lets the evil be: this fair mortal thing, awaited in the divine realm, must pass, and cannot stay. If he comes in time he will see all virtue, all beauty, all nobility, bound in one form in wondrous unity. Then will he say that these rhymes of mine are mute, and that my wit is overcome by excess of light: but if he tarries in his coming, he will have cause for lifelong sorrow.

Laura's death unquestionably brought to Petrarch a deep and abiding grief; but it brought him also new poetic themes: the shock of his own loss and of the world's loss; the variations of his sorrow; scenes revisited with a new poignancy of memory; the frustration of his hope for colloquy with her, and its final fulfillment in vision; his desire for death, and for perfect companionship.

The several sonnets that tell of Laura's return to him in his dreams contain these passages:

As a lady entering her own home she comes proudly, banishing with her serenity the sad thoughts of my dark and heavy heart. . .

To the bed in which I languish she comes, so beauteous that I scarce dare to look upon her; piteously she sits on the bedside, and with that hand that I so much desired she dries my eyes. . .

And in her words she shows me what, in this journey, I should flee or follow, telling me of the dangers of this life, entreating me to uplift my soul — and only while she speaks do I find peace. . .

Then when the light of day comes upon her she returns to heaven — she who knows all the ways — and tears are on her cheeks and in her eyes.

About forty of Petrarch's sonnets are addressed to friends. They do not deal with the sentiment of friendship: friendship is assumed, and the poems speak of various matters in which a friend would find interest. Some accompany gifts; some are advisory; some reflect his love; some concern poetry and poetic problems; some are obituary. One reports a delightful visit in the Pyrenees; one urges the addressee to take the Cross; one asks for the loan of a manuscript; one denies a report of his own death.

Three *canzoni* and four sonnets deal with public affairs — the *canzoni* carrying on, probably consciously, the tradition of the Provençal *sirventés* and of Guittone's *canzone* on the battle of Montaperti. The first of the *canzoni* urges the man to whom it is addressed to employ his eloquence in support of the crusade proclaimed in 1333 by Philip VI of France. The gathering of all the diverse hosts of Christendom for the holy enterprise is set forth in a swift and spirited review; and the assurance of victory, following the standard of Christ, is confirmed by citation of the ancient victories of Salamis and Marathon. Into the second *canzone*, addressed to a newly elected Senator of Rome, all Petrarch's enthusiasm for Rome is poured. Vividly and with deep emotion he contrasts the heroic splendor of ancient Rome and the hallowed life of early Christian Rome with the present ruin and degradation: women, children, the aged, friars black and gray and white, all others involved in the general distress, and Rome herself entreat rescue and restoration. The third *canzone*, beginning *Italia mia*, is for Italy as the second is for Rome. Addressed to the rulers of Italy, it is a protest against their internecine warfare, and in particular against their use of Northern mercenaries. Ancient triumphs over the Northern barbarians are recalled; the shame and the folly of trusting to venal hearts are made clear; and the warring princes are summoned to a common love and a common valor:

> "Is not this the ground that first I touched? Is not this the nest, where I was nursed so tenderly? Is not this my fatherland, wherein I trust, benign and loving mother, that shelters now my dead?" In God's name, let such thoughts arouse your minds; and look with compassion upon the tears of the sorrowing people. And if you but show some sign of love to them, greatness will take arms against fury, and the combat will be brief, for the ancient valor is not yet dead in Italian hearts.

All three *canzoni* are great poems. The surging eloquence of the second and the third has never been surpassed by that of any other poet. One of the four sonnets concerns the crusade proclaimed in 1333. The other three, written in sequence, are a stinging attack upon the corruption of the papal court.*

Ten poems, including a *canzone*, are primarily religious. In their predominant mood the poet seeks divine aid that he may escape from the trammels of a human love which, in these poems, is represented as an evil, and that

* These three sonnets are cancelled in or cut out from many manuscripts and many copies of early editions of the poems of Petrarch, and are omitted from several late sixteenth-century and seventeenth-century editions.

he may find refuge and strength, and ultimately salvation, in acceptance of the divine summons: *O voi che travagliate . . . Venite a me*. Written from the depths of personal conflict, they are in general poems of repentance attempted, or, at the end, presumably achieved, rather than expressions of a positive love of God — though they manifest a convinced gratitude for the Redemption. An early Good Friday sonnet begins and ends thus:

> Heavenly Father, after my wasted days, after my nights spent in vain imaginings with the fell desire that in my heart was kindled when I first beheld, to my undoing, that fair face . . .
> Have pity on my unworthy suffering; bring back my thoughts to a better goal; remind them that today Thou wast on cross.

The religious *canzone* is a formal and very beautiful hymn to the Virgin.

The perpetual conflict which in its rarer phases led Petrarch toward repentance is itself the subject of the most distinctive of all his Italian poems, the *canzone* beginning *I' vo pensando, et nel penser m'assale* . . . , "I move in thought, and in my thought I am assailed . . ." The conflict is in this case threefold, the contending forces being the desire for salvation, the desire for fame, and his love. The desire for salvation first attacks the other two forces, and bids the poet rise to the attainment of a more blessed hope. The desire for fame is then presented as of ineradicable urgency:

> This from the time I slept in swaddling clothes has ever grown in me day has followed day, and I fear that with me it will go down into my tomb.

Yet the unsubstantiality and the impermanence of fame are recognized. His love is stronger still: neither consideration of his plight nor appeal for divine help serves to release him from an affection so powerful

> Ch' a patteggiar n' ardisce co la morte —
>
> That it dares to try even to make terms with death.

The conflict is inconclusive in the poem, as it was in Petrarch's life:

> E veggio 'l meglio, et al peggior m' appiglio —
>
> And I see the better, and to the worse I cling.

The *canzone* is equivalent, in its content, to the third Book of the *Secretum*: but the conflict is here set forth in compact intensity and in lines that are a series of impassioned revelations.

The undying fame of Petrarch's Italian lyrics rests upon their blending of an inner with an outer beauty — the inner beauty of a sensitive, imaginative, and reflective response to finely discriminated shadings of emotion, the outer beauty of a verbal and rhythmic artistry that has never been surpassed. The success of the blending results not only from the perfectness of Petrarch's natural sense of euphony, but also from his persistent endeavor to find the very words that will express most faithfully what he desires to express, and to combine and order them in lines that will linger and be dear in memory. Several of his work sheets, preserved now in the Vatican Library, attest the extraordinary care he spent not only in the original drafting of his poems, but also in their revision. Nor does this spending impugn in the least his creative sincerity: rather does it prove it, for the inadequacies of human speech are such that nothing short of resolute searching can suffice to find loyal expression for the subtleties of inner experience.

Yet Petrarch, even in his lyrics, is inevitably a man of letters. His poetry comes from his heart, but it comes through a mind that is steeped in older thought and older poetry, and the treasures of his memory reappear in his verse, made newly personal through their absorption into his own consciousness. There are poems, also, in which the gift of the heart is but slight, while the artist spends himself in the elaboration of concepts that are mainly formal. And Petrarch's very sensitiveness to verbal sounds, to variations in mood, and to imagined similarities betrays him, at times, into plays on words, into over-heightened contrasts, and into strained metaphors that are unworthy of his finer verse — but were appropriated all too readily by his imitators.

In 1342 Petrarch decided to make a selective collection of his Italian poems: this was, for Italian poetry, a new idea, the nearest precedent being the *Vita nova*. On the making of this collection Petrarch worked from time to time to the very end of his life. Poems were in general carefully revised when they were first admitted into the collection, and sometimes revised again when they were copied from an earlier form of the collection into a later form. Shortly before 1350 Petrarch decided to divide the collection into two parts, the second beginning with the *canzone I' vo pensando*; and he wrote, as an introduction to the whole collection, the sonnet beginning *Voi ch' ascoltate . . .** By 1358 the collection contained about 175 poems. By this time also Petrarch had decided upon certain principles of arrangement, which he observed at first very carefully, and later with less care: the order was to be basically, but not rigorously, chronological; variation in content was to be obtained by interspersing poems addressed to friends and poems on public affairs or on religion among the love poems; and variation in form was to be obtained by interspersing *canzoni*, *sestine*, *ballate*, and madrigals among the sonnets. This concern for variation in form was a notable innovation: in the earlier manuscript collections of Italian poems the *canzoni* and the sonnets are strictly separated. After 1358 the collection was gradually enlarged by the addition of groups of poems, or of single poems, to one or the other of the two parts. The writing of Petrarch's own final manuscript of the collection,

* "O ye who listen . . ." The *Voi*, in Petrarch's thought, presumably included posterity.

now one of the chief treasures of the Vatican Library, was begun in 1366, by a scribe; but in the following year the scribe left Petrarch's service, and Petrarch himself thereafter continued the process of gradual addition. The Hymn to the Virgin was given the place of honor as the final poem. The collection, itself a work of art, bears the Latin title *Rerum vulgarium fragmenta*: it is commonly referred to as the *Canzoniere* of Petrarch.*

Outside the *Canzoniere* there remain some thirty or forty poems that are certainly or probably by Petrarch, and many others that have been attributed to him without due evidence.†

Soon after 1340, probably, Petrarch wrote, in *terza rima*, the first portions of what became eventually a poem in six parts, each of which he called a Triumph. This term meant to him a composition which, by presenting a large number of persons moving processionally under the dominance of a single figure, suggested the historic triumphal processions of ancient Rome. The first of the six Triumphs, that of Love, is followed by the Triumphs of Chastity, Death, Fame, Time, and Eternity. Two or more *capitoli*, or chapters, are extant for three of the Triumphs: the other three consist each of a single *capitolo*. The poem never received final form.

The Triumphs of Love, Chastity, and Fame are in fact processional: the many persons are gathered from ancient history and mythology, the Bible, Arthurian legend, and recent Italian reality. Some persons are merely named; most receive very brief characterization; only two stories — one of them the story of Masinissa and Sophonisba — are told at any length. Such presentation inevitably challenges comparison with the *Divine Comedy*, and the *Triumphs* suffer by that comparison. The multiplication of names grows monotonous, and the processions are not well visualized.

Laura is the protagonist of the Triumph of Chastity; and her death, portrayed not factually but in symbolic ceremony, is the main theme of the Triumph of Death. The *capitolo* beginning with the words *La notte*, entirely different from all the other *capitoli*, tells of a visit of Laura to Petrarch in vision on the night following her death. In the Triumph of Time, the Sun revolves with an extraordinary velocity, speeding days and months and years in a succession so marvelously swift that the span of human life is seen to be but momentary. The fame of those whose names have been preserved by poets or historians endures for a little while; but in the end all fame is extinguished. The Triumph of Eternity is a vision of a timeless Heaven.

The *Triumphs* as a whole are not successful; but Petrarch's inability to handle his chosen theme could not wholly quench his poetry. The scheme

* The Latin title means "Scattered Poems in the Vernacular." The word *canzoniere* means simply "collection of poems." Other informal titles in occasional use are *Le rime sparse*, "Scattered Poems," and the simple form *Le rime*.

† These poems are commonly referred to as the *Rime disperse* or *estravaganti*: both adjectives mean — not literally, but in effect — "excluded."

in itself has grandeur: death triumphs over life, fame over death, time over fame, eternity over time. Many lines and tercets are of fine quality; the end of the *capitolo* on the death of Laura is deservedly famous for its serene beauty; and the *capitolo* telling of Laura's appearance to Petrarch in vision, with its long and tender conversation in the course of which Laura admits an understanding and a love never confessed elsewhere, is perhaps the most remarkable personal passage Petrarch ever wrote.

Still toiling over the unfinished poem, Petrarch, on pages still extant, copied and revised the Triumph of Eternity in January and February 1374. He died in the following July.

* * *

The humanistic influence of Petrarch, transmitted through his younger friends and devotees and through his Latin works, far outweighed all other influences in bringing about the great development of humanism that took place both in Italy and elsewhere in Europe in the hundred years following his death. Petrarch, as we have seen, was not by any means the first humanist; but his humanism was far more thoroughgoing in its scholarship than that of any of his predecessors or contemporaries; it was powered by an enthusiasm which, in its intensity, was all his own; it was illustrated in a series of classicizing Latin writings far more impressive, in the mass, than those of any other author of recent centuries; and it was reënforced by the extraordinary prestige which attended him throughout his mature life. The Augustinianism that was so deeply interwoven with his humanism tended to hold the fifteenth-century humanists close to the traditions of Christian thought, and in particular to predispose them to the exaltation rather of Plato than of Aristotle. The humanism of the fifteenth century, in turn, is one of the main sources of later literary culture: Petrarch's humanistic influence was therefore, in its ultimate results, both enduring in time and all-European in its range.

Two of his Latin writings exerted influences that were not specifically humanistic. Throughout the fifteenth and sixteenth and early seventeenth centuries the *De remediis* was one of the most popular books of Europe. The Latin text, complete or incomplete, was printed in many countries, and translations appeared in many languages. Petrarch's version of Boccaccio's Griselda story had an extraordinary fortune, both in itself and as a source for later forms of the tale. It circulated as a separate work in many manuscripts; and it was often printed as a separate work, both in the original Latin and in translations in several languages. When Chaucer wrote his "Clerkes Tale" he had before him copies both of Petrarch's Latin text and of a French translation of it.

The *Triumphs* won immediate favor. Manuscripts abound, many of them manuscripts *de luxe*, with initial miniatures for the several Triumphs. Several early editions have full-page woodcuts. Painters treated one or more of the six subjects on *cassoni* (wedding chests), on panels, on canvases, and in fresco; and the Triumph theme was treated also, in Italy and elsewhere, in engravings, in decorative bas-reliefs, in bronze plaques, in ivory, on armor, in stained glass, and in tapestries. There are many translations, in many languages. The first English translation, by Henry Parker, Lord Morley, was made soon after 1550. Shelley's *Triumph of Life*, though the content is Shelley's own, was suggested by the Triumphs, and is written in *terza rima*.

The influence of Petrarch's Italian lyrics upon later lyric poetry has been far greater than the corresponding influence of any other lyrist of any country or of any age. The course of Petrarchism in Italy will be traced in later chapters of this book. Chaucer's "Cantus Troili" marks the beginning of foreign Petrarchism, which spread into Spain and Dalmatia in the course of the fifteenth century, and thereafter, through the poetry of Italian Petrarchists as well as through that of Petrarch himself, into France and England and many other countries. Many of the poems of the *Canzoniere* have been set to music, in many periods, chiefly by Italian composers, but also by French and German composers, from Dufay to Liszt.

CHAPTER **11**

Boccaccio

GIOVANNI BOCCACCIO was born perhaps in Paris, perhaps in Certaldo, within the period 1312–1314, probably in 1313.* In 1327 his father was sent to Naples to take charge of the Neapolitan office of the Bardi. Presumably he took Giovanni with him: from 1329 to 1335 Giovanni was at work in Naples as a merchant's apprentice. From 1335 to 1341 he studied canon law in the University of Naples, and during this period his literary career began. On the completion of his law course, in June 1341, he was called home to Florence, where he wrote busily. He found maintenance, for a time, with the lord of Ravenna, to whom he presumably rendered some sort of secretarial service; and a little later he held a similar position in Forlì. But he was again in Florence when the Black Death raged there in 1348.

He wrote Italian lyrics frequently throughout his life. His lyric vein was not deep, and his *Rime* have little individual character. Dantesque and Petrarchan motifs are imitated freely, and much use is made of classic names. The best of the *Rime* reflect prettily the Neapolitan social scene. Many of them celebrate a lady whom Boccaccio calls Fiammetta, who became and remained throughout his later Neapolitan years and for some time afterward the object of at least his literary devotion. Her real name was Maria: her identity is not known.†

His several early works in Italian (other than his lyrics), listed in what is very probably the order of their composition, with dates that are at least approximately correct and with notations as to form and firstness, are as follows:

* The story of his Parisian birth is told in pseudo-autobiographical passages in two of his romances. He certainly regarded Certaldo as his home.

† In pseudo-autobiographical passages he implies that she was a natural daughter of King Robert, and that she bore the name Maria d'Aquino; but this story, long credited, is now regarded as fictional. Similarly, it is now believed that Boccaccio's narratives of the course of his love affair with her are to be regarded as being at least largely fictional.

1336–38	*Caccia di Diana*	*Terza rima*	First Italian hunting poem
1337–39	*Filocolo*	Prose	First Italian prose romance
1339–40	*Filostrato*	Octaves	First Italian romance in verse by a non-minstrel, and first work by a non-minstrel written in octaves
1340–42	*Teseida*	Octaves	First Tuscan epic
1341–42	*Ameto*	Prose	First Italian romance with considerable pastoral elements
1342–43	*Amorosa visione*	*Terza rima*	Allegory
1344–46	*Fiammetta*	Prose	First Italian psychological romance
1346–49	*Ninfale fiesolano*	Octaves	First Italian idyll

It is obvious that Boccaccio, as a writer, was remarkably versatile, and that he was to an extraordinary extent a literary pioneer.

The *Caccia di Diana* mentions some sixty Neapolitan ladies as engaging in a hunt under the command of Diana: nearly all of the several short *capitoli* are filled with a monotonous account of their prowess. The *Caccia* is quite without poetic value in itself; but it is of some interest in that its idea of the celebration of many fair ladies is derived from Dante's lost poem on the sixty fairest ladies of Florence, in that it is probably the first poem to adopt the meter devised by Dante for the *Divine Comedy*, and in that it seems to have suggested the *Caccia col falcone* of Lorenzo de' Medici.

With the *Filocolo*, though it is naïve in many respects, Boccaccio enters definitely the area of literary achievement. The familiar story he tells, that of Florio and Biancofiore, is of French origin: his immediate written sources seem to have been a lost North Italian version and the existing *Cantare di Florio e Biancifiore*. But the tale grows, under his eager and industrious pen, from minstrel brevity to a length approaching that of the *Decameron*. The central story is told with abundant verbiage, and is adorned with many inserted episodes and with much more or less relevant material of many sorts: geographical and astronomical lore; architectural descriptions; visions; interventions of classic deities; an Infernal Council (probably from an Italian version of a French source); metamorphoses; battles (one from the *Aeneid*); banquets (one developing the French motif of the Pledges of the Peacock); letters; an exposition of Biblical history and of the Christian faith; parental instructions to a prospective ruler; and two pseudo-autobiographical narratives, one of them pastoral in its terminology. Classic elements are everywhere; Ovidian influence gives an analytic and elegiac character to amatory insights; and the style is in intention classic. The name *Filocolo* is the name adopted by Florio when he sets out on his long search for Biancofiore: it is a name of Boccaccio's own devising, fashioned, he tells us — not without pride — from two Greek words meaning respectively "love" and "labor," so that taken together they mean "Love's Labor."

The best of the many episodes is that of the Thirteen Questions of Love. Florio-Filocolo and his comrades, shipwrecked at Naples, join a joyous company in a delightful garden. After various diversions hosts and guests gather around a fountain; Fiammetta is made queen for the afternoon; her subjects in turn propound love-problems; and she in each case renders a decision, which is then forensically appealed and confirmed. In two cases the statement of the problem involves the telling of a *novella*.

The *Filocolo*, like almost all of the other works of Boccaccio, had great influence. The episode of the Thirteen Questions foretokens Boccaccio's own *Decameron*, in which both of the *novelle* of the *Filocolo* are retold; elements of Boccaccio's Infernal Council were borrowed by Sannazzaro, Vida and Tasso; and Tasso found treasure elsewhere in the *Filocolo* as well. Chaucer derived his Franklin's Tale mainly from one of the Thirteen Questions, and made incidental use of material from the *Filocolo* in the opening lines of the Prologue to the Canterbury Tales, in the *Troilus*, and in the *Legend of Good Women*; Milton's Infernal Council is indebted, ultimately, to Boccaccio; and Keats re-created the reunion of Florio and Biancofiore in *The Eve of Saint Agnes*.

In the *Roman de Troie* of Benoît de Sainte-More, or in an Italian prose version of that romance, Boccaccio found the brief episode of the faithless Briseida. Though she has sworn fidelity to her Trojan lover Troilus, Briseida, compelled to go to the Greek camp, quickly forsakes him for Diomedès, and the death of Troilus in combat ensues. From this slight source Boccaccio built his romance of Troiolo and Criseida, which deals mainly with the course of their love before her departure from Troy, and with Troiolo's subsequent grief. Boccaccio brought into the story, also, a new personage, Pandaro, who, though the cousin of Criseida, acts primarily as friend to Troiolo.

Boccaccio's interest is not in the plot, as it had been in the *Filocolo*, but in these three persons, Troiolo, Criseida, and Pandaro, whom he seeks to present as ideal types. Troiolo is for him the ideal lover, Criseida the ideal ladylove, and Pandaro the ideal friend. The story, then, is one of love and friendship; and the development of the friendship theme is on the same level of importance as the development of the theme of love. Troiolo, clearly the protagonist, is individualized by his first engaging hesitancy, his wholehearted joyousness, and his desperate clinging to a forlorn hope. The character of Criseida is not much developed, and, after the requirements of the traditional narrative render her faithless, Boccaccio has little more concern with her. Pandaro is worldly-wise and humorous, and occasionally cynical; but these qualities are by no means incompatible with his friendship for Troiolo, to whom he is as loyal in the time of Troiolo's despair as he had been in the time of happiness.

The word *Filostrato* is another of Boccaccio's Greek compounds: it means, he says, "a man overcome and overthrown by love." It does not figure in the text of the poem: it is explained in the formal title itself, and is applied to the author in a prose dedicatory letter.

As a work of art the *Filostrato* is definitely superior to the *Filocolo*, not only in its concentration on persons, but in its unity and in its style. There are no irrelevant episodes, and no passages of superfluous adornment. Dantesque elements are frequent; a *canzone* by Cino da Pistoia and two sonnets of Petrarch are introduced, recast in octaves. The octave itself is taken, now for the first time, from the *cantari*; and many motifs and the general character of the simple style come also from the *cantari*. The *Filostrato* was the greatest of Boccaccio's many gifts to Chaucer, from whom the story passed to still more famous hands.

The *Teseida* was a much more ambitious undertaking. Dante had said, in the *De vulgari eloquentia*, that no Italian had yet won distinction as a poet of arms: Boccaccio set out deliberately to win such distinction. His poem was to be definitely an epic: it was inevitable, therefore, that although it was to be in Italian and in octaves it should in some respects imitate the *Aeneid*, and the *Thebaid* of Statius. This it does in the form of its title, in its twelve-book length, and in the prefixed table of contents in sonnet form, which corresponds to the hexametric tables of contents often prefixed to the *Aeneid* and the *Thebaid*. There exists an autograph copy of the *Teseida* which contains an extensive commentary written by Boccaccio himself.

But though the background of the *Teseida* is amply martial, the foreground is filled with a romance which seems to have been essentially Boccaccio's own creation. Arcita and Palemone, Theban friends, captives in Athens, seeing Emilia, sister to the Queen, from their prison window, both fall in love with her. Arcita is released, but returns in disguise; Palemone escapes; and they meet and fight. Theseus interrupts the duel, and arranges that a tournament be held, in which Arcita and Palemone are to be the captains of two opposing companies of knights: the winning captain is to win Emilia. Arcita wins, but is mortally hurt. He is betrothed to Emilia, but he soon dies. In accordance with his expressed desire, Emilia marries Palemone. Like the *Filostrato*, the *Teseida* is a story of love and friendship: in this case the friends are rivals as well. The poem as a whole is tedious, especially in its martial portions; but it contains passages of excellent narrative and description. The style is still close to that of the *cantari*.

In its romantic nature the *Teseida* prefigures the *Orlando innamorato* of Boiardo. Chaucer, after using portions of the *Teseida* in several of his works, adopted its central story for his Knight's Tale; Fletcher and a collaborator made the Knight's Tale into *The Two Noble Kinsmen*; and Dryden retold it in his *Palamon and Arcite*.

Almost the whole of the *Ameto* is devoted to the events of a single springtime afternoon. The hunter Ameto and the nymph Lia go together to a woodland glade, where they are joined by six nymphs; it is proposed that the nymphs tell the stories of their lives and loves, each following her narrative with a song; Ameto presides; and the seven stories are told, at considerable length, and the seven songs are sung. In its general character, therefore, the *Ameto* renews the episode of the Thirteen Questions in the *Filocolo*, and still more closely prefigures the *Decameron*, especially in the introduction of the songs and in the fact that the story of Ameto and Lia serves as a sort of frame story. There is an underlying allegory: Ameto's association with Lia and the other nymphs typifies the refinement of native crudeness by love; and Boccaccio gives us to understand that the seven nymphs represent the seven virtues. They represent also seven particular women: most of them have been convincingly identified.* Boccaccio's sensualism, occasionally intrusive in the earlier works, here becomes much more pervasive. The prose style is laboriously classic; and the pastoral elements are derived mainly from Virgil. The chief specific influence of the *Ameto* was upon the *Arcadia* of Sannazzaro.

The *Amorosa visione* is an incoherent allegory, intended to signify the ascent, through love, from the life of the senses to the life of the spirit. The poet, with a majestic lady as guide, comes to a wall in which there are two gates: a narrow gate, leading to eternal peace, and a wide gate, leading to earthly happiness. The poet insists upon exploring first what lies beyond the wide gate, and his guide yields. They enter presently a great square hall, the walls of which are covered with frescoes representing philosophy (including poetry), glory, wealth, and love. Half of the entire poem is devoted to the description of these frescoes, which are said to be painted with a skill surpassing that of any human painter except Giotto. The description consists mainly of lists and accounts of the many persons who are depicted: scores of philosophers and poets; mythological, Biblical, classical, Arthurian, and late medieval heroes; Midas and other misers; and mythological and medieval devotees of love. The poet and his guide enter next a second hall, that of Fortune, which has a similar decoration, and then a garden in which they find a company of joyous ladies — who represent, enigmatically, real persons — engaged in singing, dancing, and gathering flowers. After his visit to this garden the poet is ready to go back and enter the narrow gate. At this point the poem stops: it constitutes only half of what Boccaccio originally intended to write.

The *Amorosa visione* has the dubious distinction of being the world's hugest acrostic. Boccaccio first wrote three sonnets, which together contain about 1500 letters, and then so wrote his poem that the initials of the succes-

* The pseudo-autobiographical narratives assigned to them are however to be regarded as being at least largely fictional.

sive tercets and single final lines of his fifty *capitoli* correspond exactly to the letters of the sonnets. The metrical form of the poem is taken from the *Divine Comedy*. In content it shows the influence of Dante, of Boccaccio's classical studies, and in particular of the *Roman de la rose*. The general idea of the frescoes comes from the French poem; but the particular idea of a hall decorated with such frescoes was presumably suggested by acquaintance with a hall in the Neapolitan Castel Nuovo which had been decorated, probably by Giotto, with frescoes representing famous heroes and heroines.

The story of the *Fiammetta* is narrated in the first person by the heroine. Her lover, Panfilo, after a period of mutual happiness, is recalled from Naples to Florence. He promises to return within four months, but he never does return. Fiammetta attempts suicide, but is rescued by her faithful nurse, who plays a large part in the story. A last report that Panfilo is about to return to Naples proves to be mistaken. Boccaccio's concern is not with this slight sequence of external events, but with the successive states of Fiammetta's hoping and suffering and remembering mind and heart. He had as model the *Heroides*, but his analysis is far more detailed, insistent, and imaginative than that of Ovid. Many of the pages of the *Fiammetta* are very effective; but its rhetorical style and its heavy freight of classic instances have lost their contemporary charm. For the *Fiammetta* (as he had done for the *Teseida*) Boccaccio wrote a commentary, in the course of which he quotes, in Latin, many passages from Ovid and other Latin poets.

The two streams which, coming down from heights near Fiesole, flow into the Arno just east of Florence are the Mensola and the Affrico — names, it occurred to Boccaccio, that might well have been the names of a nymph and her lover. From this imagination, and from certain Ovidian and other classic episodes, he wove the pattern of his eponymic idyll, the *Ninfale fiesolano*. Affrico by chance sees a gathering of Diana and a troop of her nymphs, and falls in love with Mensola. He searches for her, despite his father's sympathetic counsel; when he finds her she repulses him; his mother tries tenderly to comfort him; with the aid of Venus he finds Mensola again and wins her; she repents of her love and never returns; Affrico in his despair kills himself beside the stream that thereafter bears his name; and Diana, when Mensola's fault is discovered, turns her into the stream that thereafter bears her name.

This is the best of Boccaccio's poems, in the brook-like clarity of the narrative, in the simplicity and strength of its emotions, in the beauty of some of its scenes, and in the fresh lyric quality of many of the octaves — a quality at times very close to that of folk poetry. If it were not for the execrably bad taste of a very few stanzas, the *Ninfale* would be one of the most charming of all idylls. It presumably suggested to Lorenzo de' Medici his eponymic *Ambra*.

Various minor pieces of writing date from the period ending in 1349, among them a few Latin letters written in the *cursus*; a humorous letter in the Neapolitan dialect; a few Latin poems; and a brief biographical appreciation of Petrarch.

Boccaccio's classicism, manifested in his wide reading of the Latin authors, in his extensive use of classic material, and in the occasional Latin writings just mentioned, was not, then, a late interest for him, though his major Latin works are of his later years: his classic interest and enthusiasm began in his early youth, and never left him.

From the very start of his literary life he had evinced a great enthusiasm for Dante; and before he left Naples he had begun to develop an equally great enthusiasm for Petrarch. He was deeply stirred when Petrarch came to Naples to undergo examination by King Robert prior to his coronation; but the two men did not meet at that time. Both these devotions led Boccaccio to make copies of all the writings of Dante and of Petrarch that he could find: this faithful custom of his has preserved for us some letters that would otherwise have been lost.

The years 1350–1355, the central years of Boccaccio's literary activity, brought to him the beginnings of two new experiences: occasional and honorable employment by the city of Florence, and intimate friendship with Petrarch. Within these years he was sent as envoy, on missions of various kinds, to Ravenna, Padua, the Tyrol, and Avignon; and he held civic offices in 1351 and in 1355. When Petrarch made his pilgrimage to Rome in 1350 he passed through Florence both on his way to Rome and on his return, and accepted the hospitality of Boccaccio; and Boccaccio visited Petrarch in Padua in 1351. Theirs was one of the finest of literary friendships, distinguished, but not limited, by the fact that the older of the two friends was always a preceptor as well, while the younger was always an eager and admiring disciple.

During these same years Boccaccio continued to write occasionally in Latin verse and prose; but the great achievement of this period was the *Decameron*, the most famous of the world's hundreds of collections of short stories. Just when Boccaccio began and finished it we do not know: probably his main concentration of work upon it took place in 1351 and the two following years.

The full title of the work, in literal translation, reads thus:

> Here begins the book called *Decameron*, wherein are contained a hundred tales told in ten days by seven ladies and three young men.

The word *Decameron* itself, another one of Boccaccio's Greek compounds, is based on the Greek words for "ten" and "day."

The hundred *novelle* are set in one of the most skillfully wrought of all frame stories, a story so successful that one may even read it with satisfaction for its own sake, without reference to the *novelle* it contains. It moves from the terror of the Black Death, described at length and in vivid detail, to the placid relief of joyous villa gardens. The ten young people, with their servants, go first to one villa and then to another, spending in all two weeks in the two retreats. The Fridays and Saturdays are devoted to rest and to religious observances, the other ten days to amusements. For each of these ten days one of the company is chosen, in advance, to serve as king or queen. The amusements include wandering through villa grounds, excursions, bathing, singing, dancing, and the playing of various games, and center in the storytelling, which occupies the late afternoons — each of the ten young people telling one story on each day. The evenings are spent in dancing and in the singing of *ballate*, one of which, for each evening, is reported in full. The frame story as a whole represents the final perfection of the idea of the storytelling garden-gathering under the direction of a ruler — the idea that Boccaccio had employed first in the *Filocolo* and later in the *Ameto*.

The *novelle* are of many types. In general the king or queen, upon election, prescribes a general theme for the stories of the following day: thus the stories of the second day are to deal with the experiences of persons who through trial and tribulation come at last to unexpected good fortune, and those of the sixth day are to report instances of quickness of wit serving to avert impending disaster. But for the first day and for the ninth no theme is prescribed, and even on the other days the last narrator is free to disregard the stated theme. Even so, Boccaccio does not take his own classification very seriously. In point of fact the stories, as far as they are classifiable at all, fall into one or another of five groups: stories of trickery (the largest group), stories of adventure, stories of verbal wit, tragic stories, and stories of magnanimity.

The stories are told extremely well. They are well introduced, the plots excite and satisfy curiosity, the settings are clearly visualized, the dialogue is good, and the narrative moves surely to a definite point of conclusion. The style, now fully mature, is clear and straightforward: as varied as the *novelle* themselves, it ranges from swift dramatic simplicity to sustained dignity.

The persons of the stories, as different in their inner characteristics as in their outer circumstances, move before the eyes of the mind as the *personae* of an immense human comedy: they include kings, princes, princesses, ministers of state, knights, squires, abbots, abbesses, monks, nuns, priests, soldiers, doctors, lawyers, philosophers, pedants, students, painters, bankers, wine-merchants, innkeepers, millers, bakers, coopers, usurers, troubadours, minstrels, peasants, servants, simpletons, pilgrims, misers, spendthrifts, sharpers, bullies, thieves, pirates, parasites, gluttons, drunkards, gamblers, police — and lovers of all sorts and kinds.

The *Decameron* is in the main a book of laughter — laughter that runs the full gamut from gentle merriment to raucous obscenity. Yet the changes of mood are so frequent, and there is here and there so much seriousness, even somberness, that there is no monotony.

Among the most famous individual stories are those of The Sanctification of Ser Ciappelletto,* The Three Rings, Andreuccio Befooled, The Count of Antwerp, Bernabò of Genoa (the *Cymbeline* story), Gillette of Narbonne (the *All's Well That Ends Well* story), The Vengeance of Tancred, Isabella and the Pot of Basil, The Eaten Heart, Nastagio and the Wild Hunt, Frederick and the Falcon, Chichibio and the Cranes, Guido Cavalcanti Among the Tombs, Brother Cipolla and the Relics, Calandrino and the Heliotrope, The Magnanimity of Nathan, A Garden in January (the Franklin's story), Messer Torello and the Saladin, and The Patient Griselda.

The *Decameron* is like the central point of an hourglass through which, converging from many sources, the sands of narrative pass, to be dispersed into the vast field of later fiction. This is not to minimize Boccaccio's inventive powers: some of the stories are presumably his own, and even those for which immediate or ultimate sources are known or postulated are completely re-created by Boccaccio's narrative mastery and the vividness of his human understanding.

The influence of the *Decameron* has been extraordinarily great. It has served as a general model for many later story collections, in Italy and elsewhere; and nearly a thousand translations, imitations, and adaptations of particular *novelle* have been recorded. The chief German, Spanish, and French imitators were Hans Sachs, Lope de Vega, and La Fontaine. Chaucer, oddly enough, seems not to have known the *Decameron*, though he tells a few of the same stories. Among the English, Irish, and American writers who have made use of material derived directly or indirectly from the *Decameron* are Gower, Lydgate, Painter, Greene, Shakespeare, Ben Jonson, Beaumont and Fletcher, Dekker, Thomas Heywood, Middleton, Massinger, Mrs. Aphra Behn, Otway, Dryden, Swift, Pope, Goldsmith, Byron, Keats, Leigh Hunt, Tennyson, George Eliot, J. M. Synge, Longfellow, and F. Hopkinson Smith. Boccaccio's material has been used not only in prose but in narrative verse, comedy, and tragedy, as well as in opera and in painting. Among the English and American painters who have treated subjects derived directly or indirectly from the *Decameron* are Hogarth, Millais, Cope, Holman Hunt, Leighton, and J. W. Alexander.

The *Decameron*, the high climax of Boccaccio's literary career, was followed immediately by a sorry anticlimax, the *Corbaccio*. This, the last of

* These are merely convenient English titles: Boccaccio's are much longer.

Boccaccio's works of Italian fiction, is in form a pseudo-Dantesque vision and in substance a bitter misogynistic invective.

During the last twenty years of Boccaccio's life his friendship with Petrarch became still more intimate. In the winter of 1358–59 Petrarch, who had long wanted to have someone make a Latin translation of Homer, met in Padua a man who seemed to him to be a possible translator — a slovenly and altogether unpleasant Calabrian adventurer, Leonzio Pilato, who called himself a Greek and professed a learning he did not in fact possess. Boccaccio, on hearing from Petrarch about Leonzio, got the University of Florence to call Leonzio as a professor of Greek; obtained, with Petrarch's help, a manuscript of Homer; and for the two years that Leonzio remained in Florence endured him in his own house. During the academic year 1360–61 Leonzio translated the *Iliad*, reading his translation piecemeal and commenting on it confusedly to Boccaccio and the other two members of his university class; and during the following year he dealt similarly with the *Odyssey*. Leonzio's Latin was very inadequate, and his translations proved disappointing to Boccaccio and to Petrarch; but for Boccaccio, at least, they were better than nothing.

In or about 1363 Boccaccio went to live in Certaldo; but this did not prevent occasional visits to Florence, or occasional Florentine employment: in 1365 he was sent as envoy to the papal court in Avignon, and two years later he was sent as envoy to congratulate the pope on his return to Rome. In 1373 the government of Florence established a public lectureship on the *Divine Comedy* and invited Boccaccio to be the first lecturer; and, despite increasing illnesses and infirmities, he accepted the invitation. His lectures, held in the church of Santo Stefano, were given on weekdays (holidays excepted), as regularly as his health permitted, from October until, probably, the Spring of 1374. He died at Certaldo on December 21, 1375.

During his last twenty years Boccaccio continued to write both in Italian and in Latin, though Latin had now the preference. His last important writings in Italian were a *Trattatello in laude di Dante* and an incomplete commentary on the *Divine Comedy*. The *Trattatello* is a eulogy, not a biography (though it is sometimes referred to as Boccaccio's Life of Dante); and it is notable both for its expression of Boccaccio's ardent admiration of Dante and for a digression on the nature of poetry. The voluminous commentary on the *Divine Comedy*, of great but uneven value, was probably a development of Boccaccio's Florentine lectures on Dante.

In Latin, in these same years, Boccaccio wrote several eclogues and other poems, and four learned works: the *De casibus virorum illustrium*; the *De claris mulieribus*; the *Genologia deorum gentilium*; and an elaborate geographical dictionary.

The full meaning of the title of the first of these four works is "On the

Reversals of Fortune that Befell Certain Illustrious Men and Women." Cast in the form of a vision, the book contains the stories of about a hundred persons, from Adam to some of Boccaccio's own contemporaries. The narration, at times monotonous, is at its best very dramatic. Chaucer's Monk's Tale, with its several "tragedies," indicates its general source in its very title: "Heere bigynneth the Monkes Tale, de Casibus Virorum Illustrium." Lydgate's *Book called I. Bochas descriuing the falle of Pryncys pryncessys and othir nobles* is a paraphrase of a French translation of the *De Casibus.*

In a companion work Boccaccio tells the stories of about a hundred famous (or infamous) women, from Eve to Queen Joan of Naples. The mood varies: there are occasional echoes of the festivity of the *Decameron* or of the misogynism of the *Corbaccio.* There is praise of simple family life; and there is novel praise of women who participate in manly activities, in the study of the classics, in poetry, and in the arts. The *De claris mulieribus* gave Chaucer the general scheme and some details for his *Legend of Good Women.*

The geographical dictionary, intended to facilitate the reading of classic authors by providing explanations of their geographical allusions, sets forth its contents and its plan of organization in its title, "On Mountains, Forests, Springs, Lakes, Rivers, Ponds and Marshes, and on the Names of the Sea." Many of the entries that concern places known to Boccaccio are very interesting and very personal.

The *Genologia deorum gentilium*, the most massive and the most erudite of the works of Boccaccio, is a mythological encyclopedia within which he presents in a genealogical arrangement all the mythological lore in any way accessible to him. He gave his encyclopedia two remarkable adornments: some fifty quotations in Greek — the first Greek entries in any humanistic work — taken from Leonzio Pilato's translation of Homer; and a series of elaborate genealogical trees, one for each of the thirteen Books that form the main part of the *Genologia*: these trees are the earliest secular genealogical trees properly so called. For his younger contemporaries, including Chaucer, and for scholars of the next few generations, the *Genologia* was a mine of information.

The last two Books of the *Genologia* are of much greater literary value than the first thirteen. The concluding Book is a defense of the *Genologia* itself with regard to utility, accuracy, order, completeness, truth, good faith, clarity, and modesty. Still more important is the next-to-last Book, which is a defense of poetry. In it Boccaccio first satirizes his accusers — jurists, doctors, and theologians — and then enumerates and refutes the several charges brought against poetry: charges of nullity, mendacity, foolishness, immorality, and obscurity, the charge that poetry is but a poor imitation of philosophy, and the charge that poetry had been condemned by Plato, St. Jerome, and Boethius. The defense is vigorous, now medieval in its legalistic technicality or in its reliance on allegory, now modern in its perception and eloquent phrasing of permanent critical truth. One chapter begins thus:

> For poetry, which the negligent and the ignorant despise, is a certain fervor of exquisite invention, and of the eloquent expression, in speech or writing, of what you have invented. This fervor, which comes from the bosom of God, is granted at birth, I believe, to only a few minds: wherefore, since it is so wondrous a thing, poets have always been very rare. The effects of this fervor are sublime, as thus: it arouses in the mind a desire for utterance; and it leads to the devising of new and beautiful inventions, to the orderly composing of what has been devised, to the adornment of the composition with a new fabric of words and sentences, and to the covering of truth with a becoming veil of fiction.

CHAPTER 12

Contemporaries of Petrarch and Boccaccio

THE BEST of the many minor lyrists of the mid-fourteenth century was Fazio degli Uberti (c. 1307–c. 1370), an exiled descendant of that Farinata who had once saved Florence. His love poetry is warmly personal, quietly imaginative, and clear and graceful in its style. He knew deep suffering; and some of the lines that express that suffering go far beyond conventionality. His several political *canzoni* are vigorously Ghibelline. He wrote also a long geographical treatise in *terza rima*, the *Dittamondo* (that is, the *Dicta mundi*, or "Book of the World").

The Florentine Antonio Pucci (c. 1310–1388), a bell founder by profession, held civic employment from 1334 to 1369. As bell ringer he had to swing the six-thousand-pound bell of the Palazzo Vecchio; as a town crier he went about on horseback, stopped here and there, blew his silver trumpet, and then, when enough people had gathered, read his proclamation.

He was a prolific versifier, and he turned his facile hand to many kinds of verse. For his dozens of humorous sonnets he adopts, in general, a form called in Italian the *sonetto caudato*, the "tailed sonnet," in which the fourteenth line is followed by a short line which rhymes with the fourteenth, the poem then closing with a couplet which has a new rhyme. There had been much earlier experimentation in the enlargement of the sonnet: this particular form, which was destined to become the normal form for later humorous sonnets, seems to have been devised by some unknown poet early in the fourteenth century.

Pucci's most imaginative poems are five legendary *cantari*, intended for public recitation. His listening audiences, in little city squares, must have found them precisely to their taste: adventures abound, with plentiful deeds of mighty courage, menacing giants, helpful fairies, transformations, clever replies, and a prevailing good humor. The "pound of flesh" motive makes its first Italian appearance in one of these *cantari.*

Florentine sights and sounds and events fill several poems in *terza rima*: a vivacious description of the great market place that was the center of the popular life of Florence; poems on a flood, on a famine, on a pestilence, on petty wars, and on the expulsion of a would-be tyrant; a poem on the fair ladies of Florence; and a labored summary of Villani's *Chronicle* — a summary that becomes an enthusiastic expansion at the point at which Dante is mentioned.

In Pucci's *Contrasto delle donne* the deeds and characters of a long series of Biblical, mythological, and other women are debated in alternate octaves by a misogynist and a champion of feminine excellence. In his *Noie* the old Provençal genre of the *enueg* reached its fullest and most jovial development. The poem consists of about a hundred tercets, each of which (aside from those that are merely introductory), beginning with the words *A noia m' è*, sets forth pungently some type of behavior that "annoys" the poet. Among the persons who misbehave are those who go to sleep in church, or scorn a gentleman who happens to be ill-dressed, or break off friendships for some slight offense, or talk incessantly, or boast of imaginary deeds, or, if invited to the tavern, bring uninvited guests along with them, or come to table with their hands unwashed, or crack nuts with their teeth, or blow into their soup, or, when walking with a companion, keep stopping to talk with other people, or give you an invitation and leave you to pay the bill, or look over your shoulder when you are writing or reading a letter, or ask "Who hit you?" when you have a black eye, or go singing and laughing along the street after they have reached the age of forty-eight.

Meanwhile the Franco-Venetian epic came to its culmination in the work of Niccolò da Verona, of whose identity we have no certain knowledge. While he expected minstrels to make use of what he wrote, he was himself an amateur, well educated, and proud of his authorship. He was able to invent plot, and to delineate character. In his *Prise de Pampelune*, "The Capture of Pamplona," the setting is still the Christian-Islamic struggle in Spain. His *Pharsale*, derived from Lucan, is Roman, not Carolingian, in its theme. This poem he dedicated, in 1343, to Niccolò d' Este, who seems thus to have become the first member of the house of Este to serve as patron to an epic poet: such Este patronage was to be renewed in each of the next two centuries.

In Umbria, in these same years, the *lauda* had given rise to what must have been definitely a religious drama: this we know from the dated inventories of certain confraternities. The earliest such inventory, made in Perugia in 1339, lists, for instance, these properties: veils, robes, beards, wigs, gloves, books, little boxes for the Magi to carry, a star, a cross, a lance, nails, and two pairs of wings for angels.

* * *

Among the several men who at this time were writing excellent religious prose were Iacopo Passavanti and the unknown author of "The Little Flowers of St. Francis."

After busy years as professor of theology and preacher in other cities, the Florentine Dominican Iacopo Passavanti (c. 1302–1357) was made prior, in 1345, of the monastery of Santa Maria Novella, in Florence; and there he proved himself a skillful administrator, a counsellor so wise that his advice was sought by many leading citizens, an eloquent preacher, and a fearless witness to the truth as he saw it. His *Specchio della vera penitenza*, "The Mirror of True Penitence," is a treatise based upon a series of Lenten sermons delivered in 1354. It is impressive throughout in its moral dignity and its religious urgency: its most notable portions, from the literary point of view, are the *exempla* with which the preacher makes memorably evident the dangers of sin and its fearful consequences.

A lost Latin collection of Franciscan stories, written in large part — perhaps by a certain Ugolino di Montegiorgio — late in the thirteenth century and completed by an unknown continuator soon afterward, was translated into Italian, about the middle of the fourteenth century, by an unknown author, probably a Florentine, who called his version *I fioretti di San Francesco*. The little book, the most widely and fondly known, today, of all saints' legends, consists of about fifty chapters, the first forty or so concerned directly with St. Francis, the rest with St. Anthony of Padua or with early Franciscans of the region of Ancona.* While the stories were undoubtedly regarded by their first compilers as records of fact, they have historical value only in their revelation of the figure of St. Francis as seen and loved by his early followers. They have much of the nature of folk tales; but for all their naïveté they possess an inner illumination that has never faded. The simple narrative flows with a limpid and altogether charming tenderness. Among the most famous chapters are those that tell of St. Francis' exposition of the nature of perfect joy, of his preaching to the birds, and of his conversion of the wolf of Gubbio.

During this period anonymous Tuscan authors were writing Carolingian romances in simple prose, their sources being mainly Franco-Venetian poems.

Matteo Villani, a younger brother of Giovanni, continued the *Cronaca*

* The printed editions of the *Fioretti* usually contain also several other short Franciscan compilations; but these, though interesting, lack the fine quality of the *Fioretti*.

for the years from 1348 to 1363; and after his death his son Filippo wrote a few additional chapters, carrying the narrative through 1364. Far more vivid than the *Cronaca* is an incomplete work that covers the vicissitudes of Rome from 1327 to 1354, written ruggedly in the Roman dialect by an unknown eyewitness. About half of the extant portion of the book is devoted to the career of Rienzi; this portion, published under the title *Vita di Cola di Rienzo*, has been the main source for modern literary re-creations of Rienzi.

* * *

Rienzi's own letters are (except, of course, for the Latin works of Petrarch and Boccaccio) the most interesting Latin writings of this period. About fifty of them remain: the addressees include the emperor, successive popes, high officers of church and state, Petrarch, and other persons of some note. Most impressive of all are the circular letters addressed to several Italian states. In one of them he writes:

> With you and with all her statesmen we desire to restore the ancient unity of Holy Italy, long since laid prostrate, riven to this day by strife on strife, deserted by those who should have governed her in peace and justice; to set her free from the perils of her abandonment; to restore her to the pristine state of her ancient glory; and so to augment that glory that, tasting the sweetness of peace, she may through the grace of the Holy Spirit flourish as she has never flourished hitherto.

Nor can one readily forget the triumphant magniloquence of his favorite signature:

> Candidatus Spiritus Sancti miles, Nicolaus severus et clemens, liberator Urbis, zelator Italie, amator orbis, et tribunus augustus.

CHAPTER 13

Writers of the Late Fourteenth Century

THE PAPAL COURT returned to Rome in 1377; but this return was presently followed by the Great Schism (1378–1417), during which the authority of the Roman popes was contested by antipopes resident in Avignon. The dominant *condottiere* of the time was the Englishman, Sir John Hawkwood.

In Florence the fine open Gothic hall now called the Loggia dei Lanzi, designed as a place from which public gatherings could fittingly be addressed, was built soon after 1375. Gian Galeazzo Visconti, lord of Milan, founded the great Cathedral in 1386, and began the Certosa of Pavia ten years later.

In music the *Ars nova* now attained its fullest development, through the genius of the first famous and prolific Italian composer, the blind Florentine Francesco Landini. He was a man of general as well as of musical culture — he wrote the words for many of his compositions — and was held in high and well-deserved honor in his own time.

Chaucer was in Italy on official business in 1373 and again in 1378.

* * *

Franco Sacchetti (c. 1330–1400) was born in Dalmatia, of Florentine parentage: for most of his life his home was in Florence. He took an active and an honorable part in the political affairs of his city, holding office occasionally, and serving occasionally as envoy. His reading, wide but quite unsystematic, ranged from the Bible and the Church Fathers, through some of the familiar classic authors, to Dante and Petrarch. His thinking was marked by an eminently practical common sense, and by a deeply religious high-mindedness that was grieved constantly by the religious, moral, and political conditions of his strife-torn Italy.

His lyrics, though there are a few delightful poems among them, are as a whole more remarkable for their variety in form and content than for any genuinely lyrical inspiration. They include sonnets, *canzoni*, *sestine*, *ballate*, madrigals, *cacce*, *frottole* (long rigmaroles chiefly in short lines), and a few oddities; and they show a marked liking for experimentation in the use of unusual kinds of rhyme. Sacchetti was closely associated with the musicians of the *Ars nova*, and many, possibly all, of his *ballate*, madrigals, and *cacce*, were written to be set to music (Sacchetti himself wrote the music for two of his *ballate*). The poems of these three types show Sacchetti at his lyric best. A pastoral *ballata*, beginning

> O vaghe montanine pasturelle,
> Donde venite sì legiadre e belle?
>
> O gentle mountain shepherdesses,
> Whence come you, so charming and beautiful?

is very pretty indeed. A few lines from one of his three *cacce* may serve to illustrate both the quality of these particular poems and the general nature of the *caccia* form:

> Passando con pensier per un boschetto,
> donne per quello givan, fior cogliendo,
> "To' quel, to' quel" dicendo.
> "Eccolo, eccolo!"
> "Che è, che è?"
> "È fior alliso."
> "Va là per le viole."
> "Omè, che 'l prun mi punge!"
> "Quell' altra me' v'aggiunge."
> "Uh, uh! o che è quel che salta!"
> "È un grillo." . . .
> "No' staren troppo,
> che 'l tempo si turba!"
> "E' balena!"
> "E' truona!" *

The *caccia*, as this example shows, is a composition in free verse, the lines mostly short, telling of an exciting outdoor activity, and enlivened by shouts and cries and bits of conversation. The word *caccia* means "hunt," and most

* "As I was walking, deep in thought, through a little wood, women were going through it picking flowers, saying 'Pick that one, pick that one.' 'Here it is, here it is!' 'What is it, what is it?' 'It's an iris.' 'Go over there for violets.' 'Ouch, a thorn is pricking me!' 'That other girl is reaching them better.' 'Oh dear, oh dear! What's that that's jumping?' 'It's a cricket.' . . . 'We shall be staying too long, for it looks like rain!' 'It's lightning!' 'It's thundering!' "

of the *cacce* describe hunting scenes. Others, by various authors, deal with fishing, bird-catching, marketing, battles, a fire, the chase of a thief, an amorous pursuit, a country holiday. The genre was short-lived: the earliest *cacce* were probably written about 1350, the latest about 1450. Only about twenty have survived.

In Italian prose Sacchetti wrote a series of expositions of the Gospel passages appointed to be read in Lent. He gave them no title: they are now called *Sposizioni di vangeli.** Many of them are in question-and-answer form; several contain illustrative *novelle.*

Sacchetti's liking for *novelle* led him, about 1390, to begin the writing of his major work. He called it *Il libro delle trecentonovelle*; but of the three hundred stories that he wrote, or planned to write, only about two hundred have come down to us. He wrote the book, so he says, to lighten the misery of the times by providing some diversion and some laughter; and he wrote it simply and for simple folk. He wrote it, also, for himself, in a nostalgic re-creation of the days of his youth and of his strength. He sought no courtliness of style, but wrote rather as if he were actually telling his stories, in his own colloquial idiom, to a group of Florentine listeners. Nor did he seek any elaborateness of structure: there is no frame story, and no thematic organization.

Some of the stories are traditional; but the great majority are, or have the appearance of being, stories of persons whom Sacchetti had known, of strange happenings or comical tricks he had witnessed, or of witty replies he had heard — or similar stories that might have been told, credibly, to him. One does not often move, in the *Trecentonovelle*, amid the great of the earth; one moves rather amid throngs of ordinary men and women — ordinary in station, but marked, quite constantly, by curious and amusing characteristics. Sacchetti was always finding, or inventing, such "characters"; and the essence of his most typical stories lies in the reactions of such "characters" to odd chances or mischances that befall them. The stories are relatively brief, often anecdotal. They are full of lively dialogue; and they are pungent, photographic, and phonographic. Maurice Hewlett, whose opinion in such a matter is well worth consideration, rates Sacchetti, as a teller of tales, above Boccaccio. Among the best stories are those of Bernabò Visconti, the Abbot, and the Miller; the Ambassadors from the Casentino; Marabotto and Sciversmars; Sacchetti (himself) and the Soothsayer; Giotto and the Coat of Arms; Dante and the Blacksmith; Dante and the Muleteer; Pucci's Garden; the Priest who played Chess; Bonamico and the Beetles; and the Bear in the Church.

Tuscan minstrels — called, by this time, *cantastorie*, "story-singers" — were now naturalizing the Carolingian epic in Tuscany. As they had done in

* They were formerly called *Sermoni evangelici.*

the case of the earlier *cantari*, they used Tuscan as their language, and they composed in octaves. They divided their epics into *canti*, each canto being of a length suitable for singing in the course of an hour or so. While the Christian-Islamic conflict still provides the general background, while valor in defense of the Christian cause is still a dominant motive for armies and for individual heroes, and while the traditional religious accents are still to be heard (each canto, in the general practice, begins with a religious invocation), the *cantastorie* now greatly developed themes of adventure, gave a larger place to amatory episodes, introduced many fantastic elements, and lapsed willingly into occasional humor. Roland is of Italian birth; the arrogance and power of the traitorous Maganzesi have increased; and Charlemagne's imperial dignity has almost vanished.

There remain half a dozen Tuscan epics written certainly or probably before the end of the fourteenth century, all by anonymous *cantastorie*. The two that were destined to be most influential are the *Orlando* and the *Spagna in rima*. In the *Orlando*, typical in its plot, Roland, insulted by the traitor Gano, leaves the imperial court and wanders eastward. Coming to an abbey beset by three giants, he slays two of them and converts the third, Morgante, who thereafter, armed with a big bell clapper, accompanies him. In the East, Roland gives aid to certain pagan kings in their local conflicts, and now and again is slightly touched with love. Emissaries of the Maganzesi, however, reveal his identity: he is imprisoned, and is about to be put to death, when a band of Christian knights, seeking him, comes to the rescue. He returns with them to Paris, just in time to save the city from a besieging Saracen army. The *Spagna*, a better poem, deals with Charlemagne's campaigns in Spain, with the battle of Roncevaux, and with the death of Roland.

* * *

The most dynamic Italian prose of the fourteenth century is to be found in the nearly four hundred letters of St. Catherine of Siena — letters not written with her own hand, but dictated to devotees who served her as secretaries. Caterina Benincasa, born in 1347, mystic and ascetic from her childhood, became a Dominican tertiary about 1363. For some time she ministered in Siena to the sick; but about 1375 she began to go to other Tuscan cities, and to exert much influence in public affairs, and especially in the affairs of the Church. It was she who, going to Avignon, nominally as an emissary of Florence, persuaded Gregory XI to return to Rome. After his death Urban VI called her to Rome, and there, as his champion, she spent herself in futile efforts to heal the catastrophic Schism. She died in 1380.

She was utterly "in-willed" — to use a word of Dante's devising — with the will of God as she felt and understood it, and she was driven utterly by a limitless love of God from which there sprang a limitless love for all those whom He had created. She was intensely concerned for the spiritual well-being of a great many individual persons, and she was intensely and especially concerned that the Church should become worthy again of its supreme vicariate. Her letters are direct emanations of her powerful will, her limitless love, and her intense concern. Whether she speaks to humble folk or to pope, king, or queen, she speaks as one having complete authority: her sentences are quite constantly imperative in content and in form. Yet her use of her authority is so perfectly selfless, so reasonable, so tender, even in reproof, that it opens the gates of mind and heart: it was in fact welcome and in some measure effective in all but the darkest corners of the dark world in which she shone.

Among her best-known letters are the several addressed to Gregory XI, the several addressed to Queen Joan of Naples, one addressed to Sir John Hawkwood, one describing the death of a certain Niccolò Tuldo, and two describing experiences of her last days of suffering and vision. To Sir John she wrote in this vein:

> Dearest and sweetest brother in Christ Jesus, it would be a great thing now if you would withdraw a little into yourself, and reflect how great are the pains and anguish which you have endured by being in the service and pay of the devil. Now my soul desires that you should change your way of life, and take the pay and the cross of Christ crucified, you and all your followers and companions. . .*

The letter on the death of Niccolò Tuldo, the most famous of all the letters, too powerful and too poignant to admit of fragmentary quotation, tells of her consolation of the doomed man, of his insistence that she promise to be with him at the place and moment of his execution, and of her fulfillment of that promise. Her last letters tell of "the terror of demons" that beset her exhausted body, and of mystic experiences that even her clarity could only faintly suggest.

• • •

Giovanni Sercambi (1348–1424), a prominent citizen of Lucca, and an otherwise unknown Ser Giovanni, probably a Florentine, both wrote inferior collections of *novelle* within this period. Each of the two collections has a frame story; each derives some of its stories, more or less completely, from the *Decameron*; and each is largely scurrilous.

Sercambi's collection has no title. The frame story tells of the journeyings of a company of men and women who leave Lucca in order to avoid a plague that was raging in Tuscany in 1374. Choosing one of their number as

* The translation is by Vida D. Scudder.

leader, they go south to Naples, east to Brindisi, north to Venice, west to Genoa, and then back to Lucca, visiting about a hundred towns in the course of their travels. The *novelle* are told sometimes upon the way and sometimes in the towns: all are told by Sercambi himself, as one of the company. The collection was completed by 1387. It contains about 150 *novelle*, a few of which are of some interest as representing early or peculiar forms of traditional stories.*

Ser Giovanni's collection, begun in 1378 and finished after 1385, derives its title, *Il pecorone*, "the Numskull" — a title probably not due to the author — from the fact that so many *pecoroni* appear in the book. The futile frame story tells of a chaplain and a nun who on twenty-five successive days meet in a convent parlor, each telling the other one story on each day. About half of their stories are fictional; the other half are drawn from the *Cronaca* of Giovanni Villani. Many of the tales are stupid, but a few are definitely good. The best, that of Giannetto and the Lady of Belmonte, embodies the "pound of flesh" motif in an excellent plot, from which Shakespeare derived, directly or indirectly, the "pound of flesh" portion of the plot of *The Merchant of Venice.*

* * *

The leading humanist of this period, and the strongest link between Petrarch and the humanists of the following century, was Coluccio Salutati (1331–1406), Chancellor of Florence from 1375 until his death. An energetic disciple of Petrarch, he followed his master's example in his scholarly enthusiasm for classic culture, in his persistent collection of manuscripts, and in his outpouring of letters and other works in Latin. As Chancellor of Florence it was his duty to compose the official letters of the city; and he fulfilled this duty in a style and a spirit so classic as to set new standards for official correspondence. Anyone who attacked Florence verbally, in Salutati's time, came off second best. His major work, the *De laboribus Herculis*, opens with a defense of poetry, and continues with a vast assemblage and systematic presentation of classic Herculean lore. Medieval in its constant use of allegorical interpretation, the *De laboribus* is decisively humanistic in the range and the enthusiasm of its exploration of classic authors.

In 1397, on the initiative of Salutati, the Byzantine scholar Manuel Chrysoloras was called to the University of Florence as Professor of Greek. His three-year service marked the beginning of a substantial and enduring interest in Greek studies, opening thus a second field for humanistic research and imitation.

* The similarity of Sercambi's frame story to that of the *Canterbury Tales* has been noted; but the general opinion is that the likenesses are merely coincidental.

CHAPTER 14

The Militant Humanists

WITHIN THE FIRST sixty years of the fifteenth century the Sforza family succeeded the Visconti as rulers of Milan; Venice greatly enlarged her dominion on the mainland; Cosimo de' Medici became in 1434 the *de facto* ruler of Florence; and the House of Aragon came into possession of the Kingdom of Naples. Two important ecumenical councils were held: the Council of Constance (1414–1418) put an end to the Great Schism, and the Council of Basel, Ferrara, Florence, and Rome (1431–1443) led to a short-lived union of the Greek and Roman Churches. Both councils were of great cultural importance, the first because it brought together Northern and Italian scholars, and the second because it brought several Greek scholars to Italy. A new Islamic thrust resulted in 1453 in the fall of Constantinople. A good many Greek scholars came to Italy as refugees, but Greek studies were already so well established in Italy that the contribution of the newcomers was of secondary importance. Other events, taking place outside of Italy, were of world-wide significance: overseas exploration began with the Portuguese rediscovery of the Madeiras and the Azores; and German printers, about the middle of the century, invented the process of printing from movable type.

These same decades witnessed an extraordinary outburst of genius in the fine arts. In architecture Brunelleschi, reacting from the outworn Italian Gothic tradition and turning again to the monuments of ancient Rome, established concepts and patterns that were to endure, with various modifications, for centuries. His own work culminated in the superb dome of the Florentine cathedral. In sculpture Jacopo della Quercia, medieval in certain limitations, was modern in his tremendous vigor; Ghiberti's "gates of Paradise" combined grandeur and supreme grace; Donatello, greatest of them all, entering to some extent into the Roman tradition, was yet more concerned with vigor and with realism, especially in the rendering of character; and Luca della Robbia, companion to the others in the dignity of his marbles, created in his terra cottas a new medium for pure loveliness. Painting, which had no clear Roman tradition to resume, though it borrowed certain decorative elements from Roman art, saw the last perfect flowering of the medieval spirit in Fra Angelico; surged forward into vigorous modernity with Masolino and Masaccio; and found a new human charm with Fra Lippo Lippi.

* * *

Comparable in its profusion to the simultaneous development in the fine arts was the very great development of humanism, which now so fired the ambitions and absorbed the energies of Italian men of letters in general that few authors, and none of them of the highest order of ability, devoted themselves exclusively to writing in the vernacular.

To call the typical writers of this period "humanists" is to recognize their community in the enthusiastic and scholarly study of the classics, in the undertaking of extensive philological and editorial labors, and in the writing of Latin works of their own in classicizing form and style. Most of them were employed either as teachers, or as secretaries or chancellors in papal or princely courts or in city governments. And they were militant in their assertion of the importance of their own studies and their own services. But their several patterns of life and work were by no means identical. Individual likenesses and differences will appear in the following pages, in which only a few of the many militant humanists will find mention.*

Leonardo Bruni (1374–1444) was born in Arezzo, and was often called, accordingly, Leonardo Aretino; but he became a Florentine by education and by choice. For some years he served as a papal secretary, and in that capacity he attended the Council of Constance. Thereafter he made his home in Florence, busied primarily with his writing, but taking a wise and honorable part in the public life of the city. He served as its Chancellor from 1427 to his death. The most important of his many and varied Latin works was his *History of Florence*, which covers the history of the city from its Roman origins to 1402. He is careful as to facts, judging his sources critically and supplementing them by the use of documents; he seeks the causes of the events he narrates; and he tries to see those events in due perspective — characteristics which, in their combination, entitle him to be considered as the first modern historian. He sought to achieve a classic dignity of style;

* The classic phrase *studia humanitatis* was applied, in this period, to a group of studies comprising grammar, rhetoric, poetry, history, and moral philosophy; but the word *humanista* came into use only in the latter part of the fifteenth century, and then with reference only to university teachers of the "humanities," as just listed. The word "humanist" in the broader literary sense and the word "humanism" in the literary sense are of nineteenth-century coinage.

and he enlivened his pages, in the classic fashion, by the introduction of numerous imaginary harangues, many of which are devoted to the exaltation of liberty. Bruni first, among the humanists, translated from the Greek, making Latin versions of the *Nicomachaean Ethics* and the *Politics* of Aristotle, several of the dialogues of Plato, and several works by other authors. He wrote in Greek a treatise on the political constitution of Florence. In Italian he wrote lives of Dante and of Petrarch, and one *novella* (on a classic theme).

The career of Poggio Bracciolini (1380–1459) was similar to that of Bruni in that Poggio, born in Southern Tuscany, became a Florentine by education and by choice, served for some years as a papal secretary, attended the Council of Constance, and toward the end of his life served as Chancellor of Florence. At one time he spent four lonely years in England. His distinctive contribution to the cause of humanism was his persistent and repeatedly successful effort to discover missing classic works. In the years 1415–1417 he found, in various Burgundian, Swiss, and German monasteries, manuscripts of Lucretius, the *Silvae* of Statius, a complete Quintilian, several orations of Cicero, and missing works or portions of works by other authors. He wrote voluminously, always in Latin, and almost always with vivacity and brilliance. Of all the thousands of humanist letters and hundreds of humanist dialogues his are easily the best. His long dialogue *De varietate fortunae*, moving from reflection upon the ruins of ancient Rome, and Stoic in its spirit, is his ablest single work. His wit ran to uncurbed excesses in his fierce polemics, directed usually against other humanists. He wrote an *Historia florentina* covering the period from 1350 to 1455, and a very famous *Liber facetiarum*, a collection of jests and amusing anecdotes.

Francesco Filelfo (1398–1481), born near Ancona, served in his youth as a subordinate in the Venetian foreign service, spending some time in Constantinople, where he studied Greek, and visiting Hungary and Poland. After his return to Italy he taught for a few years in the University of Florence; but he made enemies there, and left the city in hostility and fear. He soon established himself in Milan, where he remained for most of the rest of his arrogant and extravagant life, patronized first by the Visconti and then by the Sforza. Utterly unprincipled, he used his verbal facility in venomous invectives against his rivals and his enemies, or as a means of extracting favors or gratuities either from those to whom he paid fulsome tribute or from those whom he threatened with insult if they did not buy him off. His literary output was enormous, but pedestrian. He alone among the humanists of this period wrote extensively in Latin verse: his poems include odes, satires, epigrams, and an epic on the rise of the Sforza family. His excellent knowledge of Greek served him for several translations, and for the writing of some Greek verse. Unwillingly, at the desire of a Visconti duke, he wrote in Italian a perfunctory and incomplete commentary on the *Canzoniere* of Petrarch.

The Roman Lorenzo Valla (1407–1457) taught in his youth in Pavia and elsewhere in Northern Italy; served for ten years as secretary to King Alfonso of Naples; and then, returning to Rome, spent the rest of his life there as a papal secretary. Keenly critical in his thinking, he attacked what seemed to him to be undue assumptions of authority or of tradition in the fields of philosophy, religion, law, and philology. In his first work, the dialogue *De voluptate*, he maintains that the desire for pleasure is the central human motive; that man, being both body and spirit, naturally and rightfully seeks, as body, the normal human pleasures and, as spirit, the eternal blessedness; and that the two types of pleasure are perfectly compatible. In a later dialogue, the *De libero arbitrio*, he wrestles with the perpetual problem of free will, concluding that the will is free in that it is not conditioned by divine foreknowledge, and that its relationship to the will of God remains a mystery that reason cannot solve. With essentially modern methods of historical and textual criticism he proved that the document asserting the Donation of Constantine was unauthentic; and that the Apostles' Creed was the work not of the Twelve, but of the first Nicene Council. He compared St. Jerome's translation of the New Testament with its Greek original, and dared to attack the infallibility of the Latin version. The best known of all Valla's writings is the *De linguae latinae elegantia*. In this work his scorn for medieval barbarisms, his enthusiasm for classic Latin, and his determination to find authority not in the grammarians but in the best classic practice enabled him to establish standards of linguistic and stylistic excellence still higher than those attained by the other humanists of his own day. His philosophical and religious works, highly esteemed by Erasmus, Luther, and Calvin, served in the following century to give aid and comfort to the Protestant cause: it was Erasmus who first published Valla's work on St. Jerome's translation of the New Testament. But Valla himself, for all his criticism, was loyal to the Church.

Enea Silvio Piccolomini of Siena (1405–1464), often called Aeneas Sylvius, began his active life as a highly gifted youth, interested in everything he saw, much amused by mankind, and unscrupulously ambitious. He came first into prominence at the Council of Basel, which sent him on a mission to James I of Scotland. He then spent several years beyond the Alps, serving first an antipope and then the Emperor Frederick III, whose court, thanks to the presence of Piccolomini, became the seedbed of humanism in Germany. In these early years he indulged in Latin love poems, and wrote, in Latin, both a disreputable Plautine comedy, the *Chrisis*, and the most undeservedly famous of his writings, the *Historia de duobus amantibus*, a Boccaccesque *novella* of some length, which gained wide circulation not only in its original form but also in Italian, French, German, and English versions. In the very next year, however, seeing the political error of his ways, he made submission to the Pope in Rome, took orders, and embarked upon an ecclesiastical career in which he advanced swiftly through bishopric and cardinalate to the papacy, which he achieved, as Pius II, in 1458. Throughout this longer portion of his life he wrote extensively, seriously, and very well indeed. The most notable of all his works is his long autobiography, wide-ranging in its experiences, its descriptions, and its comments. Its first Book includes a very interesting account of his early adventures in Scotland and England. His letters and dialogues are picturesque and lively. He was the leading orator of his day. The most spectacular scenes of his life are recorded by Pinturicchio in frescoes that still glow convincingly on the walls of the library of the Cathedral of Siena.

Leon Battista Alberti (1404–1472), born of a prominent Florentine family, held a papal secretaryship and lived in Rome for the greater part of his mature life, but spent the years 1434–1443 chiefly in Florence. He was primarily a humanist; but he was atypical both in his extraordinary versatility and in his championship of the Italian language as a worthy literary medium. He was an athlete (he excelled in racing, jumping, vaulting, climbing, ball-playing, fencing, archery, and horsemanship), a great architect, a sculptor, a painter, a musician, a mathematician, a scientist and inventor (he experimented in the field of optics, and developed several measuring devices), and an engineer (he tried to raise one of the sunken Roman ships in the Lake of Nemi); and he was skilled in astronomy and the law. He was, indeed, a pre-incarnation of Leonardo.

In his architecture he made eager, scholarly, and imaginative use of Roman principle and Roman design. The three structures that chiefly evidence his greatness are the so-called Malatesta Temple in Rimini, the Rucellai palace in Florence, and Sant' Andrea in Mantua. In Sant' Andrea the traditional Gothic columnar piers and groined vaults are replaced by massive rectangular piers and barrel vaults, suggested by those of the great Roman baths, the whole so ordered and so proportioned that the resulting structure is one of the noblest churches of the Italian Renaissance, perhaps the noblest of them all. It represents the initiation of the architectural system that was ultimately to find its most grandiose embodiment in the new St. Peter's.

Alberti wrote voluminously, both in Latin and in Italian. The most extensive of his Latin works is his very scholarly, very personal, and very influential treatise *De re aedificatoria.* Based upon a thorough and precise examination of extant monuments of Roman architecture and upon a critical study of Vitruvius, the work benefits by Alberti's experience as a successful innovating architect, and embodies confidently his firm convictions as to the nobility of a creative art concerned at once with scientific perfection and with the attainment of beauty. His *Intercoenales*, "Dinner Entertainments," is a collection of about twenty dialogues and other short pieces, largely in the mood and the manner of Lucian, which treat various aspects of life, sometimes with sympathy, oftener with satire, and always thoughtfully. Other Latin writings include an early allegorical comedy; an expert and enthusiastic treatise on the nature and the care of the horse; and a treatise on justice which inveighs impressively against pettifoggery and against cruelty in punishment, and argues that punishment should be designed not to crush but to amend.

The most important of Alberti's writings in Italian is his long dialogue *Della famiglia*, written during his stay in Florence. The conversation, which has a proud human quality of its own, is carried on chiefly by men of the Alberti family, who evince a just appreciation of their honorable family tradition. The first Book, an educational classic, discusses the responsibilities of the old to the young and of the young to the old, and in particular the education of children. That education is to be physical and social as well as mental. Great stress is laid upon bodily discipline, exercise of many kinds, and the maintenance of health — all this in order that the *corpus sanum* may then serve its mature master well for activities of a higher order. The youth is to be initiated into architecture, sculpture, painting, and music, and is to be led into the love of nature, animate and inanimate. He is to gain much from association with men, growing thus in obedience, prudence, honor, self-control, and self-reliance. He is to be moderate, and never idle, and he is to be prepared, even to the extent of learning the rudiments of a trade, to withstand the onslaughts of ill-fortune. More formally, he is to be trained in the reading and writing of Italian, Latin, and Greek. Alberti's educational theory, like his architectural theory, is derived in the first instance from ancient sources, but is developed freely in accordance with his own personal experiences and convictions.

The second Book of the *Famiglia* discusses marriage, exalted as a union of minds and wills; the third, on the general management of the household, affirms, but in no miserly spirit, the excellence of thrift, and becomes eloquent in its praise of villa life; and the fourth deals with friendship.

Among Alberti's other writings in Italian the most interesting are two early treatises, one on sculpture and one on painting, which are the first Renaissance treatments of these themes, and his last and mellowest work, the *De iciarchia*, "On the Headship of a Family." In this he goes over again some of the ground he had covered in the *Famiglia*; but he now has in mind in particular the training of men who are to exercise power in the state, and are therefore to be responsible for the liberty and dignity of the state itself, and for the welfare of its citizens. He exalts the family as the pattern for the state, and self-mastery as the chief excellence of the individual man. In some respects, even in some details, he anticipates ideas that were to be set forth by Castiglione, a century later, in his *Book of the Courtier*.

Alberti's most dramatic gesture in his championship of the Italian language as a literary medium was the *certame coronario*, the "contest for the crown," which he devised and carried through, the costs being borne by Piero de' Medici, son of Cosimo. Alberti's purpose was to prove that Italian verse could treat worthily of worthy themes. The theme chosen for the contest was Friendship. On the appointed day, October 22, 1441, the contest was held in the crowded Cathedral. The Council was then in session in Florence, and the judges were ten papal secretaries, all of them humanists, and generally disposed to scorn the vulgar tongue. The prize was to be a silver crown in the form of a laurel-wreath. Eight poets, including Alberti, presented their poems, in Italian, on the stated theme. The poems, unfortunately, were of slight intrinsic value; but two of them are of interest as being the first attempts to write Italian verse in classic Latin metres. Alberti's poem, written in unrhymed Italian hexameters, begins thus:

> Dite, o mortali che sí fulgente corona
> Ponesti in mezo, che pur mirando volete? *

The syllables are treated as long or short according as they would be long or short in the corresponding Latin words: any reader familiar with Latin scansion will see that these Italian lines may be scanned as if they were Latin. We do not know how they were actually read. At the close of the contest the judges, alleging that four of the competitors had shown equal merit, refused to award the crown, and directed that it be given to the Cathedral. The decision was ill received: it was generally believed that the judges had been moved by envy.

Many other men engaged with some distinction in humanistic activities, most of them combining scholarship with writing in Latin. Of the few whose humanism manifested itself chiefly in ways other than those of the pen, the two most eminent were the two great educators, Guarino of Verona (1374–1460), who taught chiefly in Ferrara, and Vittorino da Feltre (1373–1446), who taught chiefly in Mantua. Their careers were very similar: both maintained schools under court patronage in North Italian cities; both based their teaching upon Greek principles; both were concerned with physical, moral, and religious education as well as with mental education; both lived with their pupils; both were men of lovable and democratic personality; and both had great influence upon those whom they taught, and upon later educational theory and practice.

During these years many Greek scholars came to Italy, either to attend

* "Say, oh mortals who have set in your midst so resplendent a crown, what is it that you seek as you gaze?"

the second Council, or for other reasons; and several of them stayed on. The two who won greatest distinction and had greatest influence were Gemistus Pletho, a philosopher, and in particular an exponent of Neo-Platonism; and Bessarion, who transferred his ecclesiastical allegiance to the Roman Church, in which he became a cardinal.

The greatest of the several patrons of the period were Cosimo de' Medici, Pope Nicholas V (who in his early days had drawn up a plan of library classification for Cosimo), and, for the Greeks, Cardinal Bessarion. All three of these men, as well as others — some of them rulers, such as Federigo di Montefeltro, Duke of Urbino, and some of them private citizens — assembled fine collections of manuscripts. Under Nicholas V the Vatican Library grew from almost nothing to a collection of over a thousand volumes; and Bessarion's collection, bequeathed to the city of Venice, became the nucleus of the Venetian Library of St. Mark's.

Within this period humanism was introduced into England. Humphrey, Duke of Gloucester, the first English patron of the new learning, called three or four of the lesser Italian humanists to England, and corresponded with some of the greater ones. Toward the end of the period five Oxford men went to Italy to gain humanistic knowledge at first hand: all of them studied with Guarino, or were in some way associated with him. The most learned of the five, John Free, stayed on in Italy, where he was known among humanists as Phreas. The four who returned, and Free through his writings, did much to further the acceptance of humanism in England.

CHAPTER 15

Contemporaries of the Militant Humanists

THE EXCITEMENTS of humanism so lured Italian men of letters into the exclusive or almost exclusive use of Latin throughout this period that relatively little writing was done in Italian. Even the production of the love lyric in the traditional forms was slight. The poetry of the two chief conventional lyrists, Buonaccorso da Montemagno and Giusto de' Conti, is interesting chiefly because it marks the beginning of a thoroughgoing Petrarchism. The influence of Petrarch had been felt and shown by many minor lyrists of Petrarch's own century, but it had not dominated them completely: the verse of Buonaccorso and Giusto is much more strictly imitative, both in theme and in phrase.

Leonello d' Este (1407–1450), pupil of Guarino, friend of Alberti, and Marquis of Ferrara, was in a minor way, for his lesser state, very much what Lorenzo de' Medici was so soon to be for Florence. He was a successful ruler, he was a generous patron, he wrote Latin letters, and he wrote a few sonnets. The only two of these sonnets that have survived are remarkably imaginative and vigorous in thought and expression. The theme of blindness wrought by love is common enough: but in no other poem has it ever found such vivid realization as in Leonello's sonnet beginning *Lo amore me ha fatto cieco.*

The Florentine tradition of the humorous sonnet was carried on with great success by the barber known as Il Burchiello, a person of sufficient importance to be banished when Cosimo de' Medici returned to Florence. His life, like that of many another laughing poet, was spent in poverty and varied misery. One of his sonnets is a debate between Poetry and the Razor, each protesting that the other takes too much of Burchiello's time. Another, an early specimen of nonsense verse, begins thus:

Fried nominatives, universal maps,
And Noah's Ark astrand betwixt two poles
Were singing "Glory Be" with all their souls
Because the dishes weren't as round as caps.

The most noteworthy lyric development of the period was the adoption of the *strambotto* for use as a written literary medium. The form adopted was the Tuscan form, which consists, as we have seen, of eight eleven-syllable lines, rhyming ABABABCC.* The one series of *strambotti* written certainly within this period in Tuscany is known as the *Rispetti per Tisbe*. By an unknown author, it is of no great intrinsic interest; but the *strambotti* of the Venetian Giustinian, which may or may not have been earlier than the first written Tuscan *strambotti*, are the work of a true poet.

Leonardo Giustinian (1388–1446) was a Venetian patrician, a pupil of Guarino, learned in Latin and in Greek, and busy all his mature life with the responsibilities of public office. Yet he took delight in the popular songs that he heard about him, and with genial facility he wrote similar but more finished songs of his own, writing in a generalized Venetian dialect, and composing the music for his own words. He adopted two quite different forms, the *strambotto* and the *canzonetta.*

In his thirty-odd *strambotti* he caught the folk spirit so perfectly that several of them have entered into the folk repertory and have been perpetuated by folk voices, sometimes with folk variations, in many parts of Italy. One of the most widely known is this:

Se li arbori sapessen favellare
E le lor foglie fusseno le lingue,
L' inchiostro fusse l'acqua dello mare,
La terra fusse carta e l'erbe penne,
Le tue bellezze non potria contare.
Quando nascesti, li angioli ci venne;
Quando nascesti, colorito giglio,
Tutti li santi furno a quel consiglio —

If the trees could speak and their leaves were tongues, and if the water of the sea were ink, the land were paper, and the grass were pens, they could not tell all your beauties. When you were born, the angels came; when you were born, bright lily, all the saints gathered together there.

His *canzonette*, most of them in *ballata* form, are lighthearted in tone, and sprightly in their metrical structure. Most of them are vivacious songs of amorous pleading, pleasantly marked by the uncommonly happy use of some of the commonest of floral and other metaphors. Several are long dialogues,

* See pp. 9–10 and 76. The purely lyric and quasi-folk character of the first written *strambotti* indicates that they were modeled directly upon the folk *strambotti* rather than upon the metrically identical stanzas used in *cantari* and epics by Tuscan *cantastorie.*

between lover and lady, lover and servant, or mother and daughter: these have a gay *novella* quality.

Giustinian wrote also some seventy *laude*. These poems, though in their general manner they have much in common with his secular verse, bear evidence also of his more serious literary culture. One of them is modeled definitely on Petrarch's *Vergine bella*.

Laude were being written elsewhere as well. Among those who were writing them in Tuscany, the finest and most distinguished person was Lucrezia Tornabuoni, devoted wife of Piero de' Medici and devoted mother of their children, and the first woman known to us by name who wrote Italian verse. Her best known *lauda*, beginning *Ecco il re forte*, "Behold the strong king," is a spirited evocation of the triumphal descent of Christ into Limbus.

Within this period the *lauda* in definitely dramatic form, written for performance, reached what is on the whole its most significant development in the Florentine *sacra rappresentazione*.

The *sacre rappresentazioni* were acted by members of religious associations, usually young men and boys. Different portions of the stage represented different localities, and the actors passed obviously from one point to another as the course of the action shifted from one locality to another. The supposed time of the events represented covered, in some cases, as much as several years. There was no division into acts or scenes. The metrical form adopted was the ABABABCC octave, which was already in use in the Tuscan religious *cantari*. Each play opened with a prologue delivered by an "angel." The subjects were in general the same as those of the *laude*; but Old Testament stories and legends of saints and martyrs were more popular than narratives of the Passion. The plays of this period are by no means devoid of reverence, but the earlier ascetic enthusiasm has given place to a familiar placidity, and the religious effect is educational rather than exciting.

Most of the *rappresentazioni* are anonymous. Of the two or three identifiable men who wrote such plays in this period the only one who is of even minor literary note is Feo Belcari (1410–1484), author of the *Abramo ed Isac*, one of the earliest plays, and one of the best.

* * *

The voice most eagerly listened to at this time in Italy was that of the Franciscan friar Bernardino da Siena (1380–1444). Wherever he went thousands on thousands crowded into city squares to hear him. He spoke without notes, but a devotee once made in shorthand, and later transcribed, a word-for-word record of a series of some fifty sermons preached in the great Piazza del Campo of Siena — a record that serves almost to make us members of the huge and intent audience. Though Bernardino was in his own experience a mystic, he devoted his preaching mainly to matters of everyday conduct, attacking the sins that were inevitably the besetting sins of the human units of his listening mass, and exhorting them to live in honesty, justice, peace, religious observance, and family love; and though he was learned in theology and followed the scholastic pattern in the organization of his thought he spoke without the slightest rhetorical pretension, holding his hearers not only by his candent sincerity and his outreaching affection but also by his use of the very idiom of their own daily speech, spiced often with a homely wit, and by his free and vivid use of anecdotes, fables, *novelle*, reminiscences, and other stories of many kinds, told expertly. His version of the familiar story of The Prior, the Novice, and the Ass is often quoted. Many other stories, some of them unique, are equally perfect, among them The Lion Holds Court, A New Way to Learn the Lord's Prayer, and The Will of Lippotopo. His curiously sunken face still looks out patiently from scores of Italian frescoes and altarpieces of his century.

Similar in its general scope to the *Famiglia* and the *De iciarchia* of Alberti is the *Vita civile* of Matteo Palmieri (1406–1475), a substantial Florentine citizen who rendered good service to the city-state he loved, both in his tenure of responsible civic offices and in missions to the heads of other states. Well educated, he wrote some minor historical works in Latin; but he preferred Italian for the works on which he spent most care. The *Vita civile*, written just before Alberti's *Famiglia*, treats in dialogue form the training of the ideal citizen. Its first Book deals with the education of children; the second expounds prudence, fortitude, and temperance; the third is devoted to justice; and the fourth deals with concerns of the private citizen and with the obligations of the state in respect to the promotion of the general welfare and to civic embellishment. In later years Palmieri, who greatly admired Dante, wrote in *terza rima* an imitative vision of his own, *La città di vita*, "The City of Life," in which, with more industry than inspiration, he undertakes, under the guidance of the Cumaean Sibyl, a journey in the course of which he seeks to illustrate Neoplatonic theories as to the source and fate of human souls.

Several single *novelle* were written in this period. One of these, the anonymous *novella* of *Ippolito e Leonora*,* contains several of the elements that were to go into the making of the story of Romeo and Juliet: the lovers (in this case Ippolito Buondelmonte and Leonora de' Bardi) are of hostile families; they fall in love at a festival; they are brought together through the intervention of a religious person (in this case an abbess); access to Leonora's room is gained by use of a rope ladder; there is a secret marriage; the lover falls foul of the law; and at the end (which in this case is without tragedy) the hostile families are reconciled.

* Often unjustifiably attributed to Alberti.

The Florentine *cantastorie* Andrea da Barberino has the honor of having given more diversion to more Italians for more centuries than any other man who ever wrote: for two of his prose narratives, *Guerrino il Meschino* and *I reali di Francia*, have been the delight not only of the throngs who have heard them read or recited in public squares, but of numberless listening families to whom, in the long evenings, someone has been able to read at least the substance of the alluring pages, and for whom crude illustrations, from primitive woodcuts to modern colored lithographs, have been windows into romance.

Guerrino is Andrea's own creature, and his story, in its fantastic totality, is of Andrea's own invention, though its elements reflect a multiplicity of sources. Adventures and misadventures succeed each other endlessly; duels and battles galore are fought and won; monsters are slain, prisoners released, treacheries thwarted, and temptations withstood; journeys range to the fabulous Orient, to the marvels of a Sibylline cavern, to Hell and to the Earthly Paradise; and through it all Guerrino moves, upright and unshatterable, from a nameless childhood slavery (whence the epithet *Meschino*) to the discovery of his royal parentage, the release of his parents from imprisonment, marriage with the Persian princess of his heart, happy years of kingship, and a saintly death at the age of fifty-six.

I reali di Francia, "The Royalty of France," is a lengthy compilation, amplification, and pseudo-historicization of Carolingian material, based chiefly on earlier Italian prose versions of Carolingian stories. Thanks to Andrea, Italian audiences may still applaud the Carolingian heroics of their puppet shows. And Guerrino, in cheap editions, is still following thousands and thousands of his compatriots across the seas.

CHAPTER 16

Lorenzo de' Medici

COSIMO DE' MEDICI died in 1464, leaving his power to his elder son Piero, who administered faithfully and ably the affairs of his family and of his city. Piero and his wife, Lucrezia Tornabuoni, had two sons, Lorenzo, born in 1449, and Giuliano, born four years later. On Piero's death in December 1469, Lorenzo entered upon his great inheritance. He had been prepared for his life's work by parental care, by his mother's insistent religious training, by the best of private education, and by early participation in civic and diplomatic responsibilities; and he was qualified for it by the keenness of his own mind and the boundlessness of his own energy. He was soon called *Il Magnifico*; and in the years of his magnificence he proved himself to be the greatest Italian statesman of his time, one of the greatest poets of his time, and the greatest cultural patron of all time.

There were five major and rival states in the Italy of his day, each centering in a city, but each holding dominion over much territory and many cities: to the north, Milan, ruled by the Sforza; to the northeast, Venice, still a merchant oligarchy in republican form; then Florence, whose broad dominion followed irregularly the course of the Arno, from the Apennines to Pisa and the sea; then Rome, and the States of the Church; and to the south, the Kingdom of Naples, under the House of Aragon. There were many minor states, some of them cultural centers, such as Ferrara, Mantua, and Urbino. Beyond the Alps, France, with weak hereditary claims on both Milan and Naples, was biding its time: invasion was sure to come if the major Italian states should be sufficiently enfeebled by internecine strife. The two cardinal points of Lorenzo's foreign policy were the maintenance of a balance of power and a *modus vivendi* among the major Italian states, and the maintenance of friendly relations between Florence and France. War broke out in Italy more than once; and more than once, taking his liberty in his hands, he carried persuasion to his enemies. While his life lasted, Italy, though grievously troubled, remained free from long-continued warfare and from French invasion.

Even before his father's death Lorenzo had played the part of the young prince, and had begun to write princely, if Petrarchan, verse. The lady of his *fino amore* was Lucrezia Donati; and it was apparently in her honor, though nominally in honor of his recently arranged betrothal to Clarice Orsini, of the great Roman family, that, early in 1469, he gave a memorable tournament in the Piazza Santa Croce. It was a very gentle and a very gorgeous tournament. The prize, a silver helmet wrought by the goldsmith Pollaiuolo, was awarded to Lorenzo, who had certainly deserved it on the ground of the beauty of his costume and the brilliance of the whole affair, and may well have deserved it on other grounds also, since he delighted in physical exercise and physical prowess. In 1475 Giuliano, following his brother's example, gave in the Piazza Santa Croce a memorable tournament of his own, in honor of his lady, Simonetta Cattaneo.

Three years later Lorenzo faced his one fierce and almost fatal crisis within Florence. Members of the rival Pazzi family formed a conspiracy — involving, among others, the Archbishop Salviati — to assassinate both Lorenzo and Giuliano. The scene of the attack was the Cathedral; the moment was a certain point in the celebration of the Mass on an April Sunday. Giuliano was killed; Lorenzo, slightly wounded, fought off his assailants until he was enabled to escape. The enraged populace, loyal to Lorenzo, wrought swift and terrible vengeance upon the chief conspirators, including the archbishop. Pope Sixtus IV excommunicated Lorenzo, laid Florence under interdict, and attacked Florentine territory, in alliance with the King of Naples. Milan and Venice sided with Florence; fighting came to an end in 1479; and in the following year excommunication and interdict were withdrawn, after Lorenzo had personally won over the King of Naples, and after the taking of Otranto by the Turks had convinced the Pope of the necessity for Italian unity.

Lorenzo's later years, though strenuous always, and beset by ill health, were at least less perilous. His marriage to Clarice Orsini was in the main a happy one; and he evidently tried to be a good father to their three sons, Piero, Giovanni, and Giuliano. Clarice died in 1488. In 1489 Giovanni, being then thirteen years of age, was made a cardinal.

Lorenzo loved the country, and spent as much time as he could in one or another of the Medici country places. His favorite villas were one at Poggio a Caiano, ten miles west of Florence, and one at Careggi, in the foothills just north of the city. To Careggi he went in the Spring of 1492, knowing that he had not long to live. There, shortly before his death, he was visited by Savonarola, who, according to Politian, an eyewitness, gave him his blessing.

It was a momentous year. In January, Ferdinand and Isabella had entered Granada; in August, the Spaniard Rodrigo de Borja was to achieve the papacy as Alexander VI; and in October, Columbus was to behold what he thought to be Cathay.

Within the radiance of Lorenzo's patronage an extraordinary group of highly gifted men carried on many kinds of creative activity. Among them were the humanists Landino, Ficino (also a philosopher), Politian (also a poet), and Pico della Mirandola; the poets Luigi Pulci and Matteo Franco; the architects Giuliano da San Gallo and Benedetto da Maiano (also a sculptor); the sculptors Antonio Pollaiuolo and Verrocchio (also painters), Desiderio da Settignano, Andrea della Robbia, and, in his early youth, Michelangelo; the painters Botticelli, Ghirlandaio, Filippino Lippi, and, in his youth, Leonardo da Vinci; the musicians Squarcialupi and Heinrich Isaac; and the scientist Toscanelli.

Giuliano da San Gallo built for Lorenzo the beloved villa of Poggio a Caiano. Benedetto da Maiano as architect designed the finest of all the Florentine *palazzi*, that of the Strozzi, and made several fine portrait busts, and the pulpit in Santa Croce which is perhaps the loveliest of all pulpits. Pollaiuolo was a realist with a predilection for classic themes; Verrocchio, a supreme realist, whose statue of the Venetian *condottiere* Colleoni is one of the two or three greatest of all equestrian statues, was yet capable of a strong and refined grace, the secrets of which he transmitted to his pupil Leonardo; Desiderio and Andrea, working one in marble and the other in terra cotta, sought exquisiteness, especially in the rendering of childhood.* Among the painters the most poetic, sensitive to every wind that blew through the thought of Florence, was Botticelli, who could be, with conviction, as otherworldly as Dante, as pagan as Politian, or as penitent and foreboding as Savonarola. Ghirlandaio, prosaic but exceedingly skillful, peopled his frescoes in Santa Maria Novella and Santa Trinita with the chief men and women of Laurentian Florence; and Filippino Lippi, generally similar to Ghirlandaio, attained at times his Botticellian best. Squarcialupi, organist of the Cathedral, was also a collector and preserver of the music of the Italian *Ars nova*. After his death Lorenzo wrote a Latin epitaph for him, and called the Flemish composer Heinrich Isaac to take his place. Toscanelli, expert in mathematics, geography, and astronomy, observed and recorded the successive positions of several comets, listened avidly to the reports of men who had knowledge of far countries, and wrote in 1474, to a Portuguese correspondent, a letter in which he maintained that the most direct passage to Eastern Asia would be not by the African route that the Portuguese ex-

* The unidentified sculptor of the superb bust of Dante now in the National Museum of Naples was quite probably a Laurentian Florentine.

plorers had been following, but by a direct crossing of the Atlantic in the latitude of Spain.

The two most constant scenes of Lorenzo's patronage were the Medici palace itself and the Garden of San Marco,* which has been called the first modern Art Museum and the first modern Academy of Art. Here Lorenzo gathered pieces of ancient and of modern sculpture, together with models and drawings by many artists. An aging sculptor, Bertoldo di Giovanni, was put in charge, and young artists were welcomed as visitors. There is evidence that Leonardo da Vinci was one of those who took advantage of this opportunity. In 1489 the garden was made more formally a place of teaching; and in that year or the next Michelangelo Buonarroti, then a boy of fourteen or fifteen, became a student there, and revealed immediately his brilliant promise. Lorenzo, much impressed, took the boy into his own household, where he had the opportunity of listening and maturing at the very center of the Laurentian circle. And Michelangelo, far more than Piero or Giovanni or Giuliano, was the son of Lorenzo's poetic mind.

Within Lorenzo's circle versatility became usual. Not only did many men engage in both architecture and sculpture, or in both sculpture and painting, or in all three arts, but there were many other instances of gifts and skills combined. Ficino was the singer of the group; the learned Politian could turn to the writing of light verse; Botticelli inscribed his Nativity in Greek. Each activity, furthermore, received some influence from the activities that were going on beside it. Painting was greatly influenced by humanism and by contemporary Italian poetry; humanism lost its aloofness; and Italian poetry resumed its full literary dignity, welcomed classic elements, reflected the new Platonism, became more pictorial than ever, and in many cases sought musical fulfillment.

In Lorenzo himself, despite the tremendous pressure of his public responsibilities, poetic energy so surged that it would not be denied. His princely status tended indeed to give him poetic freedom, or at least to enlarge the poetic freedom he would in any case have attained: for in that status he was above convention. Even when he was writing consciously within the area of lyric tradition he was never kept by it from making any variation or any innovation that occurred and appealed to him. His mind was well stocked with older verse; but his mind was irrepressibly active in its liberty. He wrote what he chose to write, in the way in which he chose to write it. He was the prince of his own poetic soul.

In the exercise of his princely freedom he wrote verse of many different kinds, some of them familiar, some renewed, and some quite new. He wrote sonnets, *canzoni*, *sestine*, *ballate*, carnival songs, *laude*, meditative separate *capitoli* in *terza rima*; longer poems, some in *terza rima* and others in octaves;

* A large garden near the Convent of San Marco, not the garden *of* that convent.

and a *sacra rappresentazione*. In prose he wrote a commentary on forty of his sonnets; a preface to an anthology of Italian poetry; two *novelle*; some brief *Ricordi*; and, inevitably, thousands of letters.*

The background of the sonnets is in general Petrarchan, but the individual poems bear in almost every case the impress of Lorenzo's authorship. Many of them have, like this one, a distinctive and lovely woodland setting, in which Lorenzo's thought wanders in glad freedom:

Oh streamlet clear, within your murmuring
I hear forever but my lady's name.
Well I believe that some glad day she came
And mirrored her dear beauty in your spring;
And you that cannot that fair image bring
In all your course, amid the woods to gleam,
Can only sing her memory, little stream,
And I alone can hear the song you sing.
Ah, far more fortunate, oh streamlet clear,
Are mine own eyes, for since the joyous day
When first they mirrored her most lovely grace
They keep her image, be she far or near:
No other sight can drive that sight away,
Nor shadow darken it, nor light efface.

One stately sonnet on the mutability of fortune ends with the solemn line:

Sola sta ferma e sempre dura Morte —

Death alone stands firm and forever endures.

Country and poetry alike brought him welcome relief from the burden of statecraft:

Let whoso will in courtly show be blest,
Or find in splendid edifice his joy —
His arts for pleasure or for gold employ,
The while a thousand cares his soul molest.
A meadow green, with lovely flowerets drest,
A little brook that glides a-murmuring by,
A bird that bears its song of love on high —
More gently these do lull my thoughts to rest.
The shadowy woods, the rocks, the lofty hills,
The darksome caverns and the nimble deer
And the swift-fleeing timorous woodland fay —
Each in my mind some gentle thought instills
Of the bright eyes that shine in memory here,
But fade 'mid pomp and palaces away.

In or shortly after 1480 Lorenzo began the writing of an extensive com-

* The *Nencia da Barberino*, which, though until recently regarded as Lorenzo's, is probably not his, will be discussed in Chapter 18.

mentary on many of his sonnets. The finished portion, after a long introduction, contains about forty sonnets, with three or four pages of comment for each one. In its general character, with its poems set amid longer passages of surrounding prose, the *Comento* resembles the *Vita nova* and the *Convivio*. Both those works were certainly in Lorenzo's mind: in its main theme, the vicissitudes of Lorenzo's love, the *Comento* is closer to the *Vita nova*; but in its discursive character it is closer to the *Convivio*. The introduction contains an exposition of the nature of true love, a well-organized and forceful defense of the Italian language as a literary medium, and a just appreciation — beginning "The brevity of the sonnet does not permit the presence of a single word that is without purpose" — of the prerogatives and the difficulties of the sonnet. Throughout the commentary proper Lorenzo digresses with the utmost freedom, treating now one and now another theme brought to his mind by something in the particular poem he is discussing. Thus he considers, among other things, the beauties of soul, body, and voice; the nature of nobility; the points of a fine horse; the symbolism and the powers of hands; obstacles to the attainment of perfection; requisites for a good painting; the four humors; the inhibitive perplexities of prudent men; the supremacy of sight over the other senses; the values of song; and the identity of beauty, goodness, and truth.

Lorenzo's *canzoni* and *sestine* establish his ability to handle complex metrical forms; but they seem labored as compared with his sonnets. Most of the many poems that are in *ballata* form were written to be sung by groups of dancers or in Carnival processions. Several of these *ballate* are obscene, and Lorenzo has been accused of trying by such songs to corrupt his populace: the truth seems to be rather that finding similar songs already in currency he chose, readily enough, to write in that low vein, as at various times he chose to write in so many other veins.

Celebration of the pre-Lenten season, with tolerated excesses of boisterous merrymaking and with more or less haphazard pageantry, had been going on in Florence long before Lorenzo's time; but within his time, and probably on his initiative, Florentine Carnival celebrations became more spectacular and more artistic. Carnival songs were set to music even by Heinrich Isaac; and expert ingenuity went into the planning of costumed processional groups and the making of elaborate floats.

Lorenzo's two best Carnival songs stress the idea of the swift passing of youth and the consequent urgency of immediate joy. One, called "The Song of the Seven Planets," must have been written for use on or around a float or series of floats bearing representatives of the seven planetary spheres, the position of highest honor being assigned to Venus. The other, called "The Song of Bacchus," is Lorenzo's best known single poem. The processional group for which it was written had apparently four elements: a float bearing

Bacchus and Ariadne; Silenus, fat and bibulous, astride an ass; a float bearing Midas; and an attendant throng of nymphs and satyrs. The several stanzas of the song are vivacious in description and pointed in their incidental comment; but the power of the poem lies in its refrain, in which Lorenzo contrived the ultimate phrasing for his recurrent theme:

> Quant' è bella giovinezza,
> che si fugge tuttavia!
> Chi vuol esser lieto, sia:
> di doman non c'è certezza —

> How fair is youth, which is forever fleeing! Let whoso will be joyous: of tomorrow there is no certainty.

After Carnival, Lent: two seasons perennially opposed, yet springing both from the basic human desire for fullness of life. And Lorenzo, capable of sharing in the facile ways of Carnival, was in his great intellectual vitality capable also, beyond the measure of most men, of intense rational desire for a transcending life.

His nine *laude* as a group constitute a remarkable body of religious poetry, mature, very thoughtful, and marked by striking metaphors and by many memorable lines and stanzas. The themes include the praise of Mary, the crucifixion, the resurrection, summons to conversion, the love of Christ, and the soul's search for God. Some of the poems are general in their content; some mingle general and personal elements; and the two that treat of the love of Christ and the soul's search for God give every evidence of being completely and profoundly personal. The first, opening with the refrain

> Poi ch' io gustai, Gesú, la tua dolcezza,
> l'anima piú non prezza
> del mondo cieco alcun altro diletto —

> Since I have tasted Thy sweetness, oh Jesus, my soul no longer cares for any of the delights of the blind world —

culminates in lines that mean:

> Let my heart ever burn with Thy sweet fire, until at last nought save Thyself remaineth in my breast.

The second opens with the refrain:

> O Dio, o sommo bene, or come fai,
> che te sol cerco e non ti truovo mai? —

> Oh God, oh supreme good, why dost Thou so ordain that I seek Thee only, and yet find Thee never?

The search, exhausting and desperate, moves from the vain effort to find God within the range of his earthly manifestations to the renunciation of all that is commonly called life and to the rhapsodic expectation of the attainment of complete divine blessedness. The poem is intensely mystic, but its mysticism, though so deeply felt, is highly intellectual: it is indeed one of the world's greatest expressions of intellectual mysticism. It is the most personal, the most moving, and the greatest, of all the poems of Lorenzo.

Of the seven *capitoli* in *terza rima* one is a free translation of the First Psalm, and the others are all in one sense or another philosophical. Throughout Lorenzo's lifetime, Ficino was bringing Platonism into the forefront of Florentine thought, and Lorenzo was bound to have some interest in Ficino's work. Three of the *capitoli* are free translations of hymns contained in Ficino's Latin translations of the Neoplatonic *Pimander* and *Asclepius*, and another is a free translation of a Neoplatonic poem in the *Consolation of Philosophy* of Boethius.

The *Corinto*, the first Italian pastoral idyll, is the longer Italian equivalent of Marlowe's *The Passionate Shepherd to his Love*. It is the plea of the shepherd Corinto, sung in the woods at night, which he bids the winds carry to Galatea. What joy, if she would only be kind!

> Then I would gather flowers in the vale
>   And shower them down upon your lovely head;
>   And at your laughter, throughout all the dell
> New fragrant flowers, yellow, white, and red,
>   Would blossom where the ones I gathered grew:
>   Your golden hair should be all garlanded,
> But yet no flower be so fair as you.
>   And all around the amorous birds would sing,
>   And rippling streamlets in their gentle flow
> Echo our gladness in their murmuring.

Nor should she scorn his brownness, or his feats of strength and skill, or his humble wealth in cattle and sheep and milk and strawberries and fruits and honey. The closing lines bring the first Laurentian development of the "Gather ye rosebuds" theme, and they bring it in a specifically Laurentian form. Going into his garden, Corinto had seen, among his roses, some in full blossom, some just budding, some still within the bud, and some with petals already fallen on the ground: as the roses pass, even so youth passes. In the last line of all he bids Galatea pluck the rose of youth:

> Cogli la rosa, o ninfa, or che è il bel tempo.*

The first of the six *capitoli* of the *Altercazione* reports an imaginary debate

* Lorenzo presumably derived the motif of the several symbolic stages of the rose from an anonymous poem called *Rosae*, formerly attributed to Ausonius. When Lorenzo and his retinue entered the lists in the tournament of 1469 this same motif constituted one of the main decorative elements in Lorenzo's own costume, in the costumes of several of his attendants, and in the trappings of some of the horses.

between Lorenzo and an old shepherd, Alfeo: Lorenzo stresses the evils of city life and maintains that pastoral life is happier, while Alfeo so stresses the hardships of pastoral life as to challenge Lorenzo's preference. At the beginning of the second *capitolo* Ficino appears, and Lorenzo asks him to judge between Alfeo and himself, and to tell them where true happiness is to be found, whether in human life or in divine life. Ficino then launches into a long Platonic disquisition on imperfect and perfect happinesses, or "goods." These range from goods of fortune and bodily goods to the supreme good, which is the contemplation of God through love. This long disquisition, which extends almost to the end of the fifth *capitolo*, is hardly more than a translation, now exact and now quite free, of a Latin letter *De felicitate* which Ficino had written to Lorenzo at Lorenzo's request. The sixth *capitolo* is a long prayer, in which, paraphrasing a Latin prayer by Ficino, Lorenzo asks that he be enabled to attain to the supreme good.

The *Simposio* (sometimes called *I beoni*, "The Drinkers"), Platonic only in its mocking title, is a Rabelaisian account of the flocking of drinkers to a tavern where a cask of wine has just been broached.

The *Uccellagione*, "The Partridge-Hunt," is a delightful poem, in about fifty octaves, narrating the experiences of a day spent in hunting with falcons — the main aristocratic sport of both the Middle Ages and the Renaissance. The hunters make an early start: the eastern sky is red; the tips of the mountains are touched with gold; sparrows are chattering; the fox is returning to its den; the peasant is going out to his field; and the air is clean, cool, and crystal clear. The master of the dogs calls them around him (one entire stanza is filled with their names). The huntsmen ride along together, joking, and not without mishap, until they reach the valley where the hunt is to take place; and there, in more or less quarrelsome rivalry and with more or less success, they spend a day that never lacks for variety or for amusement. Then they ride back together, in moods that range from enthusiasm to disgust; supper is begun in hungry silence, but presently all the happenings of the day have to be talked noisily over; and at last they go off for a long night's sleep. One seems to have been watching and hearing all the sights and sounds of the day, and to have felt the coolness of the Tuscan breeze and the warmth of the Tuscan sun.

From a little stream called the Ambra which flows past the hill of Poggio a Caiano the name Ambra passed into use as a name for the villa that crowned the hill. It was presumably the sight of this hill partially surrounded, in the course of a winter flood, by the waters of the river Ombrone that suggested to Lorenzo the figure of an embrace by a river-god; and it was presumably this imagination, together with memories of Boccaccio's *Ninfale fiesolano* (with memories also, perhaps, of a recent poem by Luca Pulci), that led him to the writing of his eponymic idyll, the *Ambra*. The poem opens with a long and fine description of winter sights and scenes: the trees leafless, save for the snow-laden evergreens; long nights, with Orion triumphant; cranes patterning the sky or sleeping in some sheltering valley while a sentinel keeps watch against the eagle; streams turned to ice; Mount Morello, cloud-wreathed, with snowy slopes, defending Florence from the north winds. But then, when a south wind melts the snow, the mountain streams, unlocked, rush down in boisterous torrents, overflow their banks, mingle their waters and the noisy tidings of their sources, and flood the plain: the shepherd, from his humble housetop, watches all his poor wealth as it is swept away. It is in such times that the river embraces the hill. Then comes the story, told in Ovidian mood and manner, of Ombrone's pursuit of the nymph Ambra, whom on a summer day he had seen bathing in his waters. She flees toward the Arno; Ombrone appeals to the god of the greater river to help him; Arno, in answer, floods the course of Ambra's flight; she then, appealing to Diana, is saved by being turned to stone; and it is left to Ombrone only to wish that his surrounding waters may by a wintry wind be locked into an enduring crystal embrace.

The first of the two rhapsodies linked under the title *Selve d'amore** is devoted to Lorenzo's contentment in bondage to a late love. The contrast between the peacefulness of bondage and the destructiveness of forces unconfined is illustrated by three successive similes of Homeric breadth, picturing the stream between its banks and the stream in flood, the life-giving wind and the tempest, fire controlled and the raging forest fire.

The second *selva*, much longer than the first, tells of his lady's absence, the poet's memories of happiness, his delight in the imagination of her return, his grief as he realizes that this imagination is illusory, his imagination of her amorous memories, his final joy in the expectation of her actual return. The stanzas devoted to the first imagination of her return develop with exuberant fancy the idea that on her coming winter will give way to a miraculous spring: flowers will bloom, trees will put forth their leaves, bird-song will be heard again, pastoral life will resume its springtime course, there will be dancing under the elms. Pan, satyrs, fauns, nymphs, and river-gods will accompany her; and, when she reaches the city, women and maidens of gentle heart will throng to welcome her and will be blest by her presence. There are many digressions, among them a portrayal of the Golden Age — the first Renaissance dreaming of that ancient dream.

Lorenzo's *Rappresentazione di San Giovanni e Paolo* was performed in 1491 by a religious association, Lorenzo's youngest son, Giuliano, then ten years old, taking part, with other boys, in the performance. Music for the

* The word *selve* as used in this title does not have its usual meaning of "woodlands," but the literary meaning of "improvisations," the meaning in which the Latin *sylvae* had recently been used by Politian, as will appear in the following chapter.

play was composed by Heinrich Isaac. The titular saints are not the biblical John and Paul, but martyrs of the fourth century. The play has the general features of the *sacra rappresentazione.* There is no division into acts and scenes; occurrences which were separated, historically, by some thirty years, succeed each other in telescoped immediacy; and the scene shifts from Rome to Dacia and to Asia Minor. Two battles are fought upon the stage, and there is one celebration with banqueting, buffoonery, music, and dancing. There are visions, miracles, prayers, conversions, harangues, triumphal returns, and deaths. In addition to the dozen personages who are named there are many others: courtiers, counsellors, astrologers, servants, an angel, a trumpeter, a messenger, a captive king, a treasurer, an informer, and an executioner. Constantine, about to abdicate, instructs his three sons as to the cares and responsibilities of empire (Lorenzo was undoubtedly thinking of his own public burdens and of his own three sons). Julian the Apostate laments the decline of the Roman Empire, and echoes Constantine's convictions as to the duties of a ruler to his people. The last line of the play gives a famous phrasing to the traditional last words of Julian: divine vengeance for the execution of John and Paul has overtaken him, and he exclaims, as he dies,

> O Cristo Galileo, tu hai pur vinto! —
>
> Oh Galilean Christ, Thou hast conquered at last!

Lorenzo's two *novelle*, unimportant in themselves, provide evidence of his literary versatility. His *Ricordi* are brief reminiscent notes, biographically valuable, but without literary character.

Among the few letters of Lorenzo that have been published there are two that are well known. The earlier of the two was written to Frederick of Aragon, one of the sons of the King of Naples. Lorenzo and Frederick had met recently in Pisa; they had had some talk of Tuscan poetry; and Frederick had asked Lorenzo to make for him a collection of Tuscan poems. The collection made in response to this request (a collection often referred to as the *Raccolta aragonese*) is the first general anthology of Italian lyric poetry. It contains about 450 poems, by some thirty different poets, among them Giacomo da Lentino, Pier della Vigna, Guittone d'Arezzo, Guinizelli, Guido Cavalcanti, Dante, Cino da Pistoia, Lapo Gianni, Boccaccio, Fazio degli Uberti, Sacchetti, Buonaccorso da Montemagno, and, in accordance with Frederick's desire, Lorenzo himself. (The *Canzoniere* of Petrarch was doubtless already familiar to Frederick.) With the anthology Lorenzo sent to Frederick a carefully written prefatory letter, in the course of which he characterizes with just discrimination the poetry of most of the authors concerned, giving his highest praise to Cavalcanti, with whom he evidently felt a close poetic kinship. For the Tuscan language as a poetic medium he makes this enthusiastic claim:

> One can imagine nothing that is noble, flowering, charming, or adorned, nothing that is acute, distinguished, ingenious, or subtle, nothing that is lofty, magnificent, or sonorous, nothing, finally, that is ardent, spirited, or exalted, of which one cannot find numberless and shining examples not only in Dante and in Petrarch, but also in these others whose poetry you have brought to life again.

Lorenzo's other well-known letter was written, shortly before he died, to his sixteen-year-old son Giovanni, who was then just leaving Florence to enter upon the duties of his cardinalate. It is a fine letter: high-minded in its appreciation of the potentially beneficent dignity and influence of the College of Cardinals and in its assertion that realization of the potential beneficence requires upright individual living on the part of the members of the college ("if all cardinals were good, all popes would be good, and peace would prevail in Christendom"); wise in its recommendation of a modesty appropriate to Giovanni's youth and of deference and circumspection in his dealings with the Pope; realistic in its recognition of the temptations of life in Rome ("the sinkhole of all evil"); practical in its suggestions as to the avoidance of excessive display (though collection of antiquities and of fine books would be in order) and of excessive freedom in conversation, the maintenance of health ("rough food, plenty of exercise, early rising"), and planning in the evening the actions to be taken on the next day; pervaded with concern for the interests of Florence and of the family; and marked with clear evidences of paternal pride and affection. Giovanni may well have remembered this letter when, twenty-one years later, he was promoted to the papacy.

* * *

Di doman non c' è certezza. Two years after Lorenzo's death the precarious political structure of Italy fell apart; Charles VIII of France marched his army down the peninsula to Naples and back again; and though Italy suffered no definite loss at this time, the way was opened for the French conquest of Milan in 1499, and for the disastrous invasions of the following century. Lorenzo had been succeeded in Florence by his inept son Piero; Piero's humiliating submission to Charles roused the Florentines to decisive wrath, and he and other members of his family were driven from the city. The government was taken over by the Great Council, which for four years remained under the domination of Savonarola. Then indeed the morrow's change was manifest: Laurentian brilliance passed suddenly into a fanatical gloom; carnival songs gave way to hymns of penitence; and the gauds of luxury were heaped upon the "bonfires of vanities." And on the morrow's morrow, in the same great square that had witnessed these bonfires, Savonarola was burned at the stake.

CHAPTER 17

Florentine Humanists

HUMANISM, so imperiously dominant in the earlier part of the century, was still a major force in the cultural life of Laurentian Florence, but it was not nearly so dominant or so imperious as it had been. In particular, the earlier humanistic scorn for use of the Italian language as a literary medium had all but disappeared: while humanists still wrote primarily in Latin, they wrote also, readily enough, in Italian, and in various ways they showed respect for earlier and for contemporary writers in Italian.

Of the four chief humanists of the Laurentian circle, two, Landino and Ficino, were older than Lorenzo, and two, Politian and Pico della Mirandola, were younger.

Cristoforo Landino (1424–1498), a grandnephew of the organist Francesco, held the chair of poetry and oratory in the University of Florence from 1458 on. His main Latin writings are three philosophic treatises, each Platonic in spirit, and reflecting Landino's close association with Ficino. The most important of the three is the *Disputationes camaldulenses*, written in or shortly before 1475. Its four Books tell of an imagined four-day gathering supposed to have been held in the monastery of Camaldoli in the summer of 1468, Alberti, Ficino, and the young brothers Lorenzo and Giuliano de' Medici being among the several members of the group. Their conversations include a debate on the relative merits of the active and the contemplative life, and a discussion of the *summum bonum.*

Landino's main work in Italian is his edition of the *Divine Comedy*, published in Florence in 1481. The values of this edition, however, lie not in the elaborate commentary but in the preface and in the illustrations. The first several pages of the preface are devoted to comprehensive and enthusiastic laudation of Florence, past and present, for its military valor, its learned men and theologians, its churches and its hospitals, its poets, orators, musicians, painters, sculptors, and jurists, its far-flung commerce, its agriculture, its villas, its situation, and its great families. The latter part of the preface contains an impassioned discussion of the nature and origin of poetry, considered supreme among the arts, as being directly inspired by God, who is Himself the supreme poet, the world being his poem. It had been planned that the book should have, at the head of each canto, an engraving designed by Botticelli, who however prepared designs for the first nineteen cantos only: engravings were made from these designs.* The volume was regarded as a triumph of patriotism, scholarship, and the printer's art; and the city of Florence, in token of its appreciation, gave Landino a house in the Casentino.

Marsilio Ficino (1433–1499) was drawn in his youth, by his meditative and idealistic nature, to the study of philosophy, and in particular to the study of Platonic doctrines as set forth by the Latin Neoplatonists. Soon he was studying Greek, and giving evidence, through minor writings, of eager productivity. Cosimo de' Medici became much interested in him, and with an extraordinary combination of foresight and generosity established his lifetime scholarly program and his lifetime scholarly security by giving him, in 1462, a large supply of Greek Platonic and Neoplatonic manuscripts and a villa at Careggi. There Ficino lived and wrote prolifically; and his villa became a familiar gathering place for men interested in philosophic discussion under Ficino's guidance.† His primary task was to make the works of Plato and the Neoplatonists available in complete and reliable Latin translations. He wrote commentaries, also, on many Platonic and Neoplatonic texts; and he wrote many original works, nearly all of them Platonic, or Neoplatonic, in the distinctive character of their thought.

His Commentary on the *Symposium*, the most important, from the point of view of literary history, of all his works, was first written in Latin in 1469: in or before 1474 Ficino translated it into Italian, calling it *Il libro dello amore*. The *Symposium* itself has the form of an account of a banquet at which the guests speak in succession on the subject of love, the culminating speech being that of Socrates. Ficino's Commentary is cast in a corresponding form: the preface states that on the initiative of Lorenzo de' Medici a banquet was held, on an anniversary of Plato's birth and death, in the Medici villa at Careggi, Landino and Ficino being among the guests. After dinner one of the guests reads the *Symposium* aloud, and asks the others, except Ficino, to expound, one by one, the several speeches. As a commentary on Plato the work has little value; but in spite of its conformity with the sequence of Plato's speeches the *Libro dello amore* is in reality an exposition of Ficino's own conception of the nature of what he calls Socratic love.

* Many copies of the book are extant, but very few have the complete set of engravings. Botticelli's famous large drawings for the *Divine Comedy* were done at a later time: some of those for the first cantos are reminiscent of the earlier designs.

† The name "the Platonic Academy," applied later to Ficino and his companions, is misleading: the group never had any formal organization.

Socratic love, for Ficino, is always the desire of beauty; and the beauty desired is always, ultimately, the beauty of God. The Socratic love that one particular person bears to another is love of the beauty of God as reflected in that other person. Such love has nothing to do with sex, or with any sense except the senses of sight and hearing. A man, therefore, may bear it either to a man or to a woman. The particular form of love that Ficino seems to have most constantly in mind is the love of an older man for a younger man, the older man seeking, through his love, to educate the younger man in virtue. Ficino's version of the ascent of love, corresponding to that described to Socrates by the wise Diotima, has in its five stages these several objects:

Love of the visible beauty of a single person.

Love of the synthetic idea of perfect visible beauty.

Love of beauty of the soul, manifested in the moral and intellectual virtues, which are various forms of truth.

Love of angelic beauty, which is spaceless and eternal, but differentiated.

Love of the infinite and unitary beauty of God.

The *Libro dello amore* is the main source of the literary Platonism of the late fifteenth century and the sixteenth century. In Italy it was summarized in a *canzone* by Benivieni; that *canzone* was then expounded in a prose commentary by Pico della Mirandola; and from Ficino's work itself or from one of its derivatives its ideas were transmitted to Bembo, to Castiglione, and to other writers. In England Spenser's *Foure Hymnes* appear to reflect specifically the *canzone* of Benivieni and the commentary of Pico. Chapman drew directly on the Latin text of Ficino's commentary for passages in four of his poems.

The most massive of the original works of Ficino is his *Theologia platonica de immortalitate animorum.* The main purpose of human life, he argues, is contemplation, by which he means a progressive spiritual experience culminating in the immediate vision of God; such contemplation can be attained in this life only rarely and momentarily; therefore the soul must have before it an immortal life in which the attainment may be perpetual. The hierarchy of being, as here set forth, consists of five essences, which Ficino calls God, the Angelic Mind, the Rational Soul, Quality, and Body. The soul, then, is the central and linking essence:

> This is the greatest of all the miracles of nature. For everything else under God is in itself one single being, but the soul is, at one and the same time, all things. It has in itself the images of the divine things from which it is itself derived, and the ideas and patterns of the lower things which in its turn it, in a sense, produces. And since it is the center of all things it partakes of the powers of all things . . . so that it may rightly be called the center of nature,

the middle term of all things, the series of the world, the likeness of all things, the knot and the bond of the universe.

Ficino was conscious of a double consecration: he was consecrated to Platonism (which for him always included Neoplatonism) not only by his commitments to Cosimo de' Medici, but also by his firm belief in the dignity of man and by his ardent conviction that Platonism was rich in religious truth and power; and he was consecrated to Christianity not only formally — he took holy orders in 1473 — but by a strong sense of mission, springing from his desire to win men to the love of God. Quite naturally, then, he sought to weave his Platonism and his Christianity together into a single system, and to enrich and reënforce Christianity by the introduction of all elements of Platonism that were in his judgment consonant with it. In a sense, he undertook to do for Christianity and Platonism what Thomas Aquinas had done for Christianity and Aristotelianism. But Ficino's Platonic theology, despite its philosophic earnestness and its poetic enthusiasm, was too esoteric to have lasting religious influence. Yet whenever one turns to him one has the rewarding sense of being in the presence of a fine mind and a pure and loving spirit.

Angelo Ambrogini, the most brilliant of all Italian humanists — called in Latin, Politianus; in Italian, Poliziano; and in English, Politian — was born in 1454 in the Tuscan town of Montepulciano.* While still a small boy he was sent to Florence, and there for some time he lived in ragged poverty, managing nevertheless to get an excellent education and to demonstrate his classical precocity. He was fascinated, from the first, by the study of Greek; and when he was only about sixteen he translated four books of the *Iliad* into Latin verse. He dedicated the translation to Lorenzo de' Medici, who presently began to give him some help, and in 1473 took him into his own household, where he served as a secretary and, later on, as tutor to Lorenzo's sons Piero and Giovanni. In 1479 he lost favor with Lorenzo's wife, Clarice Orsini, and, later in the year, with Lorenzo himself; and he was dismissed. For some months he wandered from place to place in Northern Italy; but in the summer of 1480 he was taken again into Lorenzo's favor, though never again into that of Clarice, or into the Medici household. In the Autumn of 1480 he was made professor of Greek and Latin literature in the University of Florence; and for the rest of his life he was occupied mainly in work connected with his university courses. He died in 1494.

From about 1470 to the end of his life he wrote many short poems in Latin and in Greek. His favorite form in Latin, and his only form in Greek, was the epigram — a single stanza, often only a line or two and seldom more than twenty lines in length. He was a wit, an exceedingly clever chooser and user of words, a brimming treasury of classical allusions and

* The appellation Politianus came from the Latin name of this town, Mons Politianus.

reminiscences, and a master of Latin metrics. Of his somewhat more than a hundred and fifty epigrams, a third of them in Greek, many are addressed to friends and heads of states (several, naturally, to Lorenzo), many are epitaphs (including one for Fra Lippo Lippi and one for Squarcialupi) or inscriptions (there is one for Benedetto da Maiano's bust of Giotto), some are invectives, a few are amatory, and a few are of other kinds. He wrote also a few somewhat longer Latin poems, chiefly elegies and odes. Two of the elegies are deservedly famous, one a charming acknowledgment of a gift of violets from his lady, the other a poem on the death of Albiera degli Albizzi, a young and lovely bride-to-be. The best of his odes, on the death of Lorenzo, was set to music by Heinrich Isaac.

Chiefly within the decade 1470–1480 Politian wrote many lyrics in Italian. In this case also his preferred form was a very short one, the *strambotto*, or, as it was commonly called in Tuscany, the *rispetto*. Some two hundred *rispetti* are ascribed to him, and most of them are quite certainly his. They are written within the *strambotto* tradition, but they are not nearly so close to the folk *strambotti* as are those of Giustinian: one could hardly mistake any one of them for a folk song, and no one of them has entered the folk repertory. They are light, simple, and free from erudition; but in their smooth facility they are unmistakably the work of a skillful artist.

The best of Politian's lyrics are among his thirty-odd dance songs, written in the *ballata* form. Never has the *carpe diem* theme been treated with more exquisite grace than in a song with the refrain

> I' mi trovai, fanciulle, un bel mattino,
> di mezzo maggio in un verde giardino,

which reads thus, in a translation which, though faithful in content, cannot even faintly convey Politian's melodiousness:

> I found myself, oh maidens, one fair day.
> In a green garden, in the month of May.
>
> All round about amid the grasses green
> Were purple violets and lilies white:
> A thousand mingled colors there were seen,
> Filling the garden with their sweet delight,
> And I began to pluck the blossoms bright
> My golden locks to adorn with a garland gay.
>
> But when I'd filled my kirtle to the hem
> I spied some roses, yellow, white, and red,
> And swiftly then I ran to gather them:
> For such a lovely fragrance did they spread
> That deep into my heart the sweetness sped,
> And filled it with desire's dear dismay.

I looked, and ne'er had seen a sight so fair:
Here the green buds their crimson just disclose,
And here the full-blown petals scent the air,
And here the fading flower more softly glows.
And Love then bade me: "Go, and pluck of those
That are in fullest blossom on the spray."

For when the rose is fairest and most sweet,
Its every petal open to the sun,
Then for our garland-weaving it is meet,
Before its bloom of loveliness be gone.
So, maidens, ere the day of youth be done,
Gather the fairest rose, while yet you may.

Still another charming and spirited song, with the refrain

Ben venga maggio
E 'l gonfalon selvaggio —

Welcome May and the woodland banner — *

is a May Day song, written to be sung by a company of youths and maidens, to whom, as they weave in and out in the dance,

Love comes laughing,
With roses and lilies on his head.

Some of the other dance songs are more or less desirably humorous: two or three are cleverly anecdotic.

After Lorenzo's tournament of 1469 an account of it in octaves had been written by Luigi Pulci: after Giuliano's tournament, held in 1475 in honor of Simonetta Cattaneo, Politian undertook the celebration of that tournament. The task was probably never quite congenial to him, since his native poetic gifts were lyric rather than epic; he worked at it unhurriedly; and with the death of Giuliano in the Pazzi conspiracy the need for the completion of the poem ceased. The *Stanze per la giostra* as Politian left them consist only of an introductory canto and part of a second canto, still introductory.

At the opening of the poem Giuliano is represented as being hostile to love. Cupid avenges himself by bringing before Giuliano's eyes, in the course of a day's hunting, a deer which lures him to a glade where he finds Simonetta, with whom he immediately falls in love. Cupid then returns to the realm of Venus on the island of Cyprus. There follows a long description of that realm, especially of the garden and the woodland that lie below the mountain-top palace of Venus, and of the bas-reliefs that adorn the doors of that palace, reliefs which for the most part represent classic love myths. Cupid reports his success; and Venus, wishing to make the triumph evident, decides to inspire

* The May banner is a branch brought from the woodland and left by a lover at his lady's door.

Giuliano to give a tournament in honor of his lady, and sends him dreams that will lead him to do so. Waking, Giuliano prays to Love, to Minerva, and to Glory, asking them to help him to win martial honor and his lady's favor.

The elements of the several scenes are drawn mainly from classic sources, especially from Claudian's *Epithalamium*; but they are fused most skillfully in the music of Politian's verse. The account of the hunt is lively; the woodland enamorment is idyllic; and the description of the realm of Venus is a pictorial masterpiece: in its clarity of detail and its imaginative grace it is closely akin to the finest Laurentian painting, especially to that of Botticelli. It was probably from passages in the *Stanze* that Botticelli derived the subjects of two of his most famous paintings: the "Primavera," which corresponds to Politian's description of the garden and woodland of the palace of Venus, and the "Birth of Venus,"[1] which corresponds to Politian's description of one of the bas-reliefs of the doors of the palace. Something of the quality of the first passage may be suggested by a version of two of its opening stanzas:

> A wall of purest gold encompassing
> Confines the shadowy garden; in the vale
> Are tender trees that birds make musical,
> Singing their loves amid the leaves of spring.
> The grateful, rippling murmur there you hear
> Of running brooks — one sweet, one bitter stream —
> From out whose waters Cupid stole the gleam
> Of the golden tints that on his darts appear.
>
> Never within the garden are the leaves
> With the chill hoarfrost whitened or the snow;
> There icy winter does not dare to go,
> And there no storm the tender bushes grieves.
> Therein no restless round of seasons winds,
> But joyous Spring is ever present there,
> Who frees to all the winds her rippling hair
> And in a wreath a thousand flowerets binds.

The world of Politian's Italian lyrics and of the *Stanze* is a world without depth of thought or of emotion; but it is a world of great beauty. Entering it, one finds oneself within a perfect garden, in mid-May.

At the court of Mantua, in 1480, Politian wrote in two days his *Orfeo*, the first secular play in Italian. The story is that of Orpheus and Eurydice; the form is in general that of the *sacra rappresentazione*; the spirit is thoroughly pagan. There is a prologue, delivered not by an angel but by Mercury; most of the play is in octaves, but there is a passage in *terza rima*, and there are two *ballate*, two *canzonette*, and two bits of Latin verse. There is no unity of time, place, or action. The first third of the play is conventionally pastoral; the central third, containing the eloquent plea of Orpheus and a brief dialogue between Orpheus and Eurydice, is the best; the last third, following the catastrophe, is an unnecessary appendage, at the end of which bacchantes, having torn Orpheus to pieces, join in a riotous bacchanalian *ballata*.

After Politian's return to Florence later in 1480 his activities were mainly humanistic. He studied prodigiously, completed Latin translations of the *Histories* of Herodian and of works by other Greek authors, and published a collection of a hundred philological studies. In the years 1480–1490 he gave courses in the University on works of Quintilian, Statius, Ovid, Cicero, Virgil, Hesiod, Horace, Persius, Homer, and Juvenal. Each Autumn he gave an introductory public lecture, in Latin: the two on Virgil and the two on Homer are in hexameters. To these four lectures he gave the general name *Sylvae*, borrowing thus the name that Statius had given, with the meaning "improvisations," to his collection of occasional poems. In the first of the four, entitled *Manto*, the Theban prophetess foretells the glories of Virgil's poetical career. The second, *Rusticus*, introductory to a course on the *Georgics* of Hesiod and Virgil, follows the Tuscan peasant around his little farm in all the various tasks of the four seasons. The third, *Ambra*, so named because it was written in Lorenzo's villa, is devoted to the praise of Homer. The fourth, *Nutricia*, "Repayment to a Foster Mother" (that is, to Poetry), a remarkable survey of the whole history of poetry, begins with an imaginative account of the civilizing power of poetry in the primitive world and an exaltation of the divine nature of poetry, continues with a long review of legendary poets and of the real poets of Greece and Rome, and closes, after a brief reference to Dante, Petrarch, Boccaccio, and Cavalcanti, with an expert characterization of the several poems written up to that time (1486) by Lorenzo. The *Sylvae* as a whole are a unique combination of thorough scholarship and great poetic skill. Their best passages are in their brilliance unsurpassed in the Latin poetry of the Renaissance.

The fame of Politian as humanist spread swiftly beyond the limits of Italy. Thomas Linacre, who was to become the first great English humanist, was among his students. George Chapman translated a passage from the *Nutricia* in the dedication of his translation of the *Iliad* and a passage from the *Ambra* in the dedication of his translation of the *Odyssey*, and remade the ode on the death of Albiera degli Albizzi into his *Epicede . . . On the most disastrous Death of Henry, Prince of Wales.*

Giovanni Pico (1463–1494), of the ruling family of Mirandola (a tiny domain near Modena), drawn by the fame of the Laurentian circle, came in 1484 to Florence, where he was made very welcome. He was already proficient in Latin and Greek; in Florence he acquired a good knowledge of Hebrew, and some slight knowledge of Arabic. His knowledge of Hebrew enabled him to plunge into study of the occult rabbinical theosophic system known as the Cabala; and it was through Pico that this system made its first impact upon Christian thought.

Among his closest friends in Florence were Ficino and the minor poet Benivieni. Benivieni, as has been said, summarized Ficino's *Libro dello amore* in a *canzone*; and Pico wrote a commentary in three Books, his only work in Italian prose, on that *canzone*.

Late in 1486 Pico, then twenty-four, published a list of nine hundred *conclusiones*, or theses, and announced that he was prepared to defend them, in Rome, against all comers. The theses were of many kinds, dialectic, ethical, physical, metaphysical, mathematical, magic, and cabalistic: most of them were derived from philosophers of various times and countries; some of them were his own. As an introduction to the expected debate he prepared a Latin oration *De dignitate hominis*, "On the Dignity of Man." His main argument is that for man, alone in all creation, there are no foreordained limits of possibility: we may indeed descend, but we may also ascend until we stand not "a little lower than the angels" but in equality with them, until

> inspired with ineffable love, rapt above ourselves as burning Seraphim, filled with divinity, we shall no longer be ourselves, but shall enter into the being of Him who made us.

But the debate was not to take place. The Church found thirteen of the proposed theses to be heretical; Pico's protest brought down upon him the full force of papal wrath; and he fled to France. Soon, however, he was able to return to Florence, there to resume his hectic philosophizing. Thomas Aquinas had sought to harmonize Christianity and Aristotelianism, and Ficino had sought to harmonize Christianity and Platonism: Pico undertook to harmonize Christianity, Aristotelianism, Platonism, the Cabala, and all the other esoteric lore he possessed. The *Heptaplus*, "The Sevenfold Narration," presents his cosmogony; the *De ente et uno*, "On Being and the One," is devoted primarily to the reconcilement of Aristotle and Plato. But the task Pico had undertaken was beyond even his extraordinary powers: he achieved, in these works, nothing more than a confused syncretism.

Sir Thomas More translated three of Pico's letters, a few of his minor religious writings, including his "Twelve Rules of a Christian Life," and a biography of Pico written by his nephew. John Colet, who visited Italy late in the century, was greatly influenced both by the writings of Ficino and by those of Pico.

* * *

A minor but interesting phase of Florentine humanism was the performance of classic comedies in Latin — following a precedent set in Rome in 1468, when the *Epidicus* of Plautus was performed on the Capitoline. In 1476 the minor Florentine humanist Giorgio Vespucci had his pupils give the *Andria* of Terence, first in his own school, then in the Medici palace, and then in the Palazzo della Signoria; and several other Latin comedies were given in the following years.

CHAPTER 18

Luigi Pulci and Other Florentine Writers

THE THIRD MAJOR POET of the Laurentian circle, considerably older than Lorenzo and Politian, though most of his work was contemporary with theirs, was Luigi Pulci (1432–1484), whose family, once prosperous, was in Luigi's day debt-ridden. In or about 1460 he won the attention and the favor of Lucrezia de' Medici, whom he regarded thereafter as his rescuing benefactress, and of Lorenzo, who as the years went on found in Luigi both a boon companion and a man whom he could trust with responsible missions, personal or diplomatic. One such mission took Luigi to Naples in 1471; another took him to Milan in 1473. By that time he had made the acquaintance of the *condottiere* Roberto Sanseverino; and from about 1477 on, while never breaking with the Medici, he was engaged primarily, in a civilian capacity, in Sanseverino's service.

He was born to be merry: no one ever perceived more gleefully the endless laughableness of human beings and their ways, and no one ever found funnier words and combinations of words to display that laughableness for the amusement of his companions. But his own struggles and the injustices that beset his brothers and himself left their mark within him: they developed in him a strain of oversensitive bitterness, and his humor turned too often to mockery or insult. Though he was no scholar, he knew the Bible, Dante, and Petrarch well, and had a considerable smattering of classic lore. He did some serious thinking, especially in the field of religion, but his thinking was often not well balanced. For some years he dabbled in magic. Yet with all his variableness he remained essentially a prince of laughter; and to Lucrezia and Lorenzo he gave an unwavering and deeply affectionate devotion.

It was Lucrezia who requested him to undertake the writing of the poem that was to be his one great work. Apparently she wanted him to write an epic in the popular style that would serve to rehabilitate Charlemagne, whom the *cantastorie* had consistently treated with much indignity. She may have had in mind also the fact that Christian-Islamic conflict was by no means a thing of the past: the Turks were a constant menace.

Pulci's natural liking was for shorter forms. He was too volatile, and his life was too often interrupted with family troubles and with Lorenzo's missions, to permit him to work steadily on a single lengthy task. The first form of the *Morgante*, containing twenty-three cantos, seems to have been written in bursts of more or less intensive activity distributed over a period of some fifteen years.

Pulci made no effort to invent a new plot. He simply rewrote the old *cantastorie* epic *Orlando*. The rewriting, however, was itself creative. With the old poem before him, Pulci expanded some passages and contracted others, passed over many stanzas that did not interest him, and inserted many single stanzas and series of stanzas of his own. Whatever he touched he transformed, replacing stiffness and monotony by fluency and variety, and bringing the dull scenes and the persons of the *Orlando* into the colors and dimensions of vitality. He was always looking, moreover, for occasions for laughter, and his laughter rings in many passages, exceedingly clever in wording and in rhyme, that must have delighted his Medicean listeners. Yet there are passages in which, for the moment, a more serious epic spirit prevails—straightforward narratives of valiant combat, lamentations for the loss of cherished comrades. Pulci, like the people who still listened eagerly to the *cantastorie*, thoroughly enjoyed the world of chivalry; and while he added to it his own gay variations, he held it in affection, and, in his own way, in honor.

Each canto, in accordance with the *cantastorie* tradition, begins with a stanza of religious invocation: in these stanzas Pulci's sense of humor is silent. It was too strong for him, however, as he dealt with Charlemagne. The poor emperor finds no rehabilitation: he is as much befooled by the traitor Ganelon as ever, and quite as much the object of ridicule.

Two episodes, within the first twenty-three cantos, are entirely of Pulci's own invention. In the *Orlando* the giant Morgante, never more than a secondary personage, is mentioned for the last time less than a third of the way through the poem. But though he disappears for the time being at the corresponding point in Pulci's poem, Pulci, who was very fond of his irresistible immenseness and his good-humored fidelity, was by no means ready to let him go. He reappears in Canto XVIII with an extraordinary companion: the demi-giant Margutte (a mere fourteen feet tall), the first thoroughly developed picaresque figure in European literature. In his mocking creed, which he states at length in response to Morgante's question as to whether he is Christian or Saracen, he takes no sides. He believes primarily in what is eatable or drinkable; he boasts of having seventy-seven mortal sins and more than a thousand venial ones. His rascality, however, is richly seasoned with an effervescent wit and a rollicking ludicrousness; and there is one sin, the sin of treachery, of which, he maintains, he has never been and never will be guilty. Morgante and Margutte start for Babylon, with a camel and a camel-load of plunder acquired by Margutte. They rescue a captive damsel, daughter of a Saracen potentate; after a journey marked by strange combats and by extraordinary gastronomic prowess on the part of Morgante they restore her to her grateful father; and then go on their way — Margutte with a new load of plunder. He falls asleep; Morgante hides his boots; a monkey finds them, and keeps putting them on and off; Margutte, waking, and hunting for his boots, sees the monkey's antics, and dies of laughter.

The second new episode is that of the last exploits and the death of Morgante. With Orlando and Rinaldo he sets out on an enterprise that involves a sea voyage; a tempest rises; the mast is carried away; Morgante, with arms outstretched, holds the sails; as the ship nears land it is attacked by a gigantic whale; Morgante jumps on the whale's back and despatches it; but as he wades ashore he is bitten in the heel by a crab, and from that bite he dies.

In Canto XXIII the narrative derived from the *Orlando* ends abruptly, presumably because Pulci had reached the end of his copy of that poem, and the brief canto closes with a prophecy of the final Christian-Saracen struggle. In or before 1478, the poem having reached this point, Pulci released it for printing. Eventually he wrote five more cantos, first printed in a Florentine edition of 1483, which in its title, *Morgante Maggiore*, advertises its new completeness.*

The added cantos have as their theme the final struggle foretold at the end of Canto XXIII: the first of the five deals with a Saracen attack on Paris; in the second, Ganelon plots his final treachery; the third and fourth relate the battle of Roncevaux; and the fifth is of the nature of an epilogue. For these cantos also Pulci had a model — either the *Spagna in rima* or some closely similar version of the Roncevaux story — but he writes here with greater freedom as to action and incident.

The unity and the essentially tragic nature of the new theme lead to some elevation of mood and manner: loyalties are well summoned, and the last deeds and the deaths of Roland and Oliver and others of the band of Christian paladins are in truth heroic. Yet even here humorous elements are plentiful.

Canto XXV contains an episode of Pulci's own invention which is as distinctive as the episode of Margutte. Its central figure, Astaroth, once a chief among the Seraphim and now a highly intelligent infernal spirit, is con-

* The poem is now called simply the *Morgante.*

jured up by the Christian enchanter Malagigi in order that he may bring Rinaldo to Roncevaux. Before the ex-seraph starts on his mission he engages in a long theological discussion with Malagigi, in which he insists upon the supremacy of the First Person of the Trinity, and maintains the justice of his own damnation and that of the other fallen angels, on the ground that they sinned with full knowledge and by their own free will. With a companion devil, Astaroth finds Rinaldo and a companion knight in Egypt, and they set out together for Roncevaux, their steeds leaping all impediments. Just before they leap the straits of Gibraltar, Astaroth discourses on the antipodes, asserting that one can sail to them through the straits and that the antipodeans, still unconverted, are nevertheless eligible for salvation. But he is not above elemental trickery when the four attend, invisible, a Saracen banquet in Saragossa.

Charlemagne, still the dupe of Ganelon until he reaches Roncevaux, regains thereafter much of his imperial dignity; but it is only in the final canto, written after the death of Lucrezia, that he receives full rehabilitation: there the whole story of his life is set forth at great length, and Pulci, not without compunction, bestows on him the highest praise he can command.

In the course of the following century Morgante and Margutte found reincarnation in Folengo's Fracassus and Cingar, and in the Pantagruel and Panurge of Rabelais. The two chief English admirers of the *Morgante* were Byron, whose translation of the first canto is excellent, and George Borrow, who quotes from the *Morgante* in both *Lavengro* and *The Romany Rye.*

Pulci's best work, except for the *Morgante*, is to be found in his fifty-odd letters to Lorenzo. Many of them, written while Pulci was away from Florence on missions for his patron, are very vivid in description and characterization. Some of them, considered as diplomatic reports, are of a most unconventional gayety.

Luigi's older brother Luca and his younger brother Bernardo were both minor poets. The only work of Luca that is of any significance is an eponymic idyll in octaves, the *Driadeo d'amore*, "Love Among the Dryads," which tells a story suggested by the names of two Tuscan rivers. Bernardo wrote sonnets, religious poems, and a *sacra rappresentazione.*

The priest Matteo Franco was a humorous poet, devoted to the Medici, who gave him cordial patronage. He rather more than held his own in an exchange of stinging sonnets with Luigi; but his better sonnets are those that depict some of his parish experiences. The best of all is this dialogue of two peasant women at Mass (the translation sacrifices rhyme for the sake of accuracy):

> "Good day!" "Good day and good morrow, and
> how are you?"
> "Tell me, how long is it since Mass began?"

"It's only just begun." "Then I'm not late.
And how are you? Tell me, how's everything?"

"Well, I don't know; some things are pretty hard:
Tita and Tessa both of them at home,
Without much dowry, and they're getting on."
"And Bartolo?" "He's had a lot of trouble."

"Now that's too bad. I've troubles of my own,
But still I manage to find a bite of bread."
"You're spinning, aren't you? How does the work go?"

"The two of us, my boy and I, don't earn
Even the water in which we wash our hands.
How are your chickens now, those little ones?"
"Mostly all right,
But one has something or other wrong with its throat."
"So, so!" "Well, Mass is done, good-bye!" "Good-bye!"

Girolamo Benivieni, whose *canzone* summarizing Ficino's theory of love has already been mentioned, wrote much and varied verse. His love poems, conventionally Petrarchan in their general character, had a definitely Platonic coloring: after becoming a follower of Savonarola he rewrote some of them as religious poems. He wrote also new *laude*, one of which was sung around a bonfire of varieties in 1497.

In or about 1476 there was a time when "everybody" in Florence was singing about "Nencia." Bartolommeo Scala, the Chancellor, reported that he could not get away from the sound of this singing even late at night and in the depths of his library: so he wrote a Latin eclogue about Nencia. But the singing was the singing of *strambotti*. There exist three series or collections of Nencia *strambotti*, one containing twenty stanzas, one about forty, one fifty. All these *strambotti* are ostensibly sung by a peasant lad, Vallera, to or about a peasant girl of Barberino. They are unlike the folk *strambotti* in that they all concern two particular individuals; but many of them catch the spirit of folk poetry. They are, however, more explicitly rustic, in content and in wording, than true folk poetry would ever be: they are bits of peasant experience imagined by city-dwelling poets who, themselves sophisticated, are yet familiar with peasant ways and are both sympathetic with them and amused by them.

One has glimpses of Nencia spinning, making straw baskets or hats, in her garden, coming out with her dog and her sheep, going to the fountain, or on her way to church in her red dress, or at a country dance. Vallera offers her wild strawberries, and a nestful of little birds. He is going to Florence on Saturday to sell some wood: what can he bring her? pins? needles? some blue silk? a bead necklace? He would throw himself into the Sieve if she told him to; and if she should cut his heart open it would cry: "Nencia, Nencia bella!"

Some one started the vogue of such *strambotti*, and others, perhaps many others, took it up and added *strambotti* of their own. The two longer forms of the *Nencia da Barberino* are undoubtedly composites. The short form may be either a composite or the very sequence with which the vogue began. It is perhaps the work of an otherwise very minor poet, Bernardo Giambullari.*

* * *

The *sacra rappresentazione* continued to flourish in the Laurentian period, but it became much secularized. When St. Lawrence distributes alms, beggars scramble for the coins; the story of the Prodigal Son is enacted with much zest in his prodigality and little interest in his repentance; and in various plays servants, tavern-keepers, quacks, brigands, policemen, and soldiers mingle with personages of sacred story. In some cases even the religious subject matter is replaced by familiar secular stories, sanctified now and then by the prefixing of the title "Saint" to the name of the hero or heroine, or by the intervention of saints or angels in the course of the action. Among the *rappresentazioni* that deal thus with secular themes are the *Griselda*; the *Re superbo*, which tells the old story of the king impersonated, in his absence, by a much more beneficent angel;† and the *Teofilo*, in which, for the first time in the Renaissance, the hero sells his soul to the devil. The plays were now recited, for the most part, instead of being sung. Their authors are, in general, unknown or undistinguished.

* * *

The *Vite d'uomini illustri del secolo XV* of Vespasiano da Bisticci (1421–1498), completed toward the end of his life, must have seemed, even to his first readers, like voices out of an already distant past. He had been the greatest of the bookdealers of the Renaissance, serving popes and princes, and held by them in honor and in friendship. Books, for him, meant manuscripts, and manuscripts only; and in those produced under his exacting orders his considerable staff attained a high degree of textual fidelity together with great beauty of material, of handwriting, and of decoration. The *Vite*, about thirty in number, deal with "illustrious" men whom Vespasiano had known.‡ He wrote sadly: not only was this newfangled printing ruining a noble profession, but society as a whole was in his view becoming more and

* The traditional attribution of the longest form to Lorenzo de' Medici is not justifiable.

† In English versions of this story and in one of Longfellow's *Tales of a Wayside Inn* the king is called "Robert of Sicily."

‡ Three of his lives are of Englishmen: John Tiptoft, Earl of Worcester; William Grey, Bishop of Ely; and Andrew Hollis, King's Proctor at the papal court.

more degenerate. No writer has ever been more completely a *laudator temporis acti.*

The Dominican monk Girolamo Savonarola (1452–1498) was a Ferrarese by birth, but a Florentine by destiny. Preaching first in the monastery of San Marco and later in the cathedral, where he drew great crowds of listeners (among them the young Machiavelli and the young Michelangelo), he poured forth violent invectives against the wickedness of Italy and the corruption of the Church. After the expulsion of the Medici he played a leading part in the political reorganization of the republic, and for some time his influence in public affairs was very great. But his enemies in Florence and in the Church grew in bitterness and in strength, and finally brought about his excommunication and his martyrdom.

Despite his crusading intensity and his "bonfires of vanities" he was hostile not to classicism and literature and art as such, but only to their immoral elements. It was he who saved the Medicean library from dispersion; and he numbered Botticelli, Benivieni, Pico, and, for a time, Ficino, among his adherents.

His sermons — burning in their consecrated wrath, vivid in their reports of apocalyptic vision, frightening in their prophecies of impending doom, exalted in their assertions of inspired authority, loving with a pleading love as for benighted children — must have been of an extraordinary eloquence. We have only the imperfect transcripts of devotees, from which it is not easy to reanimate the emotional surges of the cathedral scene: but even these transcripts are deeply impressive. Among his other writings are several *laude*, composed as instruments of his prophetic and reforming mission. One can imagine them sung — carnival songs abjured — with fervent conviction.

The formative years of Leonardo da Vinci (1452–1519) were spent in Florence, within the Laurentian period, and it was there and then that his superhuman activity began. In 1483 he entered the service of the Sforza, with whom he remained until the French conquered Milan in 1499. Thereafter he had no fixed dwelling. He was again in Florence; served Caesar Borgia briefly; and spent the last three years of his life in France, under the patronage of Francis I.

As the world knows, he was supremely versatile. He was painter, sculptor, architect, mathematician, physicist, astronomer, geologist, botanist, zoologist, anatomist, and civil and military engineer; and in well nigh the whole range of his versatility he was a pioneering genius of the highest order. In the fields of art and of science alike he was an infinitely curious, persistent, and exact observer; he possessed a superlative ability to make exact records of what he had observed, both in his thousands of unequaled drawings and in his thousands of written notes; he probed the meanings and the interrelations of what he had seen and recorded; and from that probing he moved on to discovery and invention, and to well controlled generalization.

He projected some treatises, but seems to have completed only two, both brief: one on light and shade, and one on the nature of water. The long "Treatise on Painting" published under his name is not his own handiwork: it was apparently put together early in the sixteenth century by someone who had access to his manuscripts (including some now lost). Most of its material is authentic; but some of it seems to consist merely of a student's memories of a master's teaching.

His multitudinous notes, scattered through his manuscripts, are thus perhaps even more impressive than they could otherwise have been. They are such, in their incredible wealth and novelty, as to command an amazed admiration, whether for their revelation of facts, their assertion of great possibilities, their exposition of fine techniques, their insight into the ways of mankind, or the fascination of their fragmentary philosophy. In form their outstanding general qualities are lucidity, pungency, and grace. Those that are most extended are magnificently pictorial, especially his detailed descriptions of possible paintings of a tempest, a flood, and a battle. Many quiver with a sense of the marvelousness of the world and of man; some were written in moods of depression; some are triumphant in their assurance of truth attained; and some are exalted prophecies of achievement still to come. The most obsessing of all his prophecies was his prophecy of human flight — a prophecy that he himself strove vainly to fulfill.

* * *

It seems to have been within the Laurentian period that among the Tuscan folk the *strambotto*, or *rispetto*, as a Tuscan folk form, reached its final state. Thitherto it had consisted of six lines rhyming alternately, followed by a concluding couplet with a new rhyme; but now, even while Politian and Pulci and the Nencia singers were using this older form, the *rispetto*, among the folk, was changing in two ways: the fifth and sixth lines became a couplet with a new rhyme, the seventh and eighth lines remaining as a couplet with a rhyme of their own (the rhyme-scheme of the whole octave being thus ABABCCDD); and the second couplet became an echo of the first, the wording being so changed as to yield a new rhyme. The stanza in its new form is then of this type:

Bella bellina, quando vai per acqua
La via della fontana ti favella;
E 'l rusignol che canta per la macchia
E' va dicendo che sei la più bella.
Sei la più bella e la più graziosina,

Sembri una rosa colta sulla spina;
  Sei la più bella e la più graziosetta,
Sembri una rosa in sulla spina fresca.*

* "Fair one, fair one, when you go for water the path to the fountain greets you; and the nightingale that sings in the grove keeps saying that you are the fairest. You are the fairest and the most graceful, you are like a rose plucked from the thorn; you are the fairest and the most graceful, you are like a rose upon the flowering thorn." In many *rispetti*, as in this one, the rhyme is imperfect in its consonants. Most existing *rispetti* are of this type, but there are many variations.

CHAPTER 19

Neapolitan, Ferrarese, and Other Writers

THE HOUSE OF ARAGON, of Spanish origin, which had ruled Sicily since the late thirteenth century, had come into possession of Southern Italy also in 1442, under the enlightened King Alfonso. On his death in 1450 the kingdom was again divided, and Southern Italy was inherited by Alfonso's son Ferdinand, who reigned until 1494 with extreme cruelty and with a cultural patronage that was more lavish than understanding. He was followed, in seven years, by three ineffectual successors, of whom the second was driven away for a time by the invasion of Charles VIII, and the third, Lorenzo's friend Frederick, saw, in 1501, the fall of the House of Aragon.

Before the death of Alfonso the Neapolitan Humanists, with Alfonso's blessing, had formed an association which they called an Academy. The leading spirit of this Academy, and its official head from 1471 on, was Giovanni Pontano (1426? – 1503), known academically as Jovianus Pontanus. Born and educated in Umbria, he went in 1447 to Naples, which thereafter remained his home. He soon won royal favor and appointments; took part in military campaigns; was instrumental in negotiating favorable treaties; and in 1486 was made Secretary of State. His administration of this high office was vigorous, fearless, and wise: he maintained his rightful authority even against royal reluctance.

With all his involvement in public affairs, he found time to write an immense amount of Latin verse and prose. He felt exuberantly the overwhelming beauty of the Neapolitan scene — peopled, in his classicizing imagination, with a host of minor divinities — and the fascinations of the daily life of the always exciting city and of the peaceful surrounding country. The longest of his eclogues, the *Lepidina*, depicts a gift-bearing procession in honor of the wedding of the river-god Sebetus and the nymph Parthenope: countryfolk; Nereids, among them Capri and Amalfi; Tritons; nymphs of streets and squares and fountains of the city, and of its suburbs; woodland divinities and monsters, among them Vesuvius; dryads and oreads; and finally Antiniana, the nymph of Pontano's own villa, attended by a chorus of youths and maidens.

The best of all his poetry is to be found in the *De amore coniugali*, a unique and charming collection of poems of family life. Contained in it are poems of conjugal affection; poems of nostalgic imagination written in absence, and of joy in safe return and the renewal of idyllic quietness; a poem on the nurture of children; a poem of elation on the birth of a son; twelve lullabies; and two epithalamia, one for each of his daughters. The first of the lullabies begins thus:

Somne, veni; tibi Luciolus blanditur ocellis;
somne, veni, venias, blandule somne, veni.
Luciolus tibi dulce canit, somne, optime somne;
somne, veni, venias, blandule somne, veni.
Luciolus vocat in thalamos te, blandule somne,
somnule dulcicule, blandule somnicule.
Ad cunas te Luciolus vocat; huc, age, somne,
somne, veni ad cunas, somne, age, somne, veni —

Come, sleep; little Lucio invites you, with his
little eyes;
Come, sleep, do come; gentle sleep, come.
Little Lucio sings to you sweetly, sleep, good sleep;
Come, sleep, do come; gentle sleep, come.
Little Lucio calls you to his bed, gentle sleep,
Sweet little sleep, gentle little sleep.
To his cradle little Lucio calls you; hither, pray, sleep,
Sleep, come to his cradle, sleep; pray, sleep, come.

Other collections — within which there are heartbroken poems on the death of a little daughter, and on the death of Lucio just as he had reached manhood — range in mood from pagan voluptuousness to conventional genuflection.

Among the prose works of Pontano the dialogues hold the greatest interest. Most of them bring in members of the Academy as interlocutors. It was a rule of the Academy that any member might speak on any subject that occurred to him; and the course of the imagined conversation shifts, accordingly, with a sprightly variety, and with frequent humor, now playful, now satiric.

At the end of the *Antonius*, which finds the Academicians out-of-doors, a company of mountebanks appears and sets up a platform; a trumpet is sounded; a crowd gathers; a buffoon opens the show with tricks and jokes;

and a masked "poet" recites (in hexameters) a story of the wars of Pompey in Spain — until the buffoon interrupts him with more tricks and jokes.

Pontano's Latin, both in his verse and in his prose, is the most living Latin of the Renaissance. He writes it with a perfect mastery, and yet as if it were not a mastered speech, but rather his own native speech. It is as supple, in his hands, as any vernacular could be, and perfectly adequate for the vivid rendering of any contemporary sight or sound, and for the sympathetic conveyance of a sense of laughter or of a sense of tears.

Within three months after George Chapman took from Politian the substance of his *Epicede* he had to write an epithalamium — which he proceeded to fashion out of Pontano's epithalamia for his daughters.

Another member of the Neapolitan Academy won, even in his lifetime, far greater fame and influence. Jacopo Sannazzaro (1456–1530), known academically as Actius Syncerus, was born in Naples; and there he spent most of his life, in the faithful service of the House of Aragon, until that House fell in 1501. Then he chose to share the French exile of his king; but when Frederick died, three years later, Sannazzaro returned to Naples, where he lived quietly in his villa by the shore.

In Latin he wrote many elegies and epigrams, several piscatorial eclogues, and a late religious poem. In the piscatorial eclogues — the first such eclogues, though they had a partial precedent in one of the idylls of Theocritus — the scene shifts from pastures and woodlands to the ever beautiful Bay of Naples, and the shepherds and satyrs and nymphs of the more familiar bucolic poems give place to fisherfolk and Tritons and Nereids; but the familiar themes of love and loss and the familiar accents of joy and sorrow remain unchanged. The poem on the birth of Christ is an attempt to set forth the story of the Advent in a Virgilian vesture. The vesture, in its classic elegance, is incongruous; but the poem contains a few fine passages, some lyrical and some descriptive. It contains also certain passages, derived from Claudian's *De raptu Proserpinae* and from Boccaccio's *Filocolo*, that were to influence later treatments of the Infernal Council theme.

In Italian, Sannazzaro wrote Petrarchan sonnets and *canzoni*, which reflect his essentially idyllic spirit; a few humorous monologues; a few pageants, devised for the entertainment of the court; and, chiefly in the years from 1480 to 1485, his one triumphantly successful work, the *Arcadia*.

This romance — the first pastoral romance since Boccaccio's *Ameto*, to which it owes its general form and its labored style — consists of twelve chapters of prose and twelve poems, in various meters. Sincero, a Neapolitan shepherd, unfortunate in love, leaves Naples for the mountainous Greek province of Arcadia, the home, in classic tradition, of pastoral song. There he finds shepherds dwelling in hardy simplicity; lives for a while among them; takes part in their herding and their hunting; and witnesses their games, their contests in song, and their sacrifices. After a dream of evil omen he returns to Naples, through a series of wonderful underground caverns, only to find that the maiden he loved is dead. Sincero represents Sannazzaro himself; Pontano appears as the shepherd Meliseo; and other members of the Academy appear in easily penetrable pastoral disguise — but these identifications do not matter greatly in the romance, which is indeed descriptive rather than narrative. Its gentle idyllicism, largely a mosaic of elements drawn from Virgil, Ovid, Theocritus, and other classic poets, palls on the modern reader; but it found an eager welcome in Sannazzaro's own day. It circulated widely in manuscript copies even before its first unauthorized publication in 1501. The first authorized edition was published in 1504. Its influence was immediate in France, Spain, and Portugal. Sidney turned to it for the title and some of the matter of his own *Arcadia.* And the explorer Verrazzano gave the name Arcadia to the Virginian coast.

Two other members of the Aragonese circle wrote stories and poems which were destined to have direct or indirect influence on many Italian and Transalpine writers.

The *Novellino* of Masuccio Salernitano is the main *novella* collection of the fifteenth century. Written about 1460, it contains fifty *novelle*, distributed, according to their general themes, into five Parts: those of the first Part, for instance, concern ecclesiastic or monastic misconduct, while those of the last Part are stories of magnanimity. The one story that is really memorable is a *novella* in which one can discern for the first time the general outlines of what was soon to be known as the story of Romeo and Juliet. The scene of Masuccio's version is Siena; the hero is Mariotto Mignanelli, and the heroine is named Ganozza. They are married secretly by an Augustinian friar; a little later Mariotto, during a quarrel, kills his adversary, is banished, and goes to Alexandria; Ganozza refuses offers of marriage; her father insists upon an acceptance; the friar gives her a potion that will cause her to sleep, seeming to be dead, for three days; she is buried; the friar rescues her; she sets out for Alexandria; Mariotto, informed that she has died, returns to Siena, and is discovered as he attempts to open her tomb; he is executed; Ganozza returns, enters a convent, and dies soon afterward. Many of the elements of the *novella* are to be found in earlier stories — some of them in the anonymous *novella* of *Ippolito e Leonora* — but it was Masuccio who combined them; and it was from him that Luigi da Porto, early in the next century, derived his story of Romeo and Juliet.

Benedicto Gareth (c.1450–1514), born in Barcelona, was the first man of foreign birth to earn a place among the poets of Italy. He came in his teens to Naples; and there he spent most of his life, holding responsible official positions, and faithful always to the House of Aragon. To the Academicians his Catalan surname suggested *Charites*, the Greek name for the Graces: in the Academy he was known, accordingly, as Chariteus, and, in other literary circles, as Il Chariteo.

His main lyric collection — to which, in honor of his Luna (his poetic name for his lady), he gave the name *Endymion* — contains some two hundred poems in the conventional lyric forms. Petrarchan influence remains strong; but in the *Endymion*, Il Chariteo, first among the Italian lyrists, weaves into his verse a great many borrowings from the Latin lyrists, Propertius being his favorite source. The chief historical interest of the *Endymion* lies in its several instances of conceits so sharply antithetic or so harshly striking as to become definitely unpoetic. For the use of such conceits there was precedent in Petrarch; but Petrarch's rhetorical indulgences constitute only a very minor group of characteristics within the refined and glowing beauty of his verse. It was indeed natural enough that Il Chariteo and a host of later imitative poets should choose for imitation the superficially obvious and inferior elements of the master's poetry rather than its deeper and more personal and less readily imitable perfections. In the *Endymion* the poet's Moon is also, frequently, his Sun; her coldness is enough to freeze Vulcan and his fires; the sight of her beauteous eyes stops a runaway horse; after she has gone to Spain his eyes set sail to follow her, but suffer shipwreck; if both he and she are to be damned, she for her pride and he for his presumption, he will be content if only he can behold her, and the only torment he fears is that he should be deprived of that beholding.

The poems of Il Chariteo became known swiftly and widely; and their influence continues in the Italian and foreign Petrarchism of the sixteenth and the seventeenth centuries.

* * *

The Este had been lords of Ferrara since the time of Frederick II, and were to continue their lordship up to the very end of the sixteenth century. Their court was definitely aristocratic in its customs and its culture: in its most typical moments it was a homogeneous group of knightly gentlemen and cultivated ladies.

The Este dukes of the Laurentian period were Borso, who died in 1471, and Ercole I, who lived until 1505. Toward the end of Borso's life the new Este palace called Schifanoia ("Banish Care," or "Sans Souci") was completed. The decoration of its great hall was entrusted to Francesco del Cossa, whose frescoes are vigorous and delightful records of contemporary court life and court-sponsored amusements. Ercole included humanists in the circle of his patronage, caused many classic works to be translated into Italian, and developed a special liking for performances of Latin comedies in Italian translation. The *Menaechmi* was given in 1486, at enormous expense, in the palace courtyard; and ten of the other plays of Plautus and two of the plays of Terence were given at various times from 1487 to 1502.

The Este court had one other distinguishing literary interest. As earlier chapters have indicated, the Arthurian stories had long been familiar in Italy, where they had found their widest popularity in the form of prose romances, written mainly in Tuscany. Tuscan minstrels had made use of Arthurian stories in some of their *cantari;* but the sentimental refinement of these stories did not appeal to the plebeian audiences of the *cantastorie*, or even to the culturally democratic Medicean audience, nearly as much as the Carolingian tales of combat on behalf of country or of the Christian faith; and no Arthurian poems of epic length were composed in Tuscany. The Arthurian stories were however precisely to the taste of the court of Ferrara.

The high achievement of Boiardo, the one great Ferrarese poet of the Laurentian period, was the fusion of the Carolingian and the Arthurian traditions into a novel unity, and the initiation, thereby, of a new epic cycle. The fusion is announced in the very title of Boiardo's epic, the *Orlando innamorato*: the hero is still the Carolingian Roland, but he is no longer primarily a fighting paladin — he has become primarily an exemplar of Arthurian romantic love. The love theme, to be sure, had made episodic appearances in many Italian versions of the Carolingian stories; but it had never before been assumed into dominant importance.

Matteo Maria Boiardo (1441–1494), Count of Scandiano, took up residence in Ferrara, in 1476, as a highly honored and highly honorable member of the ducal court. In the latter part of his life he served with great skill and absolute rectitude as the Duke's regent in Modena and later in Reggio, where he died in the distressing year of the first French invasion.

The central figure of Boiardo's long and unfinished poem is a creation of his own, Angelica, daughter of the king of Cathay. With her brother Argalia she comes to the court of Charlemagne, where she proposes that such knights as may desire to do so shall engage in single combat with Argalia (whose weapons and armor are enchanted), and that all who are vanquished shall be taken as prisoners to Cathay, but that if anyone defeats him the combats shall cease and the victor shall win not only the victory but herself as well. The paladins one and all immediately fall in love with her; Argalia is overcome, despite enchantment; and Angelica flees, with Roland and Ranaldo in pursuit. Ranaldo drinks of the fountain of Merlin, whose waters turn love to hatred; Angelica drinks of a near-by stream whose waters inspire love; they meet; Ranaldo turns back; and Angelica, sorrowing, makes her way homeward to her castle in Cathay. There Roland finally arrives, to find the castle besieged by the Saracen king Agramante, whom he slays in single combat. The peril of Charlemagne calls Roland back to France, and Angelica, seeking Ranaldo, goes with him. She finds Ranaldo; but this time it is she who drinks of the fountain of hatred, while he drinks of the stream of love. Roland and Ranaldo challenge each other; but the duel is prevented by Charlemagne, who puts Angelica under guard, promising to give her to that one of the two rivals who shall most distinguish himself against the Saracens.

With this main plot many other plots of nearly equal importance are very skillfully interwoven. One such plot tells of the love of the Saracen knight Roger and the Christian warrior maiden Bradamante, sister of Ranaldo. Boiardo had planned to develop this plot into primacy in the latter part of his poem, to report the conversion of Roger and his marriage with Bradamante, and to establish them as the progenitors of the Este line; but at the point at which the poem was interrupted Roger is still unmarried and unconverted.

Still greater interest lies in the many single episodes for which the plots furnish occasion. Forest flights, marvelous gardens, the storming of castles, the vanquishing of armies, islands of delight, combats with giants or with dragons, rescues of maidens in distress, lands of strange people and strange customs, imprisonments and escapes, devices of fairies and magicians, and adventures and enchantments of every description follow each other in swift and captivating succession.

Boiardo's plots and episodes are to a remarkable extent creations of his own. His mobile imagination, more incessantly fertile than that of any other Italian narrative poet except Dante, leads him to invent characters as well as events, to delineate his characters with a satisfying clarity, and to depict his scenes with effective detail, and often with much beauty. He was very much in earnest about his chivalric virtues — valor, loyalty, and courtesy; but he was too perfectly of the Renaissance to treat his paladins and his enchantresses with quite the traditional seriousness. A vein of quiet humor — very different from the obvious merriment of Pulci — runs through his work, a humor of smiling amusement rather than of laughter. The traditional opening stanzas of invocation are rejected: each canto begins with an immediate continuation of the narrative, a summary of preceding events, or a passage of general introductory reflection or description. The tone of the poem as a whole is one of vernal freshness and eager nobility. *Omnia vincit amor*: but love and honor are coequal comrades.

The Ferrarese coloring of Boiardo's language rendered his work unacceptable to Tuscan readers, and in the next century the Florentine Berni rewrote it in smoother wording, but with alterations that weakened it and betrayed its spirit. But if Boiardo was unfortunate in this respect he was fortunate in his continuator: for Ariosto, writing also in the Este court, took up the unfinished narrative and completed it in his *Orlando furioso*.

Boiardo's lyrics are, with those of Lorenzo and Politian, the best of the century. They are in a general way Petrarchan, but they express the poet's own joys and griefs with accents that spring from his own imaginative mind. Few poets have ever interwoven moods of love and moods of nature with such deeply felt and directly rendered emotional simplicity. Sun and moon and stars, the coming of dawn over the sea, hills and streams and flowering meadows, lilies and roses, the song of birds in springtime leafage — these, for Boiardo, are not external adornments for his verse, but rather phases of his own poetic consciousness:

Al veder nostro il giorno non ha sole,
La notte non ha stelle senza lei —

To my eyes the day has no sun and the night has no stars when she is not here.

The poems of Antonio Tebaldi (1463–1537), known as Il Tebaldeo, are remarkable chiefly for their more than Charitean excesses: what had been occasional in Il Chariteo is chronic in Il Tebaldeo. He sins particularly by his materialization of common metaphors, giving to their elements an independent literal existence they were never meant to have. So many of the arrows of Love have pierced his heart that Love carries him around as a quiver; when Flavia slips on the snow, it turns to ice, out of jealousy for her whiteness, and dislocates her arm, but if she had only shared his ardor she would have melted the ice; her sore throat is due to celestial jealousy of her charming words; and when her nose bleeds it is because Love, being blind, had missed her heart.

* * *

Mantua, not very far from Ferrara, was becoming a cultural center of increasing distinction, especially after 1490, when Isabella d'Este, daughter of Duke Ercole, came there as the bride of the Marquis Francesco Gonzaga. Mantegna, the greatest of the North Italian painters of the time, lived and worked chiefly in Mantua from about 1460 to the end of his life: his illusionistic and yet dignified frescoes in a room of the Gonzaga castle, depicting members of the Gonzaga family and events in its recent history, are perhaps his finest achievement.

The one native Mantuan who won poetic eminence in the Laurentian period was the Carmelite monk and humanist, Battista Spagnoli (1448–1516), known generally as Baptista Mantuanus — and in England as Baptist Mantuan, or simply (in *Love's Labour's Lost*, for instance) as Mantuan. He was learned in Latin, Greek, and Hebrew; and he wrote voluminously in Latin, both in verse and in prose. His several long poems are religious or historical. Among his shorter poems are the ten eclogues, written in his youth, which now alone preserve his fame. The first four deal with happy and unhappy love, and the fifth with the niggardliness of patrons; the sixth is a debate on the relative merits of life in the country and life in the city; the last four are religious. His chief model was, inevitably, Virgil — a far greater Mantuan — but there are echoes of other classic poets, and of the eclogues of Petrarch. He was hailed by contemporaries, among them Erasmus, as a second Virgil; and his Eclogues were widely known, quoted, and imitated, in France, Germany, and England — Spenser, for instance, imitated them in *The Shepheardes Calender*. Not only that: for they, and they alone among all the poems of the Italian humanists, had the fate of serving in several countries as textbooks for use in the study of Latin.

* * *

In Venice the brothers Gentile and Giovanni Bellini were founding the glory of Venetian painting; and hundreds of printers were making the city the chief European center of publication.

In literature, however, only one work of any considerable interest was written in Venice during the Laurentian period. That work, one of the strangest ever written anywhere, was a prose romance by the Dominican monk Francesco Colonna, entitled *Hypnerotomachia Poliphili*, which means "The Strife of Love in a Dream with the Lover of Polia." The initials of its several chapters spell out its subject and the name and address of the author: *Poliam frater Franciscus Colonna peramavit. Adhuc vivit Venetiis in S. Iohanne et Paulo.** The romance was written in 1467. In the first of its two Books the narrative — allegorical, incoherent, obscure, and unedifying — tells of a dream-journey in which Poliphilus visits realms which appear to be those of Art and of Free Will. The author's main interest seems to be in the detailed description of imaginary structures and statues of classic type: he even records measurements and inscriptions. The second Book, still fictional, tells of the enamorment of the author (now awake), and quotes his highly rhetorical letters to his Polia. The romance is written in a unique language in which a pedantic Italian is enriched by the intermixture of ponderous newly coined words built up on Latin stems. The esoteric flavor of the original is well preserved in an anonymous Elizabethan translation. Poliphilus, greeted lovingly by a "Nymphe," finds his heart "strooken and inwardly pricking, secretly filled and compressiuely stuft." Foreheads may be "wrympled," eyes "cavernate," bones "remigiall," and maids "flamigerous." Yet Colonna had his ideals. Of the artistic writer he says:

> And besides his skil he must be honest, no pratler full of words, but courteous, gentle, bening, tractable, patient, mery & pleasant, full of new deuises, a curious searcher into all artes, and well aduised in his proceeding.

Surely such a writer would deserve to be "instrophiated with laurel."

* "Friar Francesco Colonna loved Polia dearly. He is living now in Venice in the quarter of Saints John and Paul."

The first edition of the *Hypnerotomachia*, published by Aldus in 1499, with nearly two hundred woodcuts, is regarded as the most remarkable illustrated book of the Renaissance. Colonna and his strange lore play a considerable part in Charles Reade's novel, *The Cloister and the Hearth.*

* * *

The most devastatingly popular poet of the last years of the century was Serafino de' Ciminelli (1466–1500), born in the town of Aquila, in the Abruzzi, and called usually Serafino Aquilano. He performed — he was a singer and a lutanist — in Rome, Milan, Naples, Urbino, Mantua, and elsewhere. To hear him sing his own *strambotti* or sonnets or dance-songs to his own accompaniment, with the look and the manner of an inspired and improvising bard, was to experience the utmost elite felicity. He was all but worshipped in his lifetime, and mourned, after his early death, in Greek, Latin, and Italian verse. Yet he had nothing to say that was worth saying; and much of his very considerable skill in rhyme and rhythm was spent, following the leads of Il Chariteo and Il Tebaldeo, in the effort to treat his listeners to farfetched surprises. The fire metaphor suffers his worst manipulations: the fire within him is such that its smoke renders him invisible, and that his sighs burn the birds that fly above him: even when he eats snow it turns to fire. He has in his heart, along with his fire, the gold of countless arrows, and the image of his lady: his heart, then, is a mint, wherein he may strike medals in his lady's honor.

The aberrations of Il Chariteo, Il Tebaldeo, and Serafino were due in part, at least, to reaction against the tameness of the more conventional expressions of fifteenth-century Petrarchism. Thanks to the corrective dictatorship of Bembo, their influence in Italy was brief. Editions of their poems were still current, however, when French and English gentlemen began to visit Italy; and the Charitean-Tebaldean-Serafinesque influence mingles, in France and England, with that of Petrarch himself and that of Bembo and his train of obedient followers. Both Wyatt and Surrey translated and adapted poems of Serafino's. If Serafino, escaped from an unhappy servitude and finding himself still alive, could laugh —

> Ah ah ah men rido tanto
> Ch' io son vivo e son di fuore —

Wyatt could echo him:

> Ha! Ha! Ha! full well is me,
> For I am now at liberty.

CHAPTER 20

Bembo

IN THE DARK DAWN of the sixteenth century, France was in possession of Milan; Florence was menaced by the machinations of the exiled Medici; Naples was in imminent danger of foreign conquest; and Pope Alexander VI was giving all possible support to his son, Caesar Borgia, who was striving to carve a principality for himself out of the States of the Church. This enterprise kept Central Italy in a turmoil of warfare, treachery, and crime until 1503, when, on the verge of success, it collapsed swiftly in consequence of the death of Alexander and the election of Julius II. In 1501 French and Spanish armies in alliance overran Southern Italy; in the division of the spoils Naples fell to France; the allies turned presently to fighting each other; the Spaniards won; and in 1504 Naples, with all Southern Italy and Sicily, became an appanage of the Spanish crown. The war of the League of Cambrai was fought in Northern Italy from 1508 to 1510, and the war of the First Holy League from 1511 to 1513. The fortunes of this latter war brought the Medici back to Florence in 1512. Cardinal Giovanni de' Medici, now the head of the family, was elected pope, in 1513, as Leo X.* He died in 1521,

* There will be in this and the following chapters so many references to certain members of the senior branch of the Medici family that this chart may be useful:

- Piero 1416–1469
  - Lorenzo 1449–1492
    - Piero 1471–1503
      - Lorenzo 1492–1519
    - Giovanni (Leo X) 1475–1521
    - Giuliano 1478–1516
  - Giuliano 1453–1478
    - Giulio (Clement VII) 1478–1534

The younger Giuliano was a socially charming pleasure seeker, and a minor poet. The younger Lorenzo was a man of some ability. His daughter Catherine was to become Queen of France.

and was succeeded, after a brief intervening papacy, by his cousin Giulio, who was elected pope, in 1523, as Clement VII. Francis I and the Emperor Charles V fought through Northern Italy in the years 1521–1525. The war of the Second Holy League, fought in the years 1526–1529, brought in 1527, as its most terrible event, the sack of Rome by an irresponsible imperial army. The immediate repercussions of that horror drove the Medici out of Florence again; but they were restored three years later, when a Spanish army, after a long and famous siege, finally overcame the valiant Florentine defense. Alessandro de' Medici, a putative son of the younger Lorenzo, was presently made the first Duke of Florence. On his assassination in 1537 the succession passed to Cosimo I, a member of a junior branch of the great family. Milan, which had changed hands repeatedly since the beginning of the century, became an imperial fief in 1535.

Turkish land forces had overrun Hungary by 1526, but they were turned back at Vienna in 1529. Turkish raiders descended occasionally upon the coasts of Italy; and the Turks were gradually stripping Venice of her possessions in the eastern Mediterranean.

Luther's defiance at Wittenberg in 1517 marked the beginning of the Protestant Reformation. Advocates of reform became active presently within the Church itself, among them Juan de Valdés, the Spanish theologian and mystic, who spent the last years of his life in Naples; Bernardino Ochino of Siena, Vicar General of the Capuchin Order, who fled to Geneva and became a Protestant; and the English cardinal Reginald Pole, resident in Italy most of his mature life, a wise man of wide and steadying influence. The Jesuit Order was founded in 1534; the Congregation of the Inquisition was established in 1542; and lists of prohibited books were published by various authorities from about 1540 on. The Council of Trent met first in 1545, but its sessions were soon interrupted.

Yet this stormy half century witnessed in Italy as a whole not a diminution but a surging increase of all forms of cultural activity. There were major changes in the localization of that activity. Florence, though still very productive, could no longer claim hegemony. Naples and Milan were stifled. Ferrara and Mantua continued to flourish; and Urbino had a brief eminence. Venice came into its own; and Rome, under Julius II and Leo X, reached its highest cultural excitements and achievements. There the Apollo Belvedere was found in 1503 and the Laocoön in 1506; and in the latter year the cornerstone of the new St. Peter's was laid.

The titanic power of Michelangelo dominated the triple field of architecture, sculpture, and painting. In architecture Bramante shared his eminence, and several other men were worthy co-workers. Andrea del Sarto continued the tradition of Florentine painting, bringing to it a softly glowing poetic quality; Raphael endowed churches and palatial homes with madonnas and saints of perfect grace and gentleness, and attained monumental grandeur in his frescoes in the Vatican; Giorgione and Titian enriched Venice with penetrant characterization and a new luxuriance of color; and in Correggio beauty justified sentimentality. Classic themes were treated more and more frequently; and even the greatest painters painted many individual portraits. In the clever hands of Benevenuto Cellini goldsmithery approached the status of a fine art.

Changes of a general nature were taking place in the field of literature. Humanism continued, and there were still men who preferred to write in Latin; but scorn for the vernacular was disappearing, and evidences of the humanistic spirit were entering pervasively into the more serious forms of writing in Italian. The works of Greek literature were becoming available in Italian. The number of men and women engaged in writing was much greater than it had ever been before, and a remarkably high proportion of them attained at least secondary excellence. Literary groups of various sorts came into existence in several cities: some of them called themselves "academies." While certain cities were still points of literary concentration, literature was becoming national rather than local. Writers were moving about from place to place more than ever before; and the leading writers of the period, to a remarkable extent, were acquainted with each other, and carried on correspondence with each other. It came to be realized that letters written in Italian might be works of literary art; and men began to write such letters with care, and to collect their own Italian letters for publication. Interest in the drama was developing very rapidly. Petrarchism pervaded the field of the lyric not only in this period but throughout the century; and throughout the century editions of Petrarch poured from the presses.

Early in the century there came into use a new lyric form, consisting typically of a single stanza in which long and short lines are freely mingled. This form has the look of a *canzone* stanza, and it was called at first *canzone* or *canzonetta*; but the name *madrigale* was soon applied to it, though it is quite unlike the Petrarchan madrigal. Upon the basis of this new madrigal, composers developed a new and very successful form called also "madrigal": but the word "madrigal" as a musical term was presently used to cover not only settings of lyric madrigals, but also musically similar settings of lyrics of other types.

Adrian Willaert, the last of the great Flemish composers, came to Italy in 1516, and was thereafter the main figure in the musical world; but a vigorous generation of native Italian musicians was already beginning to develop the new "madrigal" into a medium with which their successors were soon to win European musical leadership.

Pietro Pomponazzi, the outstanding philosopher of the period, taught at the Universities of Padua, Ferrara, and Bologna, expounding a Stoic Aristotelianism that was far removed both from orthodox Christian doctrine and from the Platonism of Ficino. In Florence the tradition of Ficino was carried on, with diminishing distinction, by Francesco Cattani da Diacceto.

Printing continued to thrive, especially in Venice. The most famous of all Italian printers, Aldo Mannucci, known as Aldus Manutius, issued his first book in 1495. He was a humanist by training, and had taught as a humanist before he settled in Venice. His greatest service was in the production of well edited and inexpensive classic texts. He was an innovator in typography: it was he who introduced italic type. He was an innovator, also, in respect to format: whereas earlier printers had produced, generally speaking, large volumes, Aldus first brought small portable books into fashion. He worked mainly for the benefit of scholars; and scholars — among them Thomas Linacre — were glad to work as editors for him.

The issuance of hand-written news reports (forerunners of the newspaper) designed for relatively general reading seems to have begun within this period.

These same decades, largely as a result of the very wars that made them so disastrous, were decades in which, more than at any earlier time, France and Spain came into direct and impressive contact with Italian culture. French and Spanish gentlemen, coming into Italy in their armies, or on diplomatic missions, or on other errands, now saw with their own eyes both the magnificent ruins of ancient Rome and the contemporary cultural magnificence of Renaissance Italy. Many of them read Italian works, old or new, that were then current; and some of them formed friendships with Italian writers. Englishmen were not far behind: Sir Thomas Wyatt visited Italy in 1527. Italians, in their turn, as refugees, as envoys, or as artists, began to frequent the French court, and, in lesser numbers, the Spanish and the English courts, carrying with them their pride in Italian art and Italian poetry. Petrarchism received a new impetus in Spain, and began to appear in France and in England, where Wyatt, soon followed by Surrey, wrote the first English sonnets. In Italy itself the Renaissance, now at its culmination, was soon to decline; but in northern and western Europe the Renaissance was just gathering its strength.

* * *

Pietro Bembo, whom his contemporaries were to regard as the foremost figure of their literary world, was born in Venice, of a noble family, in 1470. When his father, Bernardo Bembo, was sent in 1474 as envoy to Florence, where he remained for most of the next five years, he took the young Pietro with him; and the boy thus grew naturally into such a knowledge of the Florentine speech and such a sense of familiarity with Laurentian

Florence as he could hardly have acquired otherwise. He made the most of a thorough classical education; and throughout his manhood he was able to write with perfect freedom in Latin, and with competence in Greek. From 1498 to 1500 Bernardo served as envoy to Ferrara; and again his son, now a young man of high promise, accompanied him.

By this time Pietro had begun the writing of Italian lyrics in the conventional Petrarchan forms — sonnets, *canzoni*, and *ballate*. His poems were thoroughly Petrarchan in content also, and they were Petrarchan not only in their phrasing and their imagery but also in the consistent refinement of their good taste. They were thus in clear-cut contrast with the distorted Petrarchism of Il Tebaldeo and Serafino; and their unmistakable elegance tended in itself to discredit the excesses of the recent fashion. Bembo's Petrarchism, however, was essentially imitative, and without any warmth of inspiration. The most famous of his poems is a sonnet beginning

> Crin d' oro crespo e d' ambra tersa e pura —
>
> Hair of rippling gold and of amber clear and pure —

in which he details his lady's beauties and attractions: after her hair her eyes, her laughter, her lips, her teeth, her words, her hands, her singing, her wisdom, her charm, her modesty. These, he concludes, in a line taken, almost without change, from Petrarch, are

> Grazie, ch' a poche il ciel largo destina —
>
> Graces that on few women heaven freely bestows.

In Ferrara also he wrote most of his first ambitious work, the *Asolani*, finished in 1502 and published in 1505. It is a dialogue on the nature of love set in a connecting narrative. The scene is the palace of Asolo,* then the residence of Caterina Cornaro, the former queen of Cyprus. There are many guests, among them a group of six young people: Perottino, Gismondo, Lavinello, and three young ladies. These six meet in a well-shaded garden, by a fountain, on three successive afternoons: each of the three Books reports the conversation of one of the three afternoons.

On the first afternoon Perottino, taking love first as a general principle of life and then in its ordinary acceptation, maintains that love is evil and is the source of all life's woe. He is interrupted freely by the others, and he varies his argument occasionally by singing songs of his own composition — some of them of the new madrigal type — which he introduces to illustrate points he wishes to make. This pattern of interruption and of occasional singing continues through the second Book and the first half of the third.

* In the mountain country north of Venice. Browning went often to Asolo; made it the scene of "Pippa Passes"; and finished there the collection of lyrics to which he gave the name *Asolando*.

On the second afternoon Gismondo, taking love in the same two senses, engages first in a detailed refutation of the arguments of Perottino, and then proceeds to maintain that love is good and is the source of all that is good in life.

On the third afternoon the Queen and some of the other guests join the group of six; and Lavinello, in his turn, maintains that love may be either good or evil: good if it is worthy love of a good object; evil if it is love of a bad object, or unworthy love of a good object. Love is the desire of beauty; and beauty, whether visible or of the mind, is a grace which arises from the good proportion, the compatibility, and the harmony of various elements. Love seeks visible beauty through sight, and beauty of the mind through hearing, and may return in thought to the enjoyment of either type of beauty. Love that seeks its object thus is worthy; but if it seeks its object otherwise it is unworthy. This conclusion is reached about halfway through the third Book. What remains is of a quite different character: instead of expressing views of his own, Lavinello reports, without interruption, a conversation he has had that very morning with a holy hermit, on the top of the hill on which the palace stands. This hermit tells Lavinello that if love is to be truly good it must be the desire not just of beauty, but of true beauty, and that true beauty is not human and mortal, but divine and immortal.

Bembo's thought is not original: the ideas of the first two books and the first half of the third are derived largely from Petrarch; those of the hermit's conversation come largely from Dante; and a merely superficial Platonism makes its appearance here and there. The dialogue, however, was intended not as a serious philosophic study, but as a sophisticated breviary for the fashionable world in which the young Bembo was well content to move. For the modern reader there is little inherent appeal in the *Asolani*, though there is real beauty in the *mise en scène*, and there are a few passages that approach eloquence.

The style is something new. Bembo, always essentially imitative, and always mindful of his classics, wanted for his Italian prose a model comparable to that afforded by Petrarch for his Italian verse; and he found what he wanted in the classicizing prose of Boccaccio, especially in the *Ameto.* But while Bembo took his vocabulary and the general character of his style from Boccaccio, he out-classicized his Tuscan model. The Italian of the *Asolani*, is, indeed, a new classic language, learned and used as one would learn and use Latin itself. The resulting style has a labored stateliness, and conveys the feeling that what is said was, to the writer, precious; but it moves very slowly, and its artificiality tends to make the content seem unreal.

In 1501 Bembo prepared for Aldus the text of the famous edition of the *Canzoniere* of Petrarch which Aldus published in that year, and in 1502 he prepared the text of the first Aldine edition of the *Divine Comedy*.

From 1506 to 1511 Bembo was a member of the court circle of Urbino, which under Guidobaldo, duke from 1482 to 1508, and his wife, Elizabetta Gonzaga, rivaled Ferrara in social, artistic, and literary brilliance. There Bembo lived and wrote as a humanist and a courtly poet, reading and studying extensively and deeply in the great library, and taking a large and willing part in the social life of the court. In 1512 he moved to Rome. In 1513 Leo X made him a papal secretary; and for Leo he composed papal documents and letters in a Latin of the highest elegance. In 1521, weary and in ill health, he resigned his secretaryship, and went to live in Padua.

His second major work, the *Prose della volgar lingua*, "Discussions of the Italian Language," which, like the *Asolani*, is a dialogue set in a connecting narrative recounting conversations supposed to have been held on three successive days, was written chiefly in Urbino and in Rome. The setting of the dialogue is the home of Bembo's brother Carlo in Venice, the imagined date is 1502, and the interlocutors are Carlo, Giuliano de' Medici, and two other well-known gentlemen.

In the first Book it is argued that Italian is preferable to Latin for current literary use, and that the language of Florence as employed by Petrarch and Boccaccio is the form of Italian which should be chosen for such use, rather than the spoken language of the papal court (as a minor author had recently asserted), rather than another Italian dialect, and rather than the language of contemporary Florentine writers. The second Book, which opens with a brief review of early Italian writers through Petrarch and Boccaccio, is devoted mainly to consideration of the primary qualities of literary style: these are said to be *gravità*, "dignity," and *piacevolezza*, "pleasantness"; and there is a discussion of the means whereby these qualities may be obtained. The third Book is an exposition of grammatical rules.

This dialogue was even more influential in Italy than the *Asolani*, since it established a single, clearly defined type of language as being proper for literary use. It did not put an end to theorizing, but in practice most of the verse of the century was written in a language that is essentially Petrarchan, and most of the prose in a language that is essentially Boccaccesque.

In Padua, Bembo lived contentedly for many years, enjoying his own rich library and his own collection of pieces of ancient sculpture, visited often by friends and admirers, preparing his *Prose* and his *Rime* for publication, busy with his studies and with his very extensive correspondence. In 1530 he was made the official historian of the Venetian republic, and in the course of his remaining years he wrote in Latin a lengthy history of Venice from 1487 to 1513. In 1539 he was made a cardinal; and from that time until his death in 1547 he lived usually in Rome.

The greatness of Bembo's influence upon his contemporaries was out of all proportion to the inherent value of his own writings. By the time of his retirement to Padua he had become the literary arbiter of Italy. He was a man of notable position both by birth and by his successive appointments; he had been a leading figure in every group in which he had moved; his learning was great; his taste was sure; and his precepts were stated with confident authority and supported by weighty argumentation. Other writers, among them even Ariosto, sought his counsel and deferred to it; and a host of younger poets regarded themselves as his disciples. His dominance was indeed as complete as that of Malherbe in France a century later, or that of Dr. Johnson in eighteenth-century England. In 1531 a young Venetian, Antonio Broccardo, who was clinging in his own verse to the Charitean manner, dared to speak ill of Bembo and to criticize the master's *Rime*: the reaction of Bembo and his devotees and his venomous ally, Pietro Aretino, was so violent as to drive poor Broccardo to his death.

Bembo's dictatorship, however, was beneficent, on balance, in its literary results. His own Petrarchism was indeed pale and cold, and his own prose style was ponderous and artificial. But he did rescue the Italian lyric from Chariteanism. Niccolò Franco (a very minor poet) said of him:

> Che se non eri tu, mastron di tutti,
> Tutti sariemo stati Tebaldei! —
>
> For if it had not been for you, master of us all,
> We should all have been Tebaldeos!

And he did establish the literary language of Florence as the standard literary language of Italy: a service that was of critical importance at a moment when the habit of prolific literary production was spreading to all parts of Italy, and a service that could hardly have been rendered except by a non-Florentine who had himself attained a perfect mastery of the language of Florence and was himself a man of great authority — hardly, in short, by anyone except Pietro Bembo.

CHAPTER 21

Ariosto

ESTE PATRONAGE, already highly honored by the poetry of Boiardo, was now to be still more highly honored by the poetry of Lodovico Ariosto. He was born in 1474 in Reggio, where his father then held, for Duke Ercole, the captaincy of the citadel. After the death of his father, in 1500, Ariosto found himself laden with heavy financial burdens, and entered the service of the Este. In 1502 he was captain of the citadel of Canossa. From 1503 to 1517 he was employed as a secretarial and diplomatic attaché by Cardinal Ippolito d'Este, younger son of Duke Ercole and brother of Alfonso, who succeeded his father in 1505. The Cardinal kept Ariosto busy with many missions — to Milan, Mantua, Bologna, and to Florence, and especially to Rome. Tension between Rome and Ferrara was high during the papacy of Julius II, and the missions to Rome were not only difficult but very dangerous. In 1518 he entered the service of Alfonso. From 1522 to 1525 he served with great skill and wisdom as commissioner for a wild and bandit-ridden mountain district known as the Garfagnana. When he left that post he was able to retire from official duty, and to build a modest house in Ferrara, inscribing over the door the Latin distich:

Parva sed apta mihi sed nulli obnoxia sed non
Sordida parta meo sed tamen aere domus —

A small house, but large enough for me; to none unfriendly; not mean; and won by my own earning.

There he lived contentedly until his death in 1533.

He began to write verse about 1494. For some ten years he wrote, almost exclusively, Latin lyrics, chiefly in forms used by Horace and Catullus, and influenced greatly, though not exclusively, by those two poets. His Latin verse does not rival that of Politian or that of Pontano in grace and fluency, but it has a compact firmness of texture that is quite its own. His Italian lyrics, written from time to time throughout his life, but chiefly after his decade of Latinity, are respectably Petrarchan; but of no great excellence.

In 1506 Ariosto turned to a very different kind of poetry, in which he was to prove, among Italians, supreme. Boiardo, at his death, had left his epic unfinished: Ariosto undertook to complete it, and made his continuation, in its poetic essence, a new thing. The pattern of Boiardo's two-word title is repeated in Ariosto's title *Orlando furioso*: the adjective implies that Roland, still enamored, is by jealousy driven to furious madness. And as Boiardo's denomination of *Orlando* as *innamorato* had announced the fusion of the Carolingian and the Arthurian traditions, so Ariosto's *Orlando furioso*, by its reflection of the title, *Hercules furens*, of one of the tragedies of Seneca, announces that the tradition is again enriched, this time by the fusion of the classic tradition with the already fused medieval traditions.

The opening lines,

> Le donne, i cavallier, l' arme, gli amori,
> Le cortesie, l' audaci imprese io canto,

echo Virgil's *Arma virumque cano*, but include courtesies with valorous deeds, loves with arms, and ladies with knights.

For the construction and the adornment of his poem he drew on the whole world of poetry and romance that he knew and loved. He drew much from Italian versions of Arthurian romances; much from Boiardo; much from classic poets; and much, though more incidentally, from Dante and Petrarch and other Italians. But his derivation was never imitative: whatever he derived he re-created, fusing it all, together with many inventions of his own, in the unity of his art.

The underlying plot of the *Orlando furioso* is still the Christian-Saracen struggle. At the outset the Saracens, under Agramante, are besieging Paris. Rinaldo (Boiardo's Ranaldo) is sent to England to get reënforcements, and on their arrival the Saracens are driven off. Soon, however, they make a second general attack, which is repulsed only by divine intervention. Meanwhile the English knight Astolfo carries the war into Africa, ravaging the Saracen countries with the help of a magically equipped army of Ethiopian Christians. The Saracens attack Paris for the third time, but are defeated. Agramante embarks for Africa, but his fleet is destroyed by a magically created Christian fleet. Three pagan heroes fight a tremendous triple duel, on the island of Lampedusa, with Roland, Oliver, and Brandimarte: the success of the Christians in this combat puts an end to pagan power and ensures the peace of Christendom. Two variations from the earlier Italian tradition are noteworthy: Charlemagne, so long a figure of indignity, becomes again imperial; and the treachery of the House of Maganza fades into insignificance.

Roland is the hero both of the underlying plot and of the main personal plot. Boiardo had left Angelica under guard, at the court of Charlemagne, to be given to that one of the two rivals, Roland and Ranaldo, who should most distinguish himself against the Saracens. In the new poem she soon escapes, pursued by Rinaldo:

> She fled through woods and deserts all obscure
> Through places uninhabited and wast,
> Nor could she yet repute her selfe secure,
> But farther still she gallopeth in hast.
> Each leaf that stirres in her doth fear procure,
> And maketh her affrighted and agast:
> Each noise she heares, each shadow she doth see,
> She doth mistrust it should *Renaldo* be.*

Later, Roland also leaves the Christian camp to follow her. After a series of most remarkable adventures he finds proof that she has fallen in love with a young Saracen private soldier, Medoro, and that she has married him and set out with him for Cathay. This knowledge drives Roland mad; and for a long time he rages through France and Spain, uprooting forests and slaying beasts and men. Once he comes across Angelica and her Medoro, but he does not recognize her, nor she him: a magic ring enables her to escape his blind fury. Finally Astolfo goes on a divinely ordained mission to the moon, where he finds Roland's wits. He brings them back to earth; Roland is overpowered and made to inhale them, and thereupon resumes his place as the foremost Christian champion.

Next in importance among the personal plots, as in Boiardo, is that which tells of the love of Roger and Bradamante. They meet occasionally and briefly, only to be swept apart by tides of misfortune; and each seeks the other through a series of strange adventures. Roger is for a time held captive by an old magician, from whom Bradamante rescues him. Toward the end of the poem Roger is shipwrecked, vows to turn Christian if he survives, and is cast upon an island where he finds a hermit who instructs him in the Christian faith, and baptizes him. The impediment of Roger's paganism thus removed, Roger and Bradamante are finally married, at the imperial court. On the last day of the wedding festival the only surviving Saracen hero, Rodomonte, appears, and challenges Roger, as a renegade, to mortal combat: with Roger's victory in that combat the poem ends. Boiardo had planned to establish Roger and Bradamante as the mythical progenitors of the house of Este. Ariosto, writing also in Ferrara, carries out Boiardo's plan, and finds many opportunities to narrate the history of the great family and to pay a courtier's tribute to the Este of his own day.

Other plots tell the pathetic stories of Brandimarte and Fiordiligi and of

* Canto I, Stanza 33, in the Elizabethan translation of Sir John Harington (the initial "She" replaces Harington's "That," which refers to "Angelica" in the preceding stanza).

Zerbino and Isabella, and the troubled story of the Saracen lovers Mandricardo and Doralice. Rinaldo, cured of his love for Angelica by a belated draft of the fountain of Merlin, has his own long series of adventures, as does Astolfo.

As in the *Orlando innamorato* so also in the *Furioso* there are many episodes — shorter narratives that are in reality complete in themselves. To many of his episodes Ariosto gives a considerable development, weaving them into one or another of his continuing plots. Some of them are classic stories told again: Virgil's Nisus and Euryalus reappear as Cloridano and Medoro; Angelica, like Andromeda, is exposed as prey to a sea monster, and is rescued by Roger as Andromeda had been rescued by Perseus; and Olimpia, deserted by Bireno as Ariadne had been deserted by Theseus, is thereafter rescued by Roland from Angelica's sea monster. The story of Ginevra and Ariodante was destined to become the story of *Much Ado About Nothing.* The "bower of bliss" of the sorceress Alcina, to whom her own sorcery gives false youth and beauty, is a greatly developed version of an enchanted garden found in the *Orlando innamorato.* To Alcina's far-off and very beautiful island she lures her victims, lets them dwell for a time in a palace and a realm replete with sensuous delights, and then turns them into trees or beasts or stones or fountains. There Roger, in his turn, is borne, and charmed; but thanks to the intervention of a friendly enchantress he escapes from the wiles of Alcina — and the beasts, stones, fountains, and trees (among them the myrtle that had been Astolfo) are restored to their original knighthood.

Hundreds of persons of many kinds move through the swiftly changing scenes of the poem, among them Carolingian knights and Saracen heroes (of whom Rodomonte is at once the fiercest in battle and the most boastful), warrior maidens, kings, shepherds, traitors, magicians, giants, dwarfs, amazons, hermits, Enoch, Elijah, St. John, Sleep, Silence, Discord, Pride, and Jealousy.

Various beasts and various fantastic creatures play their auxiliary parts, notably the steeds of the paladins — Roland's Brigliadoro ("Golden Bridle"), Rinaldo's Baiardo, and the rest — and most notably the Hippogriff, a winged horse that bears its rider swiftly through the air. And there are many much needed magic properties: a ring that dispels all enchantments and confers invisibility; a shield that dazzles and stuns those toward whom it is turned; a horn whose blast terrifies the blower's enemies; a golden lance that never fails. Even that most unchivalric weapon, an arquebus, breathes its devilish fire.

Boiardo had replaced the traditional canto-opening stanzas of invocation by summarizing or reflective stanzas: Ariosto adopts the latter plan. The last canto, by exception, begins with several stanzas in which he imagines that a great throng of the companions of all his courtly and literary life, many of whom are mentioned by name, are gathered on the shore to greet him as his ship comes into harbor.

Whatever the particular impulse that led Ariosto to undertake the writing of his epic may have been, he certainly wrote it with a view primarily to the delectation of the Este court; and to the lords and ladies of that court the poem must indeed have brought as great delight as any courtly composition ever brought to any courtly group. The world of the *Furioso*, with all its fantasy, was still not utterly foreign to their own world. Social structure was still aristocratic; courtiers still sought expertness in horsemanship and swordsmanship, despite the hateful innovations of arquebus and cannon; offended honor still demanded satisfaction (at Barletta, in 1503, thirteen Italians had challenged thirteen Frenchmen, and had bested them); vicissitudes of fortune were matters of spectacular experience; courtly life was lived in a marvelously decorated palatial luxury; and science, still in its unregarded infancy, had not yet drawn its curtain between fact and fiction. And poetry was itself a cherished resource in the long afternoons. But delight in the *Furioso* spread swiftly far beyond Ferrara; and though the court life of the Renaissance is now a thing of the distant past the poem offers even to modern readers a delight which, though less immediate and complete than the delight it first conveyed, may still be very great: for the *Furioso* glows with a radiant poetic energy — an energy that manifests itself most clearly in the sheer beauty of the poem, in its reality, in its humor, and in its variety.

The Renaissance cult of the beautiful had no more ardent devotee than Ariosto. He loved the beautiful in every form — the natural beauty of field and forest and stream and mountain crag, human beauty, the beauty that painters and sculptors and architects were creating all around him, beauty of song and lute and dance, and all poetic beauty, old and new. As a result, beauty pervades the poem, suffusing even scenes that would be distressing in another's narrative: suffering and death are veiled in affection and tenderness. Yet his beauty has strength even in some of its quieter phases, and it becomes obviously vigorous in his gleaming descriptions of knightly prowess, whether in battle or in single combat, and in other scenes of strenuous human action, or of flood or tempest. His love of beauty brings him into close artistic kinship with the painters of his day. His most immediate pictorial relationship is with the Ferrarese Dosso Dossi, who shared consciously Ariosto's delight in the ways and the appurtenances of chivalry; but Ariosto, far greater than Dossi, is more closely companioned in spirit by the great Venetians, especially Giorgione and Titian, whose canvases, in their imaginativeness, in their sensuousness, and in their richness of color express a vitality as exuberant as that of Ariosto's epic.

With the greatest painters, also, Ariosto shares the ability to convey a sense of the reality of all that he depicts. His scenes, his people, and his adventures exist in actuality — even when they have been called into existence by enchantment. His endlessly varied country is a practicable country of growing and thriving nature, its shores washed by seas that can be driven into raging storm; his knights and ladies are individual and knowable persons; and their adventures enter into memory with the convincing vividness of actual experiences. He attains his reality just as Dante does, through the combination of an extraordinary power of visualization with an extraordinary power of expressing things mentally seen. Everything has appeared to him in sharp outline and in strong relief, clearly detached from a background that has its own distinctness. In the case of his persons the effect of reality is enhanced by the skill with which he renders thoughts and emotions: his psychology is not profound, and he has little interest in the minute variations of suffering or of joy; but he knows mankind well, and he endows his men and women with the moods and the passions whose interplay in the living human spirit he has himself observed.

Ariosto's humor is of much the same type as Boiardo's, but it is freer, more expansive, and more contagious. It is not immaculate. Many of the adventures are humorous in themselves: some of them are purely comic. But in its more characteristic expressions Ariosto's humor is gently ironic. The world of the poem, though not utterly foreign to the courtly world he knew, was nevertheless so far from being identical with it that there lay between a middle country of likenesses and unlikenesses; Ariosto, moving happily in that country, found many an opportunity to exalt the olden ways with an irony that warns one not to take the exaltation too seriously; and he treats contemporary follies with an irony that flashes but does not wound.

The larger constructive humor of the poem centers in the person and the adventures of Astolfo — a true and valiant knight despite his limitations and despite the smiles and laughter that attend him. By providential favor he is enabled to raise an army and an enchanted fleet. To provide horses for his army he goes to the top of a stony hill, and sets stones rolling down as in an avalanche. As they roll over and over they acquire, little by little, necks and heads and legs and tails, till they finally stand snorting, eighty thousand one hundred and two strong, in the plain below. For his fleet he fills his hands with the leaves of various trees — laurel, cedar, olive, palm — and, going to the shore, casts them on the waves, where they are transformed, very prettily, into fully equipped vessels of kinds as diverse as the trees from which they came. It is Astolfo who, in company with St. John, ascends in a celestial chariot to the moon, where he is to recover Roland's wits:

> at last his guide him brings
> Vnto a goodly valley, where he sees
> A mighty masse of things strangely confus'd
> Things that on earth were lost, or were abus'd. . . .

The precious time that fooles mis-spend in play,
The vaine attempts that never take effect,
The vows that sinners make, and never pay,
The counsels wise that careless men neglect,
The fond desires that lead us oft astray,
The praises that with pride the heart infect,
And all we lose with folly and mis-spending,
May there be found unto this place ascending. . . .

He saw great store of baited hooks with gold,
And those were gifts that foolish men preferd
To give to Princes covetous and old,
With fondest hopes of future vaine reward;
Then were there ropes all in sweet garlands rold,
And those were all false flatteries he hard,
Then heard he crickets songs like to the verses
The servant in his masters praise reherses. . . .

But last, the thing that no man thinks he needs,
Yet each man needeth most, to him was shown,
By name mans wit . . .

It seem'd to be a body moist and soft,
And apt to mount by ev'ry exhalation,
And when it hither mounted was aloft,
It there was kept in pots of such a fashion,
As we call jarrs, where oyle is kept in oft:
The Duke beheld (with no small admiration)
The jarrs of wit, amongst which one had writ
Vpon the side thereof *Orlandos* wit.

This vessell bigger was than all the rest,
And ev'ry vessell had ingrav'n with art
His name that erst the wit therein possest:
There of his own the Duke did find a part . . .

Astolfo takes his own before he goes,
For so th' Evangelist doth him permit,
He set the vessels mouth but to his nose,
And to his place he snuft vp all his wit:
Long after wise he liv'd, as Turpin showes,
Vntill one fault he after did commit:
By name the love of one faire Northerne lasse,
Sent up his wit into the place it was.*

Ariosto's variety is attained not casually, but as a main objective. He had in the foreground of his mind his Este audience, and he was bound never to weary them. So his scenes shift frequently, even within single cantos; and heroes and heroines are left in jeopardy or in the midst of some great enterprise while the poet turns to other creatures of his who are ready for a rescue or a triumph that must not be too long delayed.

* From Canto XXXIV, Stanzas 72–85, in Harington's translation. The "Duke" is Astolfo.

To Ariosto himself and to his contemporaries the classicism of the poem was an added joy — as it may well be, though with less sense of novelty, to modern classicists. Ariosto's classicism appears not only in his deliberate re-creation of classic stories, but also, more briefly, in his use of various classic motifs and devices. Astolfo, as myrtle, is bruised and laments after the manner of Polydorus; harpies infest Ethiopian banquets; the magic shield flashes as the Gorgon's head had flashed. There are many classic similes and turns of phrase. All these classic elements brought, to the first listeners and readers, an elite pleasure through recognition. But the poem is classic not only in such distinguishable elements but also in its whole spirit — in its willing and essentially serene acceptance of all the bounty that life has to offer.

In its verbal and its metrical artistry the *Orlando Furioso* is one of the most perfect of Italian poems. Ariosto avoided the linguistic uncouthness of Boiardo by study of the writings of the great Florentines; and he had a fine natural sense for choice wording and for rhythmic rightness. His phrases give that impression of inevitable ease that comes only from the combination of sure instinct with patient care. His verse is smooth and fluent, and has a disciplined resonance of its own.

Like so many other Italian writers, Ariosto spent many years in the completion of his poem. The first edition appeared in 1516; a second edition, thoroughly revised, appeared in 1521; and a third and definitive edition, much enlarged and again thoroughly revised, appeared in 1532.

The fame of the poem has been very great. In Italy some two hundred editions were published before the end of the sixteenth century, and the number of insignificant imitative epics was perhaps equally large. On higher poetic levels its influence appears in Bernardo Tasso's *Amadigi*, and to still better purpose in the *Gerusalemme liberata* of Bernardo's son Torquato. Translations and imitations multiplied in sixteenth- and seventeenth-century France and Spain. In England there have been several translations, beginning with that of Sir John Harington; Spenser owes much of the *Faerie Queene* to Ariosto; the very Italian title appears in Robert Greene's play, *Orlando furioso;* Shakespeare's *Much Ado*, as we have seen, derives its plot, ultimately, from the Ginevra episode; and minor use of portions of the poem was made by Milton and by Byron.

Even while he was hard at work on the *Furioso* Ariosto found time and energy for another major literary enterprise. Duke Ercole had developed a special liking for performances of Latin comedies in Italian translations: Ariosto himself, as a youth, had taken part in at least one such performance. It is then no wonder that he should have undertaken to write original comedies in Italian based on Latin models. So he wrote, in Italian prose, his *Cassaria*, first performed in 1508, and *I suppositi*, first performed in 1509. These and Ariosto's two later comedies are in five acts; the scene, which does not change, is a street with houses; slaves play a large part in the action, and the heroines only a slight part; many events are reported rather than enacted; there are many monologues; impersonations and recognitions are plentiful; and various motifs and details are borrowed directly from Plautus or from Terence. Each of the plays is preceded by a prologue; and when they were performed *intermezzi*, with music and dancing, intervened between acts.

In the *Cassaria*, the first Italian comedy of any importance, the scene is laid in a city of ancient Greece. Two young men are in love with two slave girls; their owner will not sell at a price the young men can pay; each of them has, however, a resourceful slave; and through the trickery of these two slaves money is found for the purchase of one of the slave girls, and the other is given outright to her lover. A chest, *cassa*, of gold figures largely in the trickery. The scenery, which was painted by a minor court painter and was much admired, represented a landscape with houses, churches, steeples, and gardens — more Ferrarese, evidently, than Grecian.

In *I suppositi* the scene is laid not in an ancient city, but in contemporary Ferrara, and contemporary allusions are introduced; but the play is still essentially Plautine and Terentian.

Both plays have many witty lines, but neither attains characterization or any other real dramatic excellence. Both plays, written originally in prose, were soon rewritten in a curious type of unrhymed eleven-syllable verse, devised in imitation of the meter of Latin comedy. Ariosto handled it skillfully, but it grows monotonous.

The *Suppositi* had a memorable performance in 1519 in Rome, in a great hall in the palace of Cardinal Cibo, a nephew of Leo X. The Pope himself was present, with a train of cardinals and ambassadors; and the Pope himself, according to a letter written a few days afterward, "Took his place at the door, and quietly, with his benediction, gave permission to enter, as he saw fit." The scenery, which represented Ferrara, was painted by Raphael. Certain Frenchmen who were present were scandalized by some of the jokes — but the Pope laughed. A translation by George Gascoigne, called *Supposes*, was performed in London in 1566. To Gascoigne's play a somewhat later play, *The Taming of a Shrew*, was much indebted; and from this play Shakespeare, in his turn, derived his own *The Taming of the Shrew*.

Plautine and Terentian influence persists in the two later plays, the *Negromante*, finished in 1520, and the *Lena*, performed in Ferrara in 1530; but these plays are more modern in their approach to the comedy of character and in their frank and satiric depiction of contemporary credulity and corruption. Toward the end of his life Ariosto began a fifth play, *Gli studenti*, which was to have university students as its principal figures; but he did not live to finish it.

In 1514 and in later years Ariosto wrote seven satires in *terza rima.* They are really letters in verse, some of them confidential letters; and though they were undoubtedly known to some extent among his friends he never published them. While they continue in form and in their reflective character some varieties of the earlier *capitoli* in *terza rima*, they are new, and neo-classic, in their likeness to the satires of Horace — satires usually urbane rather than bitter, and written in a pleasant mingling of seriousness and jest. Typically, they proceed from some situation or event in the poet's own life, and wander freely into more or less relevant comments on various persons and places and environments.

The excesses and injustices and vices and follies that were spoiling the public life of Ariosto's time were constantly present to his mind; but the resentment with which he viewed them was tempered with amusement. He has much to say of the ills of courtiership — this, for instance, with regard to flattery:

> A fool is he who doth his lord gainsay,
> Although he should aver he hath espied
> The sun at midnight, or the stars by day.
> And if he choose to praise or to deride
> An absent one — then tuned to the same key,
> A chorus loud is heard on every side.
> And he who dares not through humility
> His mouth unclose, applauds with pliant face,
> And says with every feature, I agree.*

As he prepares to go on a mission to Rome he thinks of the loss of liberty of those who serve the Roman court, and moves into an invective that is closer in mood to Juvenal than to Horace. One of the satires deals with the choice of a wife. Two reflect his experiences in the Garfagnana:

> If forth I walk or in my castle stay
> Complaints and cries and brawls salute my ear,
> Thefts, murders, hates, and ires attend my way.
> So that with brow now clouded and now clear
> Some I must e'en entreat, some threat and blame,
> One there condemn, absolve another here.
> Whole sheets I daily write — despatches frame —
> Succour or counsel craving from the Duke . . .
>
> Assassins roam abroad in gangs so bold
> Whoso is sent to capture them must hide
> Stuffed in a bag, his flag, nor dare unfold.
> Most wise who near the castle doth abide . . .
>
> Think if Apollo, when on him I call,
> Will to these caves from classic Delphi haste,
> To hear unceasing noise of strife and brawl.

* This translation and the next are by Ellen M. Clerke.

The teacher he wants for his son, he writes to Bembo in the latest of the satires, must be good as well as learned:

Dottrina abbia e bontà, ma principale
sia la bontà, ché non essendo questa
nè molto quella alla mia estima vale —

Learning and goodness let him have, but chief
Let goodness be, for if there be not this
The other counts not much, 'tis my belief.

CHAPTER 22

Michelangelo and Other Poets

MOST OF THE MANY men and women who wrote lyric verse at this time were docile Petrarchists, in the Bembist sense, with little of their own to say; but the one great lyric poet of the period, Michelangelo Buonarroti, was too powerfully individual to be subservient to Bembo or to anyone else, and was in spirit more closely akin to Dante than to Petrarch.

Born in 1475, he had in his teens been taken by the discerning Lorenzo into the Medici household; and his thought and his art were indelibly impressed with the influences of Laurentian thought and Laurentian art. In particular, he came to share with firm conviction the current Florentine admiration for Dante; he stored in his mind the Platonic lore of Ficino; and the examples of Lorenzo and of Politian gave to him or reënforced in him the impulse to write lyric poetry.

In the years just before and just after the turn of the century the already recognized greatness of his work as sculptor won him many commissions in Florence and elsewhere. The series of his monumental enterprises began in 1505, when Julius II called him to Rome, employing him first to design and execute the pope's own tomb — a project which, shrinking gradually in its scope and attended by tragic frustrations, pursued the sculptor for forty years. Rome shocked him. A sonnet written probably soon after 1505 begins thus:

> Here helms and swords are made of chalices:
> The blood of Christ is sold so much the quart:
> His cross and thorns are spears and shields; and short
> Must be the time ere even His patience cease.*

Presently Julius diverted him, much against his will, to the painting of the

* All the translations from the sonnets of Michelangelo are by John Addington Symonds.

Sistine ceiling. The physical difficulties he encountered, high on his scaffolding, are listed in a humorous sonnet which contains this quatrain:

> My beard turns up to heaven; my nape falls in
> Fixed on my spine; my breast-bone visibly
> Grows like a harp: a rich embroidery
> Bedews my face from brush-drops thick and thin.

For some years after the death of Julius, Michelangelo worked mainly on the ill-fated tomb. About 1523 Clement VII employed him to add to the church of San Lorenzo in Florence a new sacristy which should contain the tombs of Lorenzo the Magnificent and other members of the Medici family. This project, also, was only partly carried out: the only tombs that Michelangelo brought close to completion were those of the younger Giuliano and the younger Lorenzo. The tomb of Giuliano bears the reclining allegorical figures of Day and Night, that of Lorenzo the similar figures of Dawn and Evening. It must have been while his thoughts were busy with this work that he wrote, in rhythmic prose, these lines:

> The Day and the Night speak, and say:
> "We with our swift course have brought Duke Giuliano to his death.*
> It is but just that he should take vengeance upon us as he does.
> And his vengeance is this:
> That as we have slain him,
> So he by his death has taken the light from us, and by the closing of his eyes has sealed our eyes, which shine no more upon the earth.
> What, then, would he have done with us, if he had lived?"

Heartsick over the state of Florence after the siege, Michelangelo in 1534 left his city, never to return, and went to Rome. Some ten years later, when the sacristy of San Lorenzo was at last opened to the public, an insignificant poet wrote, of the figure of Night, a quatrain of which the meaning is:

> Night, whom you see so sweetly sleeping, was carved by an Angel in this stone, and because she sleeps, she lives: wake her, if you believe it not, and she will speak to you.

To which Michelangelo, from Rome, replied:

> 'Tis sweet to sleep, sweeter of stone to be,
> While ruin and dishonor hold their sway.
> To see nought, to hear nought, is gain to me.
> Wake me not, therefore: speak you softly, pray!

* Giuliano held the title of Duke of Nemours.

In the years immediately following his return to Rome he painted, again in the Sistine Chapel, his "Last Judgment," Dantesque in its general inspiration and in some of its details. In 1547 he was made architect of St. Peter's, whose unequalled dome is his crowning achievement. He died in 1564.

In the course of his life he completed about two hundred poems, and he left many poetic fragments, some of them written on sheets on which he had made drawings. Some of the poems are early; but most of them seem to have been written after his return to Rome, from about his sixtieth to perhaps his eightieth year. Most of the completed poems are sonnets or madrigals: a few are in other forms.

Michelangelo's poems are in general heavily freighted with deeply meditative thought. His approach to poetry was sculptural. Within the untouched block of marble he felt the presence of an imagined statue that his strong and patient chisel must release: within an inchoate mass of thoughts and words he felt the presence of an imagined poem that he must similarly release — and at times he wrought for that release as if he were working with a chisel rather than a pen. Yet with all their difficulties his poems constitute a unique and varied treasure: the best of them — and there are many in which he finds perfect expression for his demanding thought — attain a nobility quite comparable to that of his greatest creations in sculpture and in painting.

His experience in the practice of those other arts enters into the making of his poems, giving them their most distinctive imagery — as in the sonnet that begins

> The best of artists hath no thought to show
> Which the rough stone in its superfluous shell
> Doth not include: to break the marble spell
> Is all the hand that serves the brain can do.

They are enriched also — but never through mere imitation — by evidences of the love and understanding with which he had read the poetry of Dante, of Petrarch, and of Lorenzo de' Medici.

He was the one true Platonist among the Italian poets of his century — the only one, that is, to whom love meant specifically the searching for the divine immanence and the ascent to the divine that had been set forth by Ficino. Michelangelo's Platonism appears most clearly in poems written chiefly after 1534 to a Roman youth, and in other poems written still later to Vittoria Colonna. These three short passages, from three different sonnets, are typical:

> Love wings and wakes the soul, stirs her to win
> Her flight aloft, nor e'er to earth decline;
> 'Tis the first step that leads her to the shrine
> Of Him who slakes the thirst that burns within.

Lo, all the lovely things we find on earth
Resemble for the soul that rightly sees
That source of bliss divine which gave us birth.

True love is that which the pure heart hath known,
Which alters not with time or death's decay,
Yielding on earth earnest of Paradise.

Perhaps the most perfectly poetic expression of his Platonism is to be found in this sonnet:

This heart of flesh feeds not with life my love:
The love wherewith I love thee hath no heart;
Nor harbours it in any mortal part,
Where erring thought or ill desire may move.
When first Love sent our souls from God above,
He fashioned me to see thee as thou art —
Pure light; and thus I find God's counterpart
In thy fair face, and feel the sting thereof.

As heat from fire, from loveliness divine
The mind that worships what recalls the sun
From whence she sprang, can be divided never:
And since thine eyes all Paradise enshrine,
Burning unto those orbs of light I run,
There where I loved thee first to dwell for ever.

Two fine late sonnets are devoted to impassioned praise of Dante. One begins:

From heaven his spirit came, and robed in clay,
The realms of justice and of mercy trod:
Then rose a living man to gaze on God,
That he might make the truth as clear as day.

And the other:

No tongue can tell of him what should be told,
For on blind eyes his splendour shines too strong.

The coming of old age brought no slackening in the vigor of Michelangelo's thought or of his feeling. Many of the late poems express the tension between his continuing power of heart and mind and the impairment of his bodily strength. The last poems of all are deeply and nobly religious. One of them ends with this tercet:

Painting nor sculpture now can lull to rest
My soul, that turns to His great love on high,
Whose arms to clasp us on the cross were spread.*

* Michelangelo's poems were not published in his lifetime, though many of them circulated in manuscript. They were first published in 1623 by a grandnephew, also named Michelangelo Buonarroti, who modified them to suit himself. They were not published in their true form until 1863.

The poems of Michelangelo have found great favor with English and American translators of the nineteenth and twentieth centuries — among them Wordsworth, Southey, Symonds, Emerson, Longfellow, Norton, and Santayana.

Among the lesser poets of this period Giovanni Guidiccioni (1500–1541) is perhaps the best. He was a man of considerable eminence and of high integrity. He served the papacy admirably in various responsible positions, and during the last years of his brief life he held a bishopric. Most of his love poems and his religious poems rise only a little above the usual Petrarchistic level, but some of his madrigals have much grace and freshness. He is remembered chiefly for a series of a dozen sonnets written, in the distressing years from 1526 to 1530, on the state of Italy: they are the noblest of the many Italian patriotic poems of the century. One of them, beginning

Degna nutrice de le chiare genti,

reads thus in literal translation:

> Worthy nurse of the illustrious race that in days less somber triumphed o'er the world, once the sure and joyous abode of the gods, home now of tears and lamentation,
>
> How can I without profound sorrow hear thy grievous cries, or behold thy supreme empire fallen utterly, all thy grandeur spent, and thy renown?
>
> Enslaved as thou art, thou dost retain such majesty, and thy name doth so resound within my heart, that I bow down and adore thy scattered vestiges:
>
> What must it then have been to behold thee in the midst of all thine honors throned as queen, thy glorious and venerable tresses crowned with gold?

Two great ladies, Veronica Gambara (1485–1550) and Vittoria Colonna (1492–1547) wrote, in this period, verse that is commendable but not impressive. Each was highly educated; each was, in poetry, a disciple of Bembo; each was devoted to her husband and mourned him after his early death; each had a host of literary friends; and each moved in honor among rulers of church and state. Veronica Gambara, in her widowhood, administered and defended very capably her husband's little state of Correggio, where she twice entertained the emperor Charles V. There remain some fifty poems of hers, mostly sonnets, which seem to have been written as a diversion, or in the furtherance of her ambitions, rather than from any poetic urge. One of the best of them pleads for a reconciliation between Charles V and Francis I (whose admiration she had also won).

After the death of her husband, Vittoria Colonna of the great Roman family turned to thoughts and works of piety, living austerely, often in convents, in Rome and elsewhere, and ministering to the needy. She was deeply troubled by the current ecclesiastical corruption, and listened with great sympathy to Juan de Valdés and to Ochino; but, influenced largely by Cardinal Pole, she remained loyally within the Church. With all her religious interests, she fulfilled the responsibilities of her station in life, and maintained a wide range of distinguished literary friendships — with Sannazzaro, Bembo, Guidiccioni, Castiglione, Bernardo Tasso, and, in her last years, with Michelangelo. The earliest of her poems, an affectionate letter in *terza rima* written to her husband while he was in a brief captivity, is more appealing than anything she wrote thereafter. Her *Rime*, nearly all of them sonnets, are divided into two parts. The first part, containing about a hundred poems, consists almost wholly of poems in which, idealizing her lost husband beyond recognition, she expresses her devotion to him, praising him especially for his valor, and presenting him as a saint in heaven. The second part contains about two hundred religious poems — one of them a long Triumph of Christ, in *terza rima*, which follows the pattern of the Petrarchan *Triumphs*. Her verse is dignified, honorable, and earnestly sincere, and it has its moments of success; but as a whole it is monotonous.

The long series of Italian humorous poets reaches its apex in the Florentine Francesco Berni (1497 or 1498–1535). The active years of his life were spent, chiefly in Rome, in busy secretarial service to various officials of the papal court. He would have liked scholarly and literary freedom in a free Italy whose churchmen were worthy of the faith they professed; but fate held him in restless servitude, in a time of national disaster, and in an environment of corruption that is reflected, in more ways than one, in his own work. His only escape was through laughter.

The two poetic forms he chiefly used were the tailed sonnet, to which he gave, at times, a long series of three-line extensions (one sonnet has twenty-one such extensions), and the *capitolo* in *terza rima*. His sonnets range from sheer fun to stinging satire, from which neither pope nor poet was secure. The Dutch Hadrian VI, who for a year followed Leo X, had the unpardonable fault of not being an Italian, and the attendant fault of repressing all the splendors and the festivities of the papal court, incurring thus the indignation of the whole Roman literary coterie: and then came Clement VII, of whose papacy Berni has this to say:

A papacy composed of cautiousness,
  Of much consideration and discourse,
  Of "well," and "but," and "if," and "no," and "yes,"
  Of scores of words that haven't any force,
Of much advice and many a feeble guess,
  Of vague ideas and hints without a source,
  Of fine replies and efforts to impress
  Without a single penny to disburse,
Of leaden feet and of neutrality,
  Of patience and a mock of empty show,
  Of faith and hope and likewise charity,
Of innocence, and always lying low,
  Of something very near to idiocy

(Though quite as far as that I wouldn't go);
Forgive my saying so,
But just a little more of such complaint
Will make us think Pope Hadrian was a saint.

But when Clement lies ill, Berni mocks his incompetent doctors: all the symptoms (duly enumerated) are good, but since the doctors have once said that there was no hope, they will see to it that their prediction comes true. A certain papal underling, Ser Cecco, thinks himself indispensable to the court: Berni deflates him in a sonnet in which rhymes are replaced by pitiless repetitions of the name Cecco and the word *corte*. Domenico d'Ancona was proud of his long beard, but his reforming bishop gave orders that any bearded members of his suite who held or hoped to hold benefices must sacrifice their beards: so Domenico's beard came off — and Berni wrote a laudatory epitaph for it. He despised Petrarchism, and parodied Bembo's sonnet on the beauties of his lady in a sonnet in which pearly eyes are set in a fair golden face, eyebrows are of snow, and teeth are of ebony.

Several of Berni's thirty *capitoli* are devoted to the rollicking praise of things trivial or ruinous: there are *capitoli* in praise of gudgeons, of eels, of thistles, of peaches, of jelly, of primero (an old card game), of debt, and of the plague. One is a *capitolo* in praise of Aristotle — whose work would have been quite complete if only he had written a cookbook! The conventional theme of a bad night's lodging is treated in a jocose catalogue of the manifold discomforts of a night spent in the sorry home of a vainglorious and poverty-stricken country priest. The most violent of all the *capitoli* is a blistering attack on the Dutch pope and his foreign courtiers.

Berni's only large-scale undertaking in Italian verse was his rewriting of the *Orlando innamorato* of Boiardo. The Ferrarese coloring of Boiardo's language had rendered his work unacceptable to Tuscan readers, and Berni proceeded to put it into smoothly flowing Tuscan. By so doing he gave the story three centuries of popularity that it would not otherwise have had — it was only in the nineteenth century that Boiardo's own text came again into literary favor — but he quite failed to share or to convey the chivalric spirit that pervades the original poem. Fortunately, he made no attempt to impose his own brand of humor upon his version. He inserted two passages of his own: a few distressed stanzas on the sack of Rome, and a very interesting passage of autobiography and self-characterization.

* * *

Several men, among them some of the best poets of the period, elected still to write exclusively or almost exclusively in Latin.

Andrea Navagero (1483–1529), of noble Venetian birth, was a humanist, a naturalist, and a diplomat. For Aldus and for his successor he edited Quintilian, Virgil, Lucretius, Ovid, Terence, the orations of Cicero, and Horace; he served for some years (just before Bembo) as the official historian of Venice; and he served for a time as librarian of the Library of St. Mark's. He was greatly interested in all forms of plant and animal life, especially in plants. In his garden on the island of Murano he cultivated both native and exotic plants, and carried on serious botanical study and experimentation; and at his villa on the mainland he maintained with great care a plantation of trees. He spent four years in Spain as ambassador to Charles V.

His Latin poems, called *Lusus*, "Playful Pieces," are among the very best of the Renaissance. Their Latinity is sensitive and resourceful; their graceful imaginings are often original; and the poet's knowledge of the ways of growing things endues his little idylls with a more than ordinary truth to nature. One of his finest poems is an autumn scene in which, the harvest in and the new planting done, peasants gather for dance and song and sacrifice to Ceres, whose protection they seek for the newly sown seed. In another charming poem a cool and shaded fountain invites the weary wayfarer to rest. Most of the poems are love poems of Catullan grace. His Hyella is dearer to him than life or soul or sight, and he to her; he wishes that there were something dearer still than life or soul or sight, so that Hyella might be even dearer than that still dearer thing. The best known of all his poems, beginning

> Florentes dum forte vagans mea Hyella per hortos —
>
> While my Hyella was by chance wandering in her flowering gardens —

has been translated or adapted in England by half a dozen poets, from Thomas Lodge to Thomas Moore.

Navagero's few Italian poems, on the other hand, are insignificantly Petrarchistic. Yet his interest in Italian verse was sufficient to lead him, while in Spain, to encourage the Spanish poet Boscán to try his hand at the standard Italian meters; and Boscán's resulting *Sonetos y canciones a manera de los italianos* gave a new and long enduring Petrarchistic orientation to the Spanish lyric.

Navagero's letters from Spain, written in a straightforward and unpretentious Italian prose, are very interesting. Of special interest to Americans is a letter written from Seville in 1526 in which he gives an account of certain imports from the New World, and of certain Indian youths who had been brought to Spain.

The most prolific of the Latin lyrists of the period was Marcantonio Flaminio (1498–1550), born in Venetian territory. Some of the lyrics contained in his eight books of poems are delightful — notably a series of "Idyllic Epigrams" — but the Muses were not always generous to him. His more characteristic poems are tinged with sadness. In the latter part of his life he turned to the writing of religious verse, translating thirty of the psalms into stately Latin, and writing hymns which follow early Christian models, and are of much nobility.

Longer and more ambitious poems were written by Marco Girolamo Vida (c. 1485–1566). He was born in Cremona, but most of his active literary life was spent in and near Rome, where he served the Church in various offices. In 1532 he was made Bishop of Alba, and thereafter devoted himself austerely to the efficient administration of his diocese. He wrote Latin verse of many kinds; but his reputation rests on three particular poems.

He comes closest to poetry in his early *De ludo scacchorum*, an ingenious and amusing description in classic terminology of a game of chess between Apollo and Mercury: there are several English translations of this poem, among them one by Goldsmith. Much more important is his *De arte poetica* (published in 1527) — the first of the many sixteenth-century treatises on poetry. The first of its three Books contains a brief review of the history of poetry, a general plan of education, and an exaltation of the poet's ministry; the second describes the good poem, the *Aeneid* being the obvious exemplar; and the third discusses matters of style. The treatise is marked rather by fidelity to Horace and to Quintilian than by any inherent excellence.

Vida's most famous work, the *Christias*, is an epic in six Books, the narrative extending from the calling of the Twelve to Pentecost: as Virgil had written of the founding of the Roman State, with Aeneas as hero, so Vida attempts to write of the founding of the Roman Church, with Christ as hero. But Vida was no Virgil. The *Christias* has stylistic elegance and religious dignity; but it is devoid of poetic inspiration. Nevertheless, it was immediately influential, and was long held in high honor. The Infernal Council in the first Book of the *Christias*, composed largely of materials drawn from Boccaccio and Sannazzaro, led directly to the treatment of the same theme by Tasso; and through Tasso elements of Vida's Council enter *Paradise Lost*. Pope, in the *Essay on Criticism*, apostrophizes Vida thus:

> Immortal Vida; on whose honour'd brow
> The Poet's bays and Critic's ivy grow:
> Cremona now shall ever boast thy name
> As next in place to Mantua, next in fame!

Pope published, in 1740, a large anthology, entitled *Selecta poemata italorum*, containing Latin poems by about twenty-five Italian authors, among them Politian, Pontano, Sannazzaro, Bembo, Ariosto, Navagero, Flaminio, Vida, and Castiglione.

* * *

In 1501 a fragmentary classic statue — a torso, with part of a head — was dug up in Rome, and placed on a pedestal outside the palace near which it had been found. Presently it was nicknamed Pasquino (there are varying guesses as to the source of the name), and became the chief locus of anonymous Roman satire, both learned and popular. Verses were attached to the statue, or to its pedestal, or to the wall behind it. This could be done at any time; but it very soon became customary to dress the statue up once a year, on April 25, to represent some pagan divinity or classic personage, and on these occasions great quantities of verses appropriate to the year's impersonation poured in. Most of the festival poems were obsequious; but some of them, like most of those attached at other times, were satiric. In 1510, when Pasquino represented Hercules, an Italian quatrain read:

Hercul, già da tua maza et brava mano
Varii monstri gustorno amara morte:
Hor qua richiede uno huom di te più forte,
Tanti cerbari pasce in Vaticano!

Hercules, once from your club and your brave hand various monsters met bitter death: now here there is need for a man stronger than you, so many Cerberuses are feeding in the Vatican!

Before 1527 several annual selections of April pasquinades were published. Pasquino sometimes carried on dialogues with other Roman statues, and with one in Venice. He still stands in Rome, badly battered, in the Piazza di Pasquino. For three hundred and fifty years he said his say: since the ending of the temporal power of the papacy he has been silent.

* * *

Teofilo Folengo (1491–1544) chose to write his one great work and some of his lesser works neither in Italian nor in normal Latin, but in Macaronic Latin — a jocose artificial language in which the syntax, the inflection, and most of the words are normal Latin, but a great many Italian words, given Latin endings, are introduced. Thus in the line

Sol maris interea stancus se tuffat in undis*

the Italian word *stanco*, "weary," appears with a Latin ending and the Italian verb *tuffare*, "to dip," is inflected as if it were a normal Latin verb. Macaronic Latin had been used in verse before Folengo's time among the students of the University of Padua; but Folengo alone raised it to the status of an artistic literary medium.†

* "The weary sun meanwhile dips into the waves of the sea."

† Such verse was called "macaronic" because it reminded students of a dish called in Venetian *macaroni* and in Latin *macarones*, which Folengo defines as "a kind of coarse, rough, rustic pudding made of flour, cheese, and butter" — not the modern *maccheroni*, but rather what is now called *gnocchi*. The origin of the word *macaroni* itself is unknown.

Born in Mantua and named Girolamo, Folengo was the youngest of several brothers. With little vocation for the monastic life, he nevertheless followed the example of four of his brothers by becoming a Benedictine monk: on his reception into the Order at Brescia, in 1509, he received the name Teofilo. The first edition of his highly unmonastic masterpiece, the *Baldus*, was published, under the pseudonym Merlin Cocai, in 1517. In this edition the poem consisted of seventeen Books: a second and much improved edition, published in 1521, has eight additional Books. The *Baldus* is a humorous epic, strongly influenced by Pulci's *Morgante*, and containing some elements derived from Boiardo. Baldus, though of noble birth, is brought up in a rustic home and in rustic ways. He has as comrades the gigantic Fracasso (a reincarnation of Morgante), the picaresque Cingar (a reincarnation of Margutte), and the dog-man Falchetto (derived from a minor old Italian romance). Their misdeeds lead to the imprisonment of Baldus: his comrades continue to move on through various rustic and plebeian scenes. Cingar by trickery releases Baldus; and the four then set off on a long series of extraordinary adventures, coming eventually to the most fantastic of Other Worlds — and at the very last to a pumpkin as big as a mountain, in which poets and other dispensers of lies suffer diabolical dentistry.

The poem is notable for its irrepressibly riotous comedy, for its plebeian realism (which at times degenerates into extreme vulgarity), for its frequent satire, directed most fiercely against unworthy monks, for its brilliant characterizations of certain minor figures, for its cleverly devised incidents (one of them borrowed by Rabelais, who knew the *Baldus* well), for its elements of literary imitation and literary parody, for its evident acquaintance with the *Praise of Folly* of Erasmus, for its expressions of family affection and of loyal comradeship, and for its anarchical love of liberty — all loosely gathered into an inconsistent and kaleidoscopic whole, and all enhanced by the persistent rhythmic humor of the Macaronic hexameters.

In the second edition of the *Baldus* there were printed also two minor works in Macaronic Latin verse: the *Zanitonella*, which is a collection of short realistic poems of rustic life, and the *Moschaea*, "The Battle of the Flies" (and the Ants), which is an imitation of the pseudo-Homeric *Batrachomyomachia*.

In 1524 both Teofilo and his brother Giambattista sought and obtained release from their vows. Teofilo served for some time as preceptor in a Venetian family; and during these years he wrote two new works, the *Orlandino* and the *Caos del Triperuno*, "The Chaos of the Three-Phase Man." The *Orlandino*, a short poem in Italian, in octaves, has as its subject the Italian birth and the youthful exploits of Roland; but the treatment is burlesque, and the poem, otherwise negligible, is mainly a medium for the unrestrained satiric venting of Folengo's bitterness against monastic misgovernment. The

Caos, a medley of prose and verse, and of Italian, normal Latin, and Macaronic Latin, is an account of an allegorical journey, among personifications.

In 1530 the two brothers applied for readmission to the Benedictine order, and were told that they might be received at the end of three years of hermitage. Teofilo, furthermore, was warned against further indulgence in his Macaronics, and was requested or required to write a purely religious poem. The brothers spent their hermitage together in a deserted monastery at the western tip of the peninsula of Sorrento, and there Teofilo wrote his long religious poem, *La humanità del figliuolo di Dio*, penitent but uninspired, and some shorter religious poems in Latin. In 1534 the brothers were again received into the Order. But in 1539 or 1540 there appeared, without date and with a fictitious name for the place of publication, a third edition of the *Baldus*, extensively revised and greatly improved, especially in point of style. A letter printed in this edition implies that the revision had been made before the end of 1530. At his death Teofilo left, probably with Giambattista, the material for a fourth and final edition of the *Baldus*, again much revised and improved, which was printed in 1552.

CHAPTER 23

Machiavelli and Guicciardini

NICCOLÒ MACHIAVELLI was born in Florence in 1469. His childhood and youth were uneventful. Life really began for him on July 14, 1498, when he entered the service of the Florentine government as Secretary of the Ten. The highest governmental body, at that time, was an elected commission called the *Signoria*: subordinate to this body was an elected commission known as the Ten, which was in effect a War Department having some of the functions of a Department of State. The duties of its employed Secretary included not only the conduct of an extensive correspondence, but also extensive travel on official missions. The position was neither highly paid nor highly honorific; but it was in fact a position of great responsibility. Machiavelli held it for fourteen years; and no man ever filled any government position with more devotion and energy than he manifested. He became so well known because of the way in which he carried on his work that he was and is still often referred to simply as "the Florentine Secretary."

In 1498 Florence was trying to suppress the rebellion of Pisa; and the Florentine army was composed of mercenary troops, led by *condottieri*: like all such armies it was spiritless and ineffective, and its *condottieri*, like most such men, were grasping, unreliable, and ready for treachery. Machiavelli's duties took him often to the camp before Pisa; and what he saw there served to establish in him a passionate and lifelong conviction that the employment of mercenary troops was a fatal and disgraceful error, and led him to work in season and out of season for the creation and training of a citizens' militia.

Whenever he went on an official mission he sent back letters stating what he saw and heard; and at times, upon his return, he prepared a general report on his mission. The earliest of these reports is a short *Discourse to the Ten on Pisan Affairs*, written probably in 1499, in which ability to observe, ability to set forth his observations clearly, and ability to proceed from facts to logical recommendations are all evident. Within the first four years of his service he was sent on missions to several Italian cities, and once, with another Florentine official, as an envoy to Louis XII.

In 1502 Arezzo rebelled briefly against Florence: Machiavelli was sent to the city, and after his return wrote a short treatise — his first piece of unofficial political writing — *On Dealing with the Rebels of the Val di Chiana.* This treatise begins, surprisingly, thus:

> Lucius Furius Camillus entered the Senate, after having conquered the rebellious peoples of Latium, and said: "I have done all that war can do; now it is for you, oh Conscript Fathers, to assure your future safety as regards the rebels." And the Senate generously pardoned the rebels, excepting only the cities of Velletri and Anzio. The first was demolished, and its inhabitants deported to Rome; the second . . . was colonized by new and loyal inhabitants. This was because the Romans knew that halfway measures were to be avoided, and that peoples must either be conquered by kindness or reduced to impotence.

Machiavelli, then, was already engaged in correlating the results of his own keen observations with the results of an intense and enthusiastic study of Roman history. This correlation was to be a permanent and determining element in the formation of his political philosophy.

The year 1502 saw the culmination of Caesar Borgia's almost triumphant effort to carve a principality for himself out of the States of the Church; and Machiavelli, as envoy from Florence, was with him for a time in June and again throughout the last three months of the year.* Caesar Borgia, completely concentrated on the achievement of his purpose, was consummately efficient, undeceivably shrewd, and utterly ruthless, wielding violence and fraud with equal skill. Yet he gave to the region under his control a better government, in respect to the administration of justice, than it had had for centuries; and his plans for his new state included the foundation of a university. His distrust of his own *condottieri* and his decision to organize a native militia as the main source of his military strength commended him in particular to Machiavelli, on whom Caesar's personality and the series of extraordinary successes that brought him so close to the attainment of his goal made an indelible impression. The immediate literary result of Machiavelli's mission to Caesar was a detailed description of the treachery by which Caesar got rid of his treacherous *condottieri*: the chief and much later literary result was the evaluation of Caesar in *The Prince.*

In the years 1503–1512 Machiavelli was sent on many missions to many Italian cities, thrice to France, and once to the Emperor Maximilian. This last

* At this same time Leonardo da Vinci was serving Caesar as a military and civil engineer. The two keenest observers of the period, Leonardo and Machiavelli, were then moving in the same orbit: there is no evidence, however, that they ever observed each other.

mission and one of those to France resulted in a "Report on Affairs in Germany" and a "Portrait of the Affairs of France" that are packed with detailed and notable observations.

Machiavelli's burning conviction of the necessity of creating a citizens' militia led in 1506 to the passage of an ordinance authorizing its establishment; and both before and after the passage of that ordinance Machiavelli busied himself indefatigably with the actual raising of the militia. During these same years, also, he was sent frequently to the army before Pisa; and from 1507 on he was virtually in charge of the long-drawn-out campaign, which he brought at last to a successful conclusion in 1509.

In 1512, in the war of the first Holy League, Florence, against the urgent and realistic advice of Machiavelli, allied herself with France as against Spain and the papacy; and, when the French evacuated Italy, the Medici, who had adhered to the Spanish party, reëntered Florence with the support of seasoned Spanish troops, which had easily crushed an attempted defense by Machiavelli's untried militia. The three Medici who came again into their city were Cardinal Giovanni, his younger brother Giuliano, and his nephew Lorenzo. The Cardinal returned presently to Rome (where, in the following year, he attained the papacy), leaving the other two as his representatives in Florence, and relying chiefly on Lorenzo. Machiavelli was dismissed from office and banished for a year to a certain distance from Florence. He went therefore to live in a simple house he owned in the village of Sant' Andrea, on a hilltop some ten miles south of Florence, and about two miles from the little town of San Casciano.

His manner of life at Sant' Andrea is described in a famous letter written late in 1513 to his friend Francesco Vettori. Rising with the sun, he goes to a wood he is having cut down, looks over what has been done, and listens to the troubles of his workmen. Then he goes to a spring, and then to a grove, where he reads a little poetry. "Then," he writes,

> I go to the inn, on the highroad: I talk with the passers-by, I ask them what is going on in their towns, I listen to all sorts of things, and I make note of men's varying likes and fancies. Dinner-time comes, and with my family I partake of such humble fare as my home and my fields afford. After dinner I go back to the inn: and there I find the innkeeper, and usually a butcher, a miller, and a baker or two. With these men I vulgarize myself all the afternoon playing at cards or dice; and we are constantly quarreling and calling each other names, and usually the stake is a farthing, and yet you can hear us shouting even from San Casciano. . . When evening comes I go home and go into my study; and on the threshhold I lay aside my daytime garb, covered with mud and mire, and robe myself fairly and honorably; and thus fittingly attired I enter the ancient courts of the men of old, wherein, received by them in friendliness, I feed on that food which alone is mine and for which I was born; and I am not ashamed to talk with them and to ask them their reasons for their actions. And they of their kindness answer me; and for four hours of

time I feel no weariness, I forget all trouble, I am not afraid of poverty, death does not dismay me: I enter wholly into the spirits of those with whom I am holding converse.

To Machiavelli his loss of office brought grievous distress; but it brought him also, for a dozen years, the leisure that alone made possible long study and mature reflection, and the writing of great works that might not otherwise have been written.

The most comprehensive product of Machiavelli's years at San Casciano was his *Discorsi sopra la prima deca di Tito Livio*, "Discourses on the First Ten Books of Livy." This work, begun in 1513 and completed late in 1517 or in 1518, is not, as its title would seem to imply, a running commentary on Livy's text: it is a general treatise on the state, in which constant use is made of material drawn from Livy. The first of the three Books discusses the foundation and the organization of the state; the second the expansion of the state; and the third a considerable variety of special topics. The typical chapter considers some governmental problem suggested by a passage or passages in Livy, points out the significance of the passage or passages in question, adds pertinent illustrative material from recent Italian experience, and proceeds to the deduction and statement of a general principle.

In the preface to the first Book, Machiavelli contrasts the general current imitative enthusiasm for antiquity with the current failure to derive governmental wisdom from the recorded governmental experience of antiquity, and states that he intends "to enter upon a path not yet trodden by any man," bringing that experience, supplemented by modern instances, to bear upon contemporary problems.

His opening chapter consists of a strictly logical analysis of the various ways in which states are founded. His discussion of this subject, in which he introduces Rome, Athens, Venice, Alexandria, Florence, Ragusa, and the cities of Palestine as examples, with a reference to contemporary conditions in Egypt, is, in its brevity, the first significant study in comparative history.

The very title of his second chapter, "On the Several Kinds of Republics, and on the Nature of the Roman Republic," makes it immediately clear that while his discussions are in general to cover both republics and principalities his main concern is with the republic. In this chapter he advances a cyclic theory (derived from Polybius) of merely natural governmental mutation, the several phases being, in terms of governing persons or bodies: (1) a just and prudent elected prince; (2) hereditary princes, degenerating into tyrants; (3) liberating *optimates*, governing for the common good; (4) a degenerating oligarchy; (5) a well-administered popular republic (following a new liberation); (6) a degenerating popular republic — and then the cycle begins again. The cycle may however be arrested by the creation of a mixed form of government which finds effective place for some type of princely authority, for the *optimates*, and for the people: such a mixed form of government, instanced in Sparta and in Rome, constitutes the perfect republic.

The ninth chapter, one of the most important of all for the understanding of Machiavelli's thought, contains this passage:

> Seldom or never does it happen that a republic or kingdom is well established at its foundation, or thoroughly reformed at a later time, except by the action of a single man . . . Consequently a wise founder of a state, who intends to govern not for his own advantage but for the common good, must seek sole power; nor will anyone of understanding mind condemn him for any extraordinary action that he may take for the sake of the establishment of the kingdom or republic. . . He must however be so prudent and of such good intent that he will not leave to another by inheritance the authority he has assumed: because, since men are more prone to evil than to good, his successor might use for the purposes of his personal ambition methods that the founder had used with good intent. Moreover, while the action of a single man is good for the initial task of organization, the thing he has organized will not last long if it remains the burden of a single man: it will endure only if the responsibility for its maintenance is shared by many men.

In the eloquent tenth chapter good government is characterized as one in which the prince is secure among citizens who are secure; the state is full of justice and of peace; the senate has its due authority and the magistrates their due honors; the rich may enjoy their wealth; personal nobility and excellence are exalted; and quiet and prosperity prevail. Those who are called to rule have before them two paths: one will give them security in life and glory after death; the other, the path of tyranny, will make life for them a series of perilous emergencies, and their memory will be eternally infamous.

Several of the other ideas developed in Book I may be briefly noted. Human nature does not change. Religion is indispensable as a mainstay of the state: the discussion of this subject leads to a powerful indictment of the Church for its failure to maintain the true religion of its Founder, and in particular for its prevention of the unification of Italy — the Church being itself too weak to undertake that unification, but too jealous and too strong to allow any other state to undertake it. Actions such as those of Philip of Macedon are cruel in the extreme, and are repugnant not only to Christianity but to humanity itself: any man should shun such deeds, and live rather as an obscure citizen than as a king owing his kingship to such destruction. Few men are either thoroughly good or thoroughly evil: even a man who is evil in most respects may hesitate to commit a great immediate evil even though it would produce results of great ultimate public benefit. Since human desires and dispositions are the same in all times and all places, the examination of the past enables one to foresee political trends and possibilities.

Among the ideas developed in Book II are these. The general lessening of the love of liberty is due very largely to the difference between ancient religion, which exalted mundane power and glory, and the Christian religion, which esteems the contemplative life more highly than the active life, and exalts humility and the endurance of injury: yet the fundamental difficulty lies rather in human pusillanimity than in Christianity itself, since Christianity authorizes the exaltation and the defense of one's fatherland. The sinews of war are not money, but good soldiers: if you lack good soldiers neither money, in any quantity, nor favorable location, nor popular support will suffice for your defense. Expansion is ruinous to a republic that is not soundly organized. Halfway measures are fatal. Idleness and peace lead to disunion: war and the fear of war lead to union. A requisite victory is sufficient: to press for more than a requisite victory is to invite disaster.

Among the ideas developed in Book III are these. Newly acquired liberty cannot be maintained without severity. Unity of command is a military necessity. Poverty (by which, in this instance, Machiavelli means contentment with possessions so moderate as to require the continuance of labor) makes for better citizenship than does wealth: the example of Cincinnatus is cited with glowing praise. Strong men and strong republics maintain their equanimity alike in good and in bad fortune (one may even "lose gloriously"): weak men and weak republics are insolent in good fortune and abject in bad fortune. Deceit is in itself detestable; but in the conduct of war deceit may be laudable and glorious — not, however, the fraudulent violation of a pact, for such a violation, even if it brings you power, can never bring you glory. When the fatherland is in peril there should be no question of what is just or unjust, of what is merciful or cruel, of what is laudable or ignominious: setting aside all other considerations one must follow single-mindedly whatever course of action will maintain the safety of the fatherland and its freedom.

In the *Discorsi*, as has been shown, both republics and principalities are treated, the republic being regarded as the better form, the principality being regarded as a possible alternative, and as an indispensable initial phase for a republic. Not long after he had begun the *Discorsi* Machiavelli became so keenly interested in the special problems of the principality, and particularly in the problems of the new principality, that he dropped the longer work for a time and wrote, within the year 1513, the shorter and far more famous work commonly called in Italian *Il principe* and in English "The Prince." Machiavelli gave it the Latin title *De principatibus*, "On Principalities."

The *Discorsi* were written as a pioneering essay in political science, and with reference to a general rather than to a particular and immediate utility. As he wrote the *Prince*, though his intent was equally scientific, Machiavelli was aware that what he was writing might be of practical value to a prince, especially to the prince of a new or newly won state: it should then be of immediate value to the Medici. It was dedicated to the young Lorenzo. Yet it is not to be assumed either that Machiavelli would have advised the Medici to imitate all the actions that he reports, or that he thought the validity of his findings limited to the current situation: what he is doing is to point out objectively that certain lines of action lead to certain results. He undoubtedly hoped, also, that the Medici, after reading the *Prince*, would call him back into the service of the state.

In the *Prince*, as in the *Discorsi*, constant use is made of both classic and modern instances; but in the *Prince* the modern greatly outnumber the classic instances. The twenty-six chapters (each titled in Latin) fall into four groups: the first eleven discuss types of principalities and methods for their acquisition and maintenance; the next three discuss military matters; Chapters XV–XXIII discuss the relations of the prince with his subjects; and the three final chapters constitute a conclusion.

Principalities are classed as hereditary or new; and new principalities (which alone are discussed at length) are classed as additions to old states or as entirely new. One of the early chapters is devoted to a scathing critique of the actions and policies of France with regard to Italy; and another long chapter is devoted to a detailed review of the career of Caesar Borgia, a review that approves Caesar's use of violence and fraud as necessary to the attainment of his purpose, but includes references also to Caesar's effort to give good government to the region under his control, and to his establishment of a good system for the administration of justice. Another notable chapter, "On Those who Have Attained Principality through Crime," excludes from approval men who have attained power by means of a succession of fearful crimes, and by such crimes alone.

Within the chapters of the first group are to be found the ideas and sayings now to be quoted or summarized. Defeated enemies should either be treated generously or destroyed: for men will take vengeance for slight injuries, but cannot take vengeance for grave injuries. Republics that have been accustomed to freedom can be subdued only by their destruction as states; for in such republics there is great vitality, great hatred (for an invader), and great desire for vengeance, and the memory of their former freedom will never let them rest. All armed prophets have succeeded; all unarmed prophets (here Machiavelli was thinking of Savonarola) have failed. Anyone who thinks that new favors will make a man forget old injuries is mistaken. A new prince should carry through at the outset whatever cruelties he may judge to be necessary, and thereafter be free to do what he can for the benefit of his subjects, rather than refrain from initial cruelty and thereby find himself obliged to be cruel repeatedly. Men tend to be as much obligated by the benefits they confer as by the benefits they receive.

The three chapters on military matters present a powerful indictment of the use of mercenary troops and a powerful argument for the development of a citizens' militia.

The chapters on the relations of a prince with his subjects are introduced by a paragraph in which Machiavelli — perfectly conscious of his sharp break with the idealism of earlier political theorists — says that since he is writing with a practical purpose he will seek to deal with the *verità effettuale* of things — that is, with things as they actually are — and not with things as they are often fancied to be. The difference between the way men live and the way they ought to live is so great that a prince who seeks to follow the latter way cannot maintain himself. A prince cannot avoid certain attitudes and certain actions for which he will incur blame: he should however endeavor to limit such attitudes and actions to those which are inevitable if he is to maintain his power. It would be well that a prince should be both loved and feared: but if he has to choose it will be better for him to be feared than to be loved. To be feared, however, is not necessarily to be hated, and the prince should avoid giving cause for hatred — most of all he should abstain from seizure of property. Though the maintenance of good faith is in itself desirable, the prince should on occasion be ready to make use of fraud: if all men were good, this rule would not be good; but since men are evil and cannot be relied on to keep faith with you, you are not bound to keep faith with them. A prince wins esteem by showing himself a true ally or a true enemy — neutrality is fatal. He should encourage all good activities (at this point Machiavelli is thinking of the first Lorenzo de' Medici), including commerce and agriculture; he should provide festivals; and he should mingle with groups of his people, insofar as he can do so without loss of dignity.

In the three concluding chapters Machiavelli looks beyond the confines of the single state to the conditions and the needs of Italy as a whole. There exists, he says, a marvelous opportunity for new leadership. The King of Naples, the Sforza, and other Italian princes have lost their states through failure to observe such policies as are set forth in the *Prince;* and their loss is not to be attributed to ill fortune. Fortune does indeed play a great part in the affairs of men — it may be said that fortune controls half our actions, leaving us in control of the other half — but fortune favors the bold.

The final chapter is magnificent from beginning to end. If, for the display of the abilities of Moses, of Cyrus, and of Theseus, it was necessary that the Israelites should be enslaved in Egypt, the Persians oppressed by the Medes, and the Athenians scattered, so now for the display of the ability of a great Italian spirit Italy must needs be in her present plight, more enslaved than the Hebrews, more oppressed than the Persians, more scattered than the Athenians, without a head, without order, beaten, despoiled, torn, overrun, in utter ruin. Then let the Medici, mindful of their illustrious past, rise to this present opportunity. There is plenty of valor in Italy; it is only leadership that has been lacking. They will find a surging response:

> This occasion, then, must be grasped, so that Italy, after so long a time, may behold a redeemer. No words can tell with what ardor, with what thirst for vengeance, with what resolute faith, with what devotion, with what tears, he would be received in all those regions that have suffered from these foreign floods. What doors would be closed to him? What cities would refuse him obedience? What envy would stand in his way? What Italian would deny him homage? This barbarian dominion is a stench in our nostrils. So then let your illustrious House undertake this emprise with the spirit and the hope with which just emprises are undertaken; so that under your banner this our own native state may be ennobled, and so that under your auspices the prophecy of Petrarch shall be fulfilled:
>
> Greatness will take arms against fury, and the combat will be brief, for the ancient valor is not yet dead in Italian hearts.

But no such leadership was to be found among the Medici. Giuliano died in 1516, and Lorenzo three years later. Pope Leo then designated his cousin, Cardinal Giulio, as his representative in Florence.

After the single year of his banishment, Machiavelli was free to return to Florence; but for most of the rest of his life he chose to live at Sant' Andrea, going to Florence only occasionally.

In 1518, or possibly even earlier, he began work on his third major treatise, *L'arte della guerra*, "The Art of War," which he finished in 1520. In its seven Books he sets forth in dialogue form, and with illustrative diagrams, all the military convictions, general or technical, that he had derived from his study of Roman and contemporary military procedures. His basic conviction is that mercenary troops are an unmixed evil, and that military service is a compelling moral obligation that rests upon all citizens. All the activities that are carried on in a state for the sake of the common good of its citizens and all of the ordinances by which they are enabled to live under the rule of law and in the fear of God are futile unless the state is always adequately prepared for military defense. The final pages contain a striking series of military maxims, and a bitter invective against the folly and the weakness of the princes of Italy.

In 1519 Cardinal Giulio de' Medici, on behalf of Pope Leo, invited Machiavelli (similar invitations were extended to some other men) to submit to him a memorandum on possible improvements in the government of Florence; and Machiavelli, taking the invitation very seriously, responded with a document which bears the title *Discorso sopra il riformare lo stato di Firenze.* The form of government that Machiavelli here advocates is not a principality but a republic: specifically, he proposes that the Pope and the Cardinal retain control of Florence during their lifetime, but that they make provision whereby after their deaths the city should become a true republic, stronger and more perfect in its organization than the previous Florentine republic had been. This proposal, it may be noted, is perfectly consistent with the view expressed in the *Discorsi* that a principality is a normal initial phase for a republic. The conclusion reads in part:

> I believe that the greatest honor a man can have is the honor that is freely given to him by his native state; I believe that the greatest good a man can do, and the one that is most pleasing to God, is the good that he does for his native state. Nor is any man so highly esteemed for any action of his as are those who with laws and institutions have reformed republics and kingdoms . . . Heaven, then, gives not to any man a greater gift than this, nor can it show to any man a more glorious way; and among the many favors that God has given to your House and to your Holiness, this is the greatest — this gift of the ability and the opportunity to win immortal fame, and thus to surpass by far your paternal and ancestral glory.

But the Pope and the Cardinal were not to be persuaded.

In 1520 Machiavelli received from the Cardinal and the Signoria the first commission given him since 1512: he was sent to Lucca to negotiate the settlement of a difficult financial matter. During his stay in Lucca, which lasted for several months, he became so greatly interested in the career of Castruccio Castracani, who had been lord of Lucca and had conquered much of Tuscany in the early part of the fourteenth century, that he proceeded to make Castruccio the hero of a brief *Vita*. This "life," however, is a piece of fictionalized biography: it tells the story of a largely imaginary person to whom Machiavelli attributes the name and some of the chief exploits of the actual Castruccio, adding or substituting circumstances derived from the Life of the Syracusan tyrant Agathocles by Diodorus Siculus, and still other circumstances that appear to be of Machiavelli's own invention. Machiavelli's Castruccio emerges vividly as a sort of fourteenth-century Caesar Borgia, exceedingly able and completely ruthless, ready to conquer either by violence or by fraud, and dying, a victim of fortune, when very close to the completion of his desired conquest.

In November 1520, the University of Florence, which was controlled by the Cardinal, commissioned Machiavelli to write a history of Florence; and for the next four years the writing of the *Istorie fiorentine* was his chief occupation. He accepted too readily the statements of earlier writers; and he was so anxious to support his own conclusions that he could not be bound by hampering minor facts. But there are respects in which his *History* marks substantial progress: discarding the year-by-year procedure of the chroniclers, he seeks to link his events in a logical chain of causes and effects; and he is more concerned with civil strife — the civil strife that had so constantly kept Florence in turmoil and in peril — than he is with warfare. Each of the eight Books opens with a chapter devoted to general political reflections; and in these introductory chapters and in the course of the narrative many of Machiavelli's favorite ideas recur. The work as a whole, indeed, is written not with scholarly objectivity, but with an underlying effort to derive "rules" of political behavior, and with pressing implications for contemporary action. While it is significant, though not impeccable, as history, it is in its broadest aspects Machiavelli's final essay in political science.

In the long range of Machiavelli's political writings — a range that begins with his earliest reports, rises to its twin peaks with the *Discorsi* and the *Prince* and ends with the *Istorie fiorentine* — the two constant objects of his thought are, first, the state, and, second, the individual man of outstanding ability.

The two qualities he chiefly seeks in the state are strength, and concern for the well-being of the general body of its citizens. The provision of conditions under which such well-being can be attained is the primary function of the state. Such provision is impossible, however, unless the state is strong: strength, therefore, is so absolutely prerequisite that actions may be taken for its sake — especially during the establishment of a new regime, or in times of peril — which in themselves, or if undertaken for private ends, would be evil. There are, for the state, two possible forms: the republic and the principality. The republic is decidedly preferable; but principality — provided always that the prince is concerned for the well-being of the general body of his citizens — is a possible alternative, and principality is a necessary initial phase in the establishment or the reëstablishment of a republic.

For outstanding individual ability in any field Machiavelli's word is *virtù*. Only through the exercise of *virtù* can great things be accomplished. If *virtù* is used to a good end, the result, for the individual man concerned, is that which, Machiavelli avers, all men desire: namely, glory. But the conditions of life do not permit the unobstructed exercise of *virtù*: *fortuna*, an extra-human force that may be favorable or adverse, is always present, always a potential thwarting enemy. The greater the *virtù*, the greater the chance that it will prevail over fortune, but there is never any certainty that it will so prevail: fortune controls, on the whole, about half of the realm of human action. *Virtù*, *fortuna*, and *gloria* are the three protagonists of the great political drama, as Machiavelli sees it.

His intense interest in *virtù* is one of the main causes of his interest in principality — since principality affords obviously the most spectacular opportunities for individual achievement. His enthusiasm for *virtù* leads him to admire even *virtù* that is tarnished by the use of violence and fraud; but he never abdicates the right to distinguish the excellence of the *virtù* as such from the evil nature of the tools it may take in hand: it is the *virtù* that he admires, not the tarnishing evil in itself. Moreover, evil when misused — that is, evil that is used for purely selfish ends, or is used in hideous excess —

defeats itself: for such misuse precludes the attainment of *gloria*, which is the end to which *virtù* is but the means.

Thoroughly realistic in his appraisal of the political actions of his own day, Machiavelli is definitely less than realistic in his acceptance of the ancient Roman stories as having a weight equal to that of his own observations; and he is less than realistic, also, in his constant striving to ascend from his particular data to the formulation of "general rules" of political conduct. Beyond those general rules he does not go: he makes no attempt to combine them in a synthetic philosophy. Yet to him more than to any other man the general modern concept of the state as an organized force is due.

The compelling hold of the *Discorsi* and the *Prince* upon the reader is due in part, no doubt, to the sheer shock of their realism; but it is due mainly to the pervading presence of an intense and highly individual vitality — in other words, to Machiavelli's own *virtù*. The specific qualities of that *virtù* are keenness of observation; scientific objectivity; utter frankness; the power to set before you, swiftly and surely, significant actions of men of his own time, and to recall Roman achievements to renewed and illumined memory; the unrelenting search for generalizing interpretation; the mastery of a vigorous and unadorned prose, which ranges from a style that is fiercely compact in its insistence on essentials to a style that is probingly analytic, yet never loses itself in excessive subordinations; and an eloquence, springing ultimately from the recognition of greatness, or from patriotic suffering and patriotic hope, that is most frequently to be found in prefaces and conclusions, but may suddenly glow at any point at which Machiavelli himself is deeply stirred.

His political writing, extensive and demanding though it was, did not exhaust Machiavelli's literary energy. At various times he wrote two comedies, the *Mandragola* and the *Clizia*; a *novella*, the *Belfagor*; a dialogue on the Italian language; a few minor bits of prose; and several poems.

Both of Machiavelli's comedies are in prose. Both are brief: each is about half as long as a typical Shakespearean comedy. Each has a prologue, five acts, and stanzas to be sung or recited between the acts. Both follow the confining patterns of Roman comedy: the action takes place within twenty-four hours; the scene does not change; servants have much to say and to do; and soliloquies abound.

The *Mandragola*, "The Mandrake," is the most famous and the most powerful play of the Italian Renaissance. It is, fundamentally, a satire on bourgeois folly and on ecclesiastical corruption. Three buildings frame a little Florentine *piazza*: in the center the church of a monastic order; at one side the house of the elderly jurist Nicia, who is called "the greatest fool in Florence," and his beautiful and virtuous young wife Lucrezia; and at the other side the house of Callimaco, a well-to-do young man who is in love with

Lucrezia. The success of his desires is brought about by means of a stratagem devised by the parasite Licurgo. The Italian comedies of the Renaissance are in general plays of plot and of farcical fun, with characters that are conventional comic types rather than individualized persons. Machiavelli in the *Mandragola* outdoes other Italian dramatists of his day and of many later days in the ingenuity and the skillful development of his plot, and his farcical details — medical Latin, feigned deafness, disguises of feature, form, and costume — are handled with somewhat more than the usual zest: but his superiority lies in the fact that he achieves effective individual characterization in most of the persons of his play. Not in all of them: Nicia, a figure drawn from the *novella* tradition, is preposterously gullible; Lucrezia's mother, who plays a minor and a sorry part, is also, essentially, a *novella* figure; Callimaco is the ordinary stage lover; and his servant Siro is insignificant. But the other persons are individuals who are to be found here and here alone. Licurgo, by no means the typical parasite, has a diabolical resourcefulness surpassing that of the parasites of Roman comedy, and one has the impression that he devises and carries through his stratagem not so much for the sake of reward as because he has a liking for Callimaco and because he enjoys the game for its own sake. Lucrezia is genuinely virtuous, genuinely religious — until she is disillusioned —, sensible, a good mistress of her household, and "capable of ruling a kingdom." It takes the combination of her husband's commands, her mother's insolent urging, and, most of all, the pious assurances of her confessor, Fra Timoteo, to overcome her protests and persuade her to yield to a stratagem she does not understand. Even a silly unnamed woman of the people, who appears only in a single scene with Fra Timoteo, is sketched most skillfully. But as Fra Timoteo's church dominates the stage, so Fra Timoteo dominates the play. Having been deceived by Licurgo, who promises lavish almsgiving, Fra Timoteo becomes the willing and cynically efficient instrument of further deception: yet he hears confession, says his prayers, reads saints' lives, redds up his church (replacing the soiled veil of a miracle-working image of the Madonna), and laments that the number of votive offerings has dropped so sadly. The play is obviously the work of one who had long been a keen observer of his fellow men, and had learned to think ill of most of them. The dialogue is vivacious; and to Italians its realistic Florentinism is very amusing.

The *Clizia* is an adaptation of the *Casina* of Plautus. In this case the would-be deceiver is himself confounded; the long-lost father of Clizia, the titular heroine, turns up, wealthy, in the last act; Clizia, who never appears upon the stage, is affianced to the insipid hero; and all ends well. But the play lacks the dramatic vigor of the *Mandragola*.

The *Belfagor* is a clever reworking of a story of Oriental origin. Following an Infernal Council, the archdevil Belfagor is sent up to earth to find out whether marital life is really as full of difficulties as sinners report it to be: after an adventurous career he seeks refuge in the place he came from.

In the *Discourse on Our Language* Machiavelli maintains that the speech of Florence is the one and only language that is thoroughly suitable for Italian literary use. The whole dialogue is colored by Machiavelli's intense loyalty to Florence. The opening sentence runs thus:

> Whenever I have been able to work for the honor of my native city, even with difficulty and with danger, I have done so gladly; for a man has no greater obligation in life than his obligation to his fatherland, from which he has received, first, his existence, and then all the good things that fortune and nature have conferred upon him: and this obligation is especially great for a man whose fatherland is especially noble.

When Cardinal Giulio de' Medici, in 1523, was elevated to the papacy as Clement VII, he sent Cardinal Silvio Passerini to Florence as his representative and as guardian of two possible Medici heirs. In 1525, when Florence lay in the path of a probable imperial invasion, Machiavelli was at last taken back again into the official service of the city. He was sent on several missions in the course of the year, and early in 1526 he was put in charge of the erection of new fortifications for Florence — but he was so hampered by indecision on the part of Pope Clement that not much could be done. Early in 1527 the imperial army moved southward, without pausing to attack Florence. The sack of Rome began on May 6; the news of it reached Florence on May 11; Cardinal Passerini and the two possible Medici heirs fled; and on May 16 Florence was again proclaimed a republic — and Machiavelli found himself distrusted and discarded. He was taken seriously ill on June 20, and died two days later. If he had lived three years longer he would have had the satisfaction of seeing his militia defend Florence with magnificent valor — though unsuccessfully — in the siege of 1530.

The political writings of Machiavelli, especially the *Prince*, have made an immeasurably great impression upon later political thought and literary imagination. The Englishmen who have felt his influence most strongly are Edmund Spenser (in his *Veue of the Present State of Ireland*), Sir Walter Raleigh (in many of his works), Francis Bacon, and James Harrington (in his *Oceana*). In Bacon, who says that "we are much beholden to Machiavel and others, that write what men do and not what they ought to do," the influence of both the *Discorsi* and the *Prince* is widely and deeply pervasive.

Hosts of writers, from his own times to ours, have attacked Machiavelli or defended him. The *Prince* was first published in 1532, with the sanction of Clement VII; but its indictment of the Church was too strong for the Counter Reformation to tolerate. The attack was opened by Cardinal Pole — who spoke of the *Prince* as *Satanae digito scriptum* — and was continued immediately by other Catholic writers. All the works of Machiavelli were listed as forbidden books in the *Index* of 1559. Later attacks were made, sometimes on religious grounds, as by John Donne, and sometimes on political grounds, as by Bodin and Frederick the Great. Many such attacks have been based upon an inadequate knowledge and understanding of Machiavelli; and some of the hands held up in holy horror have been far from stainless.

Closely associated with these attacks, but due in part to extraneous causes, was the development, first in France and then in Scotland and Elizabethan England, of the popular idea of Machiavelli as a Satanic figure, embodying not only the vices that he had diagnosed, but also other vices — avarice for instance — charged against him quite unreasonably. There are some four hundred references to such a Machiavelli in the Elizabethan drama: Marlowe introduces "Machiavelli" as the speaker of the Prologue in *The Jew of Malta*; Shakespeare's Richard III can "set the murderous Machiavel to school." It is in the main from this Elizabethan misusage that the English adjective "Machiavellian" has taken the blackness of its implications.

Defenders of Machiavelli, in various periods, have often argued, quite unjustifiably, that he was in reality revealing the evil ways of tyranny in order that men might be moved to strike for liberty: Alfieri and Foscolo are among those who have taken this position.

Modern scholarship, still busily concerned with Machiavelli, seeks to elucidate and to evaluate impartially rather than to praise or blame. Lord Acton writes:

> He is the earliest conscious and articulate exponent of certain living forces in the present world. Religion, progressive enlightenment, the perpetual vigilance of public opinion, have not reduced his empire, or disproved the justice of his conception of mankind. He obtains a new lease of authority from causes that are still prevailing, and from doctrines that are apparent in politics, philosophy and science.

And again:

> The authentic interpreter of Machiavelli is the whole course of later history.

* * *

Francesco Guicciardini, born in Florence, in 1483, of a family that had consistently supported the Medici, as a young man showed much ability in the practice of law. Early in 1512 the Florentine government sent him as ambassador to Spain, where he remained for two years. During that time the Medici regained control of Florence, and on his return he was taken into their service. Leo X appointed him governor of the cities of Modena, Reggio, and Parma, and later commissioner general for the papal army: Clement VII made him governor of the Romagna, and again commissioner general for the papal army. The ousting of the Medici from Florence in 1527 led to his retirement from public life; but on their return he too returned, serving as counselor to the first Medici duke, Alessandro, and, briefly, to the second, Cosimo I. But his efforts to preserve some remnants of the former liberty brought him into disfavor, and in 1537 he retired to his villa, where he died in 1540.

Thus his career was similar, in its general pattern, to that of Machiavelli. Both men served Florence and the Medici: but Machiavelli's service was rather for the city, and Guicciardini's for the family. The offices held by Machiavelli were humbler than those held by Guicciardini, but Guicciardini's service, though energetic and efficient, was less ardent than that of Machiavelli. Both men wrote notable official reports, and discourses related to particular situations; and both men, especially when they were in disfavor, wrote both political and historical works. But whereas Machiavelli was primarily a political scientist, Guicciardini was primarily a historian.

The first of his three most important political writings is a dialogue in two Books, written shortly before 1527, and entitled *Del reggimento di Firenze*, in which he proposes what he thought to be a sound plan for the government of Florence. The interest of this treatise lies not so much in its specific proposals as in its basic attitudes. His judgment of current political motives is devastating: even those men who make public profession of their love of liberty and of democracy are usually moved, he thinks, by the desire for power. No a priori theories are of practical value: one must try to construct a government that is adapted to the particular local and personal conditions that will inevitably determine its success or failure. In his references to what seem to him to be the bitter necessities of statecraft he is at one with Machiavelli.

This dialogue was followed, during Guicciardini's retirement in 1527–1530, by his *Considerazioni sui Discorsi del Machiavelli* and by the final form of his *Ricordi politici e civili*. In the *Considerazioni* Guicciardini examines, one by one, some forty chapters found in various parts of the *Discorsi*. The two men are in agreement in their fundamental realism, in their indignation at the degeneracy of the papal court, and in their desire to see Italy set free from the invading barbarians. But Guicciardini, whose historical sense and learning were far superior to those of Machiavelli, convicts him, at many points, of errors in his interpretation of historical data, and denies the possibility of deriving from history or from experience rules of action which will have anything like a universal validity. Circumstances always differ: all one can do, therefore, is to attack each given problem as a new problem, bearing in mind, to be sure, such knowledge of previous happenings as may be clearly relevant, but relying chiefly upon analysis of the immediate situation. Guicciardini is thus more completely realistic than Machiavelli.

The collection known as the *Ricordi politici e civili* consists in its final form of some two hundred aphorisms, which range over the whole field of life as seen by one of the most observant and illusionless of men. Some are political; others are concerned with the traits and the ways of humanity in general. They are singularly impressive, not only for the keenness of their insights, but also for the finished clarity of their compact style. Among them are these:

> It is a great mistake to speak of human affairs absolutely and without discrimination and as a matter of rule; for almost all of them have distinguishing and exceptional features.
>
> I know no one who is more disgusted than I am by the ambition, the avarice, and the loose living of priests . . . But the positions I have held with several popes have compelled me, for the sake of my personal interest, to desire their greatness; and if it had not been for this I should have loved Martin Luther as myself.
>
> You should always deny anything that you do not want to have known, and affirm whatever you want to have believed; for even though there be plenty of evidence to the contrary . . . affirmation or denial that is sufficiently vigorous will often confuse those who hear you.
>
> It sometimes happens that rash men accomplish greater things than discreet men: this comes about because the discreet man . . . relies chiefly on reason and not much on fortune, while the rash man relies chiefly on fortune and not much on reason — and enterprises favored by fortune are sometimes incredibly successful.
>
> Those who talk about "the people" are talking about a creature that is mad, full of a thousand errors and a thousand confusions, without taste, discrimination, or stability.
>
> The best of all good works . . . is to do no harm to anyone, and to help everyone as much as you can.
>
> It is a remarkable fact that we all know that we must die, and yet we all live as if we were to live forever . . .

In the *Ricordi* Guicciardini neither seeks nor attains synthesis: he does not even avoid occasional inconsistencies. But the personality from which they come is clearly marked. The main motive force in life, for Guicciardini, is the desire for honor, by which he means neither power nor wealth, but the satisfaction that comes from knowledge that one has rendered good service to one's state, and from such recognition of the excellence of that service as others may manifest. The qualities indispensable for honorable achievement are discretion and courage: a discretion that analyzes with the utmost practicable thoroughness the pros and cons of every course of action possible in a given situation, and that adapts itself readily to changed conditions; and a courage that will come to resolute decisions, will strive in full strength to carry them out, even in the face of danger, and will not be cast down by errors, or by failures due to inevitable misfortune.

In the historical field Guicciardini's first essay was his *Storia fiorentina*, a history of Florence from 1378 to 1509, finished in 1509, remarkable chiefly for its studies of the characters and careers of Cosimo and Lorenzo de' Medici, Savonarola, and Caesar Borgia. In the course of the years 1527–1531 Guicciardini did some work on a second history of Florence, known as *Le cose fiorentine*, "Florentine Affairs," which, however, he never finished. There remain two virtually complete Books, which carry the story from the origins, through the period of Guelf and Ghibelline strife, to 1402, together with fragments and notes for two other Books.

His last and most famous work is the *Storia d'Italia*, completed after his final retirement. Its twenty Books cover the history of Italy from 1492 to 1534. While it has traditional features — the events of each year are treated separately, and imaginary orations are introduced — it is of lasting significance. Guicciardini's estimates and interpretations are based rather upon men's motives, as he detects them, than upon their actions. He is readily responsive to heroism; and he is unhesitatingly severe in his criticism of conduct that seems to him to call for severity. His portraits of three popes, Julius II, Leo X, and Clement VII, are admirable. Other particularly noteworthy passages are the solemn preface, and a special study, in Book IV, of the development of the temporal power of the Church. Earlier Italian histories of recent events had been essentially histories of particular states: Guicciardini's survey comprehends constantly the whole of Italy, and looks frequently beyond the Alps. His mood and manner resemble those of Tacitus rather than those of Livy. The style has great dignity; but the sentences are often of extraordinary length, as a result of Guicciardini's determination to assemble in each sentence all data that are pertinent to its specific subject and to clarify all the motives operating in the action concerned.

The *Storia d'Italia* and the *Ricordi* have been widely known. In England, some fifty passages derived from Fenton's translation (of a French translation) of the *Storia* were inserted in the second edition of Holinshed's *Chronicles*. Raleigh was well acquainted with the *Storia*. Bacon regarded Guicciardini as the most admirable of modern historians: he made extensive use of the *Storia* (which he read in an Italian edition) in many of his writings, drawing from it, in particular, illustrative instances of political behavior; and on the *Storia* he modeled his own *History of the Reign of King Henry the Seventh*.

CHAPTER 24

Castiglione and Other Prose Writers

WHEN ONE OPENS *The Book of the Courtier* Florentine republicanism and Machiavellian realism fade from one's thought, and one dwells untroubled for a time at the most gracious of all the courts of the Italian Renaissance.

Baldassare Castiglione was born in 1478 near Mantua; and after youthful years spent in study and in knightly training he entered first the service of the Mantuan Marquis Federigo Gonzaga, and then, in 1504, the service of Guidobaldo da Montefeltro, Duke of Urbino. In 1506 he was sent to England to receive from Henry VII, on behalf of Guidobaldo, the insignia of the Order of the Garter; and in 1507 he was sent on a mission to Louis XII. Guidobaldo died, much lamented, in 1508, and was succeeded by his nephew, Francesco Maria della Rovere, with whom Castiglione remained, serving from 1513 to 1516 as envoy to the papal court. In 1516 Leo X dispossessed Francesco Maria and gave the duchy to his own nephew Lorenzo. Castiglione then returned to Mantua, whence, after two quiet years, he was sent again to Rome, as envoy from Mantua to the papal court. In 1524 Clement VII sent him as envoy to the imperial court in Spain; and there, highly esteemed, he died in 1529.

In 1508, shortly after the death of Guidobaldo, Castiglione began the writing of *Il libro del cortegiano*, moved, as he says in a dedicatory letter, by his memories of Guidobaldo and of the delightful company of men and women who had frequented the ducal court. Castiglione's strenuous duties left him little time for writing, and it was not until his return to Mantua that he was able to devote himself to the perfection and completion of his book. It was virtually finished in 1518; but it was not published until 1528.

The *Cortegiano* purports to give an account of conversations held in the palace of Urbino in March, 1507. It is, like the *Asolani*, a dialogue set in a connecting narrative. Nineteen men and four ladies take part in the discussions, the number of the interlocutors being thus large beyond any precedent. They are all real persons: some of them were resident at the court at the time indicated; the others were presumably there as visitors. Among them are the Duchess (Elisabetta Gonzaga), her friend and companion Emilia Pia, Francesco Maria della Rovere, Giuliano de' Medici (still, at that time, in exile from Florence), and Bembo. Duke Guidobaldo's ill-health prevented him from taking any part in evening gatherings: he is referred to with glowing praise in the opening pages of the *Cortegiano*, but he does not appear as an interlocutor. Nor does Castiglione himself appear: he was in Urbino, in point of fact, at the time indicated, but he prefers to feign that he was still in England.

It was customary, so he tells us, for the gentlemen and ladies of the court to gather after supper in the apartment of the Duchess, where the evenings were spent in conversation, badinage, the discussion of ingenious "questions," music, dancing, witty games, and other pastimes. On the evening of March 8 it was proposed that some one of the company be required

> to fashion in words a perfect courtier, setting forth all the conditions and particular qualities requisite for a man deserving of this name, everyone being allowed to contradict anything thought to be inappropriate.

This proposal found favor; and Emilia Pia, as mistress of ceremonies, assigned the task of exposition to Count Ludovico da Canossa (a learned, able, and honorable diplomat), whose discussion of the qualities requisite in the perfect courtier — together with many interruptions, some serious, some jocose — occupies the evening, and fills the first Book of the *Cortegiano*.

As prerequisites for perfection in the courtier — he insists that it is the *perfect* courtier with whom he is concerned — Count Ludovico specifies noble birth, intelligence, good looks, "a certain grace," goodness, and integrity. The proper profession of the courtier is that of arms: the perfect courtier must therefore have courage without boastfulness; he must be expert in the use of weapons, in horsemanship, and in all kinds of knightly exercise; though not easily provoked, he should be ready for the duel if his honor is clearly involved; and he should be good at many kinds of manly sport — hunting, swimming, jumping, running, and playing ball. Whatever he does he should do with grace — grace that must be so complete as to seem perfectly natural, even nonchalant, and must be utterly without affectation. This matter is treated with a fervor that proves Castiglione's intimate kinship in spirit with his friend Raphael, in whose art a wonderfully disciplined grace reigns supreme. The perfect courtier should be graceful even in his choice and use of words, both in speaking and in writing: this pronouncement brings on a long debate on the question as to just what type of language one should employ. One of the interlocutors takes the strictly Bembist view, namely, that one should imitate the language of Florence as used by Petrarch and Boccaccio: Count Ludovico favors a language less imitative, more modern, and more broadly based, free to make use of living terms, whether Tuscan or non-Tuscan, that have in point of fact established themselves in current speech. The perfect courtier, moreover, should have a good knowledge of literature, music, and painting. Arms and letters are complementary fields: even the glories won by military prowess can endure only in "the sacred treasury of letters" — and men of letters owe thanks to men of arms for providing them with noble themes. The perfect courtier should be well versed in Latin and in Greek, his knowledge embracing poets, orators, and historians; and he should himself be able to write well in verse and in prose, especially in Italian. With conviction Count Ludovico speaks of the values of skill in music and in painting. Painting, indeed, is a natural response to natural beauty:

> for the fabric of the world — which we behold with the vast firmament so splendid with its bright stars and with the Earth in its midst, girt with the seas, varied with mountains, valleys, and rivers, and adorned with such divers trees and beautiful flowers and grasses — is as it were a great and noble painting composed by the hand of nature and of God: he who can imitate it seems to me worthy of great praise.

A debate on the relative merits of painting and sculpture — in which mention is made of Raphael and Michelangelo — is presently interrupted by a late arrival. Two of the ladies dance to charming music; the Duchess rises; and the evening is over.

On the second evening Federico Fregoso leads a discussion that deals with a series of miscellaneous topics, including outdoor games, vocal and instrumental music, conversation, dress, friendship, card games, chess, dignity, and self-control. In all activities affectation and excess of any kind are to be avoided: one should maintain "a certain honorable mean" in all one's way of life. It is suggested that the company turn to the consideration of humor, and the merry Bernardo Bibbiena is designated as the leader of this portion of the discussion, in the course of which so many jests and anecdotes are related that the second half of the second Book becomes in effect a jest-collection.

The third evening and the third Book are devoted to a discussion, led by Giuliano de' Medici, of the qualities requisite for the perfect court lady: these include affability, modesty, culture, and fidelity. The discussion includes a debate on the relative nobility of men and women, and some consideration of courtly love. Excellence in the court lady is said to be essential for the attainment of excellence by the courtier, since desire for such praise and love as an excellent court lady can bestow spurs the courtier to deeds of valor and of skill, and to high achievement in every sort of courtly activity.

On the fourth evening Ottaviano Fregoso first maintains that excellence in a courtier is not a sufficient end in itself, but rather a means enabling him to fulfill his primary purpose:

> So then the purpose of the perfect courtier . . . [is] so to win the favor and the confidence of his prince as to be able always to speak the truth, with no fear of danger from giving offense, with regard to any matter as to which it is important that the prince be informed; and that in case he should find the prince disposed to an unworthy action he should dare to speak in opposition . . . and thus the courtier, having in himself the worthiness these gentlemen have attributed to him, together with readiness of mind, pleasantness, prudence, and knowledge of letters and of many other things, will always be able to show his prince how much honor and advantage result . . . from justice, from liberality, from magnanimity, from clemency, and from the other virtues that befit a prince; and, on the other hand, how much dishonor and harm result from the vices that are opposed to these virtues.

The qualities desirable in the prince himself are then considered: he should be just, pious, and generous; he should love his subjects; and he should promote public works. Castiglione recognizes explicitly the fact that he is engaged not in a description of things as they are, but in a statement of ideals. The discussion of the prince includes a debate on the relative merits of the principality and the republic: Bembo favors the republic, and Ottaviano the principality. The debate ends with Ottaviano's advocacy of a mixed state, in which, the power remaining with the prince, representatives of both the *optimates* and the people should be authorized to give effective counsel. The Turkish menace is mentioned, and hope is expressed that the young princes of France, of England, and of Spain will lead Christendom in a new crusade.

As the discussion of princely qualities closes, the theme of love comes up again, and Bembo is requested to treat that theme. This he does, restating some of the ideas set forth in his own *Asolani*, but going beyond them into a formal exposition of Platonic love. Love is the desire of beauty; and Bembo has much to say, accordingly, of the nature of beauty as a divine emanation which in varying manners and degrees permeates the universe. His exposition culminates in a restatement of the several stages of the "ladder" of love. The two lowest stages consist in the contemplation of external beauty: first the contemplation of the beauty of some one woman; then the contemplation of human beauty as a universal whole. The next two stages consist in the contemplation of internal or spiritual beauty: first the soul's contemplation of its own essence, luminous with divine light; then the soul's contemplation of all such spiritual beauty as a universal whole. The last stage is one of mystic union with the divine:

> Then the soul, kindled by the most holy fire of true divine love, flies to unite itself with the angelic nature; and not only does it wholly transcend sense, but

> it has no longer any need of the use of reason: for, transformed into an angelic being, it understands all things that are intelligible, and without any veil or cloud it beholds the vast sea of pure divine beauty, and receives it into itself, and enjoys that supreme blessedness that lies beyond the comprehension of sense.

At the end of his exposition Bembo, in rapture, offers an eloquent prayer to the Divine Love. The whole company has been profoundly impressed: the lady Emilia relieves the tension by plucking the hem of Bembo's robe, and bidding him take heed lest if he lose himself in such thoughts his soul should escape from his body. Another debate begins; but the Duchess desires that it be postponed until the next evening. The new day, indeed, has already come:

> So then, the shutters being thrown open on the side of the palace that looks toward the high summit of Mount Catria, they saw that the east was already overspread with a fair rosy dawn; and that all the stars had vanished, save only Venus, sweet mistress of the heavens, who rules the bounds of night and day. And from that star there seemed to come a gentle breeze, which, filling the air with a keen freshness, was beginning to stir the sweet singing of gladsome birds amid the murmuring woods of the near-by hills.

In style, in design, and in tone the *Cortegiano*, itself a courtly creation, is free from affectation, and maintains faithfully "a certain honorable mean." The style is a mean between the commonplace and the elevated: its naturalness and simplicity are those of cultured speech. The book as a whole has a governing plan; but that plan is not so forced upon the reader as to produce a feeling of undue formality: the transitions are handled so well that the sequence of thought appears to spring naturally from the easy flow of conversation. Similarly, while many of the speeches of the discussion leaders are of some length, the technique of interruption is used with such great skill that the reader is never oppressed by any sense of monotony. The material of the book is serious in itself, and is developed with a serious thoughtfulness; but the seriousness is constantly controlled and relieved by touches of humor.

Humor indeed pervades the book, appearing not only in the section devoted to jests, but as a constant unifying grace. Yet one is aware of a deep underlying sadness in Castiglione's own spirit. Most clearly perceptible in certain pages of the dedicatory letter and of the introduction to the fourth Book (pages in which he mourns the loss of several of the interlocutors who had been dear friends of his), his sadness is yet deepest in his consciousness of the discrepancy between his own ideals and the surrounding reality, and in his presentiment that the graciousness of the court life he had loved and championed was destined all too soon to vanish.

Ideally, the four Books should be read on four successive long and leisurely evenings. If that is done, the reader will retain the sense that he has been for a time in a truly courtly company of men and women, well worth his acquaintance and his memory. And there will form gradually in his mind a sense of companionship with Baldassare Castiglione, who in his own day and ever since has seemed, to his princes, his friends, and his readers, to be himself the perfect courtier. In his portrait in the Louvre one may see him as Raphael saw him.

The *Cortegiano*, in the original Italian and in translations, brought to Spain and France and England a code of social refinement, touched with the glamor of Italy, which greatly influenced both literature and life. The *caballero*, the *honnête homme*, and the *gentleman* owed much to Castiglione's perfect courtier; and their ladies owed not a little to Castiglione's Duchess and Emilia Pia. Castiglione's Bembo was, moreover, for France and England, one of the main expositors of the concept of Platonic love. In literature the influence of the *Cortegiano* was in part immediate and in part diffused through the life it had already influenced. Don Quixote, as he instructs the governor-designate Sancho Panza, is mindful of the first part of the fourth Book; Rabelais borrows a jest; and Corneille's conception of character reflects knowledge either of the *Cortegiano* itself or of courtly ideals derived therefrom. In England the *Cortegiano* was well presented in the translation of Thomas Hoby, who says of it, in his dedicatory letter:

> to Princes and Greate men, it is a rule to rule themselves that rule others . . . To men growen in yeres, a pathway to the behoulding and musing of the minde, and to whatsoever elles is meete for that age: To yonge Gentlemen, an encouraging to garnishe their minde with morall vertues, and their bodye with comely exercises, and both the one and the other with honest qualities to attaine unto their noble ende: To Ladyes and Gentlewomen a mirrour to decke and trimme themselves with vertuous condicions, comely behaviours and honest enterteinment toward al men: And to them all in general, a storehouse of most necessary implements for the conversacion, use, and training up of mans life with Courtly demeaners.

Ascham was one of the earlier sponsors of the *Courtier*. The writers who for their own varying purposes drew from it most deeply were Spenser, Lyly, Sidney, and Burton.

Castiglione's verse, small in amount, is of good quality. His fine sonnet on the ruins of Rome, beginning

> Superbi colli e voi sacre ruine,
> Proud hills and you, sacred ruins,

reappears in the *Antiquitez de Rome* of Du Bellay and thence in Spenser's *Ruines of Rome*; and Milton made worthy use of Castiglione's Latin elegy *Alcon* both in *Lycidas* and in the *Epitaphium Damonis*.

* * *

At some time not far from 1520 Luigi da Porto (1486–1529), a gentleman-soldier of Vicenza, took into his hands Masuccio Salernitano's undistinguished story of two ill-starred Sienese lovers, and based upon it his one masterpiece, finished in 1524 and first published in 1530. He chose Verona as his scene; he gave to his hero and heroine the singing names of Romeo and Giulietta; and he called their rival families the Montecchi and the Cappelletti.* His chief variation from Masuccio comes in the tragic denouement: Romeo reaches the tomb of Giulietta before she wakes, believes her dead, and drinks his poison; she wakes; they spend the waning night in loving lamentation; as Friar Lorenzo enters, just before dawn, Romeo dies; and Giulietta presently takes her own life. The idea of this denouement came to Da Porto from Ovid's tale of Pyramus and Thisbe. Other elements of the *novella* were taken from Boccaccio and from the anonymous *Ippolito e Leonora*; and several are due to Da Porto's own invention. The whole story is woven together very skilfully; the chain of motivation is complete; the narrative proceeds with an excellent naturalness; the hero and heroine are movingly real; the other persons are clearly individualized; and the style is pleasant in its slightly formal simplicity.

It is no wonder that later storytellers turned to Da Porto's *novella* again and again, with more or less invention, and with more or less success. The main sixteenth-century versions succeed each other thus: †

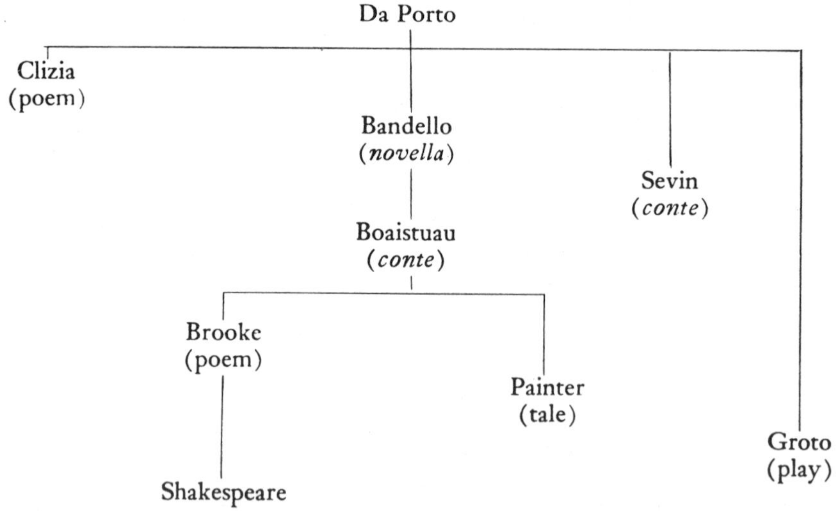

* In point of fact, though the Montecchi existed as a family in Verona in the twelfth century, the name seems to have been used thereafter only as the name of a local political faction; and the Cappelletti, neither a family nor Veronese, were a local political faction in Cremona.

† Clizia is the pseudonym of Gherardo Boldieri, a writer wholly unimportant except

The secondary interrelationships of these several versions are more complicated than the diagram indicates. Bandello drew, in all probability, upon Clizia; Boaistuau drew upon Sevin, and, to some extent, directly upon Da Porto; Groto drew upon Clizia and Bandello, and probably upon Boaistuau. Elements due in the first instance to Clizia, Bandello, Sevin, Boaistuau, and Brooke reappear in Shakespeare: Brooke's poem is Shakespeare's only certain source, but at several points Shakespeare is in exclusive agreement with Da Porto. It was Da Porto who created the story as a whole, and his own version is by far the best of all the pre-Shakespearean versions.

The largest and most influential of the *novella* collections of the sixteenth century was that of the Lombard Matteo Bandello (c. 1480–1561). In his youth he became a Dominican monk, and as such he visited various parts of Italy; but in and after 1506 he lived the life of a courtier, employed at times as an envoy and at times as a secretary, chiefly in Milan and in Mantua, and finally in France, where, in 1550, he was made Bishop of Agen.

He began to write *novelle* at about the time he became a courtier, and continued to write them, now and then, until the last years of his life. Three Parts, containing together some two hundred *novelle*, were published, in three volumes, in 1554; and a fourth Part, containing about thirty *novelle*, was published, after Bandello's death, in 1573. The collection has no title other than *Novelle*; and there is no frame-story or plan of organization. Each *novella* is supposed to have been told in some company in which Bandello was present, and to have been written down by him from memory; and each is preceded by a dedicatory letter. Some of the stories are historical, legendary, traditional, adventurous, romantic, tragic, or anecdotal; some are tales of magnanimity; and some report witty sayings. The great majority, however, are tales of trickery — which often brings horrific vengeance. They are in general the reverse of edifying. In time they range from antiquity to Bandello's own day; in scene they range all over Europe, with excursions into Asia and Africa. Among the *novelle* that may be regarded as having some special interest are those that tell of Timbreo and Fenicia (the *Much Ado* story), Romeo and Juliet, Lattanzio and Nicuola (the *Twelfth Night* story), Edward III and the Countess of Salisbury, Rosmunda, Henry VIII, and the origins of the House of Savoy.

In 1559 Pierre Boaistuau published, under the title *Histoires tragiques extraites des œuvres italiennes de Bandel*, free translations of six of the *novelle* (including that of Romeo and Juliet): and in the years from 1559 to 1570 François de Belleforest published four volumes containing translations of some seventy of the *novelle*. Both men treated the Italian text very freely

---

for his minor part in the development of this story. Sevin was a minor French writer. Bandello will be discussed and Boaistuau mentioned in the present chapter; and Groto will be discussed in a later chapter.

indeed, omitting, abridging, expanding, and adding to suit their own tastes. In 1573 or soon thereafter all the *novelle* of the fourth Part appeared in an anonymous French translation. It did not take long for Bandello's *novelle* to reach England, where several men translated one or more of them, either from the Italian or, more commonly, from Boaistuau or Belleforest. Twenty-five of the many stories contained in Painter's *Palace of Pleasure* come from Bandello. The thirteen *Tragicall Discourses* of Geffraie Fenton are all derived from Bandello, through Belleforest. The various English translations, especially those to be found in the *Palace of Pleasure*, were in their turn much used by the Elizabethan dramatists. Among the plays that owe their themes, in some sense, to Bandello are Shakespeare's *Much Ado About Nothing*, *Romeo and Juliet*, and *Twelfth Night*, Massinger's *The Picture*, Webster's *Duchess of Malfi*, and Beaumont and Fletcher's *Maid of the Mill* and *Triumph of Death*.

Innovations of considerable interest appear in the *novella* collection, entitled *Le piacevoli notti*, of Giovan Francesco Straparola. Of Straparola himself little is known: he was born in Lombardy; he published a volume of slight verse in 1508; and he published the first of the two Books of the *Piacevoli notti* in 1550 and the second in 1553. His *novelle* are set in a frame-story which, though conventional as a whole, has some features of its own. The scene is a villa on the island of Murano; the "Delightful Evenings" are the last thirteen nights of a Venetian carnival season; and the large company consists of thirteen ladies and many gentlemen. The entertainment begins on each evening with dancing, which is followed by the singing of a madrigal. Then comes the storytelling, each story ending with a riddle in verse. There are in all about seventy-five stories. Most of them are drawn from literary sources and are of the usual types; but two are told in dialect, one in the dialect of Bergamo and one in the dialect of Treviso, and about twenty are folk tales. It is the inclusion of these folk tales that gives the collection its chief distinction: for this is the first appearance of a considerable group of folk tales in modern European literature. Among them are versions of the stories of Beauty and the Beast, Puss in Boots, and The Dancing Water, the Singing Apple, and the Speaking Bird.

* * *

Within this period four men (in addition to Machiavelli and Guicciardini) wrote historical works of some note.

The Lombard Pietro Martire d'Anghiera (1459–1526) spent most of his life in Spain, in the royal service. He heard reports made to the Council of the Indies; relevant correspondence passed under his eyes; and he was acquainted with Columbus, Vespucci, Cabot. and other explorers. The knowledge he thus acquired was embodied in his Latin *Decades de orbe novo*, which begins with the first voyage of Columbus and was kept up even to the year of Pietro's death. He handles his unique sources of information with a keen intelligence and a clear sense of historic values.

The Venetian patrician Marin Sanudo (1466–1535) is best known for his vast diaries, which cover the years from 1496 to 1533, and fill some sixty monumental volumes. Into these diaries he poured everything, Venetian, Italian, or European, that seemed to him to have any bearing on the life of Venice: all sorts of daily happenings, trivial or important; anecdotes; accounts of public works and of festivals; descriptions of customs and of costumes; extensive commercial information; public and private letters; election data; reports of ambassadors and commissioners; records of meetings of governmental bodies; and all the poems he could get hold of (he was himself a minor poet) that dealt in any spirit with public affairs, local or general. As a result, his diaries constitute an amazingly vivid record of the life that surged around him, and an immense mine of general historical information. The Italian in which he wrote is highly colored with forms of his own Venetian dialect.

The Florentine Jacopo Nardi (1479–1563), in his youth a follower of Savonarola and an eager official of the Florentine republic, was so active, in the years 1527–1530, in the short-lived reëstablishment of that republic, as to win the honor of an exile from which he never returned. Living sadly in Venice, he wrote a history of the rise and fall of his republic from 1494 to 1530. He writes in general with a quiet nostalgic idealism; but on the rare occasions when he is stirred to severity the sheer simplicity of his utterance, proceeding as it does from an immaculate honorableness, gives to his judgments a quality that is almost Dantesque. In his youth he had written two so-called comedies, *L'amicizia* and *I due felici rivali*, which mingle characterestics of the *sacra rappresentazione* and of Roman comedy.

An epicurean humanism pervades the life and work of Paolo Giovio (1483–1552), born at Como. First a physician, later a bishop, he lived mainly at the papal court. Falling eventually into papal disfavor, he retired to his luxurious villa on Lake Como, where he had gathered, among other things, a remarkable collection of portraits. He wrote almost exclusively in Latin. His largest work is a bulky "History of his Own Times," which covers the period from 1494 to 1547. His best works are his several Lives of prominent men of his own time, which served as a model to many later biographers, and the series of inscriptions, called *Elogia clarorum virorum*, which he composed for portraits contained in his own collection. Each of these *elogia* consists of a paragraph of prose followed by a bit of verse. Among the men thus eulogized are Thomas Linacre and Thomas More.

Polidoro Vergilio of Urbino (c. 1470–1555) entered the papal service in his young manhood. In 1502 he went to England, on papal business; and in England he remained for nearly all the rest of his life. Known there as Polydore Vergil, he enjoyed association with More and other English humanists, and published several learned works. The most important of these, the monumental *Anglica historia*, first published in 1534, had a profound influence on English historiography, and through derivative English chronicles furnished Shakespeare with materials and judgments for his historical plays.

CHAPTER 25

Comedy and Tragedy

TOWARD THE END of the fifteenth century, while interest in the medievally rooted *sacra rappresentazione* was diminishing rapidly, interest in the Roman drama had become very active. Comedies of Plautus and of Terence had been performed in Latin in Rome and in Florence, and in Italian translation in Ferrara.

Just before 1500 and in the early decades of the sixteenth century there were written in Italian a number of plays, none of them of any great importance, which in various ways combined features of the *sacra rappresentazione* and of Roman comedy. They were called "comedies" and "tragedies," but they were in reality mixed forms that did not, strictly speaking, deserve those names. Their plots were taken, in several cases, from *novelle*, oftenest from the *Decameron*. Among these mixed plays were the two "comedies" of Jacopo Nardi, mentioned in the preceding chapter.

The Ferrarese performances, which continued into the first years of the new century, seem to have provided the stimulus for the writing of the first "modern" comedies in Italian — the first, that is, to break away entirely from the traditions of the *sacra rappresentazione* and to conform closely to Roman models. The earliest of these comedies is the *Formicone* of Publio Filippo of Mantua, written not later than 1506. It is only because he was a pioneer that Filippo deserves mention; his comedy is of no inherent interest. As so many of the succeeding comedies were to do, it follows the Roman pattern: five acts; a public street as the unchanging scene; servants prominent among the characters.

Next came three comedies that have been mentioned in previous chapters: the *Cassaria* and the *Suppositi* of Ariosto, performed in 1508 and 1509 respectively; and a little later, probably, the *Mandragola* of Machiavelli.

In 1513 a comedy by Bernardo Bibbiena, called *La Calandria*, was performed in Urbino. Bibbiena, the humorist of the *Cortegiano* and a favorite of Leo X, built his play with materials derived from Plautus and from the *Decameron*. His fun and his wit were in the main disreputable: but that did not prevent Leo X from making him presently a cardinal.

The first modern comedies followed Roman models; but Giangiorgio Trissino (1478–1550), the author of the first "modern" tragedy — the first, that is, to break away entirely from the traditions of the *sacra rappresentazione* and to look, instead, to the classics — followed Greek models, and sought to conform to doctrines found in the *Poetics* of Aristotle. Especially influential not only upon Trissino but also upon his successors were the master principles set forth in the famous sentence

> Tragedy, then, is an imitation of an action that is serious, complete, and of a certain magnitude; in language embellished with each kind of artistic ornament, the several kinds being found in separate parts of the play; in the form of action, not narrative; through pity and fear effecting the proper purgation of these emotions; *

together with the vital principle of the unity of action; and the statement — not advanced as a principle — that in the practice of the Greek stage "tragedy endeavours, as far as possible, to confine itself to a single revolution of the sun, or but slightly to exceed that limit." Aristotle makes no reference to unity of place.

Trissino, a wealthy patrician of Vicenza, exiled from Venetia in 1508 because of his imperial sympathies, took up residence in Rome in 1514. There, in the following year, he wrote his *Sofonisba*, taking as subject Livy's story of the Carthaginian Sophonisba, the Numidian king Syphax, and the Numidian prince Masinissa. Sophonisba, though betrothed to Masinissa, has by her father been given in marriage to Syphax, on condition that he resist the Roman enemy; the Romans and the vengeful Masinissa defeat Syphax; Sophonisba entreats Masinissa to save her from Roman slavery; this he tries to do by marrying her; the Roman commanders rule that she must follow Syphax into captivity; and Masinissa then sends her the fatal liberating potion. In its general structure the play follows Greek practice and precept. The chorus is continually on the stage, participating freely in the dialogue, and marking by its choral songs the main divisions of the action (there are a prologue, three "episodes," and an epilogue, but there is no division into acts); the unities of action and of time are maintained (not that of place); the catastrophe is reported, not witnessed; and the stated purpose of the play is the effective stirring of pity and fear. There are some borrowings from Sophocles and from Euripides. For his dialogue Trissino adopted the Italian eleven-syllable line, which bears some resemblance to the iambic trimeter of Greek tragedy. He used it, however, without rhyme; and the *Sofonisba* is, in consequence, the first substantial Italian composition in blank verse. Clas-

* Butcher's translation.

sicizing innovation appears also in three of the four choral songs. One of the four is a regular *canzone*, but the other three are the first Italian Pindaric odes. Unfortunately Trissino's classicizing industry was not accompanied by any slightest gleam of poetic inspiration. The play is lifeless: the dialogue is unfelt, and the wording is commonplace. Yet its pioneering is of historical importance, and in its own century it was held in high esteem. In France versions were soon made both in prose and in verse, and French imitations soon followed.* Of all Trissino's innovations in the *Sofonisba* the only one that proved successful was his decision to write in unrhymed hendecasyllables: this type of blank verse has remained the standard metrical medium for Italian tragedy.

Through papal influence Trissino soon regained his status in Venetia. Much of the rest of his life was spent in his villa near Vicenza, where he served as a generous and an honored host to many writers and artists.

He wrote many Italian lyrics, among them three more Pindaric odes, and the first Italian Horatian ode (written about 1519) — a translation of one of the odes of Horace (*Donec gratus eram tibi*) in a form which imitates the form of that particular ode. He tried to reform the Italian alphabet by introducing the letter k and the Greek epsilon, omega, and zeta to represent certain sounds: several of his writings were printed with these letters so used. In 1529 he published the first four Divisions of a treatise entitled *La Pωεtica*: these Divisions deal with linguistic matters and with versification. Two more Divisions, published only after Trissino's death, are an expanded paraphrase of the *Poetics* of Aristotle.

The main effort of Trissino's literary life was the writing of his epic, *L'Italia liberata dai Goti*, on which he toiled for some twenty years before its publication in 1547. The epic, in his view, was the noblest kind of poetry: Homer was the greatest of the Greeks. The traditional Italian epic, as represented by the *Orlando furioso*, was to Trissino an object of scorn. So he set out to show what an Italian epic might properly be. He took his theme — the liberation of Italy from the Goths by Justinian and Belisarius in the sixth century — not from the world of medieval romance, but from the Byzantine historian Procopius. His dignity never lapses; he borrows plentifully from Homer; pagan divinities are translated into similarly named Christian angels. For the traditional octaves he substitutes, again, unrhymed hendecasyllables. But his *Liberata* is as dull as his *Sofonisba*. At the very end of his life he turned again to the drama, this time to comedy: his *I simillimi*, published in 1548, is in content a pedestrian imitation of the *Menaechmi*, but in form it follows Aristotelian precept and the practice of Aristophanes.

When Trissino first went to Rome, he found a kindred spirit in the Floren-

* The several French and English Sophonisbas of the seventeenth and eighteenth centuries owe little or nothing to Trissino beyond the vogue of the subject.

tine Giovanni Rucellai (1475–1525), who was among the courtiers of Leo X. As a result, Rucellai began forthwith the writing of Trissinian tragedies: his *Rosmunda* was almost contemporary with the *Sophonisba*; his *Oreste*, begun immediately thereafter, was never quite completed. These plays follow, in general, the Greek models, though both are in five acts; and both, like the *Sofonisba*, are written for the most part in blank verse. The subject of the *Rosmunda* is taken from early medieval history. Rosmunda, daughter of Comundo, King of the Gepidae, had been about to marry Almachilde; Alboin, King of the Lombards, slays Comundo and marries Rosmunda, but at the wedding feast forces her to drink from a cup made of her father's skull; and Almachilde wreaks due vengeance. With this Gothic medievalism Rucellai mingles elements of the *Antigone* of Sophocles. The *Oreste* is a reworking of the *Iphigenia in Tauris* of Euripides. Both plays show an incipient — but only an incipient — dramatic sense. Such slight poetic promise as they contained was well fulfilled, some years later, in a long didactic poem, *Le api*, "The Bees," which is a fresh and graceful paraphrase, freely modernized and expanded, of the fourth Book of Virgil's *Georgics*.

The example of Trissino and Rucellai was followed, with variations of some interest, but with no greater dramatic success, by Alessandro Pazzi de' Medici (1483–1530), a member of a minor branch of the great family. In the years 1524 and 1525 he translated three Greek tragedies into Italian and wrote one tragedy of his own, *Didone in Cartagine*, based upon Virgil's story of Dido. This play, though its characteristics are still essentially Greek, shows elements that are derived from Seneca: in this respect he anticipated a later dramatic preference. His most valuable literary service was the preparation of an edition of the Greek text of the *Poetics* of Aristotle, accompanied by his own Latin translation. The posthumous publication of this book, in 1536, marks the beginning of the vogue of Aristotelian critical ideas in Italy (since the last two Divisions of Trissino's *Pωetica*, though written earlier, were not published until much later).

In contemporary opinion Pietro Aretino (1492–1556) would probably have been regarded as the leading man of letters of the period, after Bembo. Born in Arezzo, he lived in Rome under Leo X and through the first years of Clement VII: from 1527 on he lived in Venice. He called one of his portraits by his friend Titian (the one in the Pitti Gallery) *una terribile maraviglia*: he was himself a terrible marvel, not only in semblance but in reality. He was terrible in the viciousness of his life and of his writing, especially in the extraordinary system of blackmail that underlies his voluminous correspondence. He was called "the scourge of princes": even the Emperor was among his victims. He was marvelous in the extent to which he imposed himself upon the fearful but admiring imagination of his contemporaries, and in the extent to which, despite his viciousness, he retained the tolerance or the at least apparent friendship of many decent people; and he was marvelous in his polygraphic fertility.

In addition to his letters (of which he collected some three thousand for publication) he wrote pasquinades; lyrics of many different kinds; satires; four unfinished epics; prose dialogues; the *Giudizi*, annually issued prognostications of what would befall certain persons and certain places in the year ahead; a treatise "On the Humanity of Christ"; an exposition of Biblical mysteries; pious lives of Mary, of St. Thomas Aquinas, and of St. Catherine of Siena; a prose paraphrase of the Penitential Psalms; various miscellaneous compositions; five comedies; and a tragedy.

The earliest of his comedies, *La cortigiana*, "Life at Court," was (in its first form) written in Rome in 1525; the second, *Il marescalco*, "The Farrier," was written in 1526 or 1527 for the court of Mantua; and the rest were written in Venice, *La Talanta* (a personal name) in 1541, *Lo ipocrito* in 1542, and *Il filosofo* in 1544. All are in prose and in five acts; all have twenty or more characters; all except the *Marescalco* are confusingly intricate; and all breathe corruption. Their dialogue is vivacious; and they offer picturesque glimpses of everyday street life, in which such folk as a fishmonger, a peddler of trinkets, an old-clothes man, and a vender of chapbooks mingle with the inevitable parasites, pedants, braggart soldiers, and rascally servants. The *Cortigiana* presents a devastating picture of the lower levels of life in papal Rome, and sets forth in some detail the means of obtaining advancement in the papal court. The Hypocrite, an unctuous and unscrupulous friar who is constantly mouthing *carità*, serves at least to anticipate the far greater figure of Tartuffe. The Philosopher rejoices in the name Plataristotele.

Two years after the writing of the *Filosofo* Aretino entered the field of tragedy with his *Orazia*, "The Tragedy of the Horatii," which is Senecan rather than Greek in its general character. The story is Livy's familiar story of the combat of the Horatii and the Curiatii, of the bitter lamentations of the Horatian sister wedded to one of the Curiatii, of the fatal wrath of the triumphant Horatius against his sister, and of the final clement punishment of Horatius. Aretino, writing in this instance with more artistic patience than usual, attains a considerable degree of tragic dignity: the central situation, in which a relentless patriotism slays an unyielding love, is well handled. But the moralizing dialogues are too many and too long; too much of the essential action is reported by witnesses; and the final *deus ex machina* is very mechanical indeed. With all its limitations, however, the *Orazia* is the best Italian tragedy of the sixteenth century.

One of the more noteworthy comedies of the century, the anonymous *Gl'ingannati*, "The Mistaken Ones," performed in Siena in 1531, is in all probability the ultimate source of the main plot of *Twelfth Night*.

All of the plays thus reviewed were written for educated spectators or readers. The tragedies seem not to have been acted at this time. The comedies were acted by amateur players, usually courtiers or students or members of some literary group: now and then, however, there was participation by a popular entertainer, or by some man whose success in amateur acting had led to occasional engagements for which he received compensation. Performances were given, usually, in great palace halls.

* * *

Meanwhile, quasi-dramatic activities were going on also on a much humbler level, among the popular entertainers of the public squares. Present in all periods, they seem at this time to have attracted an unusual amount of general attention. They were commonly called *montambanchi* or *saltimbanchi* or *ciarlatani*. The *-banchi* of the first two names are the benches on which these entertainers performed: *montambanchi*, "bench-mounters, mountebanks," is a general term, while *saltimbanchi*, "jumpers on benches," has reference to the tumbling, the somersaults, and the various gymnastic feats that figured largely in their performances. The word *ciarlatani*, (related to a verb meaning "to prattle"), "charlatans," has reference to their activities as venders of quack medicines and miscellaneous trifles, which they extolled in partially improvised rigmaroles. They sang songs, also, and played on simple instruments; they sang or recited narratives in verse; they told stories and jests and riddles; they danced; they played tricks; they impersonated; and when two or three of them were working together they put on comic dialogues or crude farces. Impersonators at this time imitated, in particular, peasants of a given region or types characteristic of a given city. Such impersonators occasionally performed for private patrons — popes among them. There came to be, also, some semi-popular writing of comic dialogues and farces.

* * *

The country around Padua was one of the chief centers of popular and semi-popular dramatic activity; and acquaintance with the dialectal productions of this region determined the general character of the plays of the Paduan dramatist Angelo Beolco (1502–1542), commonly called Ruzzante. Much of his life was spent among peasants: his primary occupation was indeed the management of farms belonging to his family. His delight in the rough simplicities, the rough humor, and the rough dialect of his peasants served to give direction to his natural dramatic instincts: his plays are written almost wholly in rustic Paduan, and the majority of his characters are Paduan peasants. He wrote, in some cases, at least, for performances to be given in the carnival season; and, being by nature an actor as well as a writer, he acted in his own plays, taking usually, and with great success, the recurring part of a peasant called Ruzzante. He sometimes received compensation for his services; and he and a few of his companions made up what may have been the first company of Italian actors — their association, however, was intermittent and short-lived. With variations in personnel they played, occasionally, in Venice and elsewhere — most happily in one of the villas of Beolco's patron and friend, Luigi Cornaro.

Seven of Beolco's comedies and three dramatic dialogues have been preserved. The first two comedies, written probably before 1520, are slight affairs in verse: the later comedies are in five acts, and in prose. Of these the *Moschetta* and the *Fiorina*, written probably in 1520 and 1521, are the most original, the liveliest in plot and wit, and the most distinctive in their earthy naturalism. The three one-act dialogues are of the same character and quality. In the next comedy, the *Anconitana*, Plautine elements make their appearance; and the last two comedies, the *Piovana* and the *Vaccaria*, written not later than 1533, are based respectively upon the *Rudens* and the *Asinaria* of Plautus: Plautus, however, is Paduanized not only in language but also in the replacement of slaves by Paduan peasants and in the introduction of scenes and developments that are of Beolco's own invention. The dominant figure, in comedies and dialogues alike, is that of the peasant Ruzzante, garrulous, boastful, cowardly, now shrewd, now stupid, malicious, witty, vulgar, agile, and given to singing and to dancing about the stage.

But Beolco, though he turned his peasants to such good comic use, was in reality deeply troubled by the hardness of their lives. In two generally humorous "orations" in rustic Paduan, each delivered before a cardinal of the Cornaro family, he pleads the peasant cause. Let the Cardinal spend his wealth not on statues or objects of art or suchlike baubles: let him rather alleviate the lot of his peasants. Specifically, Beolco asks that there be an impartial administration of the justice that seems always to be on the side of the wealthy; that peasants be allowed to say their say; that taxes be lowered; and that moneylenders be restrained from usury. "We who sweat," he says, "we never have a thing; and the others, who don't sweat, are the ones who eat": *nù, che à se suòm, à no n' haom mè, e gi altri, che no se sua, el magne.*

CHAPTER 26

Poetry of the Mid-Sixteenth Century

DURING THE FOUR middle decades of the sixteenth century little political change occurred in Italy. Charles V had possessed himself of Lombardy, as an imperial fief, in 1535: on his abdication in 1556 it became an appanage of the Spanish crown. From this time on, for some two centuries, both Lombardy and Southern Italy (with Sicily), constituting together roughly half of Italy, were Spanish provinces, oppressively administered, and Spanish influence was strong elsewhere in the peninsula. In 1559, with Spanish support, Emanuele Filiberto, Duke of Savoy, gained possession of most of Piedmont, and in 1562 Turin became his capital. In 1569 Cosimo I, Duke of Florence, won for himself and his successors the quasi-royal title of Grand Duke of Tuscany. Turkish coastal raids continued; and Turkish and Venetian fleets met in battle.

The Council of Trent, which resumed its sessions in 1551–1552 and again in 1562–1563, consolidated most of the efforts of the Counter Reformation. Many reforms were effected and several basic dogmas were proclaimed. The Church, its authority firmly established, became the dominating force in the life of Italy.

Michelangelo saw the early stages of the realization of his design for the dome of St. Peter's; and Jacopo Sansovino built the elaborate library of St. Mark's. Palladio sheathed the old Gothic city hall of his native Vicenza in magnificent classic arcades; designed for Vicenza, also, the first complete permanent theater, the Teatro Olimpico; and built many palaces and churches in various Venetian cities.

In sculpture Michelangelo found no worthy successors. The lesser men who followed him sought either colossality or elegance. The glow of Renaissance painting was fading fast, except in Venice. There the aging Titian was still growing in insight and in power; Tintoretto combined Leonardo's dramatic mastery of light and shadow, Michelangelo's sweeping fearlessness, and the perennial beauty of Venetian color; and Paolo Veronese filled his canvases with all the pomp and circumstance of contemporary Venetian luxury.

Palestrina, the greatest of Italian composers, published his first collection of masses, his first collection of madrigals, and his first collection of motets in the years from 1554 to 1564. It was probably about 1570 that an unidentified Italian instrument maker, seeking a more refined form of the viol, made the first violin.

In the field of literature the number of men and women who wrote prose and verse of good quality was greater than ever; but the earlier surge of genius had subsided. Very little important work was done in Latin; but classic influence continued to make itself strongly felt in what was written in Italian. The formation of academies continued. Activity increased in the field of the drama, and began in the field of literary theory. The pressures of the Counter Reformation and the assertions of theorists began to restrict literary freedom.

The stream of French and English visitors continued: Du Bellay was among those who came from France.

* * *

The leading poet of the period, Luigi Tansillo (1510–1568), born at Venosa in Southern Italy, spent most of his life in the military service of the Spanish viceregal government, serving both on land and at sea. The life he lived and the scenes he saw were for him a constant source of poetry, which he wrote with verve and with facility. His lyrics are in the main Petrarchistic; but they show a reaction against the puristic restraint of Bembo, a reaction which is in part a manifestation of true lyric energy and in part a reversion to the conceits of Il Chariteo. In the two sonnets that are the most famous of his love poems he makes effective use of the Icarus motif to express his soaring aspirations. The second of the two is in substance as follows:

> Since I have spread my wings unto my fair desire, the more of space I behold beneath me, the more proudly I offer my feathers to the wind, and scorn the world, and rise toward heaven.
>
> Nor does the fate of the son of Daedalus lead me to descend: rather do I the more strive upward. That I shall fall, dying, to earth I know full well; but what life can equal my death?
>
> I hear, in my flight, the voice of my heart, saying: "Whither, oh rash one, are you bearing me? Turn downward, for too great daring is wont to end in grief."

> "Fear not the mighty fall," I make reply, "cleave the clouds boldly, and die content, if heaven destines us for such an illustrious death."

In some of his other lyrics Tansillo shows a liking for wild nature — "valleys hostile to the sun; proud cliffs that threaten heaven; deep caverns whence night and silence never depart" — and for "broken and grass-grown walls where once men dwelt." He wrote also a considerable number of longer poems, among them the bacchanalian *Il vendemmiatore*, "The Vintager"; the *Stanze a Bernardino Martirano*, a realistic account of naval life; the *Clorida*, a vivacious description of villa life on the Bay of Naples; and two didactic but occasionally humorous poems, *La balia*, "The Nurse," and *Il podere*, "The Farm." His verse had much influence, both in Italy — especially upon Giordano Bruno — and, chiefly through the anthologies presently to be mentioned, in France and Spain.

Three other Neapolitan gentlemen wrote Petrarchistic-Chariteau verse of varying quality, and were well represented in the anthologies. Angelo di Costanzo (1507–1591), whose sonnets aim at epigrammatic effects, was famous in his own day, and came into a renewed vogue among the Arcadians of the eighteenth century. Berardino Rota (1509–1575), a hyperbolist in much of his verse (his eyes were an ocean, his heart an Aetna), wrote also some simpler and finer poems of grieving love — as well as Italian eclogues and competent Latin epigrams and elegies. Galeazzo di Tarsia (1520–1553), a better poet than the other two, found expression in his few and carefully worded sonnets for unmistakable depths of feeling. Exiled for a time, he greeted Italy, on his return, with a poem which, while reminiscent of Petrarch's Latin salutation, has clear and worthy accents of its own.

The two chief Northern Italian poets of the period, Bernardo Tasso and Luigi Alamanni, both knew exile, both were in the first instance lyrists, both included odes of classic type among their lyrics, and both wrote verse of other kinds, including, in each case, two epics.

The home of the Tasso family was in Bergamo. Bernardo (1493–1569) earned his living honorably as courtier and secretary to a series of patrons. His longest service was with Ferrante Sanseverino, prince of Salerno (an imperial fief within the province of Naples). His duties took him, at various times, to Tunis, Spain, France, Flanders, and Germany. One brief period of idyllic family happiness, from 1542 to 1544, was spent at Sorrento, where Bernardo, released from his usual duties for a time in order that he might be free to devote himself to literary work, found a home overlooking the Bay. There, in 1544, his far more famous son, Torquato, was born.

The first collection of Bernardo's verse, *Il libro primo de gli amori*, appeared in 1531: other similar collections followed from time to time. Most of his poems are sonnets, and most of his sonnets are Petrarchistic. Two groups, however, are more distinctive: his poems of conjugal love, which in their heartfelt simplicity tell of a complete happiness; and his pastoral sonnets, which bring a successful classicizing novelty into the content of the conventional form.

A still more noteworthy innovation appears in Bernardo's several Horatian odes, the first original Italian poems written in quasi-Horatian forms. These odes consist typically of a good many short stanzas in which seven- and eleven-syllable lines are mingled. The stanza is most frequently of five lines, as in this Ode to the South Wind:

Perche con tanto orgoglio
O nimico de giorni allegri, e chiari
Turbando l'aere, e i mari
Fai ch' ogni duro scoglio
Pianga con alta uoce il suo cordoglio? *

Bernardo was as much concerned with the classicizing content of his odes as with their structure; but the lighter forms he devised, particularly the one just illustrated, were his greatest gift to later poetry. Among his later odes are some that are religious; these he called "sacred odes, or psalms."

In 1540 some Spanish gentlemen proposed to Bernardo that he write a poem on the adventures of "Amadis of Gaul"; and it was presumably with a view to enabling Bernardo to carry out this suggestion that Sanseverino in 1542 released him for a time from his other duties. But the two years at Sorrento were all too brief; and the lengthening poem underwent many vicissitudes before its publication in a hundred cantos, under the title *Amadigi*, in 1560. It was based upon the best of the Spanish prose romances of chivalry, *Los quatro libros del Virtuoso cauallero Amadis de Gaula*, by Garci Rodriguez de Montalvo, first published in 1508.† The story, that of the adventures, the constant love, and the marriage of Amadis and Oriana, is familiar to English readers through Southey's translation of Montalvo's *Amadis*. Bernardo, much influenced by the classicizing tendencies of his time, began his poem with the idea that it should be written in blank verse, and that it should deal with the unified action of a single hero: but on the insistence of Sanseverino he abandoned blank verse in favor of the traditional octaves; and somewhat later, becoming convinced that his readers would prefer variety to unity, he interwove with the main plot two minor plots of his own invention. He multiplied episodes, also, but tried to prevent excessive breach of unity by having them narrated by primary characters. Throughout his years of labor he was tormented by conflict between the opposing pressures of his hope for remunerative popularity and his desire to conform to the urgings of

* "Why with such pride, oh enemy of bright and happy days, troubling the air and the seas, dost thou cause every rocky cliff to lament in a loud voice its distress?"

† It seems probable that this Spanish version was derived from an earlier Portuguese version, now lost. Many of its elements are ultimately of Old French origin. "Gaula" is not France, but Wales.

classicizing mentors. There are many instances of Spanish borrowings from Italian writers: the *Amadigi* is the most notable of the few instances of Italian works derived from Spanish sources. It is far inferior to the *Furioso*; but it is the best of the many romantic epics written by Italians whose work was done between that of Ariosto and that of Bernardo's son Torquato. Bernardo's second but unfinished epic, the *Floridante*, develops one of the minor plots of the *Amadigi*.

The Florentine Luigi Alamanni (1495–1556) became in 1522 one of the leaders of an anti-Medicean conspiracy, and on its discovery was obliged to flee for his life, taking refuge in France. In 1527 he returned to Florence; but after 1530 he went again into exile. Nearly all of the rest of his life was spent at the French court. He won and retained the lavish favor of Francis I (to whom he read Dante), of Henry II, and of Henry's wife Catherine de' Medici. He was the chief representative of Italian culture in France, so well contented as to be rather an expatriate than an exile, so prosperous as to be the patron of many less fortunate displaced Italians.

In 1532 and 1533 Alamanni published a collection of his poems, containing both lyrics and poems of many other kinds. The best of the lyrics are those that express Alamanni's love for Italy and his hopes and prayers for the liberation of Florence. The most interesting metrically are a group of eight poems called "hymns," which are in fact Pindaric odes of the Trissinian type.

His prolific and versatile productivity continued throughout his life. His most substantial works are the *Coltivazione* and two epics. The *Coltivazione* is a long didactic poem in blank verse, classic in its precepts, on the care of fields and gardens. The first of the two epics, *Gyrone il cortese*, retells the old French story of *Gyron le courtois*: Gyrone is presented as the embodiment of all chivalric virtues. The later epic, the *Avarchide*, is an attempt — foredoomed to failure — to blend romantic and classic materials and procedures in an Italian *Iliad*. The subject is a siege of Bourges (Avaricum in Latin) by King Arthur; the heroes of the Trojan war reappear with Gallic names; and the "destroying wrath" is that of Lancelot.

The extremes of metrical classicism were reached by the Sienese Claudio Tolomei (1492–1555). His basic idea, like that of Leon Battista Alberti a hundred years before, was that Italian metrical usage, in which the character of the line depends upon respect for its natural verbal stresses, should be supplemented by the following of classic metrical usage, in which the character of the line depends upon varied arrangements of syllables regarded as "long" or "short." Tolomei, however, went far beyond Alberti in the development and the proclamation of his theory. In his *Versi, et regole de la nuova poesia toscana*, published in 1539, he sets forth rules for the determination of length or shortness in Italian syllables, and presents illustrative poems, composed by himself and by some of his converts, in which various classic lines and strophes are imitated.

Annibal Caro (1507–1566), born in Civitanuova (near Ancona), lived chiefly in Rome, where he served as secretary to a succession of members of the Farnese family. Rome was just the place for him: he was a thorough classicist, an archaeologist, and a collector of Roman antiquities. Most of his lyrics are Petrarchistic, finely chiseled, slight in content, and crowded with classical allusions. He is known and honored chiefly for his very successful translation of the *Aeneid* — written in retirement at the end of his life. The concision of the Latin text is replaced by a fuller fluency, which serves however to give complete clarity to Virgil's thought; the wealth and purity of the language are, to Italians, a delight; and the blank verse is handled with an artistic freedom that has never been excelled. Equally fine in quality is his prose translation of the *Daphnis and Chloe* of Longus.

Caro wrote also, about 1544, a clever prose comedy, *Gli straccioni*, "The Ragged Ones." The "ragged ones," drawn from life and bearing their true names, represent two elderly brothers, Giovanni and Battista Canali, who were familiar figures in Caro's Rome, where they were pressing a legal claim. They were inseparable; they had always the same ideas, and were given to echoing each other, with slight verbal variations; and they chose to wear shabby and ragged garments. Caro's portraiture is not unkindly; and at the end of the play the brothers win their case, and become well-dressed and generous.

For Gaspara Stampa (c. 1523–1554), Paduan by birth, Venetian by residence, life and love alike were fated to be both brief and tragic. Her joys and her griefs are expressed in her sonnets, madrigals, and elegies with an uninhibited directness that is unique in the poetry of the women of her century. Her last poems, written in despair, implore divine aid with an intense simplicity.

• • •

Shortly before and after 1530 there had been published, in convenient small octavo format, anthologies of early Italian lyric verse, under titles such as *Rime di diversi antichi autori toscani*. In 1545 the enterprising Venetian publisher Gabriele Giolito published a similar anthology of recent lyric verse, under the title *Rime diverse di molti eccellentiss. auttori nuovamente raccolte, libro primo*, in which about a hundred poets were represented, some by one or two poems only, some by several or by many poems. Among them were Bembo, Ariosto, Guidiccioni, Veronica Gambara, Vittoria Colonna, Navagero, Castiglione, Aretino, Bernardo Tasso, Alamanni, Tolomei, and Caro — also Della Casa and Doni, who are to be mentioned in the next chapter. Instantly successful, this *Libro primo* was reprinted in each of the two following years; and a *Libro secondo*, containing poems by some of the same authors and by some others, appeared in 1547. Other publishers followed suit; and by 1570 more than a score of these little volumes had appeared, in original or reprinted editions. In the earlier anthologies poetry of Bembo and his contemporaries predominated; but in the *Rime di diversi illustri signori napoletani e d'altri nobiliss. intelleti nuovamente raccolte*, published by Giolito in 1552, Tansillo and his Neapolitan companions are represented.

Foreign visitors, in these same decades, took home with them copies of these anthologies and copies of current editions of Petrarch: it was almost wholly through these editions and these anthologies that the poetry of Petrarch and the Petrarchistic Italian lyric of the sixteenth century came to the knowledge of foreign visitors. Before the end of the sixteenth century Petrarchism had become the lyric fashion in Spain, Portugal, France, England, and Dalmatia, and had made some impression in Flanders, Scotland, Hungary, Poland, and Cyprus. Later still it was to touch Germany, Bohemia, Rumania, Russia, and Latin America. In England the publication of Petrarchistic verse began with Tottel's *Miscellany* (1557), which contains the somewhat earlier poems of Wyatt and Surrey. Nearly all the sonnet sequences of the last two decades of the century — notably Sidney's *Astrophel and Stella*, Spenser's *Amoretti*, and the sequences of Watson, Daniel, Constable, and Lodge — are, in varying degrees, Petrarchistic.

CHAPTER 27

Prose of the Mid-Sixteenth Century

IN THE BORDERING FIELDS of fiction and of the drama the leading writer of the mid-century was Giambattista Giraldi (1504–1573).* Ferrarese by birth, he served in the University of Ferrara from 1532 to 1563, first as a professor of medicine and philosophy and later as a professor of the humanities. Thereafter he taught in other universities, in Piedmont and in Lombardy.

He began the writing of *novelle* in 1528, and kept on, from time to time, until 1565, when he published *Gli ecatommiti*, "The Hundred Stories"—*ecatommiti* being a coinage of Giraldi's own, based on the appropriate Greek words. The stories are told, chiefly on shipboard, by members of a company traveling from Rome to Marseilles to escape the pestilence that followed the sack of Rome, which is described in merciless detail in a long proem. An introductory group of *novelle* is followed by ten *Deche*, each containing the stories told on a single day. The stories of greatest interest are that of Oronte and Orbecche, on which Giraldi based his own most famous tragedy, and those of Disdemona and the Moor and of Iuriste and Epitia, which are the ultimate sources of *Othello* and of *Measure for Measure.*

Before the collection was published the Council of Trent had finished its work, and the shadow of ecclesiastical repression was falling more and more darkly upon all Italian effort. Giraldi accordingly prefixed to the *Ecatommiti* a Latin inscription with this meaning:

> In these *Ecatommiti* of mine, in which I have endeavored to condemn vice, to support morality, and to honor the holy authority of the Pope and the dig-

* In some of his Latin verse Giraldi called himself Cynthius; the Italian equivalent Cinzio was often prefixed or appended to his full Italian name; he was often called Il Cinzio; and to the Elizabethans he was known chiefly as Cynthio.

> nity of the Roman Church, all things, in my intention, are pious, holy, and conformable to the statutes, ordinances, decrees, and constitutions of the early Fathers and of the Supreme Pontiffs. If by chance anything contrary to such intention has escaped me (which I very much doubt, since I have taken the utmost care), let it be considered as null, void, unsaid, and completely cancelled.

In Ferrara, still the main Italian center of dramatic enthusiasm, Giraldi in 1541 wrote and produced his *Orbecche*, the first Italian tragedy actually to be performed. While he was not unmindful of Greek theory he chose to follow Senecan rather than Greek practice: the *Orbecche*, therefore, and all of his eight other tragedies, are grandiloquent and heavily sententious. Giraldi had a liking for horrors, and he interpreted Aristotle's "pity" as meaning "horror." In the *Orbecche*, accordingly, horror is piled on horror. The first four deaths take place off stage and are narrated by a messenger (played by the principal actor): the death of Orbecche takes place upon the stage. There is a divergence from precedent in Giraldi's choice of a subject taken not from history or from mythology but from one of his own *novelle*. Two of Giraldi's later tragedies have classic themes: all the others are based on *novelle* of his own. In the *Altile* and in two other plays the ending is fortunate for the potential victims, though fatal for the villains: Giraldi calls the *Altile* a *tragicommedia*.

His two *Discorsi*, written in 1543 and 1549, discuss the composition of comedies and tragedies and the composition of epics. The precepts they set forth are mainly classic, but Giraldi's most noteworthy assertions, made in the second *Discorso*, are that the writings of Italian poets are excellent; that Italian has its own proper forms of poetry; and that Italian poets should not be constrained to walk exclusively in classic paths.

The Florentine apothecary Anton Francesco Grazzini (1503–1584) wrote also in the fields both of fiction and of drama. In the Academy of the Umidi, of which he was a founder, he bore the name Il Lasca, and it is by that name that he is generally known.* Chiefly between 1540 and 1550 he wrote seven gay comedies, each in prose and in five acts, in which the Florence of his own day provides the setting, and the general temper of the action is Florentine. His modernization was deliberate: ancient writers, he says in one of his prologues, "saw their own times; but our times are of a different sort. We have different customs, a different religion, and a different manner of life; and so we should construct our comedies in a different fashion." His practice was, however, less rebellious than his theory. There is an Elizabethan translation, called *The Buggbears*, of one of his comedies, *La spiritata*, in which the heroine, to avert marriage with an undesired suitor and to win paternal consent to the marriage she desires, feigns amusingly that she is possessed of

* *Umido* means "wet." *Lasca*, "roach," is the name of a fish of the carp family.

an evil spirit. His *novella* collection, entitled *Le cene*, "The Suppers," was probably written, for the most part, after 1550. The frame-story is of the familiar type: four young men and four ladies, with their host and hostess, meet for supper on each of three successive carnival Thursdays. There is music, of course, and, by way of novelty, a merry snowball fight. Ten stories were to be told on each of the three evenings; but only about twenty are extant. Most of them are stories of trickery, told with a fresh and comic vivacity. Florentine scenes abound — streets, gates, the Arno and its bridges, shops, churches, the palace of the Medici, even the Sacristy of San Lorenzo, with its Medicean tombs.

This period, also, had its Lorenzo de' Medici (1514–1548), a member of the junior branch of the family: he was commonly called, because of his smallness, Lorenzino. He became a boon companion of Duke Alessandro; but as the months passed Alessandro revealed himself more and more unmistakably as an execrable tyrant; and in 1537 Lorenzino assassinated him. Escaping from Florence, he found refuge in Venice, then in Constantinople, then in France, and then again in Venice, where vengeance finally overtook him. Contemporary judgments of his action varied according to political alignments: adherents of the ducal regime regarded him as a murderous traitor; Florentine exiles and French sympathizers hailed him as a Tuscan Brutus. While in France, he undertook the task of setting his action before the world in the light in which he wished it to be judged, and composed accordingly his eloquent *Apologia*. He claims that his purpose was to set Florence free. Liberty is the most desirable of blessings, tyranny the most hateful of evils; Alessandro, in his dissoluteness, his avarice, and his cruelty, was a worse tyrant than Nero; tyrants are better dead, whatever the manner of their taking off. The style of the *Apologia* is as intense as the conviction that pervades it: Lorenzino writes with a driving incisiveness that is not unlike that of Machiavelli. He wrote also a few lyrics, two or three of which are of a very unusual intensity in feeling and in utterance.

* * *

Many treatises in Italian prose, on a great variety of subjects, were written in this period. About half of them are dialogues, and about half are continuous *discorsi*: the shorter discourses are in effect essays.

The most prolific writer of such treatises, and the dominant figure — a lesser Bembo — in the literary world, was Sperone Speroni (1500–1588), a learned Paduan gentleman. Among the subjects of his score of dialogues are love, the care of the family, discord, usury, languages, rhetoric, the active and the contemplative life, Xenophon, Virgil, history, and fortune. His *Dialogo sulle lingue*, written about 1540, is a strong defense of the worth and adequacy of the vernacular: it was only natural that Du Bellay should find in it a large part of the material he used presently in his manifesto, *La deffence et illustration de la langue françoyse.* Speroni's many *Discorsi* treat such subjects as soldiery, self-love, man, methods of study, calendar reform, the solitary life, printing, art and nature and God, the soul, honor, death, calumny, the emotions, the virtues, fortune, painting, sobriety, and the creation of Adam. He wrote also, in 1542, his *Canace*, a tragedy notable only because of its innovations: its choice of a mythological subject; its mingling of seven- and eleven-syllable lines, the short lines predominating; and its extensive use of what Aristotle calls *peripeteia* — change by which an action intended to produce a certain effect produces actually the opposite effect.

The most famous of the treatises of this period is the *Galateo* of the Florentine cleric Giovanni Della Casa (1503–1556). The subject of the treatise, written in the years 1551–1555, is "behavior that should be adopted or avoided in polite society." * The little book is still valuable — if not for the practical social instruction that the late Renaissance sought and found in it, at least for its comments on habits of which some are obsolete and some are not, for the pleasant ease with which most of it is written, and for its common sense, its plentiful humor, and its general amenity.

Della Casa begins by asserting that good manners, though not so laudable as liberality or constancy or magnanimity, are nevertheless a virtue, or very like a virtue, and are most important for the winning of esteem. He then launches into a detailed review of the elements of good and bad manners. He is more immediately concerned with the correction of what is bad than with the praise of what is good. At table, for instance, you should not gobble or guzzle or chew noisily or misuse your napkin or lean on the table or talk with your mouth full (and if you are the host you should *not* say to your guests: "You're not eating anything," or "Do try a little of this, or this"). In conversation you should avoid irreverence, indecency, lies, boasting, backbiting, puns, ridicule, and oversubtlety; you should not talk about your troubles, your children, or your dreams; and you should not laugh at your own jokes. If you set out to tell a story, this is *not* the way to begin:

> So-and-So, who was the son of So-and-So, who used to live on Watermelon Street — you knew him, didn't you? — he married that Gianfigliazzi girl — the scrawny one, who used to go to mass in San Lorenzo — what, you didn't? — you must have known him — that goodly upstanding old man who used to wear his hair long — don't you remember him?

Forms and ceremonies, really unnecessary and chiefly of foreign importation, have indeed established themselves, but should not be overdone. In company, don't cough, sneeze, blow your nose noisily, whistle, breathe in people's

* The word *Galateo* is fashioned from the name of Della Casa's friend Galeazzo Florimonte.

faces, nudge the people you are talking to, or sing if you have no voice; and when others are talking don't walk around the room or read letters or trim your fingernails or drum on the table or hum or turn your back or go to sleep. Don't engage in drinking contests (a pernicious foreign innovation); don't tie your stockings or comb your hair in public; don't wear a toothpick on a chain; don't rub your hands; don't appear in a nightcap. In general, conform to local customs in dress and in other respects, be neat, be considerate, don't keep people waiting, don't try to get the best of everything, don't be proud, don't contradict, don't find fault, don't be gloomy, speak pleasantly, talk clearly, and not too little or too much.

The *Galateo* won immediate and enormous popularity. Some fifty translations exist, in French, Spanish, English, German, and Latin. In the first English translation, by Robert Peterson, published in 1576, the title runs thus: *Galateo of Maister John Della Casa, Archebishop of Benevento. Or rather, A Treatise of the Manners and Behaviours, it behoveth a Man to use and eschewe, in his Familiar Conversation. A Worke very necessary & profitable for all Gentlemen, or Other.*

Della Casa wrote also many poems, some in Italian and some in Latin. The octave of his best-known sonnet, a sleepless man's invocation to sleep, reads, in translation, thus:

> Oh Sleep, oh placid son of quiet, dewy, shadowy Night, oh comfort of weary mortals, sweet oblivion of the weight of ill that makes life hard and grievous: bring succor to this heart that languishes and finds no rest, and relief to these frail and tired limbs! Come swiftly, Sleep, spread your dark wings, and hover over me!

In 1548 Luigi Cornaro (1467–1566; mentioned in an earlier chapter as the patron of Ruzzante), being then eighty-one years of age, wrote the first of his four *Discorsi della vita sobria*: the second was written five years later; the third five years after the second; and the fourth at the age of ninety-five. In his youth Cornaro had impaired his naturally weak constitution by intemperance. When he was just over thirty-five, tortured in body and sunk in melancholy, he was assured that he could not live unless he mended his ways immediately and completely. Thereafter he led the regular and abstemious life which, for the benefit of others, he describes in his *Discorsi*, even in dietary detail. He was never ill; he was very active; his senses remained perfect; his voice grew stronger and more melodious; his memory never failed; he gained in clarity of judgment; and he was always sure that the best was yet to be. There are many, he says, who can bear witness to the happiness of his life:

> And they will bear such witness, first, because they see . . . the prosperous state of my health; how I mount my horse without any help; and how I can climb not merely a flight of stairs but an entire hill, on foot, and vigorously.

> And then, how cheerful I am, how good-humored, and content, and free from perturbations of the mind, and from all troublous thoughts: instead of which joy and peace dwell ever in my heart, never departing thence. Moreover, they know how I spend my time, so that I never weary of life through being unable to spend it constantly with the highest delight and pleasure; for I have occasion very often to converse with many honored gentlemen, noble in intellect and courtesy and learning and in every kind of excellence. And when I lack their company I devote myself to the reading of some good book; and when I have read enough, I write, endeavoring thus, and in every other possible way, to be of some benefit to others . . . I never knew the beauty of the world till I grew old.

He was confident that death, when it came, would come to him peacefully — as it did come to him, at the age of ninety-nine.

His treatise has found admirers and translators in many lands. Addison says of the *Discorsi*:

> The Treatise I mention has been taken Notice of by several Eminent Authors, and is written with such a Spirit of Cheerfulness, Religion, and Good Sense, as are the natural Concomitants of Temperance and Sobriety.

The first English version was made by George Herbert. More than a hundred editions of this or of later versions have been published in England: and many have appeared in this country, the first in 1788.

Giambattista Gelli (1498–1563) was a Florentine shoemaker and an amateur moral philosopher. He thought it most unfortunate that there should be so great a difference between the large store of knowledge possessed by the learned and the small store possessed by common folk; and he did his best to make available to his fellow artisans what seemed to him to be important in the learned writings, ancient or modern, with which he had gained familiarity. The earlier of his two treatises, *I capricci del bottaio*, "The Fancies of the Cooper," published in 1546, consists of ten soliloquies, which discuss such matters as health, old age, the fear of death, and immortality, and attack the learned for their pride and their desire to hold their knowledge as a possession of their own caste. Learning does not ensure moral excellence:

> When learning finds a man who is wise and good it makes him wiser and better, and when it finds a man who is foolish and bad it makes him more foolish and worse.

Gelli's second treatise, the *Circe*, published in 1549, consists of ten dialogues in which the interlocutors are Ulysses, Circe, and eleven Greeks whom Circe has transformed into animals: an oyster, a mole, a serpent, a hare, a goat, a hind, a lion, a horse, a dog, a calf, and an elephant. Circe promises to restore the eleven to human shape if they so desire; Ulysses urges upon them, one by one, the unique prerogatives of man, who alone can attain true felicity; the first ten prefer to remain as animals rather than to resume the miseries of human life; the elephant (who had once been a philosopher) is persuaded, and celebrates his rehumanization in a Ficinian hymn of praise to the Creator. Both treatises received English translations before 1570.

Among Gelli's other writings are two comedies, twenty short lives of Florentine artists (the longest and the best is a life of Michelangelo), and several lectures, given in the Florentine Academy, on Dante and on Petrarch.

The Florentine Anton Francesco Doni (1513–1574), an unfrocked priest, restless, bizarre, and quarrelsome, earned a hand-to-mouth living as a literary hack, toiling in Florence, in Venice, and in other cities. Of all the numerous books he published in a variety of literary forms, the two that are best remembered are *I marmi*, "The Marble Steps," and *I mondi*, "The Worlds." The steps, those of the Cathedral of Florence, are the supposed scene of a long series of conversations, in which, from time to time, about a hundred different interlocutors take part. Their amusing talk rambles freely, delighting in fantastic ideas (the earth revolves!), among the arts, the troubles, and the foibles of mankind. Several *novelle* and several poems appear within the conversations. The other treatise, also in dialogue form, describes seven imaginary *mondi* and seven imaginary *inferni*. The sixth *mondo*, called alternately *mondo pazzo* and *mondo savio*, "the mad world" and "the wise world," is a utopia which in a general way echoes that of Sir Thomas More: it is presumably the first instance of an Italian work influenced by an English work.

* * *

The first treatise in Italian on the art of poetry — the first, and one of the best, in a long series of such treatises — is *La poetica* of Bernardino Daniello of Lucca (?–1565), published in 1536. It is a dialogue set in a connecting narrative. In the first of its two Books, after an introductory assertion that both genius and training are necessary for the poet, the chief speaker states that poetry is a kind of imitation of nature and that the poet should provide both instruction and pleasure, and then discusses at length the first two of the three essential poetic procedures, namely invention (the choice of a theme) and disposition (the ordering of the material). The second Book is devoted to consideration of the third essential poetic procedure, elocution (linguistic and stylistic artistry), with extensive discussion of words, figures of speech, and rhythm and rhyme. The whole treatise is richly illustrated with quotations from Petrarch and from Dante.

In 1548 Francesco Robortelli (1516–1567) published an improved edition of the Greek text of the *Poetics*, accompanied by his own Latin translation and a learned Latin commentary, cautious and well-reasoned; and in 1549

Bernardo Segni (1504–1558; also an historian) published an annotated Italian translation, with a brief commentary. Other editions and commentaries followed presently, together with several treatises, in Italian or in Latin, on the art of poetry. Of the treatises published before 1570 the most elaborate were the two written by Antonio Minturno (c. 1500–1574), Bishop of Ugento: his Latin *De poeta*, in six Books (1559), and his somewhat shorter Italian *Arte poetica* (1563). In the earlier treatise Minturno maintains that a poet should be free from laws and restraints, and should be true to his own nature. In the later treatise, while much of the detail remains unchanged, Minturno, now greatly influenced by the Counter Reformation and converted to Aristotelianism, thinks and writes in terms of moral purpose and of Aristotelian precept; condemns, in particular, the Italian romantic epic as a non-heroic poetic form; and asserts with a pontifical dogmatism the permanence and the universality of the basic Aristotelian principles. Minturno's treatises were widely known, and left their impress upon the thought of Torquato Tasso, of Ronsard, and of Sir Philip Sidney, who studied the *De poeta* carefully, made use of it in his *Apologie for Poetrie*, and was influenced by it in the writing of his *Arcadia*.

Giulio Cesare Scaligero (1484–1558) spent his youth in Northern Italy as a soldier and a student, especially as a student of medicine. In 1525 he went, as a physician, to France, where, turning presently from medicine to literature, he remained for the rest of his life. He wrote always in Latin, under the name Scaliger. His *Poetices*, published three years after his death, is an unsystematic manual written for the use of prospective Latin poets. It reviews ancient and recent poetic theories; but it presents no unified theory of its own. Scaliger is among the moralists: the end of poetry, for him, is the creation of good impulses which, in their turn, will produce good actions.

The most acute of all the treatises of the period on the art of poetry is the voluminous commentary on the *Poetics* by Ludovico Castelvetro (1505–1571) of Modena, published, with the Greek text and an Italian translation, in 1570. Castelvetro was an able scholar, and did his own thinking. He was, however, one of the most contradictious of men: he had no respect for the opinions of his contemporaries, and frequently pointed out their errors. His disagreement with received opinions of the Church brought him a summons from the Inquisition: rather than face that tribunal he fled to Switzerland, where his last years were spent. His interpretation of Aristotle is more penetrating than that of any of his predecessors; but his emphases and some of his deductions are his own. Earlier theorists had in general failed to make any distinction between the art of poetry and the art of rhetoric: that distinction is clear in Castelvetro. Earlier theorists had maintained that poetry has two functions, to give pleasure and to give moral instruction — a doctrine based on Horace, and reënforced, as regards the moral function, by the pressures of the Counter Reformation. Castelvetro maintains, on the contrary, that the single function of poetry is to give pleasure, and that the provision of instruction is none of its proper business: any utility that may spring from poetry is merely incidental. The range of auditors, moreover, to whom poetry should purvey its pleasure is not limited, as earlier theorists had generally assumed, to persons of cultivation, but includes "the crude multitude." There is nothing mysterious about the poetic art: the idea that poets are possessed with a divine fury is nonsense: it originated in ignorant admiration, and has been fostered, for selfish reasons, by poets themselves. But though Castelvetro was capable of liberalizing ideas such as these, he was capable also of trivialities, and of pronouncements which, however logical in their derivation, were in effect restrictive. It was he who first, in a concise and authoritative formula, consecrated the unities of time and place:

> La mutatione tragica non puo tirar con esso seco se non vna giornata e vn luogo —
>
> The tragic process cannot cover more than one day and one place.

He was indeed so much concerned with these two minor unities that he regarded the major unity of action as being relatively unimportant. With all his limitations, he wins from H. B. Charlton the verdict that "he is the most illuminating critic of the art of poetry between Longinus and Dryden."

* * *

Of all the writings of this period the two that are best known outside of Italy are Vasari's "Lives of the Painters" and the autobiography of Benvenuto Cellini.

Giorgio Vasari (1511–1574), of Arezzo, was an industrious painter and architect, well esteemed in his own day, who worked in many cities, but chiefly in Florence and in Rome. His most popular painting, of which many copies were made, was one representing a group of six poets: Dante, Petrarch, Guido Cavalcanti, Boccaccio, Cino da Pistoia, and Guittone d' Arezzo.

In the course of a conversation that took place in a cardinal's palace in Rome in 1542 or 1543 — Giovio, Tolomei, Caro, and Vasari himself being among the guests — Giovio said that he had always wanted to write a treatise about Italian artists from Cimabue on, and sketched, with many inaccuracies, what he had in mind. Vasari, asked by the cardinal what he thought of the idea, approved it heartily — provided someone who knew about art should help Giovio. The cardinal and Giovio and the rest then requested Vasari to prepare an outline. This he did; but Giovio, when he saw it, urged Vasari himself to write the book, and after some persuasion he agreed to do so. This was the origin of *Le vite de' più eccellenti pittori, scultori e architettori*, published first in 1550, and again, in a revised and enlarged edition, in 1568.

The book contains some two hundred biographies, grouped in three Parts, which correspond to the three stages in the development of Italian art as Vasari saw it: the stage of childhood (roughly, the late thirteenth century and the fourteenth); the stage of vigorous youth (roughly, the fifteenth century); and the stage of modern perfection (roughly, the sixteenth century). Michelangelo, to whom the longest of all the *Vite* is devoted, is, for Vasari, the supreme artist.

The series of biographies is preceded by a substantial treatise on architecture, sculpture, and painting, which are here grouped, for the first time, as *le arti del disegno*, "the arts of design," and by a general preface to the Lives themselves. In the course of this preface Vasari compares the rise and fall of ancient art to a process of birth, growth, aging, and death, and with reference to Italian art expresses the hope that those who read his Lives

> potranno ora più facilmente conoscere il progresso della sua rinascita —
>
> may be able now more easily to understand the process of its rebirth.

A similar phrase, *dalla rinascita di queste arti sino al secolo che noi viviamo*, "from the rebirth of these arts to the century in which we are living," occurs in the special preface to the second Part; and at the end of that preface the art of painting is said to have received from Masaccio *la sua nuova rinascita*, "its new rebirth." The metaphor of rebirth had been used earlier in a variety of applications: these are the first instances of its use with reference to the *renaissance* of the arts.

Vasari is often mistaken in his facts; but the wonder is that such a pioneering work should have come as close to accuracy as it did. He is usually sound in his critical appraisals, except in his overestimation of some contemporary work (including his own). He writes with an appealing enthusiasm, in a style that varies from a rather heavy formalism to a very attractive conversational informality. His artists are to him living individuals, and he succeeds in making them live for his readers. He is fond of anecdoes; and portions of some of the biographies have the tang — and at times the quoted dialogue — of good *novelle*. Such, for instance, are his accounts of Giotto's drawing of the perfect ○; of the rivalry of Brunelleschi and Ghiberti with regard to the construction of the dome of the Florentine cathedral; and of Leonardo's decoration of a peasant's shield.

Benvenuto Cellini (1500–1571), the most famous of goldsmiths and of autobiographers, was born and grew up in Florence. His father persisted in trying to make him a musician; but Benvenuto had no liking for music, and was not long in setting himself to learn the goldsmith's craft, in which he advanced so swiftly that after he went to Rome in 1523 his extraordinary skill was soon recognized, and he won the favor and the patronage of Clement VII. During the sack of Rome in 1527 he took part, as a bombardier, in the defense of the Castel Sant' Angelo. His whole life was stormy, despite his constant artistic successes, partly because of the jealousies of other artists, but chiefly because of his own unbridled speech and his frequent recourse to violence. Again and again he left Rome, more than once in flight, and again and again he returned. In 1538 he was imprisoned, on a false charge, in the Castel Sant' Angelo. When he was released, a year later, through the intercession of Francis I, he went to Paris, where the king proved to be a very generous patron. Even so, however, troubles pursued him; and in 1545 he returned to Florence, entering the ungrateful service of Duke Cosimo, for whom, turning often now to sculpture, he did much of his latest work.

Of all his goldsmithery only a single surely authentic piece remains, the large salt and pepper stand of gold that he made for Francis I: figures of the Sea and the Land, the Sea holding a ship for the salt and the Land a temple for the pepper, are seated somewhat precariously upon creatures of the sea and of the land respectively, the whole resting upon an elaborate base. Cellini's most famous statue, the theatrical Perseus in the Loggia dei Lanzi in Florence, is essentially a work of goldsmithery in the large.

At the age of fifty-eight, Benvenuto made up his mind to write the story of his life, and started to do so; but the writing took too much time from his work. Fortunately, he found a boy to whom, while working, he could dictate. His *Vita*, accordingly, has the character not of a formal composition, but of a story told, and told with the uninhibited forthrightness of an untutored Florentine genius. He had a natural gift for narration, and he had a great story to tell.

So he talks, with a constant seasoning of amusing boastfulness, of his Florentine childhood; of his flute-playing; of life and work in Rome as a papal favorite; of merrymaking and jealousies among the thronging artists; of ancient treasures brought to light in excavations; of the sack of Rome; of quarrels and killings and escapes and pardons and returns; of necromancy; of adventurous journeys; of long imprisonment; of pieties and of visions; and of the many vicissitudes of his years in France and his final years in Florence. The most famous chapters are those that tell of his prowess during the siege and sack of Rome; of his attempt to escape from imprisonment in the Castel Sant' Angelo; and of the successful casting of the Perseus, under extraordinary and exciting difficulties. The narrative is rich in memories of all sorts of men and women, among them priests and cardinals and popes, a king who called him *mon ami*, a rascally friar who read him sermons by

Savonarola, a friendly jailer who thought himself a bat, and an extraordinary assortment of artists, soldiers, brigands, and knaves. But the central figure is always Benvenuto himself, tireless, fearless, shameless, ingenious, choleric, vindictive, superstitious, a little crackbrained, and always an enthusiast for the art in which he knew his own supremacy.

CHAPTER 28

The Pastoral Play and the Commedia dell'arte

SEVERAL OF THE WRITERS mentioned in the two preceding chapters wrote comedies or tragedies in addition to their non-dramatic works. The Florentine notary Giovanni Maria Cecchi (1518–1587) may fairly be called the first Italian playwright, in the sense that he was the first Italian writer whose literary activity was busily and almost exclusively dramatic. He wrote about twenty regular comedies, the earlier ones quite in the spirit of his Italian predecessors, the later ones restrained by the influence of the Counter Reformation. Some are free adaptations from Plautus and Terence; some are based on *novelle*; and some reflect current Florentine incidents. They were written swiftly: no one of them, he says, took him more than ten days. They are overly complex, but lively in action and in dialogue. He wrote also many "farces" — shorter plays, which are not bound by the usual dramatic conventions, and may be either comic or moralizing in purpose; various minor dramatic pieces; and, in his later years, some fifteen religious plays.

* * *

The pastoral theme, dear to poets and romancers and sophisticated listeners in many lands and in many ages, has been cherished most of all in Italy — Virgil's country. Many uses of the theme have been mentioned in earlier chapters. The humanistic eclogues are pastoral; Boccaccio's *Ameto* is in part pastoral; Lorenzo's *Corinto* is the loveliest of Italian pastoral idylls; there are pastoral elements in the *Orfeo* of Politian; the *Nencia da Barberino*, in its own unique way, is pastoral; Sannazzaro's *Arcadia* gave to the pastoral theme a greater vogue than it had had since classic times; Boiardo, Castiglione, and many others wrote eclogues; and the pastoral theme was finding new media in the lyrics of Tansillo, Bernardo Tasso, and Tolomei. Meanwhile tragedy, still novel, had adopted a five-act form, and was being written in blank verse — sometimes in long lines only, sometimes in a mixture of long and short lines — with choral songs between the acts; and Giraldi was writing "tragedies" with happy endings.

Under all these circumstances it was virtually inevitable that there should come into existence, taking its place beside tragedy and comedy, a third major dramatic form, the pastoral drama: and it is not surprising that the new form should have made its first appearance in Ferrara. The first pastoral drama, the *Sacrificio* of the Ferrarese Agostino Beccari (? – 1590), was acted before Duke Ercole II in 1554. Its plot interweaves three stories of pastoral love, which end happily, and it is light in spirit. It is in five acts, and in blank eleven-syllable verse, with interspersed songs. Undistinguished in itself, it served to suggest the form of later and more successful pastoral plays.

* * *

By the middle of the century the multiplication of performances of comedies had brought with it, as a natural consequence, the rise of acting as a profession, and the formation of regular companies of professional actors. The earliest date for which the existence of such a company is definitely attested is February 15, 1545: on that day, in Padua, eight men contracted to give comedies under the management of one Maphio dei Re. They are to work together in fraternal love; they must obey Maphio, going wherever he bids them go; their savings are to be kept in a common chest, the three keys of which are to be held by three different men; they are to be supported if they are ill and brought to justice if they desert; they are to buy a horse to carry their luggage; and they are not to gamble, except for food. The most famous of the early companies, the *Gelosi*, appears first in Milan in 1568: their name, "The Jealous Ones," reflects their claim to skill, fame, and honor. The membership of these early companies was made up largely of men and women who had been popular entertainers. Their repertoire consisted mainly, at first, of recently written comedies (occasionally they gave tragedies or tragicomedies); but they developed almost at once a dramatic type of their own, known as the *commedia dell'arte*, "the comedy of the profession," which quickly became more popular than formal comedy. Its two distinguishing characteristics were, first, the fact that plays of this sort were not written out, but were improvised upon the basis of an outline, and, second, the fact that most of the characters were stock characters, some of them masked.

Before each performance of a comedy of this type the manager decided upon a plot, new or old. If the plot was new, he prepared an outline of it: such outlines came to be known as *scenari*. Each outline was divided into as many acts and scenes as the play was to have, and indicated very briefly what the general course of the action in each scene was to be; but it did not give the actual words that were to be spoken. When the outline was ready, the manager read and explained it to his company, and then either distributed copies of it or posted one or two copies where the actors could see and study them. If the plot was old, all he had to do was to review an old outline with his actors, and distribute or post copies. None of the earliest *scenari* have come down to us; but they were certainly of the same character as the several hundred later *scenari* that are extant, and bits of such later *scenari* may safely be regarded as typical of the earlier ones. *La vedova costante*, "The Faithful Widow," opens, for instance, with a scene for which the *scenario* reads simply thus:

> Isabella dalla finestra fa scena amorosa con Orazio; viene a basso, si danno la mano di sposi e partono.*

Isabella's father, a widower, has a friend, also a widower, who also has a daughter. The two men meet in Scene III, for which the *scenario* reads simply:

> Fanno scena d' amicizia; dopo discorrono di accasar la lor figliola; risolvono pigliarne una per uno; si danno la parola; e allegri partono.†

Each *scenario* ends or begins with a list of the necessary stage properties. *La bellissima commedia in tre persone* ends with this list:

> Un bambino.
> Carta e calamaio da portare in tasca.
> Un stiletto.
> Una chitarra.‡

Among the properties listed in various other *scenari* are beards, clothes and headgear of every description, necklaces, bracelets, rings, flasks, cabbages, plates of macaroni, sacks, moneybags, chests, medicines, dentists' tongs, packs of cards, wands, cardboard horses, lanterns, torches, ladders, swords, daggers, blunderbusses, cudgels, and stones to throw.

Most of the *dramatis personae* of the *commedia dell'arte* are stock characters who reappear in play after play with the same traits and the same costumes: in some cases even the names are constant or fairly constant.

* "Isabella from her window has a love scene with Horace; she comes down, they promise to marry, and *exeunt*."

† "They have a friendship scene; they talk about marrying off their daughters; they decide each to marry the other's daughter; they pledge themselves to do so, and *exeunt* in good humor."

‡ "A baby; paper and an inkhorn that can be carried in a pocket; a stiletto; a guitar."

The basic stock characters, at the start, were lover, lady, manservant, maidservant, Pantalone, the Doctor, and the braggart captain. The manservant and Pantalone wore masks, and the Doctor wore a partial mask; the others were not masked. Lover, lady, and maidservant dressed in ordinary costumes of the day, the others in stock costumes specific to their parts.*

The lover does not differ greatly from the lover of written comedy. He is well-dressed, and speaks in a supposedly correct Tuscan, often flowery in its style. He is often a student, and is usually short of funds.

In written comedy the lady had played a rather small part: she seldom appeared on the stage, and her hopes and fears were generally reported by her maidservant. In the *commedia dell'arte*, however, the leading lady — who also speaks in Tuscan — is released from tradition. She is as much on the stage as anyone else; and her newly found freedom expresses itself in energetic activity — not always dignified.

The maidservant, as a result of her mistress's promotion, had at first a diminished importance; but she soon became an appropriate opposite number for the manservant, rivalling him in wit and in resourcefulness.

The manservant has the stock name Zanni, a Northern Italian dialectal form of Gianni, itself an abbreviation for Giovanni. The word could be used also as plural, and was sometimes applied to a whole troupe of comedians. Zanni's characteristics are derived from three very different sources: the slaves of classic comedy, as continued in the servants of written Italian comedy; the mountebanks; and the hulking porters from Bergamo and thereabouts who did much of the heavy outdoor work in Venice and in other Northern Italian cities. Zanni speaks, in the early comedies, in the dialect of Bergamo, and his original costume is that of the Bergomask porters — a loose blouse and hood and wide trousers, all made of sacking. He wears a black mask, and a short sword-like stick. He fetches and carries, eats ravenously, and lies, bribes, extorts, and intrigues, on his master's account or on his own, with an endless and shameless resourcefulness. Continuing the *lazzi* — the antics — of the mountebanks, he jests, sings, dances, performs acrobatic feats, plays practical jokes, tumbles down, engages in mock fights, drubs and is drubbed, and indulges in all the usual devices of slapstick comedy.

Pantalone,† sometimes called *Il Magnifico*, is a lean and elderly Venetian merchant, and speaks in the Venetian dialect. He wears a red doublet and hose, a long black cloak, a little woolen cap, and Turkish slippers. He is usually well-to-do, and avaricious. He is a great talker; but for all his inquisitiveness and his commonplace bourgeois wisdom he is very gullible,

*The following descriptions rest in part upon evidence which, while of certain validity only for a later period, is in all probability valid for this period also.

† The origin of the name is unknown.

and is usually made ridiculous in the course of the play — often as the result of a foolish love affair.

The elderly Doctor, commonly named Graziano, hails from Bologna. He is usually a lawyer, sometimes a pedant, sometimes a doctor of medicine. He dresses in black, and wears a doctoral robe, a big ruff, and a skull cap. A partial mask comes down over his nose. He may speak — with a plentiful admixture of erratic Latin — in Bolognese, or in some other Northern Italian dialect, or in Tuscan. He pretends to know a great deal, but is actually absurdly ignorant. Like Pantalone, he is usually made ridiculous in the course of the play.

The braggart captain, a familiar figure in Latin comedy, was familiar also in Italian written comedy — and in contemporary Italian life. He was sometimes a Spaniard and sometimes a Frenchman (it was not always safe to make fun of Spaniards). If he was a Spaniard, he might speak in Spanish. He tells extraordinary tales of his deeds of valor; but he runs off at the first sign of a fight. He is often a parasite, ready to do anything for the sake of a dinner. He thinks himself irresistible to the ladies.

To the actor the *commedia dell'arte* brought some special facilities and some special difficulties. It involved little or no strain on the memory, and it did not necessitate individualized characterization. But the improvisation of the dialogue and the details of the action, even though phrases and stage business could be repeated to some extent, called for an extremely quick and inventive wit — a type of wit in which most of the early actors had had much practice in their days as popular entertainers. To the spectator, also, this kind of comedy brought some loss and some gain: there could be no beauty or grace in the wording of the play, and no real portrayal of character; but the acting was likely to be natural and vivacious, and elements of exciting surprise might always vary the pleasantly familiar pattern.

The *commedia dell'arte* was to continue to be the favorite form of dramatic entertainment in Italy for two hundred years. Its development and its foreign influence will be treated in later chapters.

CHAPTER 29

Torquato Tasso

THE LAST DECADES of the century were distressful with Spanish misgovernment and exploitation, with religious intolerance and persecution, with increasing brigandage, and with famine and pestilence. The Turks were pressing forward by sea and by land, and captured Cyprus in 1571. Within the same year Venice and her allies were victorious off Lepanto, in the lower Adriatic; but the possible fruits of victory were lost through jealousies. In the land fighting, which continued, in Hungary, to the end of the century, Italy was not directly involved; but the Turkish menace still troubled Italian consciousness.

The magnificent compositions of Palestrina — masses, motets, offertories, litanies, hymns, Lamentations, Magnificats, and madrigals — were pouring forth in a marvelous profusion.

The Calabrian Bernardino Telesio — whom Francis Bacon called "the first of the new men" — began in 1565 and finished in 1586 the publication of his *De rerum natura*, in which, rejecting the domination of Aristotle, he dares to maintain that philosophy should be based not upon ratiocination but upon observation: *non ratione, sed sensu.* His doctrines aroused bitter opposition, and the *De rerum natura* was soon placed on the Index.

In literature this period was in general one of exhaustion: to the inhibiting political and religious pressures there was added the pressure of Aristotelian authoritarianism. Two men only, Tasso, who conformed, and Bruno, who rebelled, reached greatness. The learned and still active Accademia della Crusca was established in Florence in 1583.*

Montaigne, the most distinguished of the foreign visitors, kept a detailed and very interesting journal of his travels in Italy in 1580 and 1581: from this journal, some of it written in a very passable Italian, he was to draw much material for his later essays.

* *Crusca* means "bran": the Academy is then the Academy of the Sifters.

This period, which corresponds closely to the reign of Queen Elizabeth I (1558–1603), witnessed the culmination of Italian influence in England, not only in literature but in many other respects as well. Particular literary influences stemmed both from writings of earlier periods and from contemporary writings. Such works as those of Machiavelli and Castiglione influenced deeply not only English literature but English political and cultural life. Hundreds of translations from the Italian were made. A good many books were published in Italian by English printers. Italian music and musicians were very popular: several collections of Italian madrigals were published in England. Italian fashions were copied, Italian manners imitated, Italian goods bought, Italian medicines taken. Italian influence appeared to some extent in architecture, and more generally in garden design. The Italian language was much studied and much used: the Queen wrote and spoke Italian, and liked to hear it spoken by her courtiers, and by envoys from other lands.

* * *

Torquato, the son of Bernardo Tasso, was born in Sorrento in 1544. In his early boyhood he attended a Jesuit school in Naples; and a little later he engaged in Greek and Latin studies under his father's direction. Still another type of education came to him presently in Urbino, where he shared the instruction given to the Duke's young son in courtly customs and in knightly skills. In the autumn of 1560 his father sent him to the University of Padua, where, after a year spent in the reluctant study of law, he entered eagerly upon the study of philosophy and eloquence. He was much with Speroni, who gave him friendly literary counsel. In Padua he began the frequent writing of lyrics; and there too he wrote his first substantial poem, the *Rinaldo*, which he published in 1562, being then eighteen years old.

The *Rinaldo* is a romantic epic in octaves, in twelve cantos. The single hero, Rinaldo (Orlando's cousin), leaves his home in search of glory; sees Clarice, sister of the King of Gascony, falls in love with her, and resolves to win her by proving his prowess; has a long series of adventures on land and sea; and at length rescues Clarice from a Saracen captor and marries her. Essentially juvenile, the *Rinaldo* has little interest in itself; but it is noteworthy not only as an evidence of Tasso's precocity but also for its anticipation of some of the features of the masterpiece that was to come. In the earlier as in the later epic Tasso is concerned equally with knightly prowess and with love; and he displays a fertile imagination, predisposed to find its resources in the world of magic. He proves himself also to be skillful in description and in the handling of the octave; and he discards the irrelevant stanzas with which earlier writers of epics had introduced individual cantos.

The preface that accompanies the *Rinaldo* reveals both a fear of adverse criticism — a fear that was to pursue Tasso pitilessly all his life — and a really remarkable thoughtfulness as to the general structure of his poem. He will not follow those who insist on being completely Aristotelian: he will however observe those precepts of Aristotle that do not hinder the giving of pleasure. He will hold his poem to the unity that comes from having a single hero and, in a general sense, a single action; but he will endue that single action with plentiful elements of variety.

In 1565, on the completion of his university studies, Tasso entered the service of Cardinal Luigi d' Este, and went accordingly to Ferrara, where he was to live — though with many absences — for most of the rest of his life. In 1572 he passed from the service of the Cardinal to that of the Duke, Alfonso II.

The idea of writing an epic which should have as its subject the liberation of Jerusalem seems to have come to Tasso in his boyhood and never to have left him: he was certainly working on such an epic during his first years in Ferrara. But he took his theme and his art very seriously, and was much more concerned with the achievement of perfection than with the early fulfillment of his plan. The poem must be his own: yet it must conform in spirit to its high religious theme, and it must be a truly heroic epic, obedient to the canons of literary theory in so far as those canons were surely sound. His own evaluation of those canons is to be found in his *Discorsi dell'arte poetica, et in particolare del poema heroico*, written, apparently, in the years 1567–1570.

The first of the three *Discorsi* deals with the epic poet's choice of his theme. It is assumed that the poem must be both verisimilar and marvelous. For the sake of verisimilitude, the theme must be taken from history. For the sake of marvelousness, the theme must be taken from Christian, not from Pagan, history. The marvels of pagan history are ruled out on the ground that pagan religion is itself unveracious; but since the Christian religion is veracious the poet may rightly make use of marvels proceeding from actions of God, of angels, of demons, of saints, of enchanters, and of enchantresses. The Christian religion, also, surpasses pagan religion in the majesty of its supernal and infernal councils, its prophecies, and its ceremonies; the perfect knight must possess Christian zeal; and the consideration of a Christian theme is of benefit to the reader. The Christian theme chosen for the poem must be not one that is an unalterable object of faith, but one that allows the poet some freedom of invention. It must be neither too ancient nor too modern. The action set forth must be noble and illustrious in itself, and of great significance in national or imperial history or in the advancement of the Faith.

The second *Discorso* is concerned with the general character of the poem. It must have unity of action, but that unity may be either simple or composite: composite unity is that in which, while there are many elements, they are so carefully interrelated that each is necessary to the perfection of the whole. Thus, while such multiple actions as those of the *Orlando furioso* violate the principle of unity, it is possible for a poet to make use of a similar variety of elements, provided they are firmly interwoven. Just as the world itself manifests variety in unity, so there may be fashioned a truly unified poem in which one may find, as in a little world,

> dispositions of armies, battles on land and sea, stormings of cities, skirmishes and duels, tournaments, descriptions of famine and of drought, tempests, conflagrations, prodigies, celestial and infernal councils, seditions, discords, wanderings, adventures, enchantments, deeds of cruelty, of daring, of courtesy, and of generosity, and loves requited or unrequited, now happy and now sad.

The third *Discorso* is a detailed treatment of style.

In 1573 Tasso turned aside from his main task to write the most perfect of pastoral plays, the *Aminta.** In form it follows the *Sacrificio* of Beccari, though with some variations. It is in five brief acts, and has a chorus (of shepherds) which sings at the end of each act, and takes part in some of the scenes. The plot is of the simplest. The shepherd Aminta loves, unrequited, his former playmate Silvia, who is absorbed in the pleasures of the hunt. Proofs of his devotion are of no avail. Finally, hearing that Silvia has lost her life in the chase, he throws himself over a precipice. Silvia, returning safe and sound, hears what he has done, and is moved to pity, love and remorse. She goes to seek his body, and finds him alive instead, bruised and unconscious, but not seriously hurt; and all ends happily. Among the minor characters are the shepherd Tirsi, friend of Aminta; Dafne, an older confidante of Silvia; Nerina, a companion of Silvia; and a satyr, from whom Silvia is rescued by Aminta. Something of the spirit of the play may be seen in this passage, in which Dafne is speaking to Tirsi:

Nor am I sure
That Silvia is as simple as she seems
In word and deed. For only yesterday
I came upon her, where the meadows lie,
Bending above a clear and tranquil pool,
As if to see how beautiful she was,
And how she best might gather o'er her brow
Her lovely hair, and how adorn her hair
With filmy veil, and how bedeck her veil
With flowers she had gathered. And anon
She 'd take a lily or a deep red rose
And hold it to the whiteness of her neck
Or to her rosy cheek, as if to make
Comparison of their hues. Then she would flash

* Usually Englished as Amyntas or Amintas.

A smile that seemed to say: "I vanquish you;
And I shall wear you not for my adorning,
But solely to your shame, that you may find
How far you are outshone." As she was thus
Adorning and admiring, she by chance
Looked where I stood; and, finding I had seen,
Blushed and arose, and let her flowers fall.
I laughed to see her blush; she blushed the more
To hear me laugh; and yet, having her locks
But partly gathered up, with furtive glance
She sought the pool again — until, afraid
That I espied her spyings, she was pleased
To leave her hair unbound, and was content
To see herself so fair, though unadorned.

The *Aminta* holds to the pleasant middle ground between tragedy and comedy. The unified action moves naturally; Aminta and Silvia, personal within the pastoral convention, win sympathy; there are moments of sorrow that one knows cannot be final; sweetness prevails. The style is limpid and yet most carefully wrought; and the whole play glows with poetry. Its artistic affiliations are with music rather than with visual art. The body of the play is written in blank verse in which eleven- and seven-syllable lines are mingled: the longer and more dignified line is the more frequent, the shorter line being used chiefly for certain quasi-lyrical effects. One of the choral songs presents a new lyric form, known later as the *canzone libera*, the "free *canzone*": it has no formal stanzaic structure; eleven- and seven-syllable lines follow each other in free succession, responding to the poet's immediate impulses; and rhymed and unrhymed lines are mingled freely.

The *Aminta* was first performed, in a sylvan pleasure-place of the Este, in the summer of 1573, by the Gelosi, playing under the direction of Tasso himself. Many other performances followed, and many imitative pastoral plays were written. It was soon translated into French, English, and other languages; and its influence — reënforced by that of Guarini's *Pastor fido* (which is to be considered in Chapter 31) — led to the writing of several English pastoral poems and plays. Among later Italian poets the one who owed most to the *Aminta* was Leopardi, who derived from it his own form of the *canzone libera*, and the two musical names Silvia and Nerina. Delibes's ballet *Sylvia*, first performed in 1876, is still calling forth new choreographic designs.

Soon after writing the *Aminta* Tasso began work on a tragedy, which he then called *Galealto, re di Norvegia*; but at this time he wrote only a first act and two scenes of a second act. Then he turned again to the "heroic poem," known to us as the *Gerusalemme liberata* (though Tasso himself had thought of it — at least in 1570 — as *Il Gottifredo*), on which he had been toiling for so many years; and early in 1575 he brought it to completion. His chosen theme, the liberation of Jerusalem in the First Crusade, is stated thus in the two opening lines:

> Canto l' arme pietose e 'l Capitano
> Che 'l gran sepolcro liberò di Cristo —

I sing of the pious arms and the Captain who liberated the great sepulchre of Christ.

In the Spring of the year 1099 the Christian army, under the command of Godfrey of Bouillon, moves southward from its encampment at Tortosa, and invests Jerusalem. The defenders are reënforced by an Arabian army; general battles are fought and single combats take place outside the walls of the city; the fortunes of war favor now the Christians, now the Saracens; Heaven and Hell intervene; enchantments abound; the Christian army storms the city; the surviving defenders retire into the Tower of David; an Egyptian army appears; battles rage around the city and about the Tower; and at last the Christian victory is complete.

Historical and imaginary events are interwoven; and historical and imaginary persons are mingled in the development of the story. Godfrey, the official hero of the poem, has the wisdom, the personal valor, the dignity, and the piety appropriate for the commander of the crusading army.

The chief imaginary hero and heroine are Rinaldo, the leading Christian champion, and the Saracen enchantress Armida. This Rinaldo is not the Carolingian Rinaldo, but an imaginary Rinaldo d' Este: his assignment to the Este family enables Tasso, like Boiardo and Ariosto before him, to sing the praises of his ducal patrons. As the result of a fatal quarrel Rinaldo leaves the Christian camp. Armida, seeking to weaken the Christian forces by prolonging his absence, brings him, by enchantment, into her power; but she falls in love with him and transports him to her "bower of bliss" in the Fortunate Islands, where he in turn falls in love with her, amid the luxurious beauties of her enchanted palace and garden. Into that garden come two knights sent by Godfrey to recall Rinaldo to his duty:

> When they had passed all those troubled ways,
> The garden sweet spread forth her green to show,
> The moving crystal from the fountains plays,
> Fair trees, high plants, strange herbs, and flow'rets new,
> Sunshiny hills, dales hid from Phoebus' rays,
> Groves, arbors, mossy caves, at once they view;
> And, that which beauty most, most wonder brought,
> Nowhere appear'd the art which all this wrought.
>
> So with the rude the polish'd mingled was,
> That natural seem'd all, and every part
> Nature would craft in counterfeiting pass,
> And imitate her imitator art.

Mild was the air, the skies were clear as glass,
The trees no whirlwind felt nor tempest's smart,
But ere their fruit drops off, the blossom comes;
This springs, that falls, that rip'neth, and this blooms. . . .

The joyous birds, hid under greenwood shade
Sung merry notes on every branch and bough;
The wind, that in the leaves and water play'd,
With murmur sweet now sung, and whistled now;
Ceased the birds, the wind loud answer made,
And while they sung it rumbled soft and low:
Thus, were it hap or cunning, chance or art,
The wind in this strange music bore his part.*

Responding to the summons, Rinaldo returns to the Christian camp. There he overcomes an enchantment that has frustrated the siege, and fights valiantly in the storming of the city and in the last battle. Tasso's Armida (unlike Ariosto's Alcina, a sorceress beautified by magic only) is young and beautiful in her own right. She is brokenhearted when Rinaldo leaves her; her love changes to wrath; and she returns to aid the defenders of Jerusalem. But after the final battle Rinaldo saves her from self-destruction; and they are reconciled.

Equal to Rinaldo in valor is the Italian Tancred, an historical figure whom Tasso endows with an unhistoric personal nobility. After an early battle he meets the Saracen warrior maiden Clorinda at a fountain at which both have sought refreshment, and falls in love with her: she flees as other Christian knights approach. When they are drawn aside for a moment from the press of a later battle, he has time only to declare his love before they are swept apart. They meet once more, under the walls of Jerusalem, by night, in single combat, neither knowing the other's identity; and in that combat Tancred wounds Clorinda mortally. Before she dies she asks for baptism:

"Friend, thou hast won, and, as I pardon thee,
Do thou too pardon, not this fearless clay,
But my dark soul. Ah, pray for it, and free,
By baptism, all my secret sins away."
In that faint voice's gentle tones there stole
Such soft unearthly music on his ear,
As quenched all rage, and, gliding to his soul,
Forced to his eyes a sympathetic tear.

A short way off, a little murmuring rill
Burst from the mountain's bosom; there the knight
Hastened, his helmet from its source to fill,
Then sad returned for the great pious rite.
He felt his hand shake, while he sought to bare
Her, as yet, unknown features to the light:

* From the Elizabethan translation by Edward Fairfax.

He saw, he knew her, and stood rooted there.
  Ah, recognition! Ah, heart-rending sight!
Yet died he not, for in that hour of strife
  He summoned all his fortitude, the pain
He felt suppressing, while he gave new life
  To her with water whom his sword had slain.
But while he spoke the sacred words, a ray
  Of joy ecstatic lit Clorinda's face;
Dying, she smiled, and, reborn, seemed to say,
  "Heaven opes its portals — I depart in peace."
Her snowy face a lovely pallor wears;
  Of lilies, blent with violets, such the hue;
Her eyes are fixed on heaven, and Heaven appears
  With tender ruth, the penitent to view.
Then, raising up her cold and ungloved arm,
  She gave the knight her hand, as earnest deep
Of peace in lieu of words, and in that form
  The maiden passed away, as if asleep.*

Among the historical persons of the poem are Godfrey's brother Baldwin, Tancred's cousin Bohemond, Raymond IV of Toulouse, Peter the Hermit, and Solyman, Sultan of Nicaea. Among the imaginary crusaders are an Odoardo — thought by Tasso to have been an English baron — and his warrior wife Gildippe, inseparable even in death. Among the imaginary Saracens is the gentle Erminia, princess of Antioch, skilled in healing, who is enamored of Tancred: she cures him of his wounds, but he does not learn of her love.

The most famous portions of the poem, in addition to the account of Armida's bower and the story of Tancred and Clorinda, are those that tell of the Infernal Council and of the enchanted forest. To the theme of the Infernal Council, already treated by Boccaccio and Vida, Tasso, echoing them and still other writers, gives an elaborate development and a livid splendor. Pluto, resolved to thwart the Christian menace, convokes his fiends and his monsters:

Th' infernal trumpet with its raucous blast
Summons the denizens of eternal night:
Tremble the caverns, shadowy and vast;
Resounds the mournful air, bereft of light.

In an eloquent speech he reminds his comrades of the state from which they have fallen, urges them to a renewal of conflict, and gives them his commands. Vida's Satan had begun his corresponding speech with the words *Tartarei proceres*, "Tartarean princes"; Tasso's Satan begins with the words *Tartarei numi*:

Tartarean gods, more worthy of your thrones
Yonder above the sun, where ye were born . . .

* From the translation by Sir John Kingston James.

Whence Milton:

> Princes, Potentates,
> Warriors, the Flower of Heaven — once yours, now lost . . .

For the storming of Jerusalem the crusaders must have a wooden tower and other wooden machinery; and the only place where wood can be found is a forest some few miles from the city. A Saracen sorcerer, therefore, with his most powerful spells, fills that forest with terror. The hewers of wood first sent there, stricken with a strange dismay, turn back at once. Chosen knights, though touched with like dismay, press on, only to be overwhelmed by a tremendous thundering sound. A single brave and boastful knight endures this sound, but stops before a wall of fire, with monsters at its battlements. Tancred penetrates the wall of fire, reaches a glade, and draws his sword to cut a cypress tree: but the cypress speaks, and with the voice of Clorinda implores a pity he cannot refuse. At last Rinaldo attempts the forest. For him, however, the enchantment has been changed: there is no terror, now, no overwhelming sound, no wall of fire, but luring beauty and woodland melody. He comes to a circle of trees around a queenly myrtle; from the surrounding trees there issue nymphs who in dance and song surround him; then, issuing from the myrtle, a semblance of Armida pleads with him. When he raises his sword, nevertheless, to cut the myrtle, the semblance turns into a hundred-armed giant; the nymphs turn into monsters; the earth quakes; and a tempest rages. But he cuts down the tree: giant and monsters vanish, the earth is still and the sky serene — and the forest is disenchanted.

Both in its form — which clings to the octave, resisting blank verse — and in its general character the *Gerusalemme liberata* holds to the tradition of the *Orlando furioso*. Its theme, like that of the *Furioso*, is taken from the unending Christian-Saracen conflict; it is concerned equally with knightly prowess and with love; feminine valor is afield; episodes flourish; enchantments abound; beauty pervades; and classical elements, in action, in phrase, in simile, are plentiful.

The *Gerusalemme*, however, is refined and chastened by the influences of current literary theory and of the Counter Reformation. Many of the differences between the *Gerusalemme* and the *Furioso* correspond to the assumptions and the precepts of Tasso's own *Discorsi . . . del poema heroico*. The *Gerusalemme* is, in Tasso's sense, an heroic poem. Its theme is taken from history; from Christian history; and from a phase of Christian history that is not an unalterable object of faith, and is neither too ancient nor too modern. The action set forth is noble and illustrious in itself, and of great significance; yet the quantitative substance of the theme is not too large. The poem is relatively brief (twenty cantos); and it has a true unity of action of the composite type: its many elements are firmly interwoven. Its dominant dignity is relieved by certain gentler qualities, but not by any touch of humor.

The poem is Christian as well as heroic. The narrative tells of the triumphant culmination of a high Christian enterprise; and the knights who are fighting for the Cross do so, in their best moments, with the exaltation of the Faith. Baptism is a holy rite; prayers rise, and are answered; and the motif of divine intervention is reverently handled. Only in the episode of Armida's bower of bliss does a pagan sensuousness for a time obscure Christian values.

The *Gerusalemme* is still further differentiated from its predecessors by certain traits of Tasso's own poetic nature, especially his emotionalism. Tasso was deeply interested in the feelings of his personages; and the portions of the poem that are most specifically Tassian are those in which he gives voice to the varying emotions of his several lovers — joy, grief, hope, despair, desire, uncertainty, enthrallment in bower dalliance, anxiety for a fighting or a stricken champion, pain of absence. Tasso is indeed so preoccupied with such matters that in much of the poem the hearty vigor of the *Furioso* is replaced by a sweetness that tends characteristically toward melancholy.

Tasso, like Ariosto, loved all forms of beauty. Less precise than Ariosto, Tasso was content with a generalized visual beauty, and was not concerned with the exact definition of line and form and color. Beauty of sound, however, pervades the *Gerusalemme*. Tasso's gardens and woodlands are alive with bird-song and with other sounds of nature; and he introduces melody of human voice and instrument as well. The artistic affiliations of the *Gerusalemme*, indeed, like those of the *Aminta*, are with music rather than with painting.

Tasso's style, intimately classic, is a meticulously wrought artifact, less natural and more finished than that of Ariosto. It is in some small degree impaired by a fondness for verbal conceits, finely spun subtleties, and rhetorical antitheses. Yet his style, as a whole, flows with an extraordinary verbal and rhythmic felicity, which has appealed, in Italy, even to the unlearned. Stanzas of the *Gerusalemme* have been sung by Venetian gondoliers and by Tuscan peasants.

The year 1575 proved to be the chief turning point in the life of Tasso. Up to that time, though he had known sorrow and anxiety, he had in the main lived in comfort, in happiness, and in honor; but the succeeding years brought him almost unrelieved and often intense suffering in body and in mind. With all his genius, Tasso was sadly lacking in self-confidence; and he had an inordinate fear of public criticism. Consequently, instead of arranging at once for the publication of his epic, he submitted it to several friends for private criticism. Their comments proved to be pedantic, censorious, and exceedingly painful to Tasso. In particular, they condemned the abundance of episodes and enchantments, and what they regarded as an excessive interest in love affairs. Tasso defended himself as best he could; but he came to the distressed conviction that he must eventually yield to his critics and rewrite the poem.

Other troubles pressed upon him. He began to suffer from ill health. He was beset with a groundless fear that some of his religious opinions were heretical. He fancied himself surrounded by enemies and by spies. By the summer of 1577 he had come dangerously close to insanity, and was placed in a mild confinement. He soon escaped, however, and made his way, after long wanderings, to his sister's home in Sorrento. The quiet affection of that home brought about some improvement in his mental health; and in the Spring of 1578 he returned to Ferrara. But flights and wanderings took him presently, in pitiful succession, to Mantua, Padua, Venice, Pesaro, and Turin. Early in 1579 he reappeared at Ferrara, at a time when the court was engaged in festivities celebrating the marriage of the Duke. No one could spare attention for Tasso, whose resentment flared into a violent insanity. He was then confined in the asylum of Sant' Anna, where he remained for seven years, at first chained, but presently with increasing freedom.* Among his visitors were Montaigne, and the friendly Prince Vincenzo Gonzaga, who in 1586 persuaded the Duke to let him take Tasso to Mantua. From this time on Tasso suffered no recurrence of violent insanity, but he never regained full mental health. New flights and wanderings took him to Bologna, Loreto, and Florence; to Mantua again; and repeatedly to Naples and to Rome. Wherever he went, though he was often a very trying guest, he was received with friendliness. Late in 1594 he returned finally to Rome, at the request of Clement VIII, who was planning a poetic coronation on the Capitol for him; but before that ceremony could be held Tasso fell gravely ill. He died on April 25, 1595.

Prior to his confinement in Sant' Anna, Tasso had not rewritten his epic, nor given it a formal title, nor authorized its publication. In Sant' Anna, however, he was helpless; and in 1580 an unscrupulous publisher brought out a very incorrect edition of the first fourteen cantos of the poem, under the title *Il Goffredo.* To some of Tasso's friends it seemed that under these circumstances the whole poem, as it then stood, should be published as correctly as possible. A complete — but imperfect — edition was accordingly published in 1581, without Tasso's sanction, by one of his friends, who, remembering the title of Trissino's *L'Italia liberata dai Goti*, gave Tasso's poem the title *Gerusalemme liberata*, by which it has ever since been known. Within the same year another friend brought out (apparently with Tasso's permis-

* The familiar story, most notably developed by Goethe in his *Torquato Tasso*, that Tasso's confinement in Sant' Anna was due to a love affair with the Duke's sister Leonora is groundless.

sion) an edition based on an autograph manuscript. Thereafter editions multiplied swiftly. The *Gerusalemme* came immediately to be known and loved in other lands. In England a partial translation appeared in 1594, and a complete translation by Edward Fairfax in 1600. Milton, among the English poets, found most treasure in Tasso's cantos.

In 1586, when Tasso was released from Sant' Anna and became the guest of Vincenzo Gonzaga at Mantua, he resumed poetic activity; but the years in Sant' Anna had all but quenched his poetic genius. He turned first to his unfinished tragedy, and by the end of the year he had completed it, giving it as title the name of the hero, *Torrismondo*. The plot, Scandinavian in locale and medieval in period, is of Tasso's own invention, but the theme is, in essence, that of the *Oedipus rex* of Sophocles. The play has dignity; but the action is forced, and the style is in general rhetorical and verbose. In 1587 Tasso turned again to his epic, and began to rewrite it in accordance with the criticisms that had come to him from his friends some ten years earlier. He removed certain episodes entirely, altered and allegorized such love affairs and enchantments as he retained, added historical, Biblical, and Homeric elements, and held his style to a monotonous aridity. He spent five years in this task, and published the rewritten poem in 1593, under the title *Gerusalemme conquistata*. But the *Conquistata* is no more than a pitiful ghost of the *Liberata*. During his last years Tasso undertook also, quite without inspiration, the writing of a few new poems of some length, most of them religious.

Before and after and even during his years in Sant' Anna, and even while he was working on his major poems, Tasso produced an almost continuous series of lyrics and of miscellaneous writings in prose. He wrote nearly two thousand lyrics: almost all of them are in the conventional forms, but a few are odes or *canzonette*. He was so thoroughly nurtured on Petrarch and on the classic lyrists that elements of their verse inevitably affected his own; but he used these elements, in all naturalness, for the perfection of his own artistry. There is evident, also, a familiarity with the lighter verse, largely in madrigal form, written, in Tasso's own time and somewhat earlier, to be set to music: but whereas such verse is in general insignificant as poetry, much of Tasso's corresponding verse is exquisite.

In the love poems one finds no depth of feeling, but many of them are of great beauty. Highly impressionable, Tasso could be stirred to poetry by impressions either strong or slight; and whenever he was so stirred he sought to render not the impressing actuality but the essence of the impression, as perceived and transmuted by an imagination that preferred the gently vague to the definite, and made little difference between the real and the unreal. And he sought always so to render that essence as to bring out the beauty that had been manifest to him, and so to choose his words and fashion his phrases and his lines as to give to his poem a rhythmic and musical beauty of its own. Close as he is to music in the *Aminta* and the *Gerusalemme*, he is even closer in the lyrics: poetry could hardly identify itself with music more perfectly than in some of Tasso's madrigals and *canzonette*.

The most distinctive of his lyrics are those written in Sant' Anna (the nature of his insanity was not such as to preclude literary activity). Many of these poems are pleas for release, or for intervention that might lead to release. They vary greatly in mood; but together they record, in a form that is poignantly beautiful, one of the most tragic experiences in the history of poetry. In a *canzone* to the Duke he writes:

> To you from the depth of my prison I raise and turn my heart, my mind, my eyes; to you I bend my knees . . . Turn your merciful eyes, and you will see him who was once your servant . . . with dread death upon his countenance.

And in a companion *canzone* to the Duke's sisters:

> To you . . . I tell . . . the bitter story of my suffering, renewing your memory of me, and of yourselves: your kindnesses, the years I spent with you, what I am now, what I once was, what I implore, where I am, who brought me hither, who imprisoned me.

And in a sonnet to the Duchess:

> The great palaces and the fair halls resound with song; and I alone make my dark prison resound with weeping. Is this the faith that had been promised me? Are these the triumphs I had desired? Alas! do you then, Lady, call the prison "pity" and the bier "reward"?

His single *invictus* begins and ends thus:

> Who challenges the stars amid which Fate
>   Holds firm her head — and upon us her feet?
>   I do: . . .
> Though the sun shine not, nor air breathe, for me,
>   And though my spirits, limbs, and senses fail,
>   My strength of faithfulness is still unbowed.

Tasso's *Dialogues* are about thirty in number: more than half of them were written in Sant' Anna. His thought is never profound; he draws heavily on classic sources; and he is often prolix. Yet he writes with urbanity; and the less formal introductory portions of some of the dialogues make very pleasant reading. Of his other formal prose writings, which include discourses, treatises, and orations of various kinds, the most important is a revised, enlarged, and moralized form of his *Discorsi dell'arte poetica.*

All but a very few of Tasso's 1700 letters were written in 1575 or later — about four hundred of them in Sant' Anna. As a whole, therefore, they reflect his experiences in the years of his distress, and some of them bear evidences of his mental unbalance. A few, less personal, are in effect treatises of one sort or another: one of the early letters, for instance, written in France, is a long disquisition on that country and its customs. Tasso's epistolary style, though in the longer letters it tends to become labored, is in general clear and graceful. Certain letters are of great beauty: such are his last letter to his sister Cornelia, and a letter written shortly before his death to one of his friends. These, and many others, one reads with deep compassion.

CHAPTER 30

Giordano Bruno

FILIPPO BRUNO, born in 1548 at Nola, near Naples, studied in the University of Naples, and in 1565 entered the Dominican order, in which he received the name Giordano. In the monastery his continuing and eager studies ranged from St. Thomas to Aristotle, the Neoplatonists, the classic Latin poets, and various modern writers. As the years passed he manifested tendencies regarded as dangerous; and in 1576, rather than face a trial, he fled (eventually discarding the monastic habit). A long series of wanderings took him to Toulouse, where he taught for two years, and finally, in 1581, to Paris. He had shown himself, by this time, to be learned, brilliant, enthusiastic, uncontrollable, critical of others but not of himself, and quite unable to steer his own course in life.

Soon after his arrival in Paris he gave a very successful course of lectures on the attributes of God; continued his development of a system of mnemonics (a lifelong obsession with him) which won the interest and patronage of Henry III; and in 1582 published his single comedy, one of the strangest of his many strange works.

Its strangeness begins on the title page, which reads thus:

> *Candelaio*: comedia del Bruno Nolano, academico di nulla academia, detto Il Fastidito. In tristitia hilaris: in hilaritate tristis.

The mock academic name Il Fastidito means "The Disgusted One." The Latin motto ("Laughing in sadness, sad in laughter") is a good key to Bruno's complex character.

Between the title page and the comedy itself there intervene a burlesque sonnet, a mocking dedication, a long Argument, an *Antiprologo* and a *Proprologo* (words of Bruno's invention), and a prologue by a beadle. Strange in their torrential and at times hardly coherent style, these introductory elements are strange in content also. One of the first sentences in the dedication reads:

> To whom shall I dedicate that which — under the influence of the celestial Sirius, in these hottest days and most lambent hours, called Canicular — the fixed stars have caused to rain into my brain, the wandering fireflies of the firmament have sifted upon me, the dean of the twelve signs has swept into my head, and the seven wandering lights have breathed into my inner ears?

The dedication is largely scurrilous, yet it contains this sentence:

> Time takes all things away, and bestows all things; everything changes, nothing is annihilated; there is but one that cannot change. One only is eternal, and can endure eternally as one, in its own likeness, in its own identity.

The play itself moves in an atmosphere of unrelieved depravity. Every single character is disreputable. Even the title is an evil epithet. Bruno certainly deplored, and at some points he clearly satirizes, the kind of life he depicts; yet he seems to depict it with a bitter gusto. He was at least *in hilaritate tristis*. His play has three protagonists: an unworthy lover, a miser who seeks to increase his gold by alchemy; and a pedant. All three, in the end, are victimized by a gang of sharpers and ruffians. The elements of the plot are largely conventional, though certain incidents and certain combinations are novel. The characters are sharply defined, as types, by their own words and actions, and by the ways in which they are treated and discussed by other characters, but they are not individualized as unique persons. The chief distinction of the play lies in the vitality of its dialogue, which is often vehement, often witty — and at times seriously reflective.

Early in 1583 Bruno crossed the Channel, bearing letters of recommendation from the French king to his ambassador, the Marquis of Mauvissière,* in whose household Bruno lived, rendering some secretarial service, while he was in England. Poggio Bracciolini, Enea Silvio Piccolomini, Castiglione, and a few minor Italian writers had already visited England; but Bruno was the first major Italian writer to come to England as a refugee, the first to write extensively while in England, and the first to enter into noteworthy association with English men of letters. He became well acquainted, in particular, with Philip Sidney and Fulke Greville. Before he had been long in England he took part, in Oxford, in certain disputations in which, according to his own account, his arguments confounded his opponent. But his "patience and humanity," he says, were met with "incivility and discourtesy," and his public lectures on the Immortality of the Soul and the Fivefold Sphere were stopped.

In 1584 and 1585 Bruno published the six philosophical treatises in Italian

* But the British ambassador in Paris wrote, at the same time, to Sir Francis Walsingham: "Doctor Jordano Bruno Nolano, a professor in philosophy, intendeth to pass into England; whose religion I cannot commend."

prose which are, aside from his comedy, his best known works. Each consists of a series of dialogues; each has a dedicatory letter; and each (with one exception) has one or more introductory poems. The first three treatises, all of them metaphysical, are dedicated, in heartfelt gratitude, to the Marquis de Mauvissière.

La cena de le ceneri, "The Ash Wednesday Supper," is a defense of the Copernican system, supplemented by statements of the essential elements of Bruno's own thought. In the traditional view the universe was geocentric and finite; Copernicus saw it as heliocentric (the Earth being reduced to planetary status) but still finite; Bruno — following Lucretius and the fifteenth-century philosopher Nicholas of Cusa, whose conceptions appealed irresistibly to his own powerful imagination — saw it as infinite, without center and without boundaries, and strewn with an infinite number of worlds. The *Supper* consists of conversations held on five successive evenings by four interlocutors, of whom one, Teofilo ("The Lover of God"), speaks as an intimate of Bruno, while another, Smitho, probably represents an actual English Smith.

The first of the five dialogues contains a general appreciation of Copernicus and a general statement of the cosmology of Bruno. In the second dialogue, which is in part a satiric picture of English manners, Teofilo tells of an invitation extended to himself, Bruno, and others to come to dinner on Ash Wednesday at the home of Sir Fulke Greville, and recounts various difficulties and discourtesies experienced in reaching the house and the table. In the third and fourth dialogues Teofilo reports the after-dinner discussion, in which two English "doctors" assail the Copernican system, which is valiantly defended by Bruno, who furthermore asserts that the universe is infinite, that its infinitely numerous stars and planets are in every respect similar to the Sun and the Earth, and that the constituent elements of life are deathless. In the final dialogue Teofilo gives some further information as to Bruno's philosophy.

Much of the material is technical, but the passionate exuberance of Bruno's own convictions compels, in the more characteristic passages, a corresponding passionate exuberance of style. Humor plays around the fundamental seriousness: one of the English doctors begins his argument only after

> looking at his own gold chain and at Bruno's breast — where some buttons may have been missing — straightening up, taking his arms off the table, shaking himself a little, puffing a bit, twisting his moustache, arching his eyebrows, distending his nostrils, glancing around, and putting his left hand on his left side in order to be in a good fencing position.

The treatise *De la causa, principio e uno*, "On Cause, Principle, and Unity," consists, similarly, of five dialogues: the first is introductory, and is in part an apology for the strictures on English manners contained in the *Supper*; the remaining four represent conversations held on successive days, this time in the home of the Marquis de Mauvissière. These four dialogues are devoted to an abstruse — but at times eloquent — discussion of the metaphysical concepts indicated in the title. The dialogues are preceded by three Latin poems in elegiac distichs and two Italian sonnets. These poems are difficult, and unconcerned with formal beauty, but tense with Bruno's own thought and feeling. The second Latin poem, addressed "To his Own Spirit," is in substance as follows:

> Mountain, though the earth hold thee, pressing thy deep roots downward, thou canst rise with thy summit toward the stars.
>
> Mind, from the supreme heights a kindred mind calls to thee, that thou be a dividing mean betwixt the low deities and Jove.
>
> Lose not thy rights; nor, downward hurled and falling to the depths, plunge to the waters of black Acheron.
>
> Rather let thy nature seek its home in the sublime; for if God touch thee thou shalt be a glowing fire.

The general pattern of the treatise *De l'infinito universo e mondi*, "On the Infinite Universe and its Worlds," is the same as that of the two preceding works. One of the introductory sonnets ends thus — the soaring motif comes from the two sonnets of Tansillo mentioned in Chapter 26, but the application is Bruno's own:

> Wherefore I spread my sure wings to the air; nor do I fear any barrier of crystal or of glass, but I cleave the heavens and rise to the infinite.
>
> And while from my globe I soar to other globes, and further penetrate the ethereal field, I leave behind me that which others behold from afar.

This treatise is in effect a finely reasoned debate between Bruno and defenders of the views of Aristotle. It is at times highly technical; but at times it soars upward on the "sure wings" of Bruno's vision, as in this passage:

> I declare that the universe is infinite in respect to its entirety, since it has no margin, no boundary, no surface; I declare that the universe is not infinite in respect to its totality, since each of its parts, in so far as we can examine them, is finite, and each of the innumerable worlds that it contains is finite. I declare that God is infinite in respect to his entirety, since he is without any limitation — and every attribute of his is one and infinite; and I declare that God is infinite in respect to his totality, since he is wholly in the whole world and is infinitely and totally in every part of it.

With his next treatise, which is commonly known as the *Spaccio della bestia trionfante*, Bruno turns from metaphysics to ethics. Its full title reads, in literal translation: "The Banishment of the Triumphant Beast, Proposed by Jove, Enacted by the Council, Revealed by Mercury, Reported by Sofia, Heard by Saulino, Registered by the Nolan." Sofia is Wisdom; Saulino speaks for Bruno. The *Banishment*, dedicated to Sidney, is a discussion of the vices and the virtues, and is designed as a relatively simple approach to the more esoteric doctrine of the later treatise, already planned, *On Heroic Enthusiasm.* Jove, grown old, repentant, and fearful that Fate will depose him and his companions, proposes reform; and noting that reminders of Olympian misdeeds remain among the stars, he calls a council of the gods to consider the banishment of the constellations, and their replacement by virtues long since banished from both heaven and earth. The council accordingly reviews the constellations, and decides where to send them, and what virtues shall occupy their places. Thus the Little Bear is to be sent to Berne, or to the Roman family of the Orsini (the Italian word for "bear" is *orsa*), or to the ursine English, and is to be replaced by Truth; the Dragon is to be replaced by Prudence; Arcturus by Law; and Hercules by Fortitude. The discussion is lively, imaginative (the Northern Crown is to be reserved for whatever hero shall bring peace to Europe), often seriously and sometimes eloquently philosophic, often humorous, and often intensely satiric. The Olympians comment mercilessly on those pedantic worshippers who exalt the catechism and disregard virtuous actions; on the idea that divine glory can be enhanced by any human act or attitude; on the idea that there is any inherent conflict between nature and divinity; on the traditional stories of the creation and the deluge; on the adoration of relics; on miracles (such as Orion's ability to walk on the waves of the sea); on the idea of a dual nature (such as that of Chiron); on the idea that the Greeks are the chosen people of the gods. The council meeting ended, its members adjourn to supper: the Southern Fish is to be expertly cooked for them, with Roman sauce.

The *Cabala del cavallo pegaseo*, "The Cabala of the Pegasean Steed," ostensibly in praise of asininity, is a satire on pretentious ignorance and on obscurantism.

The last of the six treatises, *De gli eroici furori*, "On Heroic Enthusiasm" — dedicated, like the *Banishment*, to Sidney — is also the most elaborate. It is in two Parts, each consisting of five dialogues. Tansillo, whose poems Bruno greatly admired, is one of the two interlocutors of the first Part. The treatise contains about seventy-five poems, nearly all of them sonnets, and nearly all of them Bruno's own — four are by Tansillo. The discussion proceeds, in general, by the quotation of the several poems, each quotation being followed by questions and explanations.

What Bruno means by heroic enthusiasm and enthusiasts is clearly stated in a long passage in the third dialogue of the first Part. There are, he says, two kinds of enthusiasts:

> While some only display blindness, stupidity, and irrational impetuosity . . . others by divine abstraction become in reality superior to ordinary men. And

these again are of two kinds, for some . . . speak and perform wonderful things, without themselves understanding the reason . . . while others, being skilful in contemplation and possessing innately a clear intellectual spirit, have an internal stimulus and natural fervour, excited by the love of the divine, of justice, of truth, of glory . . . [Enthusiasm of this type] is a glow kindled by the intellectual sun in the soul, and a divine impetus which lends it wings, with which, drawing nearer and nearer to the intellectual sun . . . it . . . has the perception of divine and internal harmony.*

Of the divine object itself Bruno says:

> But in the simplicity of the divine essence, all exists in totality, and not according to any measure, and therefore wisdom is not greater than beauty and majesty, and goodness is not greater than strength: not only are all the attributes equal, they are one and the same thing . . . But where there is infinite wisdom there cannot be other than infinite power . . . Where there is infinite goodness there must be infinite wisdom . . . Where there is infinite power there must be infinite goodness and wisdom.

Bruno insists upon the difficulties, the inner conflicts, the sufferings, even the perils, that are involved in the effort of the will-driven mind to attain a goal so infinitely high. The effort is itself heroic, and deserves honor even though it fail. In this connection Bruno quotes the second of the two sonnets in which Tansillo had made use of the Icarus myth: but whereas Tansillo had used the myth to suggest the loftiness of his aspiration as a mortal lover, Bruno applies it to the soaring of his own heroic enthusiasm.

The poetic character of the treatise is indicated at the outset by a brief discussion of kinds of poetry and of the "rules" of poetry. Bruno's position, definitely anti-Aristotelian, is that there are many different kinds of poetry; that the "rules" are merely derivative from poetry; and that the only poets to whom "rules" are useful are those who have no inspiration of their own. Some of the poems by Bruno contained in this treatise have fine passages; but it is obvious that most of them were written not for their own sakes, but as texts for philosophic explication.

Late in 1585 the Marquis de Mauvissière was recalled, and Bruno returned to France; but new wanderings, beginning in the following year, took him to Marburg, Wittenberg, Prague, Helmstedt, Frankfort, and Zurich, and again, in 1591, to Frankfort. During these years of wandering he published a score of works, all in Latin, in the fields of philosophy and mnemonics.

The most important of these works — the most important, indeed, from the philosophical point of view, of all the works of Bruno — is the Latin poem, in eight Books, entitled *De immenso et innumerabilibus, seu de universo et mundis*, "On Immensity and Innumerability, or on the Universe and its Worlds." Each of its chapters in verse is followed by a prose commentary: several of the commentaries are illustrated with diagrams. As the subtitle

* This and the following quotation are taken from the translation by L. Williams.

indicates, the *De immenso* has a particular correspondence with the Italian dialogue *De l'infinito universo e mondi*; but it resumes, revises, defends, and supplements all of Bruno's earlier thought. Bruno's Latin verse is in general hard reading. The prose of the commentaries is often more eloquent:

> Only the infinite is perfect . . . This is the one unbounded whole, God, and universal nature: whereof there can be no perfect image or similitude save infinity itself. Whatever is finite is imperfect. Every world of sense is imperfect, and in it good and evil, matter and form, light and darkness, sorrow and joy commingle, and all things are in change and in motion; but in the infinite all things attain to the order of unity, of truth, and of goodness.

With the *De immenso* are associated two lesser works, similar to it in form, known usually (their actual titles are very long) as the *De minimo* and the *De monade*. The *De minimo* is a supplemented restatement of the material of the *De la causa*. The *De monade* is a series of variations on the concept of the unit. Its chief interest, however, lies in this personal passage:

> I have fought, and that is much; and I had thought that I might win . . . I see that victory lies in the hands of fate . . . but the centuries that are to come will not deny that I had no fear of dying, that I yielded to none in constancy, and that I preferred a courageous death to a craven life.

In 1591 a Venetian patrician, Giovanni Mocenigo, invited Bruno to come to Venice to instruct him in the art of memory — an art in which Bruno was thought to possess almost magic powers — and with fatal unwisdom Bruno accepted the invitation. A few months passed quietly; but in the Spring of 1592 Mocenigo, angered because Bruno was determined to return to Frankfort, denounced him, as a heretic, to the Venetian Inquisition. Imprisonment and inconclusive interrogations followed. In 1593 he was extradited to the Office of the Inquisition in Rome, where he remained a prisoner, in the Castel Sant' Angelo, for seven years, undergoing a long series of interrogations. The charges brought against him were based mainly on heretical positions, such as his belief in an infinity of worlds, which he had maintained in his writings. Throughout most of the long period Bruno, admitting that some of his utterances had been erroneous, showed a willingness to abjure whatever he might be officially ordered to abjure: but he accompanied his statements of such willingness by new defenses of the positions that were regarded as heretical. At the end he refused absolutely to abjure, asserting the soundness of the positions he had maintained. He was then declared to be an impenitent heretic and condemned to be delivered to the Secular Court for punishment; and it was ordered that his books should be burned, and listed in the Index. When the verdict was read to him he said: "Perhaps you who bring this sentence against me are in greater fear than am I who receive it." He was burned at the stake in the Campo di Fiori, in Rome, on February 17, 1600.

CHAPTER 31

The Drama in the Late Sixteenth Century

MANY COMEDIES and tragedies were written at this time — among them Tasso's tragedy and Bruno's comedy — but in general these plays fell short of distinction. The ablest of the writers of comedies was the Neapolitan Giambattista Della Porta (1535–1615), an amateur scientist who wrote, in Latin, on astronomy, refraction, distillation, fortification, rural economy, ciphers, mnemonics, physiognomy, chiromancy, pneumatology, and thaumatology: he found time, nevertheless, to write some thirty comedies, of which about half are extant. The elements of his plots are taken largely from Plautus, from Italian *novelle*, and from earlier Italian comedies, and his personages include the usual pedants, braggarts, and parasites; but he shows much ingenuity in the combination of his elements; his plots are clear; his dialogue is vivacious; and some of his stock characters are very amusing. His plays were well known in England: Middleton's *No Wit, No Help Like a Woman's* is based on Della Porta's *La sorella*, "The Sister."

The ablest contemporary writer of tragedies was Pomponio Torelli (1539–1608) of Parma, whose *Merope* is the first notable version of that favorite tragic theme.

The most striking figure in the dramatic world of the time was Luigi Groto (1541–1585), commonly called, from his blindness and his birthplace (near Venice), Il Cieco d'Adria. In spite of his blindness he acquired an excellent education; wrote tragedies, comedies, and lyrics; served on occasion as an envoy of his native city; and in a performance of the *Oedipus rex* given in Palladio's theatre in Vicenza played with notable success the part of the blind seer Tiresias. One of his half-dozen tragedies, *La Hadriana*, retells the story of Romeo and Juliet: Groto follows in the main the *novella* of Luigi da Porto, but he transfers the scene to Adria and the imagined time to antiquity, changing names and various details accordingly.

The only play of this period that rivaled the success of the *Aminta* was, like the *Aminta*, a pastoral play: *Il pastor fido*, "The Faithful Shepherd," by the Ferrarese Giambattista Guarini (1538–1612). Guarini, like Tasso, was a courtier resident usually at Ferrara, but sometimes elsewhere. The *Pastor fido*, written in the years 1580–1589, with great care and much revision, was called by its author a *tragicommedia pastorale*. It is similar in form to the *Aminta*, though it is three times as long. It is in five acts, with choruses (of shepherds, hunters, nymphs, and priests); and it is written — except for the choral songs — in blank verse, with eleven- and seven-syllable lines intermingled. The scene of the play is in Arcadia. The faithful shepherd, Mirtillo, is in love with Amarilli, who returns his love, though betrothed by paternal arrangement to Silvio, who — himself loved by Dorinda — cares only for the hunt. Through the scheming of the cynical Corisca, who wants Mirtillo for herself, Amarilli, though innocent, is convicted of an offense for which the penalty is death; but Mirtillo claims and is accorded the right to die in her stead. The intervention of a blind seer sets all right, and the faithful pair are wedded. Meanwhile the wounding of Dorinda by a stray arrow from Silvio's bow has led to their happiness; and at the end Corisca repents.

In spite of its complexity the play is firmly and clearly constructed; and in the refined fluency of its verse it is a not unworthy companion to the *Aminta*. Except in the forced scenes in which catastrophe impends, the general spirit is that of comedy. Yet Guarini's play lacks the singular charm of the *Aminta;* it is obviously, even if brilliantly, artificial; and its attractiveness for modern readers is impaired by the inordinate length of many of its speeches.

The immediate Arcadian appeal of the *Pastor fido* was even greater than that of the *Aminta*. It was soon translated into many languages; and numerous imitations and adaptations followed, in Italy and elsewhere — among them, in England, Fletcher's *The Faithful Shepherdess*.

* * *

The Gelosi were still the most famous of the companies of professional actors. Their best known members, after 1575, were Francesco and Isabella Andreini: Francesco played often the part of the braggart captain; Isabella played the leading lady. The Gelosi acted in many North Italian cities, and made three tours in France. Other similar companies came into activity: the Desiosi, "The Desirous Ones," whom Montaigne saw in Pisa; the Uniti; and the Confidenti, who visited Spain.

Within this period the *commedia dell'arte* acquired a new stock character,

Arlecchino, "Harlequin," a special type of manservant who was destined to become in Northern Italy the most popular of all such characters.* He wears a tight cap, a black mask, and tight-fitting doublet and hose, and carries a short sword-like stick. His doublet and hose were at first covered with patches of various shapes and colors: this arrangement evolved later into the regular parti-colored costume that has given his name its adjective value. He has the general characteristics and engages in the typical activities of the Zanni, and is further distinguished by cowardice, superstition, perpetual hunger, and pennilessness. In the first decades of his existence he was usually stupid: later on he was usually witty.

Either at this time or shortly afterward there came into existence another stock character, Brighella, also a special type of manservant, who was to become Arlecchino's most frequent companion in mischief-making. He wears a white beret, a black mask, and a white suit with green trimmings.

Several companies of Italian players (no company, however, that can be identified by name) visited England before the end of the century. It is therefore very probable, though it has not been proved, that plays of the *commedia dell'arte* type were given in England. Some at least of the stock characters were certainly known to English writers. References to them begin in 1590, when a "Harlicken" is mentioned in the preface of a comedy by Nash. Jaques's lines on "the lean and slipper'd pantaloon" assume familiarity with the figure of Pantalone.

* A mischievous devil known by names such as Alichino and Herlequin appears in various medieval Italian and French writings: it seems probable that the name Arlecchino reflects a memory of that devil.

CHAPTER 32

Marino and Other Poets

AFTER FOUR CENTURIES of enlightened patronage the line of the Este in Ferrara came in 1597 to a childless end, and most of the Ferrarese territory was added to the States of the Church. The most notable Italian prince of the early seventeenth century was Carlo Emanuele of Savoy, who was also the most generous patron of the Italian men of letters of his day. For a time he seemed to be ready to take the lead in a movement for the liberation of Italy; but in the end he could not cope with the powers he had challenged, and his duchy fell under French control. Northern Italy suffered from a French invasion, and from a dreadful pestilence (the pestilence described in Manzoni's novel *I promessi sposi*). Venice, in spite of Spanish and Papal pressure, retained more independence than any other state.

Unhappy though this period was, it witnessed a remarkable renewal of creative vitality, chiefly — but by no means exclusively — in the fields of music and science.

The most familiar architectural enterprise of the period was, however, unfortunate: when the new St. Peter's, as designed in the shape of a Greek cross, was virtually complete, Pope Paul V decided that the plan should be changed to that of a Latin cross; and the nave was accordingly extended frontwards, and finished by the present commonplace façade.

The earlier and finer works of the baroque sculptor Bernini were done within this period. The one vigorous innovator in painting was the realist Caravaggio, who rendered with an uncompromising power subjects taken from low life, and gave his saints the likenesses of common folk. Guido Reni, whose paintings for the most part present gracious but insipid religious or classic persons or scenes, attained a single great decorative success in his Aurora.

With Monteverdi, the leading composer of the time, secular music made very great advances. The combination of poetry and music in the development of the opera will be discussed in Chapter 35. This same period saw also the beginnings of the oratorio.

Italian philosophy reached one of its noblest heights in the comprehensive thought of Campanella; and Italian science reached its apogee in the achievements of Galileo. Campanella and Galileo, as men of letters, will be considered in Chapters 33 and 34.

In 1638 and 1639 John Milton spent about a year in Italy, visiting many cities, and making his longest stays in Florence and in Rome. In Florence he "contracted a familiar acquaintance with many persons eminent for their rank and learning, and regularly frequented also their private academies." In Florence, also, he "visited the famous Galileo grown old, a prisoner to the Inquisition for thinking in astronomy otherwise than the Franciscan and Dominican licensers thought." *

* * *

The rise and collapse of the reputation of the Neapolitan Giambattista Marino (1569–1625) constitute a classic instance of the unreliability of contemporary judgments as to literary excellence. In his own day he was regarded, almost universally, as a supreme poet; † but later generations have relegated him to a much lower level of significance. He was supported chiefly by the patronage of persons who thought themselves illuminated by his flashy presence — among them Carlo Emanuele of Savoy and Maria de' Medici, Queen of France. He lived and wrote at the French court from 1615 to 1623, when he returned in triumph to Naples, where he died.

Poetry, for Marino, was a means of obtaining personal glory; and the specific object of poetry, in his definition, was to produce surprise. So he set himself to the production of surprise by all the devices he could muster: strange metaphors, far-fetched conceits, hyperboles, antitheses, incongruities, strings of synonyms, even puns. The scores of poets whose works he ransacked range from the ancients to Italians of the fifteenth and sixteenth centuries, and to recent and contemporary French and Spanish poets — among them Ronsard, Malherbe, Montemayor, and Lope de Vega. Yet his works show a vigorous imagination, a real descriptive gift, and a fluent musicality.

In 1602 Marino published two volumes of *Rime*: the first volume contains

* Before going to Italy Milton had written in Italian five sonnets and a madrigal. While his knowledge of Italian was good, it was not good enough to justify him in attempting to write Italian verse: these poems are quite unidiomatic, and are imperfect metrically at certain points.

† Browning in *The Ring and the Book* represents his Giuseppe Caponsacchi as a dissenter, who says:

I doubt much if Marino really be
A better bard than Dante after all.

some four hundred sonnets, classed as amorous, seaside, woodland, heroic, sad, moral, religious and various poems; the second contains some two hundred madrigals and a few poems in other forms. Many of the madrigals are graceful, and there are charming pictures among the seaside poems. Yet in one of the seaside sonnets his lady lets her hair wave on the waves in waves of gold: fishes, kindled with a sweet fire amid the waters, dart into the lovely snare, and, captive, say, in a language of love which only the poet can understand, " 'Tis sweet to die in such a glorious net." Two later verse collections were published in 1619: *La galleria*, a series of poems on real and imaginary works of art, and *La sampogna*, "The Shepherd's Pipe," a series of voluptuous mythological and pastoral idylls.

Finally, in 1623, Marino published in Paris his one long poem, the *Adone*, on which he had been working for some twenty years. The central story is simple enough: Venus, loving Adonis, brings him to Cyprus; through the jealousy of Mars he is compelled to flee; after many adventures he returns, and becomes King of Cyprus; but the persistent jealousy of Mars leads presently to his death. All this could easily have been told within the limits of a brief mythological idyll; but Marino inflated it into twenty cantos (in octaves) by the introduction of masses of heterogeneous material: the myth of Cupid and Psyche, and several other myths; descriptions of palaces and gardens; a journey of Venus and Adonis to the Moon, Mercury, and Venus; autobiographical passages; the discoveries of Galileo; the wars of Henry IV, Louis XIII, and the Dukes of Savoy; the marriage of Louis XIV; a contest between a nightingale (a "feathered voice") and a lutanist; a game of chess (taken from Vida); and the funeral games of Adonis, in which members of the Colonna, the Orsini, and other great Italian families take part. The earlier portions of the account of the contest between the nightingale and the lutanist are not without beauty; but at the end the nightingale, having died of exhaustion, is buried in the lute, and one of its feathers serves as quill for the writing of the epitaph.

Several English poets, among them Drummond and Crashaw, were much attracted by Marino, and translated some of his poems.

The fashion set by Marino was adopted, inevitably, by most minor contemporary poets, whose search for new surprises resulted in excesses even worse than those of their model. Man is a steed, God the rider; and if the steed is obedient God will give him the oats of eternity and a stall of stars. Mary Magdalen's hair is a Tagus (being of the golden color of that river) and her eyes are suns: so, in her weeping, she bathes the body of Christ with suns and dries it with a river.*

Outside of Italy the influence of Marinism was felt, more than elsewhere,

* Such extravagance is called, in Italian, sometimes *marinismo* and sometimes *secentismo*, as being characteristic of the seventeenth century (that century is usually called, in Italy, *il Seicento*, "the 1600's").

in Spain, where it appears first in a minor poet, Carrillo, who had spent some time in Italy, and then in the highly fashionable verse of Góngora.*

Among the poets who did not succumb to Marinism the most prominent was Gabriello Chiabrera (1552–1638) of Savona (near Genoa). His boyhood and youth were spent in Rome; but thereafter, though he visited many Italian cities, he lived chiefly in Savona, engaging often in civic and diplomatic service. His vast production includes several hundred lyrics; eclogues; epitaphs; short narrative poems, chiefly on mythological or biblical subjects; four epics; two tragedies; and several satires. In all this mass of verse the only groups of poems that retain any considerable interest are his *canzonette*, his Horatian odes, and his satires — and in the first two cases the interest is almost wholly in form rather than in content.

The *canzonette*, intended — in general, at least — to be sung, are poems written in short lines, and, typically, in several brief stanzas. One of them, for instance, begins thus:

La violetta,
Che in su l' erbetta
S' apre al mattin novella,
Di', non è cosa
Tutta odorosa,
Tutta leggiadra e bella? †

The stanzaic structure varies from poem to poem; and whereas earlier poets had made use of eleven- and seven-syllable lines almost exclusively, Chiabrera introduces also lines of four, five, six, eight, and nine syllables, usually in some sort of combination.

Most Italian words are stressed on the next-to-last syllable, and most Italian lines, in consequence, have their final stress upon the next-to-last syllable: Chiabrera makes more play than earlier poets had done with lines having their final stress on the third syllable from the end or on the last syllable, as in this stanza, in which the final stress rests on the third syllable from the end in each of the first five lines, and on the last syllable in the last line:

In van lusinghimi,
In van minaccimi,
Figlio di Venere;
Quel giogo impostomi
Dolce o spiacevole,
Io più nol vo'.‡

* Spanish *gongorismo*, however, is not identical with Marinism; and French *préciosité* and English euphuism, while in some small measure similar to Marinism, were not derived from it.

† "The violet that amid the grass opens fresh in the morning, tell me, is it not a thing all fragrant, all charming and lovely?"

‡ "In vain you flatter me, in vain you threaten me, son of Venus; that yoke that you have placed upon me, (whether it be) sweet or displeasing, I will have no more of it."

These *canzonette* served to establish in Italy a new set of lyric forms charmingly appropriate for lighthearted verse. They were not without precedent: *canzonette* had been written by Giustinian in the fifteenth century; much of the poetically unpretentious verse written to be set to music in the sixteenth century had been written in short lines and stanzas; and the Horatian odes of Bernardo Tasso had given literary status to the short stanza. All of these precedents, presumably, were familiar to Chiabrera; but the particular influence that was strongest with him was not Italian but French: Chiabrera's *canzonette* reflect knowledge of the odes of Ronsard both in general and in particular instances.

Chiabrera's Horatian odes imitate those of Horace neither in the merely general manner of Bernardo Tasso, nor, as Tolomei had prescribed, through the adoption of an artificial scheme of long and short syllables. The stanzas of each Italian ode imitate the strophes of a particular type of Latin ode through the use of unrhymed lines of different lengths that are arranged according to the pattern of the Latin type in question, and follow that type also, at least approximately, in the usual distribution of their verbal stresses: when such a stanza is read it gives an effect similar to that received from the reading of a Latin strophe of the type in question if that strophe is read with its normal verbal stresses and without regard to the rules of scansion. One of Chiabrera's Alcaic stanzas, for instance, reads thus:

Apransi rose, volino zefiri,
L'acque scherzando cantino Tetide;
Ma nembi, d'Arturo ministri,
Quindi lunge dian timore ai Traci.*

Chiabrera's best work is to be found in his thirty brief satires, written, in blank verse, in the latter part of his life. Like the satires of Horace, Chiabrera's are not violent, but are mild and amusing in manner even when they are seriously critical or tinged with sadness. Horace had called his satires *Sermones*: Chiabrera chose for his the name *Sermoni*. In them he treats such themes as his own way of quiet life; the slackness of Italian youth; feminine fashions; legal pettifoggery; avarice; the vanity of rank; moderation; life as a comedy in which we play parts that show what we should like to be. In one *sermone* he imagines what is happening on the Florentine Marmi — those Cathedral steps that Doni had made the scene of many conversations. The flower of the Florentine nobility will be there, and the flower of the commonalty too, when they have finished their trading in the New Market. Someone is reading out a letter brought by courier from France; someone else declares that Holland is fitting out a fleet that is to be commanded by an English *milorte*; Nanni is afraid that the *scirocco* has ruined his grapes; Bindo

* "Let roses open, let zephyrs fly, let the waters gaily sing of Thetis; but let clouds, ministers of Arcturus, far from hence give fear to the Thracians."

tells of a grand Spanish lady just come to lodge at the "Campana"; the painter Bronzino is there, and the musician Peri; someone is talking about the discoveries of Galileo. Just one thing could spoil it all: the coming of a poet who would insist on reading his latest madrigal, and then a sonnet, and then a *canzone*. There's nothing to do, in such a case, but flee.

Wordsworth admired Chiabrera greatly, and translated several of his epitaphs.

Alessandro Tassoni (1565–1635), Modenese by birth, lived chiefly in Rome, where he served as secretary to one or another cardinal; but he spent three years in the service of Carlo Emanuele; and he returned finally to Modena. He wrote two prose works of some interest: a miscellaneous mass of *Pensieri diversi*, philosophical, scientific, literary, and political; and a series of *Considerazioni sulle rime del Petrarca* in which his main concern is to attack the follies of Petrarchism. But his fame rests upon his mock-heroic epic, *La secchia rapita*, "The Captured Bucket," the first and best of many Italian mock-heroic epics. There had been plenty of humor in the *Morgante*, but Tassoni's humor, unlike that of Pulci, mocks the epic tradition itself. He writes in the conventional octaves: his poem, in twelve cantos, is relatively brief.

The petty warfare between the neighboring cities of Modena and Bologna which provides Tassoni with his general theme is basically historic. In 1325, after Bolognese depredations in Modenese territory, Modenese raiders forced an entry into Bologna, and carried home as trophy a wooden bucket from a public well. Bologna tried unsuccessfully to get it back: it still hangs in the *campanile* of the Cathedral of Modena. But Tassoni, making fun of history as of everything else, assigns this warfare to the middle of the thirteenth century, thus enabling himself to bring in King Enzo, a son of Frederick II, as one of his characters; and with deliberate anachronistic satire he introduces, with or without disguise, various persons, customs, and conditions of his own day. The poem opens with an account of the first Bolognese attack and of the Modenese victory, pursuit, seizure of the bucket, and triumphal return. Bolognese ambassadors then request that the bucket be sent back, offering a border town in exchange; but the request is refused. Bologna declares war: the Modenese send for help to the Emperor Frederick, make alliances, enroll their own troops, and then devote themselves to festivals and dances. The Bolognese, meanwhile, make their alliances. Jove now takes cognizance of the affair, and calls a general council of the gods, at the end of which Pallas, Apollo, Bacchus, Venus, and Mars decide to enter the conflict — Pallas and Apollo on the side of the learned and poetic Bologna, the others on the side of Modena. Venus, visiting King Enzo in a dream, summons him to Modena. The hostile armies gather, and are duly reviewed. Combat is joined, and Enzo is captured by the Bolognese. A truce is arranged, and the Modenese offer to exchange the bucket for Enzo and four captive knights; but the offer is refused. An enchanted island floats down a river that runs through the battlefield; and its occupant challenges all knights to single combat. Thanks to enchantment he wins joust after joust, but is finally unhorsed by the Modenese Count of Culagna: it then appears that such a victory could have been won only by the most cowardly of all knights on earth. The Count is presently defeated in an undesired duel. Peace is finally arranged by a papal Legate: Bologna keeps Enzo and Modena keeps the bucket.

The poem is pervaded by an exuberant, satirical, and often brilliant humor —humor that is all-inclusive and respects no limitations whatsoever. There are passages in which the humor is sustained and cumulative, and others in which an apparent seriousness finds its climax in a sudden hilarious absurdity. The outstanding passages of the former type are the account of the council of the gods and the account of the duel of the Count of Culagna. Most of the gods, when the summoning bell rings, drive to the council in their coaches, with much pomp of liveried attendants: Apollo (wearing the Spanish Order of the Golden Fleece) comes in a light traveling carriage drawn by six swift jennets; Neptune comes on a dolphin. There are absentees: Diana is doing her washing, and the Fates are baking. To the assembly, gathered in the magnificent council hall of the supreme palace, Jove enters, preceded by drums, trumpets, a hundred pages and other servants, and by Hercules, as captain of the guard. But the subsequent proceedings are disorderly in the extreme, despite Jove's thunderbolt and spectacles.

The Count of Culagna (said to be the son of Don Quixote's son Phlegethon the Fair), having issued a challenge under the mistaken impression that the man challenged would not be able to fight, does his best to get out of the duel, feigning sickness, and making his will, with his friends and servants around him; but three potent draughts of malmsey bring him to life and to the field of honor. Struck in the gorget by his opponent's lance, he is unhorsed, and seeing a redness upon his doublet he thinks himself mortally wounded, and surgeons and a confessor are called to his tent; but the surgeons can find no wound, and the redness turns out to be a ribbon that had come untied.

CHAPTER 33

Campanella

GIOVAN DOMENICO CAMPANELLA, born in 1568 at Stilo, in Calabria, showed himself as a boy to be an eager student and a precocious poet. In 1582 he entered the Dominican order, taking the name Tommaso. During the next seven years, spent in various southern monasteries, he read omnivorously in the field of philosophy, dissatisfied with everything he read until he came upon the writings of Telesio. An unfortunate friendship led him to a lasting belief in astrology and to the conviction that he himself, born under the beneficent influence of six planets in the ascendant, was destined to be the reformer of the world. In 1589 he wrote, in Latin, his first major philosophical work, the Telesian *Philosophia sensibus demonstrata*, "Philosophy Demonstrated by (the evidence of) the Senses"; and late in the year he went to Naples, where he discussed many subjects with many men, and continued his studies and his writing. In 1591, however, the publication of his *Philosophia* led to his first imprisonment, from which he was released in the following year. Ordered to return to Calabria, he went instead to the University of Padua. In 1593, charged by the Inquisition with improper theological disputation, he was tortured, condemned, and imprisoned: in his prison he wrote two political treatises in which he set forth for the first time his lifelong dream of a universal government under religious authority. In 1594 he was transferred to a Roman prison, where he was again tortured, and went on writing. In 1595 he abjured his heresies, and was placed in a Roman monastery, where for two years his incredible productivity continued. Then, however, he was again imprisoned, and ordered, on his release, to return to Calabria. There, inspired by portents and prophecies and surrounded by malcontents, he headed a conspiracy designed to overthrow the Spanish rule and establish Calabria as a religious republic under his leadership. Arrested by the Spanish authorities in 1599, together with some of his fellow conspirators, he was taken, with them, to Naples; and his twenty-seven-year ordeal of continuous imprisonment began. At the outset he underwent repeated torture, and escaped execution only through a pretense of madness maintained unbreakably for more than a year. Eight of his prison years were spent in an underground dungeon. Nevertheless he experienced an intensification of his own religious devotion, and he continued to produce philosophical works at an astounding rate, and to write poetry. There were periods in which he was treated with somewhat less severity, and he was at times allowed to receive visitors, and to give some instruction. In 1626 he was released: after a single month, however, he was sent to Rome, where he was tried by the Inquisition, and again imprisoned. In 1628, through papal intervention, he was at last set free. He was still eager to work for reform, to engage in theological discussion, and to give political advice; but suspicion and hostility beset him, and in 1634, in order to avoid a new trial, he fled to France. He was warmly welcomed; but hostility and misery soon overtook him. In the Spring of 1639 he read in the stars the imminence of his own death, which the propitiatory rites he then performed failed to avert.

All of the poems written by Campanella before his imprisonment in Rome in 1594 have been lost: it seems probable that most of them were in Latin. His surviving lyrics, all in Italian, are for the most part in the standard forms; but three are in free unrhymed imitations of Latin elegiac distichs. One of the three, beginning

> Musa latina, è forza che prendi la barbara lingua,*

contains these two lines, later to be quoted by Carducci:

> Musa latina, vieni meco a canzone novella,

and

> può nova progenie il canto novello fare.†

The few surviving poems that were written in Rome or, just afterward, in Calabria, reflect prison sufferings; attack the defenders of Greek philosophy; urge the transcendent importance of devotion to God; and express belief in the properly universal rule of the Church.

Campanella's other surviving lyrics, were composed, with only two or three exceptions, during the first eight years of his long Neapolitan imprisonment. The earliest of these poems reflect the experiences of the collapse of the Calabrian conspiracy and those of the early days of imprisonment. The

* "Latin muse, you must needs take the barbarian language"—that is, "you must needs speak now not in Latin, but in Italian, a language derived from barbarian sources." Campanella, like many others of his time, thought of Italian as a blend of Latin and the languages of the early northern invaders.

† "Latin muse, come with me to (the making of) a new song," and "the new song may (serve to) make a new people."

failure of the Calabrian people to support the conspiracy led to the writing of this sonnet:

> The people is a beast of muddy brain,
> That knows not its own force, and therefore stands
> Loaded with wood and stone; the powerless hands
> Of a mere child guide it with bit and rein:
> One kick would be enough to break the chain;
> But the beast fears, and what the child demands,
> It does; nor its own terror understands,
> Confused and stupefied by bugbears vain.
> Most wonderful! with its own hand it ties
> And gags itself — gives itself death and war
> For pence doled out by kings from its own store.
> Its own are all things between earth and heaven;
> But this it knows not; and if one arise
> To tell this truth, it kills him unforgiven.*

Other poems pour bitter scorn upon those conspirators who had turned traitors, or resound with praise of those who had been faithful under torture. There are damning indictments of their tormentors; and there is gratitude for their assigned advocate, "a lamp alight against the shadow of death." There are appeals for help, human and divine; and there are assertions of confidence: "the sword of Heaven is toiling for me."

Somewhat later are poems on a variety of themes, largely political or religious. The prisoner attacks hypocrites, sophists, heretics, and workers of miracles; and inveighs against those who are forever exalting the merely fabulous heroes of ancient Greece while disregarding the glories of modern Italy — Columbus, who "makes a bridge, for Caesar and for Christ, between two worlds"; Americo Vespucci, name-giver for the new world; and Telesio, *splendor della natura*. A fine series of Holy Week poems ends with this sonnet:

> If Christ was only six hours crucified
> After few years of toil and misery,
> Which for mankind He suffered willingly,
> While heaven was won forever when he died;
> Why should He still be shown on every side,
> Painted and preached, in nought but agony,
> Whose pains were light matched with his victory,
> When the world's power to harm Him was defied?
> Why rather speak and write not of the realm
> He rules in heaven, and soon will bring below
> Unto the praise and glory of His name?
> Ah foolish crowd! This world's thick vapours whelm
> Your eyes unworthy of that glorious show,
> Blind to His splendour, bent upon His shame.

* This translation, and the following translations of complete sonnets, are by John Addington Symonds.

In a series of three extraordinary psalms in *canzone* form Campanella wrestles fiercely with the problem of evil, especially the problem of the evil that holds him in its unrelenting grasp. One stanza reads thus:

> Oh let eternal Love be moved again to pity, and let infinite Wisdom stir the unbounded Power that of itself beholds the dire distress of my long hell: six on six years spent in suffering — the affliction of every sense; my frame seven times racked; the curses and the lies of fools; the sun denied to my eyes; nerves rent, bones wrenched apart, flesh torn; the woes of my pallet; the irons, my blood shed, the cruel fear; food scant and foul — and in hope worthy of Thy lance and shield.

The questioning *Perchè? Perchè? Perchè?* rings desperately through the three poems; and the answers that Campanella strives gallantly to perceive and to construct lead only to new questioning. Yet if release be granted him he will undertake to bring all nations to the school of the liberating, true, and living God; to destroy false and self-seeking cults; to establish the throne and the standard of reason, deposing cowardly vice; to humble the arrogant; and to call enslaved souls to liberty.

Most of his still later poems were composed in his underground dungeon; and most of them are specifically, even technically, metaphysical. But metaphysics, for Campanella, is not an intellectual exercise, but a means for the attainment of the knowledge of God and for the regeneration of the world. The three qualities of God which are the supreme determining principles of the living universe are Power, Wisdom, and Love — *Possanza, Senno, Amore.* The three besetting woes of the world are tyranny, which is false power, sophistry, which is false wisdom, and hypocrisy, which is false love. To his three supreme principles Campanella devotes long and detailed *canzoni.* In these and in similar *canzoni* on Beauty and on the Supreme Good, and in some related shorter poems, the processes of analysis and exposition tend to stifle the poetic spirit: yet one is conscious always of an urgent, if austere, apostleship that is striving to understand, to teach, and to reform; and there are passages in which the nobility of the thought finds clear and perfect rhythmic wording.

Among the later poems that are not metaphysical are two sonnets on the universe as a stage; and this modernization of the parable of the Good Samaritan:

> From Rome to Ostia a poor man went;
> Thieves robbed and wounded him upon the way:
> Some monks, great saints, observed him where he lay,
> And left him, on their breviaries intent.
> A Bishop passed thereby, and careless bent
> To sign the cross, a blessing brief to say;
> But a great Cardinal, to clutch their prey,
> Followed the thieves, falsely benevolent.

At last there came a German Lutheran,
Who builds on faith, merit of works withstands;
He raised and clothed and healed the dying man.
Now which of these was worthiest, most humane?
The heart is better than the head, kind hands
Than cold lip-service; faith without works is vain.
Who understands
What creed is good and true for self and others?
But none can doubt the good he does his brothers.

Other poems voice again his well-nigh unbearable sufferings. One of these (written in elegiac distichs), a poem to the springtime sun, unseen, but imagined in all its life-giving power, ends thus:

Tu miserere, Dio, tu che sei larghissimo fonte
di tutte luci: venga la Luce Tua —

Do Thou have mercy, oh God, Thou who art the inexhaustible fountain of all lights: let Thy Light come to me.

Another, from the deepest depths of all, begins with the lines

Temo che per morir non si migliora
lo stato uman: per questo io non m'uccido;

but though the Omnipotent is still silent the poem ends in faith:

Stiamci come Dio vuol, poiché non erra.*

Among these later poems, also, are four strange and magnificent odes: one on the powers of man, and three in which all creatures, on earth and in heaven, are summoned, in a mood of the highest exaltation, to praise the Lord.

After Campanella had virtually stopped writing Italian poems he gathered all that he could into a collection, called *La cantica*, in seven Books: this collection has not survived. In 1613 he gave to a visiting German friend a selective collection containing about ninety poems, nearly every one accompanied by a succinct comment in Italian prose: this collection was published in Germany in 1622, under the title *Scelta d'alcune poesie filosofiche di Settimontano Squilla.*† It remained almost unknown until the nineteenth century.

Campanella was concerned with poetry not only as a creative poet but also as a theorist. Before 1600 he wrote a treatise on poetry, the *Poetica*, in Italian prose; and about 1612 he rewrote it in Latin prose, under the title *Poeticorum liber unus.* While it is one of the more original of the Italian treatises on poetry, it has little continuing importance. Campanella's preoccu-

* "I fear that death brings no betterment to the human lot, and for this reason I do not take my life . . . Let us remain as God wills, since he errs not."

† Campanella called himself *settimontano* because of seven protuberances, or "mountains," on his head. *Squilla*, "bell," is a synonym for *campanella*.

pation with reform made it inevitable that he should attribute to poetry a primarily moral, almost a religious, function. Many of the examples are taken from Dante, for whom Campanella had a great admiration.

The one work by which Campanella has been widely known is his utopia, "The City of the Sun," which he wrote in Italian prose, in prison, probably in 1602, calling it *La città del sole*. About 1609 a somewhat revised form of the work was attached as an appendix to Campanella's *Aforismi politici*, which was itself included in a loosely unified collection of philosophical works, some of them in Italian and some in Latin. Five or six years later, while preparing this collection for publication in Latin as a single composite work, Campanella translated the *Città del sole* into Latin prose, calling it *Civitas solis*. Under this title, accordingly, it appeared in the *Philosophia realis*, which was first published, in Germany, in 1623, and reissued, with some revision, in France, in 1637. In the course of the nineteenth century the Latin form of "The City of the Sun" was translated into Italian, French, English, and German: the original Italian form was first published only in 1904.

The *Città del sole* shows acquaintance with Plato's *Republic*, with More's *Utopia*, with Doni's *Mondi*, and with many other works; but it is essentially a creation of Campanella's own powerful and comprehensive imagination. In form, it is a dialogue between a knight and a Genoese sea captain just returned from a voyage around the world: the knight, however, merely asks the questions that elicit the captain's account of the City of the Sun, which he had found in the interior of a great tropical island. The city is built in a series of seven concentric rings. There is an outer wall; and inner walls separate the several rings from each other. There is a temple in the focal circle.

The city is governed by a priest-philosopher known as Sun, or Metaphysician. His three chief officials bear the curious titles Pon, Sin, and Mor, which are intended to suggest the words *possanza*, *senno*, and *amore*. Pon is in charge of defense; Sin is in charge of the sciences, the men of learning, and the liberal and mechanical arts; and Mor is in charge of eugenics, education, medication, agriculture, food, and dress. Sun himself must be expert in all fields:

> None can be Sun save one who knows all the histories of nations, and rites and sacrifices, and republics and inventors of laws and arts. Then he must know all the mechanical arts . . . and all the sciences, mathematical, physical, and astrological. . . . But most of all is it necessary that he be a metaphysician and a theologian, knowing well the root and test of every art and science; the likenesses and differences of things; the Necessity, the Fate, and the Harmony of the world; Power, Wisdom, and divine and universal Love; and the grades of beings and their correspondences with the things of heaven, earth, and sea; and he must study deeply in the prophets and in astrology.

Pon, Sin, and Mor have subordinate officials charged with special responsibilities: thus the staff of Sin includes officials known respectively as Grammarian, Logician, Physicist, Physician, Politician, Economist, Moralist, Astronomer, Astrologer, Geometer, Cosmographer, Musician, Master of Perspective, Arithmetician, Poet, Orator, Painter, and Sculptor.

All property is owned in common; and there is accordingly no occasion for arrogance, wealth, inheritance, rapacity, avarice, intrigue, hypocrisy, or graft. The Solarians have a great love for their city, and are bound together in strong mutual friendship. The vast wall surfaces are utilized in an immense scheme of visual education: they are painted with mathematical figures, maps, and alphabets; and with representations of minerals, lakes, seas, rivers, liquids, herbs, trees, fish, birds, reptiles, insects, animals, the mechanical arts and their inventors, the inventors of laws, sciences, and arms, Moses, Osiris, Jove, Mercury, Mahomet, Christ and the Twelve Apostles, Caesar, Alexander, Pyrrhus, and many other persons. Children between the ages of three and seven learn through guided walks along the walls, with intervals of play and running about, and visits to the offices of artisans, tailors, painters, goldsmiths, and so on. The next three years are devoted to the study of the natural sciences, with intervals of exercise and of public service. Thereafter the course of study concentrates on mathematics, medicine, other sciences, and the mechanical and agricultural arts.

The captain goes on to describe in similar detail many phases of the life of the city: dormitories, refectories, food, dress, eugenic regulations, public works, the prevention and if necessary the conduct of war, agriculture, navigation, medical care (disease is uncommon), justice (crime is rare), philosophy, and religion. The religion of the Solarians is natural, not revealed; but it seems to the knight, as the captain describes it, to be not far from Christianity. Its holy laws are summed up in the distich:

Quel che non vuoi per te non far ad altri,
e quel che vuoi per te fa tu il medesimo —

That which thou dost not wish for thyself, do not unto others; and that which thou wishest for thyself, do thou likewise.

The *Città del sole* is impressive as an idealistic imaginative achievement; it is particularly interesting in its insistence on the importance of the sciences in life and in education; and some of its elements are still thought-provoking. It is naïvely monastic, however, in its underlying assumption that an entire people could live in loving contentment under a regime of absolute, though benevolent regimentation. In the figure of the governing priest-philosopher, who must be possessed of universal knowledge, one discerns something of what Campanella himself would have liked to be as head of his Calabrian republic and as reformer of the world.

He wrote in all about a hundred works, of which only about half survive.

Those of central importance are the purely philosophical works, especially the *Del senso delle cose*, "On the Living Quality of Things," and the *Metaphysica*. Other works deal with religion (notably the vast *Theologia* and the *Quod reminiscentur*, a program for world-wide conversion), political theory and practice (notably the *Monarchia di Spagna*, of which English translations appeared in 1654 and 1660), astronomy (notably the *Apologia pro Galilaeo*, an able defense of the Copernican system), astrology, mathematics, physiology, medicine, the government of the family, the interpretation of dreams, fortification, rhetoric, and poetry.

Campanella's philosophy is a blending of Telesian and Platonic elements, interwoven, with intuitions and intensively achieved concepts of his own, into a powerful eclectic system. His underlying philosophic assumption is that there can be no conflict between the facts of nature and philosophic verity. His most essential tenets are the belief that the three qualities of God which are the supreme determining principles of the universe are power, wisdom, and love; the belief that individual human power, wisdom and love, derived from the corresponding divine qualities, begin with and expand from the exercise of individual strength, the knowledge of self, and the fundamental instinct of self-preservation; and the belief that cognition is the proof and the characteristic activity of being: *cognoscere est esse.*

CHAPTER 34

Galileo and Other Prose Writers

GALILEO GALILEI, the founder of modern physical science, was born in Pisa in 1564. His education included a thorough study of the classic languages and literatures. He was deeply interested in poetry, and was an expert lutanist. In 1581 he began the study of medicine at the University of Pisa; but he turned presently to mathematics and physics, and by 1583 the extraordinary series of his experiments had begun. From 1585 to 1589, living chiefly in Florence, he continued his research, and supported himself by giving private lessons. In 1588 he gave two public lectures on the form, location, and size of Dante's Inferno. From 1589 to 1592 he held the chair of mathematics in the University of Pisa, perfecting his scientific method, and advancing swiftly in the establishment of physical laws. He aimed consistently at the complete mastery of isolated facts, or groups of closely related facts, through minute observation, controlled experimentation, the formulation of hypotheses, and the subjection of these hypotheses to renewed experimentation: he made no effort to unify the entire field of knowledge in a philosophic synthesis. His first scientific publication, the *De motu*, "On Motion," is of this Pisan period. Within this period, also, he wrote a burlesque *capitolo* on the requirement that the University professors should wear gowns. Either at Florence or at Pisa, in all probability, he wrote his keenly and sometimes violently critical *Considerazioni sul poema del Tasso*: he greatly preferred the *Orlando furioso*. To Aristotelianism, in science or in poetics, he was implacably hostile, winning thus the enmity of some of his Pisan colleagues.

In 1592 he was appointed to a professorship in the more liberal University of Padua. His long service there culminated, in 1609 and 1610, with the invention of the telescope (on the basis of suggestions derived from a Dutch spyglass), and his discovery, in quick succession, of the mountains of the Moon, the nature of the Milky Way and the nebulae, and four of the satellites of Jupiter — which he called *le stelle medicee*, "the Medicean stars." These discoveries he published immediately in an announcement written in enthusiastic, even poetic, Latin prose, entitled *Sidereus nuncius*, "Sidereal Message."* Before the year 1610 was over he had discovered also the rings of Saturn, the phases of Venus, and the nature of sunspots. To a friend he wrote:

> I render thanks infinitely to God who has deigned to make me the first beholder of things so marvelous, and hidden throughout the centuries.

But his colleague in philosophy at Padua refused to look through his telescope; and a Pisan professor attempted to prove, on logical grounds, that such things could not be. Late in 1610 Galileo returned to Tuscany, as Philosopher and Mathematician to the Grand Duke Cosimo II, and as Professor of Mathematics in the University of Pisa.

The discoveries of Galileo had the effect of advancing the Copernican system from the status of an a priori mathematical theory to that of a theory telescopically confirmed and verifiable: they came therefore as a perilous shock to the guardians of established philosophical and theological dogma. In 1616 the doctrine that the earth moves was formally condemned by the Inquisition, and Galileo was warned to abandon it. Three years later Orazio Grassi, a Jesuit, published a discourse on comets, which led Galileo and one of his disciples to write an opposing discourse on comets, to which Grassi replied in a Latin work entitled *Libra astronomica ac philosophica*, "The Astronomical and Philosophical Balance," in which he attacked Galileo on many counts. To this attack Galileo replied, in 1623, in *Il saggiatore*, "The Assayer's Balance" (the implication being that Galileo's balance, unlike Grassi's *Libra*, was a precision instrument). It consists of a long epistolary introduction and some fifty sections, or "assays." Each of these sections begins with a verbatim quotation of a portion of the text of the *Libra*, and then proceeds, sometimes briefly and sometimes at considerable length, to demolish the assertions and arguments contained in the passage quoted. Among the sections of greatest interest are one in which Galileo, defending his own achievement, tells of his invention of the telescope; one in which he discusses the infinite variety of observable phenomena and the consequent folly involved in claiming complete knowledge in any field; and another in which he insists upon the insignificance of constantly repeated assertions as contrasted with experimental demonstrations of fact. The *Saggiatore* is as masterly in its Italian prose style as it is in its scientific content. It is of a limpid clarity in expression, completely free from rhetorical disfigurement,

* *Nuncius* in this case means "message," not "messenger."

rich in apposite imaginative illustration, and enlivened with a humor that is now placid and now ironic.

The same literary qualities distinguish the *Dialogo . . . sopra i due massimi sistemi del mondo*, "Dialogue on the Two Principal Systems of the Universe," published in 1632. The systems in question are, naturally, the Ptolemaic and the Copernican. The interlocutors are two contemporaries of Galileo, who defend the Copernican system, the one with scientific precision, the other with a glowing enthusiasm, and a third person, perhaps real, perhaps fictional, named, by Galileo, Simplicio, who defends the Ptolemaic system with arguments based on the authority of Aristotle. Their talks, dramatic in their underlying intensity, are held on four successive days, in the Venetian palace of one of the interlocutors. The idolatry of Aristotle — not Aristotle himself — is dismissed with contempt:

> How can you doubt that if Aristotle could see the new discoveries in the heavens he would have changed his opinions, revised his writings, and adhered to the better-founded doctrines, disowning those followers of his who are of such poor brain that they are too easily induced to maintain the authority of every word of his — without realizing that if Aristotle were what they imagine him to have been he would be a man of indocile brain, of stubborn mind, of barbarous spirit, and of tyrannous will, regarding all other persons as stolid, and insisting that his own decrees should be placed above the evidence of the senses, above the results of experimentation, above nature herself?

Many portions of the *Dialogo* are technically scientific, and many contain diagrams or other illustrations. As the dialogue reaches its conclusion the Copernican system inevitably stands out as triumphant.

Latent enmity now became active, insidious, and powerful: even Pope Urban VIII, who had been friendly to Galileo, was led to believe that he had himself been caricatured in the person of Simplicio. Galileo was summoned to Rome to appear before the Inquisition. Nearly seventy, losing his sight, his health failing, he was ultimately broken by the long ordeal of menacing interrogation, and was brought to abjure the doctrine he had in fact so gloriously fortified. He was condemned to confinement for three years, and the *Dialogo* was placed on the Index. The physical conditions of his confinement were not severe. After some time spent under restriction in Roman and Sienese dwellings, he was allowed to live in his own villa at Arcetri, near Florence; but even there he was subject to constant surveillance by the Inquisition, whose officers controlled and limited his communication with friends and disciples. Yet there, in the blindness now come upon him, he completed and dictated his last major work, the *Discorsi e dimostrazioni matematiche intorno a düe nuove scienze*, published in Leiden in 1638, in which virtually all the physical theories which he had developed during his lifetime are assembled and restated. The "two new sciences" are specifically mechanics and the science of motion. From the point of view of the physicist this is the most important of all the many works of Galileo. It is highly technical, in text and illustration, but it has literary qualities as well. It is in dialogue form: the three interlocutors of the *Dialogo* reappear, and their talks are again held on four successive days. The style is still of distinguished vigor and clarity. In his last years Galileo was allowed somewhat greater freedom, and had the comfort of loyal companionship and correspondence. He died in 1642.

Fra Paolo Sarpi (1552–1623) — called by an English biographer "the Greatest of the Venetians" — took the name Paolo when, at the age of thirteen, he entered the Servite order: his baptismal name had been Pietro. Throughout his youth and young manhood he studied prodigiously in virtually all fields of knowledge, his main interests being theology and the sciences. He seems to have discovered the circulation of the blood; but he did not publish his discoveries. Somewhat later his main interest shifted to political history and theory, centering on the problem of the respective authorities of the Church and of the secular states. Partly because he was profoundly loyal to his own Venice, where alone in Italy the light of liberty still shone, and partly because of his own religious idealism and his strong sense of individual human dignity, he reached and thereafter maintained unswervingly these convictions: that in the Church as the body of all believers laymen as well as ecclesiastics had the right to say their say and exercise their influence; that ultimate human religious authority rested not with popes but with general councils, and that above even that authority rose the divine law itself; and that while the Church had absolute authority, on earth, in purely spiritual matters, it had no right to exercise temporal authority, or to interfere with the temporal activities of established states.

Early in 1606, Sarpi, as an expert in canon law, was appointed a special adviser to the Venetian government. In the Spring of that same year a bitter conflict of authority between Venice and the Church caused the Pope to lay an interdict on Venice. The firmness of the Venetian resistance, led by Sarpi, resulted eventually in the withdrawal of the interdict. From the point of view of certain extremist elements in Rome, however, Sarpi was too dangerous a force to be allowed to remain active. In October 1607, he was set upon in Venice by a band of assassins, who, leaving him stabbed, apparently, to death, escaped to Rome, where they found refuge in a cardinal's palace. Sarpi recovered, however, amid the surrounding admiration, gratitude, and concern of all Venice.

When he was able to work again he wrote his *Istoria particolare delle cose passate tra 'l Sommo Pontefice Paolo V e la Serenissima Republica di Venezia.* By virtue of its ample legal and historical knowledge, its scrupulous factual accuracy, and the compelling clarity and calmness of its style this *History* was exceedingly effective. An English translation is entitled *A Full and Satis-*

factorie Answer to the Late Unadvised Bull, Thundered by Pope Paul the Fift, Against the Renowned State of Venice.

His largest and greatest work was the *Istoria del Concilio di Trento*, written in the years 1610–1618. He spared no pains in the achievement of accuracy and comprehensiveness; and while his convictions as to the nature of the Council and its actions are clearly perceptible, they appear, in the main, not as polemic assertions but as conclusions naturally drawn from the facts stated. Going back to the days of Leo X and coming gradually to the time of the Council itself, he then studies the Council as a human phenomenon, properly subject to a critical analysis, and traces in detail the stages by which it arrived at its absolutist outcome. The long and intricate discussions of the Council are summarized with a masterly clarity; and the chief personages of the story, with their varying interests, excellences, and weaknesses, are brought revealingly to life. Leo X, notable for his cultural patronage and his kindly disposition, "would have been a perfect pope, if to these things he had added a little knowledge of religious matters and a somewhat greater inclination to piety." The style of the *Istoria*, though keen in its expression of human insights and in its occasional imagery, is chiefly impressive by its cogent calmness. Milton in the *Areopagitica* made extensive use of "Padre Paolo the great unmasker of the Trentine Councel."

The life of Traiano Boccalini (1556–1613) of Loreto, spent mostly in Rome or in minor official positions in the Papal States, was lighted by twin flames: love of Italy and hatred of Spain. His one ponderous work, the *Comentarii sopra Cornelio Tacito*, begun about 1590 and completed toward the end of his life, is not a systematic commentary, but a series of political discussions, suggested by passages in Tacitus, in which, with a wealth of modern instances, he considers various forms of government and the duties of princes, and, following the example of Tacitus, castigates the tyrannies of his day. He is at one with Machiavelli in many of his judgments:

> There is no cord or chain that can hold a prince to his word, no binding knot save his own interest and utility.

But he does not share Machiavelli's admiration of the Romans, "who filled the world with plunderings, slaughter, fire and flame," and offered "a wicked example of insatiable passion for power."

Long before he had finished the *Comentarii*, and probably about 1605, he began the writing of what he called *Ragguagli di Parnaso*, "Dispatches from Parnassus." These "dispatches" imitate in form the hand-written general news reports initiated a century earlier, which by this time had gained a wide currency. Boccalini's Parnassus is a considerable realm, ruled by Apollo, and peopled by scores of poets and other worthies, together with personifications of various states and of other human interests. The "dispatches" were at first circulated privately, some of them being such that they might have given serious offense to men powerful in Italy. But their popularity among those who received them was so very great that Boccalini ventured, in 1612, to publish a selection of a hundred of them, chosen from among those that were least likely to prove dangerous. The immediate success of this volume led to the publication of a similar selection in the following year. Many other dispatches remained in manuscript after Boccalini's death: a collection of about thirty of these was published in 1614 under the title *Pietra del paragone politico tratta dal monte Parnaso*, "Political Touchstone Brought from Mount Parnassus." About seventy others were first published in 1948.

All of the dispatches are satiric. Some of the themes are literary, others political. The satire is sometimes merely playful, sometimes bitter: its violence is greatest in the anti-Spanish dispatches included in the *Pietra del paragone*. Among the events reported are the condemnation of a Spartan who had taken three words to say what he might have said in two (he was condemned to read one of the histories of Guicciardini, but after getting through the first page begged for a life sentence to the galleys or for death instead); the arrival of a mule train laden with gold as a reward to Tacitus for praising Nero; a day of mourning for the invention of saucers; Tasso's presentation of the *Gerusalemme liberata* to Apollo; a discussion by the people of Mytilene as to whether, their prince having died, they should choose a new prince or institute liberty; the pompous arrival and ignominious departure of the Admirable Crichton; a justification of the invention of artillery on the ground that its horror would serve to bring about the ending of war; a reproof of princes for their neglect of disabled veterans; the failure of Plato and Aristotle, in a public debate, to reconcile their philosophies; the trial of Tacitus for having invented thought-penetrating spectacles; an inquiry by Thomas More as to when heresies would cease; a weighing of many states in the balance under the direction of Lorenzo de' Medici (France had gained thirteen million pounds in the last fifteen years; England had lost six million; the addition of her Italian provinces serves to *decrease* the total weight of Spain; Lorenzo, to increase the weight of Tuscany, puts in the brain of Duke Ferdinand — and the balance breaks); the condemnation of a philosopher who had advised a reduction in taxes; the erection of a statue (by Praxiteles) to a dentist; a convention of hypocrites; and instructions to a cardinal on methods of obtaining the papacy.

The *Ragguagli* were very popular throughout the seventeenth century both in Italy and elsewhere: translations appeared repeatedly in France, Spain, Holland, Germany, and England. It is altogether probable that both Swift and Addison were acquainted with them.

* * *

Straparola had included several folk tales, along with *novelle* of other kinds, in his *Piacevoli notti*: the first European book which is truly a collection of folk tales is *Lo cunto de li cunti*, "The Story of Stories," written in the Neapolitan dialect by Giambattista Basile (c. 1575–1632), and published, after his death, in 1634. Basile, born in Naples, was an honorable soldier and courtier, serving various masters on land and sea, and fulfilling faithfully and unselfishly the duties of the several minor governorships that he held in the latter part of his life. He wrote some verse in Italian and some in Spanish; but the only works for which he is remembered were written in his own Neapolitan dialect.

Lo cunto de li cunti is a collection of fifty stories set in a frame story: a prince and his wife, a Moorish slave who has won marriage by deceit, are entertained on five successive afternoons by ten women, each of whom on each day tells one story—except that on the last day the rightful princess appears as a substitute for the tenth woman and by telling her own story unmasks the slave's deceit, with appropriate results. The storytelling is preceded, on each day, by a dinner; and before dinner, on the second and later days, there is music, dancing, or the playing of games. Many familiar folk tales appear in this collection, among them Cinderella, Puss in Boots, Snow-White-Fire-Red, Beauty and the Beast, The Three Oranges, and The Dancing Water, the Singing Apple, and the Speaking Bird. Many of them begin with the formula *Era na vota*, "Once upon a time there was. . ." The stories are told without alteration of their traditional substance, but the manner of the telling is highly individual, in its vividness, in its sympathy, in its irrepressible verve, in its references to Neapolitan persons, places, and customs, and in the rampant Marinism of its style. Sunrises and the coming of night, in particular, are reported with an extraordinary Marinistic virtuosity:

> When the Sun with the golden broom of its rays had swept away the refuse of the Night from the fields sprinkled by the Dawn . . .
>
> When the Night had risen to light the candles of the catafalque of heaven for the funeral of the Sun . . .

The general likeness of the pattern of *Lo cunto de li cunti* to that of the *Decameron* led the publisher of the first edition to refer to it, in his preface, as *Il Pentamerone*; and this name is still commonly used as a brief and distinctive title for the "Story of Stories."

CHAPTER 35

Early Opera

THE FINAL RENAISSANCE manifestation of the humanistic spirit appeared late in the sixteenth century, with surprising results, in the field of music. In Florence about 1580 an informal group of musicians and other men interested in music, known as the Camerata (the word is generally used to designate a club of students), undertook intensive study of the statements about Greek music made by ancient Greek writers. Among the members of the group were the musicians Vincenzo Galilei (the father of Galileo), Jacopo Peri, and Giulio Caccini, and the poet Ottavio Rinuccini (1562–1621). The Camerata became convinced (mistakenly) that in the Greek performance of tragedies not only the choruses but also the individual parts had been sung, and that the music for these parts had been concerned mainly with the heightening of the expressive effect of the poetry it served. In the Italian tragedies and pastoral plays of the sixteenth century the choruses had regularly been sung, by several voices; but the individual parts had been spoken. The members of the Camerata, however, believing that Italian music should conform to what they thought to have been the Greek precedent, determined to devise a type of music which should be appropriate for the single-voice singing of individual parts.* This determination led them to the invention of what we know as recitative — *recitar cantando*, it was then called, and it was defined as "a mean between speech and music." The first recorded experiments in recitative were two compositions, now lost, written about 1590 by Vincenzo Galilei (who died in 1591): a setting of Dante's story of Count Ugolino, and a setting of portions of the Lamentations of Jeremiah.

The next step was the production, in 1594, of a short play entitled *Dafne*,

* They were presumably confirmed in their interest in the development of music for the single voice by the fact that among the professional or quasi-professional singers of the time there was growing, without reference to humanistic premises, a demand for the provision of music that would give them a better chance for the display of their individual abilities.

with words by Rinuccini and music by Peri. Since the *Dafne* is the first play written to be set completely to music, with the individual parts to be sung in recitative, it may fairly be called the first opera.* Peri's music for the *Dafne* is lost, but it is certain that in preparation for it he studied the natural inflections and cadences of speech, making them the basis of his recitative. Rinuccini's text, which has survived, is interesting mainly because of its firstness. The scene is a woodland glade. The persons of the play are Venus, Cupid, Apollo, Daphne, and a messenger; and a chorus of shepherds and nymphs takes part occasionally in the dialogue, and marks by stanzaic songs the ending of the four main portions of the action (neither in the *Dafne* nor in Rinuccini's later plays is there any formal division into acts). The first two of these portions are merely preliminary to the last two, which tell the familiar story of Apollo and Daphne. In the choral lyrics Rinuccini shows himself to be a follower of Chiabrera. A second performance, for which the play was somewhat altered, was given in 1597. According to an early writer, "the pleasure and astonishment created in the spirits of the spectators by this new spectacle were inexpressibly great."

In October 1600, for the festivities attending the marriage of Henry IV of France and Maria de' Medici, two plays of the new type were written, the *Euridice*, with words by Rinuccini and music chiefly by Peri, and the *Rapimento di Cefalo*, "The Deification of Cephalus," with words by Chiabrera and music chiefly by Caccini. The *Euridice* is the first opera of which the music is extant: most of the music of the *Cefalo* has been lost.

The *Euridice* is a much better play than the *Dafne*: it is longer, more substantial, and more varied. The stage setting again represents a woodland glade: for the central scene it was made, apparently by lighting devices, to represent the court of Pluto. The interlocutors, in addition to Orpheus and Eurydice, are three shepherds, a messenger, Venus, Pluto, Prosperina, Rhadamanthus, and Charon. There are two choruses, one of shepherds and nymphs, and one of infernal shades and deities. The scene in the lower world is well done; but the fact that the *Euridice* was written for a wedding festival made it necessary to provide a happy ending: the release of Eurydice is therefore unconditional — and the rest of the play falls flat. Musically, the recitative shows a tendency to blossom briefly into lyric passages which, while not yet arias, are of *arioso* character.

The performance of the *Cefalo* was remarkable chiefly for its extraordinarily elaborate stage setting and for its machinery, which was particularly convenient in providing transportation from and to Olympus.

In these first operas the music was subordinate to the words. But with the

* The *Dafne* was called a *favola per musica*, "a story for music," and similar though varying terms were applied to other early plays of this type. The term *opera* (which in itself means simply "the work") seems to have come into use about 1650. In Italian the word *melodramma* is used as a synonym for *opera*.

entrance of Monteverdi into the field of operatic composition music in its turn won priority. Monteverdi, though he retained recitative as the musical norm for individual parts, gave his recitative a much greater freedom by treating it rather as a musical expression of the spirit of the words concerned than as a mere heightening of verbal inflections and cadences; and he went well beyond Peri in his development of *arioso* passages.

His first opera, performed in Mantua in 1607, was the *Orfeo*, with insignificant words by a ducal secretary. In the following year he composed the music for a third play by Rinuccini, the *Arianna*. Most of the music is lost; but the poignant "Lament of Ariadne," beginning *Lasciatemi morire*, is still sung. The *Arianna* is the best of the plays of Rinuccini. The fixed scene represents a rocky shore on the island of Naxos. Theseus and Ariadne are the protagonists; Theseus has his counsellor and Ariadne her confidante; there are three messengers; Bacchus, Venus, Cupid, and Jove appear; and there are choruses of fishermen, of the soldiers of Theseus, and of the soldiers of Bacchus. Dramatic tension is reached in the conflict in Ariadne's heart between her longing for the home she has left and her love for Theseus, and in the conflict in the heart of Theseus between his love for Ariadne and his fear that his duty to Athens will require him to abandon her. The coming of Bacchus, a *deus ex nave*, brings the play to its happy ending. Many passages, both in the individual parts and in the choruses, are of a gentle poetic beauty. Rinuccini was by no means a great poet; but he was more successful, especially in the *Arianna*, than any other librettist of the seventeenth century.

Between 1608 and 1640 operas were written and composed by many poets and musicians, and were performed in many Italian cities. The range of subjects widened; comic elements crept into some *libretti*; the poetic text became more and more subservient to the music; *arioso* passages developed into arias; and the designing of stage settings and machinery became more and more elaborate (even Bernini was called upon for such designing). Until 1637 all performances were given privately, usually under courtly or academic auspices: in that year, in Venice, the public was for the first time admitted, on a paying basis, to an operatic performance.

Comic opera — as distinguished from opera having incidental comic elements — made its first appearance in 1639, in Rome, with the performance (at which Milton was an honored guest) of *Chi soffre speri*, "Let Sufferers Hope," the words by Cardinal Giulio Rospigliosi (later to become pope as Clement IX), the music by two minor composers. Comic characters of various kinds, together with mythological and pastoral figures, mingle with the persons of the main romantic plot. The sights and sounds of a street fair are represented in amusing detail.

* * *

The leading playwrights of this period were Michelangelo Buonarroti and Giambattista Andreini.

This Michelangelo Buonarroti (1568–1646), usually called *il Giovane* (that is, "the Younger"), was a nephew of the great Michelangelo, whose memory he did his best to honor: he founded the Galleria Buonarroti, and he first published his uncle's *Rime* (rewriting them, however, to suit his own quite inferior taste).

Chief among his writings is the enormous *La fiera*, "The Fair," a comedy written in free verse, performed in 1618. It is divided into five *giornate*, "days," each of which is divided into five acts. While there are a few characters who move through all the five days, the interest of the play lies not in what happens to these characters, but in the individual scenes, which afford vivid pictures of all sorts of persons mingling in the crowded activities of the fair. The Academy of the Crusca, of which Buonarroti was a member, had already started work on its great dictionary; and one of Buonarroti's main purposes in writing the *Fiera* was to record, with a view to later dictionary use, a mass of locutions specific to particular groups or types of people.

The *Tancia*, a comedy of rustic life, written mainly in octaves, is a much better play; but although there is in this instance a coherent plot, and although the dialogue is lively, the interest is again largely linguistic. Both dramatic and linguistic complications arise from the (eventually frustrated) desire of a young gentleman to marry a peasant girl: his city talk is past the comprehension of the peasants, who misunderstand him comically.

Giambattista Andreini (1578–1652), the son of Francesco and Isabella Andreini, was himself an actor, and a member first of the Gelosi and later of the Fedeli, "The Faithful Ones." He lived and acted chiefly in Mantua, under the patronage of Duke Vincenzo Gonzaga; but from time to time he went on tour in Italy or France or Germany. Most of his plays are run-of-the-stage comedies, conventional in their corruption and in their dramatic devices, but with some clever variations in their use of stock materials. He would hardly be remembered, however, if he had not written the devout *Adamo*, first given in 1613, which he called a *sacra rappresentazione*. The human persons of the play are, necessarily, Adam and Eve alone. The supernal and infernal persons include God the Father, the Archangel Michael, a guardian Cherub, Lucifer and several of his demons, the World and the Flesh and other allegorical figures, and the Serpent. There is an angelic chorus; and there is also a chorus of "igneous, aerial, aquatic, and infernal spirits." The play opens in Eden (a very formal garden, according to the illustrations in the first edition). The first Act tells of the creation of Adam and Eve and of an Infernal Council; in the second Adam and Eve express their gratitude to God, Adam names the animals, and the Serpent persuades Eve to taste the forbidden fruit; in the third Adam also tastes, and Michael expels Adam and Eve from Eden; in the fourth, after another Infernal Council, Lucifer dispatches the Flesh and the World to tempt Adam and Eve still further; and in the last Act, that temptation failing, there is a battle between the hosts of Heaven and those of Hell, and Michael assures Adam and Eve that because of their repentance they will be received into Heaven. The play is written in free verse, in a style which, though often extravagant in its rhetoric, is at times vigorous. The choruses were sung; the staging was very elaborate. The long-debated question as to whether the *Adamo* did or did not influence Milton is still unsettled.

In 1611 Flaminio Scala published the first collection of *scenari* for the *commedia dell'arte*, under the title *Teatro delle favole rappresentative*. About fifty *scenari* are included: among the characteristic titles are "The Dentist," "The Doctor in Despair," "Carpets from Alexandria," "The Two Pretended Gypsies," "The Crazy Princess," and "The Enchanted Tree."

Pulcinella, the last of the famous stock characters of the *commedia dell' arte*, came into existence, in Naples, probably between 1610 and 1620: he seems to have been invented by the actor Silvio Fiorillo. Pulcinella speaks the Neapolitan dialect, in a squeaky voice. He has an enormous nose and an enormous stomach, and is usually somewhat hunchbacked. He wears a black mask, a peaked hat or cap, a white jacket, and white trousers; and he carries a sword-like stick. He is a general funmaker: his traits are not as precise as those of the other main stock characters, though the fun he makes results often from his absurd blunders in speech or in action. His marital troubles are perpetuated in the Punch and Judy shows of the puppet theatre.

CHAPTER 36

A Stagnant Interval

THROUGHOUT THE REST of the seventeenth century Spanish control was crumbling, French influence was increasing, and the strength of Venice was declining. The Turks took Crete from Venice in 1669, and, driving westward again, besieged Vienna in 1683. One of the worst of all pestilences, starting in Naples in 1656, spread through Italy and over Europe.

The later sculpture of Bernini perpetuated restless moments of baroque emotionalism; but Bernini as architect designed the magnificent colonnades that embrace the approach to St. Peter's. Salvator Rosa, the leading painter of the period, was also its leading poet.

The opera — its *libretti* devoid now of poetic interest — continued to captivate Italian audiences, and extended its field to France and Germany. It became more and more a vehicle for soloists, the aria assuming musical centrality. Stage settings and mechanical devices were often highly spectacular. The violin was reaching perfection in the hands of the aging Niccolò Amati and the young Antonio Stradivari; and the evolution of the sonata was under way.

Torricelli, a pupil of Galileo, carried forward his master's work in physics, and invented the barometer. Malpighi made great advances in physiology. Redi, a poet as well as a scientist, will be considered presently.

The exiled Crashaw found monastic refuge and an early death in Italy. John Evelyn, visiting Italy just before the middle of the century, recorded his experiences and impressions in his admirable *Diaries*.

* * *

Italian literary production fell, in this period, to its lowest level. Only two writers rose much above mediocrity; and of these two, one was primarily a painter and the other primarily a scientist.

Salvator Rosa (1615–1673) spent his poverty-stricken youth in Naples; but he lived most of his tempestuous life in Rome, among loyal friends and implacable enemies. As a painter he depicts by preference, and with a driving and prolific energy, the wilder aspects of nature and of human nature — forests, craggy mountains, rocky shores, storms, ruins, bandits, battles, and scenes of human tragedy. His canvases, much sought after by English *milordi*, had their share in the stimulation of English romantic taste.

His six satires in *terza rima* release an energy not unlike that which gives life to his paintings. There is no amused aloofness here: rather has a new Juvenal come to judgment. In the first three satires, which constitute a trilogy, Rosa deals with the low state of Music, Poetry, and Painting in his time. His indignation is directed both against the incompetence and shamelessness of those who ply the arts and against the wealthy patrons who lavish gold upon such protégés while the masses suffer; and this second phase of his attack leads him naturally into indictment of heedless and grasping governors:

> The thousands that swore faith to you are to be seen half-naked on the streets, begging their bread. . . .
>
> You throw away your gold . . . and yet to one utterly bereft, who cannot stand upright for very need and hunger, you refuse a wretched farthing. . . .
>
> How many swagger about in velvet, with cape and sword, and brandish lances, in whose hands the mattock would be more fitting! How many lowly folk scrape the soil, men for whom fate has cut the nerves of their wings, who harbor thoughts magnanimous and sublime!

Music pervades the court —

> *Do re mi fa sol la* you sing as you go up the stairs; *la sol fa mi re do* you sing as you come down —

and infects the church:

> How scandalous, in sacred choirs, to hear vespers grunted, the mass barked, the *Gloria* brayed!

The satire on poetry contains a devastating analysis of the exaggerations and the absurdities of Marinism, quoting lines from some of its worst examples, and reproaches poets, in particular, for their unbounded adulation. If you must write, Rosa bids them,

> Tell rather that the zeal of faith is spent, and that for the price of a loaf of bread honor is sold, and liberty, one's soul, and heaven. . . .
>
> Tell fearlessly of the dreadful cries that rise from the earth, moaning in vain under the insults and the plunderings of faithless tyrants. . . .
>
> Tell how a poor fellow who rents four sods must pay in usury, after the injuries of tempest and of drought, the half of what remains.

Painters are attacked for their ignorance, their slovenliness, and their triviality —

> Painting pumpkins and hams all day long, coppers, pots, pans, rugs, birds, fish, greens, and flowers and fruit —

for their dishonesty, their servility, and their arrogance, and for still other faults.

The fourth satire, *La guerra*, deals with the evils of war, and then goes on to scourge the depraved manners and morals of modern life in general. The fifth is Rosa's personal defense against the attacks of his enemies. The sixth, *La Babilonia*, is a fearful indictment of the corruption of the Roman court. With all their stinging power, the satires suffer from prolixity, and from a heavy overweight of classic references.

Francesco Redi (1626–1698) of Arezzo was one of the busiest men of his century. He was, by profession, a physician: he served successive Medici grand dukes and many patients in Florence, and requests for advice came to him even from far countries. His scientific experimentation was done chiefly in biology. It was he who first impugned the theory of spontaneous generation; and he anticipated some of the methods and insights of modern bacteriology. He was an expert linguist, and was greatly interested in Italian dialects: for many years he lectured in the University of Florence on the language of Tuscany. He was also thoroughly well read in the classics and in early Italian poetry; and he collected French, Provençal, Catalan, and Italian manuscripts (preserving thus, among other things, the original manuscript of the autobiography of Cellini).

Quite inevitably — though he had no depth of poetic feeling — he turned his clear head and his clever hand to the writing of Italian verse. His poems in the conventional forms, pleasantly free from Marinism, are interesting chiefly for their revival of the lyric concepts of Dante and other early Tuscans and for their reversion to the theme of the Platonic ascent. The one poem of his that has attained some measure of fame is the thousand-line dithyramb, *Bacco in Toscana*, in which Redi's connoisseurship in verse and his connoisseurship in wine are gayly mingled. Following in a merely general sense the Greek dithyrambs (choral songs of praise to Bacchus), Redi imagines that Bacchus himself has come to the Tuscan hills, with Ariadne and a rout of satyrs and bacchantes; and that he tells Ariadne, with an agile wit, about dozens of Tuscan wines, commending some, and condemning others:

> Se vi è alcuno, a cui non piaccia
> La vernaccia
> Vendemmiato in Pietrafitta,
> Interdetto,
> Maledetto
> Fugga via dal mio cospetto,
> E per pena sempre ingozzi
> Vin di Brozzi,
> Di Quaracchi e di Peretola —

> If there is anyone who doesn't like the white wine that is harvested in Pietrafitta, let him flee away from my presence, interdicted, maledicted; and for punishment let him ever guzzle the wine of Brozzi, of Quaracchi, and of Peretola.

Other beverages are banned — among them water, lemonade, German beer, English cider, chocolate, tea, and coffee:

> Never shall I make use of chocolate or tea; such medicines shall never be for me: I'd rather drink poison than a cup full of bitter and evil coffee.

Bacchus samples as he goes along, and toward the end he reaches a swaying incoherence, which does not prevent him, however, from giving his verdict that the wine of Montepulciano is king of them all. The dithyramb is in freely rhymed verse, and gains an intriguing variety in form from the interweaving of lines of different rhythmic character and of different length, many of them very short. The linguistic brilliance of the poem is heightened by the pat use of rare words and by several comic coinages. Redi worked on the poem for several years, and published it, finally, in 1685, with an elaborate commentary.

* * *

By this time the *commedia dell'arte* had begun to deteriorate. For the several parts of the stock characters there were now booklets containing appropriate speeches that could be used in almost any play. The actors accordingly memorized such speeches, and did less and less actual improvisation. *Scenari*, also, as they multiplied, became increasingly repetitious, and novelty was limited, more and more, to the minor variation of situations that were in themselves hackneyed. Yet the *commedia dell'arte* continued to be very popular both in Italy and in France — where it had a considerable influence upon the early work of Molière. It has exercised an enduring influence upon Italian literary comedy.

* * *

It was very possibly within this period, though it may have been somewhat earlier, that a new and charming lyric form, the *stornello*, came into existence in Italian folk poetry.* The place and manner of its origin are unknown. The *stornello* consists, typically, of a short opening line, usually an invocation to a flower, followed by two eleven-syllable lines. The first and third lines rhyme; and the second line, while it differs from the first and third in its last stressed vowel, agrees with them, exactly or approximately, in the sounds that follow that vowel — as in this Umbrian example:

* The word *stornello*, as used to designate this lyric form, has no English equivalent.

Fior de ginestra!
Tutta s'infiora la campagna nostra
Quando s'affaccia Nina alla finestra.

Flower of the broom!
When Nina looks from out her window frame
Through all the fields the flowers straightway bloom.

There is also a rare two-line variety of the *stornello*, which is imitated by Browning in the snatches of song he introduces in his *Fra Lippo Lippi*. Sometimes the first line is of full length and without the floral invocation, as in this example, which is also Umbrian — and evidently later (perhaps only a little later) than the construction of Bernini's colonnade:

So' stata a Roma e so' stata a San Pietro,
E so' rivata fima al colonnato:
Ho ripensato a vo' — so' torna' 'ndietro.

I went to see St. Peter's, 'way to Rome:
I got to where those rows of columns loom —
Then I remembered you, and came back home.

Other translations follow (an attempt being made to retain the half-rhyming effect of the second line):

Flower of the rose!
Of you I think as soon as sun doth rise,
Of you I think until the day doth close.

Oh lily red!
The moments I'm with you so swiftly speed:
I say and say, and leave so much unsaid.

I stand and gaze and gaze upon the sea,
And all the boats they seem to come this way,
Save only his, that comes not back to me.

Stars by the score!
Come, count them, love: as many as there are,
The sorrows that you bring to me are more.

Flower of the cotton!
Sooner the Turk will cease to be a heathen
Than you and I make peace for all we've fought on.

Flower of love!
My name is written on the shifting wave,
And yours is written on the sky above.

CHAPTER 37

Metastasio and Other Arcadians

SPANISH MASTERY came to an end in Italy in 1713, when, as a result of the wide-ranging struggle for the Spanish succession, Spain ceded Lombardy, Southern Italy, and Sardinia to Austria, and Sicily to the Duchy of Savoy, which was then promoted to the rank of a kingdom. In 1720 Savoy and Austria exchanged Sicily and Sardinia: the young Italian kingdom was thereafter known as the Kingdom of Sardinia, though Piedmont remained its basic territory. In 1734 Charles of Bourbon, son of the King of Spain, conquered Southern Italy and Sicily, and made them into a new kingdom, detached from Spain, and influenced by Austria. In Tuscany the line of the Medici died out in 1737, and the succession passed to the Austrian Hapsburg family. Italian independence remained in the Kingdom of Sardinia, where strength was waxing, in Venice, where strength was waning, and in Rome, where there was no strength. Thus, in effect, most of Italy remained under a foreign control which had now become Austrian instead of Spanish. But throughout the eighteenth century Austrian control was milder than that of Spain had been, and Vienna itself was a center of Italian cultural activity.

The architect Nicola Salvi worked for many years, with collaborators, on the superb baroque Fountain of Trevi in Rome — finished, after Salvi's death, in 1762. A new Renaissance came to Venetian painting in the vigorous, imaginative, and splendidly glowing frescoes and canvases of Tiepolo, in Longhi's proud portraits and gay and gracious scenes of fashionable life, and in Canaletto's views of the city whose unique beauty he so well discerned and rendered. Most of the magnificent antiquities and futurities of Piranesi, the greatest of Italian engravers, had been done by 1760.

Opera was increasingly the rage throughout Italy, especially in Venice, Rome, and Naples. The methods and style of Alessandro Scarlatti set the norm for eighteenth-century opera in general. Pergolesi wrote his delightful *La serva padrona*, and, just before the end of his short life, his still living *Stabat mater*. Tartini defined the bases of modern violin technique. The continuing evolution of the sonata and the concerto was bringing them close to formal perfection. In 1711 Bartolommeo Cristofori made public his invention of the pianoforte.

Foreign literary influences became stronger than ever in Italy. Rolli's translation of *Paradise Lost* and of a passage from Hamlet will be mentioned in the course of the present chapter. *Julius Caesar*, the first of the plays of Shakespeare to be wholly translated into Italian, appeared in Italy in 1756. Many contemporary English works were translated, among them Dryden's *Alexander's Feast*, Addison's *Cato*, and Pope's *Rape of the Lock* and *Essay on Man* — also *Robinson Crusoe*, *Gulliver's Travels*, *Pamela*, and *Tom Jones*. The *Tatler* and the *Spectator* were well known and soon imitated in Italy.

Addison traveled through Italy in 1701, visiting by preference places associated with the classic poets, and after his return to England published his immediately popular *Remarks on Several Parts of Italy*. Gray spent several months in Italy in 1739 and 1740.

* * *

During the decades just prior to 1690 Queen Christina of Sweden (who had renounced her throne and was living in Rome) had been a gracious hostess to many men of letters; and some of them, after her death in 1689, decided to continue their association and to formalize it in an Academy, to which they gave the name Arcadia. Their first meeting was held in October 1690, in a Roman garden. The specific interest of the new Academy was in poetry; and its express purpose was "to exterminate bad taste, and to see to it that it shall not rise again, pursuing it continually wherever it may nest or hide itself, even in the most unknown and inconsiderable towns and villages." The particular object of attack, accordingly, was Marinism; and the substitute proposed was, as the name Arcadia suggests, a pastoral simplicity. The pastoral character of the Academy was emphasized in many ways. The Panpipe was chosen as emblem; the official terminology was pastoral; each member took a pastoral name; and the Infant Jesus (since it was to shepherds that He had first revealed Himself) was invoked as tutelary deity.

The powdered simplicity of the Arcadia, however, is not to be dismissed as a merely amusing affectation: it was, in its essence, an expression of a profound and thwarted desire for something better than the actual life of the time, for some relief from moral depression and political subjugation. No actual escape could be foreseen; and escape was sought, therefore, in enactment of the peaceful pastoral dream that had already been dreamed so often by classic and by Italian poets. Before 1600 Arcadian "colonies" had been established in Bologna, Ferrara, Venice, and several other cities; and by the middle of the eighteenth century colonies were everywhere. The chief activity of the Arcadians consisted in the production, the reading, and the discussion of poetry: but Arcadian membership included hundreds of men and women who could not by any stretch of the imagination be regarded as poets — among them artists, musicians, actors, scientists, princes, popes, and other dignitaries.

The Arcadia rendered good literary service in condemning Marinism and in promoting the restoration of a classic taste; but the quality of Arcadian verse was in general very poor. Nearly all of it was imitative, though the models were various. Some writers played the Panpipe; some turned again to Petrarch and the Petrarchists, with a curious predilection for Angelo di Costanzo; some smote the Pindaric lyre; and some imitated Chiabrera's light *canzonette.*

The Florentine Vincenzo da Filicaia (1642–1707), Polibo Emonio in Arcadia, wrote primarily in the Pindaric style, treating "heroic" subjects with a highly rhetorical sonority. In his religious and patriotic poems one perceives, beneath the rhetoric, an honorable sincerity of feeling and of purpose. He is best known for a fine sonnet that is freely rendered thus by Byron in two stanzas of *Childe Harold's Pilgrimage*:

Italia! oh Italia! thou who hast
The fatal gift of beauty, which became
A funeral dower of present woes and past,
On thy sweet brow is sorrow plough'd by shame
And annals graved in characters of flame.
Oh, God! that thou wert in thy nakedness
Less lovely or more powerful, and couldst claim
Thy right, and awe the robbers back, who press
To shed thy blood, and drink the tears of thy distress.

Then might'st thou more appal; or, less desired,
Be homely and be peaceful, undeplored
For thy destructive charms; then, still untired,
Would not be seen the armed torrents pour'd
Down the deep Alps; nor would the hostile horde
Of many-nation'd spoilers from the Po
Quaff blood and water; nor the stranger's sword
Be thy sad weapon of defence, and so,
Victor or vanquish'd, thou the slave of friend or foe.

The Roman Paolo Rolli (1687–1765), Eulibio Brentiatico in Arcadia, brilliant in his youth as poet and improviser, went in 1715 or 1716 to London, where he lived for some thirty years, returning then to Italy. While in London he engaged in many activities, among them the teaching of Italian in the family of the Prince of Wales (later George II) and in other noble families, and the writing of *libretti* for Handel and other composers.

His *Rime*, published in London in 1717, contain poems of many kinds: they show him to be in particular the prince of canzonettists. His *canzonette*, written in a variety of short lines and in a variety of short stanza forms, have a lilt that calls at once for music: Rolli himself, indeed, wrote music for some of them. Their charm is not merely formal, for they breathe a sentiment that has life for all its lightness, and they are imbued with a sense of idyllic beauty. Goethe knew by heart the song of absence beginning *Solitario bosco ombroso*, "Lonely, shadowy wood." Still more distinctive are Rolli's Catullian *Endecasillabi*, in which he paints delightful indoor and outdoor pictures of the social elegance in which he moved, with its ribbons and feathers and brocades and pearls and diamonds, its hairdressing *à la Pompadour*, its gilt and crystal coaches, its rich banquets, its masked balls in lavish candlelight, its Kensington, and its Thames, where among a multitude of vessels there are light craft that carry "the fair nymphs of this proud shore, their blond hair adorned with trembling flowers." A group of convivial songs, suggested by gatherings "on the hills of Mary-le-bone," bears the name *Le Meriboniane*. In other lyrical forms, and in his *libretti*, Rolli was less successful.

Through his long English residence he became naturally a living link between the literatures of his two countries. He translated *Paradise Lost* into Italian blank verse, accompanying it with a Life of Milton; and he included in one of his volumes a very good translation, also in blank verse, of the soliloquy of Hamlet — the first Italian translation of any Shakespearean passage. Its first lines are:

Essere o no, la gran question è questa:
Qual nella mente è forte più? Soffrire
Colpi e saette d' oltraggiosa sorte;
O prender l'armi contro un mar d'affanni . . .

In a pamphlet written in English, entitled *Remarks upon M. Voltaire's Essay on the Epick Poetry of the European Nations* — the first piece of writing in English published by an Italian author — Rolli defended Milton, Tasso, and Italian literary taste in general against Voltaire's dispraise.

* * *

Many Italians, some of them peasants, some of them highly educated, have possessed the ability to improvise in verse: it was in the eighteenth century that this ability was most deliberately cultivated and most fanatically exalted in literary circles. Many amateurs engaged in improvisation, and there were both men and women who made it an avocation or a profession. In general, the subject of the expected poem was assigned only in the presence of the audience: to respond impressively under such conditions required a great natural facility, a high degree of controlled excitability, and the possession of an ample stock of poetic commonplaces. The performances of the most successful improvisers must have been remarkable indeed: but the few bits of improvised verse that have been preserved are of no value. Rolli, as has been said, was an improviser in his youth; and Metastasio, as will appear presently, improvised in his boyhood. The most famous improviser of the Arcadian period was Bernardino Perfetti (1681–1747), Alauro Euroteo in Arcadia, a Sienese professor of civil and canon law. Deeply religious, he thought his ability a divine gift: he took communion before his performances. A letter written in Rome by the visiting Charles de Brosses contains this passage:

> We gave Perfetti, as subject, the Aurora Borealis. He thought, with bowed head, for a good quarter of an hour, while a harpsichord played softly. Then he rose, and began to declaim quietly in octaves, stanza by stanza, still accompanied by the harpsichordist, who struck chords while Perfetti was declaiming, and played continuously during the intervals between the stanzas. At first these followed each other slowly enough. Then, little by little, the poet's animation increased, and as he warmed to his task the harpsichordist played more loudly. Toward the end the poet was declaiming like a man inspired, poet and accompanist going on together with an amazing rapidity.

By order of Pope Benedict XIII, and after trial performances before twelve Arcadians, Perfetti received the laurel crown in the Capitoline Palace in May 1725, amid the acclamation of a great throng of fashionable admirers.

* * *

The one creative mind among the founders of the new academy was that of the jurist Gian Vincenzo Gravina (1663–1718), Calabrian by birth, Roman by residence, Opico Erimanteo in Arcadia. He composed the "laws" of Arcadia in compact Latin sentences, following as model the Roman Laws of the Twelve Tables; but while he agreed heartily with his fellow shepherds in their reprobation of Marinism, his juristic realism made him impatient of pastoral trivialities, and he ultimately withdrew from the Academy.

His strong literary interests and convictions bore good fruit in four treatises devoted to literary theory. In the first of these, the *Ragionamento sopra l'Endimione* (the *Endimione* was a pastoral drama by Guidi, an Arcadian poet), Gravina protests against current Aristotelian pedantry. Here first he praises Homer, his praise initiating the modern era of Homeric admiration. In the *Discorso delle antiche favole* he maintains that "poetry is an enchantress, but a salutary enchantress"; that poetry gives compelling power to truths that are essential for man's adjustment to nature and to God; and that poets and artists, as bringers of truth, through imagination, into untutored minds, are founders of civilization. The *Della ragion poetica*, "On the Nature of Poetry," has much to say of Homer, stressing especially the political, religious, and moral purposes of the *Iliad* and the *Odyssey*. Among the Italians, Dante receives the most extensive treatment and the highest praise. The fourth treatise, *Della tragedia*, is in part an application to the drama of ideas already more generally expressed, and in part a specialized discussion of dramatic values and techniques.

Lodovico Antonio Muratori of Modena (1672–1750), Leucoto Gateate in Arcadia, a scholar of great distinction and of prodigious productivity, holds an important place in the field of literary theory by virtue of his treatise entitled *Della perfetta poesia italiana*. Muratori, like Gravina, insists upon the nobility of the poetic function and upon the basic importance of truth as the source of poetry; but he differs from Gravina in recognizing that inner, or poetic, truth may be quite other than outer truth. His major aesthetic contribution lies in his exaltation of the imagination as the dominant factor in poetic creation: imagination, however, needs the companionship of intellect and the control of judgment. His aesthetic theory had great influence on the Swiss critics Bodmer and Breitinger, through whom it passed into the formation of German Romanticism.

* * *

Several Arcadians attempted tragedy, but the only one who attained any real success was the Marquis Scipione Maffei (1675–1755) of Verona, Orildo Berenteatico in Arcadia. For his single tragedy, the *Merope*, first performed in 1713, he chose the same subject that had been treated by Torelli late in the sixteenth century. His most important and beneficial innovation was the suppression of the chorus. He dispenses, also, with the "messenger": narration, when necessary, is assigned to one of the active persons of the play. Despite absurdities that result from a strict observance of the unities of place and time, and despite occasional lapses into inconsistency, the *Merope* is still a readable, even a stirring, play — clearly the best Italian tragedy written before the days of Alfieri. It was greatly admired and very influential both in Italy and elsewhere. In France it was approved, disapproved, and imitated by Voltaire; in Germany it was read thoughtfully by Goethe and discussed by Lessing; in England it was praised by Goldsmith.

Opera, long devoid of poetic value, though musically and scenically vigorous, was attacked, as an essentially hybrid form, by both Muratori and Maffei. Their hostility made no impression on the opera-mad public; but another Arcadian, Apostolo Zeno (1668–1750) of Venice, Emaro Simbolio in Arcadia, made a deliberate effort to improve the quality and status of the *libretto*. Chiefly in the years 1718–1728, when he held in Vienna the post of "poet and historian" to the Austrian Emperor, he wrote some seventy *libretti*, doing his best to make them dramatically sound, unified at least in action, and dignified in personages, sentiments, and style. He had, however, two fatal limitations: he was no poet, and he had no interest in music. His effort, therefore, was in itself an honorable failure; but it opened the way for the triumphant success of the greatest of Italian librettists.

Pietro Trapassi, born in 1698 of a humble family in Rome, was singing and improvising in public by the time he was ten. Gravina became interested in him, adopted him, changed his surname to Metastasio (Italian *trapasso* and Greek *metastasis* both mean "a passage from one place to another"), saw to it that he was well educated in the classics, in philosophy, and in law, and before long put a stop to his improvising. At fourteen he had written a tragedy; a volume of his poems was published in 1717; and in the following year he entered Arcadia as Artino Corasio. In 1719 he went to Naples, where his text for a dramatic and musical entertainment brought him the patronage of Marianna Bulgarelli, famous on the operatic stage as La Romanina. It was on her urging that he wrote the *Didone abbandonata*, the first *libretto* written in more than a hundred years in which the poetry was itself notably good. Six other *libretti* followed in the next six years.

In 1730 Metastasio was called to Vienna to be court poet in succession to Zeno; and there he remained until his death in 1782. His first decade in Vienna, when he was working under the active and friendly patronage of the Emperor Charles VI, was the time of his finest productivity.

Metastasio was both lyrist and dramatist: in spirit, indeed, he was more intimately lyric than dramatic. His most charming poems are five *canzonette*, the first two written in Naples, the others in Vienna. These last three, addressed to a real or fictional Nice, are the most perfect of all Arcadian *canzonette*—simple and yet just touched with individual reality, light-hearted and yet gently pensive, and as singable as verse can be. The first and most famous of the three, called *La libertà*, celebrates, with an amused relief, the poet's escape from amorous captivity:

Grazie agl' inganni tuoi,
Alfin respiro, o Nice;
Alfin d'un infelice
Ebber gli dei pietà:
Sento da' lacci suoi,
Sento che l' alma è sciolta;
Non sogno questa volta,
Non sogno libertà. . . .

Thanks to your deceits at last I breathe again, oh Nice; at last the gods have had pity on an unhappy wight: I feel, I feel that my heart is loosed from its snares; no dream, no dream, is liberty this time. . . .

Metastasio's *libretti* have been published as plays, and are readable as plays: some of them have even been acted without more than incidental music. They were designed, however, as portions of productions in which poetry and music were to be coequal; and they can be rightly appreciated only in the light of their special purpose. In their kind they have never been surpassed. Their subjects are taken, in general, from ancient or oriental history or legend, the basic stories being modified to suit Metastasio's own dramatic sense and the anticipated desires of his audience. There is, typically, a central conflict — as between love and duty, or friendship and justice, or the claims of family and of fatherland. The endings are not violent, except in certain cases in which a villain meets his due fate; and the usual mood, even when it is one of anxiety, is of an anxiety that is confident of relief. The plays are all in three acts, and are well constructed. Unity of action is generally observed, but is occasionally infringed by the introduction of romantic episodes. In most cases the action takes place within a day, a night, and the following day. Unity of place, however, is only regional: there are many local changes in scene. Characters are typical rather than individual; and their sayings are often reflective and sententious. Language and style are kept strictly within the limits of poetic propriety, and are governed always by the sense that they were to be fulfilled in music. "I cannot write anything that is to be set to music," Metastasio wrote, "without imagining what the music might be"; and as he worked he turned frequently from his writing table to his harpsichord.

His reform consisted first in his maintenance of a general poetic dignity, and second in his restoration of the recitative — which in recent operas had been largely sacrificed to the aria — to its normal dramatic importance. But while Metastasio kept the aria within bounds, he used it lavishly, skilfully, and delightfully within those bounds. Most of the scenes, written as a whole for recitative, culminate in arias, which, as they came from Metastasio's pen, are, as it were, tiny *canzonette*, of just a stanza or two. They are of various kinds — many are sentimental, many point a moral — but they are all perfectly singable. There are more than twelve hundred such arias in the whole series of *libretti*. This stanza may be taken as typical:

> L' onda che mormora
> Tra sponda e sponda,
> L' aura che tremola
> Tra fronda e fronda,
> È meno instabile
> Del vostro cor.*

The best of his *libretti* is the *Attilio Regolo*, which retells, worthily, the classic story of the moral heroism of Regulus, who, captured in the First

* "The wavelet murmuring 'twixt bank and bank, the breeze trembling 'twixt leaf and leaf, is less inconstant than your heart."

Punic War, is sent to Rome, with a Carthaginian ambassador, to be released if a proposed treaty is approved, but under oath to return to death in Carthage if it fails. Yet for the sake of Roman honor and greatness Regulus, though surrounded by the appealing love of his children and by the eagerness of all Rome for his release, opposes the treaty, and refuses to break his oath or to submit to prevention of his return. The play is noble throughout, and superb in its culmination. The final words of Regulus, spoken as he prepares to go aboard the ship that will take him to his fate, are these:

Romans, farewell! And let our last farewells
Be worthy of us all. Prais'd be the gods,
I go, and leave you Roman. Oh, preserve
That mighty name: and you shall be
Arbiters of the earth, and the whole world
Shall become Roman. Oh ye guardian gods
Of this dear land, oh ye who watch above
The children of Aeneas, I commend
To you this race of heroes. Oh protect
This soil, these roofs, these walls! Ever therein
Let constancy abide, and faith, and glory,
Justice, and valor. And if baleful stars
Menace the Capitol, here, ye gods, am I:
Let Regulus be the victim; let the wrath
Of heaven fall on my devoted head,
And Rome be spared . . . What, do ye weep? . . . Farewell!

It is no wonder that such words were sacred to the Italians of the resurgent generations that were soon to come.

Metastasio drew plots and elements of plots from many sources — among them Guarini, Maffei, Corneille, Racine, and Addison (the *Cato*) — but he always re-thought and re-created whatever he thus derived. Dozens of composers have written music for his *libretti*: among them, in his lifetime, Caldara, Jommelli, Leo, Paisiello, Pergolesi, Piccinni, Sacchini, Domenico Scarlatti, Johann Christian Bach, Gluck, Handel, Hasse, and Mozart, and, later, Cherubini, Cimarosa, Rossini, Mendelssohn, and Dvořák.

Metastasio wrote also, chiefly in the decade 1730–1740, the *libretti* for eight oratorios. There have been critics who consider them his best work (Monti was sure that the angels would learn them by heart). They follow in general the pattern of the secular *libretti*; but they are written in two parts instead of three acts, and arias appear somewhat more frequently. The best known are the *Passione di Gesù Cristo*, the *Betulia Liberata* (which tells the story of Judith), and the *Isacco*. One of the arias in the *Passione*, typical both in its simplicity and in its religious sincerity, reads thus:

Dovunque il guardo giro,
  Immenso Dio, ti vedo:

Nell' opre tue t'ammiro,
Ti riconosco in me.
    La terra, il mar, le spere
Parlan del tuo potere:
Tu sei per tutto, e noi
Tutti viviamo in te —

Wherever I turn my glance, illimitable God, I behold Thee: I marvel at Thy works, I recognize Thy presence within me. Earth, sea, and heavens speak of Thy power: Thou art everywhere, and we live wholly in Thee.

CHAPTER 38

Vico

GIAMBATTISTA VICO, born in Naples in 1668, was of a mind too phenomenal to submit to the normal processes of education: he sought and received guidance from certain teachers, but in the main he taught himself. With extraordinary comprehensiveness, thoroughness, and reflectiveness he studied in many fields, especially in philosophy, law, theology, the Latin language, and Latin and Italian literature. The two authors who meant most to him in his early years were Plato and Tacitus: later on he came to hold Bacon and Grotius in equal honor.

In 1699 he won a competition for the professorship of rhetoric in the University of Naples — on a salary so small that he was unable to live much above the level of poverty. Rhetoric, as Vico taught it, was far from being merely a matter of style. He defined eloquence as "wisdom effectively set forth"; and he was in fact more concerned with wisdom itself than with forms of utterance. A man who had been one of his students wrote:

> He touched in passing, as it were, on the beauties of language, the origins and meanings of words, and on beauty and dignity of expression. But as there came before his mind the images of human passions . . . he would begin penetrating into the most secret recesses of the human heart, to reveal the springs of human actions; and, then, after reviewing our duties according to our varying relations with God, with ourselves, and with our fellow men, he would go on to indicate the main lines of moral philosophy and of universal law.

Vico's earliest writing was in Italian verse; but neither his early poems nor the few (some of them philosophic) that he wrote in later years show any real poetic gift. He too was an Arcadian: his pastoral name was Laufilo Terio.

With his appointment as professor there began a long series of orations and treatises, in Latin, in which the dynamic quality of his thought became ever more clearly manifest. It fell to him, as Professor of Rhetoric, to give a public oration, in Latin, on a general subject, at the beginning of each academic year. Seven of the orations he gave are extant, the first dating from 1699 and the last from 1708. These early compositions make it clear that Vico was already moved by the desire to synthesize all knowledge, and that he believed profoundly in the providence of a creative and beneficent God. In these orations, as in his later treatises, whether in Latin or in Italian, Vico's style is highly individual — tense, compact, sometimes cryptic, and very striking. One is often aware of a driving, prophetic exaltation, of fires burning within a strangely wrought containing form.

In the first oration Vico maintains that knowledge begins not with evidence brought in by the senses, but with the study of one's inner self. It is by the process of thought that the individual attains the certainty of his own existence, the sense of his own dignity, the sense of his own divinity; and it is through the difficult process of self-knowledge that one may move on to attain knowledge of God. The second oration, juristic in tone, outlines the universal law of moral life. The mind must distinguish between the true and the false; the senses must not dominate. Reason must be the beacon, the guide and the ruler of life. The third oration deals in particular with the principles by which the *societas litteraria*, the society of men of humane learning, should be governed. Pure truth must be set forth without pretense, and with learning that is solid and not vain. The polemic spirit is unjustifiable; what is needed is a serenity that will enable one to grasp truth wherever it may be found. The fourth oration asserts that humane learning reaches its greatest usefulness and its highest honor in the promotion of the common civic good, and that the service of one's fellow men is a right means of ascent toward God. The thesis of the fifth oration is that states have exercised greatest power and enjoyed greatest fame when humane learning has most flourished within them. Examples are taken, in a remarkable sweep of historical perspective, from Assyria, Greece, Rome, the kingdom of Theodoric, the empire of Charlemagne, the monarchies of Spain and France, and the Arabian empire. The sixth oration, definitely educational, insists on the necessity of virtue, knowledge, and eloquence as means of overcoming man's separation from his fellow men.

The last and most important of the seven orations bears the title *De nostri temporis studiorum ratione*, "On Educational Method in Our Time." Comparing ancient and modern educational practices, to the advantage now of the ancient and now of the modern, Vico reviews the fields of mathematics, physics, medicine, moral and civil philosophy, poetry, Christian theology, the practical arts, and jurisprudence. In his treatment of this last field Vico for the first time traces the history of Roman jurisprudence from its origins to the days of Theodosius and Valentinian, stressing both its relation to actual custom and its philosophical and well-nigh sacred character. In general, Vico criticizes the narrowness of the Cartesian logical approach, and insists on the values of the imagination and of common prudence. He deplores the current overemphasis on the natural sciences, and the consequent depreciation of linguistic, literary, historical, legal, and political studies; and he urges the attainment of educational completeness.

Vico's first extensive philosophical treatise, published in 1710, bearing a title that means "On the Ancient Wisdom of the Italian Race, Discoverable from the Origins of the Latin Language," shows him to be already greatly interested in the problem of social origins, particularly in its linguistic aspects; but it is essentially a statement of his own metaphysical theory. Truth, in Vico's thought, is that which is knowable; and truth, in that sense, is a product of the making mind. For the all-making mind of God, truth is coextensive with the whole creation; for the mind of man truth consists only in what his mind itself creates.

When a chair of civil law in the University of Naples became vacant in 1717, Vico set his hopes on obtaining the succession to it, both because his major special interest was in the field of law and because the much larger salary would have relieved him from the extreme oppressions of his poverty. His writings of the next few years show an alternation or a combination of two motives: his increasingly strong desire "to unite in one principle all knowledge, human and divine," and his special desire to prove himself qualified for this professorship.

The year 1720 saw the publication of the first of Vico's two greatest works, the *De uno universi iuris principio et fine uno*, "On the One Principle and One End of Universal Law." The body of the work consists of more than two hundred propositions, most of them briefly stated, many of them accompanied by discussions, some of which are of very considerable length. The first forty or so are metaphysical, the rest juridical. Among the metaphysical propositions are these:

> Man consists of mind and body, and is knowledge, will, power . . . and since his mind has no spatial boundaries, but is spiritual, while his body . . . is bounded, he is a finite knowledge, will, and power which seeks the infinite.
>
> But the infinite being is God; therefore man desires to unite with God; therefore the principle of human nature is from God; therefore man is from God.

The juridical portion of the *De uno* first sets forth certain underlying ethical and social principles, and then devotes itself to a long and detailed study of the evolution, the varieties, and the values of Roman law, with many generalizations, and with occasional treatments of such matters as the origin of language and the nature and vicissitudes of states. The cyclic theory which Vico was to develop later is first suggested here:

> There is a certain hitherto unnoticed reversion (*recursus*) of states to the conditions under which they came into being.

A year later Vico published his *De constantia jurisprudentis*, "On the Consistency of the Jurist." This work, supplementary to the *De uno*, but less definitely legal, is divided into two parts, entitled *De constantia philosophiae* and *De constantia philologiae*. Philosophy, in Vico's thought, is the science of the things of God, and philology the science of the things of man: it includes, therefore, not only linguistics but also literature, mythology, customs, institutions, and all other products of man's own creativity. The first chapter of the second part, entitled *Nova scientia tentatur*, "A New Science is Attempted," promises the development of a new science of humanity, which is to be based, in particular, upon research into the origins of civilization. A second supplementary work, which appeared in 1722 under the guise of *Notae* on the *De uno* and the *De constantia*, illustrates the method proposed for such research by a special study of the *Iliad* and the *Odyssey*, considered as sources of "philological" information.

The formal competition for the professorship of civil law, held finally in 1723, was won by an entirely unqualified and unworthy candidate. Vico was bitterly disappointed; but he came later to be thankful that he had been left free to devote himself to the development of his "new science."

This "new science" is at last proclaimed in its full grandeur in his culminating work, written in Italian and published in 1725, the *Principj di una scienza nuova d'intorno alla comune natura delle nazioni*, "Principles of a New Science Concerning the Common Nature of Nations." The rest of Vico's life was devoted mainly to the drastic revision, enlargement, and perfection of this work. A second edition was published in 1730, and a third in 1744, just after Vico's death.*

In its final form the *Scienza nuova* consists of a preliminary "Idea of The Work," five Books, and a Conclusion. The "Idea" is presented in an allegorical frontispiece and an elaborate explanation of that frontispiece.

The first Book, entitled "Establishment of Principles," is introductory. It begins with a heavily annotated chronological table covering the prehistoric period: there are separate columns for Hebrews, Chaldeans, Scythians, Phoenicians, Egyptians, Greeks, and Romans. Next comes a series of about a hundred propositions laid down as axioms (most of them annotated), the validity of which is to be assumed throughout the work. They cover a multiplicity of human traits and attitudes — psychological, philosophical, religious, sociological, political, military, linguistic, poetic, and historical. Among them are these:

> Uniform ideas originating among entire peoples unknown to each other must have a common ground of truth.

* All quotations from the *Scienza nuova* are taken from the translation by T. G. Bergin and M. H. Fisch.

> . . . the Egyptians reduced all preceding world time to three ages, namely, the age of the gods, the age of the heroes, and the age of men. . .
>
> In every pursuit men without natural aptitude succeed by obstinate study of technique, but in poetry he who lacks native ability cannot succeed by technique.
>
> Men at first feel without observing, then they observe with a troubled and agitated spirit, finally they reflect with a clear mind.
>
> The first authors among the Easterners, Egyptians, Greeks and Latins, and, in the second barbarism, the first writers in the modern languages of Europe, were poets.
>
> The nature of peoples is first crude, then severe, then benign, then delicate, finally dissolute.

The institutions of religion, marriage, and burial are regarded as the "three eternal and universal customs" that mark the emergence of mankind from barbarism. After this emergence man desires first "his own welfare along with that of his family"; then "his own welfare along with that of his city"; then "his own welfare along with that of the nation"; and finally "his own welfare along with that of the entire human race":

> In all these conditions man desires principally his own utility. Therefore it is only by divine providence that he can be held within these orders to practice justice as a member of the society of the family, of the state, and finally of mankind. . . . Our new science must therefore be a demonstration . . . of the historical fact of providence, for it must be a history of the forms of order which, without human discernment or intent, and often against the designs of men, providence has given to this great city of the human race.

This science undertakes to describe "an ideal eternal history traversed in time by the history of every nation in its rise, progress, maturity, decline and fall."

Since Vico is so basically concerned with prehistory, and since virtually all the evidence that was available to him as to the beginnings of civilization had been conveyed by early poets, he proceeds, in Book II, entitled "Poetic Wisdom," to a thorough examination and evaluation of all that evidence:

> We shall show . . . how the founders of gentile humanity by means of their natural theology imagined the gods; how by means of their logic they invented language; by morals created heroes; by economics founded families, and by politics, cities . . .

and so on for physics, cosmography, astronomy, chronology, and geography. Poetry, in Vico's thought, began as an expression of the pre-rational imagination of primitive man as stirred by the phenomena of thunder and lightning. The first poets created Jove.

Book III, which is in effect an immense Corollary to Book II, is entitled

"Discovery of the True Homer." After an exhaustive review of all the many pieces of evidence he succeeds in gathering, Vico comes to the conclusion that Homer was not "a particular man in the world of nature," but "an idea or heroic character of Grecian men insofar as they told their history in song." To this synthetic Homer, Vico gives the most enthusiastic praise: for his creation of poetic fictions and heroic characters; for his comparisons, his descriptions, and "his sentences filled with sublime passions"; for the clarity and splendor of his style; for having been the organizer of Greek civilization, the father of all other poets, and the source of all Greek philosophies; and for "having been the first historian of the entire gentile world that has come down to us."

Even the second and third Books are in reality introductory: in the fourth, entitled "The Course of Nations," Vico comes at last to the formulation and elaboration of his symphonic conclusions, which, in an introductory paragraph, are announced thus:

> We shall now . . . discuss the course the nations take, proceeding . . . upon the division of the ages which the Egyptians said had elapsed before them . . . namely, the successive ages of gods, of heroes, and of men. For the nations will be seen to develop in conformity with this division by a constant . . . order of causes and effects . . . through three kinds of natures. From these natures arise three kinds of customs; and in virtue of these customs three kinds of natural laws of nations are observed; and in consequence of these laws three kinds of . . . commonwealths are established.

There are also three kinds of language and three kinds of jurisprudence. But these triads

> all lead to one general unity. This is the unity of the religion of a provident divinity, which is the unity of the spirit informing and giving life to this world of nations.

The three kinds of commonwealths are the divine, the heroic, and

> human governments, in which, in virtue of the equality of the intelligent nature which is the proper nature of man, all are accounted equal under the laws.

Human governments have themselves three phases. Beginning as aristocratic commonwealths, they develop into popular commonwealths; in popular commonwealths the ambition of the powerful and the prevalence of private interests lead to ruinous factionalism, sedition, and civil war; and as a means of salvation from such ruin the state becomes a monarchy — which Vico believes to be "the form of government best adapted to human nature when reason is fully developed." Throughout the fourth Book great emphasis is placed upon the part played by jurisprudence in the development of the state.

In the brief fifth Book, entitled "The Recurrence of Human Things in the

Resurgence of the Nations," Vico discovers in the Christian era the same cycle — divine, heroic, human — which he had found in the prehistoric and the ancient world: the three successive phases of the cycle appear in the early Christian centuries, in the feudal era, and in modern times. Thus Vico has unfolded

> not the particular history in time of the laws and deeds of the Romans or the Greeks, but . . . the ideal of the eternal laws in accordance with which the affairs of all nations proceed in their rise, progress, mature state, decline and fall, and would do so even if . . . there were infinite worlds being born from time to time throughout eternity.

The Conclusion summarizes the entire argument, tracing again, in all its essentials, the whole course of human experience.

The *Scienza nuova*, an amazing achievement of intellectual power and determination, offers the first panoramic survey of the social evolution of mankind: the word "evolution," to be sure, is not there, but the concept is omnipresent. It is an evolution out of bestial barbarism, made possible, in its earlier stages, through the development of the faculty of imagination, and, later, through the development of the faculty of reason. It is an evolution driven by all the basic human needs — physical, societal, communicative, cognitive, economic, political, philosophic, religious — an evolution as multiform in its manifestations as in its origins. It is an evolution that operates not merely here and there, but in all nations, and not at random, but in an unsuspected and yet unmistakable cyclic pattern. It is an evolution wrought out by man himself; yet over it all an all-wise providence presides.

In the years from 1720 to 1725 several North Italian men of letters had sponsored a plan for the publication of a series of autobiographies by contemporary Italian scholars: these autobiographies, to be written in Italian, were to be accounts not primarily of events, but rather of each man's studies, of his special literary interests, and of the works he had published or had in preparation. Vico, asked to contribute such an account of his own life, did so in 1725. His *Vita** proved to be exactly the sort of thing the sponsors had in mind; and it was published in 1728, as an example for other scholars (the general project, however, was not carried out). Vico's *Vita* is essentially a record of his intellectual growth and efforts. It contains his own analyses and interpretations of his several works. He writes with the care and the objectivity of an experienced historian, and he writes very well indeed, and more simply than in his orations and treatises.

In 1735 Vico was appointed Historiographer to the new King of Naples — an appointment which gave him some slight financial relief. He retired in 1741, and died in 1744.

* The word "autobiography" and the corresponding words in other languages appear to have come into use only about 1800.

As Vico's philosophy and philology embraced the thought of all mankind, so his influence has made itself felt in many nations and in many fields — law, economic and political theory, philosophy, history, and literary criticism.* Until the final decades of the eighteenth century, however, his work was not well known except among Neapolitans, who regarded him, in particular, as an authority in jurisprudence. The one notable contemporary foreign critic who honored Vico and quoted from him was the Spaniard Luzán (who had been much in Naples). Toward the end of the century the *Scienza nuova* came to the knowledge of Goethe and of Herder, and through them passed into the stream of German thought. In the nineteenth century Vico came to be widely recognized as one of the greatest of modern thinkers. Foscolo was a Vichian enthusiast; and the *Scienza nuova* was one of the books in which Mazzini and other patriots of the Risorgimento found most inspiration. De Sanctis owed much to Vico, and Vico's thought was deeply pondered and freely renewed in the mind of Croce. The chief French disciple and exponent of Vico was Michelet, who made an abridged translation of the *Scienza nuova*, and wrote glowing pages on Vico in the preface to his *Histoire romaine*. In England, Coleridge was the leading apostle of Vico's thought, which, largely through him, influenced Thomas Arnold and other historians. In Ireland, within our own century, extraordinary uses of Vico's name and ideas have been made by Joyce; and Yeats has written seriously on Vico, quoting his dictum that "We can know nothing that we have not made" — an idea which recurs in Yeats' later poetry.

* The substance of this paragraph is derived from the chapter on "Vico's Reputation and Influence" in the Introduction of Fisch and Bergin's translation of the *Autobiography*.

CHAPTER 39

Goldoni and Carlo Gozzi

NO FURTHER important political change took place in Italy until the Napoleonic storm broke suddenly at the very end of the eighteenth century.

Guardi, a lesser Canaletto, continued to produce pleasing views of Venice. The vogue of opera was as great as ever; but the musical ability of the composers was in general below that of their predecessors, and *libretti* fell into insignificance.

The experiments of Spallanzani opened the way for the development of modern bacteriology. The many terms derived from the names of Galvani and Volta bear witness to the fundamental importance of the discoveries of these two men in the field of electrical science.

Foreign literary influences became more effective than ever in Italy. The influence of the French Encyclopedists was very strong. Among the English works translated in this period were *Hamlet*, *Othello*, *Macbeth*, *Coriolanus*, Thomson's *Seasons*, Gay's *Fables*, Young's *Night Thoughts*, Richardson's *Clarissa Harlowe*, Gray's *Elegy* and *The Bard*, Johnson's *Rasselas*, "Ossian," and Sterne's *Sentimental Journey*.

Goldsmith visited Northern Italy in 1755. Sterne traveled in Italy in 1765 and 1766; but the Italian portion of the book he entitled *A Sentimental Journey Through France and Italy* was never written.

* * *

Venice was at this time the capital of the European dramatic world. There were seven theaters in the city, among them Sant' Angelo, San Luca, and San Samuele (their names indicate merely the parishes in which they stood). They were built with tiers of lavishly decorated boxes above, and a bare pit below, wherein plebeians stood, or sat on wooden benches. The theatrical year lasted from early October to Ash Wednesday, and was divided into two seasons: the Autumn season which ended on December 15, and the Winter or Carnival season which began on December 26. Each company of actors, typically at least, leased a theater for an entire season, or for several seasons. During the spring and summer these companies went on tour on the mainland.

In the 1740's the *commedia dell'arte* still dominated the comic stage, and Venice clung to it, vapid and degenerate though it was. It stirred a facile laughter; it made no demands upon the mind; and it suggested a comfortable continuity with the good old times. But it was soon to be replaced.

Carlo Goldoni was born in Venice in 1707. Before he was twelve he had written his first comedy. After some schooling in Perugia and in Rimini he returned to Venice, where his father taught him a little medicine, his father's patients a little trickery, and his uncle a little law. Then, for a more serious study of the law, he was sent to Pavia to enter the Papal College there; but he had to wait for three months before his admission could be arranged. During this time he had access to a private library which contained a large collection of classic, English, Spanish, and French comedies. The classic comedies were not new to him: he now reread them eagerly, admiring their authors' skill in plot and style, but thinking that he might hope to do better in respect to interest, distinctive characters, fun, and happy endings. He could not read the comedies in foreign languages; but he was sorry to find that comedy had flourished so much more plentifully in other lands, and he resolved to do what he could to raise Italian comedy to a worthy level. During a vacation he read for the first time the *Mandragola* of Machiavelli: he found its indecency revolting, but he greatly admired its treatment of character, and lamented the lack of Italian comedies comparable in their treatment of character, but decent.

His career at Pavia came to a sudden end as the result of an ill-judged satire; but he continued, amid many adventures, in his study of the law. He spent two years as Coadjutor to the magistrate in Chioggia; got his degree at Padua after a night of gambling; won his first case in Venice; and fled soon afterward from an unhappy engagement. In Milan he read his first *libretto* to a group of pitiless professionals—and burned his manuscript. Soon thereafter he saw courteous siege and stark battlefields in Lombardy; and Austrian deserters robbed him of all his worldly goods save a tragicomedy, which won him employment as playwright with a company of Venetian actors. Their road led hither and yon across the peninsula, bringing him at length to Genoa, where he found a devoted wife. Returning to Venice, he served there for a time as Genoese consul. The chief event of his consulship was the loss of six thousand *livres* to a swindling captain, who had persuaded him to enlist as auditor of an imaginary regiment. From Rimini, where he had enjoyed

Spanish patronage, he fled with his wife before an Austrian advance. Their baggage had been confiscated, their driver deserted them, and Goldoni forded a swollen stream with his wife on his back, saying to himself: "Omnia bona mea mecum porto." Fate brought him eventually to Pisa, where for a time he practised humdrum law, and adorned the local Arcadian colony as Polisseno Fegeio. There, in the summer of 1748, the Venetian actor-manager Medebac, then on tour, found him, and persuaded him to come back to Venice as playwright for Medebac's company, which had leased the theater of Sant' Angelo. So Goldoni at last entered definitely upon his true profession.

Up to this time he had composed some ten comedies, and a few plays of other kinds. He had determined to write regular comedies of character and manners; but the *commedia dell'arte*, as he well knew, was too strongly entrenched in public favor and in professional custom to be replaced abruptly, and the managers for whom he had worked had wanted plays of the familiar type. His early comedies, accordingly, had been in some cases mere *scenari*, and in other cases *scenari* with one or more of the parts written out: only one play had been fully written out. In every case two or more of the familiar masked characters were retained.

All of the plays that he wrote in Venice in and after 1748 were fully written out; and in nearly all of those that he wrote for Medebac, in the years 1748–1753, two or more of the masked characters were retained. His first year with Medebac went fairly well. Some of his plays failed, but others met with considerable success, notably a comedy called *La putta onorata*, "The Respectable Girl." This latter play had been written in reply to one called *Le putte di Castello*, current in another theater, in which the character of the women of the Venetian populace was slanderously misrepresented. Goldoni, in *La putta onorata*, came to their defense with conviction and brilliance, and won thereby a following among the Venetian populace that he never lost. This play, the last of the Carnival season, was written wholly in the Venetian dialect: Goldoni continued for many years the custom thus begun, his last play of the season being written in Venetian.

The following year, 1749–50, proved to be very difficult. A rival playwright, Chiari, was writing for a company which was playing in San Samuele, and the competition became acrimonious, especially when Chiari in a play called *La scuola delle vedove*, "The School for Widows," ridiculed Goldoni's successful *Vedova scaltra* of the preceding year. Chiari's antagonism was purely one of personal rivalry, for he, like Goldoni, favored the replacement of the *commedia dell'arte* by a comedy of character and manners. To make matters even worse, Darbes, the Pantalone of Medebac's company, and one of the best actors of the century, left suddenly to go to the court of Poland. Regular boxholders were giving up their boxes for the following season. Something desperate had to be done. So Goldoni, on the last night of the

Carnival season, pledged his word, in a sonnet recited by the leading actress, that for the next theatrical year he would write and the Medebac company would produce sixteen new comedies — one for every week of the double season. This extraordinary pledge served its purpose; boxes were taken again, and the public looked forward to the new year with much excitement. When Autumn came only seven of the sixteen comedies were written. More than once, in the course of the year, Goldoni had to release for rehearsal the first act of a comedy of which the rest had not been written. Ten days before the end of the Carnival season he did not even have a subject for the last of his promised plays. Meanwhile, excitement had become intense. Of the première of the sixteenth play Goldoni wrote long afterward, in his *Mémoires*:

> The crowd was so extraordinary that . . . the price of the boxes was tripled and quadrupled; and the applause was so tumultuous that passers-by wondered whether it betokened satisfaction or a general riot. I was sitting quietly in my box, surrounded by my friends, who were weeping for joy. A throng of people came to find me . . . took me in spite of myself to the Ridotto, marched me from room to room, and made me accept congratulations I would have preferred to escape. . . . It was a tribute to my fulfillment of my pledge.

The quality of the sixteen comedies is on the average remarkably high. They include several notable plays, among them *Pamela nubile*, "Pamela Unmarried," the first of Goldoni's comedies in which no masked character appears, and the final play, *I pettegolezzi delle donne*, "Women's Gossip," which is perhaps the best of the sixteen.

The next two years passed with alternating success and failure. In 1753, on the expiration of his contract with Medebac, Goldoni signed a contract with the Vendramin brothers, who owned and operated the theater of San Luca. Masked characters linger in some of the comedies that Goldoni wrote for his new employers in 1753 and 1754, but not in any of those that he wrote for them thereafter.

When Goldoni left Medebac, Chiari took his place. Their rivalry went on, more or less actively, for several years. When Goldoni, seeking new themes, wrote *La sposa persiana*, "The Persian Bride," Chiari capped it with *La schiava cinese*, "The Chinese Slave," and Goldoni's *Filosofo inglese* was followed by Chiari's *Filosofo veneziano*. Chiari's *Plautus* was followed by Goldoni's *Terence*; and in *I malcontenti* Goldoni caricatured Chiari.

In the course of the year 1757 a third and not unworthy combatant made his appearance: Carlo Gozzi, a lover of the good old days and the good old ways, took up the cudgels, in a satirical publication, for the *commedia dell' arte*, and denounced both Goldoni and Chiari as upstart radicals. Goldoni, however, proceeded to write some of his best comedies. The years 1757–61 saw the production not only of some excellent Italian plays, but also of two plays in the Venetian dialect, *I rusteghi*, "The Tyrants," and *Le baruffe chiozzotte*, "Quarrels at Chioggia," which are generally regarded as his masterpieces.

Early in 1761 Gozzi entered the dramatic arena. In the course of the controversy Goldoni, defending his departure from the *commedia dell'arte*, had maintained that the merit of his plays was proved by the throngs that came to see them. To that assertion Gozzi had retorted that throngs proved nothing as to merit, and that he would undertake to attract still larger throngs by a dramatization of "the fairy tale of the Love of the Three Oranges, a tale told by grandmothers to their grandchildren." So he made the old story into a *scenario* and had it produced in San Samuele, in true *commedia dell'arte* fashion, by a company of which Sacchi, one of the best actors of the century, was manager. It had a great success, due in part to Sacchi's acting and in part to the fact that one of the characters was a caricature of Goldoni, and another a caricature of Chiari.

This play had two quite unexpected results. In the first place, it led to a reconciliation between Goldoni and Chiari. In the second place, Gozzi suddenly found himself to be a successful playwright, with a vein of his own; and having made that discovery he proceeded to exploit it during the next few years — moving somewhat away from the traditions of the *commedia dell'arte*, ironically enough, as he became conscious of his own very real dramatic gifts.

Early in 1761 Goldoni received an invitation to go to Paris, to serve as playwright of the *Comédie italienne*. He was growing weary of controversy, and he wanted to see Paris — but he loved Venice. He finally agreed that he would go, but only after one more year. In the course of that year he continued to write excellent and successful plays; but Gozzi's fairy tales still held the double charm of novelty and real dramatic excellence.

He reached Paris in the summer of 1762, and there he stayed for the rest of his life. He had gone there under an extraordinary misapprehension: for what the *Comédie italienne* really wanted him to do was to revive the *commedia dell'arte* — so he had to go through the old struggle all over again. He was still under contract with the Vendramin brothers to supply them with several plays a year, on the understanding that these might be plays written in the first instance for the *Comédie italienne*, provided they were thoroughly rewritten for Venetian use. Thus *L'éventail*, "The Fan," written in French in 1763, was rewritten in Italian as *Il ventaglio* and sent to Venice in 1764. Another fine play, *Le bourru bienfaisant*, "The Beneficent Grumbler," was written in 1771.

Five years later Goldoni wrote a last and unsuccessful comedy. Thereafter, though the stairways of Versailles were a hard path for him, he supported himself by teaching Italian to the young ladies of the royal family, until the King pensioned him. In 1783 he began the writing of his *Mémoires*. Then came the Revolution. In July 1792, the Convention cancelled his pension. He died on February 6, 1793. On the next day, before his death was known, Marie-Joseph Chénier persuaded the Convention, on the ground of Goldoni's essential democracy, to restore his pension. Three days later, his death being known, the Convention voted a pension to his widow; and in June a benefit performance of *Le bourru* ordered by the Convention and attended by the Convention *en masse* yielded a large sum for her.

All in all, Goldoni wrote about a hundred and fifty comedies. Most of them are in prose, but a few are in verse. Nearly all of them fall into one or another of three general classes: comedies retaining masked characters, who speak in the dialects they had always used; comedies of character and manners without masked characters, written in Italian; and comedies written entirely in the Venetian dialect.

Those of the first of these three classes continue obviously one of the main features of the *commedia dell'arte*. They differ from that type of comedy, however, in that the dialogue, completely written out, is itself a result of dramatic consideration; and they differ from it also, to some extent, in the handling of the masked characters: Pantalone, for instance, becomes, in certain cases, an individualized and sensible person, and Arlecchino and Brighella, though close to their prototypes, have a larger range of mental resourcefulness. Many of these plays, moreover, mark a great advance over earlier Italian comedy both in plot and in the treatment of characters who are not masked. Even in his student days Goldoni had formed the habit of observing men closely, especially those who seemed to him to have curious and amusing personalities. As he grew older, also, he came to observe more and more thoughtfully the whole Venetian and Italian society of his day — its customs, its pleasures, its frivolities, its problems, its weaknesses, its errors. The perceptions and the understandings provided by these habits of observation give both charm and substance to his plays, in many of which he does not hesitate to use his comic gifts in smiling but effective criticism of those features of the life around him which he regarded as lamentable. He managed also to achieve, at all times, a surprising variety in theme and treatment.

The best plays of this first class are *La vedova scaltra*, *La famiglia dell' antiquario*, and *Il bugiardo*. The "clever widow" is courted by four suitors: a monosyllabic Englishman, who sends her jewelry; a gaily polite Frenchman, who sends her a portrait of himself; a loftily dignified Spaniard, who sends her a copy of his family tree; and an Italian Count, who sends her a love letter. After intricacies due to Arlecchino's mixing of messages, the heroine cleverly tests the sincerity of the four men, and accepts the Count. In the *Famiglia dell'antiquario* the head of the house, Anselmo, who has wasted his fortune in incorrigible antiquarian expenditures, is befooled again and again by Arlecchino and Brighella, who sell him an old kitchen lamp as an eternal light found in the tomb of Ptolemy in the pyramids, a lock of contemporary hair as a tress from the head of Lucretia, and a scribbled collection of modern Greek folk songs as the original manuscript of a treaty of peace between Athens and Sparta. The main plot concerns a struggle for domestic and social supremacy between Anselmo's aristocratic wife and her daughter-in-law, wife of Anselmo's ineffective son Giacinto, and daughter of the *nouveau riche* Pantalone. Neither will yield, despite elaborate negotiations: at the very end of the play Pantalone brings the problem to a precarious solution. The *Bugiardo*, "The Liar," is a lively adaptation of the *Menteur* of Corneille.

Less successful than these three plays, but notable for various reasons, are *Il cavaliere e la dama*, in which Goldoni makes his first direct attack on cicisbeism (the then current social convention by which every married lady of fashion had her *cavaliere servente* — a recognized social escort); *Il teatro comico*, which contains a play within a play, and presents effectively Goldoni's main convictions as to the structure and the acting of comedy; *Il poeta fanatico*, a gentle satire on the Arcadian Academy; and *Le donne curiose*, "The Inquisitive Women," a play on Freemasonry — a subject suggested to Goldoni by the English consul, Joseph Smith.

In his comedies of the second general class Goldoni, unhampered by the conventions of the *commedia dell'arte*, continues with increasing maturity his genial depiction and criticism of character and of society. These plays are often similar in form and spirit to those of Molière. Most of them are later than most of the plays with masked characters: a few are new versions of plays in which masked characters had originally appeared. The plays of this class include many that are of high excellence, among them *Il vero amico*, *La locandiera*, *La villeggiatura*, *Un curioso accidente*, and *Gl'innamorati*.

The *Vero amico* is a love story that comes out wrong, inflexible loyalty to a strict code of friendship having triumphed over love. Most of the comic relief is afforded by the heroine's father, one of the most amusing of all stage misers.

In the *Locandiera*, "The Mistress of the Inn," the best known of all the plays of Goldoni, the heroine, Mirandolina, has become the owner of an inn through the death of her father, who had urged her to marry Fabrizio, a faithful servant. She prefers, however, to remain mistress of her own sometimes fanciful but generally sensible devices. Two noblemen, a proud and penniless marquis and a newly rich count, have lodged at the inn for the chance of courting her: she keeps them dangling at courting distance, for the good of the inn and for the fun of it. A new arrival, taunting the marquis and the count on their infatuation, declares himself a woman-hater, and acts accordingly. This puts Mirandolina on her mettle, and she cleverly brings him to a complete submission, which, when he realizes her wiles, is followed by a fury from which she is saved by Fabrizio and the count, with the marquis valiant in the background. Having had her fling and learned her lesson, she decides to marry her worried but devoted Fabrizio.

The *Villeggiatura*, "In Villa," for all its humor, is in reality a serious, even a bitter, criticism of cicisbeism and of fashionable villa life. *Un curioso accidente* is a pleasant love story, in which a tyrannical Dutch father is finally outwitted. It is the best of Goldoni's several "exotic" comedies — plays in which the scene is not Italian. *Gl'innamorati* tells of a pair of lovers, Fulgenzio and Eugenia, who, though very much in love, are both so quick to take offense that they have little peace except in their occasional moments of reconciliation: but all ends in a happy betrothal.

Other plays of comparable interest are *La bottega del caffè*, "The Coffee-Shop," a play of bourgeois life in which a young merchant is brought by gambling to the brink of ruin, and an irrepressible scandalmonger makes general and complicated trouble; *Pamela nubile*, a serious play derived, with free alterations, from Richardson's novel; *La dama prudente*, in which a husband and wife, equally unable to endure the polite tyranny of cicisbeism, seek refuge at last in the simplicities of a small mainland town; *La guerra*, "War," an impressively realistic play, based on Goldoni's still vivid recollections of the warfare he had witnessed in his youth; and *Le smanie della villeggiatura*, "Villa Mania," the first of a sequence of three plays in which Goldoni satirizes again the socially compulsory extravagances of the villa season.

Goldoni is at his very best in his comedies of the third class, those written in the Venetian dialect. Quite unhampered, here, by literary or stage conventions of any sort, he could satisfy fully and in his own novel ways his constant desire to be true to life; and the life he chose to reflect in these plays was life that he knew thoroughly and loved dearly, the simple, homely, and fundamentally honest life of the common people of Venice. Later literature can show no realism that is more real than that of Goldoni's Venetian comedies. There is no inherent reason why realism should deal by preference with the unlovely: Goldoni's faithful realism deals with phases of life which, for all their ruffled surfaces, are essentially of good report. His realism resulted in two notable innovations in technique: in the conventional comedies a few actors move in pairs on different planes of dramatic importance, and their speeches are often leisurely and balanced; but in the Venetian comedies the characters are more numerous and more variously related, and their speeches are short, crisp, and often interrupted.

Best of all, among these plays, are *I pettegolezzi delle donne*, "Women's Gossip"; *I rusteghi*, "The Tyrants"; *La casa nova*, "The New House"; and *Le baruffe chiozzotte*, "Quarrels at Chioggia."

One of the stage settings in *I pettegolezzi* is a quayside, with boats in view; and men come ashore from a *tartana* (a small craft with a lateen sail). Among the twenty-one characters are the master of the *tartana*, sailors, a porter, an Armenian vender of dried fruits, a Neapolitan street Arab, an old-clothes-woman, a washerwoman, and a seamstress — also Pantalone and Arlecchino (who do not appear, however, in the later Venetian comedies). The play is a sunlit, colorful, and chattering "school for scandal" in humble Venetian life.

I rusteghi recounts the domestic experiences of four crusty old cronies who, though subtly individualized, are at one in their ancient bourgeois principles: they think that their wives and children should be neither seen nor heard, and rule them, or try to rule them, with iron hands. They arrange a marriage between the son of one of them and the daughter of another, but forbid the two to meet. The one wife who is both clever and rebellious contrives a meeting of the two young people (who are well pleased with each other), defends them in the storm that breaks when that meeting is discovered, tells the four tyrants exactly what she thinks of them, and succeeds in bringing about the formal betrothal.

La casa nova opens with a scene in which masons, carpenters, painters, and an upholsterer are making over an apartment for a bride and groom. The bride's would-be aristocratic follies and the groom's extravagances lead them into manifold troubles, from which they are rescued by a beneficent uncle, Cristofolo, who beneath an alarming gruffiness has a heart of gold.

Goldoni in his youth had spent two years as Coadjutor to the magistrate in Chioggia, a fishing town at the southern end of the Venetian lagoon; and the sights and sounds of those two years, cherished in his memory, went into the making of the *Baruffe chiozzotte*, in which the prevailing dialect is the special Chioggian variety of Venetian. Most of the several men of the play are fishermen: their womenfolk gather to wait and worry for them, making lace and gossiping. An idling boatman buys a slice of roast pumpkin for one of the lacemakers, Lucietta, who is betrothed to Titta-Nane, an absent fisherman; jealousies and name-callings follow; and when the *tartana* comes in and unloads its cargo, and the returning fishermen find out what has happened, there is a general shouting, stones are thrown, a knife is drawn, pistols are brandished (no one is hurt), and Titta-Nane and Lucietta scorn each other. All concerned are summoned to the chancellery by the Coadjutor, to whom they give their evidence, one by one, in a most amusing sequence of scenes (no one is punished). Quarrels break out once more; but the Coadjutor brings about the reconciliations that lead to the happy ending.

Of the plays Goldoni wrote in France the two best are *Il ventaglio* and *Le bourru bienfaisant*. The *Ventaglio* (not extant in its original French form) is a unique and altogether admirable comedy, in which Goldoni has made use of the main techniques of his Venetian plays: the participation of numerous characters, and the constant succession of short, crisp speeches. The setting represents a village square, with an inn, a cobbler's shop, an apothecary shop, a two-story villa, a café, a dry goods shop, and the house of a villager. When the curtain rises all the characters are on the stage: the innkeeper working at his accounts, the cobbler tapping, the apothecary pounding in his mortar, Candida — the heroine — and her aunt on the villa terrace, their servant sweeping around the door, Evaristo — the hero — and a Baron sitting at a table and drinking coffee, the café waiter serving them, a Count reading to himself, the owner of the dry goods shop sewing, the villager ready to go hunting with Evaristo and the Baron, and Giannina — the villager's sister — spinning. For a few moments the stage remains silent — except for the tapping and the pounding; and then the swift action starts. Candida accidentally drops her fan from the terrace, it breaks, and Evaristo buys a new one for her at the dry goods shop; but before it reaches its destination it passes through the hands of Giannina, the cobbler, the innkeeper, the cobbler again, the Count, the Baron, the Count again, and Evaristo again, and is the cause of a delectable series of misunderstandings. At the end Candida, fanning herself happily, is assured that her new fan really comes from Paris.

The *Bourru bienfaisant* is a very skillful conventionalization of the *Casa nova* for the French stage. Géronte, the surly but beneficent uncle, becomes a much more dominant figure than Cristofolo had been. The *Bourru* lacks the vivacious realism of its Venetian original, but it is in other respects an even better comedy.

Goldoni's work marks, for Italy, the establishment of a direct relationship between the drama and life. He was not a man of many books, and the instances in which he derived characters or situations from other playwrights are relatively unimportant. His characters are drawn from all the social levels of the life he observed so faithfully. It is in his plays that the common people first came into their own, finding in him a champion ready to assert their value and to treat them with understanding, with affection, and with a gaiety that has, for them, no sting.

His general method of construction seems to have been to receive or create in his mind certain individual characters, to bring them together in some amusing relation, and to see what would then naturally happen to them — the plot thus shaping itself. Sometimes, indeed, his characters get themselves, momentarily, out of comic control, even into dangers from which it takes a skillful dramatic effort to rescue them. And there are plays in which the characters refuse to converge in a conventional solution, and the play has to end without a satisfactory denouement — an artistic blemish, but a striking testimony to Goldoni's resolution to be true to nature.

Within the limitations of his own honest simplicity, and within certain limitations imposed on him by Venetian ordinances (which, for instance, forbade the representation of ecclesiastics on the stage), he sought also, though genially rather than passionately, to influence the life of his day, through a criticism of its undesirable features expressed not in diatribes but in humorous portrayals, pointed occasionally by speeches — always in character — of unmistakable frankness. His own instinctive and convinced morality keeps his plays clean with a cleanness that is itself a protest against theatrical and social immorality.

First and always, Goldoni was a humorist. Humor of character and humor of situation, as revealed in action and in speech, are alike constant. His humor is cumulative, growing from scene to scene as humor of character is brought out more and more brilliantly by successive novel situations, which themselves grow out of each other with irresistible increases of heart-warming fun. Goldoni had, indeed, as resourceful and delectable a sense of sheer fun as any dramatist who ever wrote. His humor has no extension into profundity: it is essentially simple, genial, and serene. He gave good pleasure to thousands on thousands of persons in his own day, and his giving of good pleasure has never ceased.

Editions, translations, and adaptations of his comedies have multiplied: the *Locandiera* alone has been translated half a hundred times, and into a dozen or more languages. Many of his plays still hold their places on the stage. Italian players have brought them to America — Duse the *Locandiera*, Novelli the *Bourru bienfaisant* — and several of the comedies, the *Ventaglio* oftener than any other, have been acted here by amateur enthusiasts.

His *Mémoires*, written in French in his old age, are among the best of autobiographies. The swiftly moving story of the vicissitudes of his boyhood and youth is told with a reminiscent zest that has much of the appeal of his own comedies; and his comments on many of his own plays and on his experiences as playwright are of much interest.

* * *

Goldoni's chief rival, Carlo Gozzi (1720–1806), was a bizarre Venetian aristocrat who in happier days might have enjoyed a life of indolent pleasure; but his family fortune was swiftly vanishing, and he could not help realizing the decadence of the very society whose traditions he cherished and defended. And when the *commedia dell'arte*, so long the favorite form of public entertainment in Venice, was threatened by the innovating bourgeois realism of Goldoni and the pretentious inanities of Chiari, Gozzi rose to do battle for the masks and what they represented.

The course of the controversy, as has been said earlier in this chapter, led to the production in 1761 of Gozzi's *L'amore delle tre melarance*, designed to prove that people would go to see anything, no matter how absurd, if only it were novel. For this play, in accordance with the practice of the *commedia dell'arte*, Gozzi wrote only a *scenario* (and a few bits of dialogue which parody Chiari and Goldoni): later on he wrote a detailed "reflective analysis" of it. Taking the fairy tale of The Three Oranges from Basile's *Lo cunto de li cunti*, Gozzi retained all the essential features of the familiar story, exaggerating its absurdities and yet endowing it with a new, if strangely laughable, vitality. All of the characters are in some sense comic. Among them are four stock characters: Pantalone, Brighella, Tartaglia, and Truffaldino (Tartaglia is distinguished chiefly by his enormous spectacles and his stuttering — *tartagliare* means, in Italian, "to stutter"; and Truffaldino is a variant of Arlecchino). Tartaglia, son of the King of Goblets (a playing-card suit), sets out, with Truffaldino as his companion, to rescue the maidens imprisoned in the Three Oranges; the first two maidens perish when Truffaldino is too thirsty to obey orders; but the third, Ninetta, survives, and after her traditional tribulations becomes the bride of Tartaglia. Among the other characters are the King of Goblets, his ambitious niece and her fellow conspirator Leonardo, the magician Celio, a caricature of Goldoni, and the malevolent fairy Morgana, a caricature of Chiari. Gozzi's hostility to Chiari and to Goldoni is vented, throughout the play, in merciless and exceedingly clever satire.

Stimulated by this initial success, Gozzi proceeded to write, in the years 1761–1765, nine other *fiabe*, "fantastic plays," deriving his main plots either from fairy tales or from stories of oriental origin. All nine were written out, with some provision for incidental improvisation. Pantalone, Tartaglia, Brighella, and Truffaldino appear in every case, speaking in their various forms of prose. The other characters speak, for the most part, in pedestrian verse. The best of these plays are *Il re cervo*, "The King Turned Stag"; *Turandot*; and *L' augellino belverde*, "The Pretty Little Green Bird."

The *Re cervo* presents a series of transformations amid which the King and his faithful Queen suffer and rejoice with a surprising measure of emotional reality.

Turandot is based upon a story that goes back to an old Persian romance. Turandot, the proud and cruel daughter of the Chinese Emperor, will marry only a suitor who solves her three riddles: those who fail in the attempt are put to death. At last a foreign prince, Calaf, succeeds; but he in turn, hesitant to marry one who does not love him, proposes a riddle to Turandot: if she fails to answer rightly she must marry him; if she does answer rightly he must die. She answers rightly; but she saves Calaf from death.

The plot of the *Augellino belverde*, like that of "The Three Oranges," is taken from one of the stories retold by Basile, that of the Dancing Water, the Singing Apple, and the Speaking Bird; and the *Augellino*, like the earlier play, has a particular satiric purpose, the object of the satire being, in this case, the newfangled ideas of the French Encyclopedists. The two chief characters of the *Augellino* are Renzo and Barbarina, twin children of Tartaglia and Ninetta, and the King and Queen of Monterotondo. Through the machinations of a wicked grandmother the twins had been exposed to death as infants; but they had been rescued and brought up by Truffaldino, a cynical sausage-maker, and his generous wife Smeraldina, who has lavished a mother's affection upon them. They, however, have imbibed the French philosophy from books that Truffaldino had bought, by weight, to get paper for the wrapping of his sausages; and they are persuaded that all human actions are motivated by self-love. Truffaldino, unwilling to support the twins any longer, turns them out of his house. They get good counsel from the noseless statue of Calmon, an old philosopher. Renzo, for his sister's sake, secures the Singing Apple and the Dancing Water, but in his attempt to capture the Little Green Bird he is turned to stone. Barbarina, for her brother's sake, faces the same perils, and is successful. These experiences cure them of their false philosophy. In the final scene the Apple sings a recitative and an aria while the Water dances; Barbarina is betrothed to the Little Green Bird, who now resumes human form; Renzo is betrothed to a *ci-devant* statue; the wicked grandmother is turned into a turtle; and Calmon is promised a new nose. Throughout the play there is an extraordinary intermingling of serious attack on the philosophy of self-love, an effective assertion of the worth of selfless love, a constant stream of absurdities, and a plentiful supply of trivial fun in word and in action.

In Italy the spell of Gozzi's *Fiabe* was soon broken: recently, however, Gozzi has returned to the Venetian stage. In 1777 and 1778 the *Fiabe* were translated into German; and it was in Germany that they had their only considerable influence. They won early admiration from Goethe, Schiller (who remade *Turandot* into a serious drama), Lessing, and the Schlegels. To these and to other early Romanticists, Gozzi's blending of the fantastic and the serious made an impressive appeal. For Friedrich Schlegel, Gozzi stood by the side of Shakespeare. *Turandot* and "The Three Oranges" have come to life again in operas by Puccini and Prokofiev.

Gozzi's memoirs, written mainly in 1780, are entitled *Memorie inutili della vita di Carlo Gozzi scritte da lui medesimo e pubblicate per umiltà*, "Useless Memoirs of the Life of Carlo Gozzi Written by Himself and Published out of Humility" — but they yield little evidence of humility. Two of the chapters are self-portraits — one a physical portrait, the other a "moral" portrait; and the narrative and its many interspersed reflections are concerned primarily with the impact of an unfriendly world upon a well-intentioned Carlo Gozzi. The story of his youth is entertaining; the account of the absurd and disastrous plight of the whole Gozzi family is vivid; and the chapters devoted to his controversy with Goldoni and Chiari have a special interest. In the *Memorie* as in Gozzi's other writings one finds humor mingled with seriousness — a seriousness that becomes violent when he attacks current philosophic and social degeneracy.

CHAPTER 40

Parini and Other Writers

GIUSEPPE PARINI was born in 1729, of a humble family, in the village of Bosisio on the shore of the little Lake of Pusiano in the beautiful region just south of the Lake of Como. Most of his life, after his childhood, was spent in Milan; but he revisited his birthplace from time to time. For some years he earned a precarious living by private teaching and by copying legal papers. In 1752 he published a slender volume of merely Arcadian verse, which won him a welcome into Milanese literary circles. In 1754 he was ordained, but he remained always in the status of an abbé. In 1754, also, he entered, as tutor, the household of the ducal Serbelloni family. This residence, which continued for eight years, gave him a perfect opportunity to observe from within the futile and overbearing life of the aristocracy, and served to confirm the native democracy of his spirit. The duke called him "that peasant from Bosisio"; the duchess was capable of petty cruelty; and Parini's service came at last to an unhappy ending.

It was during his years with the Serbelloni that his distinctive poetic activity began. He turned first to the writing of odes — similar in form to the current *canzonette*, but differing from the *canzonette* by their general seriousness in content, and by the refinement of their artistry. Three odes were written in the years from 1756 to 1761. In the first, *La vita rustica*, he celebrates the beauty of his own little lake and its surrounding hills, and the peacefulness of the free and simple life of his village. He prays that no hostility may invade that peacefulness, and he praises those peasants who by the use of new methods increase the yield of their vines and the fertility of their fields. With such life the prisoning gold and honors and fears of city life cannot compare. The second ode, on "Salubrity of the Air," again contrasts country and city, but in this case with a particular civic urgency: Parini is attacking the disease-breeding carelessness of the Milanese authorities with regard to unsanitary conditions in and around the city. The third ode, *L' impostura*, is an attack on hypocrisy in public and in private life.

In these same years Parini began the composition of his unique masterpiece, a long poem in blank verse entitled *Il giorno*. The "day" is the day of a young gentleman of fashion; and the poem, ostensibly a course of instruction in the ways of spending fashionable hours, is in reality a satire upon the actual life of the aristocracy. The poem is divided into four portions: *Il mattino*, *Il mezzogiorno*, *Il vespro*, and *La notte*.

At dawn, when the cock crows, and the toil of peasant and smith begins, the *giovin signore*, who has spent the night at soirées, at the opera, and at cards, is ready at last for the sweet closing of his eyes. He sleeps until the sun is high; then valets hasten to open blinds — and instruction begins:

> Raise then your fair form, lean upon the pillows that, gently yielding, softly support your shoulder, and with your right forefinger, lightly, lightly, rub your eyes, dispelling what may remain of the Cimmerian mist: then, forming with your lips a little bow — sweet to behold! — silently yawn.

A servant asks whether he will drink coffee or Caribbean chocolate; and Parini comments:

> Surely 'twas needful that from its ancient domain a nation should go forth, and with audacious sails, amid wild storms, strange monsters, fears, dangers, and inhuman hunger, should pass the boundaries so long inviolate; and it was but right that Cortes and Pizzarro should esteem as less than human the blood that flowed in human bodies beyond the seas, until at last, flashing and thundering, pitilessly they hurled Mexican kings and noble Incas from their high ancestral thrones — since thence came new delights, oh gem of heroes, to your palate.

Presently come his dancing teacher, his music teacher, and his French teacher, with their sheaves of gossip. A servant is despatched to bear a morning greeting to the lady whom the *giovin signore* serves as *cavaliere servente*. His hairdresser dresses his hair elaborately (he may while away the time by dipping into some prettily bound little French book) and powders him profusely; a jeweler offers him costly pseudo-Parisian trinkets; and he receives the miniaturist who is painting for him a miniature of his lady. Most elegantly dressed, equipped, and perfumed for the day, he may — while his coach is kept waiting — write precious missives, or engage in other occupations, until at last he is ready to set out to dine with his lady.

In similar vein the three later portions of the *Giorno* lavish precepts for Midday, for Evening, and for Night. The scene of the *Mezzogiorno* is laid in the home of the lady. The *giovin signore* is taught precisely how to make his bow on entrance. Dinner — prepared by "a great mind from the land where Colbert and Richelieu were once illustrious" — is eaten with ritual delicacy; the lady tells of the day when a long-faithful servant, having dared with his plebeian foot to insult her lapdog, which had playfully bitten him, was forthwith expelled, and thus reduced to hopeless beggary; and the *giovin signore* is encouraged to display his learning.

The *Vespro* opens as the sun is setting:

> From highest hills and lofty cliffs the sun sends its last greetings to departing Italy, and seems to long to behold you once again, my lord, before Alp or Apennine or the curving sea shall hide you from its eyes. All day long it has seen only the bent and weary bodies of the scythe-bearing reapers of your fields . . . and dusty peasants leading home carts laden with your harvests, and on canals and fertile lakes the hairy chests of oarsmen bringing their cargoes for your comfort and your luxury. These were ignoble sights: now let the sun behold him who, served by all, serves none.

The *giovin signore* and his lady drive out together; they call maliciously on a lady who has been having convulsions; and they join the haughty procession of rival coaches on the Corso — remaining until night equates grandees and commoners in its darkness.

The *Notte* takes the bored pair to a thronged and opulent soirée, where a varied company passes in swift review. Card play begins:

> Now through the fortunate hall around a hundred tables sit the goddesses and the heroes who are the highest glory and hope of Italy . . . On every brow thought gravely reigns; and a majestic silence surrounds all.

Hero and heroine are last seen as ambrosia and iced nectar are brought in, and the *giovin signore* gives his lady his exquisite handkerchief to serve as napkin.

The *Mattino* was published in 1763, and the *Mezzogiorno* two years later. The *Vespro* and the *Notte* were never quite completed, and were not published in Parini's lifetime.

Throughout *Il giorno* Parini's abounding irony treats trivialities as if they were matters of high moment, and pettiness as if it were magnificence. The constant target of his attack is the caste system as a whole, its injustice, its cruelty, and its absurdity. The special features of current aristocratic manners that most stir his indignation are cicisbeism and the affected preference for everything French, with a corresponding depreciation of everything Italian. His irony is the more effective because of the perpetual elegance of his poem, an elegance as insistent as that of the luxury by which he had been surrounded. Parini's poetic elegance, however, is genuine, not factitious: it is the result of an inner gentility, a deep absorption of the qualities of the best classic and Italian poetic style, and an endlessly patient refining care. His verse is extraordinarily rich in overtones for those who are familiar with the poetic patrimony of Rome and Italy. The greatness of his poem is enhanced by his fine sense for the ordering of words in such a way that they linger pleasantly in one's memory, and by his ability to make beauty visible — the beauty of unspoiled morning and evening, even the very different beauty of the lights and colors and patterns and the formal grace of the aristocratic society whose total impact on life he so deplored.

The years from 1762 to 1769 were very difficult for Parini: their happier aspects were the success of the *Mattino* and the *Mezzogiorno* and the tutoring of the young and responsive Carlo Imbonati. In 1769 Parini was appointed professor of literature in the Palatine Schools of Milan, and thereafter his life was busily professional. He loved his teaching, and he was loved and admired by his students. He served on educational commissions, and he was influential in various phases of the cultural life of Milan. Yet he never escaped hardship. He was beset by ill health; his salary was small; and his frankness aroused troublesome hostilities.

He wrote constantly, in many forms of verse and in prose. His finest work — aside from the *Giorno* — was done in the several odes that he wrote at various times from 1764 to 1795.

The first of these odes, *L'educazione*, was a birthday gift to his pupil, Carlo Imbonati, who had just recovered from a serious illness. The opening stanzas picture affectionately the boy's return to health, while in the rest of the poem Parini imagines that Chiron is talking to his pupil Achilles. The centaur's precepts reflect Parini's own principles of education:

> From the soul alone spring noble deeds: illustrious blood avails nought to a languishing spirit. . .
> The first altar must be raised within the soul. . .
> Let loving disposition . . . make you a constant defense for the needy, a faithful lover, and an indomitable friend.

The next ode, *Il bisogno*, "Need," is the most powerful of all. Suggested by Beccaria's treatise on "Crimes and Punishments" (which will be mentioned later in this chapter), it nevertheless voices Parini's own profound sympathy with those who suffer from dire poverty, and may thereby be driven to wrongdoing:

> Ah then the unfortunate breaks the common laws; transgresses all bounds; invades what others own; and eats with bloodstained hands his stolen bread.

Some of the later odes deal with subjects such as vaccination, education for women, and the "guillotine" fashion, imported from France, of leaving off a veil and wearing a red ribbon around the neck; some express a tempered tenderness; and some give praise to men who well deserved it. In the most personal of all the odes, *La caduta*, "The Fall," Parini tells of slipping and falling as he was walking through the streets of Milan in bad winter weather.

An acquaintance helps him to rise, picks up his hat and cane, puts an arm around him, and advises him henceforth to play the courtier, and thus acquire wealth enough to enable him to set up his own coach. Parini replies indignantly, defending his personal and poetic dignity — and limps home alone. The last ode is addressed *Alla musa.* Unlike the others it is not in *canzonetta* form, but consists of a succession of Horatian Sapphic stanzas; and it breathes throughout a Horatian serenity.

When the "liberating" French entered Milan in 1796 Parini and other Milanese liberals took places in the republican municipal government, ready to fight for the realization of their promised liberties, hoping against hope for the establishment of a true democracy. Before long, however, Parini resigned his municipal position, giving to those who were poorer than he the pay he had received. His last years were spent quietly in the rereading of his favorite authors — Dante, Ariosto, Machiavelli, Euripides, and Plutarch — and in meditation on the "Last Supper" of Leonardo da Vinci. When the Austrians retook Milan in the Spring of 1799 Parini was menaced, but not harmed: he prophesied their reactionary excesses. He died before the end of the summer.

* * *

Among the lesser men who wrote Italian verse in this period the two most interesting were Giovanni Fantoni (1755–1807) and Lorenzo Mascheroni (1750–1800).

Fantoni (Labindo in Arcadia) was called the Tuscan Horace; and his odes are indeed successfully Horatian both in form and in content. His best poems are patriotic. He writes in honor of Admiral Rodney and of Franklin, and refers to Washington's defense of liberty: but for his celebration of the Peace of 1783 he merely borrows — gracefully enough — Horatian hearth-fire and Horatian wine.

Mascheroni, Professor of Mathematics in the University of Pavia, Dafni Orobiano in Arcadia, is remembered mainly for a poem in excellent Italian blank verse, *L'invito a Lesbia Cidonia,* in which he invites an Arcadian countess to visit the University. The illustrious faculty will welcome her; and he, Dafni Orobiano, will guide her eagerly through the Museum of Natural History, with its sections for minerals, fossils (here the nautilus sets out on its first poetic voyage), birds, insects, creatures of the sea, beasts, and reptiles; the Museums and Laboratories for Physics, Astronomy, Chemistry, and Anatomy; the Library; and the Botanical Garden. The *Invito,* by far the best of the several "scientific" poems of the period, derives a remarkable vitality from Mascheroni's constant sense that everything he describes is in reality a phase of life.

* * *

Giovanni Meli (1740–1815), born in Palermo, a physician and chemist, chose to write in the Sicilian dialect. His best work, *La buccolica*, was composed in the peaceful beauty of the village of Cinisi, where the mountains approach the sea, and the villagers toil in the fields or as fishermen. In this work several eclogues and idylls are grouped in four parts, *La primavera*, *L'està*, *L'autunnu*, and *L'invernu*. The sympathetically observed and shared realities of these poems are in welcome contrast to the artificialities of Arcadian verse. The first song, in each of the four groups, is seasonal: Spring invites to love; Summer is a time of reaping and pasturing; grapes and olives ripen in the Autumn; Winter brings storms and a shivering desire for warmth. One of the idylls begins thus:

Già cadevanu granni da li munti
L'umbri, spruzzannu supra li campagni
La suttili acquazzina: d'ogni latu
Si vidìanu fumari in luntananza
Li rùstici capanni: a guardii a guardii
Turnavanu li pècuri a li mandri . . .

Now the long shadows were falling from the mountains, sprinkling the light misty rain over the fields; everywhere, in the distance, one saw smoke rising from rustic huts; the sheep in flocks were returning to their folds.

Meli, with all his understanding of his peasantry, was himself a cultured poet. He handles his dialect with sensitive skill, often refining it slightly: its soft fluency accords well with his prevailing moods. He is a worthy successor to Theocritus.

* * *

Among the abler writers of this period who wrote mainly in prose the most incessantly industrious was Gaspare Gozzi (1713–1786), the elder brother of Carlo. He lived the life of a superior hack writer, trying his hand at almost every current form of prose, verse, and drama: much of his work is valueless, but much is redeemed by the excellence of his native gifts and the general strength of his literary conscience. An elaborate *Difesa di Dante* had much to do with the renewal of Italian appreciation of the great poet: to this *Difesa* Gozzi appended a translation of Pope's *Essay on Criticism*.

The first really noteworthy Italian periodical to show the influence of the *Tatler* and the *Spectator* was the *Gazzetta veneta*, written by Gozzi for a society of merchants, and published twice a week from February 1760, to January 1761. To the commercial information which was the reason for the gazette's existence Gozzi added brief and well-told *novelle*, fables, dialogues, miniature essays, and literary and artistic critiques, always with reference to the day-by-day life of Venice. When his employers cancelled his contract he began at once, and kept up for another year, the publication of a new bi-weekly, *L'osservatore*, in which the field observed is broadened to include human traits and manners as a whole. The portraits of typical characters are among the very best of their kind; and the dialogues are written with originality and with verve.

A score of *Sermoni*, satires in which the general mood is one of humor rather than one of violence, are Gozzi's best work in verse. Some of them deal reproachfully with the besetting social evils of the time, especially the passion for luxury and for social display, and the heedless disregard of parental responsibilities; some are concerned with the low estate of poetry and of criticism; and some, in which the satiric element is slight, report Gozzi's personal trials and hopes. Loyal to older virtues and simplicities, and distressed by the life in which he was fated to move, Gozzi writes as a high-minded, true-hearted, protesting, and lonely gentleman.

The life and work of Giuseppe Baretti (1719–1789) constitute one of the most remarkable of all the many literary links between Italy and England. He was born and spent his boyhood in Turin, but thereafter he never had a fixed home in Italy. Throughout his life he was warmhearted and hotheaded; he had a genius for friendship, but his quickly flaring temper and the outspoken fearlessness of his resentments and his criticisms made him many enemies. In 1751 he left Italy for London, where he soon became an active member of Dr. Johnson's circle. His extraordinary linguistic ability enabled him presently to write in excellent English: in 1753 he published *A Dissertation upon the Italian Poetry*, a defense of Italian literature against the attacks of Voltaire; and in 1760 he brought out his *Dictionary of the English and Italian Languages* (which, in successive revisions, remained the best Italian-English and English-Italian dictionary until 1915).

In 1760 he traveled with a young Englishman through parts of England, Portugal, Spain, and France. He then returned to Italy, where he began to publish an account of his travels in the form of *Lettere familiari a' suoi tre fratelli*; but the protests of a Portuguese diplomat prevented completion of the publication. Praise and dispraise are mingled in Baretti's impressions of England; the balance, however, is decidedly favorable. In his "letters" from Portugal he describes, among other things, a bullfight, royal parsimony, the destruction wrought by the earthquake of 1755, inns, barbers, maskers, dances, Portuguese scenes and persons and customs, and various aspects of Portuguese culture — which he did not admire.

In 1763 Baretti went again to Venice; and there, beginning in October, he wrote and published once a fortnight, for a year, under the pseudonym of Aristarco Scannabue, "Aristarchus the Ox-Slaughterer," a periodical devoted to literary criticism and called *La frusta letteraria*, "The Literary Whip." His criticism is based less upon general principles than upon his passionate personal and national loyalties and antipathies. The Gozzi brothers, for instance, are highly praised; and anything that suggests French influence or bears any sign of French approval is anathema. Goldoni is severely treated. The value of the *Frusta* lies not so much in its judgments — though some of them, including favorable judgments of Cellini, Metastasio, and Parini, are certainly sound — as in the scourging vigor of its prose.

In 1766 Baretti returned to London, where he made his home for the rest of his life. There, in the year of his return, Samuel Sharp published his *Letters from Italy*, which seemed to Baretti to be filled with calumnies against his always beloved native land; and he therefore wrote in reply *An Account of the Manners and Customs of Italy*, which was published in 1768. Of this book Dr. Johnson said:

> His account of Italy is a very entertaining book; and, sir, I know no man who carries his head higher in conversation than Baretti. There are strong powers in his mind. He has not, indeed, many hooks, but with what hooks he has he grapples very forcibly.

In 1769 Baretti was set upon, in the Haymarket, by half-a-dozen ruffians, one of whom, in the ensuing struggle, he killed, in self-defense. At his trial, which resulted in acquittal, Dr. Johnson, Burke, Garrick, Goldsmith, and Sir Joshua Reynolds were among those who appeared as character witnesses on his behalf.

Among the more noteworthy of his later publications were a complete English version of his *Lettere familiari*, and a powerful *Discours sur Shakespeare et sur Monsieur de Voltaire*, in which the English poet is defended valiantly and Voltaire, as a critic of literatures of which he had little knowledge, is thoroughly demolished.

Several Milanese gentlemen, much influenced by French thought, were working together, at this time, for economic, political, and social reform. Pietro Verri (1728–1797), the leader of the group, was primarily an economist. He wrote several cogent treatises on economics and related subjects; and in 1764 — while Baretti in Venice was still publishing his *Frusta* — he started a periodical called *Il Caffè*, "The Coffeehouse," to which several members of his group contributed. It was modeled on the *Spectator*: but while some of its articles were of a literary character it was devoted mainly to the promotion of reform — and in the two years of its existence its impact upon administrative practices in Milan and upon Italian social consciousness in general was very considerable.

From Verri's group there came one and only one work that combined great literary vitality with social urgency: the brief treatise *Dei delitti e delle pene*, "On Crimes and Punishments," written by the Marquis Cesare Beccaria (1738–1794), and published in 1764. Beccaria was led to the writing of this book by his shocked sense of the inhumanity of criminal procedure and punishment as practiced throughout most of Europe in his day:

> lamentations of the weak, victims of cruel ignorance and wealthy indifference; barbarous torments inflicted with prodigal and useless severity for crimes imaginary or unproved; the squalor and the horrors of imprisonment, made still more intolerable by that most cruel of executioners, [prolonged] uncertainty as to one's fate.

Moving from a general discussion of the nature of law, he explores such subjects as the obscurity of laws, arbitrary arrest, the credibility of witnesses, secret accusations, the death penalty, the relation of the punishment to the offense, and the prevention of crime. He treats with special fullness and special indignation the use of torture to extract confession, the imprisonment in the same "caverns" of men who have been proved guilty and men who are awaiting trial, and the shattering results of long legal delay. A deep sense of the inherent dignity of man pervades the work. There is no liberty, Beccaria says, when the law permits a man "to cease to be a person and to become a thing." He is able even to put himself in the place of the criminal, and to quote what the criminal might say if he had the ability to express the feelings that impelled him toward crime:

> What are these laws that I must respect? . . . Who made these laws? Rich and powerful men, who have never deigned to visit the squalid hovels of the poor, who have never shared a piece of mouldy bread amid the cries of famished children, and a wife's tears.

The concluding and summarizing sentence is this:

> Unless punishment is to be an act of violence by one or by many against an individual citizen, it must be public, prompt, necessary, as light as may be possible under the given circumstances, proportionate to the offense, and in accordance with the dictates of the law.

Few books have ever been written in which such persistent logical analysis is powered by such vigorous assertion of the rights of human beings, however hapless they may be. Beccaria's style is robust and tense, so wrought as to give clear and effective expression to his compelling ideas, and eloquent when he turns from exposition to pleading. The treatise was immediately and very widely influential. It was translated into a score of languages, and led to the revision of several penal codes. The first English translation appeared in 1767: a reprint of that translation issued in New York in 1773 is, with a single unimportant exception, the first translation of an Italian work to be published in this country. The influence of Beccaria's thought is manifest in the American Bill of Rights.

The abbé Ferdinando Galiani (1728–1787), perhaps the most diminutive, physically, of all men of letters, was educated and began his career in Naples, where he gave early evidence of possessing not only keen intelligence and competence in public affairs, but also an inexhaustible fund of sparkling wit. His first notable work was a substantial treatise on money, written in Italian prose. In 1759 he was sent to Paris as Secretary of the Neapolitan Embassy, and there he came into his own. He was faithful and successful in his official work; but the life he loved was led in the *salons* of Paris, chiefly in that of Mme d'Épinay. His irrepressible wit made him a general favorite; and he deserved and won the friendship of Diderot and other French thinkers and writers of the time. In 1764 a sudden removal of all restrictions on the export and import of grains caused hunger and rioting in regions that were adversely affected, and led Galiani in the next few years to write, in French, his best known work, the *Dialogues sur les bleds*, "Dialogues on the Grain Trade," in which he argues cogently that general principles should never be applied without careful adaptation to particular local conditions, and that the grain trade should be regulated accordingly. He wrote this treatise not in conventional economic form, but as a series of dialogues that flash with incessant wit: it was read and relished, accordingly, by the whole reading world of France. Voltaire said that Plato and Molière seemed to have combined to produce it, and that it was "as amusing as our best novels and as instructive as our best serious books."

In 1769, much to his distress, Galiani was recalled to Naples. There too he was busied with official duties, and there too he radiated *bons mots*; but he missed Paris dreadfully, and kept up an active correspondence, in French, with his Parisian friends, especially Mme d'Épinay. His letters perpetuate his extraordinary combination of wit and wisdom. He discusses, briefly and always lightly, even when convictions underlie his humor, all sorts of subjects: religion, morals, politics, economics, education, cats, wills, the world of 1900 as he foresaw it, an imaginary statue of himself. In his letters, or in bits of conversation otherwise preserved, one hears him saying such things as these:

> Paris is the café of Europe.
>
> The French cannot think without talking, and they think only in order that they may talk.
>
> An isolated truth is as useless as a mushroom alone in a meadow.
>
> Liberty under the *Contrat social* means the right to interfere in other people's business.
>
> The man who is really to be feared is not the rascal or the knave: it is the honest man who is mistaken — *l'honnête homme trompé*.

CHAPTER 41

Alfieri

VITTORIO ALFIERI was born in Asti, in Piedmont, in 1749, of a noble, wealthy, and honorable family. In his boyhood, as he wrote long afterwards in his *Vita*, he was

> usually taciturn and placid, but at times very loquacious and vivacious; often alternating between opposite extremes; obstinate and restive against constraint; very ready to accept affectionate counsel.

Even then, he says, there began to develop in him the melancholy disposition which he regarded as his dominant characteristic. The language of his home was French: the Piedmontese nobility scorned Italian. At the age of nine he was sent to the Royal Academy in Turin, a school for sons of the nobility. The eight years spent there were years of "ill-health, idleness, and ignorance." In the course of these years, however, the boy for the first time gained some acquaintance, at first surreptitiously, with a few Italian authors. It is noteworthy, in view of the intense unity of Alfieri's own best writing, that he disliked Ariosto's frequent dropping of one line of action to take up another, and that he regarded Metastasio's arias as unwelcome interruptions.

On his graduation from the Academy Alfieri, at seventeen, became his own master. He had developed a driving inner energy, which, however, was as yet wholly undirected. He plunged into a long series of travels, which took him, in the next six years, through Italy, France, England, Holland, Switzerland, Austria, Hungary, Bohemia, Germany, Denmark, Sweden, Finland, and Russia; then again to Western Europe and England; and finally to Spain and Portugal. Restless and bored, he traveled with no fixed purpose, seeing little of what was really worth seeing. He was fortunate in the making of a few faithful friends; unfortunate in his love affairs; and very proud of his fine horses. His slight literary knowledge, however, was measurably increased, and his political convictions were formed and strengthened. Within these years he read Voltaire, Rousseau, Montesquieu, and other French authors; but his greatest literary experience was the discovery of Plutarch:

> But for me the book of books . . . was Plutarch — the lives of the truly great. Some of them . . . I read over and over again, with such transports of outcries, weeping, and even fury that anyone who might have been listening in the next room would certainly have thought me mad. As I read of certain great deeds of those greatest of men, I would spring to my feet, again and again, in great agitation; and tears of grief and rage flowed from my eyes at the thought that I had been born in Piedmont, and at a time and under a government such that nothing noble could be done or said, and could hardly — and then uselessly — be felt or thought.

In 1772 Alfieri bought a house in Turin, and began to lead the typical life of a young and wealthy aristocrat. With some of his friends he formed a club which had no serious purpose, but encouraged some ephemeral writing; and for the amusement of this club his first compositions were written. One day early in 1774, merely to kill time, he dashed off, in bad Italian verse, two acts of a play on Cleopatra; and some months later he developed it into a full length tragedy. In June 1775, the *Cleopatra* was performed in Turin, and was well received. Alfieri had no illusions as to the quality of his play; but the whole experience marked a turning point in his life. His intense energy, so long wasted, had now found a firm and perfectly appropriate direction. In one of his letters he writes:

> Da quel giorno in poi volli, e volli sempre, e fortissimamente volli —

> Ever since that day I have willed, and willed always, and willed most intensely.

He was resolved to write great dramatic poetry in Italian; yet his knowledge of the Italian language and of Italian literature was very inadequate: French was still the language of his thoughts. He decided to go to Tuscany, to learn "to speak, to listen, to think, and to dream in Tuscan"; and in the Spring of 1776 he went to Pisa, traveling lightly, he says, with only three horses, two servants, pocket editions of Italian poets, a guitar, "and many hopes of future glory." After three months in Pisa and three in Florence he was talking freely in Tuscan, and beginning to think in Tuscan. He went back to Turin for the winter; but in the Spring he returned to Tuscany — this time with eight horses — going first to Siena, and then, in the Autumn, to Florence, where for the next three years he made his home. Thereafter he was able to write correct and pure Italian, and to write verse that was not unworthy of the Italian poetic tradition. But he wrought out a style that was all his own.

Wholly his own, also, was the process he followed consistently in the composition of his tragedies. That process had three successive phases, for which Alfieri uses the terms *ideare*, *stendere*, and *verseggiare*. The first phase consisted in the writing of a two- or three-page outline of the play. The second phase consisted in writing out the whole play in Italian prose, with all possible fervor, with the uncritical inclusion of whatever ideas came into the writer's head, and with no concern as to wording. The third and most laborious phase consisted in turning the prose into verse, with constant revaluation and pruning of the prose material, and with great formal care. The completion of this task was followed by revision, and sometimes by a complete rewriting. He generally allowed a considerable amount of time to intervene between the first and second phases of the process, and between the second phase and the third. One of his tragedies, for instance, was *ideata* in January 1777, *stesa* in July 1778, and *verseggiata* in 1779. Between phases of his work on a given play Alfieri frequently carried forward a play or plays that had been begun previously, or started a new play: toward the end of 1777, for instance, he had on hand three plays that were versified but clearly needed revision or rewriting; four that were only written out in prose; and one that had recently been *ideata*. This way of doing things, curious as it was, had two advantages: it enabled Alfieri, while a play was still in an unfinished state, to review it with a freshly critical mind; and it enabled him to turn freely from one type of creative activity to another, and thus to write as and when his restless spirit moved.

All in all, in the years from 1775 to 1787, he completed nineteen tragedies. The first of them all, the *Filippo*, is also one of the best. The historical originals of Alfieri's protagonists are Philip II of Spain; Charles, Philip's son by his first wife; and Philip's third wife Isabella, who before her marriage to Philip had been betrothed to Charles. The clashing passions that dominate the play are the fearfully vindictive tyranny of Filippo and the deep and essentially blameless love that Carlo and Isabella strive vainly to repress. Carlo is strong and clear-sighted; the gentle Isabella is easily and fatally entrapped by Filippo's cunning.

In the years from 1781 to 1785 Schiller was working independently on his *Don Carlos*. There have been several comparisons of the two plays: Carlyle's, in *The Life of Frederick Schiller*, is perhaps the best. Of Alfieri's Filippo as compared with Schiller's Philipp, Carlyle says:

> Without the aid of superstition, which his rival, especially in the catastrophe, employs to such advantage, Alfieri has exhibited in his Filippo a picture of unequalled power. Obscurity is justly said to be essential to terror and sublimity; and Schiller has enfeebled the effect of his tyrant, by letting us behold the most secret recesses of his spirit: we understand him better, but we fear him less. Alfieri does not show us the internal combination of Filippo: it is from its workings alone that we judge of his nature. Mystery, and the shadow of its horrid cruelty, brood over his Filippo: it is only a transient word or act that gives here and there a glimpse of his fierce, implacable, tremendous soul;

> a short and dubious glimmer that reveals to us the abysses of his being, dark, lurid, and terrific, "as the throat of the infernal Pool."

Carlyle notes also the brevity of the Italian play, the fewness of its characters, the fact that Alfieri is not concerned with historical or local color, and the severe simplicity of his style. These four features of Alfieri's craftsmanship appear not only in the *Filippo* but also in his other tragedies; and they all result from his own intensity of feeling and his determination to make his plays concentrations and conveyors of intensity. He sought brevity as a definite objective. The *Filippo* in its versified form contained about 1900 lines: the successive rewritings reduced that number to about 1400. One of the tragedies has less than 1100 lines, and only one has more than 1500. By contrast, *Don Carlos* has more than 5000.

The *Filippo* and a few of the other tragedies have each six named characters: in the remaining tragedies the number is either four or five. By contrast, *Don Carlos* has twenty. Alfieri believed firmly that the persons of a tragedy should be limited to those who are themselves involved in its tragic passions and in the determination of its course of action; that every appearance and every word of a minor person not so involved serves to chill the tragic mood; and that in any art anything that is not clearly necessary is fundamentally wrong.

Alfieri's disregard for historical and local color was due to his constant concern for inner rather than outer experience, and to the fact that he was working within the tradition of the three unities: for an author who observes those unities strictly, eschewing episodes and limiting his time to a single day and night and his place to a single scene, can hardly do much with historical or local color. In the tragedies of Alfieri unity of action is absolute; unity of time is virtually absolute; unity of place is infringed in only three or four cases. The unities, thus observed, bring a most valuable reënforcement to the effect of intensity that Alfieri sought so relentlessly to produce. His tragedies, indeed, show the theory of the unities carried to its logical extreme; and to one who accepts the production of an intense and significant inner experience as the fundamental tragic purpose their stark power affords a more convincing justification of that theory than can be found elsewhere.

Alfieri's style is indeed severely simple, but its simplicity is an achieved and not a casual simplicity: it is free from decoration, compact, powerful, and slightly archaic.

The best of the early tragedies are (together with the *Filippo*) the *Antigone*, the *Agamennone*, the *Oreste*, and the *Virginia*. The *Antigone* is noteworthy chiefly for the fearlessness of the heroine, contemptuous of tyranny and of death. Clytemnestra, fiercely driven by her vainly resisted love for the iniquitous Aegisthus, dominates the *Agamennone*. The *Oreste* is more exciting and more poetic than any of the preceding plays. The ardent and fearless son of Agamemnon, thirsting for a just vengeance, is the most moving character thus far depicted by Alfieri. Clytemnestra, still bound to Aegisthus, yet stirred to a maternal love to which Orestes can respond only with wrath and bitterness, is an even more tragic figure here than in the *Agamennone*. The *Oreste* is the first of the plays of Alfieri in which friendship becomes a major dramatic resource.

Alfieri's hatred of tyranny had been evident in these earlier tragedies, but it is in the *Virginia* that he first turns to the exaltation of the struggle for liberty. Following Livy's familiar story, Alfieri brings into the Roman Forum, in a succession of increasingly dramatic combinations, the tyrannous decemvir Appius Claudius; Virginia, whom Appius is trying to get into his power; her father Virginius, an heroic soldier; Icilius, a fiery and eloquent tribune, betrothed to Virginia; and the Roman People. When Icilius appeals to the people, bidding them tremble for themselves and for their children, one hears for the first time their answering cry:

> Per noi, pe' figli, o libertade, o morte.

At the end of the play, when Virginius has given his daughter the death that alone could save her, the people are roused to a fury that dooms the tyrant and his tyranny: the sounds of the final tumult continue even after the curtain falls.

The two greatest of the tragedies of Alfieri, the *Saul* and the *Mirra*, are both compassionate probings of tormented souls. The scene of the *Saul* is a camp on Mount Gilboa; and the day and night of the play are the last of Saul's life. His faithful son Jonathan and his daughter Michal, the beloved wife of David, are with him. Saul, guilty of disobedience to divine commands, is haunted now by visions of a condemning Samuel, and is beset by an evil spirit. When that spirit masters him he trusts only Abner, his evil counsellor, and his hatred of David, whom he has driven away, is implacable. When his mind clears he rises to something of his former greatness, finds comfort in his children, distrusts Abner, and longs for David. As the play opens, David comes secretly to the camp, resolved to fight for Saul and for Israel in the impending battle. He is welcomed first by Jonathan, and then by Michal: the motives of a strong friendship and of a strong marital love, distressed by separation past and dreaded, are interwoven with the tragic passions of the play. Saul appears first with Abner, in a scene from which the following lines, spoken by Saul, are quoted:

> How many years have passed since these my lips
> Were moved to smile! My children, even they
> Whom I so truly love, stir me to wrath
> If they but show their fondness. — Turbulent,
> Intolerant, fierce, restless, anger-swayed

Am I unceasingly: to all about
A hated burden I hate most of all.
In war I long for peace, in peace for war.
Poison doth lurk in every cup I taste;
In every friend I see an enemy.
These rugs Assyrian prick my side like thorns.
Sleep is but anguish: dreams are horrible.
Nay more, nay more: who would believe it? Fear,
Quivering fear is the war trumpet's sound
To me, to me, to Saul! Now look and see
If widowed of her glory be in truth
The house of Saul. Now look and see and tell
If God hath left me desolate indeed. . .

That very voice, that very sovereign voice
That in my youth called to me night by night
When I, unknown, dreamed not of kingly power,
That very voice, grown fearful in its sound
Calls to me now by night, and overwhelms
My senses like the thunderous crash of waves:
"Saul, Saul, thy throne is lost, thy day is done."
And that same venerable, saintly face,
That once I saw in dream, ere Samuel
Had come to tell me of God's will for me,
I see again in dream, but oh how changed!
Within the chasm of a dark abyss
I seem to stand: and gazing up, behold
A hill resplendent, and the prophet, throned.
David is kneeling there before his feet,
And on his head the holy prophet pours
The consecrated oil. Then, searching down
Into my chasm, with gigantic arms
He plucks the royal crown from off my head,
And seeks to place it on the anointed locks
Of the kneeling David: who — oh wonder! — seems
The honor to deny: and weeps, and signs
That on my head the crown be placed again.
Oh David, David, can it then be true
That thou art loyal yet: art yet my son,
My faithful subject, and my friend? — Ah, rage,
That thou should'st dare to rob me of my crown!
Thou that dost dare so much, old man of evil,
Tremble! — Who art thou? — Perish him who dares
To pluck it from me! — Ah, the light is gone!

David first enters the presence of Saul at a favorable moment. Before long, however, Saul's mind is darkened again and David seeks to soothe him, as in earlier days he had done so often, by singing to him. Into the scene of this singing Alfieri introduces four lyrics of varying metrical structure: a majestic invocation, a vigorous song celebrating the youthful exploits of Saul, a gentle song of peace, and a vision of renewed martial prowess.* The spell, however, is quickly broken. Saul's wrath is rekindled, and he rushes with drawn sword upon David, who escapes. In the course of the night the Philistines rout the Israelites, and Jonathan and two other sons of Saul are slain. Tidings of the disaster serve to revive Saul's kingliness. He is left finally alone, and the play ends with his last words:

> My sons, my sons! — Father am I no more —
> Thou art alone, oh king: not one is left,
> No friend, no servant. — Art thou sated now,
> Terrible wrath of an inexorable God?
> But thou, my sword, art left: to my last need
> Come now, thou faithful minister. — I hear
> The shouts of the insolent victors: on my sight
> Flash now their blazing torches and their swords,
> Their thousand swords. — Evil Philistia,
> I die, but even as a king should die.

His sword is indeed faithful; and as the Philistines rush upon the stage the curtain falls.

In the *Mirra* Alfieri handles with unfaltering dignity the most terrible of all his themes. Myrrha, daughter of the King and Queen of Cyprus, is cursed by the gods, through no fault of her own, with a more than filial love for her father. In constant torment of soul, she struggles desperately to overcome what the gods will not let her overcome, and to keep from revealing her fearful secret — though she cannot conceal the fact of her suffering, which is increased by the loving efforts of her parents to discover its cause. The final tragedy consists not in her death, but in the fact that in the moment before her death she has been forced to confess what she had so fought to keep hidden forever.

In the *Bruto primo* and the *Bruto secondo*, the last two of the nineteen tragedies, both finished in 1787, Alfieri returns to the Roman Forum and to the championship of liberty. The first Brutus is the founder of the Roman Republic, the second is the Brutus who played a leading part in the conspiracy against Caesar. The dedication of the *Bruto primo* begins thus:

> To the illustrious and free man, General Washington:
> Only the name of the liberator of America can stand before the tragedy of the liberator of Rome.†

Alfieri stated thus his high concept of the function of tragedy:

> I believe firmly that in the theater men should learn to be free, strong, gen-

* This scene follows, in a general way, the model of Dryden's *Alexander's Feast*, but it is far finer than its model.

† A presentation copy of the play, bearing Washington's signature upon the page on which the dedication begins, is preserved in the Boston Athenaeum.

> erous, zealous followers of true virtue, unwilling to suffer violence, devoted to their fatherland, acquainted with their own rights, and in all their emotions and enthusiasms ardent, upright, and magnanimous.

He was intensely energetic in his own spirit: the foundations of his art lay in his response to similar intense energy perceived in great figures of history or legend. His essential service is in the moving presentation of men and women whose tremendous energy has enabled them to achieve or to endure beyond the common powers of humanity, whether in personal devotion, in ambition, in the cause of liberty, or in the strifes that rage within the soul. Death, never feared, is often the seal of moral victory. Yet Alfieri, though his underlying desire was always that right should prevail, is stirred by greatness in itself, whatever its direction: even his tyrants are manifestations of a force that in itself is marvelous, and, being at once marvelous and turned to evil, is profoundly tragic. The people of his heroic world, when once they are known, are not to be forgotten; and their total impact upon the memory is certainly such as to confirm a responsive spirit in generosity, in strength, and in the love of freedom. Many Italians, in the stormy years that were to come, found, in the tragedies of Alfieri, such confirmation.

For a hundred years his tragedies held their place upon the stage, and occasional modern performances revive their stark grandeur. Adelaide Ristori played Myrrha again and again, in America as well as in Europe, with what seems to have been an almost unparalleled dramatic power; and Gustavo Modena and Tommaso Salvini both played Orestes, Icilius, David, and, most impressively, Saul.

The drama of Alfieri's personal life was shared, after 1777, with the *grande dame*, known usually as the Countess of Albany, who was the wife and later the widow of the drunken Pretender, once "Bonnie Prince Charlie," who had continued to call himself "Charles the Third, King of Great Britain, France, and Ireland." Even after his death the Countess clung to the semblance of royalty: her plate bore the royal arms, and her servants addressed her as "Your Majesty." After 1786 Alfieri and the Countess were much together, first in Alsace and in Paris — where the salon of the Countess was frequented by men and women prominent in public or in literary affairs — and then, following a narrow escape from the French revolutionists, in Florence, where they maintained a common household, the Countess's salon being as popular as it had been in Paris. Their companionship gave to Alfieri a sense of inner stability he had never known before, and his literary activity flourished under her constant encouragement.

His many sonnets are of great value to those who seek an intimate understanding of his essentially tragic spirit, but, while many of them contain vigorous quatrains or tercets, few are moved throughout by a clear lyric impulse. Among the lyrics that are not sonnets the most interesting, to an

American reader at least, are the five magniloquent odes that are grouped under the title *L'America libera.* The first four were written late in 1781, soon after the news of the surrender at Yorktown reached Italy. The first deals with the causes of the Revolution; the second pictures the coming of the French fleet; and the third and fourth exalt Lafayette and Washington. The fifth ode, written in the Spring of 1783, celebrates the conclusion of the peace of Versailles.*

In the course of the dozen years during which Alfieri was working on his tragedies he wrote also a narrative poem, two prose treatises, a prose dialogue, and a few other compositions. The treatise *Del principe e delle lettere* is at once a defense of liberty and a defense of letters, conceived as being in themselves a noble instrument for the attainment and the defense of liberty. In one long chapter Alfieri discusses the specific services that may be rendered, in the common cause, by the epic poet, the writer of tragedy, the writer of comedy, the satirist, the orator, the historian, the lyric poet, and the philosopher. The chapter preceding the "conclusion of the work" is, like the last chapter of Machiavelli's *Prince*, an "Exhortation to Free Italy from the Barbarians."

In Paris, in 1790, Alfieri wrote the first and much the longer of the two Parts of his *Vita*: the second Part was written in 1803. In his Introduction he declares that he has been led to this writing by his "love of himself" — a phrase which, in his thought, covered both his self-esteem and his desire for glory. Such self-love is

> a gift which Nature gives in greater or lesser degree to all men, especially to writers, and most especially to poets, or to those who regard themselves as such. And this gift is a very precious thing, since it becomes the source of all noble action when to self-love a man joins a reasoned knowledge of his abilities and an enlightened enthusiasm for the true and the beautiful.

He believed, also, that his works would prove to be of lasting significance, and that it was desirable, therefore, that there should be made a record, and a record such as only he could make, of the spirit of the author of those works, and of the circumstances under which they were written.

His powers of observation and of memory were very great; but in the application of those powers he was concerned not with events and scenes as such, but with their effects upon his inner self: the *Vita*, indeed, is less an autobiography than an auto-psychography. Yet when he chooses to narrate or to describe he does so vividly — as for instance in his account of his escape from Paris, with the Countess of Albany and seven servants, on August 18, 1792. At the city gate, where his two heavily laden coaches were

* Alfieri sent Washington a copy of one or all of these odes, but that copy seems not to have survived.

stopped, despite the willingness of the few guards to let them proceed, by a slovenly, drunken, and furious crowd, he leaped from his coach, passports in hand, and began to shout more loudly than anyone else:

> Full of anger and fury, regardless of the immense danger that threatened us, I shouted: "Look, listen; my name is Alfieri; Italian, not French; tall; thin; pale; red hair; that's who I am; look at me; this is my passport . . . we wish to go on, and *per Dio* we shall go on."

The crowd increased, shouting: "Let's burn the coaches; let's stone them; they are trying to escape; they are rich nobles; let's take them back to the Municipality, and get justice done." But at last the opposition of the crowd slackened somewhat, the guards managed to clear the way, and the coaches moved on, amid hisses, insults, and curses. Most of the pages of the *Vita* perpetuate Alfieri's intense thoughts and intense feelings and intense efforts of will. The drama he reënacts is a drama of mind and heart; and as one follows the unfolding of that drama one does indeed gain both a fuller understanding of the conditions and the processes of Alfieri's creativity, and a reënforcement of one's belief in the potentialities of the human spirit.

During the last eleven years of Alfieri's life, years spent wholly in or near Florence, he continued to write; but the quality of his late writings is not equal to that of his earlier works. His hatred of tyranny was as strong as ever, but that hatred had now a new immediate object. He had known and attacked long since the tyranny of the single tyrant: now he had learned, from France, that the tyranny of the many could be as terrible as the tyranny of the one. This new conviction led him to write from time to time stinging epigrams, satirical sonnets, and various prose pieces in which he attacked the new tyranny. Eventually he gathered these various materials in a miscellany which he called *Il Misogallo*, "The Gallophobe." Its best elements are its dedication and its concluding sonnet. The dedication is to Italy of the past, the present, and the future:

> to that which . . . you have been so long, the chief abode of all human wisdom and excellence; to that which, alas, you are today, unarmed, divided, debased, enslaved, and powerless; and to that which some day (whenever it may come) you will indubitably rise again to be, virtuous, magnanimous, free, and unified.

In the final sonnet Alfieri makes the proud and the justified claim that when such resurgence comes it will be inspired not only by the memory of ancient Italian valor but also by his own verse.

Alfieri hated the French: but fate, with a most insidious irony, led the French, and those Italians who favored them, to exalt Alfieri as an enemy of tyranny and an apostle of liberty, and to arrange performances of his most ardent republican tragedies. In 1796 a performance of the *Virginia* in Milan was witnessed by the young general Napoleon Bonaparte, and the *Virginia* and the *Bruto primo* were given in Turin in the course of a celebration of an anniversary of the execution of Louis XVI.

Not long after his return to Florence, also, Alfieri resumed the writing of satires in the traditional *terza rima* form (he had written two or three such poems in earlier days). All in all, he wrote nearly a score of satires. Most of them are on political subjects; the others deal with social, pseudo-philosophic, or educational abuses. The best of them, *L' educazione*, is very successful in its dialogue and in the characterization of its interlocutors — an insolent and ignorant count and the cringing abbé whom he is hiring, at less than he pays his coachman, to serve as tutor to his children.

Studious throughout his mature life, Alfieri turned in 1795 to the field of Greek literature. Years before, after the completion of the *Bruto secondo*, he had sworn to write no more tragedies; but his reading of the *Alcestis* of Euripides so stirred the embers of his tragic fire that he immediately outlined and eventually completed a play of his own on the same theme. As drama the *Alceste seconda*, which is almost devoid of action, is by no means great; but it is none the less a noble poem of conjugal love — love that proves itself stronger than life, and, finally, stronger than death.

The French occupations of Florence in 1799 and 1800 caused Alfieri much distress — which was not assuaged by the efforts of a French general to pay his respects to the Italian apostle of liberty.

Alfieri's last major enterprise, carried through in the years 1800–1802, was the writing of six unsuccessful satirical comedies, four of them political theses. In the Spring of 1803, as has been said, he wrote the second Part of his *Vita*. In the Autumn of that same year he died.

CHAPTER 42

Foscolo and Other Writers

THE RAGING of the Napoleonic storm kept Italy in turmoil from 1796, when Bonaparte, hailed by many as a liberator, first crossed the Alps, to 1814, when his imperial domain shrank to the island of Elba. Rulers fled; so-called republics — the Cispadane, the Cisalpine, the Ligurian, the Tiberine, the Parthenopean — came into brief existence; "liberation" proved to be an illusion; the thousand-year-old independence of Venice came in 1797 to an ignominious end; armies surged back and forth; the Cisalpine Republic became the Italian Republic (with Napoleon as president), and the Italian Republic became a very incomplete Kingdom of Italy (with Napoleon as king, and his stepson as viceroy); Napoleon was proclaimed Emperor of the French; Italian regiments were sent to fight in Russia. When the storm was over the ousted rulers came scurrying back, and the aspect of Italy became again very much what it had been before, except that Venice and its mainland were now an Austrian province. But Italy had learned that kings could be overthrown and foreigners expelled; and the names and forms of the Italian Republic and the Kingdom of Italy gave new strength to the idea of Italian unity.

Classicism reëntered sculpture in the strict and placid art of Canova.

* * *

The poet whose verse responded most immediately — too immediately — to the political vicissitudes of the Napoleonic era was Vincenzo Monti (1754-1828). From 1778 to 1797 he lived in Rome, writing profusely, and enjoying high favor in papal circles. He often drew the subjects of his poems from current events; and when the French revolution broke out he was drawn inevitably into the vortex of the passions it aroused. In 1793 a French official named Bassville, who had come to Rome to promote the cause of the Revolution, was set upon and killed by a mob; and this occurrence led Monti to write the violently anti-Republican poem entitled *In Morte di Ugo Bassville*. Borrowing forms and ideas and phrases from Dante, he imagines that the soul of Bassville is compelled, by way of penance, to revisit the fearful scenes of the Terror — some of which, especially the massacre of the priests and the execution of Louis XVI, are vividly portrayed. But in 1797 — the "liberating" armies of Napoleon moving now from victory to victory in Northern Italy — Monti, easily converted, became in effect Napoleon's Italian poet laureate. From this time on he lived chiefly in Milan. He disowned the *Bassvilliana*; attacked the Vatican and the anti-Napoleonic coalition; wrote a hymn for a Milanese celebration of the sixth anniversary of the execution of Louis XVI; celebrated many French triumphs; hailed Napoleon as King of Italy and as Emperor; and heaped praises upon him, calling him the conqueror of fate, the new Prometheus, and the first of heroes. In 1814, after the defeated Napoleon had been sent to Elba, Monti still inveighed against the predatory powers assembled in the Congress of Vienna; but in the following year he welcomed the returning Austrians with a fulsome tribute to the divine genius of Austria.

Nevertheless, his political poems are in some measure redeemed by their frequent utterance of his love of Italy and his desire for Italian unity. The best of them is the *canzonetta Bella Italia*, which begins with the spirited stanza

Bella Italia, amate sponde,
Pur vi torno a riveder!
Trema in petto e si confonde
L'alma oppressa dal piacer —

Beautiful Italy, beloved shores, again, at last, I behold you! My heart throbs in my breast, and my soul is overwhelmed with joy —

and twice cries out:

Il giardino di natura,
No, pei barbari non è —

No, the garden of nature is not for the barbarians.

Among the best of Monti's many non-political poems are the ode *Al signor di Montgolfier*, a brilliant celebration of the historic balloon ascension of December 1, 1783, with a clear picture of the scene itself, a remarkably sure sense of its significance, and a clever review, in poetic terms, of progress in chemistry, electricity, mathematics, and astronomy; the Horatian ode *Invito d'un solitario ad un cittadino*, one of the most successful poetic assertions of the superiority of country life to city life — in the country there is nothing to fear save winter and the north wind — ; and a late essay in verse form, *Sulla mitologia*, in which he claims for mythology an enduring poetic value, and writes scornfully of the new "audacious boreal school" that would substitute its northern mists, its ghosts, and its witches for the sapphire sky of Italy and the fair fancies of classic poetry. His poetic gifts are most richly manifest and his shortcomings are least evident in his blank-verse translation of the *Iliad*, which is generally regarded as his masterpiece. He wrote also three tragedies: the *Caio Gracco*, the best of the three, tells again the story of the Gracchi, and is, like several of the plays of Alfieri, a proclamation of liberty, in Roman terms.

Monti's poems, as a whole, are alight with clarity of imagination and expression, descriptive skill, and responsiveness to beauty, and are distinguished by his master craftsmanship as a maker of verse. But he fell too easily into mere rhetoric, he made too much use of outworn conventions, and his attempts at grandeur were futile. There are echoes, in his poems or his tragedies, of Milton, Young, Gray, and "Ossian," and of several of the tragedies of Shakespeare.

One of the lesser poets of the period, Ippolito Pindemonte (1753–1828) of Verona, is of some special interest because of his English experiences and admirations. Within the years 1789 and 1790 he spent several months in England, and while there he addressed a *canzone Alla bellissima ed onoratissima fanciulla Agnese H**** and a sonnet *Per Madamigella Gray che danzava con somma grazia e pari modestia.* After his return to Italy he wrote a long prose dissertation on English gardens, and a description of English estates (in a poem on another subject) which contains this passage:

> Beautiful paths, cool grottoes, shaded seats, still waters moving slowly among grasses and flowers; thunderous waters plunging from on high, cliffs of awesome sublimity; fields and gardens, learned display and rural simplicity: harvests wave, goats cling to rocky heights, there is a lowing in the valley, a bleating on the hill; a marble bridge curves over the streamlet, and a temple gleams white amid the leafage; strange plants flourish, casting American shadows on British ground, and the birds of Europe sing on branches that Nature had prepared for other songsters; the proud-antlered deer glides through the woods, turning his head now and again to watch you; and the swan, arching his neck, swims across the silvery lake.

His Anglophile disposition did not prevent him, however, from finding amusement in the habits of the Englishman touring Italy:

> He lives with his fellow Englishmen and reads the English gazette, which follows him faithfully from place to place: and thus he thinks that he is learning all about the customs of Italy.

* * *

Ugo Foscolo was born in 1778, of a Venetian family living on the Greek island of Zante. In 1792, his father having died, his mother moved to Venice;

and there, in the next five years, the young Foscolo went on with his classical studies, read widely in Italian literature, and developed an intense love for Italy and for liberty. In Venice, also, he wrote his first poems and his first tragedy. He welcomed the coming of Napoleon with an ode entitled *Bonaparte liberatore*; but he was soon bitterly distressed by the cession of Venice to Austria and by the abject passiveness with which Venice sank into its new provincial status.

His distress led him, in 1797, to leave Venice for Milan, which remained the center of his activities for several years. Early in 1799 he published, in its first form, the first part of his novel, the *Ultime lettere di Jacopo Ortis*; but he was unable to complete the work before the Austrians, in the same year, invaded Northern Italy. He enlisted in the Cisalpine Legion; fought honorably; was wounded, captured, and liberated; and from the end of the year to the summer of 1800 was with the French troops who were besieged in Genoa. While in Genoa he wrote the first poem in which he showed unmistakably his distinctive poetic gifts. Luigia Pallavicini, a leader in Genoese society, had been injured by a fall from a runaway horse: Foscolo sends her an ode in which memories of her dancing, a lively description of her misadventure, and a prophecy of her restoration to health and beauty are ingeniously interwoven with a series of relevant scenes, in miniature, from classic mythology. The whole ode, perfect in its technique, is a charming piece of poetic goldsmithery.

With Napoleon again dominant in Italy, Foscolo, attached to the staff of a French general, was sent on missions to various North Italian cities and to Florence, where he fell in love with Isabella Roncioni, who, though she returned his love, maintained her promise of marriage to a man to whom, before meeting Foscolo, she had, against her will, become engaged. While Foscolo was in Florence he discovered, with indignation, that the publisher who had brought out the first part of his *Ultime lettere* had brought out also a second part, which had been put together by a hack writer; and early in 1801, on his return to Milan, he set about the rewriting and the completion of the book, which was published, in its final form, in 1802. The novel — the first Italian novel, in the modern sense of the word — consists of some eighty letters written in the years 1797–1799 by Jacopo Ortis, a young Venetian student, to his intimate friend Lorenzo Alderani, together with two or three letters addressed to the heroine, a few personal notes, and connecting and concluding statements by Lorenzo. In the first of the two Parts of the novel, Jacopo, overcome with grief at the cession of Venice to Austria, leaves the city and goes to a place in the Euganean hills, near Padua. There he meets a gentleman who is spoken of as "Signor T***," his daughter Teresa, and her fiancé Odoardo. Teresa — beautiful, good, and accomplished — has no love for Odoardo, but her father insists on the marriage. Jacopo falls in love with

Teresa, and she, during a long absence of Odoardo, falls in love with Jacopo. Once, and once only, they acknowledge their love; but Teresa will not fail in her promise to her father. Odoardo returns; and Jacopo, for Teresa's sake as well as his own, goes away. In the second Part Jacopo wanders from city to city in Northern Italy and Tuscany; and Teresa and Odoardo are married. Jacopo, resolved upon suicide, returns; sees Teresa again, with her father and her husband; takes leave of them, as for a long journey; and finally carries out his resolution.

The story is based in part on Foscolo's own experiences, and in part on Goethe's *The Sufferings of Young Werther.* The sufferings of Werther, however, result only from his love: those of Ortis result both from his love and from the deplorable state of his fatherland. But the grief that permeates the novel is more than personal and more than political: it is a true *Weltschmerz*, arising from a profound consciousness both of the transitoriness of all human achievement and of the inevitability of human suffering:

> I look out from my balcony now that the immense light of the sun is fading and the shadows are dispelling the faint rays that gleam on the horizon: and in the darkness of the sad and silent world I contemplate the image of the Destruction that devours all things. . .
>
> Men appear to be the makers of their own misfortunes; but their misfortunes derive from the order of the universe, and the human race in its pride and its blindness is a slave to fate. Our talk is of things that have happened within a few centuries: what are a few centuries in the vast sweep of time?

Yet though Jacopo finds the weight of his sorrows too heavy for endurance, he recognizes and exalts the value of heroic effort. After all, "the human race, precisely when it seems to be on the point of death, is reborn in new vigor." He urges those who have the gift of writing to exercise that gift by depicting the shamefulness of the oppression under which their world is crushed, and seeking to stimulate heroism in generations yet to come: it was indeed Foscolo's hope that his book might share — as in fact it did — in the task of such stimulation.

Among the most noteworthy letters in the novel are one beginning "If only I were a painter," which contains one of the finest landscape descriptions ever penned; two letters from Florence, one telling of Jacopo's reverent emotion in the presence of the tombs of Galileo, Machiavelli, and Michelangelo in Santa Croce, and another telling of his visit to the battlefield of Montaperti, peopled, for him, with the fratricidal phantoms of Guelfs and Ghibellines; and two letters, written from the mountainous Italian border, in which, as from a great height, Jacopo surveys the fates of his fatherland and of humanity.

Beyond all else, however, the novel is, fictionally, a recording of the emotions of its hero, and, in actuality, an outpouring of the turbulent spirit of its author. The style, consonant with that turbulence, is insistently tense and emphatic. The contrast between the *Ultime lettere* and the odes of Foscolo is very striking. He is indeed, in his creative life, a dual personality: in the odes he is an objective neoclassicist, delighting in sunny classic memories and concerned primarily with his artistry; while in the novel he is a romantic — not as the adherent of a literary doctrine, but because he is driven irresistibly to the utterance of the stormy passions of his restless soul.

In Milan, Foscolo wrote also a number of lyrics, among them an ode *All' amica risanata*, "To His Friend on Her Recovery," which is of quite the same character and quality as the ode he had written in Genoa, and several excellent sonnets, which express the romantic phase of his poetic being. One of them is this self-portrait:

> A furrowed brow, eyes deep-set and intent, hair fulvous, sunken cheeks, a bold aspect, lips full and mobile, slow to laughter, head bowed, neck firm, chest hirsute, limbs well formed; dress choice and plain; steps swift, and swift my thoughts, my acts, my words; prodigal, sober, kindly, blunt, forthright; adverse to the world, events adverse to me; mournful, on most days, and alone; thoughtful ever, and distrustful of both hope and fear: shame makes me craven, and wrath makes me bold; reason speaks cautiously in me, but my heart raves, rich in evil and in good. — Death, thou wilt give me fame, and peace.

In the Autumn of 1804 Foscolo was sent to Northern France as a captain in an Italian division attached to the French army that was being prepared for the invasion of England; and at Boulogne he began a translation of Sterne's *Sentimental Journey*, which he completed some ten years later, and published under the pseudonym of Didimo Chierico.

In 1806 he returned, on leave, to Milan; and there, in that year and the next, he wrote, in blank verse, his best known poem, *I sepolcri*. The writing was occasioned by the extension to Italy of a French law providing that all graves should be marked with stones identical in size and form, and should bear only such inscriptions as might be officially approved. The main elements in the thought of the poem are these: a tomb, though it be beautiful and visited by mourning friends, brings no comfort to the dead, but the sight and the care of it lead to the cherishing of memories among the living; the law is wrong in forbidding differentiation between the burial places of the evil and the good, the illustrious and the infamous; the cult of the tomb goes back to the beginnings of civilization and has attended the whole course of its development; the sight of the tombs of great men kindles the noble heart to glorious deeds; and even though tombs may at last disappear the poet renders the names of great men eternal. The poem proceeds, however, not in the manner of a formal argument, but by a series of surging lyric impulses, each giving inspired expression to some one phase of the underlying thought. The central passage, in a slightly abbreviated translation, reads thus:

To glorious deeds the tombs where heroes lie
Kindle the noble heart: holy and fair
Unto the pilgrim is the sacred ground
That shelters them. And I, when first I saw
The monument wherein the body rests
Of him who taught the prince to hold domain,
Yet in his teaching stripped the laurel leaves
From off the sceptre, and to all revealed
The tears it drips with, and its stains of blood,
And when I saw the tomb of him who raised
In Rome, unto the Gods, that mighty dome,
And his who, gazing upward, first beheld
The circling of our world and other worlds,
The unmoving sun irradiating all —
When these I saw, "Blessed art thou," I cried,
"Oh Florence, for thy dear life-giving air;
For all the streams that lofty Apennine
Pours to thee from its summits; for thy hills,
Festive with vineyards, where the moonlight rests;
For all thy gathering valleys, with their homes
And olive orchards; for the incense sweet
Rising toward heaven from thy flowery fields!
Blessed for thy first hearing of the song
That tempered wrath in the banished Ghibelline;
For giving parents and thy native speech
To him who found for Love so fair a veil:
Yet blessed most for that one single fane
That holds the bodies of our glorious dead!"
Unto these marble tombs Vittorio came,
The pallor of death and hope upon his brow,
To find a peace no living sight could give:
And now he lies among them, and his frame
Quivers with love of country, in its dust!

There are many other noble passages in the poem, and many lines and brief sequences of lines that have as much poetic scope as many an entire poem. The dignity of ancient burial ceremonies and the beauty of English suburban cemeteries are made visible. In the climax of the poem the blind Homer, groping his way among Trojan tombs, learns from them the story of the rise and fall of Ilium. Over the whole poem there brood a consciousness of the unending successions of life from the infinite past to the infinite future, and a sense of the enduring sorrow of the human lot: but through these shadows there gleams the firm assurance of the grandeur of high achievement, and of the immortality of heroism.

Foscolo was acquainted with Gray's *Elegy* and with other similar English poems, and traces of that acquaintance are discernible in *I sepolcri*; but Foscolo's purpose, as he himself makes clear in one of his letters, was quite different from that of the English poets. Young and Hervey, he says, wrote as Christians, concerned with the ideas of resignation and immortality, and Gray wrote as a philosopher, praising simplicity of life; whereas he, Foscolo,

> considers tombs in their political significance; and seeks to stimulate the political spirit of Italians by adducing examples of nations that honor the memory and the tombs of great men.

In the *Sepolcri*, also, one feels the presence of the spirit of Vico. But Foscolo's poem, assuming into itself the essence of all his learning, all his experience, and all his contemplation, is wholly his own in its fullness and its power. Classic and romantic elements are harmonized in its universality: Foscolo's dual poetic personality is here perfectly unified.

In the years 1811–1813 Foscolo wrote two tragedies, the *Aiace*, on the story of Ajax, and the *Ricciarda*, which tells a medieval story of Foscolo's own invention. They are not lacking in eloquence; but they are not well constructed, and they are ineffective in characterization.

In 1813, during a long stay in Florence, Foscolo began work upon an elaborate poem in which he intended to set forth, in mythological allegory, his thought on the significance of beauty, and to present a series of mythological pictures that might serve as models for sculptors and painters. The thematic development and the title of the poem, *Le grazie*, were suggested to Foscolo by his admiration of Canova's group of the Three Graces: the poem is addressed to Canova. Thoroughly and serenely neoclassic, the poem is artistically a continuant of the early odes. It was never completed, though many portions of it were written, and many passages were brought to an unsurpassed exquisiteness of verbal and rhythmic perfection. It consists of three "hymns": the first deals with the divine origin of the Graces and with the development of human civilization; in the second three lovely priestesses (who represent certain Florentine ladies) illustrate the beneficent influences of the Graces in music, poetry, and the dance; and the third describes the weaving of a veil that is to protect the Graces from the passions that beset humanity. The harp and the voice of the first priestess interpret the alternate joy and suffering of the human lot, in which sorrow is a guide to virtue, and may itself, by the Graces, be made sweet; and then the inspired notes reveal the function of harmony in the differentiation of the elements of the universe and in their recombination,

> Till all their dissonances, unified,
> Give forth a sound of harmony divine
> That lifts our minds above terrestrial things.

The weaving of the veil takes pleace on an island set in the midst of the ocean. The weavers are the Hours who wind the golden rays of the sun upon the spindle; the Fates who fill the shuttle with the diamond woof of destiny; Iris and Flora who bring colors of sky and earth; and Psyche who imparts her knowledge of mortality. As they weave, three Muses, Thalia, Terpsichore, and Erato, bear them company. The song of Erato, in its several stanzas, gives to the weavers the themes they are to weave into the pattern of the veil: youth, to be depicted with rosy threads; conjugal love, with threads of snowy whiteness; a warrior's filial memories, with threads of laurel; hospitality, with threads of gold; and, with cerulean threads, a mother bending over the cradle of her firstborn.

In 1815, faced with the necessity of taking an oath of allegiance to the Austrian regime if he were to remain in Italy, Foscolo preferred voluntary exile, and fled to Switzerland. Thence he made his way, in the following year, to England, where the rest of his life was to be spent. He was in general warmly received, as a poet and as a liberal (Wordsworth and Scott were among the dissidents); but his life in London, though it had its industrious and its brilliant hours, was on the whole discreditable, and was made distressful by his irresponsibility, his readiness to take offense, his incorrigible prodigality, the crushing burden of his debts, and his failing health.

He seemed to be in exile not only from Italy but also from Parnassus: he wrote no Italian poetry of any importance while in England. He did write, in English, one short poem addressed "To Callirhoe" (Caroline Russell), which begins thus:

> I twine, far distant from my Tuscan grove,
> The lily chaste, the rose that breathes of love,
> The myrtle leaf and Laura's hallowed bay,
> The deathless flow'rs that bloom o'er Sappho's clay;
> For thee, Callirhoe!

Throughout his London years Foscolo, driven always by necessity, wrote essays and reviews, in English, on literary, linguistic, historical, and political topics, for various periodicals — *The Edinburgh Review*, *The Quarterly Review*, *The New Monthly Magazine*, *The European Review*, *The London Magazine*, *The Retrospective Review*, and *The Westminster Review*.* His literary essays include discussions of early Italian poetry, of Boccaccio, of Michelangelo, of Tasso, of the Italian epic, and of "Principles of Poetic Criticism, as Applicable, More Especially, to Italian Literature"; a volume of admirable *Essays on Petrarch*; and an essay on contemporary Italian literature which was written and published under strange circumstances. In 1818, when Byron was preparing to publish the Fourth Canto of *Childe Harold's Pilgrimage*, he asked his friend John Cam Hobhouse to prepare, for inclusion in the forthcoming volume, some "Historical Illustrations . . . Containing

* Foscolo drafted his articles in Italian or in French: English versions were made by friends or by employed secretaries.

. . . an Essay on Italian Literature." Hobhouse, however, did not feel competent to write such an essay, and asked Foscolo, as a favor, for his help. Foscolo promptly produced a document of considerable length, which Hobhouse, making some additions, put into English and incorporated in his "Historical Illustrations." Foscolo's authorship was not indicated, and it was never admitted by either Foscolo or Hobhouse.

Foscolo shows himself, in his essays, to be a master — the first Italian master — of literary criticism, modern in his spirit and in his judgments. He is in complete possession of the works of which he writes; he is primarily concerned with their poetic or other literary qualities; and he brings to his interpretation a remarkable fund of historical learning and an amazingly comprehensive familiarity with the world's poetry. The *Essays on Petrarch* contain illustrative quotations from poets ranging from Sappho, Anacreon, and Dante, to Ben Jonson, Drummond of Hawthornden, Pope, and Samuel Rogers.

Foscolo died in 1827, in the village of Turnham Green. He was first buried in the Chiswick cemetery: he now rests, among his heroes, in Santa Croce.

* * *

Carlo Porta (1776–1821) was born in Milan and spent most of his life there, earning his living in the financial offices of successive governments. Primarily a humorist, he chose to give play to his humor in verse written in the dialect of Milan. His humor attains in its expression a specific realism anticipating that of the realistic novelists of the late nineteenth century; and it reveals a deep human sympathy, especially for the weak and bewildered folk who suffer through their own folly or through abuse by their superiors in strength or wit or station. In *novelle* in verse Porta tells of the *Desgrazzi* ("misadventures") *de Giovannin Bongee*; of the wiles by which *Marchionn di gamb avert*, "Bow-legged Melchior" (who plays the mandolin in a dance-hall orchestra) is entrapped into a disastrous marriage; of priests who intermingle phrases of the *Miserere* and bits of a mundane conversation of their own; and, most hilariously, of *La nomina del cappellan.* The marchioness Paola Traversa is about to select a new chaplain, the previous incumbent having died from over-exertion in taking the pet dog, Lilla, to walk. Thirty applicants gather on the appointed morning; but as the majordomo tells them of the requirements of the position — which include, among many other things, the ability to play tarots, and the readiness to go marketing and to run errands to the dressmaker and the hairdresser — more and more of the thirty drop out, until only six are left. These are admitted to the presence. One is summarily dismissed when he starts to kick the barking Lilla. Two others laugh inopportunely, and are banished because

poi che l' Altissim el ci ha post
In questo grado, e siammo ciò che siamm,
Certissimament l' è dover nost
Di farci rispettar come dobbiamm —

since the Most High has placed us in this rank, and we are what we are, most certainly it is our duty to make ourselves respected as we should be.

Three are left: but Lilla fawns upon the ugliest and shabbiest of the three, and it is upon him, therefore, that the choice falls (it turns out that he had with him some slices of sausage).

* * *

Lorenzo Da Ponte (1749–1838), born in the town of Ceneda, on the Venetian mainland, gained in his youth a considerable amount of literary knowledge, showed himself to be a facile versifier, and so misbehaved as to incur, in 1779, a sentence of banishment from Venetian territory. He took refuge in Austria; and in 1782 he won appointment as "Poet to the Italian Theater" in Vienna. During the nine years in which he held that position he wrote a score of *libretti* and other dramatic works, reaching his most memorable successes in association with Mozart, for whom he wrote the *libretti* of *Le nozze di Figaro*, *Don Giovanni*, and *Così fan tutte*. In 1791, however, he fell into disfavor, and was ordered to leave Vienna. After some wandering, in the course of which he made a very happy marriage, he found work in London, in 1793, as poet to the Drury Lane Theatre, for which he wrote several *libretti* and other plays; but by 1804, foreseeing financial catastrophe, he sent his wife and children to America, and in the spring of 1805 he followed them.

After disastrous attempts to sell groceries, first in New York and then in Elizabethtown, he returned to New York; and there, befriended by Clement Moore (the author of " 'Twas the Night Before Christmas"), he began the private teaching of Italian. He taught with energy, and with considerable success, holding *conversazioni* at which Italian was spoken, passages from Italian writers were read, and little comedies and operas of his own composition were given. In 1811, however, with high hopes of finding a quiet home, he moved to Sunbury, Pennsylvania, where he dealt in medicinal drugs and general merchandise, and did some teaching. But calamity followed upon calamity; and in 1819 he moved back to New York.

He was now seventy; but it was now that the most relatively peaceful and the most serviceable portion of his life began. He resumed his teaching, some of it at Columbia University, which gave him the title of Professor of Italian Literature; he wrote articles and pamphlets, in Italian and in English, promoting appreciation of Italy and Italian culture; and he imported and sold Italian books. In 1825 the first coming of an Italian operatic company to America brought him great joy, especially when performances of "his" *Don Giovanni* were given. Eight years later his efforts to establish Italian opera in New York on a permanent basis resulted in the erection of an Italian Opera House; but after two seasons the collapse of the operatic enterprise brought him his last great disappointment.

In the years 1823–1827, Da Ponte published, in four little volumes, his one substantial work, the *Memorie di Lorenzo Da Ponte da Ceneda scritte da esso*, of which a revised and enlarged edition appeared in 1829 and 1830. Lamartine's praise — "the most original and the most anecdotical memoirs ever offered to the public view by artistic Italy" and "the memoirs of Benvenuto Cellini are not more naïve or more diverting" — is undoubtedly excessive; but Da Ponte's narrative does possess a continuing interest, thanks mainly to the extraordinary series of experiences it relates. For American readers, in particular, it offers memorable pictures of life in New York and in Pennsylvania in the early decades of the nineteenth century, and preserves the memory of a man who did his devoted best to bring to America some comprehension of the greatness of his Italy.

CHAPTER 43

Manzoni

THE HEROIC AGE of modern Italy, known as the Risorgimento, "the Resurgence," extends from the downfall of Napoleon to the completion of the new Kingdom in 1870. The rulers who returned to the territories from which Napoleon had ousted them governed with a constantly suspicious repressiveness. Censorship was very strict, and arrest and imprisonment were frequent. But the Italian passion for liberty and for unity, stimulated by Napoleonic experiences, was now insistent, and gained encouragement from contemporary struggles in other countries. Secret societies and groups of conspirators were active. The society called the Carbonari, "the Charcoal-burners," grew swiftly in membership and in power, though membership invited death. In 1820 and 1821 revolutions, fomented by the Carbonari, broke out in Naples and in Piedmont, but were suppressed with Austrian aid; and in 1831 lesser risings in Parma, Modena, and the Papal States were also suppressed with Austrian aid. But the forces that were to achieve the final victory were gathering strength.

During the first half of the century Rossini, Bellini, and Donizetti were producing their dozens of operas — among them the *Barbiere di Siviglia*, *Norma*, and *Lucia di Lammermoor*.

The first of the great Italian magazines, the *Antologia*, began publication in Florence in 1821. Its articles were mainly literary or scientific; but the frequency of patriotic implications led to its suppression in 1833.

It was in this period that Italian literature felt the main impact of Romanticism. The presence of Romantic elements in Foscolo has already been mentioned; the relationships of Manzoni and of Leopardi to Romanticism will be indicated in the present chapter and the next; and a more general account of Italian Romanticism will be given in Chapter 45.

To English writers, Italy now meant more than ever before. During Byron's seven years in Italy, where he joined the Carbonari, he wrote the Fourth

Canto of *Childe Harold's Pilgrimage* — the most substantial tribute paid to Italy by any English poet — *The Lament of Tasso*, *The Prophecy of Dante*, most of his dramas (two of them on Venetian themes), his translation of the first canto of the *Morgante*, and much else. The last four years of Shelley's life were spent mainly in Rome and in Pisa; and in those four years he wrote most of his greatest poems, some of them touched by Dantesque or Petrarchan influence. Both Shelley and Keats, who was fatally ill before he reached Italy, are buried in the Protestant Cemetery in Rome. Wordsworth, who in his youth had had a glimpse of the Italian Lakes, visited Italy in 1820 and again in 1837: his Italian experiences are plentifully reflected in the collections called *Memorials of a Tour on the Continent* and *Memorials of a Tour in Italy*. Leigh Hunt, who went to Pisa on Shelley's invitation, remained in Italy for three years. Before leaving England he had written *The Story of Rimini* and had translated the *Aminta*; and after his return he wrote *A Legend of Florence* and his *Stories from the Italian Poets*, which did much to spread acquaintance with Dante, Pulci, Ariosto, and Tasso among English readers. Scott's hope to regain his health in Italy proved vain. In the course of conversations in Rome he said that he had formerly made it a practice to read through the *Orlando* of Boiardo and the *Orlando* of Ariosto once every year, and he expressed great admiration for Manzoni. Walter Savage Landor lived for many years in Florence, and there he wrote most of his immense series of *Imaginary Conversations*, some thirty of which have Italian interlocutors, from Dante and Beatrice to persons of Landor's own day.

Washington Irving spent several months in Italy in 1804 and 1805. Longfellow spent the whole year 1828 in Italy. Cooper and his family lived in Florence during the winter of 1828–1829, in Rome during the following winter, and in Venice in the spring of 1830. His enthusiastic recollections are recorded in a volume entitled *Gleanings from Europe: Italy*.

* * *

Alessandro Manzoni was born in Milan in 1785; and except for the years 1805–1810, which he spent chiefly in Paris, and for a few shorter absences, he lived in Milan, or in a villa near the city, through the whole of his long life. It was a good life, fortunate in its general circumstances, except for family sorrows, and fine in its controlling spirit. Manzoni was of an equable temper, upright, kindly, sympathetic, and loyal. He was a keen and logical thinker, studious, reflective, and eminently sensible.

In Paris he had yielded to the prevalent religious indifference; but soon after his return to Milan he experienced a genuine conversion, and he remained thereafter a reverent votary and loyal champion of the Christian faith. He was concerned primarily, in his religious thought, with the power of

Christianity to transmute human life, and with its effort to establish a valid sense of brotherhood among all men. His patriotism was strong and constant, but not militant. He felt that Italy's need of moral education was even greater than her need of political freedom; he believed in the forgiveness of enemies; and he saw the national problem against a world-wide background. His religion and his patriotism mingled and blended with his literary interests. He had the true artist's respect for the values of his own craftsmanship, and his work is not didactic in tone; but in the years of his maturity he wrote with a constant underlying hope that what he wrote might prove to be of more than literary serviceableness.

He was writing verse by 1801. Several poems written before his conversion are extant: they are for the most part conventionally neoclassic, though some of them, more personal than the rest, give promise of finer things to come.

Manzoni's conversion turned him to the writing of religious poetry; and in the years from 1812 to 1822 he composed his *Inni sacri*, five hymns intended rather for reading than for singing. They have as their themes the Resurrection, the Name of Mary, Christmas, the Crucifixion, and Pentecost. Each consists of twelve or more stanzas: the metrical structure varies. They are noble hymns, fervent, pervaded by a sense of wonder, Biblical in their dignity — the Latin of the Vulgate echoes often through the Italian words — and yet modern in their spirited fluency. Their horizons are wide; and they manifest a constant concern for all those who labor and are heavy-laden. Free now from neoclassic conventions, Manzoni shows special abilities in swift narrative and description, and in fresh and effective simile.

The joyous *Risurrezione* opens with the triumphant cry *È risorto!*, which is heard again in succeeding stanzas, and at last in the words of the angel at the empty tomb: *È risorto; non è qui.* In the *Nome di Maria* praise rises as from all ages and all lands: some of its stanzas are of great beauty. The *Natale* offers charming pictures of the Nativity and of the Adoration of the Shepherds. The *Passione* is a contrite prayer for forgiveness. The *Pentecost*, celebrating in its opening stanzas the first descent of the Holy Spirit and the origin of the Church, culminates grandly in a plea for the coming of the Spirit to all men.

In May 1821, Europe received the news of the death of Napoleon, once marvelously its master; and Manzoni, profoundly moved, wrote in three days the famous ode to which he gave as title the date of Napoleon's death, *Il cinque maggio*. The introductory stanzas represent the world as stunned by the departure of so mighty a spirit, and claim for the poet, never in Napoleon's lifetime subservient or injurious, the right to interpret the meaning of his life and death. His career is then synthesized. with a fine imaginative power, in several stanzas, two of which, in substance, read thus:

> All fates he knew: glory, the greater after peril; flight and victory; palace and lonely exile. Twice was he smitten to the dust; twice worshipped as divine.
>
> He named his name: two centuries, one armed against the other, turned in submission to him as arbiter of their destiny. He ordered silence; and he took his place as judge between them.

Two later stanzas picture him on St. Helena:

> How often, at the silent dying of an inert day, he stood with flashing eyes downcast, arms folded on his breast, as memories of bygone days assailed him,
>
> And he thought again of armies on the march, of ramparts shattered, of charging infantry and waves of cavalry, and of swift obedience to swift command.

The concluding stanzas, in the mood of the *Inni sacri*, represent Napoleon as accepting humbly, in his last hours, the blessing of faith. The *Cinque maggio* has been translated again and again in many languages — French, Spanish, Portuguese, German, English, Latin. The first of the German translations was made by Goethe.

Manzoni's admiration for Shakespeare (whom he read in the French translation of Letourneur) was expressed repeatedly and with the greatest enthusiasm: *sommo poeta*, he called him, *grande e quasi unico poeta*, *genio meraviglioso*, *sovrumano ingegno*. His reading of Shakespeare was done mainly in the decade following 1810; and in that same decade he read with great interest and thoughtfulness August Wilhelm Schlegel's lectures on dramatic literature and art.

His study of Shakespeare and Schlegel and his acquaintance with some of the plays of Goethe and Schiller led him, in the years 1816–1822, to the writing of two tragedies, *Il conte di Carmagnola* and *Adelchi*, which break away from the neoclassic pattern in their rejection of the unities of time and place: in each of the two plays the action covers several years, and the scene changes freely. In a Preface to the *Carmagnola*, Manzoni defends his rejection of the secondary unities, arguing very effectively indeed, and seasoning his argument with a fine quiet humor. There are many Shakespearean echoes in both plays, but they result not from definite imitation but from a long and intimate process of absorption and re-creation. In one respect Manzoni declines to follow the example of Shakespeare: the presence of comic elements in a tragedy impairs, in his judgment, the essential unity of impression, and he therefore excludes all humor from his tragedies.

The *Conte di Carmagnola* is based on episodes in the early fifteenth-century warfare of Venice and Milan. The *condottiere* Carmagnola, once in the service of Milan, is made commander of the Venetian troops, and wins a victory at Maclodio. His soldiers, in accordance with the custom of the mercenaries, set free the prisoners they have taken. In consequence of this action, which Carmagnola defends, he is recalled to Venice and sentenced to death.

Dramatically, the play is weak; but it has patriotic strength in its insistence on the evils of internecine strife. The chorus that follows the second act is a direct plea for Italian unity. Looking upon the battlefield, the chorus asks what foreigner is making war on Italy; and the answer is that the combatants are all Italian:

They are all of one land and one nation,
One speech; and the foreigner names them
All brothers, of one generation;
In each visage their kindred is seen;
This land is the mother that claims them,
This land, that their life blood is steeping . . .*

The chorus expresses its foreboding that Italy, thus weakened by internal conflict, will be attacked and enslaved by foreign invaders; foretells the horror and the shame of such warfare and such slavery; and closes with a denunciation of war and a plea for human brotherhood.

The *Adelchi*, though it falls far short of Shakespearean greatness, is in its general character more Shakespearean than any other Italian tragedy. It deals with a momentous historic event, the overthrow of the Lombard kingdom by Charlemagne. Its leading characters are Charles, the Lombard king Desiderius, his son Adelchi, raised by Desiderius to a shared kingship, and Ermengarda, daughter of Desiderius, the repudiated but still loving wife of Charles. Desiderius is single-minded in his resolution to maintain and to extend his power, warlike, contemptuous of danger, and impatient of caution. Adelchi, aware that his father's cravings are unjust and his decisions perilous, but unable to dissuade him, plays his own part loyally and heroically; and at the end, after facing, as Hamlet faced, the possibility of self-given escape, finds honorable death.

At one point in the play an emissary sent by the Church to Charles, having found the pass of Mont Cenis blocked by Lombard troops, has made his own way through the Alps; and in the presence of Charles tells thus, in part, of his journey:

Beyond the valley's end a peak arose,
And, putting faith in God, I climbed it. Here
No trace of man appeared: only the forests
Of untouched firs, rivers unknown, and vales
Without a path; and in the stillness naught
Save my own steps I heard, and now and then
The rushing of the torrents, or the sudden
Cry of the hawk, or else the eagle, launched
From his high nest, and hurtling through the dawn
Swiftly above my head; or then at noon,
Struck by the sun, the crackling of the cones

* The translation is by W. D. Howells.

Of the wild pines. And so three days I walked,
And under the great trees and in ravines
Three nights I slept. The sun was guide for me:
I rose with him, and him upon his journey
I followed till he vanished. Doubtful ever
Of my way on I went, from vale to vale
Crossing forever; or if perchance at times
I saw the accessible slope of some great height
Rising before me, and attained its crest,
Yet loftier summits still, before, around,
Above me towered: other heights with snow
Shone white from base to summit, and they seemed
Like steep, sharp tents fixed in the soil; and others
Were as of iron, standing in the form
Of walls insuperable. As evening fell
On the third day a mighty mount I saw
That overtopped the others all around:
Its slope was green, and all its crest was crowned
With verdure. Thither eagerly I turned
My weary steps. — It was the eastern face,
Sire, of this very mountain whereon lies
Thy camp, that looks upon the setting sun.

As the impulse to write historical tragedies had come to Manzoni chiefly from the reading of Shakespeare, so the impulse to write a historical novel came to him chiefly from the reading of Scott (in French translations). The particular document that gave him the basic idea for his plot was an actual proclamation, issued on October 15, 1627, by the Spanish governor of Lombardy, which reads in part thus:

> Although . . . rigorous measures have been taken to put an end to the oppressions, extortions, and tyrannical actions which certain persons dare to commit . . . nevertheless the frequency of such excesses . . . has so increased that His Excellency . . . has determined to publish the present proclamation. And . . . since experience shows that many persons . . . tyrannically practice extortions and oppress the weak in various ways, as for instance in forcing or preventing marriages . . .

Manzoni began work on his novel in 1821 and finished it, in its first form, in 1823: publication of this first form was completed in 1827. Dissatisfied with his style, Manzoni soon began a thorough revision, in the course of which he visited Florence in order to improve his own linguistic sensitiveness and to get the advice of Florentine friends. The revised edition, greatly improved in form, but hardly changed at all in content, was published, in parts, in 1840–1842. Its full title reads: *I promessi sposi, storia milanese del secolo XVII scoperta e rifatta da Alessandro Manzoni*, "The Betrothed, a Milanese Story of the Seventeenth Century Discovered and Retold by Alessandro Manzoni."

The events of the story take place in Lombardy in the years 1628–1631. Renzo and Lucia, who are already betrothed when the story opens, live in simple homes in a little village near Lecco, at the southern end of the eastern branch of the Lake of Como. Both are silk-weavers. Lucia has attracted the capricious attention of Don Rodrigo, a lawless local grandee, who is determined to get her into his power. His bravoes frighten the village curate, Don Abbondio, out of performing the marriage, and attempt to abduct Lucia. Renzo and Lucia, who have been constantly befriended by Fra Cristoforo, a Capuchin monk, escape to his convent; and since their homes are no longer safe for them he sends Renzo to Milan and Lucia to Monza. Renzo gets into trouble in a bread riot, is arrested, escapes, and makes his way to Bergamo, just over the Venetian border. Lucia lives for some time in a convent in Monza; but then, through the treachery of a privileged nun, she is carried off by the bravoes of a powerful friend of Don Rodrigo — a man referred to only as *l'innominato*, "the unnamed." This man, however, already weary of evil-doing and troubled by his conscience, is deeply moved by the entreaties of Lucia, and delays sending her to Don Rodrigo; and she, meanwhile, in her terror, vows to remain unmarried if she is saved from her peril. *L'innominato* seeks guidance from the great Cardinal Federigo Borromeo, who is visiting a near-by village; is fully converted; and sets Lucia free. She enters the service of a Milanese lady. In 1630, as a result of the passage of an army, the plague breaks out in Lombardy. Don Rodrigo dies of it. Fra Cristoforo serves heroically among those stricken in Milan, as does the Cardinal. Renzo, returning, searches the city for Lucia, and at last finds her, recovered from the plague. Fra Cristoforo before his death releases Lucia from her vow. Don Abbondio marries Renzo and Lucia, and they live in modest happiness near Bergamo.

The plot is admirable in its soundness, its clarity, its sequential naturalness, its variety, and in the interweaving of its several elements; and there is plenty of action, mounting again and again into crisis. But the novel is primarily a novel of character. All of the recurring characters live in Manzoni's mind as individuals, and their individualities are made known to the reader through the careful rendering of whimsicalities, inconsistencies, and other minor phases of personality, and growth and change result from varying associations and thrusts of fortune.

Manzoni's sympathies are unquestionably with the lowly, and it is with plain people that he is mainly concerned: Renzo, honest, industrious, excitable, easily led, with a penchant for getting into trouble; Lucia, gentle, modest, loving, strong in her sense of what is right, sorely tried, sustained by her faith; her mother, Agnese, worldly-wise, but less shrewd than she thinks herself to be, warmhearted, devoted to her daughter; Don Abbondio, a comfortable village priest, well-meaning, overanxious for his own safety, unable to resist when resistance would be dangerous; Perpetua, his loyal, domineering, and gossipy servant; and many, many others. And Manzoni is no less sure in his handling of his greater folk.

Like Dante and like Ariosto, Manzoni possessed an extraordinary power of visualization, together with the ability to convey in words what his mind's eye saw so exactly. Persons and scenes are thus presented with perfect clarity: one seems to have known the very lineaments, the very expressions, the very gestures that are described, to have beheld the landscapes through which the story moves, and to have participated in its scenes of action. Don Abbondio, walking slowly homeward in the late afternoon,

> was tranquilly reciting his prayers; and sometimes, between one psalm and the next, he closed his breviary, keeping his right forefinger in it to mark the place, and went on his way, putting his right hand in his left behind his back, bending forward, and jerking toward the wall, with his foot, the little stones that lay in his path.

A singularly keen perception of similarities flowers in the novel in scores of similes, fresh, unexpected, and illuminating, some of them brief, some of them, such as this one, more developed:

> For several months Renzo, Agnese, and Lucia remained each in the situation last described. Public events of varying importance succeeded each other without influencing their lives. But finally there came certain events, more universal and more overwhelming, the force of which reached even to them in their insignificance and to others still more insignificant than they: as a fierce whirlwind, which uproots trees, unroofs dwellings, overthrows belfries, beats down walls and scatters their debris far and wide, picks up also bits of straw hidden among the grass, or seeks the light and withered leaves lying in corners where they had been stored by lesser winds and whirls them away in its all-involving fury.

Humor pervades the novel: a quiet humor that is neither scornful nor absurd, and does not seek verbal brilliance. It is essentially humor of character, springing from Manzoni's delight in the variations of human personality. Most typically it is found in the reactions of person to circumstance or of person to person, and manifested in unconsciously and amusingly self-revealing speech. But Manzoni's humor is not incompatible with his brooding awareness of the shadows of life, nor with the sense of tragedy that prevails when he deals with the persistent evils of insolent power, or with the catastrophes of warfare, famine, and pestilence, or with riving individual tragedies.

Manzoni's style, as finally perfected, is straightforward, free from rhetorical adornment, unhurried but always living and moving, dignified in reflection, quietly graceful and constantly firm, and above all wonderfully clear. He is supremely skillful in the use of dialogue. Many passages, especially at points that are critical for the development of the story, consist wholly or almost wholly of words spoken — and spoken just as they would have come, swiftly and with frequent interruptions, from the lips of those who speak them, in courtesy, in gossip, in surprise, in perplexity or dismay, in excitement or in conciliation, in anger, in deceit, in affection, in menace or in consolation, in the endless variety of human needs and desires and impulses and hopes and fears.

The single defect in Manzoni's artistry is his failure fully to assimilate his historical material, a failure due to his own abiding satisfaction in history itself. Many pages of the book are pure history: some are laden with documentary quotations; others come in substance from historical works to which due footnote reference is made. To the general reader such pages are tiresome; but it remains true that the events of the story are placed perfectly in their historical setting.

The influence of the *Promessi sposi* in Italy was very great, both in the stimulation of the writing of other historical novels and, more beneficially, in the simplification and the revitalization of Italian prose style. Outside of Italy the novel was at once greatly admired, by Goethe, Scott, and Poe among others. Even before the publication of the revised edition translations had appeared in France, Spain, Germany, Sweden, England, and America; and the process of translation still continues.

The most interesting of Manzoni's other prose writings are two treatises in which he deals with literary problems. In the *Conte di Carmagnola*, as has already been stated, he had disregarded the unities of time and place, justifying that disregard in his Preface. Shortly after the publication of the *Carmagnola* in 1820, the French critic Victor Chauvet attacked its breach of the rule of the unities. To this attack Manzoni replied in a hundred-page *Lettre à M. C*** sur l'unité de temps et de lieu dans la tragédie*, written in 1820, and published in 1823, in Paris, in a volume that contained Fauriel's translations of the *Carmagnola* and the *Adelchi*. This "letter," in the course of which Manzoni calls himself *un bon et loyal partisan du classique*, is even more cogent in its argumentation than the Preface of the *Carmagnola*. The premises that underlie Manzoni's thought are, as always, historical and moral. He gives the name *système historique* to the dramatic system that rejects the minor unities; and he insists on the value and the power of historic truth. Actual tragedy consists not so much in deed as in the loss of an inward struggle, and the poet should reveal that inward struggle to the spectator, even though the revelation causes grief. Love does not, in Manzoni's judgment, provide a sufficient or a worthy motivation for great tragedy; and the dominant place often given to love compels the subordination of all other human sentiments, especially the noblest ones. The meaning of the principle of unity is well discussed. Tragedy, it is said, should permit and indeed welcome change and development of character in its personages. Of the writers of romances Manzoni says:

> à force d'inventer d'histoires, de situations neuves, de dangers inattendus, d'oppositions singulières de passions et d'intérêts, ils ont fini par créer une nature humaine qui ne ressemble en rien à celle qu'ils avaient sous les yeux. . . . Et cela est si bien arrivé que l'épithète de romanesque a été consacrée pour désigner généralement, à propos de sentimens et de mœurs, ce genre particulier de fausseté, ce ton factice, ces traits de convention qui distinguent les personnages de roman.

He distinguishes, however, between the *romanesque* and the *romantique*, and praises Italian critics who, developing in their own ways "romantic" ideas found in French, German, English, and earlier Italian writers, are doing good service in their attacks on outworn literary theories. From this "letter" Victor Hugo derived many of the ideas set forth in 1827 in the *Préface de Cromwell*, the manifesto of the French Romantic School.

The second of the three treatises is a letter on Romanticism, written in 1823 to an Italian friend. The *sistema romantico*, as Manzoni calls it, has two phases, one negative, one positive. In its negative phase it attacks three features of the *sistema classico*: use of mythology, servile imitation of classic authors, and observance of invalid "rules," especially the "rule" of the unities of time and place. The greater part of the letter is devoted to a detailed defense of the Romantic position in these respects. The positive phase of Romanticism, Manzoni continues, is not nearly so well developed as its negative phase. It seems to him that the general principle that underlies the *sistema romantico* is

> that poetry or literature in general should take that which is useful as its purpose, that which is true as its subject, and that which is interesting as its means.

Subjects, then, should be such as will appeal to the generality of readers through curiosity and interest derived from their own memories and impressions of life; and in treating such subjects the writer should endeavor

> to discover and to express historical truth and moral truth, not only as an end, but as the most ample and perpetual source of the beautiful.

Recognizing the fact that the concept of "the true," as applied to works of the imagination, lacks definition, Manzoni expresses the hope that Romantic theory will achieve such definition — a hope cherished because he seems to perceive in the *sistema romantico* a Christian tendency. There are those, he says toward the end of the letter, who by the term Romanticism understand "a hodgepodge of witches, of specters, a systematic disorder, a striving for the extravagant, a forswearing of common sense": if Romanticism were indeed of such a character it would deserve to be refuted and forgotten.

In a phrase that has already been quoted Manzoni calls himself *un bon et loyal partisan du classique*, and he never retracts or contradicts that statement. In terms of formal allegiance, therefore, one must accept his own self-classification as a classicist. He was indeed essentially classic in his unvarying dignity, in the serenity of his spirit, and in his fundamental respect for that which he regarded as "the true." But he departed decisively from neoclassic theory and practice in his disapproval of the use of classic mythology and the bondage of the minor dramatic unities, and in that he never engaged in literary imitation. He approved Romantic theory and practice in so far as they stood opposed to neoclassicism in these respects; his tragedies are cast in a mold that is Shakespearean and German rather than neoclassic; and for his masterpiece he adopts a new genre made popular by Scott. But he regrets the failure of Romanticism to develop a positive program; he reacts strongly against Romantic extravagances; he regards love as an inappropriate motivation for great tragedy; and there is no love-making in *I promessi sposi.* Moreover, though he wrote before the days of realism, he is a realist in his preoccupation with humble folk, in the minute fidelities of his observation and description, and in his concern for historical accuracy: but he would have abhorred the excesses to which a formulated realism was soon to lead. The truth is that Manzoni resists and rises above classification. Bound by no "ism," he was his own independently thoughtful and predominantly Christian self.

Manzoni's other writings include a third literary treatise, *Del romanzo storico*, in which his insistence on truth and his scrupulous respect for the facts of history lead him, in spite of the success of his own novel, to condemn the historical novel as a genre; a religious treatise; a philosophical dialogue; a few purely historical works; and several minor poems, two or three of them in Latin.

Well-deserved honor surrounded him in his declining years. His long life came to an end in 1873. Verdi's *Requiem* was dedicated to his memory.

CHAPTER 44

Leopardi

GIACOMO LEOPARDI was born in 1798 in Recanati, a town near the central Adriatic coast. His father was a well-meaning gentleman, a prolific and futile writer, stubbornly reactionary in all his opinions. He was also incompetent financially, and in 1803 the management of the family affairs was taken over by his wife, who ruled, in all respects, with a faithful but relentless despotism.

Even in his boyhood the traits that were to be fused in Leopardi's character were already clear. He was of a deeply loving spirit, and craved love; he was immediately sensitive to beauty, especially to beauty of nature and to musical and poetic beauty; his imagination was constantly alert and endlessly resourceful; he had an insatiable thirst for knowledge, especially for philological knowledge; and he was driven by an incessant urge toward literary or scholarly creativity. These were great gifts, gifts that held in themselves the possibilities of happiness and of suffering alike: the circumstances of Leopardi's life forbade him, after his childhood, more than momentary happiness, and burdened him with a crushing weight of suffering.

He discovered far too soon the fascinations of his father's library; and in that library, unrestrained, he spent most of the waking hours of the second decade of his life, devoting himself almost exclusively to the study of Greek and Latin authors. By 1813 he was already immensely learned, and in that year and the four following years he produced an extraordinary series of dissertations, translations from the Greek, and other scholarly works. Several of his writings were published in the *Spettatore italiano*, a Milanese journal, and won for the young Leopardi a considerable reputation, and the enduring friendship of the much older Pietro Giordani, who was regarded as one of the leading Italian men of letters of the time.

Throughout the same period Leopardi had occasionally written original Italian verse; and in 1816 he entered the field of current literary debate. The

Biblioteca italiana of Milan had published an article and a letter by Mme de Staël in which she urged Italian writers to familiarize themselves with modern foreign literature as a means of liberating themselves from traditionalism and pedantry. The editors invited replies; and Leopardi addressed to them a letter in which, exalting the classics and maintaining that "the making of a great poet requires a celestial spark and a superhuman impulse, rather than the study of authors and the examination of foreign tastes," he expresses the fear that such familiarization as Mme de Staël proposes would lead only to new imitations.

The cost of all these precocious activities was terrible. By 1817 Leopardi's health was irremediably shattered; he had contracted a distressing nervous malady; he had become somewhat deformed; and he had fallen prey to a depression from which he was never to know more than temporary relief. The failure of his health made it necessary for him to give up his philological work and to reduce greatly the amount of time he could spend in reading. Thrown in upon himself, he began to develop more and more the resources of his own mind; and he engaged more and more in the writing of original verse.

Early in 1818 there appeared in the *Spettatore italiano* certain *Osservazioni sulla poesia moderna* by Lodovico di Breme, who was a leader in the Italian Romantic movement, as will appear in the following chapter. Leopardi regarded Di Breme's ideas as pernicious, and set himself at once to the writing of a refutation, which in its final form is entitled *Discorso di un italiano intorno alla poesia romantica*. It is a vehement, even torrential, polemic, in which Leopardi writes as an ardent classicist and an ardent patriot. It is inadequate in its knowledge and its judgment of Romanticism, but its thrusts are keen and it is lighted by flashes of insight. Nature, in its perennial and simple beauty, is for Leopardi the proper object of poetic imitation, rather than the transient artificialities of civilization; and imagination, the primeval poetic gift, is still, rather than reason, the true source of poetic inspiration. The *Discorso* ends with a long and impassioned appeal to the youth of Italy — Italy, fallen now into a state of unexampled catastrophe, yet deserving of the most absolute devotion.

In the autumn of the same year Leopardi again expressed his love of Italy in the first of his major poems, the excited and exciting *canzone All'Italia*. The opening motif is familiar:

> Oh my fatherland, I see the walls and the arches and the columns and the images and the lonely towers of our ancestors, but I see not their glory, I see not the laurel and the steel that our ancient fathers bore.

A companion *canzone*, *Sopra il monumento di Dante che si preparava in Firenze*, is similar in its patriotic urgency, but less imaginative and less resonant.

In the spring of 1819 Leopardi wrote the first of several poems that he called idylls. He was fond of going to an unfrequented hill just outside Recanati, and of resting on its summit, where the height suggested an awareness of great distances, and trees and bushes grew in such a way that those distances were largely unseen: in the poet's imagination they were magnified into an infinity, the thought of which led in its turn to the thought of eternity — thoughts in which Leopardi's spirit, oppressed with present troubles, found relief. There, in presence or in memory, he composed the idyll *L'infinito* — fifteen lines of unrhymed verse that have, in the Italian, a wonderful beauty of sound. The poem reads, in translation, thus:

> Dear to me ever was this lonely hill
> And, round about, the clustering trees that shut
> So much of the horizon from my view.
> But as I sit and gaze, within my thought
> I feign, beyond them, boundless distances,
> Silences such as man has never known,
> And profound quietness, wherein my heart
> Is lost in awe. And when I hear the wind
> Rustling among the bushes, I compare
> Its single voice to the infinite silences;
> And I am conscious of eternity,
> Of ages past, and of this present age
> And the low sound it makes. And thus amid
> These vast immensities my thought is drowned:
> Sweet is the sinking into such a sea.

Life in Recanati was becoming more and more intolerable. The town itself could not provide the kind of companionship that Leopardi craved; and the continuous household despotism wore upon him grievously. As soon as he came of age, in the summer of 1819, he planned to escape; but his father, who was unwilling that Giacomo should be exposed to the perils of the outer world, learned of his plan and prevented him from carrying it out. Leopardi's earlier depression became now a despair that spread from the consideration of his own personal suffering and frustration to an inclusive conviction that all human life was doomed to suffering and to tedious futility. Yet his lovingness and his sensitiveness to beauty remained; and he found some relief from his appalling sense of tedium in literary and scholarly activities that were, in view of his physical limitations, almost incredibly incessant.

Early in 1820, after Angelo Mai had discovered Cicero's *De republica*, Leopardi addressed to Mai a *canzone* in which again he contrasts the former glories of Italy and her current shame. Several stanzas are devoted to fine appreciations of Dante, Columbus, Ariosto, Tasso, and Alfieri; but the notes of personal and universal despair prevail.

Late in the same year he wrote the idyll *La sera del dí di festa*, "Evening After Holiday." The poem opens with lines of tranquil beauty:

> Sweet and clear is the night, and the wind is still; and over the roofs and the gardens rests the quiet moon, revealing, serene in the distance, every mountain;

finds in its questioning of omnipotent nature only this answer:

> "To you I deny hope, even hope; never shall your eyes shine except with tears";

rises to agony:

> I ask how much longer I must live, and throw myself upon the ground and cry aloud and writhe;

and grows calmer, though still infinitely sad, as the solitary song of an artisan returning late at night from the pleasures of his holiday, to which the ordinary day so soon succeeds, leads the poet to think how everything in the world passes, leaving scarcely a trace of what has been.

The finest of the poems of the next three years are *La vita solitaria*, another grieving and lovely idyll; the solemn and desolate *canzone Bruto minore*; and the hymn *Alla primavera*, "To Spring," in which the unexpected stirring of the poet's cold heart lures him again into classic illusion:

> Ah, dost thou live? ah, dost thou live indeed,
> Oh holy nature? Does my dulléd sense
> Gather indeed the tones of a mother's voice?
> Time was when every river was the dwelling
> Of fair white nymphs, and every spring and pool
> A mirror for their beauty. Mystic dances
> Of feet immortal stirred the mountain heights
> And the deep forests, where the whistling wind
> Wanders today and finds no habitant.
> The shepherd, when he led his thirsty flock
> At noon, amid the haze of summer heat,
> Where flowers grow upon the riverside,
> Heard the shrill song of Pan and his woodland fauns
> Echo along the banks; or, marveling, saw
> The wave before him tremble, welcoming
> The unseen Dian, come to bathe her there
> After the dust and turmoil of the chase.

In the winter of 1822–23 Leopardi, with parental consent, spent some months in Rome. But he did not find the employment he had hoped for; Roman scholars seemed dull to him, and Rome itself a lonely vastness; and in the spring he returned to Recanati.

There, in the autumn, he wrote the unique poem *Alla sua donna*. The image he cherishes is not that of any actual woman, but that of an ideal being, seen only in dream or vision, a being perhaps incarnate in the golden age, perhaps yet to be vouchsafed to humanity, perhaps a dweller in some distant star, perhaps one of the eternal "ideas," a being so beautiful, a giver of such bliss, that if one could love her in reality life would indeed be blessed, even amid the sorrows of the human lot:

> But heaven grants no comfort for our suffering — and with thee this mortal life would be like unto that which in heaven makes one divine.

During the years from 1824 to 1827 Leopardi's sensitiveness to life was dulled, and no lyric inspiration stirred in him.

In 1824 he wrote, in prose, nearly all of his *Operette morali*: three were added in the years 1825–27, and two more, which will be considered at a later point in this chapter, in 1832. These "little works" comprise about a score of dialogues and about half as many other writings. Among the interlocutors of the dialogues are Hercules and Atlas; Fashion and Death; a Sprite and a Gnome; Nature and a Soul; the Earth and the Moon; Tasso and a Familiar Spirit; Nature and an Icelander; Fredrik Ruysch (a Dutch anatomist) and his Mummies; Columbus and one of his shipmates; Copernicus, the Sun, and the First and Last Hours of the Day; and Plotinus and Porphyry. All of the dialogues and most of the other *operette* have Leopardi's constant pessimism as their common background; but they gain a compensating fascination through their variety in persons and in devices, their imaginative vigor, the liveliness of their conversational give and take, the brilliance of their irony and of their lighter incidental humor, and the crystal clarity of their prose.

Jove, thinking that Atlas must be tired of holding the Earth, has sent Hercules to relieve him; but Atlas says that the Earth has grown so light that it is easily held. Hercules takes it in his hands, and finds that it is both light and perfectly silent: all its inhabitants must be sunk in a long sleep. In order to wake them, the two play ball with the Earth: a poor return by Atlas lets it fall, but no signs of life appear. Hercules concludes that all earth-dwellers must be just, since it is said that the just man will not be moved though the Earth should fall.

The Gnome, sent to find out what has happened to mortals, learns from the Sprite that they have become extinct, as a result of warfare and other follies. But the loss is small: the Earth is not conscious of any lack; the rivers continue to flow; the sea is not dried up; and sun and planets and stars continue on their courses as before.

In the long and closely reasoned dialogue of Plotinus and Porphyry, the latter maintains that the unhappiness of life is such as to justify suicide: Plotinus does not deny the unhappiness of life, but does deny the justifiability of seeking escape by death. Throughout the dialogue there runs the sense of a deep friendship between the two men; and at the end this sense broadens to include "kinsmen, children, brothers and sisters, parents, wife, and all those with whom we are accustomed to live." To deprive oneself of life is to deprive oneself of all this dearness, and, what is worse, it is to inflict selfishly a barbarous additional unhappiness upon those whom one holds dear. The rightful human course is very different:

> Let us live, Porphyry, and let us strengthen each other: let us not refuse to sustain our destined portions of the ills that are common to the human race. Rather let us bear each other company and give each other courage, extending our hands to each other in mutual helpfulness.

The most notable of the *operette* that are not dialogues is a charming essay *In Praise of Birds*, as the happiest of all creatures.

For three years, beginning in the summer of 1825, Leopardi was employed by the Milanese publisher Antonio Stella, and was thus enabled to leave Recanati. Residence in Milan was not necessary, and the three years were spent chiefly in Bologna, Florence, and Pisa: in all of these cities Leopardi found appreciative friends. For Stella he directed, in part, the preparation of an edition of Cicero, wrote a serviceable commentary on the *Canzoniere* of Petrarch, and compiled anthologies of Italian prose and verse.

In the spring of 1828 the mildness of the Pisan climate brought him some relief from his ill-health; the insensitiveness in which he had been existing gave way to a new sensitiveness; and the lyric impulse stirred in him again. His reawakening is reported in a poem entitled *Il risorgimento*: now, though his estimate of fate remains unchanged, he feels again both grief and pleasure — his heart is, at least, alive.* His new vitality and new sensitiveness first rise to fullness of poetry in the *canzone A Silvia*. Here and in several of the following poems there is a nostalgic return in memory to the vanished days and emotions of his early years. He gives the name Sylvia to a girl of Recanati, long since dead, who had once gently stirred his fancy, and recalls the time when beauty shone in her shy and laughing eyes, and she, happy and wondering, was crossing the threshold of youth. She was wont to sing at her household tasks; and he, leaving his studies, would come to his window to listen to the sound of her voice and of her spinning:

> I gazed at the tranquil sky,
> At streets and gardens golden in the sun,
> At the mountain there in the distance, at the sea:
> No mortal tongue can tell
> What I felt then in my breast.
> What sweet imaginings,
> What hopes, what hearts, were ours, oh Sylvia mine!
> How fair life seemed to us, and the human lot!
> When I remember all our welling hope
> Bitterness overwhelms me,
> And, disconsolate,

* Less than half of the poems written by Leopardi before *Il risorgimento* have been mentioned above: all of his later poems will be mentioned in the rest of this chapter.

I grieve anew at my hard destiny.
O nature, nature,
Why dost thou not fulfill
Thy first fair promise? Why dost thou deceive
Thy children so?

The youth that might have been so sweet was denied to both of them: to her by death, to him by fate.

For this poem, and for most of his later poems, Leopardi adopts the form of the *canzone libera*, first devised by Tasso: the several stanzas, varying in length, show various arrangements of the long and short lines of which they consist, and rhyme is used sparingly. This form lends itself admirably to the immediate and unimpeded expression of his throbbing thought and emotion.

After his contract with Antonio Stella had expired, Leopardi returned to Recanati; but this return, though it brought its own hardships, did not quench his newly found poetic vitality, and by the stimulation of his memories it provided him with a new source of inspiration. In the single year 1829 he wrote five of his finest poems: *Memories*, *The Solitary Thrush*, *The Calm After the Storm*, *The Village Saturday Evening*, and *The Night Song of a Wandering Asian Shepherd*. The first of these poems, *Le ricordanze*, weaves together many of the unforgotten sights, sounds, fragrances, dreams, hopes, fears, and sorrows that went into the early formation of the poet's spirit, and culminates in a deeply moved and moving passage of longing for youth. In the thrush of the *Passero solitario*, singing alone, on an ancient tower, while other birds speed cheerily through the free air, Leopardi sees a likeness to his own lonely singing.

La quiete dopo la tempesta and *Il sabato del villaggio* are companion pieces. Each offers first a perfectly drawn picture of simple happiness, and then, from the very nature of that happiness, derives a pessimistic conclusion. *The Calm After the Storm* opens with the line

Passata è la tempesta,

and this scene follows:

. . . See yon blue sky that breaks
The clouds above the mountain in the west!
The fields disclose themselves,
And in the valley bright the river runs.
All hearts are glad; on every side
Arise the happy sounds
Of toil begun anew.
The workman, singing, to the threshold comes,
With work in hand, to judge the sky,
Still humid, and the damsel next,
On his report, comes forth to brim her pail
With the fresh-fallen rain.

The noisy fruiterers
From lane to lane resume
Their customary cry.
The sun looks out again, and smiles upon
The houses and the hills. Windows and doors
Are opened wide; and on the far-off road
You hear the tinkling bells and rattling wheels
Of travelers that set out upon their journey.
Every heart is glad;
So grateful and so sweet
When is our life as now? *

But as this happiness springs from the fact that a period of storm-terror has just passed, so all happiness is in essence nothing more than a momentary relief from pain.

The Village Saturday Evening opens with a swift succession of beautifully drawn scenes. A girl comes in from the country with the flowers she will wear on the morrow; an old crone sits spinning out of doors, talking of the days when she too was young and gay; and after the sunset fades

The sky turns blue again; and from the hills
And roofs again the shadows fall,
Cast by the whiteness of the rising moon.
The vesper bell
Foretells the coming holiday,
Its sound gladdening the heart.

Boys play merrily on the little square; the laborer comes home, whistling, to his supper; and after all else is dark and still the carpenter in his shop, by lantern-light, works hard to finish his task before the dawn. Then the poem takes its sudden turn: the morrow, deceiving anticipation, will bring only boredom, and its own anticipation of the renewal of the weekly tasks. And youth is the Saturday evening of life.

An even greater poignancy of sorrow and a profound sense of the infinite are blended in the *Canto notturno di un pastore errante dell'Asia*. The wandering shepherd, alone with his flock, lifts his questioning to the silent wandering moon:

> Tell me, oh moon, of what good is the shepherd's life to him, your life to you? Tell me, whither tends this brief wandering of mine, whither your ceaseless circling? . . . You, surely, understand the reason of things, you, surely, see the fruit of morning and evening, of the silent and unending course of time. . . . When I gaze at the stars alight in the heavens I say to myself: "Why all these torches? What is this infinite air, this deep and infinite serenity? What means this immense solitude?" . . .

But he finds no answer.

In 1830 a group of Florentine friends made it possible for Leopardi to

* The translation is by Howells.

come to live in Florence. There he soon formed an intimate friendship with a young Neapolitan exile, Antonio Ranieri, who thereafter made a home for the constantly ailing poet, caring for him with the devotion of an admiring younger brother. There also Leopardi's last tragedy came upon him: he fell deeply in love, and he was led to think, despite his sickliness and his deformity, that his love was not unwelcome; but he was doomed to suffer a cruel disillusion. The first and finest of the poetic fruits of this experience is the ecstatic poem entitled *Il pensiero dominante.* At the advent of love, all his wonted thoughts have been banished, and in his mind only the thought of love remains. Love alone gives value to life; through love alone life may be kinder than death; to attain such knowledge of love as is now his he would be willing to live again even the life he has lived:

> What world transformed, what new immensity, what paradise is this into which thy marvellous enchantment uplifts me!

Even this wonder is in part, he knows, illusory; but this illusion is at least divine. A few months later he wrote the calmer and somberly meditative *Amore e morte* — love and death are the fairest things in all the universe — and the romantic *Consalvo*, in which, for the imagined hero, response to love is simultaneous with death. The disillusion, when it came, wrung out of Leopardi's bitterness the brief *A sé stesso*, "To Himself," as heart-rending and as terrible a poem as any poet ever wrote.

During these years in Florence Leopardi wrote also two final *operette morali*, the *Dialogue of a Vender of Almanacs and a Passer-By*, and the *Dialogue of Tristan and a Friend.* The first opens thus:

> VENDER. Almanacs! new almanacs! new calendars! Will you have an almanac, sir?
> PASSER-BY. Almanacs for the new year?
> V. Yes sir.
> P. Do you think that this new year will be happy?
> V. Oh yes sir, yes indeed.
> P. As happy as the last year?
> V. Much, much happier.
> P. As happy as year before last?
> V. Much, much happier.

The vender is led to admit that he would not want the new year to be like any one of the many years in which he has sold almanacs; that he would not want to re-live the life he has lived; and that if he were to live another life he would not want to know anything in advance about that life. And the dialogue ends thus:

> P. So . . . the life that is really good is not the life we know, but the life that we do not know . . .

This new year fate is going to treat us well, and life will begin to be happy, won't it?

V. Let's hope so.

P. Well then, show me your very best almanac.

V. Here, your lordship. This costs thirty *soldi.*

P. Here are your thirty *soldi.*

V. Thank you, your lordship. Good-bye. Almanacs! new almanacs! new calendars!

In the other dialogue the debate between Tristan (who represents Leopardi) and a friend ends with the most complete of all the expressions of Leopardi's pessimism.

In the autumn of 1833, Ranieri, his exile cancelled, returned to Naples, taking Leopardi with him. Burning still with the pain of his disillusion, Leopardi wrote, in 1834, a vengeful poem, *Aspasia*, in which accusation and relief are mingled. Soon afterward he wrote two poems suggested, or supposed to be suggested, by sepulchral bas-reliefs: the first, a quiet meditation, stresses the grief that the death of a dear one brings to the survivor; the second descends into the macabre. In Naples, also, Leopardi wrote two short satires in verse and a long poem, *Paralipomeni della Batracomiomachia*, "Sequel to the *Batrachomyomachia*," in which he presents the Neapolitans as mice, the subjects of the Pope as frogs, and the Austrians as crabs, and introduces, under absurd names, the King of Naples, the Austrian Emperor, Metternich, and other actual persons. In these same years he prepared for publication a series of about a hundred miscellaneous *Pensieri*, "Thoughts," varying in length from single sentences to brief treatises. Many are concerned with human faults and follies; others deal with such topics as youth, paternal power, friendship, standards of perfection, courtesy, tedium, old age, and death. They constitute, in effect, a minor appendix to the *Operette morali.*

The works written in Naples show an ebbing of Leopardi's creative power; but that power was to flow back in one last full tide. In April 1836, a friend invited Leopardi and Ranieri to spend some days in a villa that he owned at the foot of Vesuvius; the change proved to be beneficial to Leopardi; and he continued to live there for nearly a year. Looking seaward from this villa he could enjoy the perpetually marvelous beauty of the Bay of Naples; Pompeii was near by; the volcano towered above. In this setting he wrote his last two poems, *La ginestra*, "The Broom Plant," and *Il tramonto della luna*, "Moonset."

Vesuvius was, for Leopardi, the immense and perfect symbol of the attitude of nature toward man. Flaunting its tremendous menace in its pillar of smoke by day and its red glow by night, it displayed in its lava streams and in the ruins of Pompeii the evidence of its capacity for catastrophic cruelty. Yet life and beauty clung to its lower slopes.

The broom plant serves Leopardi as a symbol of that clinging life and beauty. The first lines of *La ginestra* picture it as growing in fragrant yellow clusters in the desert spaces that had once been alive with cities and palaces and gardens and fertile fields. To the contemplation of the contrast between vanished splendor and present desolation Leopardi invites those who think man the darling of a loving Nature — Nature that with the slightest motion can blot out the dwellers in one countryside and could with motions only less slight annihilate humanity. No better than a fool is he who proclaims felicity the lot of those whom a wave of an angry sea, a breath of pestilential air, or a quaking of the earth beneath may destroy so utterly that they are lost even to memory. But the conclusion to which the Vesuvian fact leads Leopardi — a conclusion implicit in his lifelong lovingness, and first clearly expressed in the *Dialogue of Plotinus and Porphyry* — is that men can find worthy life only in active brotherhood:

> The noble man is he who dares to lift his eyes to the facing of our common fate, and outspokenly, suppressing nothing of the truth, confesses the evil of our lot, and our low and frail estate; he who shows himself great and strong in suffering, and does not to his sorrows add fraternal wrath and hatred — worse than all else — by blaming his fellow men for his plight, but gives the blame to her who is really guilty. . . . Her he calls the enemy; and thinks rightly that against her the human company was first gathered and disposed, regards all men as federated together, and embraces all with a true love, offering and expecting prompt and valid help in the manifold perils and distresses of our common warfare.

To turn against one's fellow men is utter treachery in the face of a common foe. Only on the acceptance of such verities can there be built a firm human society that will grow in honesty, in truth, in justice, and in *pietade* — by which Leopardi means a reverent sense of the common human bond. At this point in the poem there follows a stanza of great beauty in which the poet from his mountainside again views infinity:

> Often upon these slopes, desolate with the dark lava streams that, motionless, seem yet to flow, I sit at night; and above the sad waste, in the pure blue, I see the flashing of the stars, mirrored afar in the waters . . .

The immensities of stars and nebulae confirm in him the thought of the littleness of the earth — "this obscure grain of sand" — and of the vanity of human pride. The closing stanzas of the poem contain a vivid picture of the destruction of Pompeii and Herculaneum, an equally vivid picture of the modern peasant fleeing from the advancing lava, and this last vision of Nature, towering over mankind as Vesuvius towers over the ruins of Pompeii:

> Thus, heedless of man and of the ages man calls ancient, and of the succession of progeny to ancestors, Nature stands ageless . . . Kingdoms fall the while; races and their tongues vanish. She sees not: and man boasts of his eternity.

There is a final return to the broom plant, destined, like all around it, to yield to lava streams: pliant then and only then, never bowed in supplication or upthrust in vainglorious pride.

In moonlit evenings, from his villa or from his lava fields, Leopardi may well have watched the sinking of the moon toward the horizon beyond the bay. Some such watching, it would seem, stirred him to the writing of the simpler and calmer *Tramonto della luna.* Silver light has rested on land and water, and the world has been filled with beguiling shadows; but with the setting of the moon light and shadows disappear; and darkness covers all. Even thus youth passes, and old age and death succeed. For hills and vales there will yet be sunrise, but not for youth.

Death came to Leopardi, suddenly and quietly, in the summer of 1837.

From 1817 to 1829 he had made entries almost daily on a series of large loose leaves that by the latter year numbered more than two thousand: he called the series, as a whole, his *Zibaldone*, his "Miscellany." Some of the entries are passages copied from the works of authors he had been reading; but most of them are impressions, memories, *pensieri*, reflections, questions, studies, discussions, or projects of his own. The impressions are attempts to capture and to preserve fleeting sights or sounds or sensations that had stirred him: some of these impressions found poetic use. He had never intended that his *Zibaldone* be published, and for more than half a century it remained in private hands; but the growing certainty of his greatness led eventually to national acquisition and to publication. It is an almost inexhaustible mine of information for students of Leopardi; and the more general reader may gain from the turning of its pages a sense of friendly companionship with one of the most sorely distraught and one of the noblest of all poetic spirits.

CHAPTER 45

Contemporaries of Manzoni and Leopardi

TRACES OF ROMANTICISM had appeared previously in Italian verse and prose, most strikingly in *Le ultime lettere di Jacopo Ortis*; but the Italian Romantic movement, as a deliberate effort to guide Italian literature into a new course, began only in June 1816. In January of that year the *Biblioteca italiana* had published an article by Mme de Staël "On the Method and Value of Translations," in which she urged Italian writers to familiarize themselves with foreign literatures as a means of liberating themselves from traditionalism and pedantry. To many Italian readers this article seemed to be an insulting depreciation of the literary glory of Italy, and it was immediately attacked in the *Biblioteca italiana* and in other periodicals; but three writers, Lodovico di Breme, Pietro Borsieri, and Giovanni Berchet, gave prompt support to Mme de Staël's position in substantial pamphlets, all three of which were published in Milan within the year 1816: these three pamphlets are the manifestoes of the Italian Romantic movement.

The Piedmontese abbé Di Breme (1781–1820), whose pamphlet was published in June, attacks vehemently the critics who had attacked Mme de Staël, accusing them of misrepresentation and discourtesy. Current Italian literary poverty, he says, is not to be excused by reference to past Italian literary greatness. Changing times call for new ideas and for new forms of expression. Poetry should not be "based exclusively upon the learned pondering of things dreamed three thousand years ago," but should be

> capable of expressing on its own initiative all the impressions, all the feelings, that have been generated in the sensitive and the contemplative faculties of man by our spiritual religion, by our social forms, by our dignified reverence for women, by the arts, by the immense range of knowledge we now possess. . . . and if our religious, moral, and scientific doctrines, our customs, our new desires, have thus enlarged the field of possible creation, let us measure the

whole amplitude of that horizon, let us plunge into that immensity, and let us advance courageously into the realms of the infinite that have been disclosed to us.

In June, also, Mme de Staël sent to the *Biblioteca* a letter defending herself from the attack that had been published in that periodical; and this letter was the occasion for new attacks — among them the letter by Leopardi referred to early in the preceding chapter.

In the pamphlet of the Milanese Pietro Borsieri (1786–1852), published in September, the themes that recur most frequently are the justification of Mme de Staël, the pettiness of current Italian criticism, and the value of familiarity with foreign literatures, a familiarity that makes possible the delightful contemplation of previously unknown forms of beauty, and opens previously untouched sources of invention for poetic fancy:

> Nor should we ever call truly great writers "foreigners," for their beautiful and useful works make them citizens of all countries in which they are read and studied.*

The third pamphlet, by the Milanese Giovanni Berchet (1783–1851), appeared in December. Its long title, "On the 'Wild Huntsman' and the 'Lenore' of Gottfried August Bürger, a Semiserious Letter from Chrysostom to his Son," indicates its point of departure, its fictional framework, and its somewhat humorous tone. Berchet's main insistence is that poetry should be "popular": that it should be addressed not to the fastidious few, but to the millions who intervene between the unawakened savage and the over-cultivated Parisian. If the poetic audience is to be, in this broad sense, popular, it follows that the content of poetry should be not erudite but drawn from the areas of popular tradition and popular experience. German poets have realized that the love of their fellow men is the truest of Muses, and that their art has a purpose far more sublime than the momentary delectation of a few idle readers. They have sought to make use of all the passions, all the opinions, and all the sentiments of their compatriots, and their appeal is therefore universal. In particular, their ballads, infused with an undefinable magic, present a salutary union of the marvelous and the terrible. If Italian poets will but follow such examples, Italian poetry will be enriched with new, original, and modern beauties.†

Neither Di Breme nor Borsieri ever wrote anything else of any importance, but Berchet proved himself to be an effective poet. In 1821, indignant at the

* Borsieri, arrested because of his liberal political activities, was imprisoned in the Spielberg from 1824 to 1836. After his release he spent two years in America, earning a precarious living as a teacher of Italian in New York, Princeton, and Philadelphia.

† Berchet's interest in balladry seems to have begun when in the reading of Goldsmith's *Vicar of Wakefield* (which he translated in 1809) he came upon the ballad of Edwin and Angelina.

action of the British government in ceding the Greek city of Parga to Turkey, he wrote his first elaborate poem, *I profughi di Parga*, "The Refugees of Parga." Late in the same year, forewarned of impending arrest, he escaped and went to London, where he lived until 1829. There he wrote several ballads, and a long poem entitled *Le fantasie*, "The Visions" — the dreams of an exile, in which he beholds ancient Lombard glories and contemporary Italian shame. Later, in Belgium, excited by the Italian risings of 1831, he wrote a vigorous ode entitled *All' armi! All' armi!*, with the refrain

> Su, Italia! su, in armi! venuto è il tuo dí!
> Dei re congiurati la tresca finí! —

> Up, Italy! up, in arms; your day has come!
> The orgy of the conspiring kings has ended!

Ten years later he was able to return to Italy, and to take some part in the first phase of the final struggle.

The advocates of Romanticism and the defenders of classicism continued for some time, after 1816, to urge their opposing views. But the Romanticists were in general active patriots, and in 1820 and 1821 most of their leaders were imprisoned or driven into exile; and the Romantic movement, as a coherent enterprise, came to an early end. Romanticism as a general literary attitude was much more widespread and much more important than the deliberate Romantic movement. Even Manzoni, who called himself a classicist, discussed Romanticism thoughtfully and sympathetically, and was to a considerable extent Romantic in his own practice. Even Leopardi, militantly classic in his youthful theories, was not without Romantic impulses and attitudes. Most of the lesser writers of the Manzonian period acquainted themselves to some extent with northern literature and were in differing degrees influenced by it, gaining in fact, as Mme de Staël and her champions had prophesied, a new range of poetic and fictional invention, and a new readiness to write for a popular audience. Nor did Romanticism as a general attitude cease at the middle of the century.

Italian Romanticism, in general, but not always, was saved from certain northern excesses by a deep and persistent consciousness of the validity of classic literary refinement. It was also intensely patriotic, and in a large measure it was Christian. But its most essential characteristic was a pervading sense of liberation from traditional formalism of any sort: there had come into literature a new conviction that the individual writer, however restrained by his own concepts of artistry, was free to seek and to find inspiration in his own life and in the life of which he was a part, and to choose or to create his own forms of expression.

Silvio Pellico (1789–1854), born in Saluzzo, in Piedmont, spent most of his young manhood in Milan, where during the Napoleonic regime he taught in a government school. He undertook the writing of tragedies, and won his first and only great success, in 1815, with his *Francesca da Rimini.* Formally, the play is Alfierian: it is brief, there are but four characters, and the unities are strictly observed. It is not too well constructed, and its characterization is only moderately effective; but it enjoyed an immense popularity, due in part to the fame of its story, in part to a single stirring patriotic speech, and in part to the fact that it was at times admirably performed: the role of Francesca was often played by Ristori, and Salvini played now Paolo and now Lanciotto.

In 1816 Pellico took a position as secretary to the liberal Count Luigi Porro Lambertenghi, and when the Count, in 1818, founded a semi-weekly paper called *Il conciliatore* Pellico became, in effect, its editor. The *Conciliatore* supported the progressive point of view in political, social, and literary matters — and accordingly favored the Romantic movement. The liberalism of the paper brought it under police suspicion, and it ceased publication after running for little more than a year.

In 1820 Piero Maroncelli, a young musician who had joined the Carbonari in Naples, came to Milan as an emissary of the society, and enrolled Count Porro, Pellico, and others in its membership. Before the end of the year the police learned, through an intercepted letter, of Maroncelli's activities; and both he and Pellico were arrested.

Up to this time Pellico had been a hesitant Christian; but in the distress of his first night in prison, and in particular through the thought that only divine love could bring comfort to his dear ones, he came to the decision that thereafter his Christianity should be firm and consistent, and centered on the resolution to love God and his fellow men. For four months he was held in prison in Milan. Then, in February 1821, he was transferred to Venice, where he was imprisoned first in a cell under the leaden roof of the Doge's palace and then on the island of San Michele. In February 1822, he was notified that he had been sentenced to death, but that the penalty had been commuted to fifteen years of "severe imprisonment" in the Spielberg, a prison located in Brünn (now Brno) in Moravia. Other Carbonari, among them Maroncelli, received similar sentences. In August 1830, Pellico was pardoned, escorted to the border of Piedmont, and released. Nearly all of the rest of his life was spent in Turin.

In 1832, on the advice of his confessor, he wrote the story of his experiences, entitling it *Le mie prigioni*, "My Prisons." In his brief preface his purposes are stated thus:

> To help to comfort some unknown persons by setting forth the ills I endured and the consolations that I found to be available even in my greatest misfortunes; to bear witness that in the course of my long sufferings I did not find

humanity to be so evil, so intolerable, so lacking in worthy spirits as it is commonly supposed to be; to urge noble hearts to love much and to hate no human being, but to hate only, and irreconcilably, low deceits, meanness, perfidy, and all moral degradation; and to state again a truth once well known, but often forgotten: that both Religion and Philosophy call for energetic will and for calm judgment, and that without the union of these qualities there can be no justice, no dignity, no security of principle.

Pellico's story, told simply and without vindictiveness, is necessarily a story of suffering. Conditions were bad enough in the prisons of Milan and Venice; but they were far worse in the Spielberg. "Severe imprisonment" meant that each prisoner was forced to labor, that chains linked his legs, that he had only boards for a bed, and that the food allowed him was scanty and of the poorest quality. Pellico's first cell was a "horrible cave," opening from a subterranean corridor. Twice during the day and again at midnight every cell was thoroughly searched. Each prisoner was allowed a little "outdoor exercise," but with his legs still chained, and under guard. Prisoners were forbidden to communicate with each other. No letters could be received or sent. Sickness was prevalent, sometimes fatal. Pellico suffered from one illness after another, and expected to die. Medical care was inadequate; and only when a prisoner was thought to be critically ill could regulations be relaxed.

Eventually, all the political prisoners being in shattered health, it was ordered that two should be assigned to each cell, so that one might help the other. Pellico had the joy of receiving Maroncelli as his cell-mate — but found him hardly recognizable. For months Maroncelli had been suffering from a tumor on a knee; and it became evident that only an amputation could save his life. Permission having been sought and obtained from Vienna, the operation was performed by the prison's barber-surgeon, while Maroncelli sat on the edge of his bed, with Pellico's arms around him:

> Maroncelli did not utter a sound. . . . [When the operation was over] he turned to the surgeon and said: "You have liberated me from an enemy, and I have no means of thanking you." There was a rose in a glass at the window. "Please bring me that rose," he said to me. I brought it to him, and he offered it to the old surgeon, saying: "This is all I can give you in token of my gratitude." The surgeon took the rose, and wept.

Many men and a few women live in the pages of the *Prigioni*. Some appear briefly, some frequently; some are merely described, some speak, some sing. Most of them are prisoners or jailers of some sort; but there are many others: members of jailers' families, various officials, soldiers, priests, doctors, a deaf and dumb orphan, a prophetic beggar, a Hungarian fruit-vender. In all of those with whom he has to deal Pellico looks for goodness, and he usually finds it, often in rich measure. Especially memorable is the aged jailer named Schiller, a man rough in speech and in manner, but in reality deeply sympathetic with his prisoners, and as helpful to them as he felt he could be.

The Christian gentleness of *Le mie prigioni* at first disappointed some Italian patriots, who would have preferred vituperation; but it soon became apparent that the very gentleness of Pellico's manner made it inescapably clear that the sufferings inflicted in the Spielberg were in fact inhuman. The Piedmontese historian Cesare Balbo said that the book was more damaging to Austria than the loss of a battle — a statement confirmed in effect by Metternich's futile effort to discredit Pellico's veracity. The book was soon translated into many languages. The first American translation, by Mrs. Andrews Norton, was published in 1836 for the benefit of Maroncelli, who had come to America in 1833.*

In Venice and after his liberation Pellico wrote additional tragedies and several *cantiche* — narratives in verse. In the Spielberg, where he was not allowed to write, he composed one tragedy, which he retained in his memory. After his liberation he wrote also religious lyrics, and a treatise on "The Duties of Man."

One other member of the Milanese group, Tommaso Grossi (1790–1853), born at Bellano on the eastern shore of Lake Como, won distinction in both verse and prose. A ready convert to Romanticism, he published in 1820 a long, complicated, and thoroughly Romantic *novella* in octaves, entitled *Ildegonda.* Under the double influence of Tasso and Scott, he next wrote, and published in 1826, a fifteen-canto epic poem, *I Lombardi alla prima crociata*, which, however, is hardly more than a greatly over-extended *novella.* The heroine, Giselda, on pilgrimage in the Holy Land, is captured; she and the Saracen prince Saladino fall in love; he is slain, and she in her agony renounces her faith; but she is re-baptized just before she dies. The libretto of Verdi's opera *I Lombardi alla prima crociata* is based upon this story.

The first Italian novel, after *I promessi sposi*, that possesses any excellence is Grossi's *Marco Visconti*, begun in 1831 and finished three years later. Marco, an actual fourteenth-century *condottiere*, seeks to win Bice del Balzo, who is in love with Marco's cousin Ottorino Visconti. One of Marco's retainers, ordered by him to prevent the marriage of Bice and Ottorino, fails to do so, but contrives to separate them after their marriage; and the bride dies. History and fiction are not well blended, the chain of causation is not always strong, and most of the major characters lack individuality; but

* He had been released from the Spielberg with Pellico. In America he lived chiefly in New York, giving lessons in music and in Italian. He was befriended by Andrews Norton, and at one time spent two or three months in Boston and Cambridge. He died in New York in 1846.

many episodes are exciting and well told, there are admirable descriptions, and some of the minor characters are very much alive. The two chapters that contain an account (modeled closely on passages in Scott's *Antiquary*) of a sudden tempest on Lake Como, the drowning of a young boatman, the discovery of that drowning by his father, also a boatman, and the overwhelming sorrow of the stricken father and mother as they face continuance of life in their humble cottage, constitute one of the finest episodes in Italian fiction. Several poems appear in the novel: one of them, *Rondinella pellegrina*, a prisoner's song, beginning

> Pilgrim swallow, singing every morn at my window your plaintive song, what is it that you would be telling me, pilgrim swallow?

was destined to be sung by Italian prisoners in Austrian prisons, and for a hundred years remained a popular favorite in Italy.

The leading playwright of the period, Giovan Battista Niccolini (1782–1861), born in a town near Pisa, served more than fifty years as Professor of History and Mythology in the Florentine Accademia di Belle Arti. The desire to write tragedies came to him from his acquaintance with classic tragedy, and his own first plays, written in the years 1810–1814, are Greek in subject and strictly neoclassic in form. In the *Nabucco*, "Nebuchadnezzar," written in 1815, he takes a new direction: for his nominal Nebuchadnezzar represents Napoleon, and the play is an attack on despotism.

All of the eight tragedies that Niccolini completed thereafter are medieval or modern in subject, and in all of them, largely as a result of admiration for Shakespeare, Byron, Schiller, and Manzoni, he adopts in varying degrees the increasingly popular Romantic attitudes and methods. Four are plays of tragic love: one of these, *Beatrice Cenci*, is a free adaptation of Shelley's *The Cenci*. The other four are primarily political in purpose, and draw their subjects from critical moments in the agelong Italian struggle against despotism: *Giovanni da Procida* deals with the Sicilian Vespers of 1282, *Lodovico Sforza* with the Milanese tyrant whose invitation to Charles VIII brought the beginning of foreign domination, *Arnaldo da Brescia* with the hero of a twelfth-century Roman republican revolution, and *Filippo Strozzi* with the final establishment (after Lorenzino's assassination of Duke Alessandro) of the line of the ducal Medici.

The *Arnaldo*, printed in France in 1843 and circulated clandestinely in Italy, is the best of all these tragedies. The protagonists are the fearless monk Arnaldo, who represents the cause of Italian freedom and unity, the English pope Hadrian IV, who represents the papal claim to temporal power, and the emperor Frederick Barbarossa, who represents the imperial claim to absolute dominion. None but a supreme dramatist could handle worthily the clashing of these three mighty men and these three tremendous forces:

Niccolini was by no means a supreme dramatist, but he does his loyal best with his great theme, and the resulting play has much nobility.

* * *

There remain to be mentioned two poets of this period, one of whom was touched only very slightly, and the other not at all, by the Romanticism of Northern Italy.

Gabriele Rossetti (1783–1854), born at Vasto on the central Adriatic coast, was a Metastasio reincarnate in a strangely excited world. He won early note as an improviser and as a writer of light Arcadian verse: Arcadian moods and forms and the casual habits natural in improvisation continued to characterize most of his poetry throughout his life. In 1804 he went to Naples, where he was received in Arcadia as Filidauro Labediense — and became a Carbonaro. It was he who gave poetic voice to the emotions of the Neapolitan revolution of 1820. One evening, in a group of revolutionists, he improvised a patriotic ode on the refrain

> Non sogno questa volta,
> Non sogno libertà —

lines that Metastasio had written a hundred years before on his escape from amorous captivity. His best known poem is an eloquent and more formal ode written at the most successful moment of the revolution. But political liberty proved to be only a dream after all; and in 1821 only the initiative of an English admiral's wife who admired Rossetti's poetry saved him from probable imprisonment or death. He was taken on an English man-of-war to Malta, where he remained for three years. There he wrote many religious and political "psalms," published later under the title *Iddio e l'uomo*, "God and Man."

In 1824, in the same man-of-war, Rossetti embarked for England; and there he lived for the rest of his exemplary life, teaching Italian privately and in King's College. His main concern was the preparation of a series of books in which he sought vainly to prove that there had existed in the Middle Ages a vast and ritualistic secret society opposed to all forms of tyranny, and that Dante wrote as an affiliate of that society. But he continued to write poetry, much of it patriotic, just a little of it Romantic. In 1846 he published *Il veggente in solitudine*, a long and elaborate poem in which, as a seer in an Arcadian solitude, he meditates on many themes, indulges in fantastic visions, tells many of his own experiences, and includes several of his own short early poems. Three years later he wrote a rambling autobiography, *La vita mia*, in prosaic verse.

In 1826 he had married the daughter of an Italian long resident in England. Two of their children, Dante Gabriele and Christina, wrote poetry in Italian — the language of their home — as well as in English.

With Giuseppe Gioacchino Belli (1791–1863), Roman born, one enters an utterly different area of poetry. He grew up amid hardships that served at least to make him familiar and sympathetic with the plebeian life of Rome. From time to time, after 1807, he held private secretaryships or minor offices in the Papal government. In 1827, however, becoming acquainted with Porta's poems in the Milanese dialect, he made up his mind to write of Roman life in the dialect of the common people of his city; and in the next twenty years he wrote more than two thousand humorous sonnets in that dialect. The humor ranges from bitter satire to deep compassion.

The mass of sonnets is of an extraordinary sociological completeness and of an unsurpassed vividness. They tell of the religion of the people — sacraments, commandments, Bible stories — from *La creazzione der monno* to *Er giorno der Giudizzio* — stories of the saints, miracles, relics, holy days, Hell, and Paradise; the Roman swarm of priests, friars, nuns, prelates, cardinals, and popes; experiences with the police, the courts, and the jails; overbearing officialdom; various Roman sights and scenes; amusements and festivals; disasters — tempests, burning heat and freezing cold, earthquakes, and *Er còllera mòribbus*; "sympathetic" remedies; masters and servants, tavern keepers, venders of fruit or stuffs or glassware or fish or pictures or prints, cobblers, cab-drivers, undertakers, washerwomen, a carpenter, a mason (who objects to prayers against earthquakes), a plasterer, a tailor, an exterminator, a public letter-writer, a public waker-up, a blacksmith, a potter, a ragpicker, a hangman, an umbrella-mender (who thinks that there is altogether too much good weather), a guide — how the Ingresi keep him on the run:

> E a Sampietro! e a Sampavolo! e ar Museo!
> mo a Campidojo! mo a la Fernesina!
> e curre ar Pincio! e curre ar Culiseo! * —

moneylenders, beggars, loafers, and various sinners; omens, witcheries, spirits, and superstitions galore. And they report bits of popular philosophy:

> E quanno che la notte nun c'è sole,
> contentàmose allora de la luna —
>
> And when at night there isn't any sun,
> let's try to be contented with the moon —

and

> La morte è in man de Dio. Se sa, fijola,
> dove se nasce e no dove se more —
>
> Death's in the hands of God. We know, my daughter,
> where we were born, but not where we're to die.

* *Mo* means "now," and *curre* means "run." The *Campidojo* is the Capitoline Hill, and the *Fernesina* is the Villa Farnesina.

CHAPTER 46

Mazzini

DURING THE YEARS that followed the frustrations of 1831 the continuing struggle for freedom and unity found its chief leadership in Mazzini and in the society he founded, *Giovine Italia*, "Young Italy." The early impulsive liberalism of Pius IX, elected in 1846, aroused frantic enthusiasm; but his liberalism was short-lived. Revolutionary activity rose to a new height in 1848; constitutions were demanded and granted in Piedmont, Tuscany, Rome and Naples; Milan and Venice revolted briefly; and in support of the Italian cause Carlo Alberto of Piedmont declared war on Austria. He could accomplish nothing, however, and met with crushing defeat in 1849. Early in that year — Pius IX having fled — a republic was declared in Rome; but Pius won French support, and in the summer French troops captured the city and restored him to power.

Reaction and savage repression followed throughout Italy, accompanied, however, by constant agitation and by new planning. In 1859 Piedmont, led by its new and vigorous king, Victor Emmanuel, and by his prime minister, Cavour, and supported, now, by France, forced Austria into a declaration of war; and a series of Franco-Italian victories resulted in the liberation of Lombardy and its annexation to Piedmont, though Venice was left in the hands of Austria. In 1860 — French consent being purchased by the cession of Savoy and Nice to France — Tuscany and the duchies of Parma and Modena were, in accordance with their desire, annexed to Piedmont. In the same year the unauthorized but glorious expedition of Garibaldi and his "Thousand" led to the liberation of Sicily and Southern Italy. The Kingdom of Italy — lacking Venice and Rome — was constituted in 1861, with Victor Emmanuel as its first king and Turin as its first capital: Florence was made the capital four years later. In 1866 a new war against Austria, with Prussia as an ally of Italy, brought the liberation of nearly all of the Venetian territory; and in 1870, when French troops were at last withdrawn from

Rome, Italian forces entered the city, which in the following year became the capital of a free and united nation.

In the work of Dupré, Italian sculpture gained in realism, while remaining carefully beautiful. The triumphal career of Verdi began about 1840: *Rigoletto*, *Il trovatore*, and *La traviata* are among his early operas.

Italian writers devoted themselves mainly to patriotic support of the struggle for liberation. Romanticism, sometimes whole-hearted, sometimes eclectic, dominated poetry and the novel.

Dickens' *Pictures from Italy* were drawn from observations made in 1844–1845. Throughout the years of their marriage, from 1846 to Mrs. Browning's death in 1861, the Brownings made their home in Casa Guidi, in Florence. There Browning wrote the poems, many of them Italian in scene, that are gathered in the two volumes of his *Men and Women*; and there Mrs. Browning, in her *Casa Guidi Windows*, set down her impressions of the events she witnessed. The idea of *Romola* came to George Eliot in Florence in 1860, and she returned in the following year to study the history of the city in the days of Savonarola. Swinburne visited Italy in 1864, and wrote thereafter of Siena as his "gracious city well-beloved." Meredith, already familiar with the Italian lake country, served as a correspondent with the Italian troops in 1866.

Lowell spent the autumn of 1851 in Florence and the following winter and spring in Rome, and returned to Italy in 1856 and again in 1873. His Italian experiences are reflected in his *Verses on Italy* and in his *Leaves from a Journal in Italy and Elsewhere*. Melville visited Italy in the Spring of 1857. In 1858 and 1859 Hawthorne spent more than a year in Italy, chiefly in Rome, where he began *The Marble Faun*, and in Florence. Howells' consulship in Venice from 1861 to 1865 led directly or indirectly to the writing of his *Venetian Life*, *Italian Journeys*, *Roman Holidays*, and *Modern Italian Poets*. *Indian Summer* and some of his other novels have Italian backgrounds.

* * *

Giuseppe Mazzini, born in Genoa in 1805, was the most passionately political of all the writers of the time, and the most profoundly poetic in spirit of all the many men who devoted themselves heart and soul to the cause of Italian liberation. In 1827 he became a Carbonaro — and wrote his first serious essay, on Dante as a prophet of Italian unity. During the next three years he was active as a conspirator, but his writings were primarily literary. Among them are reviews of translations of *The Fair Maid of Perth*, *Faust*, and Schlegel's *History of Ancient and Modern Literature*, and long essays on "European" literature and on the historical drama. These essays and reviews show that the young Mazzini was an enthusiastic Romanticist, that his outlook embraced all Europe, and that he believed in particular that while individual nations should have political independence they should join in a moral unity and in the production of a literature that should reveal and promote that unity:

> Thus there exists in Europe a concord of needs and desires, a common thought, and a universal spirit that is leading the nations toward one and the same goal: there exists a European tendency. Literature, therefore, if it is not to condemn itself to trivialities, must root itself in this tendency, express it, assist it, and direct it — must itself become European.

Late in 1830 Mazzini was arrested, and for about three months he was imprisoned in the fortress of Savona. There he came to the conclusion that the day of the Carbonari was over, and devised in his mind a new secret society to take its place. Early in 1831 he was released and given the choice between exile and restricted residence in a Piedmontese community. He chose exile; and in the spring, in Marseilles, in company with other exiles, he brought his *Giovine Italia*, "Young Italy," into being. Its purpose was the achievement of Italian unity, independence, and internal freedom, under a republican form of government, with Rome as capital. It was to be an organization of young men; its membership was to be as inclusive as possible — Mazzini believed firmly in "the people," and was convinced that insurrection, to be successful, must be a surging of the whole people rather than an enterprise of a few devotees — and it was to be motivated by love, not by hate. And Italy, once liberated, was to initiate a new international unity in progress and in brotherhood. The formula of initiation, composed by Mazzini, reads thus, in very small part:

> In the name of God and of Italy, in the name of all the martyrs of the holy Italian cause . . . By the duties that bind me to the land where God has placed me and to the brothers God has given me . . . by our youth slain on the scaffold, in prison, in exile; by the misery of millions . . . Believing in the mission entrusted by God to Italy, and in the duty of every man born an Italian to contribute to its fulfillment . . . I give my name to Young Italy . . . and I swear: to consecrate myself wholly and forever to the task, shared with my brothers, of constituting Italy as a Nation, One, Independent, Free, Republican . . .

In the spring of 1831, also, Carlo Alberto, who as prince had shown signs of liberalism, became king in Piedmont; and Mazzini, from Marseilles, addressed to him a firmly reasoned and impassioned letter (the masses, after all, must have leadership, and Italian unity under a liberal monarch would at least be better than tyrannous fragmentation) urging him to put himself at the head of the cause of liberation:

> Free Italy from the barbarians! Build the future! Give your name to a century! Begin your own Era! Be the Napoleon of Italian liberation! Humanity

> has said "We are through with kings," and history has confirmed that verdict: prove that humanity and history are mistaken. Compel them to write, beneath the names of Washington and Kosciusko, citizens born, "There is a name still greater than these; a throne raised by twenty million free men bears this inscription: 'To Carlo Alberto, born a king, Italy, reborn through him!'"

But Carlo Alberto, no longer liberal, was not to be moved by words, however eloquent. Mazzinian tracts now flooded Italy; "Young Italy" soon had its committees and agents in scores of cities and towns; and in 1832, still in Marseilles, Mazzini began the publication of a periodical called *La Giovine Italia.*

In 1833, driven from France, he made his way into Switzerland. There he organized a "Young Switzerland" society and edited a journal called *La Jeune Suisse*; founded still another society, "Young Europe," with a constitution which was in effect a charter for humanity; and launched a tragically ill-fated expedition into Savoy. His Swiss years were extraordinarily prolific, not only in political articles, but also in philosophical and literary reviews and essays (among them essays on the philosophy of music, on fate as a dramatic force, and on Victor Hugo); and in Switzerland he wrote, in French, a treatise entitled *Foi et avenir*, in which he maintains that his own time has witnessed the dissolution of the past, but has not yet moved forward to the building of the future. "Liberty, Equality, and Fraternity," which in France have become mere negative passions, are insufficient even in principle: liberty must be liberty under law if it is to be liberty indeed, and there must be founded a religion of humanity. And as Christ's victory began upon the cross, so the sufferings of the new faithful will make possible a new victory.

In 1837, driven from Switzerland, Mazzini took refuge in London, where he lived until 1848. The Carlyles were among the first and closest of his English friends. His main concern was with the promotion of revolution, in Italy and elsewhere in Europe. He maintained a far-flung correspondence: he had sympathizers, for instance, in Montreal, Boston, New Haven, New York, Philadelphia, Richmond, Charleston, New Orleans, Cuba, and Venezuela. Within these same years he founded a new Italian journal, *L'Apostolato popolare*, "The Apostleship of the People," and a new political organization, the *Associazione nazionale italiana*, which was designed to unify the patriotic effort; and his desire to improve conditions of life and work for the large numbers of Italians laboring in London led him to establish an Italian Workingmen's Association and a free Italian Night School. With Sir John Bowring and other kindred spirits he founded, in 1847, the People's International League, which was to take cognizance of all matters in which international coöperation could promote the progress of Humanity, and "to lay a sure foundation for that alliance of the Peoples for which through all struggles and strivings the Spirit of God has been continually preparing mankind."

During much of his stay in England, Mazzini, in a serious financial plight, earned all he could by writing for English periodicals. His command of English was none too good, and in general he composed in French and paid for the making of English versions. Much of his writing was mere hack work, but he wrote also substantial review-essays on literary topics for *The British and Foreign Review*, *The Foreign Quarterly Review*, *The Monthly Chronicle*, and *The Westminster Review*. The most notable of these essays are one on contemporary Italian literature, one on Byron and Goethe, two on Carlyle, and one on Dante. The essay on contemporary Italian literature begins with severe criticism of Monti and high praise of Foscolo; continues with a discussion of Romanticism; distinguishes the "school" of resignation — that of Manzoni and Pellico — from the "school" of action, which emanates from Foscolo and Byron; and concludes with a survey of recent Italian works in the fields of history and philosophy.

The essay on Byron and Goethe contrasts the two men as poets of the subjective and of the objective life:

> In Byron the *Ego* is revealed in all its pride of power, freedom, and desire, in the uncontrolled plenitude of all its faculties; inhaling existence at every pore, eager to seize "the life of life." . . . Goethe . . . dwells aloft alone; a mighty Watcher in the midst of creation.*

In an admirable essay on *Past and Present* and other writings of Carlyle, Mazzini first praises Carlyle for his sincerity, his idealism, his cosmopolitanism, and his artistic power; and then proceeds to discuss at great length, and with a frankness that is never unfriendly, first, Carlyle's failure to recognize the importance of collective as against individual intelligence and his consequent undemocratic insistence on the gigantic importance of great men, and, second, Carlyle's preference for contemplative patience as against forceful action. History, Mazzini maintains, is *not* the biography of great men:

> The great men of the earth are but the marking-stones on the road to humanity: they are the priests of its religion. What priest is equal in balance to the whole religion of which he is a minister? There is yet something greater, more divinely mysterious, than all the great men, — and this is the earth which bears them, the human race which includes them, the thought of God which stirs within them, and which the whole human race collectively can alone accomplish.

Carlyle's "patience" leads Mazzini to exclaim:

> Suffer in silence, do you say? no, cry aloud upon the housetops, sound the tocsin, raise the alarm at all risks, for it is not alone your house that is on fire,

* Quoted from *Life and Writings of Joseph Mazzini*, edited by Emily A. Venturi.

> but that of your neighbour, that of every one. Silence is frequently a duty, when suffering is only personal; it is an error and a fault, when the suffering is that of millions.*

Mazzini's second essay on Carlyle is a searching discussion of *The French Revolution* and of the general principles that should govern the writing of history. While the merits of Carlyle's work are gladly recognized, particularly the vividness of his descriptions, he is blamed for his failure to perceive and to interpret the significance of the Revolution in the onward march of humanity as a whole. Historians belong to one or the other of two schools: the fatalistic School of Circular Movement, and the School of Progressive Movement, derived from a new conception of Humanity.

The essay on Dante culminates in a study, based mainly on the *Monarchia*, of Dante as a prophet of Italian unity; but it contains also discerning and sensitive pages on the *Vita nova*, and it manifests a devout appreciation of the supreme quality of the *Divine Comedy*, and of the nobility of Dante's soul,

> that soul so loving, and so severe, so susceptible to all emotions, yet so profoundly sad, which by turns reflected within itself Heaven, earth, hell, things finite, and things infinite.†

These and Mazzini's other essays establish him as a literary critic of the first rank, a worthy successor to Foscolo and a worthy predecessor of Carducci and De Sanctis.

The most important of the political treatises written by Mazzini in these same years is his *Thoughts upon Democracy in Europe*, a document at once idealistic and practical, in which Mazzini recognizes the dangers of suffrage in the hands of a people unfitted for its use, and the extreme difficulty of extending political education to laborers who work fourteen or sixteen hours a day for a bare subsistence. Democracy is defined as "the progress of all through all under the leading of the best and wisest."

In 1847, Mazzini, republican though he was, addressed to Pius IX a letter urging him to assume the leadership of the Italian people, and asserting that the unity of Italy would be achieved either with him or, if he should refuse, without him.

The revolutions of 1848 brought Mazzini, in April, to Italy, and the fifteen months that followed were the most momentous of his life. The people whom he so loved and in whom he so believed gave him clamorous demonstrations of their love and trust and hope, and among the leaders there were men who shared and honored his republicanism; but to those who did not share that faith he was unwelcome. In Milan — where he started another

* These quotations are from the essay as first published (in 1844) in *The British and Foreign Review.*

† Quoted from the essay as first published (in 1844) in *The Foreign Quarterly Review.*

journal, *L'Italia del popolo* — he resisted political temptation from Piedmont, and witnessed the Piedmontese abandonment of Lombardy to the returning Austrians. He then took refuge in the Swiss city of Lugano, where in February 1849, he received from the young Goffredo Mameli the three-word message: *Roma! Repubblica! Venite!* He reached Rome early in March; and throughout April, May, and June, as the dominant force among the three elected Triumvirs, he governed the republic, ruling firmly and wisely amid unsurmountable difficulties, determined that at least the idea of Rome as a republican capital should be impressed upon the world, and inspiring his new-found fellow citizens with his convinced and meaningful eloquence:

> We must act as men who have the enemy at their gates, and yet as men who are working for eternity.

But French cannon put an end to the Republic and cleared the way for the Pope's return; and reaction triumphed throughout Italy.

Mazzini made his way to Switzerland, and in 1850 he returned to England. For the next few years — now in London, now secretly and perilously on the Continent, even at times in Italy — he spent his strength in the stimulation of the revolutionary spirit in Italy, and in the support or promotion of ill-fated local insurrections. He founded a new journal, *Pensiero ed Azione*, "Thought and Action." His resolution was concentrated, now, upon the achievement of Italian unity; and though his republican creed remained unchanged he was willing now, in theory, to accept for the time being some other program, if it should give promise of leading more surely to unification. But in practice he trusted no leadership but his own. Most Italian patriots, even some who had been his disciples, now regarded him as a failure and as an obstacle to effective national progress. With the realistic Piedmontese prime minister Cavour he came into open and bitter hostility; and at the outset of the campaign of 1859 he foretold publicly that it would end with Austria confirmed in her possession of Venice.

After the fulfillment of that prophecy he came, in disguise, to Florence, whence he wrote to Victor Emmanuel, summoning him to lead a truly national revolution. Presently, from Lugano, he issued a long and magnificent appeal "to the Youth of Italy," calling upon the young strength of the whole Italian people to rise in a supreme effort to create a united nation. And in the days when Garibaldi and his Thousand paused in Sicily, after their conquest of the island, it was largely the unremitting urgency of Mazzini that drove them on across the straits to their conquest of Naples, which ensured the union of Southern and Northern Italy. But Mazzini, still proscribed, and disheartened by the incompleteness of the new Italian kingdom, returned to London.

There, in the years from 1860 to 1868, he was regarded with disfavor by the government and by the press; but Garibaldi, receiving a hero's ovation in London, could not be prevented from paying heartfelt homage to him, and he had many English and American friends and admirers — among them the now lonely Carlyle, George Meredith, who portrayed Mazzini as "the Chief" in *Vittoria*, John Morley, who thought him the most morally impressive man he had ever met, Swinburne, who called Mazzini the master of his spirit and dedicated to him the *Songs Before Sunrise*, and William Lloyd Garrison, Carl Schurz, and Whistler. In these years Mazzini, not conspiring now, was deeply interested in many things: in religion most of all, but also in economic problems, and in such matters as abolitionism and the woman's suffrage movement in the United States, the plight of Poland, and the plight of Mexico.

In 1860 he published *I doveri dell' uomo*, "The Duties of Man," a series of chapters addressed to Italian workingmen, on God and the law of God; on one's duties to humanity, to the family, and to oneself; and on liberty, education, association and progress, and the economic problem. The mood is one of moral evangelism; the argument is simple, kindly, and persuasive.

For a collection of his writings published in several volumes in the years 1861–1871 (essays originally published in English being now translated into Italian by Mazzini himself) Mazzini prepared a series of statements of varying length designed to throw light on the circumstances under which some of the several writings were composed. These statements, gathered after his death under the title *Note autobiografiche*, constitute an autobiography which, though fragmentary, serves to illumine much of Mazzini's thought, and to preserve, in excellent narration and description, memories of experiences and of men important in the progressive advance of the People and the Nation.

In a preface to a volume of literary studies included in this edition Mazzini found opportunity to express his convictions as to the mission of art and the moral function of literature, with particular reference to contemporary and future Italian literature. The long paragraph, here translated only in part, in which he sums up these convictions is a summary, also, of much of his thought on Italy and on life:

> . . . to tell our young people of the greatness of our fathers . . . and the causes of their decline; to recall them from dismembering analysis to creative synthesis, from the habit of looking at the universe fragmentarily to the concept and the feeling of the life that pervades it, and from the materialism that sees only facts to the study of the ideas that generate them; to propose for their veneration men who have fought and suffered for the banner of Duty, and, for their blame, men who have so abused the gifts of God as to deny or to betray that banner and to make themselves slaves to egoism and to pleasure; to instill in their minds the principle that only great virtues make great peoples; to educate them to constancy in the face of obstacles, to hope in time of grief, to

> faith when surrounded by the triumphs of Evil, to affection and good will amid disillusion; to build an altar to Love and to unite upon that altar, in equal accord, the hands of Woman and of Man; to raise on high the banner of the liberation and the brotherhood of peoples, and to infuse in Italy the desire to assume the leadership in that cause — all this is the sacred obligation of every Writer.

In Mazzini's four remaining years, spent largely in Lugano, he founded a new Workingmen's Federation and a new journal, *La Roma del popolo*; wrote, after the Ecumenical Council of 1870 had proclaimed the doctrine of Papal Infallibility, an impassioned appeal "From the Council to God" (published in *The Fortnightly Review*); engaged in a futile conspiracy which had as its object the liberation of Rome; was courteously imprisoned in Gaeta, and released after the troops of Italy had at last taken Rome; visited London once more; and thereafter, his health failing, his will marvelously strong, produced a flood of articles on many subjects, but chiefly on the need for a spiritual and social regeneration of Europe. His lifelong productivity had been enormous: his writings fill nearly a hundred volumes.

After his death Swinburne wrote of him as

> the man who was to me . . . what Christ himself must have seemed to the very first disciples, and for whom I would very gladly have given all the blood of my body and all the power of my heart and mind and spirit.

CHAPTER 47

Contemporaries of Mazzini

THE MOST PROMINENT, the most prolific, and the most typically Romantic poet of the mid-century was Giovanni Prati (1815–1884), born in Campo Maggiore in the Trentino. His first success came with his *Edmenegarda*, a long Byronic poem of contemporary Venetian life, telling a tragic story of betrayal, abandonment, and expiation. Soon thereafter, in Milan, he published three collections of poems: *Canti lirici*, vague treatments of exalted themes; *Canti pel popolo*, efforts to educate the people in morality and patriotism; and the much more characteristic ballads, in which languishing maidens, minstrels, avengers, suicides, witches, and will-o'-the-wisps reappear in their familiar atmosphere of melancholy and horror.

His best work was done in his last years, when a new appreciation of classic poetry led him to acceptance of simplicity and to a greater stylistic carefulness. Several of the five hundred sonnets assembled in a collection called *Psiche* are quasi-Horatian; and his final collection, *Iside*, "Isis," contains his pleasantest poems.

Far more substantial, as poet, and far less facile, was Niccolò Tommaseo (1802–1874), one of the most remarkable men of his time. In addition to his poetry he wrote much poetic prose, a novel, a few stories, and several critical and aesthetic works, including a commentary on the *Divine Comedy*; he made collections of Tuscan, Corsican, Dalmatian, and Greek folk songs; and he wrote also, in enormous total volume, works in the fields of religion, ethics, politics, education, and lexicography. He was born in Šibenik, in Dalmatia: his ancestry was in part Italian and in part Slavic. He studied in Italy, and engaged in literary activities in Florence for several years. Knowing that his liberalism had rendered him suspect, he went for a time into semi-voluntary exile; but in 1839 he was able to return to Italy and to establish himself in Venice. He took a leading part in the revolutionary activities of 1848 and 1849; and when Austria regained control he was banished. For five years he lived on the island of Corfu: his eyesight was failing fast, but neither that nor any other misfortune could stop his productivity. Returning to Italy in 1854, he spent the next five years in Turin, and the rest of his life in Florence, where blindness closed upon him.

The central vein in all Tommaseo's activity was poetic. Poetry, as he understood it, consisted not in one element alone, but in a union of elements:

> Not the radiant image, nor the hidden idea, nor rhythmic harmony, nor is it creative love: idea, harmony, image, and the breath of fruitful love are blended, and from that blending there come forth a poem, a flower, a world.

The gift of rhythmic harmony was denied to Tommaseo — his verse is rough rather than smooth, hard rather than fluent — but the gifts of imagery, of thought, and of creative love he possessed in rich measure. His imagery and his thought are his own, often strikingly his own; and his love for individual persons, for mankind, and for God, is river-strong and ocean-wide.

His earlier poems — those written before 1850 — include many that deal with personal experiences; patriotic poems, for Italy and for Dalmatia, that are humanized by a deep sense of sacrificial suffering; a poem on Napoleon that in the intensity of its ten lines rivals *Il cinque maggio*; a very few Romantic ballads and *novelle*; an unsurpassed expression, in a poem called *Carità*, of the ideal of human brotherhood made immediate; and poems of religious grandeur, such as his hymn for "The New Year," and a poem entitled *Cristo e le cose*, "Christ and Things," in which it is said that the touch of the feet of Christ will imprint all earth forever with his virtues, the air he breathed will carry perpetual inspiration, the atoms of his body will enter into the bodies of kings and beggars alike, and all the light and warmth and spirit that dwelt in him will permeate life endlessly.

One might have supposed that Tommaseo's second exile and his simultaneous certainty of impending blindness would have halted or at least reduced his writing of poetry: they led on the contrary to a new surge of song. In his first years in Corfu, as if he were determined to record the beauties of the world before darkness fell, he wrote poems on "The Earth," "The Sea," "Light," "Colors," "Forms," and "Space"; and in a poem entitled *Vita nuova* he sought the attainment of a universal awareness that could not be impaired by the loss of any physical faculty.

Tommaseo's writings in deliberately poetic prose include a vast number of prayers and meditations, and two curious little volumes, each bearing a title that means "Sparks," and each consisting of a series of detached paragraphs. One of the two, *Iskrice*, written in Serbo-Croatian, is devoted to the praise of Dalmatian life, spirit, customs, songs, history, rights, and hopes. The other, *Scintille*, treats a great variety of subjects: some of its paragraphs are written in Italian, some in French, some in Latin, some in Greek. His novel, *Fede e bellezza*, "Faith and Beauty," is a psychological and partly autobiographical story of sin expiated through suffering and death.

Giuseppe Giusti (1809–1850), born in the little Tuscan town of Monsummano, spent most of his mature life in Florence. While he wrote several conventional lyrics of good quality, most of the poems on which his reputation rests are brilliant satires, sparkling with Tuscan wit, that spring from his great love for Italy. They consist, typically, of many brief stanzas, composed of short lines.

The first of these poems, *La guigliottina a vapore*, "The Steam Guillotine," written in 1833, reports that the Chinese have invented a guillotine driven by steam, which speeds up splendidly the process of decapitation: it would be very useful to local tyrants. *Lo stivale*, "The Boot," taking its title from the shape of Italy, recounts in a sort of cobbler's parable the sufferings of Italy from foreign legs: the boot is sadly in need of repair, and should be worn by someone who is not a coward. *Il brindisi di Girella*, "Girella's Toast" (*girella* means "whirligig"), dedicated to the memory of Talleyrand, is the comic autobiography of a shameless turncoat. *La chiocciola*, "The Snail," praises the habits of that humble creature, to the disadvantage of the greedy, the wrathful, the arrogant, and those who think ill of their own home. Lamartine had once referred to the Italians as "human dust," and, though he ultimately recanted, his despicable phrase gained wide circulation. Giusti's *La terra dei morti*, "The Land of the Dead," is a bitter attack on those who thus scorn Italy. Why bother to baptize creatures who exist but to die? What use have skeletons for liberty and glory? The barbarians would do well to suppress even our cemeteries: is not the Day of Judgment to come?

In other poems Giusti satirizes bureaucracy, avarice, the exploitation of popular ignorance, degenerate nobles and arrogant parvenus, obscurantism, hypocrisy, lazy Utopians, excessive harping on ancient glories, foreign spies, mechanized education, armchair patriots, pacifism, profiteering, abject resignation, false liberals, majority inertia, partisanship, dishonest politics, and demagoguery.

In 1845, while visiting Manzoni in Milan, Giusti had the experience that he relates in his beautifully written *Sant' Ambrogio*. Wandering into the ancient church of St. Ambrose, he finds it filled with stiffly standing Austrian troops — sent to serve as poles in the Italian vineyard; he is disgusted, but their military band plays, and plays well, Verdi's chorus *O Signore, dal tetto natio* ("Oh Lord, from our native home"); and he begins to feel a certain kinship with these foreigners. Then they sing a German anthem:

In that sad hymn, I felt the bitter sweet
  Of the songs heard in childhood, which the soul
Learns from beloved voices, to repeat
  To its own anguish in the days of dole;

A thought of the dear mother, a regret,
A longing for repose and love, — the whole
Anguish of distant exile seemed to run
Over my heart and leave it all undone: . . .
Here,
But that I turned in haste and broke away,
I should have kissed a corporal, stiff and tall,
And like a scarecrow stuck against the wall.*

The best of the many martial "hymns" written and sung in this period are those of Mameli and Mercantini. Goffredo Mameli's *Inno*, written in 1847, when Mameli was but twenty years old, opens with the lines

Fratelli d'Italia,
L'Italia s'è desta —

Brothers of Italy,
Italy has awakened.

Two years later Italy called Mameli to take part, as a volunteer, in the defense of Rome; and there death found him ready.

In December 1858, Garibaldi, then planning his part in the war that was soon to be declared, asked Luigi Mercantini (1821–1872) to write him a song that might be sung by his troops; and Mercantini responded with his rousing *Canzone italiana*, soon popularly renamed *Inno di Garibaldi*. Its first quatrain reads:

Si scopron le tombe, si levano i morti,
I martiri nostri son tutti risorti!
Le spade nel pugno, gli allori alle chiome,
La fiamma ed il nome d'Italia sul cor! —

The tombs are opening, the dead are rising, our martyrs are all risen again! Their swords in their hands, their laurels on their brows, the flame and the name of Italy in their hearts!

* * *

The most prolific and the most incorrigibly Romantic of the many men who wrote historical novels in this period was Francesco Domenico Guerrazzi (1804–1873) of Leghorn. His settings are Italian; his plots are heavy with more than the ordinary weight of Romantic horrors; and his style is rhetorical and at times convulsive. The best and the most ardently patriotic of his novels is *L'assedio di Firenze*: the siege is the famous siege of 1530, and many of the characters among the besieged and the besiegers are historical. Two love stories wind their way to tragic denouements. The book was written "with the same heart with which one would fight a battle": it became very popular, and had its share in the molding of Italian valor.

* The translation is by Howells.

Better than those of Guerrazzi are the two historical novels of the Piedmontese Massimo D' Azeglio (1798–1866): *Ettore Fieramosca*, which deals with an episode of the Franco-Spanish warfare in Southern Italy in 1503 (thirteen Italian gentlemen had challenged an equal number of Frenchmen, and in the presence of a great throng of spectators had won a complete victory), and *Niccolò de' Lapi*, which, like Guerrazzi's novel, deals with the siege of Florence in 1530. D'Azeglio's style is swift and vigorous, if undisciplined, and he had a very real gift of invention, and some ability in characterization. His most successful persons are a furious Spaniard, Diego Garcia de Paredes, of enormous strength, and a fun-loving and gallant Italian soldier, Fanfulla da Lodi.

In the years 1853–1860 there were published in Great Britain four historico-political novels written in English by Giovanni Ruffini (1807–1881). Born in Genoa, he became in his youth a Carbonaro and a close friend of Mazzini, whom he helped in the organization of the *Giovine Italia*. In 1833 he was involved in a conspiracy which was discovered and ruthlessly suppressed by the Piedmontese government. He escaped to France, and in 1837 went with Mazzini to England, where much of his later life was spent. His novels read as if they had been written by an Englishman: the *Edinburgh Review* spoke of the "easy elegance and idiomatic accuracy of style" of his first novel, *Lorenzo Benoni*. He appears to have had some friendly English help; but even so his command of English represents a remarkable linguistic achievement. *Lorenzo Benoni, or Passages in the Life of an Italian*, published in 1853, is an autobiographical novel, dealing mainly with Ruffini's experiences as a conspirator. It offers a faithful and very interesting account of conditions in Piedmont in the 1830's, and of the harried and exciting life of the conspiring patriots, men and women. Ruffini's second and best known novel, *Doctor Antonio*, published in 1855, met with great and continued favor. It is a Victorian love story, with Italian patriotic complications. The other two novels are of less importance.

The one really great novel of the period is *Le confessioni di un Italiano*, by Ippolito Nievo (1831–1861). He was born in Padua, and spent much of his life there; but the region that meant most to him was northeastern Venetia, the hilly river-strewn country between the head of the Adriatic and the Alps. Before he came to the writing of his masterpiece he had written lyrics, satires in the manner of Giusti, historical tragedies, and — of better quality — prose *novelle* and two minor novels. Italians use the word *novella* both for the type of pointed story current in earlier Italian literature and for the "short story" in the modern sense — a story, usually, of character or of customs, differentiated more and more from the older tale as the tendencies toward realism and psychologism gain strength. Nievo's *novelle*, some of which deal with peasant life, are among the first of the modern type. His first novel, *Angelo di bontà*,

"Angel of Goodness," is laid in Venice in the mid-eighteenth century, his second, *Il conte pecoraio*, "The Shepherd Count," in his own century and his own northeastern Venetian country. In each the worthy and troubled heroine comes at last into a happy matrimonial haven.

The *Confessioni di un Italiano*, written in a few months in 1857 and 1858, begins thus:

> I was born a Venetian on the 18th of October, 1775 . . . and by the grace of God I shall die an Italian when Providence shall so ordain . . . I am old now . . . in this year of the Christian Era 1858; and yet younger in spirit, perhaps, than I ever was in my stormy youth or in my weary manhood. So the fact . . . that I have lived in these years has led me to record what I have seen and felt and done and experienced from my early childhood to the beginning of my old age.

The narrator is Carlo Altoviti, tolerated in the castle of Fratta, in his childhood, as a motherless nephew of the Countess. The story opens with a masterly account of the rambling old castle and of its many occupants, every one of them strikingly characterized. Pisana, the younger daughter of the Countess, is the heroine. High-spirited, tantalizing, and unpredictable, she is the object of Carlo's childish devotion, which in her own capricious ways she encourages, and of his lifelong love, which, also in her own ways, she returns, though the course of life and love is never smooth for them. She is a unique figure, alive with an insistent and an ultimately sacrificial vitality. Carlo is himself a vital person, both in his boyish years — the account of his experience on one particular day, as given in one of the early chapters of the novel, is not to be surpassed in any other story of boyhood — and in the long years of his youth and his maturity: the reader indeed becomes Carlo, strives with him, fails with him, succeeds with him, and shares something of his final peace.

Most unfortunately, Nievo never revised the first draft of the novel. It would have been the better for much pruning and for further structural and stylistic care — and the last chapters are dreary. Had it received its due measure of perfecting artistry, it would have been a very great novel. Nievo never released it for publication. The publisher who brought it out in 1867, thinking that the author's title was too suggestive of political debate, renamed it *Le confessioni di un ottuagenario*, "The Confessions of an Octogenarian"; and it still, in common usage, bears that name.

In 1860 Nievo was one of Garibaldi's fabulous Thousand. In the following year he was drowned in a storm at sea.

Though the pen was not his natural instrument, Giuseppe Garibaldi (1807–1882), the Paladin of the Risorgimento, essayed twice, once in prose and once in verse, to tell the story of his life. That story is so amazing, and the spirit of the great Liberator is so heroic, that one reads his own narratives with a peculiar interest, despite their limitations and imperfections. The prose *Memorie autobiografiche*, written at various times, affords a straightforward account of an extraordinary series of adventurous campaigns undertaken in South America, in Italy, and in France in the course of his persistent and passionate championship of liberty, a championship now incredibly triumphant, now unbearably frustrated and disowned.* There are passages in which remembered or reflective emotion lifts his prose, for the moment, to a poetic level. His *Poema autobiografico*, a long composition in blank verse, written on the island of Caprera in 1862, after the repulse of an unauthorized attempt to liberate Rome, is essentially a prolonged outcry of righteous indignation. He wrote much other verse, most of it well forgotten. But he rose to heights of sudden eloquence in his proclamations and in his battle cries. One can sense something of the flashing magnetism that drew his devoted followers onward as he challenged them, at the outset of a long and desperate effort, with the words "I offer you hunger, thirst, marches, battles, and death," or as he led the last charge at Mentana with the shout: "Come and die with me! Come and die with me! Do you fear to come and die with me?"

* In one of his periods of eclipse he worked for a few months in a candle factory on Staten Island.

CHAPTER 48

Carducci and Other Poets

THE NEW KINGDOM had now to wrestle with multifarious and very difficult problems of internal organization and improvement. The Papacy was at first completely unreconciled to the new order, but its antagonism gradually diminished. In 1878 Humbert succeeded Victor Emmanuel, and Leo XIII succeeded Pius IX.

Verdi advanced in range and in power from *Aïda* (1871) to *Otello* (1887) and *Falstaff* (1892).

Browning returned to Italy in 1879, and spent much of the rest of his life in Venice and Asolo. Ruskin would not have been Ruskin without Italy. Henry James visited Italy frequently: his discriminating pleasures are recorded in *Italian Hours.*

* * *

Giosue Carducci was born in 1835 in Val di Castello, in northwestern Tuscany. His boyhood, from 1838 to 1848, was spent in the strange and desolate region known as the Maremma, along the coast south of Pisa. He was of a rebellious spirit, and his reading kindled in him an ardent republicanism. His first verse, satiric, was written in 1846. In 1856, now definitely a classicist, he joined with some of his friends in a violent anti-romantic polemic. He was still given to satire; and his childish religion had yielded, partly through reaction against bigotry, partly because of the religious tendencies of romanticism, to a rebellious impiety. During the school year 1856–1857 he taught in San Miniato al Tedesco; and there, in 1857, his first volume of verse, *Rime*, was published. For the next two years he studied and wrote in Florence, where he undertook the editorship of a series of pocket editions of Italian authors: poetry and scholarship were to companion each other throughout his life. His increasing prominence as scholar and writer led in 1860 to his appointment as Professor of Italian Literature in the University of Bologna, a position which he held until his retirement in 1904. He was often in Rome and occasionally in other Italian cities; and he spent long vacations in the Alps. In 1890 he was made a senator; in 1906 he received the Nobel prize for literature. He died in 1907.

He was a great teacher and a great scholar. Of his students he once wrote:

> When I am with my students I believe — oh so firmly — in beauty, in goodness, in greatness, and in the future. They do more for me than I do for them. And when I see their fine gleaming eyes fixed on me it makes me want to shout "*Viva l'Italia!*"

His first really great work as scholar was a remarkable edition of Politian, published in 1863: other scholarly works, written always with literary sensitiveness and skill, followed each other swiftly thereafter.

Gradually, over the years, some of his main attitudes and opinions changed, not so much through denial of any earlier positive beliefs as through a broadening of his thought to admit truths and values that he had not previously recognized. In literature, though he always remained primarily a classicist, he came to appreciate modern foreign literatures, and to feel their influence. In politics, though at first he had felt no allegiance to the monarchy, he came gradually, especially during the reign of Humbert and his gracious and accomplished queen, Margherita, to accept the necessity and to approve the quality of the service the king and queen were rendering. His early impiety was soon stilled; but in his abounding vitality he resented all emphasis on suffering and all asceticism, and for the greater part of his life he remained strongly anticlerical. Later years brought a growing personal faith, and some measure of appreciation of the historic mission of the Church. His own mature religion was in essence a vigorous and loving morality, touched with a quiet consciousness of the divine. He loathed moral decadence.

By 1899 he had published ten volumes of poems, which in a definitive edition he rearranged in six collections: *Juvenilia* (containing poems written from 1850 to 1860), *Levia gravia*, "Light and Serious Verse" (poems of 1861–1871), *Giambi ed epodi*, "Iambics and Epodes" (poems of 1867–1879), *Rime nuove* (poems of 1861–1887), *Odi barbare*, "Barbarian Odes" (poems of 1873–1889), and *Rime e ritmi*, "Rhymes and Rhythms" (poems of 1885–1898). In the first two collections the prevailing mood and intent are classic, but the poems show familiarity not only with Greek and Latin verse but also with the whole range of Italian poetry. There is much variety in theme and in form.

Between the *Levia gravia* and the *Giambi ed epodi*, in the definitive edition, there stands, as an independent poem, the "Hymn to Satan," an explosive manifesto of rebellion — very startling to the readers of the early 1860's — in which the repressions of traditional religion are scornfully denounced, while the natural energies of life and thought are exalted.

Most of the "Iambics and Epodes" are powerfully political and satiric: they include, in particular, bitter attacks on the still resisting Pius IX and on the insufficiencies of the Italian government. Very different from the satirical poems (though linked to them by certain references) is the *Canto dell' amore*, placed as the last poem of this group. As the poet stands in the *piazza* of Perugia, looking away over the Umbrian plain to the rising hills, evoking with his clear vision the centuries of struggle and endurance enacted in that scene, there comes upon him an intense consciousness that the bygone ages are joining in one brief insistent message:

From Umbrian hamlets nestling in the vales
 Where swift and still the darkling rivers flow,
From summits where Etruscan citadels
 Tower aloof and watch the world below;

From fields wherein the busy plowman oft
 Upturns the relics of a Roman day,
From the invader's castle, perched aloft
 Like falcon spying out the distant prey;

From answering dark turrets that defy
 The foreigner, and hold the towns in ward,
From churches raising upward to the sky
 Long marble arms in prayer unto the Lord . . .

Amid the tender green of the ripening grain,
 O'er terraced hillsides fragrant with the vine,
O'er lakes and rivers silver in the plain,
 From the distant snowy crests of Apennine;

Amid the clamor of the busy mills,
 Where open meadows in the sun rejoice,
Rises one chant among the listening hills,
 One hymn, in a thousandfold and mighty voice:

"Greeting to you who live and toil and move
 In the swift-passing yet eternal day!
Too much we hated, suffering. So love!
 Holy and fair the world shall be alway."

In the three later collections, the *Rime nuove*, the *Odi barbare*, and the *Rime e ritmi*, Carducci achieves his spiritual and poetic maturity. The earlier fire still glows, but it is under control; and negative rebelliousness is supplanted by a positive, even a serene, acceptance of all that has been and is wholesome and beautiful and good in life, and by a projection of this concept of the good life into the future. The *Rime nuove* are in familiar Italian metrical forms; the unrhymed *Odi barbare* are modeled on various types of the Horatian ode; poems of both kinds appear in the *Rime e ritmi*.

Several of the sonnets of the *Rime nuove* are among the most perfect sonnets of modern times. One of them, *Sole e amore*, is, like Leopardi's *La quiete dopo la tempesta*, a poem suggested by calm after storm — but two poems on the same theme could hardly be more different. Carducci's reads, in translation:

> Soft and white into the distant west
> The clouds are gone; the wet sky laughs again.
> The sun, triumphant, hails the labor of men
> In busy streets astir with the daily quest.
>
> High above, in the golden radiance pressed,
> The thousand pinnacles of a mighty fane
> Intone Hosanna; and in swift-wing'd train
> The circling swallows speed from spire to nest.
>
> So shines again the sun within my soul
> When love has swept away with its sweet smile
> The heavy-lowering clouds of doubt and wrong:
>
> In luminous wonder is revealed the whole
> Ideal of life — my every thought the while
> A harmony, and every sense a song.

As Leopardi had used the word *pietade* to express his sense of the common human bond, so Carducci, in these sonnets and elsewhere, uses the adjective *pio* to express his sense of the same bond, his willing consciousness of interwoven life. Leopardi's *pietade* had been for defense: Carducci's is vigorous, positive, good for its own sake, a fellowship in everyday toil and in all forms of ennobling effort. Such phrases as *il pio travaglio* and *la giustizia pia del lavoro* recur in his poems; and in one of the most famous of his sonnets he calls the ox *pio*, as a willing sharer in man's toil.

The series of sonnets is followed by several smaller groups of poems, in which, with a completely satisfying metrical mastery, Carducci chooses for his varying moods a great many different lyric and semi-lyric forms. Among the poems of these groups are freshly imaginative love poems, a most poignant and exquisitely wrought little poem written after the death of his three-year-old son, Alpine poems, poems of autumn and winter and springtime, a serenade and an aubade, childhood reminiscences — one of these, *Davanti San Guido*, "Before (the church of) San Guido," is the best-loved of all Carducci's poems — and many historical and legendary evocations. Three of the springtime poems are grouped as *Primavere elleniche*, "Hellenic Springs": in one of these — as Leopardi had done in his "Hymn to Spring" — Carducci seeks again the beauty of the classic illusion:

> Though other gods may wane, the gods of Greece
> Live on for aye. They sleep in the maternal
> Trees, on the hills, in streams, and in the peace
> Of seas eternal. . . .
> And if there summon them the enamour'd face
> Of a fair woman, or a poet's strain,
> They, laughing, from their sacred biding-place,
> Flash forth again.

Historic and legendary evocation constitutes one of the most distinctive features of Carducci's art. "The present," he once wrote, "belongs to the drama, the novel, and the newspaper; the future, to God; the past, to poetry." And elsewhere:

> Great poetry aspires ceaselessly to the past and proceeds from the past. The dead are infinitely more numerous than the living, and the spaces of time under the Triumph of Death are incomparably more immense and more tranquil than the brief moment agitated by the phenomenon of life. Hence the imagination of the poet can there freely take its flight . . . while the appearances of the present, in their continual flux, do not allow the artistic faculty so to fix them as to be able to transform them into the ideal.

The intense sensation of the past is indeed a natural thing in Italy. It comes with overwhelming power when one stands high above a plain that quivers with the life of generations: at Fiesole, looking down on Florence and the Arno; on Vesuvius, with Herculaneum and Pompeii at one's feet; on the hill of Tusculum, with Rome in the distance. Some such mountain experience as this gave Carducci the phrase by which he expresses his visualization of the past: "I stand upon the mount of centuries." From that height he directs his vision over the immense continent of experience and imagination that lies below, discerning men and scenes that shine with some rich human significance; and then, as creator, he evokes those men, those scenes, for the modern world.

The "Envoi" of the *Rime nuove* is a poem called *Congedo*, the best of Carducci's several poems on poetry, in which he sings of the creative activity of the poet under the figure of the smith at his forge — a fitting symbol for the virile strength of Carducci's own genius. Most of its stanzas follow, in a free translation:

When the bird at daybreak sings,
And the gleam of early light
Rests upon the waiting height,
    He the bellows full doth urge
Till the ruddy fire springs
    Cheerily within the forge.

Now the flame darts upward high,
Flashing with its sparks of gold,
Leaping with defiance bold
    Far above the waiting tools;
Now it sinks as though to die,
    Lurking low amid the coals.

What the flame may be, who knows?
Only He that doth the fire
Of the human heart inspire.
    But the smith, when white-intense
Every burning ember glows,
    Casts therein the elements

Of his deepest love and thought:
Treasures of his memory,
Glories of his ancestry,
    Hopes that yet shall come to pass,
All lie molten to be wrought
    In the incandescent mass.

Now the glowing bar he bends
And upon the anvil lays,
Then with shaping hammer plays;
    Strikes, and while he strikes he sings;
Strikes, the while the sun ascends
    And the forge with clamor rings.

Strikes, and lo! for liberty
Here are shields, and here are swords
That shall smite despotic lords;
    And for those that vanquish them
Here are wreaths of victory;
    Here for love a diadem.

Strikes, and lo! for sacred shrine
Here are altars with the story
Graven fair of martyrs' glory;
    Here are goblets that shall render
Dearer still the sparkling wine
    'Mid the banquet's joyous splendor.

For himself, of shining gold
Makes he then a single dart,
Hurls it upward from his heart
    Toward the sun; and its ascent
And its gleaming doth behold,
    And, beholding, is content.

Carducci's "barbarian" stanzas, like those of Chiabrera, imitate the corresponding Latin strophes through the use of unrhymed lines of different lengths that are arranged according to the pattern of the particular type of Latin strophe that is being imitated, and follow that type of strophe also, at least approximately, in the usual distribution of their verbal stresses. A typical Carduccian Alcaic stanza reads thus:

Il dittatore, solo, a la lugubre
schiera d'avanti, ravvolto e tacito
cavalca: la terra ed il cielo
squallidi, plumbei, freddi intorno; *

a typical Sapphic stanza thus:

Solenni in vetta a Monte Mario stanno

* "The dictator, alone, at the head of his saddened troop, rides on wrapped in his cloak and silent: earth and sky squalid, leaden, cold around him." This is the first stanza of an ode to Garibaldi.

nel luminoso cheto aere i cipressi,
e scorrer muto per i grigi campi
mirano il Tebro; *

and a typical elegiac distich thus:

Rompendo il sole tra i nuvoli bianchi a l'azzurro
sorride e chiama — O primavera, vieni! †

Such stanzas appealed to Carducci as affording appropriately classic forms for the expression of moods that he felt to be classic, and in particular as being at a far remove from the easy forms favored by Romantic poets. He was familiar with poems in which Chiabrera and Campanella and other Italians had made use of similar stanzas; and he was interested in the somewhat similar poems of Klopstock, Goethe, and Platen. His own consummate artistry enabled him to write in these forms more successfully than anyone else has ever done. His "barbarian" odes are of great dignity, and often of great strength and beauty. He presumably derived the term "barbarian" from Campanella's line

Musa latina, è forza che prendi la barbara lingua.

Several of the *Odi barbare* are classic in theme as well as in form, but Carducci is conscious simultaneously of the classic, the medieval, and the modern worlds, and likenesses and contrasts and resulting prophecies occur to him continually. Thus in an ode in which he celebrates the triumphs of ancient Rome — "everything in the world that is humane, great, and august is Roman still" — he prophesies that the future Italian triumph will be not a triumph of kings or Caesars over other nations, but a triumph of the Italian people, for all nations, over darkness, barbarity, and injustice. In the ode "At the Source of the Clitumnus" he pictures the quiet beauty of the unvarying peasant life that borders the gentle course of the little river, tells in superb stanzas of the rush of Umbria to arms after Thrasimene, condemns the servile fanaticism of the Middle Ages, and then returns to the normal vigor of Italian life, hailing Italy as the perennial mother of harvests, of laws, of the arts, and of new industry. Familiar legendary figures of the ancient and medieval worlds are brought together, like meeting like, in the ode "At the Urn of Percy Bysshe Shelley," written in elegiac distichs. The scene is a faraway island "resplendent with fancy":

There, leaning on their spears, Siegfried and Achilles, tall and fair,
wander singing along the resounding sea:

* "On the summit of Monte Mario the cypresses stand solemnly in the luminous and quiet air, and watch the Tiber flowing silently through the gray fields." This is the first stanza of an ode entitled *Su Monte Mario*.

† "The sun breaking through the white clouds smiles to the blue sky and calls: 'Oh springtime, come!' " This is the first stanza of a poem entitled (in Latin) *Vere novo*, "Early Spring."

To the one Ophelia, escaped from her pallid lover, gives flowers;
to the other Iphigenia comes from the sacrifice.
Under a green oak Roland speaks with Hector;
Durendal flashes with gold and gems in the sun:
Andromache calls her boy to her bosom;
Alde the fair in silence watches her stern lord.
King Lear of the flowing locks tells his sorrow to the wandering Oedipus;
with uncertain eyes Oedipus seeks ever the sphinx:
The loving Cordelia calls — "Ah, white Antigone, come!
Come, O Greek sister! Let us sing of peace to our fathers."

There also Helen and Ysolde go pensively together, and Lady Macbeth and Clytemnestra vainly dip their stained white arms into the sea. To this island Shelley, alone among modern poets, has been borne by Sophocles.

Modern history takes classic form in several odes, one of them on the nemesis that overtook the Bonapartes. At the end of this poem the mother of Napoleon vainly calls her children and her children's children:

Stands in the night the Corsican Niobe,
stands at the door whence to their baptism
her children went; and her arms,
guiltless, she lifts to the wild sea,

and calls, and calls: perchance from America,
perchance from Britain or burning Africa,
some one of her tragic sons,
freed by death, may come to her breast.

In still other odes history gives way to contemporary moods and scenes: companionship and love, a reading of Marlowe, flights of birds, a railroad station on a rainy autumn morning, Tuscan hills, Alpine meadows.

Many of the poems of the last collection, *Rime e ritmi*, were written in the Alps, and many are imbued with an Alpine clarity and breadth of vision. Some of them are purely Alpine, as for instance this rendering of noontide stillness:

> In the great circle of the Alps, over the bare gray granite, over the gleaming glaciers, noon reigns, serene, intense, infinite, in the great silence.
>
> Pines and firs, unstirred by any breath of wind, rise in the sunlight that shines through them. Only the tiny brook flowing amid the stones sings its soft lyric song.

In other poems the Alpine setting serves as Carducci's "mount of the centuries," and he brings back into a life newly interpreted noble figures of the Italian past. One of the last poems of all, the *ode barbara* (not Alpine) entitled *La chiesa di Polenta*, "The Church of Polenta," suggested by the restoration of a very ancient church not far from Rimini — a poem filled with medieval memories — ends in the imagined healing peace of the Ave Maria rung at sunset from the new belltower. The collection ends with this *stornello* (in which the *tricolore* refers to the three colors of the Italian flag):

> Fior tricolore,
> Tramontano le stelle in mezzo al mare
> E si spengono i canti nel mio core —

> Tricolored flower, the stars are setting in the midst of the sea, and all my songs are dying in my heart.

In prose Carducci wrote plentifully in three fields: literary history and criticism; Italian history and patriotism; and personal reminiscence. Whatever his theme, his prose is fresh, imaginative, and vigorous. It has always a vocal quality, as though it had been spoken, and spoken with a great and yet a natural distinction.

He was often called upon to make addresses on literary occasions. Thus he spoke in Pietole on Virgil, in Rome on Dante, in Arquà on Petrarch, in Certaldo on Boccaccio, in Lecco on Manzoni, and in Recanati on Leopardi. In such addresses the distinction of his style rises often to a disciplined eloquence, and his evocations are comparable in their insight and their power to those of his poems.

In the field of Italian history and patriotism Carducci wrote occasional essays and reports, and several *discorsi.* The best of these *discorsi,* rich in content, profoundly loyal, and irresistibly impassioned in style, are among the greatest of modern orations.

At a mass meeting held in Bologna on June 4, 1882, two days after the death of Garibaldi, Carducci out of the fullness of his mind and heart delivered extemporaneously an oration hardly to be surpassed in any time or place. Every sentence is memorable, and the successive paragraphs rise to supreme heights of eloquence. When applause greeted his preliminary words he bade his hearers refrain from any further demonstration: but toward the end the audience, moved beyond control, was shouting its assent. The opening summary of the career of Garibaldi, a summary at once solemn and resplendent, begins thus:

> The revelation of glory that appeared to us in our childhood, the epic of our youth, the ideal vision of our maturity, have closed and disappeared forever. . . . That blond head with its lion's mane and its splendor as of an archangel, that head that passed along the Lombard lakes and beneath the Aurelian walls, reawakening Roman victories and spreading fear and dismay among foreigners, lies now cold and motionless . . .

Similar sentences follow for hand and eyes and voice and heart. From this summary the orator moves through a characterization that draws upon likenesses in ancient and in modern heroism, through a fiercely satirical condemnation of the partisan politics of the new Italy for which Garibaldi had given his life, and through a marvelous telling of the legend of Garibaldi as it might be told and sung by the poets of a far distant century, to a final summoning of Italy to cast all her unworthiness into the flames of the funeral pyre:

> So and only so we may hope that in the days of trial and of peril that are to come . . . the General's spirit may return to ride at the head of our armies, and to lead us again to victory and to glory.

* * *

Giacomo Zanella (1820–1888), born in a village near Vicenza, was ordained as priest in 1843, and then taught in a church school until 1853, when his patriotic liberalism led the Austrian government to forbid his teaching. During the next four years he did much reading and studying, especially in the field of science. In 1857 he was allowed to resume his teaching, and in 1866 he was made Professor of Italian Literature in the University of Padua. In 1872 personal distresses brought him into a deep depression; and in 1875 he gave up his professorship. After his recovery he built a tiny villa for himself, in 1878, by the little river Astichello, near Vicenza; and there he spent contentedly much of the rest of his life.

In the years before his retirement he wrote by preference of the effects of scientific discovery upon the inner life of man. In the lyric *Sopra una conchiglia fossile nel mio studio*, "On a Fossil Shell in my Study," his fossil suggests to him the eons when the earth, still in its volcanic making, was peopled with strange creatures, and man was not:

> Noi siamo di ieri;
> Dell' Indo pur ora
> Sui taciti imperi
> Splendeva l'aurora;
> Pur ora del Tevere
> A' lidi tendea
> La vela d'Enea —

> We are of yesterday; only just now the dawn shone over the silent empires of the Indus; only just now the sail of Aeneas turned to the banks of the Tiber.

Man, the newcomer, treading the ashes of an ancient world, moves onward into an unknown future:

> Advance, advance, oh divine stranger; acquaint thyself with the dwelling the fates have given thee: so long as there are still slaves or tears upon the earth it is but young.
>
> Lofty and hidden in the unknown years God has set the goal for thy noble strivings. With sword and torch up the fateful slope press on, oh mortal!

In the narrative poem *Milton e Galileo*, Zanella seeks to recreate the meeting of the young Milton and the aged and blind Galileo at Arcetri. Galileo is fearful lest the power that holds him in confinement may reach out to punish his unwary visitor, but Milton is fearless. Galileo asks whether his discoveries, condemned by the Church, are gaining acceptance in the world; and Milton replies that the truth is making its way invincibly. Galileo tells of his own struggle between love of the truth and love of the Church; and Milton responds with an eloquent Protestant invective against the Church, contrasting its pomp and display with the simplicity of primitive Christianity. Galileo replies that the Church is in its nature both human and divine, and that while its human element is imperfect and subject to change, its divine element remains eternal:

> These human forms have risen with the years
> And with the years may vanish: but the tree,
> The tree triumphant, loses not its might
> For any falling of its autumn leaves,
> Because its roots are firm in depths divine. . . .

Man in his toiling needs the sustenance of faith:

> Through such faint light as comes before the dawn,
> 'Mid gleams and shadows mingled, the believer
> Moves on, his feet in the dust, but on his brow
> The living breath of a mysterious wind.

The discussions of the poet and the scientist last long into the night — the towers of Florence rising above the moonlit mist, the Arno now dark, now silver. Galileo sets forth his majestic concept of the universe. Milton, through the strange telescope, beholds in amazement the mountains and valleys of the moon. Galileo fears that the advances of science may fill man with a disastrous pride: Milton undertakes to tell in solemn warning the story of man's primal pride and fall.

Most of the poems written after Zanella's retirement are pleasant — at the best, delightful — poems of simple country life and of the thoughts it suggests. Nearly a hundred sonnets are gathered in a collection called *Astichello*; and closely associated with these sonnets is a Latin *Carmen alcaicum*. Zanella would have been quite at home on Horace's Sabine farm, and Horace would have been quite at home in Zanella's villa.

* * *

Leo XIII (Gioacchino Pecci, 1810–1903), one of the most eminent of ecclesiastical statesmen, was himself a poet. Born at Carpineto, in the mountains south of Rome, he was ordained as priest in 1837, and made Bishop of Perugia in 1846, cardinal in 1853, and pope in 1878. He began the writing of poetry, in Italian and in Latin, in his youth — he was indeed admitted to Arcadia, as Neander Heracleus, in 1832 — but most of his poems were written after 1870 and in Latin, many of them in the very last years of his long life. He handled competently the usual Latin lyric forms, and the forms of the early Christian hymns. The most interesting of his few secular poems is an excellent poetic contribution to the celebration, in 1890, of the two-hundredth anniversary of the founding of the Arcadian Academy: in the course of this poem Leo bestows high praise on Metastasio, Parini, and Alfieri. His religious poems include hymns, prayers, admonitions, poems in honor of certain saints, poems addressed to contemporaries, memorials, and meditations on his own approaching death. The best known of all his poems is a noble Alcaic ode written on New Year's Eve, 1900 — the Pope being then ninety years of age — on the need for a spiritual renewal in the coming century. Within a short time after its publication it had been translated into a dozen languages: there are at least ten English versions, among them one by Andrew Lang, from which these stanzas are taken:

Renowned in letters, famed in art,
The Age recedes: of many a thing
Won for man's good from Nature's heart
Who will may sing.

The glories of the faded years
I rather backward glancing mourn —
The deeds ill done, the wrongs, the tears
Of the Age outworn. . . .

O blinded Pride on chaos hurled!
O Night proclaimed where Light should be!
Obey thou Him who rules the World,
Man, and be free! . . .

Sow Thou the seeds of happy Peace,
All Evil drive from us afar;
And bid the rage and tumult cease
Of hateful War. . . .

My course is run, long ninety years
Thy gifts are mine; Thy grace retain;
Let not Thy servant's prayers and tears
Be poured in vain.

CHAPTER 49

De Sanctis, Verga, and Other Writers

FRANCESCO DE SANCTIS (1817–1883), born at Morra Irpina (not far from Naples), had his serious schooling in Naples; and there, in the years from 1839 to 1848, he did his first teaching. He was primarily and always a teacher, widely read, independent in his judgments, enthusiastic, eager to stir responsiveness in his students and to guide them into moral maturity. He came to regard Shakespeare as the greatest of modern poets, and Hegel as the greatest of modern literary theorists; but though he learned gratefully from Hegel he criticized as he learned, and continued the gradual development of his own literary convictions.

He took part in the brief Neapolitan uprising of 1848; and at the end of 1850 his liberalism led to an imprisonment that lasted until 1853. On his release he was exiled, and made his way to Turin, where he did some teaching and wrote for newspapers and magazines.

From 1856 to 1860 he held an appointment as Professor of Italian Literature in the Polytechnic Institute of Zurich. In a characteristic opening lecture to his students he tells his prospective engineers that every one of them has a literary as well as a scientific vocation:

> For literature is not an artificial thing: it has its dwelling within you. Literature is the cultivation of knowledge, the enthusiasm of art, the love of what is noble, gentle, beautiful; and it educates you . . . to the use and the ennoblement of your mind through the exaltation of all generous ideas. . . . Literature is not an ornament externally applied . . . it is your very self: it is the internal sense that everyone has of what is noble and beautiful, the sense that makes you recoil from any base or brutal action, and sets before you an ideal perfection that every well-born spirit strives to approach.

In the course of this same lecture he states the essence of his aesthetic theory, as it then lay in his mind:

> What matters is that once the concept is determined, the expression should correspond to the concept: the aesthetic value of a work proceeds not from the idea, but from its manifestation.

Finding that his Swiss associates were inclined to depreciate Petrarch, he rose to a discriminating defense in a series of public lectures on the *Canzoniere*, given in the year 1858–59, and published with little change, under the title *Saggio critico sul Petrarca*, in 1869. This "essay" is not without immaturities, but it is rich in insights. Its best pages are those in which De Sanctis devotes himself to the detailed aesthetic exposition of the poems that he felt to be most perfect.

The events of 1860 made it possible for him to return to Naples. In the following year he was elected as a member of the first Italian parliament, and made Minister of Education in the first Italian cabinet. From this time on he was frequently involved in governmental duties, chiefly in the field of education — though he spoke his mind freely on other matters of national concern.

From 1871 to 1877 he served as Professor of Comparative Literature in the University of Naples. He had now reached his final conclusions as to the essential nature of poetry. Earlier critics had concerned themselves with formal matters and had failed to realize the importance of the idea, while more recent critics had overstressed the importance of the idea. De Sanctis, in agreement with Hegel, but more decisively than Hegel, holds that the idea and the mode of its expression arise simultaneously in the mind of the poet, and are in truth inseparable:

> the essence of art lies in form — not form as dress or veil or mirror or what not, but form into which the idea has already entered . . . herein lies the organic unity of art. . . . That which lives, in poetry, with an immortal life, is [in this sense] its form.

Art as thus conceived constitutes its own autonomous world. That world, however, is far from constituting the whole human world, or even the whole world of the poet:

> The poet, to be sure, is not merely a poet, but a man, a citizen, a person concerned with philosophy and with religion, and he is responsible for what he writes — but on grounds that are extrinsic to art.

De Sanctis, however, though he felt the values of social integrity even more deeply than he felt the values of art, never grappled with the problem of the role to be played by art in the weaving of the whole social fabric.

The individual artist and the individual work of art have also, in his thought, their own particular autonomies, and are to be judged by the critic not on the basis of any preconceived or general rules or notions, but through a reliving of the creative experience of the artist:

> The critic may prepare himself for his criticism by long study . . . but the certainty of view through which he can distinguish that which is essential and vital in a poem can be reached only in the glow of a clear and immediate impression. . . . After that first fervor has subsided, the critic, if he is skilled in philosophic reflection, may address these questions to the [particular] poetic world that he has now before him in its verity and its integrity: what are you? and who and what is he who made you? . . . Perfect criticism is that in which these differing moments [the moments of impression and of reflection] are reconciled in a harmonious synthesis.

The process thus outlined is in fact the process by which De Sanctis prepared himself to set forth his interpretations and his judgments. Most of his critical writings are gathered in two volumes entitled *Saggi critici* and *Nuovi saggi critici*, the first published in 1865, the second in 1872. These collections contain, chiefly, essays on individual writers — Guicciardini, Meli, Parini, Foscolo, Schiller, Hugo, Zola — on groups of poems or particular poems by other writers — Monti, Manzoni, Leopardi, Prati — or on particular cantos of the *Divine Comedy*. These are essays that one may read and reread with deep gratitude. They do enable one to relive poetic experience and to understand and to feel, more fully than one could otherwise feel and understand, the poet's fused idea and mode of expression; they do transmit into the veins of one's own life the energy that had pulsed in the poet's own vitality; and they do qualify one for a readier independent penetration into other poetic experience, vision, and life.

In a long essay on Zola, De Sanctis — partly because of his reaction against pre-Hegelian idealism, and partly because of his constant delight in what seemed to him to be truly alive — welcomes literary realism, which marks, he thinks, a progressive step, a step away from unrealities spun by the imagining mind, a step toward a more complete envisagement of life. But he does not consider realism as a sufficient end in itself. Neither idealism nor realism is sufficient:

> Just as the ideal is empty and abstract unless accompanied by a keen consciousness of the real, so your realism will remain stupid and insipid unless you have a keen consciousness of the ideal.

Realism represents a transitional phase of thought:

> Humanity gains resurgence through new ideals, better realized, more conformable to nature and to thought, having even a scientific and a naturalistic basis. In the real one feels a desire for ideals that have been lost and a tendency to try to recover them. The ideal rises again: but in such measure and with such limitations as are imposed upon it by a more mature and more fully educated intelligence and by a better understanding of reality.

The greatest work of De Sanctis is his *Storia della letteratura italiana*, published in 1870 and 1871. It is indeed a history of Italian literature, but it is, even more than that, a history of the early strength, the decline and fall, and the resurgence of the Italian spirit as reflected in Italian literature. De Sanctis' dominant purpose is to render Italy, through an understanding of her moral past, the better able and the more resolute to build her moral future. This preoccupation leads him to explore with a special eagerness the work of those writers — notably Machiavelli — whose attitudes and ideas and practices seem to him to be most revealingly indicative of general conditions and of general trends.

The *Storia* is not a book for the novice: it is philosophic rather than informative; it is not always well grounded in fact; its verdicts, explicit or implicit, are not always just; its generalizations are not all acceptable. But for serious students of Italian literature the *Storia* will remain a treasury of the interpretations and the judgments of one of the finest of modern critical minds. It is based upon a thorough knowledge of the works examined; and it abounds in effective comparisons, contrasts, and perceptions of continuity, of discontinuity, and of transition. Here also, as in the *Saggi*, there are admirable aesthetic expositions of particular passages of verse and prose. And the *Storia* is in itself a work of art, filled with a life that is life both of thought and of expression: thought that is always fresh, untiring, and honorable; expression that is always personal, persuasive, and often memorably brilliant.

In the last year of his life De Sanctis returned to the question of realism and idealism in a Note written for inclusion in a second edition of the *Saggio critico sul Petrarca*. Realism, he says, has now gone too far, and is dismissing idealism as a metaphysical antique. So De Sanctis, who had never scorned the ideal even when he welcomed realism, now scorns the realistic form, and defends idealism. The ideal, as substance, is a complex of ideas and principles — beauty, justice, truth, family, fatherland, glory, heroism, virtue — that have been acquired by humanity in the course of its long evolution; and only one who feels himself to be a beast rather than a man can deride such ideals, or fail to take account of them, or act in opposition to them. The ideal as expression consists in the representation of things according to their repercussion in the mind, together with the impressions and the sentiments therewith involved; and those who through fear of offending reality set before you things in their naked crudity, as they appear to the imbecile, have neither the feeling nor the understanding of nature. Yet the ideal may become blameworthy if it leads to distortion, or forgets that individuals are individuals and not types:

> The whole question is one of measure, and there is no need to slay either the

real or the ideal, which in the last analysis are both phases of what is living, of life. Create for me things that have life — and baptize them as you will.

* * *

The turn from romanticism to realism in Italian fiction came with the work of two Sicilian friends, Giovanni Verga and Luigi Capuana. Verga (1840–1922) was born and grew up in Catania. His father had also a country home in the mountainous region south of the city, and in summers spent there the young Verga gained an intimate acquaintance with the ways of peasant speech and peasant life. Before he was well out of boyhood he had determined to be a novelist; and by the time he was twenty-five he had written three insipid historical novels and a somewhat more promising melodramatic novel of contemporary life.

Realizing that he needed to establish himself in a literary environment, he went in 1865 to live in Florence. Five years spent there gave him valuable experience, and opportunity for the completion of his *Storia di una capinera*, "Story of a Linnet," a pathetic and still popular short novel. In 1870 he moved to Milan, where he maintained living quarters until 1885, though his returns to Sicily were frequent and sometimes prolonged. In 1873 he published two novels, *Eva* and *Tigre reale*, "Royal Tigress," both of them melodramatic stories in which he depicts the unprincipled search for pleasure that marked the fashionable society in which he moved. In his preface to *Eva* he speaks with sarcasm of the blindness and cruelty of that sociey; but he writes of it as an observing artist, not as a social reformer.

In the following year he published a short story entitled *Nedda*, the first of the many realistic tales of Sicilian peasants or fisherfolk in which his genius was to find its most natural and most distinctive expression. No two human worlds could be more different than the heedlessly luxurious world of which he had been writing and the stark world of Sicilian poverty. But this Sicilian world had its own strivings, its own miseries, its own simplicities, its own violences, its own codes, its own resignation, and its own coloring; and with all its pitifully elemental endurance it was far more profoundly human than the distant world of artificial splendor.

From 1874 on he wrote now of one world and now of the other; but nothing that he ever wrote of his northern world compares in human significance or in artistic power with the finest of his Sicilian short stories or with his two great Sicilian novels. In these narratives, as in his Milanese novels, he writes as an observer rather than a reformer; but in place of the sarcasm of the preface to *Eva* there is here a deep immanent sympathy that is all the more powerful for being unexpressed.

The style of the Sicilian stories is determined by their content, and is, like that content, a new thing. The persons of the stories are Sicilian peasants or fisherfolk; the stories consist largely of words spoken; and these words are set down in an Italian that echoes the Sicilian dialect in its phrasing, in its cadences, and in its laconic simplicity. This echoing extends even into the portions of the stories that are not in direct discourse. The very structure of the stories is laconic: there is no intervention of the author, and there is virtually no formal narration or description. Persons are not introduced: they simply appear and speak and act, and one learns who and what they are as the story unfolds. Events are reported, sometimes almost parenthetically, with no more fullness than is necessary for the establishment of causation. Such a style is inherently tragic in its intensity: it is at the same time poetic in its selectivity, its vitality, and its cadences, and in its conveyance of a sense of brooding sympathy.

Among Verga's several statements of his conception of realism are these two (the first from the preface of a short story, *L'amante di Gramigna*, the second from the preface to *I Malavoglia*):

> I believe that the novel — the most complete and the most human of all works of art — will attain its triumph when . . . the harmony of its forms will be so perfect, the sincerity of its realism so evident, and its method and procedure so inevitable, that the hand of the artist will remain absolutely unseen, and the novel will have the character of an actual event, and the work of art will seem to have made itself, to have arisen and matured spontaneously, as if it were a natural phenomenon, without retaining any point of contact with its author . . . [who, like a great sculptor] will have had the courage to eclipse himself and disappear into his undying work.

> The observer of this spectacle [the spectacle of certain phases of human life] has no right to judge it: the best he can do is to withdraw himself from the field of human striving long enough to study it dispassionately, and to render the scene clearly, with its true colors, in such a way as to represent reality as it has actually existed, or would seem necessarily to have existed.

But Verga elsewhere makes it clear that the artistic process, for him, is not one of merely photographic transference, but one in which the mind of the artist, while stimulated by reality, is constantly active, though its activity is to be hidden from the reader. And it remains true — though Verga never admits it — that while the artist, in theory, is to observe and not to judge, and is finally to disappear, Verga's own stories are suffused with the underlying compassion he would not state. His realism — though certainly confirmed by acquaintance with French realism — is in essence the natural form of his own response to the insistent reality of the regional life that he knew best.

Nedda, in the story that bears her name, is a *vinta*, a woman defeated by a life in which she never had a chance to escape defeat. She has to leave her dying mother untended in order to earn in hardship the few *soldi* that are needed to provide their meagre subsistence. Her betrothed, exhausted by his toil, dies in an accident resulting from his exhaustion, leaving her to a forgivable motherhood that her village does not forgive. But no summary can fairly suggest the quality of this or of any of Verga's other Sicilian narratives, for no summary can convey their atmospheres of light and darkness, of heat and cold, their conflicting motivations, or the inevitability of the sequences of misfortune that lead so often to catastrophe.

During the six years that followed the publication of *Nedda*, Verga, though he wrote other short stories and a minor novel, was primarily concerned with the gradual development of his greatest novel, *I Malavoglia*. It began as a draft of a short story, to be called *Padron 'Ntoni* — the *'Ntoni* being a Sicilian form for Antonio, the *Padron* indicating that 'Ntoni owned and sailed his own fishing boat. But the story grew and grew as Verga's imagination busied itself more and more with 'Ntoni's family and the surrounding community, and with a long succession of possible events; and before it was done it had become not only a novel, but the first of a projected series of five novels, to be called *I vinti*, "The Defeated." The idea of the series, presumably suggested or confirmed by knowledge of the early volumes of Zola's Rougon-Macquart series, is, as stated in the preface to *I Malavoglia*, that the movement of the great stream of human life, deriving from "the vague desire of the unknown, the sense that one is not well off, or that one might be better off," carries along in its course individual lives which, though they contribute in some small measure to the total movement, are themselves destined to be cast, defeated, upon the shore. The five novels of the series were to represent the struggle for the maintenance or the expansion of life under five different sets of circumstances. In *I Malavoglia* the struggle is merely for the satisfaction of the primal needs. The intended character of the four novels that were to follow is stated thus:

> These needs being satisfied, the struggle takes the form of a desire for wealth, and will be incarnated in a bourgeois type, *Mastro-don Gesualdo*, framed in the still restricted picture of a small provincial city . . . Then it will become aristocratic vanity in the *Duchessa de Leyra*; and ambition in the *Onorevole Scipioni*, to culminate in the *Uomo di lusso*, who combines in himself all these desires, all these vanities, all these ambitions . . .

I Malavoglia was published in 1881 and *Mastro-don Gesualdo* in 1888; but the other three novels (except for a brief fragment of the *Duchessa de Leyra*) were never written.

The scene of *I Malavoglia* is the fishing village of Aci Trezza, north of Catania. The Malavoglia own their little home "by the medlar tree" and the fishing boat *Provvidenza*, which is the source of their scanty earnings. Padron 'Ntoni is the head of the family. His son Bastiano, "who had a heart as big as the sea and as good as the mercy of God" and Bastiano's good wife

Maruzza have five children: 'Ntoni, able enough, and well-meaning, but a reluctant worker, and of no inner strength; Luca, who is his father all over again; Mena, called "Sant' Agata" because of her gentle domesticity; Alessi, a stout-hearted small boy; and the baby Lia. Many other persons, of all sorts and humble conditions, share in the intimate and crowded life of the village. Grievous trouble comes to the Malavoglia first when 'Ntoni is called away for his military service, and next when, fish being scarce, Padron 'Ntoni decides to eke out his earnings by a simple enterprise: he buys on credit a boat load of beans to be taken by Bastiano, in the *Provvidenza*, to be sold in a port up the coast. But Bastiano is drowned in a storm; and 'Ntoni, released from his military service, returns as a discontented idler. As the years pass misfortunes stemming from the disastrous enterprise or from 'Ntoni's weaknesses bring distress and shame to the family; and death comes to Luca in battle, to Maruzza in a cholera epidemic, and, near the end, to Padron 'Ntoni in a heartbroken old age. The home and the boat have both to be given up, and life becomes very hard indeed. Throughout the years the thwarted love of Mena and the carter Alfio runs with a quiet dignity. At last Alessi, persistent and undefeated, buys back the house by the medlar tree and marries the chosen companion of his childhood, and the family is renewed. 'Ntoni, having served out a long sentence, comes home once, in the darkness: he is given food, and told that he may stay if he will, but he knows that he has no right to stay, and after renewing every sight within and around the house goes on alone into the night. With such materials Verga builds a world that seems to be a world of life indeed, a world into which one is drawn as a hoping and a sorrowing participant, a world which, held in memory, deepens continually one's perception of unfamiliar values, one's understanding of life, and one's own compassion.

During the years in which Verga was writing and rewriting *I Malavoglia* he published three other books: *Eros*, a novel of the same general character as *Eva* and *Tigre reale*; *Primavera e altri racconti*, a collection of a few negligible short stories; and a collection of realistic Sicilian short stories published in 1880 under the title *Vita dei campi*, "Life of the Fields," but called *Cavalleria rusticana ed altre novelle* in some of the later reprints. Some of the stories included in this collection are masterpieces — among them the rightly famous *Cavalleria rusticana*. The life depicted in these *novelle* is a primitive life of endless toil and endurance, a clinging sense of the home, slow thought, naïve faith, strong passions, and swift vengeance. The prevailing style is as starkly objective as that of *I Malavoglia*. *Jeli il pastore*, "Jeli the Herdsman," the longest of these stories, opens and continues for many pages as an unspoiled, if realistic, idyll, its slowly developing sinister elements rising only at the end into an irresistible climactic fury. *Rosso Malpelo*, the most powerful story in the collection, tells of the good and evil impulses and the rudimentary fatalistic ideas of a lonely young miner, who carries on fiercely, to a haunting end, the occupation that had killed his father.

Not long after the publication of *I Malavoglia*, Verga began work on *Mastro-don Gesualdo*. Gesualdo Motta, in his boyhood a mere laborer, is bound that he will make himself rich, and he has the knack of doing so. By the time when the action begins, in a small Sicilian city, about 1820, Gesualdo, through all sorts of enterprises, has already acquired large possessions, farms, vineyards, groves, orchards, and ready wealth:

> He takes on anything in which there's money to be made . . . he's started dealing in wheat, has he? . . . He has a try at everything, that devil. They say he's even going to bid for the lease of the public lands. . . . Do you know how much he's made building mills? . . . He's pulled himself up from nothing. I remember him when he was a hod carrier. . . He has a finger in every pie in the city.

When he had been only a master mason he had been called Mastro Gesualdo; when he had become a man of consequence he was addressed as Don Gesualdo: but those who thought of him as an upstart called him, behind his back — combining the two titles — Mastro-don Gesualdo. His rugged figure dominates the novel, which finds its unity not in the unfolding of a continuous plot but in the successive impacts of his will upon the life around him and of circumstances upon his will. He has no desire to set himself up as a gentleman or to be accepted by the gentry of the city as a social equal; but fate soon brings about his marriage to Bianca Trao, daughter of the proudest family of all, poverty-stricken in its decaying mansion. He can never change his peasant nature enough to understand his wife or to bring happiness to her, although he admires her and has for her a genuine affection, to which she, though often suffering, is able to make some timid response. As far as the gentry are concerned, his marriage results not in social acceptance, but in the development of jealousies and self-seeking schemes. He remains defiant in his still increasing financial power, though signs of trouble are beginning to appear. He is involved briefly in a local Carbonaro uprising. Years pass. There is a daughter now, Isabella, to whom Gesualdo is determined to give the best of everything: but costly convent education separates her from the longing mother whom she needs, and estranges her from her father. An epidemic of cholera brings out all that is best in Gesualdo, but plays havoc in one way or another with his interests and his hopes. Rapacious relatives and other claimants make inroads upon his wealth. Thanks to his provision of a large dowry, Isabella is married, reluctantly, to the Duke de Leyra, an extravagant nobleman of Palermo. Much of the property that Gesualdo has acquired during his long years of unremitting toil now melts away; Bianca dies; a revolutionary mob pillages his house; he is stricken with a ravaging disease. He goes to his daughter's palace in Palermo; there amid its luxuries and its formalities he is sadly out of place; there he is still besieged for financial concessions; there the ties between distressed father and distressed daughter become close at last; and there, utterly *vinto*, he dies.

Around him, throughout the novel, swirl the passions, the ambitions, and the rivalries of the intriguing gentry and the earthy resentment of the mass of peasants and laborers. The laconic intensity of *I Malavoglia* remains; but the range of imagination is greater than in the earlier novel, and the style is itself more ample and more varied. There is however some loss of structural unity. The portrayal of the human tragicomedy is in general severer here; but one feels, in certain cases, the persistence of an unspoken compassion. The realism of *Mastro-don Gesualdo* is so complete as to make most other realism seem trivial; but in the breadth and depth of its humanity it rises above the limits of any defining classification.

During the decade in which *Mastro-don Gesualdo* was written Verga wrote also another novel, many *novelle*, which he gathered in four collections, and dramatized forms of two *novelle*. The novel, *Il Marito di Elena*, "Helena's Husband," is the most mature of Verga's novels of sophisticated life. Two of the collections of short stories, *Novelle rusticane* and *Vagabondaggio*, are tales of Sicilian life. In 1883 Verga rewrote *Cavalleria rusticana* as a one-act play. Produced early in the following year (with Duse taking the part of Santuzza), it proved to be triumphantly successful on the stage; and it inaugurated the reign of realism in the Italian theater. As a work of art, however, the play is inferior to the story: the dialogue lacks the quasi-Sicilian tang of the original, the motivation is weakened, and the introduction of minor and unnecessary characters impairs the tense unity of the *novella*.* A little later Verga made also a dramatic version of one of his Milanese stories. After 1890 Verga wrote very little, and what he wrote bears witness to the fading of his once great powers.

* * *

Luigi Capuana (1839–1915), born in Mineo (not far from Catania), was one of the most active Italian men of letters of his day. His life paralleled that of Verga in so far as both men sought literary experience and fortune in Florence and Milan and returned often to their native Sicily. Much of the latter part of Capuana's life, however, was spent in Rome. He served at various times as critic for one periodical or another; and his critical essays and reviews, collected in half a dozen volumes, reflect the changing literary fashions of the last quarter of the century. At first a devotee of Balzac and Zola, he later outgrew their control; but he never outgrew his early reputation as

* The *libretto* for Mascagni's opera was written not by Verga but by two minor librettists. The prominence of the arias and choruses impairs the dramatic effect.

the Italian champion of realism. He published also six novels, some fifteen volumes of short stories, five volumes of plays in the Sicilian dialect, and four volumes of delightful fairy stories — the first entitled *C'era una volta*, "Once Upon a Time." The best of his novels and short stories have a Sicilian setting. Many of them are realistic, with a realism that tends to be pathological and quasi-scientific.

Edmondo de Amicis (1846–1908), born in Oneglia (on the Italian Riviera), was the most widely popular of the writers of the period. He served with distinction as an infantry officer in the war of 1866; and after the war he wrote for an army paper a series of sketches of military life, sentimental but skilfully descriptive, which were gathered, in 1868, in his first book, *La vita militare*. In 1872 he resigned his commission in order to devote himself to writing; and within the next few years, believing rightly that books of travel would give him an opportunity for the kind of writing he liked to do, he visited Spain, Holland, London, Morocco, Constantinople, and Paris, each of the six visits resulting in a volume or pair of volumes attractive in their clarity and their enthusiasm. In the middle eighties his interest turned to the field of education, and much of his writing, for the next ten years, was done in that field. He was sincerely concerned both to improve the quality, especially the moral quality, of education itself, and to impress his fellow countrymen with the importance and the needs of the educational effort. The first and best of his several books written with this motive was the extraordinarily successful *Cuore*, "Heart," intended for boys, and published in 1886. One of his later books, *Sull' oceano*, illustrates the hardships that beset emigrants to the Americas; and others seek to better the lot of Italian workers.

Pinocchio, liveliest of puppets, was the creation of the Florentine journalist Carlo Lorenzini (1826–1890), who took as pseudonym the name of the Tuscan village, Collodi, where he had spent much of his childhood. Many of his articles and *novelle*, generally humorous, are gathered in half a dozen volumes; but his reputation rests upon his gay and delightfully written stories for children, and chiefly upon *Le avventure di Pinocchio*, which was published in book form in 1883. The mischievous and wayward puppet, with his lie-lengthened, truth-shortened nose, has long since become familiar to children in many lands, along with his "father" Geppetto, the Cricket, the Fox, the Cat, the benevolent blue-haired fairy, the tempter Lucignolo, and the kilometric Sea-Monster. Featured in new media, he seems likely to remain a perennial source of juvenile pleasure.

* * *

In the work of Paolo Ferrari (1822–1889) Italian comedy found a merrier excellence than it had had since the days of Goldoni. In his native Modena and later in Milan he produced a swift series of comedies, generally successful in characterization and in dialogue, but often forced and confused in plot. Several were written originally in the dialect of Modena and later put into Italian. Many are Goldonian in spirit; a few renew Goldonian themes; and in one of the earliest Goldoni is himself the hero. This play, *Il Goldoni e le sue sedici commedie nuove*, written in 1851, is generally regarded as Ferrari's best comedy: its subject, as the title indicates, is that crisis in Goldoni's career which led him to pledge the writing of sixteen new comedies in a single year. The most completely comic of his comedies, written first in Modenese as *La medseina d' ónna ragaza amalèda* and later in Italian as *La medicina d'una ragazza malata*, tells of the troubles of the daughter of a touchy cabdriver and the son of a touchy clerk: the girl's illness is cured when the clerk at last consents to the proposed marriage. Several later plays, influenced by those of Augier and Dumas *fils*, deal with current social problems: here Ferrari is moralist as well as playwright, his moralism taking the form of a defense of the ruling conventions.

The Roman Pietro Cossa (1830–1884) did some teaching and held civic office; but from 1864 on he devoted himself mainly to the writing of historical dramas in verse. Most of his themes are Roman or Italian. His earlier plays followed the Alfierian model; but beginning, in 1871, with the *Nerone*, his best drama, he discarded the older conventions, proclaiming himself a realist: his realism, however, consists only in the reduction of his personages to common stature, and in the lavish use of types and accessories that he thought to be representative of the historical moment he was depicting. He called most of his plays comedies: in point of fact they show a free mingling of tragic and comic elements. With his effective choice of subjects and his sure instinct for dramatic effect he gave his audiences great pleasure; and the reader may still enjoy the *Nerone*, the *Cleopatra*, and the *Cola di Rienzo*.

CHAPTER 50

Pascoli and Other Poets

THE CLOSING YEARS of the nineteenth century and the opening years of the twentieth brought to Italy, in spite of many trials, a gradually increasing prosperity. In 1896 an Abyssinian adventure proved disastrous. A war with Turkey in 1911 and 1912 gave Libya to Italy.

Mascagni's *Cavalleria rusticana* was first performed in 1890, Leoncavallo's *I pagliacci* in 1892, and Puccini's *La Bohème*, the first of his several successes, in 1896. Marconi's first wireless transatlantic message sped from Newfoundland to Cornwall in 1901.

Gissing's impressions of Italy were gathered in his *By the Ionian Sea.* Marion Crawford lived most of his life in Italy, and wrote most of his novels there. Mark Twain took a Florentine villa for several months in 1892 and 1893, and returned to Florence for the Winter and Spring of 1903–1904. Italy was the favorite land of Woodberry's wanderings.

* * *

Giovanni Pascoli (1855–1912) was born in the village of San Mauro (not far from Rimini). Tenderhearted, sensitively responsive to all the life around him, he grew up in a simple home in which the parents and the several children were bound together by ties of the strongest affection; but before he was out of boyhood death had struck into his family six times, most terribly in the unsolved assassination of his father. In poverty and amid local turbulence Pascoli studied at the University of Bologna. Thereafter he taught, in the fields of Greek, Latin, and Italian literature, in various schools and universities: in 1905 he succeeded Carducci as Professor of Italian Literature at Bologna. Summers brought him back to the home he was finally able to buy at Castelvecchio, high in a valley among the Tuscan mountains.

He had begun to write poetry before 1880; but his first collection of poems was published only in 1891, under the title *Myricae*, "Tamarisks." This title, taken from a line in one of the eclogues of Virgil in which the "humble tamarisks" appear as symbolic of the humbler forms of rural poetry, is perfectly appropriate: Pascoli's "tamarisks" are the poems of a modest spirit, and they spring from his absorption in the simple country life he knew so well and from his fondness for all the elements of the low-lying landscapes of his youth. Groups of poems, or individual poems, have such titles as "In the Country," "Sunsets," "Trees and Flowers," "The Poplars," "The Hedge," "The River," "The Nest," "The Dog," "Snowfall," "The Old Peasant," "The Hearth Log," "Sewing," "Lullaby." Nothing was too small or too particular for him: he loved to observe minute distinctions of form or sound or action. Birds were not just birds to him: they were goldfinches or chaffinches or linnets or wrens or cuckoos or titmice or stonechats. Yet with all his perceptive and verbal exactitude he felt no sharpness of demarcation between human life and the teeming life of its environment: in his intuition, the human and the sub-human partook of the same nature and the same destiny. This sense of essential oneness led him at times to endue his quiet poems with a gently shimmering magic, and more often to infuse them with a deeply felt sense of the mystery of all life and of all death.

Many of his "tamarisks," like this "October Evening," are humble even in their brevity:

Lungo la strada vedi su la siepe
ridere a mazzi le vermiglie bacche:
nei campi arati tornano al presepe
tarde le vacche.

Vien per la strada un povero che il lento
passo tra foglie stridule trascina:
nei campi intuona una fanciulla al vento:
Fiore di spina!

Along the road you see the red berries laughing in clusters on the hedge: in the plowed land the cows are coming gravely homeward to the manger.

Down the road comes a poor man who drags his slow step through the crackling leaves: in the fields a girl is singing to the wind: "Flower of the thorn!"

Arano, "They Are Plowing," offers a contrasting scene:

In the field — the vines shine red in their rows, and the morning mist steams upward from the thickets —

they are plowing: one, with slow shouts, drives the slow cows; another sows the seed; and one, with patient hoe, turns down the ridges;

and the knowing sparrow is glad in his heart, watching it all from the rough branches of the mulberry; the robin, too: in the hedges his slender golden song is heard.

Three other collections, *Poemetti* (1897: called *Primi poemetti* in its later and enlarged editions), *Canti di Castelvecchio* (1903), and *Nuovi poemetti* (1909), renew the themes and the moods of the *Myricae*; but their range is greater, their poems are in general more elaborate, an expansion of imagery results in the composition of a number of poems that are wholly symbolic, and the sense of the mystery of life and death becomes even more pervasive and more solemn. Contemplation of the double mystery leads Pascoli to the conclusion that men will find their greatest happiness in close and loyal companionship. He seems, however, to reach this conclusion rather through his need for comfort than through intellectual conquest: his attitude toward life is one of shadowed resignation rather than of transforming energy.

Many of the poems of these three collections are memorable. In *Suor Virginia* a gentle nun is summoned mysteriously to her serene entrance into the final mystery. In *Il libro* an ancient book (the book of the mystery) lies open upon a reading desk: an invisible reader (thought) turns its pages, vainly, again and again. *Il focolare*, "The Hearth," tells of wayfarers, old and young, unknown to each other, who on a wintry night, uncertain of their course, take refuge in an empty dwelling: the hearth is bare, but a kindly storyteller begins his tale, and gradually, as they listen,

> every eye discerns on the empty hearth the faint flickering of a spark. Around the empty hearth, little by little, they cease to tremble or lament: they are warm; and it is not fire that warms them, but their sweet being together.

Un ricordo, "A Memory," recalls with extraordinary vividness the events and the emotions of the day on which Pascoli's father met his death. *La mia sera*, "My Evening," is a poem of calm after storm, of the remembered peace of being sung to sleep, and of the last anticipated quietness.

The poems contained in the five other collections made or planned by Pascoli himself are in general works of deliberate construction rather than results of compelling poetic impression. The narrative poems gathered in the *Poemi conviviali* (1904) treat perennial themes thoughtfully and imaginatively in classic and early Christian settings. In the *Odi e inni* (1906), dedicated to those who are youthful in years or in spirit, Pascoli seeks to celebrate and to stimulate worthy achievement. As their titles indicate, the three late collections, *Canzoni di Re Enzio* (1908), *Poemi italici* (1911), and *Poemi del Risorgimento* (published posthumously), are filled with evocations of persons and events of the Italian past. The poems contained in *Poesie varie*, a supplementary collection made after Pascoli's death, are for the most part of the earlier and simpler types. The most notable group, entitled *Piccolo vangelo*, "A Little Gospel," opens with a Nativity, follows Jesus in his teaching, and ends with a rendering of the scene in which he takes the children into his arms and blesses them — though Peter protests, and Judas warns him that one of the children is the son of the robber Barabbas.

Pascoli's many translations include excellent versions of Shelley's *Time Long Past*, of Tennyson's *Ulysses*, and of Wordsworth's *We Are Seven*, a poem that appealed to Pascoli very deeply because of the sorrowful losses of his own childhood.

Pascoli departs from the Italian lyric tradition not only in the profusion of his images and in his deliberate symbolism, but also in his language, in his rhythms and tonalities, and in his stanzaic forms. His predilection for the humble and his desire for minute precision, together with a linguist's pleasure in linguistic rarities, led him greatly to enlarge the Italian poetic vocabulary. Local terms and childish words are used freely; objects of many kinds are referred to with technical accuracy; dialects and the jargon of returned emigrants make occasional appearances; unfamiliar archaic words are imported for special purposes. Bird songs and twitterings are rendered just as Pascoli heard them: *scilp*, *vitt . . . videvitt*, *dib dib bilp bilp*, *virb*, *cu cu*, *chiù*. His phrasing follows the patterns of ordinary speech in its simplicities, its repetitions, its pauses, and its incompletenesses. Much of his verse could be written as prose, but as a prose of subtle delicacy. His rhythms are often unconventional. With patient artistry in the choice and the interweaving of his words, he achieves results in pure sound that contribute directly to the conveyance of mood and are in themselves novel and sometimes richly musical. He wrote freely in the familiar forms, but he wrote with equal freedom in forms of his own successful devising. These new characters and qualities made a very deep impression on younger poets: it is indeed in the poetry of Pascoli that the stream of the more recent Italian lyric takes its rise.

Latin was for Pascoli a language almost as natural as Italian, and he wrote verse in Latin as readily as in Italian. D'Annunzio called him the greatest Latin poet since the Augustan age: he is at least one of the greatest. In most of his major Latin poems his thorough knowledge of ancient and early Christian Rome serves as background for narratives, of his own invention, which are filled with imaginative life. Those most frequently republished are a group known as the *Carmina christiana*. In the earliest of the poems of this group the centurion of the Crucifixion, returned to Rome, is beset by boys begging for stories of conquest, but tells them instead of four times when he saw and heard One whom he saw last upon the Cross. In every year from 1891 to 1911 Pascoli entered one or more of his Latin poems in the annual *Certamen poeticum hoeufftianum*, and in thirteen of these years he won the highest award.*

In *Il fanciullino*, "The Child," the most delightful of his several essays, Pascoli, discussing the nature and the value of poetry, identifies Plato's "child" (the childlike spirit of which some trace survives in adult life) with

* The Dutch scholar Jacob Hoeufft (1756–1843) left to the institution that is now the Amsterdam Academy of Sciences a fund the income of which is used annually for prizes for the best Latin poems submitted for consideration.

the poetic spirit, the spirit that illumines and purifies. Pascoli himself never ceased to be, at heart, a child.

Gabriele d'Annunzio (1863–1938) was born in Pescara, on the Adriatic coast, in the province of the Abruzzi. The centers of his literary activity were first Rome, from 1881 to 1891; then Naples for a year; then the Abruzzi until 1898; then Settignano (near Florence) until 1910; and then Arcachon (near Bordeaux) until 1915. He was writing verse by the time he was ten; and throughout his life, though he wrote extensively also in the fields of fiction and the drama, he remained primarily a poet.

His first collection of poems was published, under the Latin title *Primo vere*, "In Early Spring," while he was still in school. These earliest poems are largely imitative, the dominant influence being that of Carducci: some of them are *odi barbare*. With all their immaturities they show certain characteristics that were to mark most of D'Annunzio's poetry: great linguistic and metrical facility (later to develop into an opulent virtuosity); an overloading with classic allusions; a remarkable gift for vivid description; and, most of all, an unlimited *joie de vivre*.

In almost every year for the next dozen years D'Annunzio published a new or largely new collection of verse. The first volume to bring him fame was the *Canto novo* (1882): it has been called "an explosion of colors, of lights, and of Wagnerian sonorities." One of its quieter poems, an impression of the setting of the new moon, opens with this quatrain:

O sickle of moonlight declining
That shinest o'er waters deserted,
O sickle of silver, what harvest of visions
Is waving down here, thy mild lustre beneath! *

In the *Intermezzo di rime* (1883) D'Annunzio plunges with a hectic abandon into the excesses of decadentism. The "Prelude" reads in part:

As from corrupted flesh the over-bold
Young vines in dense luxuriance rankly grow,
And strange weird plants their horrid buds unfold
O'er the foul rotting of a corpse below . . .

E'en so within my heart malignant flowers
Of verse swell forth . . .

By the time of the publication of this volume D'Annunzio, through his luxurious extravagances, his ultrasophisticated aestheticism, his overt shamelessness, and his unquestionable brilliance, had attained a histrionic prominence that he continually cultivated, and never lost.

Decadentism and a somewhat recondite aestheticism prevail in *Isaotta*

* This translation and the next are by G. A. Greene.

Guttadauro (1886), which contains, however, some pleasantly pictorial poems. The collection called *Elegie romane* (1892) gathers D'Annunzio's impressions of contemporary Rome. In the *Odi navali* (also of 1892) he begins to blow the imperial trumpet: he loved the sea and ships; he was convinced of the importance of the sea in international conflict; and he had become a propagandist for Italian naval armament. The *Poema paradisiaco*, "A Poem of Gardens" (1893), breathes in a few of its poems a momentarily redemptive longing for the home and the surrounding family love of his boyhood. His most concentrated song of joy, an alcaic ode contained in the definitive edition (1896) of the *Canto novo*, opens thus:

> Sing of joy! I would surround you with all flowers, so that you may sing of joy, of joy, of joy, the magnificent giver!
>
> Sing of the unbounded joy of living, of being strong, of being young, of biting the fruits of earth with sound white hungry teeth . . .

Between 1893 and 1900 he had written rather less verse than formerly: his only wholly new volume of verse was published in 1899 with the resounding title *Laudi del cielo del mare della terra e degli eroi*, "Praises of the Sky, of the Sea, of the Earth, and of Heroes." This collection proved to be the first form of D'Annunzio's most ambitious undertaking: the *Laudi* were to be expanded — retaining their original title — into a series of seven Books, each bearing the name of one of the Pleiades. Of the seven proposed Books, however, only four were completed: *Maia* (1903), subtitled *Laus vitae*; *Electra* and *Alcyone* (1904); and *Merope* (1912). They constitute an exuberant celebration of the joys of life as D'Annunzio felt them — joy in the perception of beauty in the actual world and in the worlds of art and poetry and legend, joy in vivid experiences of sense, joy in exciting and, at the best, heroic action. But D'Annunzio's joy is utterly self-centered, even dictatorial; and he appears to be insensitive to the joys of thought and of spirit.

In *Alcyone*, highly perfected in its artistry, all that is best in D'Annunzio comes to fulfillment. With four dithyrambs serving as its main structural elements, it gathers poems, many of them of great beauty, that renew the myriad sensations of a Tuscan summer — colors, melodies, silences, fragrances, tastes, dawns, burning noontides, starlit evenings, harvests, voices of crickets, of nightingales, of the rain, of brooks, and of the sea.

In 1882 the young D'Annunzio published a volume of short stories; and from that time on the writing of fiction served as a prose accompaniment to his writing of poetry. In his short stories — other volumes appeared in 1884 and 1886, and a final collection, *Le novelle della Pescara*, containing some old and some new stories, in 1902 — he tried to do for the peasant life of his native Abruzzi what Verga had done for the peasant life of Sicily. In sheer descriptive skill he excels Verga, and his most vivid stories, once read, are hardly to be forgotten; but his persons have no richness of individual life, and his realism, often barbaric, is unrelieved by any breath of compassion or any touch of humor.

His first novel, *Il piacere*, "Pleasure," published in 1889, was followed, before the end of the century, by five other novels, and in 1910 by a final novel, *Forse che sì, forse che no*, "Perhaps So, Perhaps Not." The Nietzschean *Trionfo della morte*, which gains from its setting in the Abruzzi, is D'Annunzio's most substantial fictional achievement. His novels as a whole, while descriptively brilliant, are weak in plot and in characterization — D'Annunzio himself, in one or another incarnation, is their single autonomous personage. Most of them are set in an atmosphere of social corruption. There is little joy in them: typically, the search for pleasure ends in tragedy.

To tragedy itself D'Annunzio turned in 1898, with the writing of *La città morta*, "The Dead City"; and from that time until 1914 almost every year brought a new play, in Italian or in French. His flair for the spectacular stood him in good stead in his writing for the theater; but he lacked the greater dramatic gifts. *La figlia di Iorio* stands out from among the other plays both because of its general dramatic excellence and because of its skillful use of exotic Abruzzian customs and superstitions. *Francesca da Rimini*, a weak play, won temporary favor as a lavish recasting of the Dantean story.

After the outbreak of the first World War, D'Annunzio urged, ardently and effectively, the entrance of Italy upon the side of the Allies; and when Italy did enter the war he at once enlisted, as a naval lieutenant. He played his part valiantly and brilliantly in operations on the Adriatic, in flights over enemy territory, and in expeditions on land. In 1919, when it seemed clear that Fiume would not be awarded to Italy, he with three hundred followers took possession of the city, overriding the orders of the representative of the Interallied Commission. He remained in Fiume as dictator until January 1921, when he withdrew in order to save the city from attack by the Italian forces that had surrounded it. From that time on until his death he made his home in a luxurious villa on the shore of Lake Garda.

During the war years and while he was in Fiume he published orations, messages, pamphlets, poems, and narratives dealing with political and military subjects; and after his retirement he published four or five volumes of reminiscences.

Arturo Graf (1848–1913), son of a German father and an Italian mother, was born in Athens. After a studious youth spent partly in Rumania and partly in Naples he found literary work and a teaching position in Rome. In 1876 he was appointed to a professorship of Romance Literature in the University of Turin: this position he held for the rest of his life.

He was profoundly concerned with the problem of human destiny. His immersion in positivist philosophy and the uncompromising honesty of his own thought left in him the tragic conviction that human life was without purpose or significance — a conviction tempered, somewhat, by a softening sense of mystery, by a poetic perception of fancied images, and by a poetic urge to find rhythmic expression for his own meditations and emotions. He renewed, in some measure, the experiences of Leopardi — with less inspiration, but with a firmer grounding in philosophy and science. His poetry is necessarily somber, and it has the qualities of a steel engraving rather than those of a painting. Yet it has a fine dignity, except when it subsides to the level of the macabre; its landscapes, though austere, are often beautiful; its imagery is often striking; and the verse has a minor music of its own.

He had written and published verse even in his boyhood; but his first important collection of poems, *Medusa*, appeared only in 1880: the Medusa of the title represents the inexorable face that life seemed to turn to him. His recurring symbol for the frustration of humanity, the figure of a ship that can find no haven, is developed most impressively in a poem called *Il vascello fantasma*, "The Phantom Frigate." Over a silent leaden sea there sails a great black ship, with a Medusa as its figurehead and a black banner at its stern, its crew aloft, emaciated, pallid, and ancient:

> The captain, with his hundred mariners, searches the sky and gazes over the ocean wastes, looking in vain for a harbor, a harbor prayed for but never attained. Thus the great vessel sails and wanders; and if at times a cloud on the horizon seems to be a mountain, there rises a breathless and a weary cry, "Land, land, land!"

In three succeeding lyric collections the clouds of Graf's pessimism lighten from time to time, and the mood of rebellion gives way to resignation, or even to resolution, as in the spirited *L'ale*, "Wings," a fine development of the idea that "the spirit of man was born with wings, and soars like an eagle." In his last volume of lyrics, *Le rime della Selva* (the *Selva* is the Black Forest, which Graf often visited), the clouds part now and then, and shafts of hopefulness shine through.

The *Poemetti drammatici* (1905) tell stories of Christ, Dante, Faust, Don Juan, and other figures of history and legend. In *La resurrezione di Lazaro* Lazarus asks:

> Master, why hast Thou wakened me? Sleep was so sweet; so sweet oblivion!

But Christ replies sternly:

> Hast thou yet merited rest and peace? Hast thou with firm faith, with serene constancy, spent all the love that a heart can hold? Hast labored enough? Hast thought enough? . . .
>
> I come to summon you to light, to life, to tasks that increase strength, to refining toil. Oh slothful spirit, timid spirit, rise from thy tomb, gird up thy loins, and walk!

Graf wrote also a few short stories, and a substantial but monotonous novel,

Il riscatto, "Redemption." In 1905 he published an essay entitled *Per una fede*, "Toward a Faith," in which, basing his thought on his sense of need for a "moral relationship" with the universe and on his gradually attained belief that there is something enduring and indestructible in the human spirit, he builds a free and undogmatic faith. For the youth of Italy he published (also in 1905), under the title *Ecce homo* (by which he meant: "This is Man"), a series of a thousand aphorisms and a few parables, designed to encourage and strengthen young men and women in their first conflicts with the sorrows and doubts and evils of life. The long preface, deeply felt, is a noble valedictory.

* * *

Two poets, the Roman Cesare Pascarella (1858–1940) and the Neapolitan Salvatore di Giacomo (1860–1934), chose to write in their own dialects.

Pascarella, like his Roman predecessor Belli, presents in sonnet form, and in the words of men or women of the Roman people, a vivid succession of Roman scenes, comic or tragic or comic and tragic at the same time. In *Villa Gloria*, the first of his two famous sonnet sequences, a veteran of the Risorgimento tells the story of the ill-fated attempt of a band of seventy young patriots, in 1867, to wrest Rome from papal control. There is no humor here: the tale is one of amazing valor and readiness to die for love of Italy. It is told as by an untutored survivor; and to that fact it owes an immediate authenticity that gives a special quality to its truly epic power. There is epic power also in the fifty sonnets of the second sequence, *La scoperta de l'America*, but in this case humor pervades the poem. It is again a man of the people who tells the story, this time to a tavern group that interrupts now and then with its questions and comments and thirsts. Columbus and King and Queen and savages all speak, naturally, the Roman dialect. Columbus says to the King:

> Io avrebbe l'intenzione,
> Si lei m'ajuta, de scoprì' l'America —

> What I mean to do,
> If you will help me, is to discover America.

When America has been reached, and the first native appears,

> "Ah quell' omo!" je fecero, "chi sête?"
> "Eh," fece, "chi ho da esse'? So' un servaggio." —

> "Oh you there!" they said to him, "who are you?"
> "Why," said he, "who should I be? I'm a savage."

But the humor serves not to impair but rather to enhance the realization of the persevering certainty, the delays, the unfailing courage, the ocean endurances, the faltering of crews, the supreme excitement of the sight of land, the brilliant return, and the cruel ingratitudes that marked an achievement proudly claimed, in the concluding sonnets, as a truly Italian exploit.

The poems of di Giacomo, written at various times from about 1880 to about 1915, are of many kinds, in theme, in form, and in mood. The most striking, but not the best, are realistic scenes of poverty-stricken and passionate low life, presented with swift and excited dialogue. Thus the twenty sonnets of *'O fúnneco verde*, "The Green Alley," bring momentarily onto the stage some of the swarms of men and women who live in a foul slum; and *A San Francisco* tells a fierce story of vengeance carried out within prison walls. But di Giacomo was by nature more inclined to sentiment than to realism, and in the majority of his poems sentiment prevails — though it is often touched with realism, is sometimes imbued with tragedy, and occasionally has recourse to the supernatural. His longest poem, *'O munasterio*, "The Monastery," is the story of a jilted sailor who becomes a Franciscan monk, but is beset by memories, longings, doubts, and fears. One night, in his cell, he starts to sing:

La luna nova 'ncopp' a lu mare
stenne na fascia d'argiento fino,
dint' a la varca lu marenare
quase s'addorme c' 'a rezza nzino —

The new moon over the sea casts a band of fine silver; in the boat the sailor is all but asleep, holding his net.

But he is interrupted by a friar who bids him be silent, since no such song, but only prayer, is fitting in the house of God. Di Giacomo's best poetry is to be found in some of the quieter stanzas of *'O munasterio*, and, more plentifully, in many wonderfully musical poems in which the themes are the lyric themes of all ages. Among the best of all are *Pianefforte 'e notte*, "Piano at Night," in which the poet, at his window, hears distant music come sighing through the darkness, gazes at the wonder of the sky, and lingers at the window, as in enchantment, after the music has ceased; and *Pusilleco*, in which the beauty of moonlight on the Bay spreads a mysterious spell over Posilipo. It is indeed moonlight rather than sunlight that illumines the poetry of di Giacomo.

In the same years in which he was writing his poems di Giacomo wrote some fifty *novelle* in Italian and a half a dozen plays in Neapolitan. Both the *novelle* and the plays are predominantly tragic; most of them have a Neapolitan setting; and many are realistic. Both before and after 1915 he wrote also, in Italian, numerous books and essays in the fields of Neapolitan history and description.

CHAPTER 51

Fogazzaro and Other Writers

ANTONIO FOGAZZARO (1842–1911) was born in Vicenza, and most of his outwardly uneventful life was spent there, or in a summer home at Oria, on the northern shore of the Lake of Lugano, at the point where the Valsolda, a beautiful mountain valley, comes down to the lake. High-minded by nature, and of a gentle disposition, he was deeply influenced by the teaching of Giacomo Zanella, who gave a somewhat modernistic direction to the boy's religious beliefs. In his youth Fogazzaro thought of devoting himself to a musical career; but his parents disapproved, and he came to recognize the insufficiency of his own talent: music therefore remained for him a constant personal resource. He was active in public affairs, and was made a Senator in 1900.

His belated literary activity began with the writing of poetry. In 1874 he published *Miranda*, a brief and sentimentally tragic romance in blank verse, and two years later, under the title *Valsolda*, a collection of pleasant lyrics, descriptive and meditative, suggested by the sights and sounds and imagined presences of his mountain valley and his mountain lake.

It was not until 1881 that Fogazzaro proved himself, with the publication of *Malombra*, to be a novelist. Inexpert in construction, and still dark with the shadows of a misty, even occult, romanticism, *Malombra* is marked nevertheless by many of the qualities that were to persist in the later novels and give them their strength and distinction. Fogazzaro is a novelist of character rather than of plot. Some of his leading characters are of a fine and sustained nobility; others suffer from perpetual conflicts between their weaknesses and their idealisms. His major characters are surrounded by a whole world of minor figures, creations of his own mind, but drawn on the basis of the keenest observation, and, in many cases, with a delicious humor that serves to lighten the central seriousness, a humor expressed in description, in dialogue, and in cleverly contrived incident — a humor gayer and more energetic than that of Manzoni, something like that of Dickens, but truer and more restrained. His characters are so much alive that they will not leave his imagination: some of them insist on reappearing from book to book. Throughout Fogazzaro's work there is evidence of his preoccupation with religious problems; the sounds of music are heard frequently; and elements of the environment reflect and deepen moods, and at times become virtually participants in the action.

In *Daniele Cortis* (1885), more firmly constructed and freer from romantic turbidness, the hero, torn between his idealism and his weakness, tries ineffectually to carry his idealism into politics: the heroine, Elena, has a richer vitality. Major and minor characters are more closely linked; and certain intermediate characters — Daniele's perplexing mother and Elena's staunchly loyal uncle — are realized most successfully. *Il mistero del poeta*, "The Poet's Mystery" (1888), a much simpler love story, has a lyric quality that becomes dramatic and very moving in the denouement, in which happiness at last attained vanishes in sudden tragedy.

Piccolo mondo antico, "A Little World of Former Time" (1895), is generally accepted as Fogazzaro's masterpiece, and as one of the greatest of Italian novels. The Lake of Lugano and its northern villages provide the setting; and the story runs through the years from 1850 to 1860, the years of the final struggle with Austria. The hero, Franco Maironi, himself a patriot, is the son of a grim and imperious pro-Austrian marchioness. In opposition to her will he has married a village girl, Luisa Rigey: the marchioness disowns him, and Franco and Luisa go to live in Oria. Franco is deeply religious, but lacking in energy; Luisa, full of energy, has a strong sense of what is right and just, but no faith. Franco leaves to take his part in the national struggle. In his absence Luisa, discovering that the marchioness thinks she has disinherited Franco, but has in reality failed to do so, plans to confront her with the evidence of her cruelty and her failure; but at the very moment when they meet cries call Luisa back to her house, where she finds that her idolized little daughter Maria — one of the most appealing of the children of fiction — has been drowned, in a disaster that might not have occurred had Luisa not been so bent upon her errand of vengeance. The pages that tell of her desperate grief and of the unsuccessful efforts of a doctor, friendly women, a kinsman, and priests to bring her some respite are, in their kind, unmatched. For a very long time she remains despondent; but at last her husband's love and faith prevail.

Fogazzaro was convinced that religion, being conditioned by the limitations and the acquisitions of the human mind, is necessarily a changing thing; that in addition to its inmost and permanent verities it has at any given time temporary vestures of creed and of form that are properly subject to modification or to rejection in favor of new vestures; and in particular that true religion and true science cannot be irreconcilable. Fully aware that the development and the championship of convictions such as these involve conflicts both within the individual and between individuals, he chose such conflicts as the general themes of his three last novels: *Piccolo mondo moderno* (1900), *Il santo*, "The Saint" (1905), and *Leila* (1910). They form a series with *Piccolo mondo antico*: the hero of *Piccolo mondo moderno* and *Il santo* is Piero Maironi, the son of Franco and Luisa; the hero of *Leila* is a disciple of Piero.

In *Piccolo mondo moderno*, Piero, religious in spirit but weak and impulsive, is torn between his religious loyalties and his love for Jeanne Dessalle, a woman of refined charm and of strong will, who is quite without religious faith. They are held apart both by legal barriers and by their fundamental religious difference. Vicenza serves as the scene of most of the action, and local politics and other local interests afford an often humorous background. Among the intermediate characters are a prankish musician, and a worthy priest, Don Giuseppe Flores, to whom Piero turns for counsel. At the end Piero disappears, leaving with Don Giuseppe a sealed account of a vision that has led him finally to respond to the call of religion. In *Il santo*, Piero, who has renounced his former world and has taken the name Benedetto, reappears as an ascetic lay evangelist, ministering selflessly to bodily and intellectual and spiritual needs, and possessed by a fervent desire for the regeneration of the Church from within. Jeanne seeks to win him back to an ordinary way of life: failing in that effort she does all she can to protect him from exhaustion and from intriguing hostility; and she is with him at the moment of his death. Fictionally, the finest scenes of the novel are those that bring Benedetto and Jeanne together. The religious interest culminates in a scene in which Benedetto, granted a private interview in the Vatican, urges the Pope to free the Church from four evil spirits that beset it: the spirit of falsehood, the spirit of clerical domination, the spirit of avarice, and the spirit of immobility. In the novel, the Pope's reply is inconclusive: actually, *Il santo* was placed upon the Index. Five years later *Leila*, milder both in its romance and in its doctrine, received the same official condemnation.

Fogazzaro published also two collections of admirable short stories; three good short plays; and four substantial volumes of essays and addresses.

One of the best novels of the period is the *Demetrio Pianelli* of the Milanese Emilio De Marchi (1851–1901), whose other novels seem to be fading, perhaps undeservedly, from memory. In his moral and literary ideals he resembles his far greater Milanese predecessor, Manzoni; but his vision of the world lacks the breadth of Manzoni's, and Manzoni's serenity is replaced by a sense of exhausting conflicts and pitilessly thwarting circumstances. His scenes are contemporary, not historical. His plentiful humor is more mirthful that Manzoni's. In *Demetrio Pianelli* (1888) the monotonous life of a government clerk becomes dramatic through contact with tragedy, through love, and through sacrifice — his simple heroism giving him a consciousness of a kind of triumph "that God does not grant to the strong or the fortunate" — and then subsides into a resignation in which a certain lingering sweetness weaves a consoling pattern.

Renato Fucini (1843–1921) was born in Monterotondo (a small town not far from Pisa), studied agriculture and engineering in the University of Pisa, and served for a few years as an assistant city engineer in Florence. Full of fun, and expert in the Pisan dialect, he amused his cronies by reading to them swiftly written humorous sonnets in that dialect. The fame of these sonnets spread rapidly; and in 1872 he published a hundred of them, using the anagrammatic pseudonym Neri Tanfucio. Most of them are cleverly composed bits of Pisan chatter, featuring ingenuities, and dealing with many phases of Pisan life: there are sonnets on politics, gas, learning to ride a bicycle, taxes, the lottery, the aurora borealis, soldiering, the police, the courts, a sleight-of-hand man, a saint's figure that moves its eyes, a play, fishermen, a doctor and a loquacious patient, the Camposanto, and the Leaning Tower.

When Florence ceased to be the capital of Italy, Fucini lost his city position; and for thirty years and more he lived chiefly in rural Tuscany — as an inspector of schools in the country around Pistoia, on his farm at Empoli, or at a villa near Leghorn. During these years nearly all of his writing was done in Italian prose. In 1877 he spent a month in Naples, where he wrote a series of remarkably vivid letters which were published in the following year under the title *Napoli a occhio nudo*, "Naples to the Naked Eye."

In 1884 he published his best known book — a collection of short stories, entitled *Le veglie di Neri*, "Evenings with Neri" (the word *veglia*, which in general means an evening gathering, designates in this case a quiet gathering in which stories are told). The stories are all of rural Tuscany — they are Tuscan in setting, Tuscan in customs, Tuscan in the freshness of their speech. Most of them, instead of continuing the merriment of the majority of the sonnets, deal with hardships and tragedies such as those that came to Fucini's knowledge in the years in which he was constantly traversing the Tuscan countryside, and with the response, usually courageous, made by humble hearts to the siege of privation and suffering. A few of the stories of the *Veglie*, however, are wholly or mainly humorous; and one is a grateful portrait of Fucini's father, a hard-pressed and devoted country doctor.

In a second collection, *All'aria aperta*, "In the Open Air" (1897), while shadows darken some of the stories, a hearty, even a hilarious humor prevails: this is indeed the best modern Italian collection of humorous *novelle*. Three stories find their fun in the prides and jealousies of little Tuscan towns. In *Il monumento*, for instance, three public-spirited citizens agree that their town needs a monument, preferably equestrian; dissension arises as to the person to be honored; great plans are made for the raising of funds; the total amount subscribed is thirty-five *lire*, the idea of the horse is given up, then the idea of a mere statue, and then the idea of buying a left-over bust of Garibaldi; the committee members vote to spend the thirty-five *lire* on a dinner for themselves, and send their order to the inn; and word comes back that they can't have all that for thirty-five *lire!* A third and smaller collection of stories, *Nella campagna toscana* (1908), is less noteworthy. Fucini's other writings include books for children and two collections of delightful anecdotic reminiscences.

Alfredo Oriani (1852–1909), born in Faenza, lived the life of a proud hermit in his Apennine villa, writing an incessant series of novels, plays, and critical, social, historical and political books and articles, and suffering from the indifference with which they were received. After his death, and in particular after the advent of Fascism, of which he came to be regarded as a prophet, that indifference gave place to extremes of admiration, which seem now to be yielding to more judicious estimates. He was primarily a thinker, greatly influenced by Hegel, wide in his range and keenly intuitive, but overconfident of his own powers, restless, and at times self-contradictory and inconclusive. Of his many books, those that seem most likely to survive are one novel, *La disfatta*, "The Defeat" (1896), and three historico-political works. Although the main persons of *La disfatta* — a scholar, the girl whom he loves and marries, and members of the diplomatic world — have their own distinctive individualities, the ideas that crowd the novel are at least as much alive. The scholar seeks persistently and in vain a faith that he can hold in intellectual honor: his defeat consists in his failure to participate fully in the onward movement of life. *Fino a Dogali*, "Even to Dogali" (1889: Dogali was the scene of the first major Italian disaster in Africa), contains remarkable historical passages, one of them a majestic evocation of the throngs of human beings who over three thousand years have traveled the Via Emilia, the great Roman highway that leads toward Bologna over the plains and under the shadow of the Apennines. *La lotta politica in Italia* (1892: *lotta* means "struggle") has as its amply developed theme the slow emergence of the concept and at last the actuality of Italian unity: united Italy was, for Oriani, a land of destiny, and of a destiny not yet fulfilled. *Rivolta ideale*, his culminating work, condemns spiritual poverty, and exalts idealism. Though his meditations have found no answers for the fundamental problems of life, though the human spirit is still a mystery, and though he foresees no diminution in the volume of human grief, he does foresee the possibility of greater human freedom. In his concluding "Appeal" he writes:

> [Those who are truly strong] create a faith, give nature a design and history a mission . . . Only through the ideal, even if it be only a phantom within a mirage, does life possess beauty. . . Light your torches then, and have no fear of their smoke in the darkness; for in the night the onward march has already begun, and the dawn is near.

* * *

Giuseppe Giacosa (1847–1906), the leading Italian playwright of the period, was born in Colleretto, in the mountains of Piedmont. His writing was done chiefly in Turin until 1888, and thereafter in Milan: he returned, when he could, to his beloved mountain valley. His first two successful plays, *Una partita a scacchi*, "A Game of Chess" (1872), and *Il trionfo d'amore* (1875), are slight but graceful romantic idylls in verse, set in the Middle Ages and in the Valle d'Aosta. They were followed by a few light comedies, of which *Acquazzoni in montagna*, "Mountain Showers" (1876), is perhaps the best. *Il fratello d'armi*, "The Brother-in-Arms" (1877), and *Il conte rosso* (1880) are again romantic plays in verse, both set in the Middle Ages and mainly in the Alps of Piedmont and Savoy; but the gentle charm of the early idylls is replaced, in these later plays, by a strenuous vigor in character and in action, and they show a great advance in dramatic imagination and resourcefulness. Each of the two plays rises to a dramatic climax. The Red Count is an historical figure; and the play of which he is the hero has historical substance and patriotic overtones.

Just before writing *Il conte rosso* Giacosa had tried his hand at a serious drama of modern social life, and while he continued for a time to write occasional comedies, he now devoted himself mainly to the writing of dramas of this type; and with *Tristi amori*, "Hapless Loves," first performed in 1888, he emerged at last as a master of the modern social drama. In this and in his two most important later plays, *Come le foglie*, "As the Leaves Fall" (1900), and *Il più forte*, "The Stronger" (1904), he takes besetting modern problems as his themes, dramatizing them as the readily possible experiences of readily possible persons. To his new task Giacosa, as dramatist, brings a faithful care in the observation of all relevant matters, great and small, together with a high degree of skill in selective emphasis, in dialogue, and in the use of incidental humor; and as a practical moralist he expresses his own healthy common sense, without preachment and without profundity. In *Tristi amori*, woven of the strains and stresses of modern life, the problem is that of the relations of a husband, deserving and perfectly trustful, but too busy in his effort to "get ahead," and his wife, who has lost her love for him and is sorely tempted to yield to the call of illicit romance. When the crisis comes she resists, deciding to remain in her home for the sake of her daughter. Her husband, brokenhearted, will work with her for the benefit of their child, but cannot forgive. His culminating words are: "Things like this have no ending: they just drag on hopelessly."

In 1891 Giacosa turned aside from his social dramas to write for Sarah Bernhardt a romantic play in French verse, *La dame de Challant*, set in sixteenth-century Lombardy. This play, of no great merit, was first produced in New York: Giacosa came over to superintend the rehearsals. In collaboration with Luigi Illica, Giacosa wrote the *libretti* for Puccini's *La Bohème*, *Tosca*, and *Madama Butterfly*. He wrote also, and gathered in two volumes, many good stories and historical and descriptive essays concerning Piedmontese mountains and valleys and castles; and he published as well his *Impressioni d'America.*

The first two plays of the Venetian Giacinto Gallina (1852–1897), pretentious and conventional comedies in Italian written before he was twenty, met with no success; but an enterprising theater manager saw possibilities in the young man — then a cellist in a theater orchestra — and asked him to write a play in the Venetian dialect. This he did, reluctantly — and found his perfect medium. In order to prepare himself for this new venture he studied, to good effect, the comedies of Goldoni; and his own first play in the Venetian dialect, *Le barufe in famegia*, "Family Quarrels" (1872), was an instantly successful free modernization of Goldoni's *La famiglia dell'antiquario.* For the next seven years Gallina was constantly writing Venetian comedies, Goldonian in their vivacious humor, but quite his own in plot and character. The setting is in every case the Venice of Gallina's day, a Venice in which, while the perennial charm remained, old and cherished ways were passing and new ways were coming in. Most of the plays of these years are thoroughly delightful. They are not trivial, and their sunshine is varied with shadow — but the sunshine still prevails. Best of them all, perhaps, is *I oci del cuor*, "The Eyes of the Heart" (1879): the protagonist, Teresa, is an old lady wonderfully courageous and cheerful in her blindness.

For several years in the eighties Gallina was overcome by despondency and illness. When he resumed activity his plays showed increased maturity, increased subtlety, and increased power; but they showed also that his courage and faith had been severely shaken. His last plays, though still comedies, are serious, vigorous, and psychologically realistic plays of personal and social conflict: they have moments of sunshine, but more of shadow. His particular object of attack is the corrupting power of money, which seems to him to have become, as he calls it in one of his titles, *La base de tuto*, "The Basis of Everything." But his dealings with that power, which manifests itself in differing circumstances and in differing combinations with other forces, still leave him room for ample dramatic variation.

At the time of his death Gallina was working on a play called *Senza bussola*, "Without Compass": he had finished the first act, and he left many pages of fragmentary notes for his own use. The hero is astray because he refuses to accept as "compass" the belief that money is everything. What the development of the plot would have been we cannot tell; but among the notes are sentences that have this meaning:

> The future will belong to men of good will, to those who have faith in what is true. . . But it will be necessary for them to renounce their own interests, and to take up their cross and defend it with the light and the courage of love.

CHAPTER 52

Writers of the Twentieth Century

IN THE COURSE of the first half of our own century Italy endured two world wars and an intervening dictatorship: yet Italian literary productivity did not diminish. Under Fascism, however, little writing was done, even in the field of fiction, that could be regarded as injurious to the regime. Among the writers of the half century Pirandello and Croce have enjoyed the greatest prominence hitherto; but the historical perspective that could alone make possible sound critical estimates of these two men and of their contemporaries does not yet exist.

Italian-English literary relationships remained close: Joyce (who once taught in Trieste, and while there wrote articles in competent Italian) made extraordinary uses of the name and the ideas of Vico; Joyce, Wilde, and Shaw were very well known in Italy; and Pirandello and Croce were very well known in England. Italian-American literary relationships became closer than they had ever been before. Certain Italian writers, voluntary exiles, made their home in this country, and played their parts well in American educational and public life. Others spent a few months or a year or two in America, and thereafter published their impressions of the nation that had welcomed them. Italian critics wrote books or essays on American authors; and some of the younger Italian novelists felt the influence of Faulkner, Hemingway, and Steinbeck. After 1945 the vogue of translations of contemporary Italian novels became very great in America, and the vogue of translations of contemporary American plays became very great in Italy.

* * *

Luigi Pirandello (1867–1936) was born in Girgenti: thus he shared the Sicilian inheritance of Verga and Capuana. Determined to be a writer, he studied for a time at the University of Rome, and then at Bonn. On his return to Italy in 1893 he established himself in Rome, where he became acquainted with several writers, Capuana among them. He devoted himself primarily to writing; but for some twenty-five years he supplemented his earnings by teaching in a Normal School. During much of this period life was very hard for him: his incessant writing, done often under conditions of extreme difficulty, was for him both a necessity and a means of escape. By 1921 he had won fame as a playwright; and in 1923 he visited Paris and New York to assist in the production of some of his plays. In 1925 he became both the financial supporter and the artistic director of a newly organized Roman theatrical company; and with that company he traveled widely, in the next three years, in Europe and in South America. He received the Nobel prize for literature in 1934.

His first book, published in 1889, was a collection of poems, and for several years thereafter he thought of himself primarily as a poet: his fifth and last collection of poems was published in 1912. His verse, however, is of little interest except in its manifestation of characteristics that were to mark his far more successful work in fiction and in the drama: a deep pessimism; a sense of humor that expresses itself in satire and in epigram; and a keen observation of "the curious course of the foolish lives of innumerable mortals."

In 1893, soon after Pirandello's return to Rome, Capuana advised him to try his hand at prose fiction, and Pirandello took the advice, with fortunate results. He began the writing of *novelle* at once; by 1922 he had written some two hundred, and had gathered them in several volumes; and in 1922 he decided to regroup them all, together with new stories, in a series to be called *Novelle per un anno*, which was to consist of twenty-four volumes, each containing fifteen stories. He continued the occasional writing of *novelle* as long as he lived; but of the projected twenty-four volumes only fifteen were completed and published.

Most of his *novelle* are stories of Sicilian peasant or petty bourgeois life; some are laid in Rome; only a few have other scenes (two are laid in New York and one in Brooklyn). They range in mood from broad comedy to macabre tragedy; but the mood of tragedy predominates. Pessimism, indeed, underlies all of Pirandello's work — a pessimism summed up, in the powerful *novella* entitled *La veglia*, "The Deathwatch," in these words, spoken by one victim to another: "I'm not suffering on my own account, or on your account. I'm suffering because life is what it is." His pessimism is shot through with a relentless humor, tending to the grotesque, which plays about all sorts of individual and social insufficiencies and absurdities, and appears insistently even in stories of suffering or squalor or injustice or sin or cruelty.

Problems concerning the nature of personality and of reality beset Pirandello, especially in the later *novelle*: problems of exhausted personality; problems of escape vainly attempted or achieved through illusion; problems of self-deceit; problems of experience in dream; problems of the survival of our earlier selves. The *novella* entitled *La tragedia di un personaggio* begins thus:

> I have long been in the habit of giving audience on Sunday mornings, from eight to one, to the characters of my future stories. . . I don't know why, but the people who flock to these audiences are usually exceedingly discontented, or afflicted with strange troubles, or involved in the most singular difficulties. . . I listen to them all patiently; I question them courteously; and I make note of their names, qualities, sentiments, and aspirations. . . It often happens that some of them are offended, even greatly offended, by my questioning, perhaps because it seems to them that I am disturbing the seriousness with which they have presented themselves to me. Patiently and courteously I try to show them that my questioning is not superfluous, because it's easy enough to want to be one kind of person or another, but it's something else to succeed in being what we want to be; and if we fail the effort can't help seeming useless and ridiculous.

Later in the same *novella* its main character, pleading with Pirandello to give him life, cries out:

> We are living creatures, more alive than those who breathe and wear clothes; perhaps less real, but more true! There are more ways than one of being born into life; and you know well that nature makes use of the instrument of human imagination to carry on its creative work.

Similar ideas appear in two other *novelle* (written in 1915), called *Colloqui coi personaggi*, "Conversations with Characters."

Pirandello's style is commonplace; but his powers of characterization and of invention are extraordinary. His plots propose situations which, though conceivable, are unique; and they come to endings that are almost always unexpected and often startling. A list of the *novelle* that are masterpieces in their kind would be very long indeed. It would certainly contain the hilarious *La giara*, in which a jar-mender, working from inside an enormous jar intended for the storage of olive oil — the jar-mender and the owner of the broken jar being both "originals" — finds himself caught in the jar when he has finished work, but comes off as victor in the ensuing contest of wills; the intensely tragic *La veglia*, already mentioned; *Alla zappa*, "To the Mattock," in which a peasant father who with the utmost pride and sacrifice has had his eldest son educated for the priesthood condemns that son, when he has proved unworthy, to the endurance of the unremitting earthiness of peasant toil; *Ciàula scopre la luna*, in which a laborer in a sulphur mine discovers the moon; and *La signora Frola e il signor Ponza, suo genero* (*genero* means "son-in-law"), in which townspeople seek in vain to discover the truth as to the mutual relations, the contradictory assertions, and the sanity of the members of a family of newcomers — and reach the conclusion that there isn't much practical difference between what is real and what is imaginary.

In 1893, the year in which Pirandello wrote his first *novella*, he wrote also his first novel (*L'esclusa*, "The Outcast"); and from time to time thereafter, but chiefly before 1915, he wrote six other novels. His great fictional ability, however, appears to better advantage in the tense brevity of his *novelle* than in the elaborateness of his longer narratives. The best known of his novels is *Il fu Mattia Pascal*, "The Late Mattia Pascal," written in 1904. Mattia, custodian of a useless library in a small North Italian town, is driven by financial troubles and constant family aggravations to seek escape. He disappears, wins a small fortune at Monte Carlo, and on his way homeward reads in a newspaper that the body of Mattia Pascal has been found in a millrace near his home and duly buried. He decides to accept his freedom, takes the name Adriano Meis, and rents a room in a tragicomic household in Rome. There the daughter of the family falls in love with him, and he with her; but he finds that his lack of a legal identity prevents the freedom he had thought to gain: he cannot marry, he cannot prosecute for theft, he cannot get the seconds he needs in order to fight a duel. There seems to be no way out of his difficulties except an apparent death. So, in the darkness of night, he leaves his hat and cane and a note on the parapet of a bridge over the Tiber, and disappears from Rome (the next day's newspapers carry an account of his suicide). He reverts to his true identity; and after his two years' absence he returns to his home town, where he lays a wreath on his grave and resumes his custodianship, but does not interfere with his wife's second marriage. The story is told very well indeed, with Pirandello's usual success in characterization. There is an undertone of concern with the problems of freedom, and the treatment of the Roman love affair is very gentle; but in the novel as a whole humor and sheer interest prevail.

Two volumes of essays, *Arte e scienza* and *L'umorismo*, both published in 1908, are in the main the fruits of Pirandello's teaching. In the essay from which the first of the two volumes takes it title Pirandello, writing as one convinced of the complexities both of human personality and of the process of artistic creation, protests vigorously and effectively against the oversimplification of the aesthetic theory of Croce (whose *Estetica* had appeared in 1902). The true basis for a science of aesthetics would be afforded by study of those relationships and laws that live in the instinct of the artist, relationships and laws to which art unconsciously but inevitably seeks to conform. Humor, as Pirandello defines it in the companion volume, "consists in the awareness of contrasts" — contrasts between life as it is and life as it ought to be, between the individual as he actually is and the individual as he thinks he is, or as he would like to be. Humor is like a two-faced statue one of whose faces laughs at the tears of the opposite face. But the laughter is not thoughtless or cruel: through that which is ridiculous the humorist sees that which is serious.

Pirandello wrote two plays in the years 1898 and 1899, and three in the years 1910–1913; but not until 1916 did he begin to write frequently for the theater. From that time on he was primarily a dramatist. More than half of his more than fifty plays are dramatized versions of *novelle* of his own; and in most of these versions the changes made in the recasting are slight: titles, plots, names, and a good many passages of dialogue reappear with little or no alteration. The dramatic versions in general lose a little of the excellence of the original narratives, through compression, in the case of one-act plays, or overexpansion, in the case of three-act plays, or concessions to theatrical effect. Much of the *novella* material that could not well be included in the dialogue of the plays is retained in stage directions as elaborate as those of Barrie and Shaw. Among the most successful instances of dramatization are the early *Lumìe di Sicilia*, "Sicilian Limes," based upon a *novella* of the same name, and *Così è (se vi pare)*, "So It Is (If You Think So)," based upon *La signora Frola*.

Pirandello's two most noted plays, however, and several of his other most distinctive plays, were written directly for the theater. The *dramatis personae* of *Sei personaggi in cerca d'autore*, "Six Characters in Search of an Author," include both the *personaggi* themselves and the members of a company of actors; but the *personaggi* are the significant figures. Among the characters who had long been pleading with Pirandello to give them life there had been six members of a tragic family — a Father, a Step-daughter, a Mother, a Son, and two younger stepchildren. They had haunted him; but he had not been able to grant their desire. Finally — so he imagines — they rebel; and, resolved to find life at other hands, they make their way into a theater in which actors are gathered for a rehearsal, and demand that the Manager become their "author" and give them the life they crave. The theme of the *Sei personaggi*, accordingly, comprises both the experience that has constituted the tragedy of the six characters themselves — an experience revealed, little by little, in the course of the play — and their effort to get the Manager and his company to give them the life they have been seeking in vain. That effort fails; and the *Sei personaggi*, therefore, while there is laughter on the stage, is doubly tragic. It is of great complexity: not only does Pirandello cause his two types of reality — the ordinary and impermanent type, represented by the Actors, and the artistic and eternal type, represented by the Characters — to confront and challenge each other, but the Characters themselves move on three different planes of artistic reality, the Father and the Stepdaughter being the most completely alive, then the Mother and the Son, and then the two younger stepchildren, who cannot speak, since they have already died. At several points, also, the Father (though quite within the logic of the play) voices Pirandello's recurrent ideas as to the nature of reality and of personality: the second passage quoted above from *La tragedia di un personaggio* reappears almost *verbatim* in a scene in which the Father pleads with the Manager. When the play was first performed, in Rome, in 1921, it was met with a wild mingling of applause and protest: its combination of novelty and of dramatic power soon won for it an international fame that it has never lost.

The tragic *Enrico IV*, "Henry the Fourth," is, in a very different way, as unusual as the *Sei personaggi*; and like that play and many of Pirandello's other plays it is concerned, fundamentally, with problems of personality and of reality. Twenty years before the action of the play begins, the hero had taken the part of the eleventh-century Emperor Henry IV in a pageant, in the course of which a rival had caused an accident that had resulted in the hero's going mad and believing that he was actually Henry IV. For his sake his family had given him such surroundings and such attendants as to foster his illusion. After some years he had recovered his sanity, but had kept his recovery to himself, pretending that he still thought himself to be Henry IV. Some years later a question as to whether he might not be curable had arisen; and he is visited by a medievally costumed group including a member of his family, a psychiatrist, the rival responsible for the accident, the woman in the case, and her daughter, who resembles her as she had been in her youth. Complications of action and of thought ensue. At the end, fearfully excited and infuriated, the hero kills his old rival, and then, terrified, realizes that he must now maintain for life his mask of madness.

Among the more remarkable of Pirandello's later plays are *Vestire gli ignudi*, "To Clothe the Naked," in which the heroine fails tragically to free herself from her past and to realize a desired personality; *Diana e la Tuda* (Tuda is a proper name), a tragedy scened in a sculptor's studio, with much aesthetic theorizing; *Lazzaro*, "Lazarus," an ethical myth; *Non si sa come*, "One Doesn't Know How," a Freudian tragedy; and *Quando si è qualcuno*, "When One is Somebody," a play with fantastic elements in which a poet, universally admired and publicly honored by his government, is forced by such admiration and honor into the maintenance of a frustrating statuesque perfection from which he tries vainly to escape.

* * *

The mood prevalent among the most characteristic younger poets of the early twentieth century was one of desolation. They had lost faith in life; their world was a world without compelling values and without dependable reality; and they lacked the energy to attempt renovation. The literary influences they felt most strongly were those of recent French poetry. Carducci's enthusiasms, D'Annunzio's rhetorical flamboyance, and Pascoli's sense of mission were alike repugnant to them: in Pascoli, however, they found a humility they could share — a humility that dealt with humble themes, in verse that was unpretentious, yet patiently woven of musical and mood-conveying sounds. The critic G. A. Borgese, contrasting them with their more radiant predecessors, called them *i crepuscolari*, "the twilight poets," and the name has found a general acceptance.

The Piedmontese Guido Gozzano (1883–1916) is the most restful interpreter of the twilight mood. His verse, limited in extent, is limpid, musical, and of a refined artistry. He is perplexed, but not distressed by his perplexity; conscious of a limiting fate, but resigned to an acceptance that is without probing or rebellion; and aware of a suffering humanity, but content, not without sympathy, to observe the persons and the experiences that come most immediately within his ken. He writes by preference, and often with much charm, of simple folk and of simple things: of children and of the people of Piedmontese hills and valleys, or of the knicknacks of an old parlor. Of himself he writes, as lying in a clover field and lulled by a children's ring-around song he wakes from semi-consciousness:

> Ma dunque esisto! O strano!
> vive tra il Tutto e il Niente
> questa cosa vivente
> detta guidogozzano! —

> But then I do exist! How strange! 'twixt All and Nothing there lives this living thing called "guidogozzano."

His longest and most memorable poem, *La signorina Felicita*, is a unique and very personal idyll, yearningly nostalgic and yet completely modern.

A dissatisfaction similar to that which produced the crepuscular mood in Gozzano and certain other poets led to a very different result in the case of the naturally rebellious Filippo Tommaso Marinetti (1876–1944), born in Egypt of a Piedmontese family. After the completion of his studies he established himself in Paris, although he called himself *invincibilmente italiano* and went often into Italy. In Paris, in the years 1902–1909, he wrote furious poems and other works in French; and there, in 1909, he and his companions issued their *Manifeste du futurisme*, which expressed a revolutionary attitude toward life and art in general, praising, in particular, speed, machines, and war. Among its pronouncements as to poetry are these:

> Courage, audacity, rebellion, are to be essential elements of our poetry.
>
> Literature hitherto has exalted pensive immobility, rapture, and sleep: we shall exalt aggressive movement, hectic sleeplessness, the quickstep, the somersault, the slap, the blow . . .

Later "technical" manifestoes were devoted to painting, sculpture, architecture, and other activities. The special manifesto for literature, issued in 1912, proclaims the autonomy of the word (*parole in libertà*), the abolition of syntax, and other similar "liberations." Futurist poetry seldom rose above absurdity. A long poem by Marinetti is entitled *Zang-tumb-tuuum*; and a collection of short poems by Ardengo Soffici (who, like some other able men, was attracted temporarily to Futurism), is entitled *Bif*§z+*18*. Futurism served to spur some less aberrant writers toward the attainment of a greater freedom than they might otherwise have sought. Its influence was mainly felt, however, not in literature but in art and music and in the stimulation of a baleful nationalism.

Other "isms" have appeared from time to time in more recent Italian poetry, but the effort of most of the poets active in the second quarter of the century was in the production of *poesia pura*. The phrase itself is of French origin; and the most obvious (though not the only) precedent for the type of poetry concerned is to be found in the work of Mallarmé and Valéry. In theory, the poet's objective is to give to an impression that seems to him to transcend common experience an expression that will render it with an utter immediacy. He builds with words that will serve, through their inherent emotional content, to suggest the nature of the impression; he abjures as unessential, and therefore unpardonable, everything that might merely decorate or explain; and he accepts only such metrical patterns as may seem to serve the expressive purpose. In practice, this "pure poetry" tends to be tense, living, and obscure: it is poetry of the elect and for the elect. Among the men who wrote this type of poetry Giuseppe Ungaretti (1888–1970) was, on the whole, the most generally esteemed: Eugenio Montale (1896–) and Salvatore Quasimodo (1901–1968) were its chief younger representatives.

* * *

The leading novelist of the earlier decades of the century was Grazia Deledda (1871–1936), through whose work her native Sardinia came for the first time into literary prominence. She began writing in her teens, and by 1900 had published several collections of *novelle* and several novels. In 1900 she married, and moved with her husband to Rome. Thereafter she published a dozen additional collections of *novelle*, and some twenty-five additional novels. In 1927 she received the Nobel prize for literature.

Most of her novels, and all of those that are generally regarded as the best, are Sardinian in setting, filled with memories of a beloved island still largely primitive in its occupations, its poverty, its beliefs, its customs, and its violences. She is therefore a regionalist, and in some degree a realist; but she is more concerned with the inner experiences of her characters than with their environment, and her realism is incidental rather than deliberate. She writes, with clear individual characterization, of Sardinian figures of many kinds — farmers, shepherds, servants, mountaineers, bandits, priests, beggars, madmen, aristocrats of fading fortune and authority, townsfolk struggling to maintain themselves in decency, or longing for a larger life. A typical portrait is that of an old shepherd:

> a gigantic old man, still strong and straight, with long yellowish hair and a thick gray beard; his face, all furrowed with wrinkles, seemed cast in bronze. He was majestic in his dark garments, over which he wore a sleeveless jacket of stained leather: he seemed a prehistoric man.

The mood of her earlier work is darkly pessimistic; but she moves gradually toward acceptance of the conditions of life, and in her latest work she emerges into tranquillity.

Among her most successful novels are *Elias Portolu*, in which the hero, returning from imprisonment for a deed of which he was innocent, falls through passion and weakness into a guilt that creates in him an intense and lasting grief from which no redemptive efforts enable him to escape; *Le colpe altrui*, "The Faults of Others," a novel of tragic perplexities, in which right and wrong seem inextricably mingled, and the conclusion, recognizing the inevitability of evil, consists in a plea for mutual forgiveness; and *La madre*, in which a young priest's bitter conflict between love and duty is the source of such unavailing efforts and such exhausting distress to his mother — the chief figure in the book — as to lead, at the moment of crisis, to her death.

Several impressive novels by men whose work in the field of fiction was not extensive were published shortly after the first World War. In the somber *Tre Croci* of Federigo Tozzi (1883–1920) of Siena, the "Three Crosses" are those that mark the graves of three brothers whose helplessness and lack of moral fiber in the face of trouble lead them into three varieties of catastrophe. The excellences of the book lie in its conveyance of a sense of fatality, in its narrative skill, and in the firmly engraved quality of the style. Tozzi's *Il podere*, "The Farm," is similar in mood and in the trend of the story; but the lonely hero, in this case, is not without warmth and tenderness, and there are passages in which the sights and sounds of farm life and of its environment in nature are finely rendered. Giuseppe Antonio Borgese (1882–1952), Sicilian by birth, cosmopolitan by experience, critic, professor, and, at the last, advocate of world unity, portrays in his *Rubè* the plight of an intellectually brilliant youth, aiming at greatness, who is tormented by a perpetual and pitiless self-analysis from which he can gain no release either through the ordinary relationships of life or through the excitements of the first World War.* The Triestine Ettore Schmitz (1861–1928), who wrote under the pen name Italo Svevo, won his only real success with *La coscienza di Zeno*, "The Confessions of Zeno." The story is in form a loosely constructed statement prepared by Zeno at the request of a psychiatrist: it is in fact a minute psychological analysis of the interplay of perpetually contradictory ideas and desires in the conscious and unconscious life of a man who habitually says the opposite of what he really thinks and does the opposite of what he really wants to do.

Riccardo Bacchelli (1891–), born in Bologna, wrote several historical novels, holding true to the Manzonian tradition in his serenity, in his humor, in his deeply interested and faithful scholarship, and in his strong stylistic conscience. His two best known books are *Il diavolo al Pontelungo*, "The Devil at Pontelungo," in which he brings to life a host of persons involved in a nineteenth-century Socialist effort, and the two-thousand page *Il mulino del Po*, "The Mill on the Po," in which, with an epic sense of destiny, he follows successive generations of a family — "as the river flows, as the years pass" — from the time of Napoleon to the end of the first World War.

Several able younger men were writing novels and *novelle* before 1950: among the most prominent were the Roman Alberto Moravia (1907–), a relentless realist, and the Piedmontese Cesare Pavese (1908–1950), whose work, much influenced by American novelists, shows a very personal mingling of realism, poetic feeling, and social sympathy.

* * *

In the immense and varied field of prose that is not primarily fictional or is not fictional at all the most indefatigable, the most assertive, and the most Protean writer of the half century was the Florentine Giovanni Papini (1881–1956). In the course of the fifty years he published more than fifty books, of many kinds, and from time to time he served as editor of one periodical or another. In 1903 dissatisfaction with things as they were led him and his friend Giuseppe Prezzolini to found a review to which they gave "the symbolic and auspicious name" *Leonardo*. In their first number they proclaimed themselves and their associates to be enthusiasts for freedom, universality of interest, and high intelligence in life, in thought, and in art; and during the four years of its existence the *Leonardo* did indeed stimulate vigorously the intellectual life of young Italy.

* Borgese came to the United States in 1931; became an American citizen in 1938; taught in various institutions of higher learning; wrote in excellent English his *Goliath*, a passionate narrative of the rise and the march of Fascism; and took a leading part in the preparation of later books looking toward effective world organization. He returned to Italy in 1948.

Papini's first book, *Crepuscolo dei filosofi*, "Twilight of the Philosophers" (1906), voices his bitter disappointment with the traditional philosophies. In the same year he published the first of four collections of *novelle*, in which his own experiences, especially his experiences in philosophic struggle, are the main sources of his invention. In 1912, being then thirty-one, he published his autobiographical *Un uomo finito*, "A Man Who Has Failed" — beautifully written memoirs of a Florentine childhood and youth dominated by an obsessive craving for certainty and for achievement, even for omniscience and for beneficent omnipotence.

Three volumes called *24 cervelli*, "Four and Twenty Minds," *Stroncature*, "Slashings," and *Testimonianze*, "Testimonies," each containing twenty-four essays, appeared in 1912, 1916, and 1918: these are perhaps the most thoroughly characteristic of all his works. In the preface to *24 cervelli* Papini writes:

> These essays deal with twenty-four men — poets, philosophers, imaginary beings, scientists, mystics, painters . . . Some of the essays are tributes of affection, some are slashings; some reveal neglected greatness, others demolish undeserved reputations. . . . [They] are for the most part impassioned, subjective, partial — lyric, in a sense — and *not* critical.

The men discussed are of many lands and many centuries, from the Taoist Kwang-Tze of the fourth century B.C. to Papini himself. His essays are, indeed, less than profound; but they express convictions, matured or sudden, that have been formed by a keen intelligence and by strong literary likings and dislikings. They are rich in incidental or more than incidental insights, they are full of surprises, and they often coruscate with wit.

During a temporary allegiance to Futurism, Papini founded, with Soffici and others, a new review, *Lacerba*, which lasted from 1913 to 1915. The next phase, for Papini, was one of poetry and of prose poems. A turn to religion, foreshadowed in some of his poems, resulted in 1921 in his most famous work, the *Storia di Cristo*. As in the case of each previous attainment of what, on discovery, he had regarded as certainty, he enters with all his energy into his new championship. The life of Christ is narrated with a highly personal ardor, and the familiar scenes of the Gospel are recreated with a vividness that is at times even too realistic. The new devotion is poured forth in proclamations, now poetic, now rhetorical, of the familiar Christian principles, or in violent invectives against those who reject and scorn them.

The most striking of Papini's many later works is his *Dante vivo*, "The Living Dante," published in 1933. Like his essays, it is impassioned and subjective. His living Dante is definitely his own Dante, and is not to be accepted as a complete or wholly accurate portrayal: but one who has already a good knowledge of Dante may gain much from the reading of this book. Many of its interpretations and appreciations are illuminating; but conjecture and paradox play too large a part. That which was purely human in Dante is overstressed: that which was divine is not adequately recognized.

Papini's steadier companion, Giuseppe Prezzolini (1882–), born in Perugia, rendered great service not only to Italian literature but to Italian culture in general through the review *La Voce*, which he founded in 1908. During the eight years of its existence it provided a forum for serious writing on many important subjects by many able men, but through all its variety one could hear the "voice" of Prezzolini himself, a voice of eminent good sense and of resolute uprightness, speaking firmly in a courageous and persistent effort to strengthen the intellectual, moral, and political life of his country. His own books include collections of excellent essays, a notable study of Croce, and a lively biography of Machiavelli.*

The Tuscan Ardengo Soffici (1879–1965), already mentioned as a temporary Futurist and as a co-founder, with Papini, of *Lacerba* — he wrote also for *La Voce* — was a painter as well as a writer, and in his writings he conveys to the reader most successfully the painter's joy in the perception of all the light and shadow and color and form that he sees in the world of nature and in the world of man. To read the scenes that constitute the volume he called *Arlecchino*, "Harlequin," is to walk with him in the Spring through the country around Florence, or to sit with him in a crowded tavern, or to look out of the window with him on endlessly varied sights seen on a journey by train from Florence to Paris:

> The magnificent rocky mountain, all gray, with clusters of cypresses here and there! I have seen it at sunset, in the Summer, all golden, and full of warm blue shadows.
>
> The straight ditches, full of water that reflects the sky; the brown sledges; men digging and ploughing amid the stubble, between rows of vines.
>
> A ravine with a white road winding along beside a torrent: in the distance, very tiny, a man and a woman walking behind a donkey laden with what seem to be two great baskets.
>
> Now the lake stretches out toward the mountains, dentate, livid, that bound it on the north. Beyond them one can begin to see snow-clad summits, and, in the sky, sleepy rose-colored clouds.

Other books, more meditative, are in the form of diaries; and one, *Kobilek*, preserves most vividly the sights and sounds that Soffici, as an infantry officer, saw and heard at his Alpine post during the first World War.

The Florentine Emilio Cecchi (1884–1966), journalist, essayist, and art critic, was also, in his youth, a frequent contributor to *La Voce*. His best writing is

* Prezzolini came to the United States in 1930 as Professor of Italian in Columbia University. Here his great "usefulness" — the quality he most sought and achieved — continued, both through his own writing (in English as well as in Italian) and through his completion of an enormous bibliographical repertory that is invaluable to students of Italian literature.

to be found in his *Pesci rossi*, "Goldfish" (1921), and *Corse al trotto*, "Trotting-Races" (1936). The essays in the first of these two volumes, clever in the Chestertonian manner, include an account of a call on Chesterton, essays on various English themes, and others that range far and wide among topics that may be slight or may be fundamental, but are treated always with a twinkling humor: differences between Orient and Occident; transformations wrought by snowfall; soldiers' songs; a country home; fragments of *Zang-tumb-tuuum* and other Futuristic productions discovered in the year 3009 and investigated with an academic owlishness; a visit to a zoo ("men of old, in order fully to recognize their status as human beings, compared themselves to the gods; modern men, applauding and congratulating themselves, compare themselves to the beasts"). The essays in *Corse al trotto* deal, in similar vein, with such matters as concerts, cats, pilgrimages, hairdressers, trapezists, and the sight of Saturn through a telescope. Cecchi — though his published impressions of America were unfavorable — was one of the main Italian interpreters of American literature.

* * *

In 1916 there was performed in Rome a play entitled *La maschera e il volto*, "The Mask and the Face," which its author, the southerner Luigi Chiarelli (1884–1947), called a *grottesco*. It was grotesque only in the extreme improbability of its plot and in that the hero is led to play a part that is at variance with his real nature. But the term *grottesco* caught theatrical fancy; and in the next few years several other playwrights, themselves classed as *grotteschi*, wrote plays that were much more definitely grotesque.

While their grotesquerie varies from author to author and from play to play, it proceeds in general from the assumption that life is itself grotesque; it relies heavily on the paradoxical and the fantastic; its characters are often abstractions rather than individuals, and include puppets, ghosts, skull-faced creatures, Death (in Alfredo Casella's "Death Takes a Holiday"), a mechanical man, and an all-green heroine; and personalities and sequences of events are presented in disorganized patches. In one of the most substantial of these plays, the tragic *L'uomo che incontrò se stesso*, "The Man Who Met Himself," by Luigi Antonelli (1882–1942), the forty-year-old hero meets his twenty-year-old self, but fails to prevent that youthful self from repeating the mistakes the older self had made.

The plays of the *grotteschi* were in general cerebral affairs, devoid of any depth of feeling; but strong emotion claims its place in the dramas of the Sicilian Piermaria Rosso di San Secondo (1887–1956), who, though "grotesque" in some respects, was not bound by the grotesque conventions. For him also life was meaningless; but he was haunted by a nostalgia for an unknown

Elysian world, and the human actuality seemed to him all the more tragic because of the impossibility of returning, in life, to that better world. The human actuality as he saw it was, moreover, a complex of passions and crimes. His characters are at the mercy of the primal forces that drive them on: they are accordingly puppets rather than individuals, abstractions who partake of human qualities that are distorted by their very isolation. In his best known play, *Marionette, che passione!* . . . , "Marionettes, What Passion! . . . ," the three essential characters, variously distressed, and brought together by merest chance, are not even named, but are referred to simply as The Lady with the Blue Fox Scarf, The Gentleman in Gray, and The Gentleman in Mourning. The Gentleman in Gray chooses escape by death: for the other two distress continues. Yet Rosso's plays, undisciplined in construction, failing often to realize the great dramatic possibilities of their themes, have a turbulence of invention that serves to give them a strangely grasping power, and in certain scenes they rise to surprising heights of dramatic impressiveness.

* * *

Benedetto Croce (1866–1952), born in a small town in the Abruzzi, was taken in his early childhood to Naples, and there all of his long life, except for a few interludes, chiefly Roman, was spent. His craving for mental occupation, his great love of books, and his Neapolitan surroundings led him first to a delving into Neapolitan history and to the writing of erudite studies in that field. He always enjoyed research, and felt that it afforded him an invaluable intellectual discipline. But after a few years he came to regard his Neapolitan studies as unduly narrow in scope, and he then determined to undertake the writing of history of a broader and deeper kind — a history covering all Italy and concerned primarily with the nation's sentiments and spiritual life. While he was patiently gathering material for such a work he thought more and more intently about the nature and function of history; and this thinking led him to write, in a single evening in 1893, an essay on history conceived as a form of art — his first venture into the field of philosophy. His general interest in historiography and his liking for literature aroused in him presently a special interest in literary historiography and criticism, and in 1894 he wrote a polemical essay on critical method and on the status of literary criticism in Italy. In the following year he engaged in the study of Marxism, which gave him a momentary faith in the possibility of social regeneration through labor (a faith quickly dispelled by his own critical analysis of Marxist theory), and a lasting awareness of the importance of the economic factor in human affairs.

Devoting himself definitely now to philosophy, he directed his attention first of all to the field that had the strongest natural appeal for him —

aesthetics. After a long period of the hardest kind of wrestling with aesthetic problems, he published, in 1902, his *Estetica come scienza dell'espressione e linguistica generale*, "Aesthetics as the Science of Expression and General Linguistics," the first of his major philosophical works. It is typical of all his philosophical writing in two important respects: while it rests upon a vast amount of reading, the thought is Croce's own thought, thought that cannot rightly be characterized by any adjective derived from the name of any earlier thinker; and the single phase of philosophy that is for the moment the object of special study is seen not in isolation but as closely interrelated with other phases. Furthermore — and this, also, proved to be characteristic of all Croce's work — the fact that he had once reached a formulation of his opinions did not prevent him from a continuous reëxamination of those opinions, a reëxamination that resulted often in new publications. His successive discussions of a given topic became in consequence more and more valuable, more and more completely and surely expressive of his maturing thought. This process of constant rethinking, in turn, led him not only to freedom from any feeling that he had reached an unassailable finality in any given field, but also to a new and liberating sense of the nature of truth, which he recognized as being not a treasure already complete and so hidden from men that they must exhaust themselves in a vain struggle to discover it, but as an endlessly growing treasure, to be created bit by bit through the perpetual effort of thinking men — an effort to which an individual man might gladly and serenely devote his whole energy, confident that whatever contributions he might make would have enduring value, either as he had made them, or as refined by the later work of other men. More and more, as his own work progressed, he looked forward, conscious of the long course of human life that lies ahead as well as of the long course of life that is already past.

With the completion of the *Estetica* Croce came to two new decisions: he would proceed to write companion works on other phases of philosophy; and he would supplement his theoretical works by particular applications of the principles he had set forth. In accordance with this latter decision he established, in 1903, a review, *La Critica*, which was to take as its province Italian literary and philosophical production since the mid-nineteenth century: Croce himself was to deal with literature, and his friend Giovanni Gentile with philosophy. The *Critica* was published uninterruptedly until 1944, and supplementary numbers appeared until 1951. Croce's essays on recent and contemporary Italian literature constitute an extraordinarily complete, searching, and luminous account of nearly a hundred years of Italian literary activity. He wrote in all more than a hundred such essays, which were eventually gathered in a series of volumes under the general title *La letteratura della nuova Italia*. Each essay is the result of an exemplary scholarly thoroughness in preparation and of Croce's own careful evaluation of the books he is considering. Among the most notable essays are those on Carducci, De Sanctis, Verga, Pascoli, D'Annunzio, and Fogazzaro. Croce's own writing, here and always, is of high literary quality, clear, firm, living, touched often with a wise humor, and eminently humane.

From 1903 to 1909 Croce was engaged also in the preparation of his projected treatises on phases of philosophy other than aesthetics. In the course of this preparation he studied with special care the work of Hegel, and published a book entitled *Ciò che è vivo e ciò che è morto della filosofia di Hegel*: discrimination between what he thought was living and what he thought was dead in the works he studied was a constant characteristic of Croce's procedure. He was strongly influenced by what seemed to him to be the living elements in Hegel, but his thought differed sharply from that of Hegel in certain central respects, and he refused to be classified as a Hegelian. He felt more closely akin to Vico, on whose philosophy he published a special study in 1911.

The treatises that rounded out his major philosophic effort, on "Logic as the Science of the Pure Concept," and on the "Philosophy of the Practical: Economics and Ethics," were both published in 1909. To his philosophy as a whole, covering the four fields of aesthetics, logic, economics, and ethics, Croce gave the name *Filosofia dello spirito*, its unifying idealistic force being the conviction that the world is solely and in very truth a manifestation of spirit.

Throughout the rest of his life Croce continued to reëxamine old conclusions — stating modified or divergent opinions in new works or in new editions of old works — and to write books on a large variety of particular topics, especially in the fields of historiography and criticism. To aesthetic theory he had returned in 1908 in a work on "Pure Intuition and the Lyric Character of Art"; he published a collection of discussions of "Problems in Aesthetics" in 1910, an "Aesthetic Breviary" in 1913, "New Essays in Aesthetics" in 1920, and a book on "Poetry and Non-Poetry" in 1923; for the fourteenth edition of the *Encyclopaedia Britannica*, issued in 1929, he wrote the long article on "Aesthetics"; and he published in 1933 a far-reaching study of "Popular Poetry and Art Poetry" and in 1936 a book entitled simply *La poesia*, which contains incisive discussions of special problems regarding the poet's creation, the reader's re-creation, and the critic's interpretation of poetry.

Croce's *Britannica* article, his simplest summary of his aesthetic theory, is intended to cover the whole field of art, and it does contain occasional references to painting, sculpture, architecture, and music; but it is in fact concerned almost entirely with poetry. His essential definition reads in part thus:

> The constant and necessary elements of a poem are a complex of images, and a feeling that animates them. Moreover . . . the feeling is altogether converted . . . into this complex of images . . . Hence poetry must be called neither feeling nor images, nor yet the sum of the two, but "contemplation of feeling" or "lyrical intuition" or . . . "pure intuition"—pure, that is, of all historical and critical reference to the reality or unreality of the images of which it is woven, and apprehending the pure throb of life in its ideality.

Other things, he says, may be found in poetry, but these other things are merely non-poetic interpolations or attachments. The basis of all poetry is human personality:

> [Feeling involves] the whole mind, with its past thoughts, volitions and actions, now thinking and desiring and suffering and rejoicing, travailing within itself. . . Those artists who embrace the creed of pure art or art for art's sake, and close their hearts to the troubles of life . . . are . . . wholly unproductive.

Intuition and expression are aspects of a single process: the poet cannot attain an intuition except by means of expressive terms or forms. Communication—the transmission of the intuition to the hearer or reader—is a subsequent affair. For Romantic theory and its continuants Croce has no sympathy. Romanticism as such is dead, but its soul, still living, consists in the tendency toward an immediate expression of passions and impressions:

> Hence it changed its name but went on living and working. It called itself "realism," "verism," "symbolism," "artistic style," "impressionism," "sensualism," "imagism," "decadentism," and nowadays, in its extreme forms, "expressionism" and "futurism." The very conception of art is attacked by these doctrines.

Croce reacts strongly against the form of artistic and literary history, originating in the Romantic period, that was still prevalent in his day:

> [That form] expounds the history of works of art as a function of the concepts and social needs of its various periods . . . This tends to obscure . . . the peculiar character of the individual work of art . . . In practice . . . this method is tempered by what may be called the "individualizing" method, which emphasizes the individual character of the works; but the mixture has all the defects of eclecticism. To escape this, there is nothing to do but consistently to develop individualizing history, and to treat works of art not in relation to social history but as each a world in itself.

In Croce's actual critical practice, while he never loses sight of the individual work of art, he often takes the individual author as his unit of consideration, and he sometimes deals with groups of authors.

From about 1920 on Croce wrote many essays on individual authors in addition to those treated in *La Critica*, as well as separate books on Goethe, Dante, and Carducci, and a single volume on Ariosto, Shakespeare, and Corneille. The least satisfactory of these works, perhaps, is *La poesia di Dante*, in which Croce seems to reduce the values of the *Divine Comedy* to those of selected lyric passages, thereby depreciating much that certainly enters into the greatness of the poem. Best of all, perhaps, is his volume on *Poesia antica e moderna*, which contains admirable essays on works of many ancient and modern writers, from Homer to Gerald Manley Hopkins. One of his many literary and scholarly diversions was the making of an Italian translation of Basile's Neapolitan *Pentamerone*.

Croce was made a Senator in 1910; and in 1920 and 1921 he served for a time as Minister of Public Instruction. On the advent of Fascism he was at first hopeful that it might bring corrective strength into a government that was greatly in need of such strength; but he soon found himself forced into decisive opposition, and it was he who in 1925 drew up, in reply to Gentile's "Manifesto of the Fascist Intellectuals," a scathing counter-manifesto. His hostility was reciprocated, but the Fascist regime never interfered with his writing. In 1937 the *New Republic* asked him to answer certain questions as to "The Future of Democracy": his reply, published in the issue of April 7, contains a piercing analysis of the inevitably evil character of any form of dictatorship, exalts liberalism — as being friendly to democracy specifically because liberalism implies "an administration that provides . . . an education of the governed for governing," and as being hostile to the democratic tendency to substitute mere numbers or quantity for quality — and expresses confidence in the future of freedom, which he thinks will never succumb in great and powerful nations that preserve their civil liberties.

After the downfall of the Fascist regime in 1943 Croce was made a Minister without portfolio, and as a member of the Committee of Liberation played a leading part in the difficult transition from monarchy to republic. He served also as President of the Italian Liberal Party until 1947, when, at the age of eighty-two, he "retired" to continue his philosophical and literary activities.

CHAPTER 53

The Literature of the Republic

SEEN AGAINST the background of the past — and particularly the recent past — the years since the end of World War II have marked a time of unusual tranquillity in Italy's national life. Italians may well be proud of this, considering the state of the country at the end of hostilities. The avowed goal of the Fascist regime had been to forge a united people, but its ultimate effect had been to bring about bitter division and finally civil war. In 1945 Italy was a country not only ravaged and defeated but, it might have been feared, also permanently divided. The plebiscite that sanctioned the new Republic yielded a verdict by no means unanimous; well over forty percent of the voters opted for a monarchy. Yet the verdict was accepted and the wounds of the country healed with suprising swiftness. Epuration never became persecution and elements potentially hostile to the Republic and even to the concept of democracy have abided by the decision of the majority. Both neofascists and Communists have defended their programs within the constitutional framework.

Ever since the new Republic came into being the country has entrusted its destinies to one political party, Christian Democracy, a unique development among the countries of the free world. The heterogeneity of the party membership might at first glance suggest instability, for along with a majority of moderates its ranks include right-wing reactionaries, clericals, and monarchists on the one hand and on the other a substantial quota of reform-minded and progressive liberals whose programs hardly differ from that of orthodox Socialists. But, beginning with Alcide DeGasperi, astute and able party leaders have turned this potential weakness into an asset by discreet courtship of other elements. The party can, for example, move slightly to the Left (indeed it has done so) and, thereby assuring itself of the cooperation of the Socialists, safely accept some defections on the Right. Thus, since the election of Giovanni Gronchi to the presidency (1955) the country has been governed by a center-left coalition, with Christian Democracy claiming the prime minister and the majority of the cabinet, which regularly includes representatives of the Socialists and other minority parties. It has never accepted the collaboration of neofascists, monarchists, or Communists, though the exclusion of the last named has signified continuous political tension, as the Communists regularly poll approximately one third of the popular vote.

Under the aegis of Christian Democracy many long overdue reforms have been effected: the great latifundia have been broken up and special programs implemented for the benefit of the long-neglected South, social services have been improved, and a number of ambitious projects in the area of public works have been undertaken. Not all Italians are satisfied with the pace of improvement: the party is recurrently accused of sluggish response to the needs of the people and there have been some cases of scandalous corruption. Nevertheless general elections have consistently returned Christian Democracy to power and its successive coalitions, though frequently suspect and always vulnerable, have probably given the nation the kind of administration and the tempo of reform acceptable to the majority of Italians.

Postwar Italy has been more fortunate than other nations in having no serious problems of foreign policy to deal with. An early participant in the movement towards European unity, the country took part in the formation of the Common Market, of which it has been a useful and cooperative member; and in 1949, overriding the objections of the Left, Italy joined NATO. She has had no further commitments, no imperialistic wars, and no colonial problems. Resurgence of aggressive nationalism has been minimal once Trieste's destiny was settled (1954). The discontent of the German-speaking population in the South Tyrol has been placated by the granting of a certain amount of autonomy to the region.

Meanwhile the prosperity of the country — in spite of the economic recessions which have been the lot of all industrialized nations — has been remarkable. Housing has improved, new roads have been built (of which the great highway running from the Swiss border to Sicily is but one example), unemployment has been held to a minimum, and the standard of living has noticeably risen. Italian industry has maintained its prestige; it will suffice to mention the internationally respected names of Fiat, Olivetti, and Pirelli. Along with industrial success has come a kind of cultural ascendancy. Italian fashions have become the international vogue and the Italian cinema, with such gifted directors as De Sica, Fellini, Antonioni, and Pasolini, has elicited the admiration of critics and public alike in all parts of the world.

* * *

It is hardly surprising that the vigor and exuberance of Italy's economic and social progress are paralleled in the field of letters. Under the regime of Mussolini the great majority of intellectuals had been frustrated. Many simply ignored, as far as was possible, the policies of the dictatorship; a few went into exile; and a number came to terms with the regime, but even this group was disillusioned by the Duce's entrance into the war. So the end of the war brought a sense of euphoric release to Italian men of letters. "It was as if we had all been seized by a great fever — but a beneficent fever," says Guido Lopez, commenting on the literary activity of the immediate postwar years. Magazines sprang up overnight and publishers eagerly sought new writers. Memories of recent ordeals supplied the themes and spurred the imagination of artists and authors.

The climate since the mid-fifties has been more tranquil as memories of the time of crisis have faded. Yet the creative vitality has endured and has produced many younger writers who in the course of time may well come to enjoy the respect now accorded to such novelists as Moravia, Vittorini, and Pavese and such poets as Ungaretti, Montale, and Quasimodo, all associated in varying degrees with the years of resistance and emancipation.

It is in the fields of narrative prose and lyric poetry that the production of the last three decades has been richest. In the sector of the novel particularly so many talented artists have emerged that a mere census would be impressive, and the variety of themes, styles, and attitudes has been so great as to make any attempt at classification difficult. We may here attempt to indicate in a general way the sundry schools or, perhaps more properly, currents that have been dominant among the prose writers, centering on the specific contributions of those whose achievement gives them preeminence in their own right. We shall also take into consideration themes of recurrent exploitation; and since the new Italy has all the colorful local variation that characterized the old, we shall also cite examples of contemporary regionalism.

* * *

First of all, however, a chronological distinction must be made if only to do justice to the older writers who had won recognition during — and in some cases before — the Fascist period and who have continued to produce notable works during the postwar years. Among those whose beginnings date back to the period of World War I and whose prestige, either because of consistent production or belated recognition, stands high in the seventies the names of Marino Moretti, Aldo Palazzeschi, Bruno Cicognani, and Massimo Bontempelli are prominent. Moretti (b. 1885), born in Cesenatico and one of the earlier *crepuscolari* poets, achieved fame as a novelist with *Il sole del sabato* (Saturday's Sunshine) in 1916; he has continued writing down to the present, turning in recent years to evocative memoirs. His friend and contemporary Aldo Palazzeschi (pen name of Aldo Giurlani, 1885–1974) has also continued to publish both verse and prose. Though he will be remembered chiefly for such works as *Il codice di Perelà* (1911, *Perelà, the Man of Smoke*), * *Sorelle Matterassi* (1934, *The Sisters Matterassi*), and his

*For works that have been published in translation the English title is regularly supplied in italics.

youthful verses, associated with both *crepuscularismo* and *futurismo*, his recent works, including the substantial postwar novel *Roma* (1953), cannot be overlooked. Bruno Cicognani (1879–1971), whose novels *La Velia* (1923) and *Villa Beatrice* (1931) assure him of a permanent place in the chronicles of the Italian novel, brought out the very ambitious *La nuora* (The Daughter-in-law) in the same year as Palazzeschi's *Roma*. The versatile Bontempelli (1884–1960) had been a pioneer spokesman for new directions in the narrative; although his significant creative work is associated with the Fascist period (he was one of the few intellectuals to give enthusiastic support to the regime), he lived to see his original and somewhat surrealistic volume of short stories honored by the Viareggo prize (1953). Enrico Pea (1881–1958) is another notable member of this age group; he continued writing his highly personal prose poems until a few years before his death. A slightly younger group should also be mentioned; it would include Bonaventura Tecchi (1895–1968), Giovanni Comisso (1895–1969), and Anna Banti (b. 1895), Gianna Manzini (1896–1974), and Leonida Repaci (b. 1898). Tecchi began publication in the early twenties but his finest novel, *Valentina Valier*, is of 1950. Comisso, gifted with a painter's perceptions, brought out one of his best works, *Mio sodalizio con De Pisis* (My Association with De Pisis) in 1954. Anna Banti's best novel, *Artemisia*, was published in 1947; Gianna Manzini's latest volume of short stories came out in 1972, and Repaci, "the fiery Calabrian," is still an important figure in Italian literary circles.

Among the men of letters of his generation Corrado Alvaro (1895–1956) is a rather special case. He too had won recognition well before World War II with *Gente in Aspromonte* (1930, *Revolt in Aspromonte*) and *L'uomo è forte* (1938, *Man Is Strong*), but his thoughtful concern for the direction and problems of the new Italy, evidenced in his works of social commentary and personal reminiscence, made him a particularly significant figure in the postwar years; one of his best novels, *L'età breve* (The Brief Age), appeared in 1946 and the autobiographical *Quasi una vita* (Almost a Lifetime) in 1951.

The mention of Alvaro suggests another distinctive figure, Ignazio Silone (pen name of Secondino Tranquilli; b. 1900). Silone will long be remembered for his *Fontamara* (1933), a novel that blended literary artistry with an anti-Fascist thesis (the book was originally published in Switzerland); its naturalistic technique looks backward to Verga and at the same time forward to the neorealists. It was followed by *Pane e vino* (1937, *Bread and Wine*), in which the same elements that characterized *Fontamara* are somewhat less successfully fused. Silone was one of the founders of the Italian Communist Party but later left its ranks; in recent years his works have abandoned political concerns to take on a certain religious flavor; *L'avventura di un povero cristiano* (1968, The Fate of a Poor Christian), dealing with the life of Pope Celestine V, may be cited as characteristic of his present interests. Silone spent many years in exile and is today a somewhat isolated figure but his contribution is significant and enduring.

Finally, the precocity of Alberto Moravia (pseudonym of Alberto Pincherle; see p. 487) requires his association with a chronologically older group; his *Gli indifferenti* (1929, *The Time of Indifference*), in which some critics have seen the existentialist posture *avant la lettre*, appeared when the author was only twenty-two. Since then he has been Italy's most productive novelist. His first book set the pattern for all that have followed; all deal with the corruptions of a venal and sex-ridden society. Among his many novels, somewhat repetitive in substance but always masterful in exposition, *La romana* (1949, *The Woman of Rome*), the story of a prostitute, *Il conformista* (1951, *The Conformist*), and *La ciociara* (1957, *Two Women*) are the most successful. Moravia is equally adept at the short story; the Roman sketches written over many years for the *Corriere della sera* (*Roman Tales*, *More Roman Tales*) are admirable for their realism and deftness of character delineation. Moravia's works have been widely translated and many of his plots have been adapted to the cinema; he is Italy's best known and most successful living novelist.

* * *

If we turn to the writers whose works may be said to exemplify the new departure in the narrative coincident with the twilight of Fascism and the dawn of the new freedom, we encounter at once the leading exponents of the fashion defined as "neorealism": Elio Vittorini (1908–1966) and Cesare Pavese (1908–1950). The term "neorealist" has been applied rather loosely to a number of writers of postwar prominence who deal, normally at least, with inarticulate and humble characters and who express themselves in a programmatically unpretentious, conversational style. More strictly defined, the term calls for an immersion on the part of the author in his narrative (usually in the first person), colloquial and often elliptical dialogue, and an oblique but perceptible social intention. It is an approach that owes much to the influence of such American writers as Steinbeck, Caldwell, and most of all Hemingway. It is fair to say too that the components of neorealism are also to be found in Verga's Sicilian novels.

Vittorini, a Sicilian, was himself a man of the people; his father was a railroad worker. In the thirties Vittorini became associated with the review *Solaria* ("a 'solarian' in those days," he recalls, "signified being anti-Fascist, European, anti-traditionalist"). His first novel *Il garofano rosso* (1934, *The Red Carnation*) appeared in serial form in that magazine. At this time too he translated a number of American works, including novels of Steinbeck and Saroyan. In 1941 he published *Conversazione in Sicilia* (*In Sicily*), which may fairly be called the cornerstone of neorealism. It is the simple account of a Sicilian employed in the North who returns to his native island to escape the "abstract furies" that have been oppressing him. The "action" of the work is a sequence of conversations with fellow travelers, the people of his home town, and finally his mother. The dialogues, scrupulously recorded without commentary on the part of the author, express the anxieties of the time — the substance is topical and latently anti-Fascist — but in their simplicity they suggest as well the dimensions of the eternal human predicament. *Uomini e no* (1945, *Men and Non-men*) depicts, in a series of short chapters, the tensions of the people of Milan in the anxious winter of 1944. *Le donne di Messina* (1949, The Women of Messina) is a long novel in which "Uncle Agrippa," a retired railway worker, travels back and forth between North and South immediately after the end of the war; it is, in a realistic idiom, an allegory of the problems of social and moral reconstruction facing the country. Other notable works of this begetter of neorealism include the novellas *Erica* (1936) and *La garibaldina* (1950); after the publication of the latter work Vittorini turned from writing to the editorial direction of *I gettoni*, a series that brought to the attention of the public the works of many significant younger writers.

As if to confirm the often observed truth that many Italian writers of innovative talent are "peripheral" (in Italian literary tradition, as indeed in her topography, the regions from Lombardy to Campania are thought of as "central," regions outside of that zone are "peripheral"), the other pillar of neorealism, Cesare Pavese, was a native of Piemonte. The same age as Vittorini, Pavese was also of humble stock, although he had more formal education than his Sicilian *confrère*. Pavese too was an anti-Fascist and, for a time, a Communist. Perhaps more significantly, he too felt the attraction of American literature; he translated *Moby Dick* and it is not hard to see the influence of Melville on his vision. Unlike Vittorini, however, Pavese was always a withdrawn and solitary person. Finding it difficult to establish and maintain close relationships, he never married, and it may be that his suicide was the result of a frustrated love affair. His tragic death seemed a sadly appropriate realization of the motifs of alienation and despair that appear in his works. In manner his novels have something in common with those of Vittorini: he normally employs the first person, his prose is lean and direct (though relieved by lyrical passages), and in his works too the theme of the return to one's roots is prominent. In his best known and most successful novel, *La luna e i falò* (1950, *The Moon and the Bonfires*), the protagonist returns from America to his native Piemonte to find it at once recognizably familiar and forever lost and alien. This concept of childhood as a lost world to which we long vainly to return is a recurrent motif in Pavese's work; it appears again in *La casa in collina* (*The House on the Hill*) and *Tra donne sole* (*Among Women Only*), both of 1949, to cite two of his more memorable stories. Pavese's tales have a mythological quotient, even though the action takes place in clearly defined contemporary time and place and the characters are well aware of their political and social *milieu*. Because of this quasi-mystical dimension and perhaps because of the circumstances of his death, Pavese has had a great influence on younger writers. Many critics regard him as the most perceptive novelist of his generation.

To this pair of innovators we may add the name of Vasco Pratolini (b. 1913), likewise classifiable in substance and to a marked degree in manner as a neorealist, although still bearing the imprint of a more traditional school. Pratolini, a Tuscan, is, as was Vittorini, largely self-taught. He too depicts the life of the lower classes — in his case those of his native Florence — and his protagonists tend to be youths or adolescents. His best known works are *Il quartiere* (1945, *The Naked Streets*) and *Cronache di poveri amanti* (1946, *A Tale of Poor Lovers*), reflecting the ferment of the years of the decline and fall of Fascism. Pratolini writes with verve and lucidity; if his work lacks the lyrical appeal of Pavese's and perhaps the sense of universal significance that Vittorini conveys, he is a more skillful narrator than either of them; his plots have a well-constructed story line and a cast of believable and interesting characters. Beginning with *Metello* (1955), Pratolini turned from the chronicling of current events to the historical novel; the protagonist of *Metello* is a Florentine worker participating in the labor movements of the late nineteenth century; the last part of the book contains a rather detailed account of the great strike of 1902. *Lo scialo* (1950, The Waste) and *Allegoria e derisione* (1966, *Allegory and Derision*) complete the trilogy of which *Metello* was the first part; in scope and focus it may be compared to Bacchelli's *Mulino del Po*.

* * *

The period of the fall of Fascism, the war, and the resistance, which provides the subject matter for the neorealists, is widely exploited by many writers, often in a manner akin to neorealism. Carlo Cassola (b. 1917) deals with humble and all but inarticulate folk, centering primarily on their personal problems but with occasional political allusions; *Fausto e Anna* (1952) and *La ragazza di Bube* (1960, *Bebo's Girl*) are typical studies. Cassola's prose, programmatically "anti-rhetorical," has a dour but compelling texture. Giuseppe Berto (b. 1914) is an interesting case; his first novel *Il cielo è rosso* (1947, *The Sky Is Red*) is a graphic depiction of war on the civilian front, but in 1964 he signified a change of direction with the publication of *Il male oscuro* (*The Incubus*), the story of his own psychiatric cure, told with a stream-of-consciousness technique in the manner of Joyce and other experimentalists.

The war in all its various phases has been the subject of many fine works of fiction. The early euphoria of its beginning is comically portrayed in *L'entrata in guerra* (1954, Entering the War) by Italo Calvino (b. 1923) but a less lighthearted tone characterizes the accounts, more or less fictionalized, of the engagements in the field. Mario Rigoni Stern (b. 1921) wrote a graphic report on the campaign in Russia, *Il sergente nella neve* (1953, *The Sergeant in the Snow*). Mario Tobino, a doctor, described the war in Libya in his *Il deserto della Libia* (1951, *The Libyan Desert*) and Ugo Pirro (pen name of Ugo Mattone, b. 1920) set the action of his compact novel *Le soldatesse* (1951, *The Camp Followers*) in the ill-starred Greek theater of operations.

Other aspects of the years of crisis provide the substance for the works of many able and perceptive writers such as Giose Rimanelli (b. 1926), known also under the name of A. G. Solari for his sharp critical comments on the contemporary literary scene, and Gino Montesanto (b. 1922), whose *Cielo chiuso* (1956, Closed Sky) reflects his own experiences in service with the co-belligerent Italian units of the Allied armies after the armistice. Guido Lopez (b. 1924) wrote of his enforced exile in *Il campo* (1948, The Camp) and Guglielmo Petroni (b. 1911), poet and novelist, drew on the experiences of his incarceration in Rome under the Nazis for his *Il mondo è una prigione* (1949, The World Is a Prison). The resistance is treated with a kind of ironic realism in *I ventitrè giorni della cittá di Alba* (1952, The Twenty-three Days of the City of Alba) by Beppe Fenoglio (1922–1963), who also wrote an account of his military service in the last days of Fascism under the suggestive title *Primavera di bellezza* (1959, Springtime of Beauty); the posthumous *Gianni il partigiano* (1969, Johnny the Partisan) has earned for Fenoglio the appellation of "the Homer of the Resistance." In manner and matter he is a neorealist. The atmosphere of the clandestine struggle is also movingly evoked in *L'Agnese va a morire* (1949, Agnes Is Going to Die) by Renata Viganò. It is notable that many of the works cited above — those of Stern, Calvino, Fenoglio, and Vigano for example — appeared in the series of "gettoni" under the aegis of Vittorini.

* * *

Some of the more memorable works dealing with the era of crisis and anxiety are not fiction but personal memoirs or reports, such as those of Lopez or Petroni cited above. In the immediate postwar period no book had a greater impact than *Cristo s'è fermato a Eboli* (1946, *Christ Stopped at Eboli*), another work in this genre, written by Carlo Levi (1902–1975). Levi, born in Torino and a painter by vocation, was confined by the Fascist authorities to a small town in Lucania. His book is an account not so much of his own experience as of the life led by the people of that region; he studies their condition and their mores with the probing but not unsympathetic eye of an anthropologist. More effectively — and poetically — than any single work of recent years, Levi's report focused the attention not only of Italians but of the western world on the long-ignored "problem of the South." The book assured an attentive audience for such works as the later and more polemical *Inchiesta a Palermo* (1957, *To Feed the Hungry*) by the crusading Danilo Dolci (b. 1924) and likewise enlarged if it did not create the public for the numerous and gifted creative writers from regions south of Rome. Another Levi, Primo (b. 1919), more than a decade later published *Se questo è un uomo* (1958, *If This Is a Man*), a report of his experiences in a German labor camp, impressive for its sober depiction of horror and brutality.

In this general category of documentation we may also include Mario Tobino's sympathetic study of the mentally disturbed, *Le donne di Magliano* (1953, The Women of Magliano) and *Donnarumma all'assalto* (1959, Donnarumma on the Offensive) by Ottiero Ottieri (b. 1924), yet another report on the South, this time in its confrontation with Northern industrialism. Ottieri has also written a rather unusual "proletarian" novel, *Il campo di concentramento* (1972, The Concentration Camp). The genre affords scope too for the mention of outstanding contributions from serious and percipient journalists, as exemplified by Guido Piovene (b. 1907) and Enrico Emanuelli (1909–1967); the former wrote an exhaustive and well-documented study of the United States, *De America* (1953) and the latter's firsthand accounts of Russia and Red China were widely read. In his time the inventive, capricious, but always lively political commentator Curzio Schuckert Malaparte (1898–1957) had a large public. More recently Luigi Barzini (b. 1908) essayed an analysis of the mentality and behavior of his compatriots; his somewhat mischievous bestseller, *The Italians*, appeared (first in the author's English version; Barzini is a graduate of Columbia University) in 1964.

* * *

Returning to the consideration of the narrative, we may note that the time of tension in the national life has served as a functional background for many distinguished writers whose works cannot be defined as "war" or "resistance" novels. In this group, aside from Calvino, of whom we shall have more to say, Natalia Ginzburg (née Levi, b. 1916) has a high place. Her brief and effective story of an unhappy marriage, *È stato così* (1947, *The Dry Heart*) brought her well-merited critical acclaim. She has continued to publish novels and stories, drawing largely on memories of her family life: *Tutti i nostri ieri* (1953, *A Light for Fools*) and *Le voci della sera* (1961, *Voices in the Evening*) have confirmed her promise. Another example is Giorgio Bassani (b. 1916); his *Il giardino dei Finzi-Contini* (1962, *The Garden of the Finzi-Contini*) is a moving evocation, Proustian in tone, of the last summer of tranquillity before the application of the Fascist racial laws destroyed the Jewish community of which he writes. Told in a restrained, somewhat old-fashioned style, this novel is certainly one of the best of the contemporary period; a like tone and quality pervade *Cinque storie ferraresi* (1956, *Five Stories of Ferrara*) and other works of this sensitive writer.

Neither Ginzburg nor Bassani is a neorealist either in matter or manner, and in this respect they are typical of a great number — perhaps the majority — of the writers of the sixties and seventies. Although neorealism, because of its novelty and the level of excellence attained by its champions, may fairly be called the most noteworthy renovating trend of the postwar period, yet much admirable work has been produced by authors writing in a more conventional manner, eschewing the "engagé" style and dealing with the familiar subjects — love, ambition, corruption — often centering on the middle classes. In some of these writers critics see legacies of Fogazzaro or D'Annunzio; they are all inheritors of the pre-neorealist tradition. Prominent in this rather large group are Guido Piovene of Vicenza and Mario Soldati (b. 1906) of Torino. The former, as noted, is a journalist and a student of social mores; as a novelist he is remembered chiefly for his *Le lettere di una novizia* (1941, Letters of a Novice), an analysis of an unscrupulous woman against a clerical and faintly decadent background. "Decadence" is a word also frequently used with reference to the novels of Soldati; he likes to probe uneasy personal situations, ambiguous characters (here he has something in common with Moravia) in a world where sensual urgencies seem to predominate. Good examples of Soldati's art are *Le lettere da Capri* (1954, *The Capri Letters*), *Il vero Silvestri* (1957, *The Real Silvestri*), and the somewhat more ambitious *Le due città* (1965, *The Two Cities*), in which a critic might fairly find traces of D'Annunzio. The name of P. A. Quarantotti Gambini (1910–1965), with his special interest in wayward and perverse adolescence, may be added to this group as well as that of P. M. Pasinetti (b. 1913), whose *Rosso veneziano* (1959, *Venetian Red*) has an appealing warmth of its own. As far as the substance of his major novels is concerned Giovanni Arpino (b. 1927) shows an affinity with writers of this stamp, although stylistically he is perhaps less traditional.

This general approach and zone of operation have also characterized certain women writers and contemporary Italy may boast of a number of women, aside from those already mentioned, who have made substantial contributions to the narrative. The work of Alba de Céspedes (b. 1911) in such novels as *Dalla parte di lei* (1949, *The Best of Husbands*) and *Quaderno proibito* (1952, *The Secret*) centers on the problems of middle-class women of today; Giovanna Zangrandi (b. 1910) is the author of a family saga of Dolomitic flavor. Lalla Romano (b. 1909) and Milena Milani (b. 1922) are also gifted and respected *scrittrici*.

In this category of the traditional novel the writers of the South are so numerous as to merit special attention. There has been, in the postwar period, a very conspicuous school of novelists centered around Naples and an equally talented contingent of Sicilians. Some of them have been concerned with "the problem of the South" while others have simply enriched their studies of universal human situations by the addition of regional color. If we may speak of neorealism perhaps we may also employ the term "neoregionalism" with reference to these artists, who have brought new techniques into a traditional mode. Michele Prisco (b. 1920) has been prominent among Neapolitan novelists; his field is the petty bourgeoisie of Naples and its province. A characteristic study is *Gli eredi del vento* (1950, *The Heirs of the Wind*), in which motifs of jealousy, avarice, and the status of contemporary woman are mingled. Prisco's contribution has been consistent and substantial; he is in process of creating a province of his own and, for scope and penetration, may be accounted a major figure of his generation. Domenico Rea (b. 1921) is at his best in the short story; the collection *Spaccanapoli* (1947) indicated his humanitarian and somewhat polemic motivation. He has pursued his study of the impoverished lower classes in *Quel che vide Cummeo* (1955, What Cummeo Saw) and successive works. Luigi Incoronato (1920–1967) is another of this group; he was until his death an editor of the review *Le ragioni narrative*, dedicated to Southern letters, as are Prisco and Rea. Incoronato will be remembered for his powerful *Morunni* (1952), written in the tradition of regionalistic naturalism. Mario Pomilio (b. 1921), born in Chieti but living in Naples, specializes in delicate crises of conscience; some see in his work the "Fogazzarian decadence" exemplified by Piovene and Soldati. His thoughtful *La compromissione* (1965, The Compromise) treats of the dilemma of a political leader who has lost faith in his party.

The older Carlo Bernari (b. 1909) is sometimes associated with the neorealists; the program of neorealism does not exclude regionalism so long as it is not romanticized. *Speranzella* (1949), a characteristic work of Bernari, takes its name from a Neapolitan quarter dear to the dialect poet Salvatore di Giacomo; in subject and treatment it shows affinities with Pratolini's *Il quartiere*. Of like flavor and with sharper social thrust are the stories in *Il mare non bagna Napoli* (1953, *The Bay Is Not Naples*) by Anna Maria Ortese (b. 1914). Other able Neapolitan authors are the colorful and *brioso* Giuseppe Marotta (b. 1902); Mario Schettini (1918–1969), esteemed for his graphic *Il paese dei bastardi* (1953, Land of Bastards); and Raffaele LaCapria (b. 1922), author of the highly original *Ferito a morte* (1961, *The Mortal Wound*), which combines local color and Fogazzarian decadence with an inventive structure that has been called "Joycean."

In addition to Vittorini, Sicily has produced a large number of significant novelists. Vitaliano Brancati (1907–1954) studied with ironic percipience the mystique of the dominant male so dear to his fellow islanders; *Don Giovanni in Sicilia* (1947) exemplifies both his intent and his artistry. Ercole Patti (1904–1976), whose facility perhaps obscures his merits, looks with a disillusioned eye on the world of the well-to-do both in his native Catania and in Rome, where he now lives. To the roll call of Sicilian novelists the name of Livia de Stefani (b. 1913) should also be added; her *La vigna di uve nere* (1953, *Black Grapes*) is a traditional tale of jealousy and vengeance but told with masterful assurance.

In recent years two other writers from this fertile island have come to the fore, each with a contribution of exceptional quality. The older, Giuseppe Tomasi di Lampedusa (1896–1957), wrote only one novel, *Il gattopardo* (1959, *The Leopard*), but its merits are such as to ensure the author an enduring place in Italian letters. It was published posthumously and many years had gone into its composition. In essence *Il gattopardo* is a capsulized history, as seen through the eyes of a cynical and wistful aristocrat, of the impact of the Risorgimento and the successive "Piedmontese" government on a land where corruption is ancient and endemic. The work is divided into a number of moments, like the acts in a play, each bringing its own illumination. It is definable as a historical novel but its penetrating commentary, fused with deft characterization and an evocative atmosphere, lend it a quality not normally associated with that *genre*.

The second major figure is Leonardo Sciascia (b. 1921) whom many critics would call the most gifted of his generation in Italy. Sciascia's prose is lean and factual; he has no lyric intention nor does he comment on the situations he presents. Dialogue predominates in his novels — as is the case with the neorealists. Yet for all his objectivity, his choice of theme and manner of composition reveal a deep concern for his native island. His books sometimes have the form and often the pace of a detective story. In his best known novel, *Il giorno della civetta* (1961, *Mafia vendetta*), he probes the roots of Sicily's hidden government; the wary mentality of the small town is the subject of *A ciascuno il suo* (1966, *A Man's Blessing*); and in *Il consiglio d'Egitto* (1966, *The Council of Egypt*) the author combines historical reconstruction, an implicit commentary on the island's destiny, and the portrayal of a true patriot. *Il contesto* (1972, *The Worm in the Bud*) is a chilling and pointed story of political corruption. Sciascia has written studies of Verga and Pirandello and essays of a historical and social nature.

There are not lacking spokesmen for other regions of the South. Francesco Jovine (1902–1950) wrote of his still feudal Molise with creative artistry; his best novel is *Le terre del Sacramento* (1950, The Sacrament Lands). The Lucanian Rocco Scotellaro (1923–1953) wrote with participant sympathy of the life of his region; he was also a poet of distinction and his early death was a great loss to Italian letters. The Calabrian Fortunato Seminara (b. 1903) is well-known for *Il vento nell'oliveto* (1951, *The Wind in the Olive Grove*), a novel of introspection against a realistic rural background. Of a younger generation another Calabrian, Saverio Strati (b. 1924), is gaining increasing recognition. Strati, a self-educated man, has lived in the North and in Switzerland; his *Tibi e Tascia* (1959) is an authentic and tender story of children — a field neglected by Italian writers since the (perhaps unjustly) forgotten Luciano Zuccoli. Strati's most recent work, *Noi lazzaroni* (1972, We Loafers) deals with the plight of Italian emigrant laborers.

Somewhat comparable to Sciascia, in intention at least, is the Sardinian novelist Giuseppe Dessì (1909–1977), who after a number of earlier novels turned to his native island for the background of his plots. Although he repudiates the Sardinia of Grazia Deledda for its stress on local color, he yet depicts the same proud and dour islanders that she had celebrated. Dessì's concise *Il disertore* (1961, *The Deserter*) is a moving portrayal of a frightened fugitive; the prize-winning *Paese d'ombre* (1972, Land of Shadows) is a work of larger scope and not without descriptive details that might have been used by Grazia Deledda. Like Sciascia, too, Dessì has written historical and critical essays and has also had some success in the theater.

* * *

All of the writers so far mentioned, though variously classifiable, have written within the broad tradition of nineteenth century realism and naturalism; even the neorealists could have been, as it were, postulated, given the theories and examples of Zola and the Goncourts. In recent years in Italy, as in other countries, a number of writers have departed from this tradition. Some, stylistically conventional, have turned to fantasy for their subject matter while others have sought to create a new kind of novel — or artifact to replace the novel — often with tools borrowed from fields far removed from the conventional limits of literature.

Among the novelists of fantasy (some critics call them "Gothic") the most prominent is Italo Calvino. He began his career with the publication of the neorealistic story of partisan warfare, *Il sentiero dei nidi di ragno* (1947, *The Path to the Nest of Spiders*) but he found his true metier in the elaboration of his fantastic trilogy, of which the individual titles may speak for themselves: *Il visconte dimezzato* (1952, *The Cloven Viscount*), *Il barone rampante* (1957, *The Baron in the Trees*), and *Il cavaliere inesistente* (1959, *The Non-existent Knight*). The settings of these fables are, respectively, the sixteenth century, the eighteenth century, and the legendary middle ages; the variously mutilated protagonists serve the purposes of allegory, satire, and pure diversion. Of like fiber is the highly acclaimed *Le città invisibili* (1972, The Invisible Cities). Not surprisingly, their creator, an avowed admirer of Ariosto, has also edited a collection of fairy stories and experimented with science fiction in *Le cosmicomiche* (1966, *The Cosmicomics*). The allegorical thrust of this anti-realistic school is notable in the case of Dino Buzzati (1906–1972); his best known novel is *Il deserto dei Tartari* (1940, *The Tartar Steppe*), a fable for our age of anxiety, with Kafka-esque overtones; his numerous short stories may also be described as moralizing fantasies and he too found science fiction an appropriate vehicle for his message. Tommaso Landolfi (b. 1906) exhibits a mixture of verbal pyrotechnics, surrealistic imagination, and a melancholy view of life; the title of his collection of short stories, *Racconti impossibili* (1966, Impossible Tales) is at once descriptive and programmatic. Goffredo Parise (b. 1929) is the author of the truly surrealistic *Il ragazzo morto e le comete* (1951, *The Dead Boy and the Comets*), although his production also includes, along with other works of fantasy, such titles as *Il prete bello* (1954, *Don Gastone and the Ladies*) which associates him with the Fogazzarian inheritance, and *Il padrone* (1965, *Boss*) which exploits the background of the contemporary industrial world. The novels of broad canvas of Elsa Morante (b. 1912) may possibly be assigned to this category; neither *Menzogna e sortilegio* (1948, *The House of Liars*) nor *L'isola di Arturo* (1957, *Arturo's Island*) lack realistic detail, but with respect to both structure and atmosphere they carry us into a dream world. The sentimental fantasies of Luigi Santucci (b. 1918) have a special religious dimension.

The conventional historical novel — another nineteenth century legacy — has not lacked cultivation, albeit with the application of new and sophisticated techniques. Aside from the cases we have cited in other connections, the contributions to this field of Carlo Alianello (b. 1901) and Luciano Bianciardi (1922–1971) are noteworthy; both have written tales of the Risorgimento period, the former from the Bourbon point of view, the latter evoking memories of the *garibaldini*.

Bianciardi has also written the realistic and forceful *La vita agra* (1962, *It's a Hard Life*).

The novel of pure humor has had few cultivators—and the critics ignore them—but Achille Campanile (1900–1977) has had a wide circle of readers for many years and his nonsense novels are masterpieces of their kind. In the immediate postwar years many Italians found Giovanni Guareschi's (b. 1908) tales of Don Camillo to their taste. Pietro Chiara (b. 1913) and Luigi Mastronardi (b. 1930) have also found provincial Lombardy a fruitful field for thier comic muse. The piquant *La vacanza delle donne* (1954, The Women's Vacation) of Luigi Compagnone (b. 1915) has a Rabelaisian flavor. Fabio Tombari (b. 1899), author of the sparkling *Tutta Frusagalia* (All about Frusaglia) of the early Fascist era, has turned to children's books, lyrical and appealing.

"Experimentalists" have not flourished in Italy as they have in France. Yet one very prominent writer in contemporary letters might fit into that category, even granting his "traditional" beginnings. This is Carlo Emilio Gadda (1893–1973), an engineer by profession and a veteran of World War I; chronologically he belongs with the older writers, but his remarkable novel *Quer pasticciaccio brutto de Via Merulana* (*That Awful Mess on Via Merulana*) published in 1957 associated him at once not only with the younger generation but with the avant garde. In technique the work enlarges the dimensions of neorealism; the tale is told in a mixture of dialects and with a sophisticated coloration of prose that is suggestive of Joyce. The plot is that of a detective story with a police inspector in the central role; the mystery is never solved but in the course of the investigation "all Rome boils as if in an immense cauldron," as Italo Calvino puts it. For perception and sophistication the work can be challenged only by *Il gattopardo* among novels of recent years; in scope it is at once narrower and deeper. Gadda was not unknown at the time of the publication of his masterpiece; his earlier works, such as *L'Adalgisa* (1944) and *Le novelle dal ducato in fiamme* (1953, Stories from the Duchy in Flames) had earned the respect of the critics but *Il pasticciaccio* — original, powerful, and, one suspects, seminal — gave him a unique preeminence. Of similar style is *L'anonimo lombardo* (revised version 1973, The Anonymous Lombard) by the young critic-moralist-novelist Alberto Arbasino (b. 1930).

Another writer who has skillfully exploited dialect is the versatile Pier Paolo Pasolini (1922–1975); his two Roman novels *Ragazzi di vita* (1955, Low Life Kids) and *Una vita violenta* (1959, *A Violent Life*) focus sharply on a class of purposeless and *au fond* pathetic adolescent idlers. Since the city he deals with is Rome, his stories attracted a wider audience than they would have if they were written in a dialect other than that of the capital, which has become fashionable in recent years. One may see in Pasolini's approach either the ultimate legacy of naturalism or the neorealistic theory pushed to the extreme. In any case, for his field of investigation and skillful use of language he is an original and significant chronicler — and a moralist as well. Pasolini is also a poet and has likewise been prominently involved with the Italian cinema.

The term "experimental" may be more properly applied to those novelists who have used methods unknown to an earlier tradition or whose substance implies a new vision of life. For example, Oreste del Buono (b. 1925), a versatile critic of sports, movies and comic-strips, has experimented with the notion of introspective memory, repudiating the conventional time structure, in *Un intero minuto* (1959, *Image of Love*). Paolo Volponi (b. 1924) has dealt with the impact of today's computerized industrial society on the individual — "the civilization of the machines," to cite the title of a current magazine. Luigi Malerba (b. 1927) and Edoardo Sanguineti (b. 1930) have used the techniques of the cinema in their fiction; unlike traditional novelists they are not so much concerned with narrative or characterization as they are with documenting a state of mind, individual or collective, typical of the uneasy culture of our times. Sanguineti is also a critic of note and — somewhat paradoxically — a Dantist. Other novelists whose works may be described in varying degree as "experimental" are Mario Spinella (b. 1918), Marcello Venturi (b. 1925), and Luigi Meneghello (b. 1922).

In the nature of things it is the novelists of the younger generation who have been in the forefront of radical innovation. Yet of all the younger novelists now active the most talented, in the opinion of many critics, is Fulvio Tomizza (b. 1935), whose approach is in no sense experimental. Yet another "peripheral" figure, Tomizza was born in Istria and spent some of his youthful years in Yugoslavia. His *Trilogia istriana* (1967) revealed a writer of unusual power and scope. His recent *La città di Miriam* (1973, Miriam's City) is a story of compassion, insight, and humor. Not only topographically may he be regarded as the heir of Svevo, but he has added to that legacy a lyricism of his own. He could be a major figure of the late twentieth century.

* * *

Although the narrative has been widely cultivated and has been distinguished by many excellent works, it is possible that a hundred years hence the literature of the twentieth century in Italy — and particularly its middle years — will be remembered chiefly for its poetry. At least four poets have come into world prominence since the end of World War II (though all began their careers somewhat earlier) and may be said to have achieved international recognition.

Umberto Saba (1883–1957), the oldest of the quartet, is a somewhat unusual figure in Italian letters. His origins are strikingly peripheral: he was born in Trieste at a time when the city was still a part of the Austro-Hungarian Empire; he was the child of a Jewish mother, Felicita Cohen, and abandoned in infancy by his Christian father, Ugo Poli. His pen name is a testimony of the affection he always retained for his childhood nurse, surnamed Saber, a simple Slovenian woman of staunch Catholic piety. Saba was unusual too among Italian poets of all ages in that he had little formal education: he did not even complete his secondary schooling. Shortly after World War I he set up a book store in his native city and, save for military service and a period of exile under Fascism, the store remained the center of his life.

Saba's inspiration is eclectic; he took his masters where he found them and drew freely from them all. His early verse, with echoes of Pascoli and Leopardi, may fairly be associated with the *crepuscolari*; he was not unwilling to learn from the French symbolists nor from his younger contemporaries Ungaretti and Montale, exponents of the new "hermeticism." Saba fuses these elements into his own style and, with regard to content, whatever his manner may be, he is personal and original. His successive volumes, of which the first was *Poesie* (1911), were combined in 1945 in the *Canzoniere* (originally published in 1921); as the years passed he published from time to time new editions of the *Canzoniere*, adding the verses published under separate titles in the intervals and editing as he progressed. The autobiographical-critical *Storia e cronistoria del Canzoniere* (1948) is an illuminating chronicle of his career. The *Canzoniere* itself (and Saba is a poet who is best appreciated when read *en bloc*) is an intimate lyrical autobiography.

The muse of this dedicated poet is highly subjective; he responds with empathy to persons, places, and even objects in his immediate line of vision, which, though egocentric, is honest and acute. So he tells us of his old nurse, his military service, his first meeting with his father, his city, and the trials he has endured. Casual, even trivial, sights or impressions will stir him. In a broken windowpane he can see how "all things take arms against you"; in a youth snatching a few apples from a fruit stall he can see all the joyous irresponsibility of adolescence; the sight of a goat in the fields can stir him to perceptive meditation:

In una capra dal viso semita
sentivo querelarsi ogni altro male,
ogni altra vita.*

(From a goat with semitic muzzle
I heard the lamenting
of all living things and their trouble.)

The exaltation of simplicity at times leads the poet into the banal and the sentimental. Yet this honesty of response, humble but very self-assured, remains his abiding strength. As his patient devotion to his craft over the long years made him increasingly skillful in the technical manipulation of assonance and cadence, his direct perceptions are set forth in a language as persuasive as it is simple. Elements of his inspiration are effectively blended in his "Ulysses," at once a confession, a credo, and an evocation:

Nella mia giovinezza ho navigato
lungo le coste dalmate. Isolotti

*Texts of the poems of Saba, Ungaretti, Quasimodo, and Montale are reproduced by permission of the publisher, Arnoldo Mondadori, Milan.

a fior d'onda emergevano, ove raro
un uccello sostava intento a prede,
coperti d'alghe, scivolosi, al sole
belli come smeraldi. Quando l'alta
marea e la notte li annullava, vele
sottovento sbandavano più al largo,
per fuggirne l'insidia. Oggi il mio regno
è quella terra di nessuno. Il porto
accende ad altri i suoi lumi; me al largo
sospinge ancora il non domato spirito,
è della vita il doloroso amore.

(From days of youth I remember sailing
past the Dalmatian shore; the rugged islets
came forth from the waves. Infrequently, upon them
sea birds, intent on prey, would alight; the beaches,
kelp-encrusted, gave slippery footing. Under
the sun they sparkled, bright as emeralds.
The tide rising or the night blotting them out,
barks bearing leeward would give them wide berth,
fleeing their treachery. And now my kingdom
is that land of No-man. The harbor kindles
its light for others. I turn out to sea
once more impelled by heart untamed and love,
laden with sorrow, of the life of man.)

The other three major poets of the era are associated with the "hermetic" movement, stressing the intimacy of the poet's vision, characterized by unusual and allusive imagery and a kind of stylistic austerity. Hermeticism was the prevailing current under Fascism, when poets saw the futility — or the dangers — of the social muse. In manner the school owed much to the French masters such as Mallarmé, Rimbaud, and Valéry. Of the great hermetic trio Giuseppe Ungaretti (1888–1970) is the oldest and may be regarded as the pioneer of the movement. Like Saba, Ungaretti was peripheral in his origins for he was born in Alexandria, Egypt, though of Tuscan stock. When he left Africa in his early twenties he established his residence not in Italy but in Paris where he attended the Sorbonne and became a friend of many of the French poets of the time; the influence of Apollinaire is immediately perceptible in his early verses. When Italy entered the war in 1915 Ungaretti volunteered and saw active service on the front. His first volume of poems — limited to eighty-seven copies and subsidized by the critic Renato Serra — was printed in 1916. Its title, *Il porto sepolto* (*The Buried Port*), is programmatically hermetic (even though the term had not yet been invented) and its contents revealed a very original talent. Ungaretti's aim was to seize the reader's attention at once; brevity is a necessary element in the impact he seeks to make. Abandoning traditional verse patterns, he employed short, staccato lines, eschewing adverbs and adjectives. Some of these earlier compositions have become the patrimony of Italians, for example, the lines from "Sono una creatura": "La morte / si sconta / vivendo" (Death / is discounted / by living), or the very characteristic (almost to the point of caricature) two line affirmation that makes up one complete poem: "M'illumino / d'immenso" (I illuminate myself / immensely). The most significant of these early verses is the poem that gives its title to the book, "Il porto sepolto," programmatic not only for Ungaretti but for all the hermetics to come:

Vi arriva il poeta
e poi torna alla luce con i suoi canti
e li disperde

Di questa poesia
mi resta
quel nulla
d'inesauribile segreto

(The poet goes ashore there
then returns to the light with his songs
and scatters them

Of this poem
there is left to me
that inexhaustibly secret
nothing)

In the Fascist era Ungaretti enjoyed a successful career as a journalist, critic, and, for a time, propagandist for the regime in Brazil. He became a member of the Italian Academy and ultimately a professor of literature at the University of Rome. As the years passed his poetic manner changed; he began to cultivate a somewhat more traditional style of verse and some of the ebullience of his early manner disappeared, giving place to a reflective melancholy. The maturing Ungaretti nourished his muse by translating Shakespeare, Góngora, and Racine; he learned to respect and employ the hendecasyllable and conceived of a great opus, made up of individual items, to which he gave the title *Vita d'un uomo* (*Life of a Man*). Many of these later poems are compositions of great verbal and musical subtlety, with a haunting suggestion of hidden, tragic significance. A fair example is "Il tempo è muto" ("Time is Silent") from *Il dolore* (1947, *Sorrow*):

Il tempo è muto fra canneti immoti . . .

Lungi d'approdi errava una canoa . . .
Stremato, inerte il rematore . . . I cieli
Già decaduti a baratri di fumi . . .

Proteso invano all'orlo dei ricordi,
Cadere forse fu merce . . .

Non seppe

Ch'è la stessa illusione mondo e mente,
Che nel mistero delle proprie onde
Ogni terrena voce fa naufragio.

(In the unstirring canebrake time is silent . . .

Remote from landfalls a canoe came straying . . .
The paddler exhausted, limp . . . The heavens
Already fallen into misty chasms . . .

Poised vainly on the brink of memories . . .
To fall perhaps was mercy . . .

He knew not

That world and mind are but the same illusion,
That in the mystery of its own high combers
Every terrestrial voice is doomed to founder.)

After the fall of Mussolini, Ungaretti lost his faith in Fascism. But retaining his professorship in Rome, he continued, though at irregular intervals, his writing of verse; the most important volume of his later years is *La terra promessa* (1952, *The Promised Land*); the title alludes to the *Aeneid* and the hero's search for a promised land — a metaphor susceptible of extension. At Ungaretti's death he enjoyed worldwide respect; his poetry preserved to the end a high level of excellence although — at least historically — perhaps the youthful verses are of greater significance than those of his later years.

Salvatore Quasimodo (1901–1968), brother-in-law of Vittorini, was born in Modica, a market town not far from Syracuse. He studied to be an engineer but at the end of his schooling he left his native island and found his vocation in journalism and literature. Most of his life he resided in Milan and was for many years a teacher of Italian literature at the Conservatory of Music in that city. He began writing verse at an early age; his first collection of poems *Acque e terre* (1930, *Waters and Lands*) was published in *Solaria* (which also, as we have noted, gave hospitality to Vittorini's early prose). *Oboe sommerso* (*Sunken Oboe*) followed in 1932 and the title poem of the collection was warmly received. The major theme of Quasimodo's first phase, lasting until the end of the war, is isolation. In the poet's terms of reference the motif centers on his nostalgia for Sicily, recalled with a rich imagery and symbolizing lost innocence or the irretrievable illusions of youth; his verse has great verbal polish and a seductive music.

Quasimodo's Sicilian inheritance gave him an affinity to the ancient Greek lyric poets and his translations of their verses, *Lirici greci* (1940), have the spontaneity of original compositions. He possesses all the intellectual austerity that is commonly associated with the hermetics, but at the same time his lyrics are characterized by a certain warm exuberance that have suggested to some critics a legacy of D'Annunzio. A typical and enduring poem of this nostalgic Sicilian is "Vento a Tindari" ("Wind at Tindari") from *Acque e terre:* the following passage illustrates its texture:

Tindari, mite ti so
fra larghi colli pensile sull'acque

dell'isole dolci del dio,
oggi m'assali
e ti chini in cuore.

Salgo vertici aerei precipizi,
assorto al vento dei pini,
e la brigata che lieve m'accompagna
s'allontana nell'aria,
onda di suoni e amore,
e tu mi prendi
di cui male mi trassi
e paura d'ombre e di silenzi,
rifugi di dolcezze un tempo assidue
e morte d'anima.

A te ignota è la terra
ove ogni giorno affondo
e segrete sillabe nutro:
altra luce ti sfoglia sopra i vetri
nella veste notturna,
e gioia non mia riposa
sul tuo grembo.

(Tindari, gentle I know you
between wide hills, leaning over the waters
of the god's sweet islands,
today you assail me
creeping into my heart.

I climb precipitious aerial cliff-sides,
made as one with the wind of the pines,
and the lighthearted band, my companions,
fades off in the air,
a wave of murmuring love receding,
and now you claim me —
you whom I erred in leaving,
and fears of shadow and silences,
shelters once of assiduous sweetness
and death of the soul.

To you unknown is the land
wherein daily I founder
and nourish secret syllables;
another light over the windows
defoliates you, robed for night,
and joy not mine finds repose
on your bosom.)

At the end of the war Quasimodo's poetry suffered a change of direction. He became a Communist sympathizer concerned with problems of social justice, and his verse reflects his new commitment. His poem "To the new moon," celebrating

Sputnik (1958), is symptomatic of this later phase; he also affirmed in a polemical lecture on "the Poet and the Politician" the significance of the poet's role in the life of the state. In 1959 Quasimodo was awarded the Nobel Prize — the first Italian so honored since Pirandello in 1934. The award was not unanimously acclaimed in Italy; many felt that if an Italian representive of the new poetry was to be recognized (and all agreed that such recognition was proper and timely) the prize should have gone more fittingly to Ungaretti or to Eugenio Montale, the third member of the hermetic triumvirate, Quasimodo's senior and — by a plurality if not a majority of critics — considered to be the most accomplished and enduring poet of his time.

Montale, born in Genoa in 1896 is certainly today a poet of truly international prominence. After some irregular schooling — he has no university degree — he served in World War I, seeing action on the Carso. For a time he trained to be a singer; most of his life, however, has been spent in journalism and collateral activities. He was one of the founders of the literary review *Primo tempo* (1922) and, since 1947, has been on the staff of the *Corriere della sera*. For many years (1929–1938) he was director of the Viesseux Library in Florence. During the years of the dictatorship Montale remained a quiet but tenacious anti-Fascist. He is something of an Anglophile; he translated T. S. Eliot's *Wasteland* and critics have found striking similarities in the style and substance of the two poets. His muse, though centered on the hermetic motifs of inner meditation, memory, and solitude, is more somber than that of Quasimodo, less aggressive than that of Ungaretti. Montale's is a quiet, inward-looking muse; his verses are gaunt to the point of obscurity, his posture essentially stoic, and his imagery — highly individual — is stark and even prosaic. Neither glowing sunrises nor aerial cliffsides capture his attention, which instead is seized by cuttlefish bones (such was the title of his first collection of verses, *Ossi di seppia*, 1925), a sea wall, an abandoned coast guard shed ("La casa dei doganieri" in *Le occasioni*, 1939), and the like. His "objective correlatives" are bleak and unassuming but they lead him to acute if not always consoling perceptions of the human predicament. Critics have found in his verses legacies of Dante and Leopardi but they have nothing of Dante's orthodoxy and not much of Leopardi's concern with musical effect. A "mottetto" from *Le occasioni* may perhaps be regarded as characteristic:

Lo sai: debbo riperderti e non posso.
Come un tiro aggiustato mi sommuove
ogni opera, ogni grido e anche lo spiro
salino che straripa
dai moli e fa l'oscura primavera
di Sottoripa.

Paese di ferrame e alberature
a selva nella polvere del vespro.
Un ronzio lungo viene dall' aperto,

strazia com' unghia ai vetri. Cerco il segno
smarrito, il pegno solo ch' ebbi in grazia
da te.

E l'inferno è certo.

(You know: once more I must and cannot lose you.
As by a well-directed shot I'm shaken
by every move and every cry and even
by every salt breath borne
from the quayside that brings the gloomy spring
to Sottoripa's shore.

A town of iron stacks and masts and riggings
looms like a forest in the dusk of evening.
A long drawn humming from the open sea
rasps like a fingernail on glass. I seek
for the lost token, the one pledge freely given
I had from you.

And Hell is certain.)

* * *

The four poets we have discussed enjoy a special and well-earned distinction, both for their originality and the consistency of their contribution over the years; there are however many other servants of the Muse whose works exemplify the healthy condition of poetry in contemporary Italy. The *crepuscolari* Moretti and Palazzeschi are still read and indeed are still writing verse. The poetry of their contemporary, Dino Campana (1885–1932), is enjoying increasing prestige; his *Canti orfici* (1914, Orphic Songs), though employing a vocabulary and a rhetoric of recognizably Carduccian and Dannunzian inheritance, yet have a music and an imagery that foreshadow the hermetics. Campana has had a considerable influence on younger poets. Arturo Onofri (1885–1928) was a more legitimate descendant of the old school, forging his own style out of Dannunzian decadence and classical discipline. Although differing greatly in manner the trio of older poets Pietro Jahier (1884–1966), Clemente Rebora (1885–1957), and Camillo Sbarbaro (1888–1967) share a preoccupation with ethical and religious matters. Jahier was a Waldensian; Rebora ended his life as a priest; Sbarbaro, a reflective, pessimistic moralist, is a forerunner of Montale.

Giacomo Noventa (1898–1960) is a special case; he wrote in his native dialect, many of his motifs are those of the nineteenth century romantics and, unlike most poets of his time, he expressed himself vigorously on public questions. Before the onslaught of the hermetics the polished verses of Vincenzo Cardarelli (1887–1959) were highly esteemed and the poems of Riccardo Bacchelli — associated with Cardarelli in the direction of the conservative review *La Ronda* — though overshadowed by his contribution to the narrative, are noteworthy for their elegant sobriety.

A fair number of poets, although contemporaries of the hermetics, have succeeded in resisting the attraction of that school. Carlo Betocchi and Sergio Solmi (both born in 1899) provide examples. Betocchi's verse has an inspiration at once Catholic and Georgic; Solmi, although he took something from the hermetics, is closer to Cardarelli in his search for simple grace and classical serenity; he is also a perceptive critic. Sandro Penna (b. 1906) and Leonardo Sinisgalli (b. 1908) have also escaped the hermetic influence; Penna's brief, sharp notations of fleeting impressions suggest Saba's manner, although Penna lacks an element of meditation. Sinisgalli is gifted with a bright deftness that occasionally verges on satire. Standing almost alone in clear opposition to the hermetic thrust is Cesare Pavese whose *Lavorare stanca* (1936, Work Is Wearying) presented a poetry of fact and even of narrative, with thematic echoes of the *crepuscolari*, patent indebtedness to Walt Whitman in its verse structure, and the exploitation of the "myth" that plays so prominent a part in Pavese's prose works.

Inevitably the influence of the great hermetic trio has been strong on the poets who have come after them. Both Alfonso Gatto (1909–1976) and Mario Luzi (b. 1914), significant poets in the seventies, can be classified as legitimate heirs of the masters, while possessing their own distinctive personalities. Gatto's poetry has a warmth and color suggestive of Quasimodo and sometimes betrays a social involvement as well. Luzi's terse lines, illuminated by the rugged kind of imagery for which Montale is famous, are closer to the true hermetic tradition; his content however bespeaks a man of faith, though hardly serene.

As the mention of Gatto, born in Salerno, suggests other southern voices (such as Rocco Scotellaro and the Apulian Vittorio Bodini [1914–1970], proud of his Bourbon inheritance), so Luzi calls to mind his fellow Tuscans and contemporaries Alessandro Parronchi and Piero Bigongiari, both born in 1914 and like him classifiable as hermetics of religious orientation. Vittorio Sereni (b. 1913), teacher, journalist (editor of the review *Questo e quello*), and war veteran, reflects the dilemmas of the contemporary world in a style growing increasingly less hermetic. Lucio Piccolo (1901–1969) is a special case; like his cousin Tomasi di Lampedusa, he is a "late bloomer." Chronologically he belongs with the generation of Quasimodo but the first of his three volumes of verse, *Canti barocchi e altre liriche* (*Baroque Songs and Other Lyrics*), was published in 1956, the title defiantly suggestive of the nature of the verses, distinguished by musical artistry but antimodern in thrust.

Italian poets born in the twenties or later have had a rich legacy to draw on; they have also had a challenging field of interest in all the complexities of a mechanized society. The most prominent of the younger poets to respond to this challenge is P. P. Pasolini whose *Le ceneri di Gramsci* (1957, The Ashes of Gramsci) indicates by its title the direction of his inspiration. A group of poets associated with Milan, Italy's greatest metropolis, are also fusing — often with highly charged language and arresting imagery — their private preoccupations with concern for the plight of twentieth century mankind; these include Giovanni Giudici (b. 1924), Giancarlo Majorino (b. 1928), and Roberto Sanesi (b. 1930), translator of Eliot and other English writers. To this list might be added the names of Nelo Risi (b. 1921), distinguished for his ironic humor, and Andrea Zanzotto (b. 1920) who, though not of Milan, shows attitudes akin to the metropolitan writers. The slightly older Franco Fortini (pseudonym of Franco Lattes, b. 1917), born in Florence, is a sensitive poet still in course of development, interesting for the influence of Brecht perceptible in his work.

Among the score of other lyric voices destined to profit by the assessment of time one may mention Margherita Guidacci (b. 1921), Luciano Erba (b. 1922), Alberico Sala (b. 1923), Bartolo Cataffi (b. 1922), Paolo de Benedetti (b. 1923), and Camillo Pennati (b. 1931).

* * *

In contrast to the abundant harvests in the fields of the narrative and verse, which are unrivaled in any comparable time span if one takes into consideration both quantity and quality, the contribution from the sector of the drama has been somewhat meager in contemporary Italy. The critic Giorgio Pullini has remarked on the paradoxical condition of the theater today, noting that although there are a number of repertories and traveling companies now active, well-staffed, well-directed, and successful (the *Teatro Piccolo* of Milan is but one example), yet more often than not they prefer to present plays translated from other languages or older Italian classics, ignoring the works of contemporary playwrights. The theater, to be sure, has always been the most neglected or the least successfully cultivated of genres in the annals of Italian letters. And it is probably true that in recent decades a good deal of talent that in another time would have sought expression in dramatic composition has been channeled into the cinema, in which, as we have noted, Italians may claim something of a primacy. Whatever the reason may be, outstanding dramatists are few. There is no figure today to rival Pirandello, whose plays still hold the stage and whose stature grows with the passing years. It could be said that there is no living dramatist either of the fertility of Roberto Bracco or the inventiveness of the *grotteschi* of the twenties. This is not to say however that Italy has no playwrights of merit.

The plays of Ugo Betti (1892–1953), for example, have enjoyed both the acclaim of the public and the esteem of literary critics; he is the most highly respected Italian dramatist since Pirandello. Betti was a magistrate and his plays, dealing with questions of guilt, justice, and atonement, reflect his professional concerns. Symbolically suggestive of universal moral problems, they are often exciting, although the characters portrayed tend to lack sharpness of definition. Among the best known of Betti's twenty-five plays are *Frana allo scalo nord* (1932, *Landslide*), *Ispezione* (1944, *The Inquiry*), *Delitto all' Isola delle Capre* (1948, *Goat Island*), and *La fuggitiva* (1952, *The Fugitive*). These and others of Betti's dramas have been presented abroad as well as on the Italian stage.

Something of Betti's ethical intention is also apparent in the work of Diego Fabbri (b. 1911). His *Processo a Gesù* (1955, *The Trial of Jesus*) attracted much attention; it deals with the question of society's guilt and, although obvious in intention and melodramatic in style, it remains a powerful drama. In other plays Fabbri pursues similar interests while casting his action in the more familiar sector of the traditional bourgeois drama. *Il seduttore* (1952, *The Seducer*) is a fair sample; in this case there is evidence of Pirandellian influence.

The engaging Eduardo de Filippo (b. 1900) is the most widely known and truly popular of living Italian playwrights both at home and abroad. His *Napoli millionaria* (1945) is a study, half comic, half moralistic, of ethical tensions under the pressures of wartime hardships; although the moral of the play is laudable its merits lie rather in the excellence of characterization and the convincing evocation of the atmosphere of time and place. Another successful play of this competent dramatist is *Filumena Marturano* (1946), later made into the film *Marriage Italian Style*. To a degree greater than any contemporary, de Filippo has the gift of creating natural and lively situations with sparkling dialogue, salted with humor in the tradition of the dialect theater.

Albertina (1945) of Valentino Bompiani (b. 1898) and *Giuditta* (1949) of Carlo Terron (b. 1910) also center on problems created by wartime stresses; the former studies the effect of separation on a young married couple, the latter, in effective human terms, poses the problem of the rights of the individual against the claims of the state. Terron, who has written more than a dozen plays, is a cerebral moralist; to *Giuditta* we may add *Lavinia fra i dannati* (1960, *Lavinia Among the Damned*) as characteristic of his work. Another notable study of human reactions in the times of air raids is *L'abisso* (1948, *The Abyss*) by Silvio Giovaninetti (b. 1901).

The hospitality of the Italian stage to the works of foreign dramatists has inevitably stimulated the younger generation of native playwrights and in recent years the influence of such innovators as Becket, Brecht, and Ionesco has been apparent. Among the avant garde writers who appeared in the sixties and are at present active, Edoardo Sanguineti and Dario Fo (b. 1926) may be mentioned. Sanguineti's theater contains such titles as *K* (1959) — the initial stands for Kafka — and *Protocolli* (1968) in which the characters are identified only as "masculine voice 1," "feminine voice 1," etc. Fo is essentially a humorist but his absurdities are not without their intellectual substratum or their social implications. Characteristic titles are *Un morto da vendere* (1962, Corpse for Sale) and *Pum pum! pum? la polizia* (1972). Another dramatist of interest, less experimental but forceful, is Giovanni Testori (b. 1923) who has presented dramas of Milanese life as well as the burlesque *Amblero* (1972, Hamblet) in a "Lombard" dialect. He is the author too of the "proletarian" novel *Il fabbricone* (1961, *The House in Milan*); his manner and zone of interest make him a kind of Milanese Pasolini.

Finally it should be noted that many of the novelists we have mentioned have also tried their hand at plays, some with considerable success. Bontempelli's *Nostra Dea*, written in 1925, still has vitality; others of the older generation who have written for the stage are Bacchelli, Alvaro, and Repaci. Among more recent writers Patti, Brancati, Dessì, Buzzati, Ottieri, and Pirro have all written plays — and the list could be extended. In all cases however their contributions to the theater are secondary to their other works.

* * *

Not suprisingly in a country whose greatest poet was also a major critic of his time, the practice of literary criticism thrives in the Italy of today. There may well be as many critics as creative writers; in many cases the categories overlap. As we have noted in passing, novelists such as Bacchelli, Alvaro, and Sciascia have made substantial contributions to literary criticism as have such poets as Quasimodo and Luzi — and more examples could be cited. Of the writers known primarily as critics many classifications have been made. Critics of criticism, using various criteria, subdivide themselves and their confrères into such compartments as Croceans and non-Croceans, ontological and historical schools, Marxists (whose prophets are the Communist martyr Antonio Gramsci [1891–1937] and the Hungarian Lukacs) and Catholics (with their own orthodoxy by no means monolithic), hermetics (owing something to the American New Criticism, assiduously studied in Italy), or variantists (Leopardi and Ungaretti are favorite exercise grounds for this group), or, recently, structuralists — to name only the principle varieties. Such categories blend into each other; one may have Crocean ontologists (most of them are), for example, or sundry eclectic mixtures. Individual practitioners are sometimes difficult to pigeonhole. It will suffice here to identify the outstanding figures in the general field of criticism and to record their specific contributions.

We may begin with the academic critics (yet another kind of distinction) and proceed to the "journalistic" which is to say the nonacademic group. As to the former, mostly university professors, while conceding that the line between research and criticism is difficult to draw, one may remark that in general they deal with figures and movements of the past, but there are many too who have written of the contemporary scene as well; the more prominent of them have essayed works of synthesis. Attilio Momigliano (1883–1952), a Crocean impressionist, wrote an illuminating history of Italian literature and a sensitive commentary on the *Divine Comedy*. Francesco Flora (1891–1962) is another critic of broad scope; his five volume history of Italian literature suggests the range of his erudition, and he is also the author of an early study of hermetic poetry and a critique of Joyce's *Ulysses*. Natalino Sapegno (b. 1901), a Marxist scholar, has published the most widely accepted commentary on the Divine Comedy; he has also in his *Compendio della storia della letteratura italiana* (1947) demonstrated his familiarity with and appreciation of the literature of our times and has collaborated in a number of encyclopedic enterprises. The hermetic Gianfranco Contini (b. 1900) is a prominent Dantist and also the editor of an anthology of twentieth century writers which is enriched by shrewd commentary. Other academic critics of stature include Umberto Bosco (b. 1900), a leading Petrarchist among other things, Giorgio Petrocchi (b. 1921), whose edition of the *Divine Comedy* is now accepted as the text of reference, Walter Binni (b. 1913), an astute student of intellectual currents, and Mario Fubini (b. 1900) who, within the Crocean framework, has produced valuable studies in literary theory.

The journalistic group — using the term in a wide sense — has naturally focussed on contemporary letters. The final volume of the *Scrittori d'Italia* of Pietro Pancrazi (1893–1952) appeared in 1953; Pancrazi was one of the most lucid of book reviewers. His work has been supplemented and continued by Emilio Cecchi (1884–1966) and Enrico Falqui (1902–1974). The latter has been called "the notary of Italian letters"; his *Novecento letterario italiano* (1970) is a massive compilation. The versatile Luigi Russo (1892–1961) belonged to both the academic and journalistic groups; he was a professor and also for many years editor of *Belfagor*, one of the best of the literary reviews. Russo's own work includes an authoritative study of Verga, an exhaustive account of the trajectory of modern criticism, and the very useful *I narratori* (revised edition 1959) which combines essential bio-bibliographical data with concise and pointed comment on writers of this century. Russo's criticism has both Marxist and Crocean facets. Giuseppe De Robertis (1888–1963) is another critic of perception and originality; he is the chief exponent of the variantism mentioned above. Mario Praz (b. 1896) deserves special mention; he is Italy's leading and one might fairly say pioneering student of English letters. His "comparatist" study of romanticism, *La carne, la morte e il diavolo nella letteratura romantica* (1930, *The Romantic Agony*) has become a kind of classic.

There are many younger critics of the contemporary scene. Carlo Bo (b. 1911), a "Catholic" critic, wrote a study of neorealism basic for the understanding of that school. Giorgio Pullini (b. 1928) has written book-length studies of the post-war novel and theater. Leone Piccioni (b. 1925) has studied prose writers and poets of today; he has recently published an all but definitive study of Ungaretti. Silvio Guarnieri (b. 1910) and Giuliano Manacorda (b. 1919) have written comprehensive works on the narrative. Oreste Macrì (b. 1913) and Luciano Anceschi (b. 1911) have devoted their attention to the contemporary poets.

* * *

An account of the activities in the sector of criticism would be incomplete without recognition of the role played by the numerous and varied magazines and reviews that have flourished in recent decades. We have mentioned a few of them in connection with individual authors or specific trends but there are many others no less worthy of note. The torch of *Solaria*, which expired in 1936, was taken up by *Letteratura* (founded in 1938): works of Montale, Ungaretti, Quasimodo, and Vittorini as well as critical studies by Walter Binni appeared in its pages. In the immediate postwar years *Botteghe oscure*, directed by Giorgio Bassani, offered hospitality to younger writers, native and foreign; the short-lived Leftist-oriented but open-minded *Politecnico*, under the aegis of Vittorini, made a significant contribution during this period. Among more recent reviews *Nuovi argomenti*, founded by Moravia, and *Officina*, under the direction of P P. Pasolini and Franco Fortini, are of particular interest. *Lo specchio* carried the very independent commentary of Giose Rimanelli; *Il caffè*, edited by Giorgio Soavi (b. 1923), poet and novelist, has also a personal approach. *La fiera letteraria*, of which G. A. Cibotto (b. 1925) was for some time the editor, and *Leggere*, under the direction of Gino Montesanto, exemplify reviews of an essentially informational nature.

Other magazines of importance include *Aretusa*, *Aut-aut*, *Il borghese*, *Menabò* (with the collaboration of Vittorini and Calvino), *Inventario*, *Il mulino*, *Il ponte* (in charge of Silvio Guarnieri), *Mercurio* (founded by Alba de Céspedes), *Nuova presenza*, *Tempo presente*, and *Paragone* (with contributions from the young critic Silvio Ramat, b. 1939). Many such publications had but a short life span; on the other hand new ones spring up with reassuring regularity. The weeklies and monthlies of general coverage also have *rubriche* dedicated to book reviews or comment on the literary scene; some very good criticism has appeared on the pages of *Epoca*, *Europeo*, *Espresso*, and like publications.

Finally, due credit must be given to the long standing journalistic tradition of the "terza pagina," regularly devoted to literary and cultural matters. The third page of *Il corriere della sera* of Milan, *La stampa* of Turin, and *Il messaggero* of Rome are the best known but no Italian daily is without this department, which provides scope for literary criticism, political-social commentary, and not infrequently memoires, anecdotes, and even short narrative pieces. Such critics as Cecchi and Falqui and such creative writers as Moravia and Montale have been more or less regular "terzapaginisti"; indeed a substantial number of the writers mentioned in our survey have appeared on the third page of one or more of the principal journals cited above.

* * *

The critical appraisal of any area of contemporary culture is likely to be hazardous and must be regarded as purely tentative. In matters of art and letters particularly, final judgment — if indeed it is ever to be reached — can only be pronounced after the passage of sufficient time to allow the virtues of any given artifact to be properly assayed — or for its flaws to become apparent. No doubt a decade or so hence some of the writers cited above who seem today most worthy of approbation will have declined in prestige, while others merely mentioned — or even overlooked — will rise in esteem. Yet if the foregoing account may be subject to revision in detail, it will at least serve to indicate two general truths concerning the state of Italian literature in the mid-twentieth century that are unlikely to be invalidated by the passage of time. First of all, the abundance of writers mentioned who have earned the acclaim of their compatriots and who have also succeeded in finding a public abroad will testify to the vitality of letters in the young Republic. Put simply, the period has produced many poets, novelists, and critics — and many good ones. And secondly, it is worth remarking that the period as a whole has been characterized by what one might call the true Italian approach — in which innovation flourishes within the framework of tradition. The recent decades have provided their share of novelty in matter and manner but there has been no repudiation of Italy's humanistic heritage.

APPENDIX

A LIST OF ADDITIONAL WRITERS

A LIST OF ENGLISH TRANSLATIONS
AND BOOKS IN ENGLISH DEALING WITH ITALIAN
LITERATURE

A CHRONOLOGICAL CHART

INDEX

A LIST OF ADDITIONAL WRITERS

For the convenience of some readers, listed here are a number of writers who, because of limitations of space, have not been treated in the body of the book.

Aleardi, Aleardo. 1812–1878. Poems.
Algarotti, Francesco. 1712–1764. Dialogues.
Astaldi, Maria. B. 1900. Historical studies.
Bellonci, Maria. B. 1902. Historical studies.
Bene, Sennuccio del. c. 1275–1349. Lyrics.
Benelli, Sem. 1875–1949. Plays.
Bevilacqua, Alberto. B. 1934. Novels.
Bigiaretti, Libero. B. 1906. Novels.
Boito, Arrigo. 1842–1918. Plays; *libretti*.
Botta, Carlo. 1766–1837. Histories.
Bracco, Roberto. 1862–1943. Plays.
Brignetti, Raffaello. B. 1921. Novels.
Brocchi, Virgilio. 1876–1961. Novels.
Camerino, Aldo. 1901–1966. Criticism; translations.
Cancogni, Manlio. B. 1916. Novels.
Cantù, Cesare. 1804–1895. History; historical novels.
Carrer, Luigi. 1801–1850. Ballads.
Castellaneta, Carlo. B. 1930. Novels.
Cavalca, Domenico. c. 1270–1342. Religious prose.
Cesarotti, Melchiorre. 1730–1808. Translator of Ossian.
Chiesa, Francesco. 1871–1973. Poems; novels.
Corti, Maria. B. 1915. Novels.
Davenzati, Chiaro. Second half of the thirteenth century. Lyrics.
Eco, Umberto. B. 1932. Criticism; *belles lettres*.
Firenzuola, Angelo. 1493–c. 1548. *Novelle*.
Flaiano, Ennio. 1910–1972. Novels.
Frescobaldi, Dino. ?–c. 1320. Lyrics.
Frugoni, Carlo Innocenzo. 1692–1768. Poems.
Gotta, Salvatore. B. 1888. Novels.
Griffi, Giuseppe Patroni. B. 1921. Plays.
Guidi, Alessandro. 1650–1712. Poems.
Lipparini, Giuseppe. 1887–1951. Novels; poems.
Martelli, Pier Giacomo. 1665–1727. Tragedies.
Molza, Francesco Maria. 1485–1544. Poems.
Montanelli, Indro. B. 1909. Journalism; historical studies.
Negri, Ada. 1870–1945. Poems.
Niccodemi, Dario. 1874–1934. Plays.
Panzini, Alfredo. 1863–1939. Novels; essays.
Rinuccini, Cino. c. 1350–1417. Lyrics.
Rovetta, Girolamo. 1851–1910. Novels; plays.
Salustri, Carlo Alberto ("Trilussa"). 1873–1950. Roman dialect verse.
Serao, Matilde. 1856–1927. Novels.
Serra, Renato. 1884–1915. Essays.
Slataper, Scipio. 1885–1915. Personal prose.
Testi, Fulvio. 1593–1646. Patriotic poems.
Varchi, Benedetto. 1503–1565. History.
Villaroel, Giuseppe. 1889–1964. Poems.
Zuccoli, Luciano. 1870–1929. Novels.

A LIST OF ENGLISH TRANSLATIONS AND BOOKS IN ENGLISH DEALING WITH ITALIAN LITERATURE

This list mentions only books (not articles), and is selective; only those translations and other works are mentioned that are thought to be of the greatest probable interest to readers of this book. The abbreviations EL and TC stand for Everyman's Library and Temple Classics respectively. The sign + following a date of publication indicates that the book in question has been reprinted since the date given. In the many cases in which a book has been published in two or more cities, only the original place of publication is mentioned.

A. BOOKS ON ITALY AND THE ITALIANS

Barzini, Luigi. *The Italians*. New York, 1964.

Olschki, Leonardo. *The Genius of Italy*. New York, 1949 +.

Salvadori, Massimo. *Italy*. Englewood Cliffs, 1965.

B. BOOKS RELATING TO ALL OR MOST OF THE COURSE OF ITALIAN LITERATURE

Bentley, Eric and others, trs. and eds. *The Classic Theatre: Six Italian Plays*, vol. 1. New York, 1958.

———*The Genius of the Italian Theatre*. New York, 1964.

De Luca, Michael and William Giuliano, eds. *Selections from Italian Poetry*. Irvington on Hudson, 1966.

De' Lucchi, Lorna, tr. *An Anthology of Italian Poems, 13th–19th Centuries*. London, 1922 +.

De Sanctis, Francesco. *History of Italian Literature*, tr. Joan Redfern. 2 vols. New York, 1931.

Everett, William. *The Italian Poets Since Dante*. New York, 1904.

Gardner, E. G., ed. *Italy, A Companion to Italian Studies*. London, 1934.

Garnett, Richard. *A History of Italian Literature*. London, 1898 +.

Hall, Robert A., Jr. *A Short History of Italian Literature*. Ithaca, 1951.

Italian Short Stories from the 13th to the 20th Centuries, tr. by various persons. EL.

Kay, George B., ed. and tr. *The Penguin Book of Italian Verse*. Penguin, 1966.

Luciani, Vincent. *A Brief History of Italian Literature*. New York, 1967.

———*A Concise History of the Italian Theatre*. New York, 1961.

Rebay, Luciano, tr. and ed. *Invitation to Italian Poetry*. New York, 1969.

Rendel, Romilda, tr. *An Anthology of Italian Lyrics, from the 13th Century to the Present Day*. London, 1925.

Roscoe, Thomas, tr. and ed. *The Italian Novelists*. London, 1825 +.

Shields, Nancy C. *Italian Translations in America*. New York, 1931.

Thayer, W. R. *Italica*. Boston, 1908.

Whitfield, J. H. *A Short History of Italian Literature*. Penguin, 1960.

Wilkins, E. H. *The Invention of the Sonnet and Other Studies in Italian Literature*. Rome, 1959.

C. BOOKS ON THE MEDIEVAL BACKGROUND OR RELATING TO EARLY ITALIAN LITERATURE

Artz, F. B. *The Mind of the Middle Ages*. New York, 1953.

Bishop, Morris, tr. *A Medieval Storybook*. Ithaca, 1970.

Bloch, Marc. *Feudal Society*, tr. L. A. Manyon. Chicago, 1961.

Curtius, Ernst. *European Literature and the Latin Middle Ages*, tr. Willard Trask. New York, 1959.

De Rougemont, Denis. *Love in the Western World*. New York, 1940.

Flores, Angel, ed. *An Anthology of Medieval Lyrics*. New York, 1962.

———*Medieval Age*. New York, 1963.

Gardner, E. G. *The Arthurian Legend in Italian Literature*. London, 1930.

Gaspary, A. R. *The History of Early Italian Literature to the Death of Dante*, tr. by Hermann Oelsner. London, 1930.

Jones, Charles W., ed. *Medieval Literature in Translation*. New York, London and Toronto, 1950.

Lewis, C. S. *The Allegory of Love*. London, 1936.

Lopez, Robert. *The Birth of Europe*. London, 1966.

Pound, Ezra. *The Spirit of Romance*. New York, 1952.

Previté-Orton, C. W. *The Shorter Cambridge Medieval History*. 2 vols. Cambridge, 1950.

Ross, James Bruce and Mary Martin McLaughlin, eds. *The Portable Medieval Reader*. New York, 1949.

Rossetti, D. G., tr. *The Early Italian Poets*. TC.

Sedgwick, H. D. *Italy in the Thirteenth Century*. 2 vols. Boston, 1912.

Southern, R. W. *The Making of the Middle Ages*. New Haven and London, 1953.

Taylor, H. O. *The Mediaeval Mind*, 4th ed. 2 vols. Cambridge, Massachusetts, 1949.

Valency, Maurice. *In Praise of Love*. New York, 1958.

Vossler, Karl. *Mediaeval Culture*, tr. W. C. Lawton. 2 vols. New York, 1929.

Weinberg, Julius R. *A Short History of Medieval Philosophy*. Princeton, 1964.

White, Lynn, Jr. *Medieval Technology and Social Change*. New York, 1966.

Wilhelm, James J. *The Cruelest Month*. New Haven and London, 1965.

———*Medieval Song: An Anthology of Hymns and Lyrics*. New York, 1971.

D. BOOKS RELATING TO ITALIAN LITERATURE OF THE RENAISSANCE

Aldington, Richard, tr. *Latin Poems of the Renaissance*. London, 1919.

Baron, Hans. *The Crisis of the Early Renaissance*. Princeton, 1955.

Bishop, Morris, tr. *A Renaissance Storybook*. Ithaca, 1971.

Blanchard, H. H., ed. *Prose and Poetry of the Continental Renaissance in Translation*. New York, 1949.

Burckhardt, Jacob. *The Civilization of the Renaissance in Italy*, tr. S. G. C. Middlemore. London, 1878 +.

Cassirer, Ernst, P. O. Kristeller, and J. H. Randall, Jr., eds. *The Renaissance Philosophy of Man*. Chicago, 1948.

Cronin, Vincent. *The Flowering of the Renaissance*. New York, 1969.

Durling, Robert. *The Figure of the Poet in the Renaissance Epic*. Cambridge, Massachusetts, 1965.

Einstein, Lewis. *The Italian Renaissance in England*. New York, 1902 +.

Ferguson, W. K. *The Renaissance*. New York, 1940.

———*The Renaissance: Five Centuries of Interpretation*. Boston, 1948.

Fletcher, J. B. *Literature of the Italian Renaissance*. New York, 1934.

Gardner, E. G. *The Arthurian Legend in Italian Literature*. London, 1930.

Garin, Eugenio. *Science and Civic Life in the Italian Renaissance*, tr. Peter Munz. Garden City, 1969.

George, William and Emily Waters, trs. *Renaissance Princes, Popes, and Prelates*. New York, 1963.

Giamatti, A. Bartlett. *The Earthly Paradise and the Renaissance Epic*. Princeton, 1966.

Greene, Thomas M. *The Descent from Heaven: A Study in Epic Continuity*. New Haven and London, 1963.

Hathaway, Baxter. *The Age of Criticism: The Late Renaissance in Italy*. Ithaca, 1962.

Hay, Denys. *The Italian Renaissance in its Historical Background*. Cambridge, 1961.

Haydn, Hiram. *The Counter Renaissance*. New York, 1950.

Herrick, Marvin T. *Italian Comedy in the Renaissance*. Urbana, 1960.

Huizinga, Johan. *The Waning of the Middle Ages*, tr. F. Hopman. New York, 1954.

Kristeller, Paul Oskar. *Studies in Renaissance Thought and Letters*. Rome, 1956.

———*Renaissance Thought: The Classic, Scholastic and Humanist Streams*. New York, 1963.

Lind, L. R., ed. *Lyric Poetry of the Italian Renaissance*. New Haven and London, 1954.

Lopez, Robert. *The Three Ages of the Italian Renaissance*. Charlottesville, 1970.

Mazzeo, Joseph Anthony. *Renaissance and Revolution*. New York, 1965.

Moore, O. H. *The Legend of Romeo and Juliet*. Columbus, 1950.

O'Kelley, Bernard, ed. *The Renaissance Image of Man and the World*. Columbus, 1966.

Priest, Harold M. *Renaissance and Baroque Lyrics*. Evanston, 1962.

The Renaissance. (Various authors). New York, 1953.

The Renaissance: A Reconsideration of the Theories and Reinterpretations of the Age. (Various authors). Madison, 1961.

Renaissance Profiles. (Various authors). New York, 1965.

Roeder, Ralph. *The Man of the Renaissance*. New York, 1933.

Scott, Mary A. *Elizabethan Translations from the Italian*. Boston, 1916.

Sellery, George Clarke. *The Renaissance*. Madison, 1950.

Singleton, Charles S., ed. *Art, Science, and History in the Renaissance*. Baltimore, 1967.

Speroni, Charles S. *Wit and Wisdom of the Italian Renaissance*. Berkeley, 1964.

Symonds, J. A. *Renaissance in Italy*. 7 vols. London, 1875–1886 +.

Taylor, H. O. *Thought and Expression in the Sixteenth Century*. 2 vols. New York, 1920.

Trinkaus, Charles. *In our Image and Likeness: Humanity and Divinity in Italian Renaissance Thought*. 2 vols. Chicago, 1970.

Tusiani, Joseph, tr. and ed. *Italian Poets of the Renaissance*. New York, 1971.

Weinberg, Bernard. *History of Literary Criticism in the Italian Renaissance*. Chicago, 1961.

E. BOOKS RELATING TO ITALIAN LITERATURE OF THE SEVENTEENTH, EIGHTEENTH, NINETEENTH, AND TWENTIETH CENTURIES

Bergin, Thomas G., tr. *Italian Sampler*. Montreal, 1964.

Borgese, G. A. *Goliath, or The March of Fascism*. New York, 1938.

Cary, Joseph. *Three Modern Italian Poets: Saba, Ungaretti, Montale*. New York, 1969.

Collison-Morley, Lacy. *Italy after the Renaissance*. London, 1930.

Colquhoun, Archibald and Neville Rodgers, eds. *Italian Tales of the Nineteenth Century*. Oxford, 1961.

Corrigan, Robert W. and others, trs. and eds. *Masterpieces of the Modern Italian Theatre*. New York, 1965.

Golino, Carlo, ed. and, with others, tr. *Contemporary Italian Poetry: An Anthology*. Berkeley and Los Angeles, 1962.

Greene, G. A. *Italian Lyrists of Today*. London, 1893 +.

Heiney, Donald. *Three Italian Novelists: Moravia, Pavese, Vittorini*. Ann Arbor, 1968.

Howells, W. D. *Modern Italian Poets*. New York, 1887.

Hughes, Serge. *The Fall and Rise of Modern Italy*. New York, 1967.

Hughes, H. Stewart. *The United States and Italy*, rev. ed. Cambridge, Massachusetts, 1965.

Lind, L. R. *Postwar Italian Poetry*. New York, 1974.

Livingston, Arthur. *Essays on Modern Italian Literature*. New York, 1950.
———*Modern Italian Literature*. London, 1911.
Ojetti, Ugo. *As They Seemed to Me*, tr. Henry Furst. Freeport, New York, 1927 +.
Pacifici, Sergio. *A Guide to Contemporary Italian Literature*. New York, 1962.
———ed. *From Verismo to Experimentation*. Bloomington, 1969.
———*The Modern Italian Novel from Capuana to Tozzi*. Carbondale, 1973.
———*The Modern Italian Novel from Manzoni to Svevo*. Carbondale, 1967.
———ed. *The Promised Land and Other Poems*. New York, 1957.
Paget, Violet. *Studies of the 18th Century in Italy*, 2nd. ed. London, 1907.
Phelps, Ruth S. *Italian Silhouettes*. New York, 1924.
Scott, Antonia and Laura Caretti, trs. *Postwar Italian Poetry*. Austin, 1972.
Smith, Denis Mack. *Italy: A Modern History*. Ann Arbor, 1959.
———*The Making of Italy, 1796–1870*. New York, 1968.
Trevelyan, Raleigh, ed. *Italian Short Stories*. Penguin, 1965.
———ed. *Italian Writing Today*. Penguin, 1967.
Tusiani, Joseph, ed. and tr. *From Marino to Marinetti*. New York, 1974.
Vittorini, Dmitri and Edwina, trs. *Italian Short Stories*. Penguin, 1972.
Vittorini, Domenico. *The Modern Italian Novel*. Philadelphia, 1930.
Wicks, Margaret C. W. *The Italian Exiles in London, 1816–1848*. Manchester, 1937.

CHAPTER 1: EARLY FOLK LITERATURE AND MINSTRELSY

Folk-Ballads of Southern Europe, tr. Sophie Jewett. New York, 1913.
Folk Songs of the Tuscan Hills, tr. Grace Warrack. London, 1914.
Italian Popular Tales, tr. and ed. T. F. Crane. Boston, 1885.
Lum, Peter. *Italian Fairy Tales Retold*. Chicago, 1967.
Out of the Heart of Italy: Folk Songs from Venetia to Sardinia, tr. Grace Warrack. Oxford, 1925.

CHAPTER *2*: ST. FRANCIS OF ASSISI

Capozzi, F. A. *A New Portrait of Francis of Assisi*. Northbridge, California, 1967.
Father Cuthbert. *Life of St. Francis of Assisi*. London, 1912 +.
Jörgensen, Johannes. *St. Francis of Assisi*, tr. T. O. Sloane. London, 1912.
St. Bonaventure's *Life of St. Francis; The Converse of Francis and his Sons with Holy Poverty;* and other writings of St. Francis. TC.
St. Bonaventure's *Life of St. Francis; The Little Flowers of St. Francis;* and *The Mirror of Perfection*. EL.
St. Francis. *The Writings of St. Francis of Assisi*, tr. by Paschal Robinson. Philadelphia, 1908.
St. Francis, Essays in Commemoration, 1226–1926. (Various authors). London, 1926.
Thomas of Celano. *Lives of St. Francis of Assisi*, tr. A. G. Ferrers Howell. London, 1908.

CHAPTER *3*: FREDERICK THE SECOND AND HIS CIRCLE

Deiss, Joseph Jay. *The Great Infidel*. New York, 1963.
Frederick the Second. *The Art of Falconry*, tr. and ed. C. A. Wood and F. Marjorie Fyfe. Stanford, 1943.
Kantorowicz, Ernst. *Frederick the Second*, tr. E. O. Lorimer. London, 1931.

CHAPTER 4: POETRY OF THE LATTER HALF OF THE THIRTEENTH CENTURY

Musa, Mark, tr. and ed. *The Poetry of Pannuccio del Bagno*. Bloomington, 1965.
Pound, Ezra. *Translations*. New York, 1953. Contains translations of Cavalcanti's poems.

Shaw, J. E. *Guido Cavalcanti's Theory of Love*. Toronto, 1949.
Underhill, Evelyn. *Jacopone da Todi: Poet and Mystic*. London, 1919.

CHAPTER 5: PROSE OF THE LATTER HALF OF THE THIRTEENTH CENTURY

Coulton, G. G. *From St. Francis to Dante*. London, 1906 +. (For Salimbene).
Da Varazze, Jacopo. *The Golden Legend*, tr. William Caxton. 7 vols. TC.
———*The Golden Legend*, tr. Granger Ryan and H. Ripperger. New York, 1948.
Gilson, Etienne. *The Philosophy of St. Bonaventura*, tr. Illtyd Trethowan. London, 1938.
Hart, H. H. *Venetian Adventurer*. Stanford, 1942 +.
Il novellino: The Hundred Old Tales, tr. Edward Storer. London, 1925.
Olschki, Leonardo. *Marco Polo's Asia*, tr. John F. Scott. Berkeley, 1960.
Polo, Marco. *The Book of Ser Marco Polo*, tr. Henry Yule. 3rd ed., rev. by Henri Cordier. London, 1926.
———*The Travels*, tr. R. E. Latham. Penguin, 1965.
———*The Travels*, tr. Aldo Ricci. London, 1931.
St. Bonaventure, *Life of St. Francis*. See list for Chapter 2.

GENERAL WORKS ON DANTE

Translations

The Temple Classics edition (6 vols; London, 1899–1906) contains translations of all of Dante's works. *The Portable Dante* (ed. Paolo Milano; New York, 1949) contains the complete *Divine Comedy* (tr. Laurence Binyon), the *Vita Nuova* (tr. D. G. Rossetti), and excerpts from the Latin works. There are many English translations of the *Divine Comedy;* see Gilbert F. Cunningham, *Dante in English*, 2 vols. (Edinburgh and London, 1965–1966).

Dante's Lyric Poetry, tr. Kenelm Foster and Patrick Boyde. 2 vols. Oxford, 1967.
De Monarchia, tr. Donald Nicholl in *Monarchy and Three Political Letters*. New York, 1954.
De Monarchia, tr. Herbert W. Schneider in *On World Government*. New York, 1957.
The Eclogues, tr. Wilmon Brewer. Boston, 1927 +.
The Eclogues, tr. P. H. Wicksteed and E. G. Gardner in *Dante and Giovanni del Virgilio*. Westminster, 1902.
La Vita Nuova, tr. Ralph W. Emerson. Chapel Hill, 1960.
La Vita Nuova, tr. Mark Musa. Bloomington, 1962.
La Vita Nuova, tr. Barbara Reynolds. Penguin, 1969.
Letters, tr. Warwick Chipman. Oxford, 1966.
Letters, tr. C. S. Latham, Boston, 1891.
Letters, tr. Paget Toynbee, Oxford, 1920 +.
The Odes of Dante, tr. H. S. Vere-Hodge. Oxford, 1963.

Concordances

Gordon, Lewis H., ed. *A Supplementary Concordance to the Minor Italian Works of Dante*. Cambridge, Massachusetts, 1936.
Rand, E. K. and E. H. Wilkins, eds. *Dantis Alagheri operum latinorum concordantiae*. Oxford, 1912.
Wilkins, Ernst Hatch, Thomas G. Bergin, and Anthony De Vito, eds. *A Concordance to the Divine Comedy*. Cambridge, Massachusetts, 1965.

Studies

Barbi, Michele. *Life of Dante*, tr. Paul Ruggiers. Berkeley, 1954.
Bergin, Thomas G. *Dante*. New York, 1965.

Cambon, Glauco. *Dante's Craft*. Minneapolis, 1969.
Centenary Essays on Dante. Oxford Dante Society. Oxford, 1965.
Chubb, Thomas Caldecot. *Dante and His World*. Boston and Toronto, 1966.
Cioffari, Vincent. *The Conception of Fortune and Fate in the Works of Dante*. Cambridge, Massachusetts, 1940.
Cosmo, Umberto. *A Handbook to Dante Studies*, tr. David Moore. Oxford, 1950.
Davis, Charles Till. *Dante and the Idea of Rome*. Oxford, 1957.
De Sua, William and Gino Rizzo, eds. *A Dante Symposium*. Chapel Hill, 1965.
Dinsmore, C. A. *Aids to the Study of Dante*. Boston, 1903.
———*Life of Dante Alighieri*. Boston, 1917.
———*The Teachings of Dante*. Boston, 1902.
Fergusson, Francis. *Dante*. New York, 1966.
Freccero, John, ed. *Dante: A Collection of Critical Essays*. Englewood Cliffs, 1965.
Friedrich, W. P. *Dante's Fame Abroad (1350–1850)*. Rome, 1950.
Gardner, E. G. *Dante*. London, 1903 +.
Gilbert, Allan H. *Dante's Conception of Justice*. Durham, North Carolina, 1925.
Gilson, Étienne. *Dante the Philosopher*, tr. David Moore. New York, 1949.
Grandgent, C. H. *Dante*. New York, 1921.
———*Discourses on Dante*. Cambridge, Massachusetts, 1924.
———*The Power of Dante*. Boston, 1918.
Haller, Robert S., ed. and tr. *Literary Criticism of Dante Alighieri*. Lincoln, Nebraska, 1973.
Holbrook, R. T. *Dante and the Animal Kingdom*. New York, 1902.
———*Portraits of Dante from Giotto to Raffael*. London, 1911.
Howell, A. G. Ferrers. *Dante, His Life and Works*. London, 1912.
LaPiana, Angelina. *Dante's American Pilgrimage*. New Haven, 1948.
Lenkeith, Nancy. *Dante and the Legend of Rome*. London, 1952.
Limentani, V., ed. *The Mind of Dante*. Cambridge, 1965.
Mather, F. G., Jr. *The Portraits of Dante*. Princeton, 1921.
Moore, Edward. *Studies in Dante*. 4 vols. London, 1896–1917.
Musa, Mark, ed. *Essays on Dante*. Bloomington, 1964.
Scartazzini, G. A. *A Companion to Dante*, tr. A. J. Butler. London, 1893.
Sedgwick, H. D. *Dante*. New Haven, 1918.
Symonds, J. A. *An Introduction to the Study of Dante*. London, 1899.
Toynbee, Paget. *Dante Alighieri: His Life and Works*, 4th ed. London, 1910 +.
———*Dante in English Literature from Chaucer to Cary*. 2 vols. London, 1909 +.
———*Concise Dictionary of Proper Names and Notable Matters in the Works of Dante*, rev. by Charles S. Singleton. Oxford, 1968.
Wicksteed, Philip H., tr. *Dante and Aquinas*. New York, 1971. First published 1913.
———tr. *The Early Lives of Dante*. London, 1904.

CHAPTER 6: DANTE IN FLORENCE

Boyde, Patrick. *Dante's Style in His Lyric Poetry*. Cambridge, 1971.
Grandgent, C. H. *The Ladies of Dante's Lyrics*. Cambridge, Massachusetts, 1917.
Grey, Nicolette. *Rossetti, Dante and Ourselves*. London, 1947.
Leigh, Gertrude. *New Light on the Youth of Dante*. London, 1929.
Ruggiers, Paul G. *Florence in the Age of Dante*. Norman, Oklahoma, 1964.
Shaw, J. E. *Essays on the Vita Nuova*. Princeton, 1929.
Singleton, Charles. *An Essay on the Vita Nuova*. Cambridge, Massachusetts, 1949.
Wicksteed, Philip H. *From Vita Nuova to Paradiso*. Manchester, 1922.

Williams, Charles. *The Figure of Beatrice*. London, 1943.

CHAPTER 7: DANTE IN EXILE

Passerin d'Entrèves, Alessandro. *Dante as a Political Thinker*. Oxford, 1952.
Wicksteed, P. H. and E. G. Gardner. *Dante and Giovanni del Virgilio*. Westminster, 1902.

CHAPTER 8: *The Divine Comedy*

Asín, Miguel. *Islam and the Divine Comedy*, tr. and abr. Harold Sunderland. New York, 1926.
Auerbach, Erich. *Dante: Poet of the Secular Worlds*, tr. Ralph Manheim. Chicago, 1961.
———"Farinata and Cavalcante" in *Mimesis*, tr. Willard Trask. Princeton, 1953.
Bergin, Thomas G. *Dante's Divine Comedy*. Englewood Cliffs, 1971.
———*A Diversity of Dante*. New Brunswick, 1969.
———ed. *From Time to Eternity*. New Haven and London, 1967.
———*Perspectives on the Divine Comedy*. New Brunswick, 1967.
Blake, William. *Illustrations to the Divine Comedy by William Blake*. London, 1922.
Brandeis, Irma. *The Ladder of Vision*. Garden City, 1961.
———ed. *Discussions of the Divine Comedy*. Boston, 1961.
Brieger, Peter, Millard Meiss and Charles S. Singleton, *Illuminated Manuscripts of the Divine Comedy*. 2 vols. Princeton, 1969.
Carroll, J. S. *Exiles of Eternity: An Exposition of Dante's Inferno*, 2nd ed. London, 1904.
———*Prisoners of Hope: An Exposition of Dante's Purgatorio*. London, 1906.
———*In Patria: An Exposition of Dante's Paradiso*. London, 1911.
Chandler, Stanley Bernard, ed. *The World of Dante: Six Studies in Language and Thought*. Toronto, 1966.
Charity, A. C. *Events and their Afterlife*. Cambridge, 1966.
Clements, Robert J., ed. *American Critical Essays on the Divine Comedy*, New York and London, 1967.
Croce, Benedetto. *The Poetry of Dante*, tr. Douglas Ainslee. New York, 1922.
Demaray, John G. *The Invention of Dante's Commedia*. New Haven, 1974.
Dunbar, Helen Flanders. *Symbolism in Mediaeval Thought and Its Consummation in the Divine Comedy*. New Haven and London, and 1929.
Eliot, T. S. "Dante" in *Selected Essays*. New York, 1932.
Fergusson, Francis. *Dante's Drama of the Mind: A Modern Reading of the Purgatorio*. Princeton, 1953.
Flamini, Francesco. *Introduction to the Study of the Divine Comedy*, tr. Freeman M. Josselyn. Boston, 1910.
Foster, Kenelm. *God's Tree*. Blackfriars, 1957.
———*The Mind in Love*. London, 1956.
Gardner, E. G. *Dante and the Mystics*. London, 1913.
———*Dante's Ten Heavens*, 2nd ed. London, 1904.
Gilbert, Allan H. *Dante and His Comedy*. New York, 1963.
Hollander, Robert. *Allegory in Dante's Commedia*. Princeton, 1969.
Kuhns, Oscar L. *The Treatment of Nature in Dante's Divina Commedia*. London, New York, 1897.
Lagercrantz, Olof. *From Hell to Paradise*, tr. Ann Blair. New York, 1966.
Lippmann, Friedrich, ed. *Drawings by Sandro Botticelli for Dante's Divinia Commedia*. London, 1896.
Mazzeo, Joseph Anthony. *Structure and Thought in the Paradiso*. Ithaca, 1958.

———*Medieval Cultural Tradition in Dante's Comedy*. Ithaca, 1960.

Orr, M. A. *Dante and the Early Astronomers*, 2nd ed. London, 1956.

Papini, Giovanni. *Dante Vivo*, tr. Eleanor Broadus and Anna Benedetti. New York, 1934.

Reade, William Henry V. *The Moral System of Dante's Inferno*. Oxford, 1909.

Santayana, George. *Three Philosophical Poets*. Cambridge, Massachusetts, 1910 +.

Sayers, Dorothy L. *Introductory Papers on Dante*. New York, 1954.

———*Further Papers on Dante*. New York, 1957.

Singleton, Charles S. *Dante Studies 1: Commedia — Elements of Structure*. Cambridge, Massachusetts, 1954.

———*Dante Studies 2: Journey to Beatrice*. Cambridge, Massachusetts, 1958.

———*The Divine Comedy: Inferno*. 2 vols. Princeton, 1970. Text, translation, and commentary.

Stambler, Bernard. *Dante's Other World*. New York, 1957.

Swing, Thomas K. *The Fragile Leaves of the Sybil*. Westminster, Maryland, 1962.

Thompson, David. *Dante's Epic Journeys*. Baltimore, 1973.

Whitfield, J. H. *Dante and Virgil*. Oxford, 1949.

Wicksteed, Philip H. *Dante and Aquinas*. London, 1913.

Witte, Karl. *Essays on Dante*, tr. C. M. Lawrence and P. H. Wicksteed. Cambridge, 1898.

CHAPTER 9: CONTEMPORARIES OF DANTE

Chubb, Thomas C., tr. *The Months of the Year*. Sanbornville, New Hampshire, 1960. Twelve Sonnets by Folgore da San Gimignano.

———tr. *The Sonnets of a Handsome and Well-Mannered Rogue*. Hamden, Connecticut, 1970. Sonnets of Cecco Angiolieri.

Compagni. *The Chronicle*, tr. Else C. M. Benecke and A. G. Ferrers Howell. TC.

Rossetti, D. G., tr. *Dante and His Circle*. London, 1874.

———tr. *The Early Italian Poets*. London, 1861.

Tusiani, Joseph, tr. *The Age of Dante: An Anthology of Early Italian Poetry*. Long Island City, New York, 1974.

Villani's Chronicle: Being Selections from the First Nine Books of the Croniche fiorentine, tr. Rose E. Selfe; ed. P. H. Wicksteed. London, 1896 +.

CHAPTER 10: PETRARCH

Armi, Anna Maria, tr. *Petrarch: Sonnets and Songs*. New York, 1946.

Auslander, Joseph, tr. *The Sonnets of Petrarch*. London, New York, and Toronto, 1931.

Bergin, Thomas G. *Petrarch*. New York, 1970.

———*Petrarch: Selected Sonnets, Odes and Letters*. New York, 1966.

———*Petrarch's Bucolicum Carmen*. New Haven and London, 1974.

———ed. *The Sonnets of Petrarch*. New York, 1965.

Bernardo, Aldo. *Petrarch, Scipio and the "Africa."* Baltimore, 1962.

Bishop, Morris, ed. and tr. *Letters from Petrarch*. Bloomington, 1966.

———tr. *Love Rhymes of Petrarch*. Ithaca, 1932.

———*Petrarch and His World*. Bloomington, 1963.

Calthrop, H. C. H. *Petrarch, His Life and Times*. New York, 1907.

Cosenza, Mario E. *Francesco Petrarca and the Revolution of Cola di Rienzo*. Chicago, 1913.

———tr. and ed. *Petrarch's Letters to Classical Authors*. Chicago, 1910.

Draper, W. H. *Petrarch's Secret*. London, 1911.

Forster, Leonard. *The Icy Fire: Five Studies in European Petrarchism*. Cambridge, 1969.

Foscolo, Ugo. *Essays on Petrarch*. London, 1823.

Foulke, William D., tr. *Some Love Songs of Petrarch*. London, 1915. Annotated with a biographical introduction.

Gail, Marzieh. *Avignon in Flower: 1309–1403*. Boston, 1965.

Mills, Edmund James. *The Secret of Petrarch*. London, 1904.

Mommsen, Theodor E., ed. and tr. *Petrarch's Testament*. Ithaca, 1957.

Parker, Henry, Lord Morley, tr. *Tryumphes of Fraunces Petrarke*, ed. D. D. Carnicelli. Cambridge, Massachusetts, 1971.

Phelps, Ruth S. *The Earlier and Later Forms of Petrarch's Canzoniere*. Chicago, 1925.

Potter, M. A. *Four Essays*. Cambridge, Massachusetts, 1917.

Rawsky, Conrad H., ed. and tr. *Petrarch: Four Dialogues for Scholars*. Cleveland, 1967.

Robinson, J. H. and H. W. Rolfe. *Petrarch, The First Modern Scholar and Man of Letters*, 2nd ed. New York, 1914.

Tatham, E. H. R. *Francesco Petrarca: The First Modern Man of Letters*. 2 vols. London, 1925–1926.

Thompson, David H., ed. and tr. *Petrarch: A Humanist Among Princes: An Anthology of Petrarch's Letters and Selections From His Other Works*. New York, Evanston and London, 1971.

Whitfield, J. H. *Petrarch and The Renascence*. Oxford, 1943.

Wilkins, E. H. *Life of Petrarch*. Chicago, 1961.

———*The Making of the "Canzoniere" and Other Petrarchan Studies*. Rome, 1951.

———tr. *Petrarch at Vaucluse: Letters in Verse and Prose*. Chicago, 1958.

———*Petrarch's Correspondence*. Padua, 1960.

———*Petrarch's Eight Years in Milan*. Cambridge, Massachusetts, 1958.

———*Petrarch's Later Years*. Cambridge, Massachusetts, 1959.

———*Studies in the Life and Works of Petrarch*. Cambridge, Massachusetts, 1955.

———*The Triumphs of Petrarch*. Chicago, 1962.

Zacour, Norman P., tr. *Petrarch's Book Without a Name*. Toronto, 1973.

Zeitlin, Jacob, tr. *The Life of Solitude by Francis Petrarch*. Urbana, 1924.

CHAPTER 11: BOCCACCIO

Translations

Available translations of the *Decameron* include those of: Richard Aldington, New York, 1971; G. H. McWilliam, Penguin, 1972; Frances Winwar, New York, 1930 +.

Coulter, Cornelia. *Geneology of the Gods*. Poughkeepsie, 1922.

Donno, Daniel J. *The Nymph of Fiesole*. New York, 1960.

Gordon, R. K. *The Story of Troilus*. London, 1934. Contains translation of *Il Filostrato*.

Griffin, N. E. and A. B. Myrick. *The Filostrato*. Philadelphia, 1929 +.

Guarino, G. A. *Concerning Famous Women*. New Brunswick, 1963. Contains translation of *De claris mulieribus*.

Hall, L. B. *The Fates of Illustrious Men* (De casibus virorum illustrium). New York, 1965.

Hutton, Edward, ed. *Amorous Fiammetta*, tr. Bartholomew Yong (1587). London, 1926.

———ed. *A Pleasant Disport of Divers Noble Personages*, tr. H. C. London, 1927. An Elizabethan translation of the Thirteen Questions of Love in the *Filocolo*.

Osgood, C. G. *Boccaccio on Poetry*. Princeton, 1930. A translation of *Genealogia deorum gentilium*, XIV–XV.

Wright, H. G., ed., *Forty-six Lives, translated from Boccaccio's De claris mulieribus* (by Henry Parker, Lord Morely). London, 1943.

Studies

Chubb, Thomas C. *The Life of Giovanni Boccaccio*. New York, 1930.

Lee, A. C. *The Decameron: Its Sources and Analogues*. London, 1909.
Scaglione, Aldo. *Nature and Love in the Late Middle Ages*. Berkeley and Los Angeles, 1963.
Young, Karl. *The Origin and Development of the Story of Troilus and Criseyde*. London, 1908.

CHAPTER 12: CONTEMPORARIES OF PETRARCH AND BOCCACCIO

Hughes, Serge. *Little Flowers of St. Francis*. 1964. See also list for Chapter 2.
Origo, Iris. *Tribune of Rome*, London, 1938.

CHAPTER 13: WRITERS OF THE LATE FOURTEENTH CENTURY

Curtayne, Alice. *St. Catherine of Siena*. London, 1929.
Jorgenson, Johannes. *St. Catherine of Siena*, tr. Ingeborg Lund. London, 1938.
Misciattelli, Piero. *The Mystics of Siena*, tr. Margaret Peters-Roberts. Cambridge, 1929.
Scudder, Vida D. *St. Catherine of Siena as Seen in her Letters*. With many translations. London, 1905.
Ser Giovanni. *The Pecorone*, tr. W. G. Walters. 3 vols. London, 1901.
Tales from Sacchetti, tr. Mary G. Steegman. London, 1908.

CHAPTER 14: THE MILITANT HUMANISTS

Ady, Cecilia M. *Pius II . . . The Humanist Pope*. London, 1913.
Alberti, L. D. *The Albertis of Florence: Leon Battista Alberti's Della Famiglia*, tr. G. A. Guarino. Lewisburg, 1971.
———*The Family in Renaissance Florence*, tr. Renée Neu Watkins. Columbia, South Carolina, 1969.
———*On Painting*, tr. John R. Spencer. New Haven, 1956 +.
———*Ten Books on Architecture*, tr. James Leoni. New York, 1966.
Boulting, William. *Aeneas Sylvius*. London, 1908.
Pius II (Enea Silvio Piccolomini). *The Commentaries*, tr. Florence Alden Gragg. New York, 1959 +.
———*De gestis Concilli Basiliensis commentariorum libri II*, tr. Denys Hay and W. K. Smith. Oxford and New York, 1967.
———*Selected Letters*, tr. Albert R. Baca. Northridge, California, 1969.
Poggio, Bracciolini. *The Facetiae*, tr. Bernhardt J. Hurwood. New York, 1968.
Valla. *Treatise on the Donation of Constantine*, tr. C. B. Coleman. New Haven, 1922.
Woodward, W. H. *Studies in Education During the Age of the Renaissance*, 1400–1600. Cambridge, 1906.
———*Vittorino da Feltre and Other Humanist Educators*. Cambridge, 1897 +.

CHAPTER 15: CONTEMPORARIES OF THE MILITANT HUMANISTS

Howell, A. G. Ferrers. *S. Bernardino of Siena*. London, 1913.
Misciatelli. See list for Chapter 13.
St. Bernardine. *Examples*, tr. and ed. Ada Harrison. London, 1926.
———*Sermons*, tr. Helen J. Robbins; ed. Nazareno Orlandi. Siena, 1920.

CHAPTER 16: LORENZO DE' MEDICI

Armstrong, E. *Lorenzo de' Medici*. London, 1911.
Lipari, Angelo. *The Dolce Stil Nuovo according to Lorenzo de' Medici*. New Haven, 1936.
Schevill, Ferdinand. *The Medici*. New York, 1949.

CHAPTER 17: FLORENTINE HUMANISTS

Dulles, Avery. *Princepts concordiae: Pico della Mirandola and the Scholastic Tradition.* Cambridge, Massachussets, 1941.

Ficino. *Commentary on Plato's Symposium*, tr. S. R. Jaynes. Columbia, Missouri, 1949.

Kristeller, P. O. *The Philosophy of Marsilio Ficino*, tr. Virginia Conant. New York, 1942.

Lord, L. E. *A Translation of the Orpheus of Angelo Politian and the Aminta of Torquato Tasso.* London, 1931.

Martines, Lauro. *The Social World of the Florentine Humanists.* Princeton, 1963.

Pico. *Of Being and Unity*, tr. and ed. V. M. Hamm. Milwaukee, 1943.

———*On Being and the One*, tr. P. J. W. Miller and *Hectaplus*, tr. Douglas Carmichael, together with *Dignity*. Indianapolis and New York, 1965.

———*On the Dignity of Man.* tr. Elizabeth L. Forbes. Lexington, Kentucky, 1953.

———*Oration on the Dignity of Man*, tr. A. R. Caponigri. Chicago, 1956.

———*A Platonick Discourse Upon Love*, tr. Thomas Stanley; ed. E. G. Gardner. Boston, 1914.

CHAPTER 18: LUIGI PULCI AND OTHER FLORENTINE WRITERS

Da Bisticci, Vespasiano. *Memoirs*, tr. W. G. and Emily Waters. London, 1926.

Einstein, Lewis. *Luigi Pulci and the Morgante Maggiore.* Berlin, 1902.

Hart, Ivor B. *The World of Leonardo da Vinci.* New York, 1962.

Leonardo. *The Notebooks*, tr. and ed. Edward McCurdy. London, 1906 +.

——— *Treatise on Painting*, tr. P. A. McMahon. 2 vols. Princeton, 1956.

Merejkowski, Dmitri. *The Romance of Leonardo da Vinci*, tr. Herbert Trench. New York and London, 1912.

Misciatelli, Piero. *Savonarola*, tr. Margaret Peters-Roberts. Cambridge, 1929.

O'Malley, C. D., ed. *Leonardo's Legacy: An International Symposium.* Berkeley, 1969.

Savonarola. *The Triumph of the Cross*, tr. O. T. Hill. London, 1868. Translated from the Latin.

——— *The Triumph of the Cross*, tr. John Procter. London, 1901. Translated from Savonarola's own Italian translation.

Vallentin, Antonina. *Leonardo da Vinci*, tr. E. W. Dickes. New York, 1938.

Villari, Pasquale. *Life and Times of Girolamo Savonarola*, tr. Linda Villari. 2 vols. London, 1888 +.

CHAPTER 19: NEAPOLITAN, FERRARESE, AND OTHER WRITERS

Boiardo. *The Orlando innamorato Translated into Prose from the Italian of Francesco Berni*, tr. W. S. Rose. Edinburgh, 1823. A full summary of the poem, with several passages in translation.

Colonna. *The Strife of Love in a Dream*, ed. Andrew Lang. London, 1890. The anonymous Elizabethan translation of the first book.

Mantuan. *The Eclogues*, tr. George Turberville (1567); ed. Douglas Bush. New York. 1937.

Masuccio. *The Novellino*, tr. W. G. Waters. London, 1895 +.

Sannazzaro. *Arcadia* and *Piscatorial Eclogues*, tr. Ralph Nash. Detroit, 1966.

CHAPTER 20: BEMBO

Bembo. *Gil Asolani*, tr. Rudolph Gottfried. Bloomington, 1954.

CHAPTER 21: ARIOSTO

Ariosto. *Orlando Furioso*, tr. Allen Gilbert. New York, 1954.

——— *Orlando Furioso*, ed. Rudolph Gottfried. Bloomington, 1963. Selections from Harington's translation (1591).

——— *Orlando Furioso*, tr. Harington (complete); ed. Robert McNulty. London and New York, 1972.

——— *Orlando Furioso*, tr. Harington; ed. Graham Hough. Carbondale, 1963.

——— *Orlando Furioso*, tr. W. S. Rose; ed. S. A. Baker and A. B. Giamatti. New York, 1968.

——— *Supposes*, tr. George Gascoigne (1556). In *Supposes and Jocasta*, ed. J. W. Cunliffe. Montreal, 1906.

Croce, Benedetto. *Ariosto, Shakespeare and Corneille*, tr. Douglas Ainslie. New York, 1920.

Gardner, E. G. *The King of Court Poets*. London, 1906.

Grillo, Giacomo. *Poets at the Court of Ferrara: Ariosto, Tasso, and Guariui with a Chapter on Michelangelo*. Boston, 1943.

CHAPTER 22: MICHELANGELO AND OTHER POETS

Michelangelo: Translations

De Tolnay, Charles. *Michelangelo: The Complete Works*. New York, 1965.

Gilbert, Creighton. *Michelangelo: The Complete Poems and Selected Letters*. New York, 1963.

Jennings, Elizabeth. *The Sonnets of Michelangelo*. New York, 1970.

Newell, W. W. *Sonnets and Madrigals*. Boston, 1900.

Ramsden, E. H. *The Letters of Michelangelo*. 2 vols. Palo Alto, 1963.

Symonds, J. A. *The Sonnets* (Michelangelo and Campanella). London, 1878 +.

Tusiani, Joseph. *The Complete Poems of Michelangelo*. New York, 1960.

Michelangelo: Studies

Clements, R. J. *Michelangelo's Theory of Art*. New York, 1961.

——— *The Poetry of Michelangelo*. New York, 1965.

——— ed. and tr. *Michelangelo: A Self-Portrait*. Englewood Cliffs, 1963.

De Tolnay, Charles. *The Art and Thought of Michelangelo*. New York, 1964.

Ludwig, Emil. *Three Titans*, tr. Ethel C. Mayne. London, 1930.

Morgan, C. H. *The Life of Michelangelo*. New York, 1960.

Stone, Irving. *The Agony and the Ecstasy*. Garden City, 1961.

Venturi, Adolfo. *Michelangelo*, tr. Joan Redfern. London, 1928.

Other Poets

Jerrold, Maud F. *Vittoria Colonna, with Some Account of her Friends and her Times*. London, 1906.

Cook, A. S. *The Art of Poetry*. Boston, 1892. Contains a translation of Vida's *De arte poetica*.

Vida. *The Game of Chess*, tr. by R. S. Lambert. Wembley Hill, 1921.

CHAPTER 23: MACHIAVELLI AND GUICCIARDINI

Machiavelli: Translations

The Art of War, tr. Ellis Farneworth. Indianapolis and New York, 1965.

The Chief Works and Others, tr. A. H. Gilbert. 3 vols. Durham, North Carolina, 1965.

Clizia, tr. Oliver Evans. New York, 1962.

The Discourses, tr. L. J. Walker. 2 vols. London, 1950 +.

The Historical, Political, and Diplomatic Writings, tr. C. E. Detmold. 4 vols. Boston, 1882 +.
History of Florence and Other Selections, tr. Judith A. Rawson. New York, 1970.
The Letters of Machiavelli, tr. A. H. Gilbert. New York, 1961.
The Literary Works, tr. J. R. Hale. Oxford, 1961.
Lust and Liberty, tr. Joseph Tusiani. New York, 1963. Contains the poems.
Mandragola, tr. Anne and Henry Paolucci. New York, 1957.
The Prince. (There are many separate translations.)

Machiavelli: Studies

Anglo, Sydney. *Machiavelli: A Dissection*. London, 1969.
Campbell, W. R. *Machiavelli: An Anti-Study*. Kingston, Rhode Island, 1968.
Cassirer, Ernst. *The Myth of the State*. New Haven, 1946.
Gilbert, A. H. *Machiavelli's Prince and its Forerunners*. Durham, North Carolina, 1938.
Hale, John R. *Machiavelli and Renaissance Italy*. London, 1961.
Muir, D. E. *Machiavelli and his Times*. London, 1936.
Olschki, Leonardo. *Machiavelli the Scientist*. Berkeley, 1945.
Villari, Pasquale. *The Life and Times of Niccolò Machiavelli*, tr. Linda Villari. 2nd. ed. 2 vols. London, 1891.
Whitfield, J. B. *Discourses on Machiavelli*. Cambridge, 1969.
——— *Il Principe, with an Essay on The Prince*. Wakefield, England, 1969.
——— *Machiavelli*. Oxford, 1947.

Guicciardini

Guicciardini, Francesco. *Counsels and Reflections*, tr. N. H. Thomson. London, 1890 +.
——— *The History of Florence*, tr. Mario Domandi. New York, 1970.
——— *The History of Florence and The History of Italy*, tr. Cecil Grayson; ed. John R. Hale. New York, 1964.
——— *The History of Italy*, tr. Sidney Alexander. New York, 1969.
——— *Maxims and Reflections of a Renaissance Statesman*, tr. Mario Domandi. Philadelphia, 1972.
——— *Selected Writings*, tr. Margaret Grayson. Oxford, 1965.
Luciani, Vincent. *Francesco Guicciardini and his European Reputation*. New York, 1936.

CHAPTER 24: CASTIGLIONE AND OTHER PROSE WRITERS

Ady, Julia Cartwright. *Baldassare Castiglione, the Perfect Courtier*. 2 vols. London, 1908 +.
Bandello. *Novels*, tr. John Payne. 6 vols. London, 1890.
——— *Tragical Tales*, tr. Geoffrey Fenton (1567); ed. R. L. Douglas and Hugh Harris. London, c. 1923.
Castiglione. *The Book of the Courtier*, tr. L. E. Opdycke. New York, 1903.
——— *The Book of the Courtier*, tr. Sir Thomas Hoby (1561); ed. W. H. D. Rouse and Drayton Henderson. EL.
——— *The Book of the Courtier*, tr. C. S. Singleton. New York, 1959.
——— *The Book of the Courtier*, tr. G. Bull. Penguin, 1968.
Da Porto. *Romeo and Juliet*, tr. and ed. by Maurice Jonas. London, 1921.
D'Anghiera, Pietro Martire. *De orbe novo*, tr. and ed. F. A. MacNutt. New York, 1912.
Giovio. *An Italian Portrait Gallery*, tr. Florence A. Gragg. Boston, 1935.
Hay, Denys. *Polydore Vergil*. Oxford, 1952.
Pruvost, Renè. *Matteo Bandello and Elizabethan Fiction*. Paris, 1937.
Straparola. *The Nights*, tr. W. G. Waters. 2 vols. London, 1894 +.

CHAPTER 25: COMEDY AND TRAGEDY

Chubb, T. C., tr. and ed. *The Letters of Pietro Aretino*. Hamden, Connecticut, 1967.
Rosenthal, Raymond, tr. *Aretino's Dialogues*. New York, 1972.

CHAPTER 26: POETRY OF THE MID-SIXTEENTH CENTURY

Jerrold, Maud F. *Vittoria Colonna*, etc. London, 1906. (For Gaspara Stampa.)
Williamson, Edward. *Bernardo Tasso*. Rome, 1951.

CHAPTER 27: PROSE OF THE MID-SIXTEENTH CENTURY

Cellini. *The Autobiography*, tr. George Bull. Penguin, 1968.
——— *The Life*, tr. R. H. H. Cust. 2 vols. London, 1910 +.
——— *The Life*, tr. Anne Macdonell. EL.
Charlton, H. B. *Castelvetro's Theory of Poetry*. Manchester, 1913.
Cornaro. *The Art of Living Long*, tr. by "able translators." Milwaukee, 1903 +.
Cust, R. H. H. *Benvenuto Cellini*. London, 1912.
Della Casa. *Galateo*, tr. Robert Peterson (1576); ed. J. E. Spingarn. Boston, 1914.
——— *Galateo, or The Book of Manners*, tr. R. S. Pine-Coffin. Penguin, 1958.
Hall, Vernon, Jr. *Life of Julius Caesar Scaliger*. Philadelphia, 1950.
——— *Renaissance Literary Criticism: A Study of its Social Content*. New York, 1945.
Herrick, M. T. *Comic Theory in the Sixteenth Century*. Urbana, 1950.
Scaliger, Julius Caesar. *Select Translations from Scaliger's Poetices*, tr. F. M. Padelford. New York, 1905.
Snuggs, H. L., tr. *Giraldi Cinthi on Romances*. Lexington, Kentucky, 1968.
Spingarn, J. E. *A History of Literary Criticism in the Renaissance*, 2nd. ed. New York, 1908 +.
Vasari. *Lives of Seventy of the Most Eminent Painters, Sculptors, and Architects*, tr. Margaret E. Foster; ed. E. H. and E. W. Blashfield and A. A. Hopkins. 4 vols. New York, 1896 +.
——— *Lives of the Artists*, tr. George Bull. Penguin, 1970.
——— *Lives of the Painters, Sculptors, and Architects*, tr. A. B. Hinds. TC (8 vols.) and EL (4 vols.).
——— *Vasari on Technique*, tr. Louisa S. Maclehouse. New York, 1960.

CHAPTER 28: THE PASTORAL PLAY AND THE *Commedia dell'arte*

Duchartre, P. L. *The Italian Comedy*, tr. R. T. Weaver. London, 1929.
Lea, Kathleen M. *Italian Popular Comedy*. 2 vols. Oxford, 1934.
Smith, Winifred. *The Commedia dell'arte*. New York, 1912.

CHAPTER 29: TORQUATO TASSO

See also Giacomo Grillo, Chapter 21 above and various books cited in General List D.
Boulting, William. *Tasso and his Times*. London, 1907.
Brand, C. P. *Torquato Tasso, a Study of the Poet and of His Contribution to English Literature*. Cambridge, 1965.
Lord, L. E. *A Translation of the Orpheus of Angelo Politian and the Aminta of Torquato Tasso*. London, 1931.
Tasso, Torquato. *Godfrey of Bulloigne, or The Recoverie of Hierusalem*, tr. Edward Fairfax (1600). Several modern editions.
——— *Jerusalem Delivered*, tr. J. K. James. 2 vols. London, 1884.
——— *Jerusalem Delivered*, tr. Joseph Tusiani. Rutherford, New Jersey, 1970.
——— *Jerusalem Delivered*, tr. J. H. Wiffen. 2 vols. London, 1824–1825 +.

CHAPTER 30: GIORDANO BRUNO

Boulting, William. *Giordano Bruno, his Life, Thought, and Martyrdom.* London, 1916.

Bruno, Giordano. *The Expulsion of the Triumphant Beast*, tr. A. D. Imerti. New Brunswick, 1964.

——— *The Heroic Enthusiasts*, tr. L. Williams. 2 vols. London, 1887–1889.

——— *The Heroic Frenzies*, tr. Paul E. Memmo, Jr. Chapel Hill, 1965.

Greenberg, Sidney. *The Infinite in Giordano Bruno, with a Translation of his Dialogue "Concerning the Cause, Principle, and One."* New York, 1950.

Horowitz, I. L. *The Renaissance Philosophy of Giordano Bruno.* New York, 1952.

Nelson, John C. *The Renaissance Theory of Love: The Context of Giordano Bruno's "Eroici furori."* New York, 1958.

Patterson, Antoinette M. *The Infinite Worlds of Giordano Bruno.* Springfield, Illinois, 1970.

Singer, Dorothea W. *Giordano Bruno, his Life and Thought, with Annotated Translation of his Work "On the Infinite Universe and Worlds."* New York, 1950.

Yates, Francis A. *Giordano Bruno and the Hermetic Tradition.* Chicago, 1964.

CHAPTER 31: THE DRAMA IN THE LATE SIXTEENTH CENTURY

Staton, W. F. and W. E. Simeone, eds. *Il pastor fido*, tr. Richard Fanshawe (1647). London and New York, 1964.

CHAPTER 32: MARINO AND OTHER POETS

Priest, H. M. tr. *Adonis: Selections from L'Adone.* Ithaca, 1967.

Mirollo, J. V. *The Poet of the Marvelous: Giambattista Marino.* New York, 1963.

CHAPTER 33: CAMPANELLA

Bonansea, B. M. *Tommaso Campanella: Renaissance Pioneer of Modern Thought.* Washington, 1970.

Campanella, Tommaso. *The City of the Sun*, tr. T. W. Halliday in *Ideal Commonwealths*, ed. Henry Morley. London, 1885 +.

——— *The City of the Sun*, tr. W. J. Gilstrap in *The Quest for Utopia* by Glen Negley and J. M. Patrick. New York, 1952. Both the Halliday and the Gilstrap translations are from the Latin and neither is complete.

——— *The Defense of Galileo*, tr. and ed. Grant McColley. Northampton, 1939.

——— *The Sonnets* (Campanella and Michelangelo), tr. J. A. Symonds. London, 1878 +.

Grillo, Francesco. *Tommaso Campanella in America.* New York, 1954.

CHAPTER 34: GALILEO AND OTHER PROSE WRITERS

Basile. *Il Pentamerone*, tr. Sir Richard Burton. London, 1893 +.

——— *Il Pentamerone*, tr. (from the Italian version of Benedetto Croce) N. M. Penzer. 2 vols. London, 1932.

Boccalini. *Advices from Parnassus.* College Park, Maryland, 1971.

De Santillana, George. *The Crime of Galileo.* Chicago, 1954.

Drake, Stillman, tr. *Discoveries and Opinions of Galileo.* New York, 1957.

Galileo. *Dialogue Concerning the Two Chief World Systems*, tr. Stillman Drake. Berkeley, 1953.

——— *Dialogues Concerning Two New Sciences*, tr. Henry Crew and Alfonso de Salvio. New York, 1914 +.

——— *On Motion and On Mechanics*, tr. Stillman Drake and I. E. Dubkin. Madison, Wisconsin, 1960.

Lievsay, John L. *Venetian Phoenix: Paolo Sarpi and Some of His English Friends.* Lawrence, Kansas, 1974.

Robertson, Alexander. *Fra Paolo Sarpi, the Greatest of Venetians.* London, 1894.

Taylor, F. S. *Galileo and the Freedom of Thought.* London, 1938.

CHAPTER 35: EARLY OPERA

Grout, D. J. *A Short History of Opera.* 2 vols. New York, 1947.

Henderson, W. J. *Some Forerunners of Italian Opera.* New York, 1911.

CHAPTER 36: A STAGNANT INTERVAL

Morgan, Lady Sydney. *The Life and Times of Salvator Rosa.* London, 1824 +.

Redi. *Bacchus in Tuscany*, tr. and ed. Leigh Hunt. London, 1825.

CHAPTER 37: METASTASIO AND OTHER ARCADIANS

Burney, Charles. *Memoirs of the Life and Writings of the Abate Metastasio.* 3 vols. London, 1796.

Mestastasio. *Dido Forsaken*, tr. J. G. Fucilla. Florence, 1952.

Robertson, J. G. *Studies in the Genesis of Romantic Theory in the Eighteenth Century.* Cambridge, 1923.

CHAPTER 38: VICO

Adams, H. P. *The Life and Writings of Giambattista Vico.* London, 1935.

Caponigri, A. R. *Time and Idea: The Theory of History of Giambattista Vico.* Chicago, 1953.

Croce, Benedetto. *The Philosophy of Giambattista Vico*, tr. R. G. Collingwood. London, 1913.

Gianturco, Elio. *Joseph de Maistre and Giambattista Vico.* New York, 1937.

Manson, Richard. *The Theory of Knowledge of Giambattista Vico.* Hamden, Connecticut, 1969.

Piovano, Pietro. *Giambattista Vico*, tr. E. Gianturco. New York, 1968.

Tagliacozzo, Giorgio, ed. *Giambattista Vico: An International Symposium.* Baltimore, 1969.

Vico, Giambattista. *The Autobiography*, tr. M. H. Fisch and T. G. Bergin. Ithaca, 1944.

——— *The New Science*, rev. tr. T. G. Bergin and M. H. Fisch. Ithaca, 1968.

——— *On the Study Methods of Our Time*, tr. Elio Gianturco. Indianapolis, 1965.

CHAPTER 39: GOLDONI AND CARLO GOZZI

There are translations of many of the comedies of Goldoni.

Chatfield-Taylor, H. C. *Goldoni.* New York, 1913.

Goldoni. *Memoirs*, tr. John Black; ed. W. A. Drake. New York, 1926.

Gozzi, Carlo. *Memoirs*, tr. J. A. Symonds. 2 vols. London, 1890.

CHAPTER 40: PARINI AND OTHER WRITERS

Farrar, J. A. *Crimes and Punishments, Including a New Translation of Beccaria's Dei delitti e delle pene.* London, 1880.

Lubbers-van der Brugge, Catharina J. M. *Johnson and Baretti.* Groningen, 1951.

Maestro, M. T. *Voltaire and Beccaria as Reformers of Criminal Law.* New York, 1942.

Parini. *The Day*, tr. and ed. H. M. Bower. London, 1927.

Rossi, Joseph. *The Abbé Galiani in France.* New York, 1930.

CHAPTER 41: ALFIERI

Alfieri, Vittorio. *On Tyranny*, tr. and ed. Julius Molinaro and Beatrice Corrigan. Toronto, 1961.
——— *The Tragedies*, tr. Charles Lloyd. 3 vols. London, 1815+.
——— *Vita*, tr. Henry McAnally. Cambridge, England, 1949.
Megaro, Gaudence. *Vittorio Alfieri, Forerunner of Italian Nationalism*. New York, 1930.
Miller, C. R. D. *Alfieri*. Williamsport, 1936.

CHAPTER 42: FOSCOLO AND OTHER WRITERS

Da Ponte. *Memoirs*, tr. Elisabeth Abbot; ed. Arthur Livingston. Rev. ed. New York, 1959.
——— *Memoirs*, tr. L. A. Sheppard. Boston, 1929.
Foscolo. *Last Letters of Jacopo Ortis*, tr. D. Radcliff-Umstead. Chapel Hill, 1970.
——— *Last Letters of Jacopo Ortis*, tr. Dale McAdoo and Anthony Winner. New York, 1968.
——— *On Sepulchres*, tr. T. G. Bergin. Bethany, Connecticut, 1971.
Radcliff-Umstead, Douglas. *Ugo Foscolo*. New York, 1970.
Russo, J. L. *Lorenzo da Ponte: Poet and Adventurer*. New York, 1922.
Vincent, E. R. *Byron, Hobhouse and Foscolo*. Cambridge, 1949.
——— *The Commemoration of the Dead, A Study of "Dei sepolcri."* Cambridge, 1923.
——— *Ugo Foscolo: An Italian in Regency England*. Cambridge, 1953.

CHAPTER 43: MANZONI

Cippico Antonio. *The Romantic Age in Italian Literature*. London, 1918.
Colquhoun, Archibald. *Manzoni and His Times*. London, 1954.
De Simone, J. F. *Alessandro Manzoni: Esthetics and Literary Criticism*. New York, 1946.
Manzoni, Alessandro. *The Betrothed*, tr. Archibald Colquhoun. New York, 1951.
——— *The Column of Infamy*, tr. Kenelm Foster and Jane Grigson. London and New York, 1964. With C. Beccaria, *Of Crimes and Punishment*.
Wall, Bernard. *Alessandro Manzoni*. New Haven, 1954.

CHAPTER 44: LEOPARDI

Leopardi, Giacomo. *Essays, Dialogues and Thoughts*, tr. James Thomson; ed. Bertram Dobell. London, 1905.
——— *Poems and Prose*, tr. by numerous translators; ed. Angel Flores. Bloomington, 1966.
——— *Poems from Leopardi*, tr. John Heath-Stubbs. London, 1946.
——— *Selected Prose and Poetry*, tr. Iris Origo and John Heath-Stubbs. London and New York, 1966.
Origo, Iris. *Leopardi*. London, 1935.
Perella, N. J. *Night and the Sublime in Giacomo Leopardi*. Berkeley, 1970.
Singh, G. *Leopardi and the Theory of Poetry*. Lexington, Kentucky, 1964.
Whitfield, J. H. *Giacomo Leopardi*. Oxford, 1954.

CHAPTER 45: CONTEMPORARIES OF MANZONI AND LEOPARDI

There are English translations of most of the novels mentioned in this chapter and in later chapters.

Belli, G. G. *Roman Sonnets*, tr. Harold Norse. Highlands, North Carolina, 1960.
Pellico. *Memoirs*, tr. M. J. Smead and H. P. Lefebvre. New York, 1844 +.

Rossetti, D. G. *A Versified Autobiography*, tr. and ed. W. M. Rossetti. London, 1902.
Vincent, E. R. *Gabriele Rossetti in England*. Oxford, 1936.

CHAPTER 46: MAZZINI

Barr, Stringfellow. *Mazzini*. New York, 1935.
Griffith, G. O. *Mazzini: Prophet of Modern Europe*. London, 1932.
King, Bolton. *The Life of Mazzini*. EL.
Mazzini, Joseph. *The Duties of Man and Other Essays*, tr. Ella Noyes et al. New York, 1955.
——— *Essays: Selected from the Writings, Literary, Political, and Religious, of Joseph Mazzini*, ed. William Clarke. London, 1887 +.
——— *Letters (1833–1871)*, tr. Alice De Rosen Jervis. Westport, Connecticut, 1930.
——— *Life and Writings*, ed. Emily A. Venturi, 6 vols. London, 1864–1870 +.
——— *The Living Thoughts of Mazzini*, presented by Ignazio Silone; tr. E. A. Venturi. New York, 1939 +.

CHAPTER 47: CONTEMPORARIES OF MAZZINI

Garibaldi. *Autobiography*, tr. A. Werner. 3 vols. London, 1880.
Horner, Susan. *The Tuscan Poet Giuseppe Giusti and his Times*. London, 1864.
Smith, Denis Mack. *Cavour and Garibaldi*, 1860. Cambridge, 1954.
——— *Garibaldi*. New York, 1956 +.
Trevelyan, G. M. *Garibaldi and the Making of Italy*. London, 1911 +.
——— *Garibaldi and the Thousand*. London, 1909 +.
——— *Garibaldi's Defense of the Roman Republic*. London, 1907 +.

CHAPTER 48: CARDUCCI AND OTHER POETS

A Selection from the Poems of Giosuè Carducci, tr. and ed. Emily A. Tribe. New York, 1921.

CHAPTER 49: DE SANCTIS, VERGA, AND OTHER WRITERS

Alexander, Alfred. *Giovanni Verga: A Great Writer and His World*. London, 1972.
Bergin, T. G. *Giovanni Verga*. New Haven, 1931 +.
Breglio, L. A. *Life and Criticism of Francesco de Sanctis*. New York, 1941.
Collodi. *Pinocchio: The Story of a Puppet*, anon. tr. EL.
De Amicis. *The Heart of a Boy* (*Cuore*), tr. Sophie Jewett. Chicago, 1912. There are English translations of all De Amicis' books of travel.
De Sanctis, Francesco. *History of Italian Literature*, tr. Joan Redfern. 2 vols. New York, 1931.
———*De Sanctis on Dante*, tr. and ed. Joseph Rossi and Alfred Galpin. Madison, Wisconsin, 1957.
Ragusa, Olga. *Verga's Milanese Tales*. New York, 1964.
Scalia, S. E. *Luigi Capuana and his Times*. New York, 1952.
Verga, Giovanni. *Cavalleria Rusticana and Other Stories*, tr. D. H. Lawrence. London, 1928 +.
———*The House by the Medlar Tree*, tr. Raymond Rosenthal. New York, 1964.
———*The House by the Medlar Tree*, tr. Eric Mosbacker. New York, 1955.
———*Little Novels of Sicily* (*Novelle rusticane*), tr. D. H. Lawrence. New York, 1925 +.
———*Mastro-don Gesualdo*, tr. D. H. Lawrence. New York, 1923 +.
———*The She-Wolf and Other Stories*, tr. Giovanni Cecchetti. Berkeley, 1958.

CHAPTER 50: PASCOLI AND OTHER POETS

Antongini, Tom. *D'Annunzio*. London, 1938.

D'Annunzio. *The Child of Pleasure*, tr. Georgina Harding. London, 1898 +.

——— *The Daugheter of Iorio*, tr. Charlotte Porter, Peter Isola, and Alice Henry. Boston, 1907.

——— *The Dead City*, tr. G. Mantellini. New York, 1923.

——— *Tales of My Native Town* (from the *Novelle della Pescara*), tr. Rafael Mantellini. Garden City, 1920.

MacClintock, Lander. *The Contemporary Drama of Italy*. Boston, 1920.

Maurino, F. D. *Salvatore de Giacomo and Neapolitan Dialectal Literature*. New York, 1951.

Pascoli. *Poems* (selected), tr. Arletta M. Abbott. New York, 1927.

——— *Poems* (selected), tr. Evaleen Stein. New Haven, 1923.

Rhodes, Anthony. *D'Annunzio: The Poet as Superman*. New York, 1959.

Winwar, Frances. *Wingless Victory*. New York, 1956. D'Annunzio and Duse.

CHAPTER 51: FOGAZZARO AND OTHER WRITERS

Gallarati-Scotti, Tommaso. *The Life of Antonio Fogazzaro*, tr. Mary Prichard Agnetti. London, c. 1925.

Giacosa. *The Stronger; Like Falling Leaves; Sacred Ground*, tr. Edith and Allen Updegraff. New York, 1913 +.

CHAPTER 52: WRITERS OF THE TWENTIETH CENTURY

There are translations of a great many twentieth-century works. A few examples are cited.

Bacchelli. *The Mill on the Po*, tr. Frances Frenaye. New York, 1950.

——— *Nothing New Under the Sun*, tr. Stuart Hood. New York, 1955.

Bishop, Thomas. *Pirandello and the French Theatre*. New York, 1960.

Budel, Oscar. *Pirandello: Studies in Modern European Thought and Literature*. New York, 1966.

Cambon, Glauco. *Pirandello: A Collection of Critical Essays*. Englewood Cliffs, 1967.

Carr, H. W. *The Philosophy of Benedetto Croce: The Problem of Art and History*. London, 1917.

Croce, Benedetto. *Philosophy, Poetry, History: An Anthology of Essays*, tr. Cecil Sprigge. New York, 1966.

Furbank, P. N. *Italo Svevo: The Man and the Writer*. London, 1966.

Holmes, R. W. *The Idealism of Giovanni Gentile*. New York, 1937.

MacClintock, Lander. *The Age of Pirandello*. Bloomington, 1951.

Matthaei, Renate. *Luigi Pirandello*, tr. Simon and Erika Young. New York, 1967.

Orsini, Gian N. G. *Benedetto Croce: Philosopher of Art and Literary Critic*. Carbondale, 1961.

Papini. *Four and Twenty Minds*, tr. E. H. Wilkins. New York, 1922.

——— *The Failure*, tr. Virginia Pope. Westport,Connecticut, 1970.

Piccoli, Raffaello. *Benedetto Croce*. New York, 1922.

Pirandello. *The Late Mattia Pascal*, tr. William Weaver. New York, 1964.

———*The Merry-Go-Round of Love and Selected Stories*, tr. Frances Keene and Lily Duplaix. New York, 1964.

———*Naked Masks: Five Plays*, tr. by various persons; ed. Eric Bentley. New York, 1952.

———*Short Stories*, tr. Frederick May. New York, 1964.

Ragusa, Olga. *Pirandello*. New York, 1970.

Riccio, P. M. *On the Threshold of Fascism*. New York, 1929.

Sprigge, Cecil. *Benedetto Croce, Man and Thinker*. Cambridge, 1952.
Staley, T. F., ed. *Essays on Italo Svevo*. Tulsa, 1969.
Starkie, Walter. *Luigi Pirandello*. London, 1926 +.
Svevo. *As a Man Grows Older*, tr. Beryl de Zoete. New York, 1962.
———*The Confessions of Zeno*, tr. Beryl de Zoete. New York, 1968.
Tozzi. *Three Crosses*, tr. R. Capellero. New York, 1921.
Vittorini, Domenico. *The Drama of Luigi Pirandello*. Philadelphia, 1935.

CHAPTER 53: THE LITERATURE OF THE REPUBLIC

For translations of individual novels, plays, etc., see text of this Chapter, passim. For critical studies see also books listed under E above.

Betocchi, Carlo. *Poems*, tr. I. L. Salomon. New York, 1969.
Biasin, Gian-Paolo. *The Smile of the Gods: A Thematic Study of Cesare Pavese's Works*. Ithaca, 1968.
Cambon, Glauco. *Eugenio Montale*. New York, 1972.
———*Guiseppe Ungaretti*. New York, 1957.
Campana, Dino. *Orphic Songs*, tr. I. L. Salomon. New York, 1968.
Dego, Giuliano. *Moravia*. London, 1967.
Montale. *The Butterfly of Dinard*, tr. G. Singh. Lexington, Kentucky, 1971.
———*Imitations*, tr. Robert Lowell. New York, 1961.
———*Poems from Eugenio Montale*, tr. Edward Morgan. Reading, England, 1959.
———*Poesie*, tr. Robert Lowell. Bologna, 1960.
———*Poesie/Poems*, tr. George Kay. Edinburgh, 1964.
———*Selected Poems*, tr. by various persons. New York, 1965.
Piccolo, Lucio. *Collected Poems*, tr. Brian Swann and Ruth Feldman. Princeton, 1972.
Pipa, Arshi. *Montale and Dante*. Minneapolis, 1968.
Quasimodo. *The Poet and the Politician and Other Essays*, tr. T. G. Bergin and S. Pacifici. Carbondale, 1964.
———*The Selected Writings*, tr. and ed. Allen Mandelbaum. New York, 1969.
———*To Give and To Have and Other Poems*, tr. Edith Farnsworth. Chicago, 1969.
Rebay, Luciano. *Alberto Moravia*. New York, 1970.
Ross, Joan and Donald Freed. *The Existentialism of Alberto Moravia*. Carbondale, 1972.
Singh, G. *Eugenio Montale: A Critical Study of his Poetry, Prose, and Criticism*. New Haven, 1973.
Ungaretti. *Life of a Man*, tr. Allen Mandelbaum. London, New York, and Milan, 1958.
———*Selected Poems*, tr. Patrick Creagh. Penguin, 1971.

A CHRONOLOGICAL CHART

ITALIAN LITERATURE /OTHER LITERATURES	POLITICAL AND SOCIAL EVENTS
1200–1250 Frederician (or Sicilian) School	
	1209–1229 Founding of Franciscans; Albigensian Crusade
1214 St. Francis, *Canticle of the Sun*	
	1215 Founding of Dominicans
	1220–1250 Reign of Frederick II
1221–1285 Alfonso the Wise	
1225–1294 Guittone d'Arezzo	
1225–1240 Guillaume de Lorris, *Roman de la rose*	
1230–1306 Jacopone da Todi	
1240–1276 Guido Guinizelli	
1255–1300 Guido Cavalcanti	
1265–1321 Dante	
	1266 Charles of Anjou becomes King of Naples
	1270 Seventh Crusade
1273–1280 Jean de Meun, *Roman de la rose*	
1293 Dante, *Vita nova*	
	1294–1303 Papacy of Boniface VIII
1304–1374 Petrarch	
1307–1321 Dante, *Divine Comedy*	
	1308–1377 Papacy in Avignon
1309 Joinville, *Histoire de Saint Louis*	
1313–1375 Boccaccio	
	1337–1453 Hundred Years' War
1341 Petrarch crowned Poet Laureate	
1344–1380 St. Catherine of Siena	
	1346 Battle of Crécy
	1347–1348 Black Death
1348–1358 Boccaccio, *Decameron*	
1362 Langland, *Piers Plowman*	
	1378 Rising of the Ciompi in Florence
	1385–1402 The Milanese expansion; Gian Galeazzo Visconti
1398–1400 Sacchetti, *Trecentonovelle*	
1400 Chaucer, *Canterbury Tales*	

ITALIAN LITERATURE
/OTHER LITERATURES

1437–1441 L. B. Alberti, *Della famiglia*

1452–1519 Leonardo da Vinci

1461 Villon, *Testament*

1464 *Farce of Maître Pathelin*

1470 Malory, *Morte d'Arthur*

1475–1564 Michelangelo

1476 Jorge Manrique, *Las coplas*

1480 Politian, *Orfeo*

1483 Pulci, *Morgante Maggiore*

1487–1494 Boiardo, *Orlando innamorato*

1499 *La celestina*

1501 Sannazzaro, *Arcadia*

1509 Ariosto, *I suppositi*

1513 Machiavelli, *The Prince*

1516 More, *Utopia*

1516–1532 Ariosto, *Orlando furioso*

1520 Machiavelli, *Mandragola*

1522 Luther's translation of the Bible

1528 Castiglione, *Cortegiano*

1533 Rabelais, *Gargantua et Pantagruel*

1534 Aretino, *Ragionamenti*

1541 Guicciardini, *Storia d'Italia*

1543 Garcilaso de la Vega, *Poems*

POLITICAL AND SOCIAL EVENTS

1414 Council of Constance

1431 Execution of Joan of Arc

1450 Invention of printing

1453 Fall of Constantinople

1455–1485 Wars of the Roses

1469–1492 Lorenzo de' Medici in power

1492 Fall of Granada; voyage of Columbus

1494 French invasion of Italy

1498 Voyage of Vasco da Gama

1517 Luther's theses

1519–1521 Conquest of Mexico by Cortes

1525 Battle of Pavia

1527 Sack of Rome by Imperial troops

1533 Pizarro's conquest of Peru

1534 Jesuit order founded

1535 Milan becomes fief of Spain

ITALIAN LITERATURE	/OTHER LITERATURES	POLITICAL AND SOCIAL EVENTS
	1544 Clément Marot, *Poems*	
		1545–1563 Council of Trent
	1549 Du Bellay, *Deffense . . . de la langue*	
	1554 *Lazarillo de Tormes*	
1554 Bandello, *Novelle*		
1558 Della Casa, *Galateo*		1558–1603 Reign of Elizabeth
	1559 Montemayor, *Diana*	1559 Treaty of Cateau-Cambrésis; half of Italy under Spanish rule
		1562–1598 Religious wars in France
		1571 Battle of Lepanto
		1572 Massacre of St. Bartholomew's Day
1575 Tasso, *Gerusalemme liberata*		
	1578 Ronsard, *Sonnets pour Hélène*	
	1580 Sidney, *Arcadia;* –1588 Montaigne, *Essays*	
		1581 Northern Netherlands declare independence from Spain
1585 Bruno, *De gli eroici furori*		
	1587 Marlowe, *Tamburlaine the Great*	
		1588 Defeat of Spanish Armada
1590 Guarini, *Pastor fido*		
	1590–1609 Spenser, *Faerie Queene*	
1594 Rinuccini, *Dafne*		
	1595 Shakespeare, *Romeo and Juliet;* 1601 *Hamlet*	
1602 Campanella, *City of the Sun*		
	1605–1616 Cervantes, *Don Quixote*	
	1606 Jonson, *Volpone*	
1610–1618 Sarpi, *Istoria del Concilio di Trento*		
	1611 King James Bible; Shakespeare, *The Tempest*	1618–1648 Thirty Years' War
	1612 Góngora, *Polyphemus and Galatea*	
	1618 Lope de Vega, *Fuente Ovejuna*	
		1620 Landing of the Mayflower
1622 Tassoni, *La secchia rapita*		

ITALIAN LITERATURE /OTHER LITERATURES	POLITICAL AND SOCIAL EVENTS
1623 Marino, *Adone*	
1625 Bacon, *Essays*	
1630 Tirso de Molina, *El burlador de Sevilla*	
1632 Galileo, *Dialogue of the Two Systems*	
1635 Calderón, *La vida es sueño;* Lope de Vega, *El major alcalde*	
1636 Corneille, *Le Cid*	
1637 Descartes, *Discourse on Method*	
	1642–1648 English civil war
	1649 Execution of Charles I
1651 Hobbes, *Leviathan*	
	1659 Peace of the Pyrenees
	1660 Restoration of Charles II
1665 La Rochefoucauld, *Maxims*	
1666 Molière, *Le misanthrope*	
1667 Milton, *Paradise Lost;* Racine, *Andromaque*	
1668–1669 La Fontaine, *Fables*	
1678 Mme. de Lafayette, *La princesse de Clèves;* –1684 Bunyan, *Pilgrim's Progress*	
1685 Redi, *Bacco in Toscana*	
	1688 Glorious Revolution
	1689–1725 Reign of Peter the Great
1697 Dryden, *Alexander's Feast*	
1709–1711 Steele and Addison, *Tatler*	
1711–1712 Steele and Addison, *Spectator*	
	1713 Peace of Utrecht; Spanish possessions in Italy pass to Austria
1715 Le Sage, *Gil Blas*	
1719 Defoe, *Robinson Crusoe*	
1723 Giannone, *Istoria del regno di Napoli*	
1725 Vico, *Scienza nuova*	
1726 Swift, *Gulliver's Travels*	

ITALIAN LITERATURE /OTHER LITERATURES	POLITICAL AND SOCIAL EVENTS
1728 Gay, *Beggar's Opera*	
1731 Prévost, *Manon Lescaut*	
1733 Pope, *Essay on Man*	
1740 Metastasio, *Attilio Regolo*	1740–1748 War of the Austrian Succession
1740 Richardson, *Pamela*	
1748 Montesquieu, *Esprit des lois*	
1749 Fielding, *Tom Jones*	
1751 Gray, *Elegy*	
1753 Goldoni, *La locandiera*	1756–1763 Seven Years' War
1759 Voltaire, *Candide*	
1760–1767 Sterne, *Tristram Shandy*	
1761 Gozzi, *Love of the Three Oranges*	
1762 Rousseau, *Social Contract*	
1763–1801 Parini, *Il Giorno*	1763 Treaty of Paris; Canada ceded to England
1764 Beccaria, *Dei delitti e delle pene*; –1766 Verri, *Il Caffè*	
1766 Goldsmith, *Vicar of Wakefield*; Lessing, *Laocoon*; –1768 Rousseau, *Confessions*	
1775 Beaumarchais, *Barber of Seville*	1775–1783 American Revolution
1777 Sheridan, *School for Scandal*	
1778 Herder, *Volkslieder*	
1782 Alfieri, *Saul*	
1786 Burns, *Poems*	
1787 B. de Saint Pierre, *Paul et Virginie*	
1789 Alfieri, *Mirra*	1789 Fall of the Bastille
1789 Blake, *Songs of Innocence*	
1790–1803 Alfieri, *Vita*	
1791 Boswell, *Life of Johnson*	
	1792 French Republic proclaimed; Battle of Valmy
1793 Monti, *La Bassivilliana*	1793 Louis XVI executed; Reign of Terror
	1797 Napoleon in Italy; Peace of Campoformio; the Cisalpine Republic; Venice given to Austria

ITALIAN LITERATURE
/OTHER LITERATURES

1798 Coleridge/Wordsworth, *Lyrical Ballads*
1800 Schiller, *Wallenstein*
1802 Foscolo, *Ultime lettere di Jacopo Ortis*
1802 Chateaubriand, *René*
1807 Foscolo, *I sepolcri*
1812–1818 Byron, *Childe Harold*
1813 Austen, *Pride and Prejudice*
1818–1820 Keats, *Odes*
1819–1847 Belli, *Sonnets*
1819 Scott, *Ivanhoe*
1820 Lamartine, *Meditations;* Shelley, *Prometheus Unbound*
1821–1822 Manzoni, *Inni sacri*
1822 Manzoni, *Adelchi*
1823–1831 Pushkin, *Eugene Onegin*
1825–1827 Manzoni, *I promessi sposi*
1827 Leopardi, *Operette morali*
1827 Heine, *Buch der Lieder*
1830 Hugo, *Hernani;* –1847 Balzac, *Comédie humaine*
1831 Leopardi, *Canti*
1832 Pellico, *Le mie prigioni*
1832 Goethe, *Faust II*
1839 Stendhal, *Chartreuse de Parme*
1841–1845 Emerson, *Essays*
1842 Manzoni, *I promessi sposi*, 2nd. ed.
1843 Carlyle, *Past and Present*
1844 Giusti, *Poesie*
1844 Zorilla, *Don Juan Tenorio*
1845 Poe, *The Raven*
1847 Brontë, *Jane Eyre*
1848 Thackeray, *Vanity Fair*
1850 Dickens, *David Copperfield;* Hawthorne, *The Scarlet Letter*

POLITICAL AND SOCIAL EVENTS

1799–1804 Napoleon becomes First Consul
1804 Napoleon crowned Emperor
1815 Battle of Waterloo
1825 First steam railroad
1830 July Revolution; accession of Louis-Philippe
1844 Morse perfects telegraph
1847 Marx, *Communist Manifesto*
1848 First War of Italian Independence; Roman Republic

ITALIAN LITERATURE /OTHER LITERATURES	POLITICAL AND SOCIAL EVENTS
1851 Melville, *Moby Dick;* –1853 Ruskin, *Stones of Venice*	
	1852 Napoleon III Emperor
1853 Wagner, *Ring of the Nibelungs*	
1855 Whitman, *Leaves of Grass*	
1857 Baudelaire, *Fleurs du mal;* Flaubert, *Madame Bovary*	
1858 Nievo, *Confessioni di un Italiano*	
1859 Mill, *On Liberty;* Tennyson, *Idylls of the King*	1859 Second War of Italian Independence; Darwin, *Origin of Species*
1860 Mazzini, *Doveri dell'uomo*	1860 Garibaldi in Sicily; union of Italy
	1861 Victor Emanuel proclaimed King; –1865 American Civil War
1862–1869 Tolstoy, *War and Peace*	
1865 Arnold, *Essays on Criticism*	
1866 Swinburne, *Poems and Ballads*	1866 Laying of the Atlantic Cable; Third War of Italian Independence; Venice annexed
1868–1869 Browning, *The Ring and the Book*	
	1870 Franco-Prussian War; Rome becomes capital of Italy
1871 De Sanctis, *Storia della letteratura italiana*	1871 Wilhelm I proclaimed Emperor of Germany
1871–1893 Zola, *Les Rougon-Macquart*	
1872 Eliot, *Middlemarch*	
1873 Rimbaud, *Saison en enfer;* –1879 Galdos, *Episodios nacionales*	
1874 Valera, *Pepita Jimenez*	
1876 Mallarme, *L'Apres-midi d'un faune*	
1877–1889 Carducci, *Odi barbare*	
1878 Collodi, *Pinocchio*	
1879 Meredith, *The Egoist*	
1880 Dostoevsky, *Brothers Karamazov*	
1881 Verga, *I Malavoglia*	
1881 Ibsen, *Ghosts*	

ITALIAN LITERATURE /OTHER LITERATURES

1883–1894 Nietzsche, *Thus Spake Zarathustra*

1885 Maupassant, *Bel-ami;* Twain, *Huckleberry Finn*

1887 Strindberg, *The Father*

1888 Verga, *Mastro-don Gesualdo*

1889 D'Annunzio, *Il Piacere*

1890 De Marchi, *Demetrio Pianelli;* Serao, *The Land of Cockayne*

1891 Pascoli, *Myricae*

1891 Verlaine, *Parallèlement;* Hardy, *Tess of the D'Urbervilles*

1895 Fogazzaro, *Piccolo mondo antico*

1895 Wilde, *The Importance of Being Earnest*

1896 Chekhov, *The Seagull*

1898 Svevo, *Senilità*

1898 Blasco Ibáñez, *The Cabin*

1900 Capuana, *Il marchese di Roccaverdina*

1900 Conrad, *Lord Jim*

1901 Mann, *Buddenbrooks*

1903 Deledda, *Elias Portolu;* –1912 D'Annunzio, *Laudi*

1903 Butler, *Way of All Flesh;* James, *The Ambassadors;* Shaw, *Man and Superman*

1904 D'Annunzio, *The Daughter of Iorio;* Pirandello, *The Late Mattia Pascal;* –1909 Palazzeschi, *Poems*

1907 Gorky, *The Mother;* Synge, *Playboy of the Western World*

1909 Benelli, *The Jest*

1909 Benavente, *Bonds of Interest*

1911 Gozzano, *I colloqui*

1912 Papini, *Un uomo finito*

POLITICAL AND SOCIAL EVENTS

1882 Signing of the Triple Alliance

1890 Italy colonizes Eritrea

1897 Marconi patents wireless

1898 Spanish-American War

1900 Humbert I assassinated; Freud, *The Interpretation of Dreams*

1903 First flight of Wright brothers

1904–1905 Russo-Japanese War

1911–1912 Italo-Turkish War; Libya ceded to Italy

ITALIAN LITERATURE /OTHER LITERATURES	POLITICAL AND SOCIAL EVENTS
1913 Apollinaire, *Alcools;* Lawrence, *Sons and Lovers;* Unamuno, *The Tragic Sense of Life;* –1927 Proust, *Rembrance of Things Past*	
1914 Campana, *Orphic Songs*	1914 Panama Canal opened; –1918 World War I
1914 Frost, *North of Boston*	
1916 J. R. Jiménez, *Platero y yo*	1916 Einstein's general theory of relativity
1917 Chiarelli, *La Maschera e il volto*	1917 October Revolution; Lenin in power
1918 Blok, *The Twelve;* Hopkins, *Poems* (first published); Mayakovsky, *Mystery Bouffe*	1918–1919 Civil War in Russia
1919 Ungaretti, *Allegria di naufragi*	
1920 Valéry, *The Graveyard by the Sea*	
1921 Pirandello, *Six Characters;* Tozzi, *Il podere*	
1921 Capek, *R.U.R.*	
1922 Eliot, *The Waste Land;* Joyce, *Ulysses;* Lewis, *Babbitt;* –1940 Martin du Gard, *The World of the Thibaults*	1922 March on Rome; Fascism in Italy
1923 Rilke, *Duino Elegeis*	
1924 Forster, *Passage to India*	1924 Murder of Matteotti
1925 Montale, *Cuttlefish Bones*	1925 Locarno treaties
1925 Dreiser, *An American Tragedy;* Feuchtwanger, *Power;* Fitzgerald, *The Great Gatsby;* Yeats, *A Vision;* –1960 Pound, *Cantos*	
1926 Gide, *The Counterfeiters;* Kafka, *The Castle*	
1927 Mauriac, *Therèse Desqueyroux*	
1928 Guillén, *Cántico;* Lorca, *Romancero gitano*	
1929 Moravia, *The Indifferent Ones*	1929 Lateran Pact
1929 Cocteau, *Les enfants*	

ITALIAN LITERATURE /OTHER LITERATURES

terribles; Faulkner, *The Sound and the Fury;* Giraudoux, *Amphitryon 38;* Remarque, *All Quiet on the Western Front;* Wolfe, *Look Homeward, Angel*

1930 Alvaro, *Revolt in Aspromonte*

1930 Crane, *The Bridge;* Dos Passos, *Forty-second Parallel*

1931 Neruda, *Residencia en la tierra;* O'Neill, *Mourning Becomes Electra*

1932 MacLeish, *Conquistador*

1933 Malraux, *Man's Fate;* Werfel, *The Forty Days of Musa Dagh*

1935 Eliot, *Murder in the Cathedral*

1936 Cardarelli, *Poems*

1936 Bernanos, *Diary of a Country Priest*

1938–1940 Bacchelli, *Mill on the Po*

1938 Cummings, *Collected Poems;* Wilder, *Our Town*

1939 Sartre, *Le Mur;* Steinbeck, *Grapes of Wrath*

1940 Hemingway, *For Whom the Bell Tolls*

1941 Vittorini, *Conversation in Sicily*

1941 Aragon, *Le Crève-coeur;* Brecht, *Mother Courage*

1942 Quasimodo, *And Suddenly It's Evening*

1942 Cela, *The Family of Pascual Duarte*

1943 Anouilh, *Antigone*

1944 Sartre, *Huis-clos*

1945 Saba, *Canzoniere*

1946 Levi, *Christ Stopped at Eboli;* Pratolini, *Tale of Poor Lovers*

1946 Warren, *All the King's Men*

POLITICAL AND SOCIAL EVENTS

1931 Republic proclaimed in Spain

1933 Hitler comes to power

1934–1935 Mao Tse Tung founds Communist Republic in North China

1935 Italy attacks Ethiopia

1936 Ethiopia annexed; Italian Empire proclaimed; –1939 Spanish Civil War

1938 Austria annexed to Germany; partition of Czechoslovakia; Munich meeting

1939 Italy occupies Albania; –1945 World War II

1943 Fall of Mussolini; Italian armistice

1946 Italy becomes a republic

ITALIAN LITERATURE
/OTHER LITERATURES

1947 Camus, *The Plague;* T. Williams, *Streetcar Named Desire*

1948 Auden, *Age of Anxiety;* Char, *Fureur et mystère*

1950 Pavese, *The Moon and the Bonfires*

1954 S. de Beauvoir, *The Mandarins*

1957 Pasternak, *Doctor Zhivago*

1958 Gadda, *That Awful Mess on Via Merulana*

1959 Lampedusa, *The Leopard*

1959 Ionesco, *Rhinoceros*

POLITICAL AND SOCIAL EVENTS

1947 Marshall Plan

1948 Proclamation of State of Israel

1949 North Atlantic Treaty; Communists rule China

1950–1952 Korean War

1953 Coal and Steel Community

1954 Treaty of London gives Trieste to Italy

1955 Warsaw Pact

1956 Suez crisis; Algeria wins independence from France

1958 European Common Market formalized

1959 Castro takes power in Cuba

1962–1963 Second Vatican Council

1969 First manned landing on moon

INDEX

Academies, 149, 167–169, 179, 245, 252, 257, 268, 293, 317. *See also* Arcadian Academy
Acton, 222
Addison, 256, 312, 325, 332
Alamanni, 246, 248
Albany, Countess of, 372–373
Alberti, 127–129, 131, 134, 148, 248
Albertus Magnus, 46, 54
d'Alcamo, 20
Aldus, 176, 180, 182, 203
Aleardi, 527
Alexander VI, 138, 177
Alexander, J. W., 109
Alfani, 73
Alfieri, 222, 365–375, 378, 382, 401, 447
Alfonso the Wise, 32
Alfraganus, 54
Algarotti, 527
Alianello, 508
Allegory, 5, 32, 47, 52–53, 57, 59, 67–68, 70–71, 75, 91, 102, 105, 127, 175, 207, 383–384
Alvaro, 521
Amati, 319
St. Ambrose, 6
America. *See* Italian authors in America
De Amicis, 458
Amor de caritate, 34
Anacreon, 385
Anceschi, 522
Andreini, Francesco, 290, 317
Andreini, Giambattista, 317–318
Andreini, Isabella, 290, 317
Fra Angelico, 123
Angiolieri, 74
Anjou, Charles of, 23, 37
Anjou, Robert of, 80, 83, 87, 89–91, 101, 107
D'Annunzio, 463–466, 484, 493, 505, 514
Anthologies, 5, 140, 146, 204, 246, 249–250
St. Anthony of Padua, 115
Antioch, Frederick of, 19
Antonelli, 490
Aquilano, 176, 181
d'Aquino, Rinaldo, 19, 20
Aragon, Alfonso of, 126, 167
Aragan, Ferdinand of, 167
Aragon, Frederick of, 146, 167, 169
Aragon, Peter of, 23
Arbasino, 509
Arcadian Academy, 246, 325–334, 344, 348, 418, 447
Aretino, Leonardo, 124
Aretino, Pietro, 184, 240–241
d'Arezzo, Geri, 78
d'Arezzo, Guittone, 26–27, 29, 33, 42, 48, 92, 95, 146, 259
Ariosto, 173, 184–195, 204, 237, 239, 248, 271, 276–277, 307, 359, 365, 389, 395, 401, 494, 508
Aristotelianism and Anti-Aristotelianism: philosophic, 24–25, 53–54, 86, 92, 99, 151, 156, 179–180, 285; poetic, 238–240, 252, 254, 257–259, 268, 307; scientific, 312
Aristotle 2, 24–25, 36, 46, 53–54, 125, 156, 202, 282, 312
Aristophanes, 239
Arnold, Matthew, 33
Arnold, Thomas, 341
Arpino, 505
Arthurian stories, 6, 8, 14, 35–37, 55, 77, 98, 105, 171–172, 186, 248
Arts of Poetry, 204, 238, 240, 257–259, 303–304
Ascham, 231
Astaldi, 527
Augier, 459
St. Augustine, 5, 24–25, 46, 54, 83, 85, 89–90, 92
Ausonius, 143
Averroes, 24, 54, 80
d'Azeglio, 433

Bacchelli, 487, 502, 517, 521
Bach, 332
Bacon, 221, 225, 268, 334
Balbo, 416
Ballads, 10, 412–413, 429–430, 499
Ballata, 10–11, 26, 29, 31, 33, 48, 74, 81, 92, 97, 108, 118, 132, 139, 141, 152–153, 181
Balzac, 457
Banti, 499
Bandello, 232–234
"Barbaric" meters. *See* Latin meters in Italian verse
da Barberino, Andrea, 135
da Barberino, Francesco, 75
Baretti, 361–362
Barrie, 482
Barzini, 504
Basile, 312, 353, 495
Bassani, 504, 523
Batrachomyomachia, 206, 408
Beaumont, 109, 234
Beccari, 264, 271
Beccaria, 358, 362–363
Becket, 520
Behn, Aphra, 109
Belcari, 133
Du Bellay, 231, 245, 254
de Belleforest, 233–234
Belli, 419, 468
Bellini, Gentile, 175
Bellini, Giovanni, 175
Bellini, Vincenzo, 388
Bellonci, 527
Bembo, Bernardo, 180
Bembo, Pietro, 150, 176, 180–184, 195–196, 200–204, 227, 229–231, 240, 245, 250, 253
del Bene, Sennuccio, 527
de Benedetti, 519
Benedict XIII, 328

Benelli, 527
Benivieni, 150, 156, 162, 164
Beolco, 242–243, 255
Berchet, 411–413
St. Bernard, 6, 46, 70, 72
St. Bernardine of Siena, 133–134
Bernari, 506
Bernhardt, Sarah, 476
Berni, 173, 201–202
Bernini, 292, 316, 319, 323
Berto, 502
Bessarion, 130
Betocchi, 518
Betti, 519–520
Bevilacqua, 527
Bianciardi, 508–509
Bibbiena, 228, 237
Bigiaretti, 527
Bigongiari, 518
Binni, 522, 523
da Bisticci, 163
Blake, 71
Bo, 522
Boaistuau, 232–234
Boccaccio, 25, 87–88, 99, 101–112, 121, 144, 146, 155, 169, 182, 204, 228, 232, 238, 259, 263, 275, 312, 384, 444
Boccalini, 311–312
Bodin, 222
Bodini, 518
Bodmer, 329
Boethius, 5–6, 44, 46–47, 54, 111
Boiardo, 104, 172–174, 186, 190, 192, 202, 206, 263, 389
Boito, 527
Bompiani, 520
St. Bonaventure, 25, 39
Boniface VIII, 24, 33–34, 47, 78
Bontempelli, 498, 499, 521
Borgese, 484, 486–487
Borgia, Caesar, 164, 177, 209, 214, 217, 225
de Borja, 138
de Born, 7, 55
de Bornelh, 55
Borrow, 161
Borsieri, 411–412
Boscán, 203
Bosco, 522
Botta, 527
Botticelli, 71, 138–139, 149, 154, 164
Bourbon, Charles of, 324, 340
Bowring, 423
Bracciolini, 125, 283
Bracco, 519, 527
Bramante, 178
Brancati, 506, 521
Brecht, 519, 520
Breitinger, 329
di Breme, 400, 411–412
da Brescia, Albertano, 21
Brignetti, 527
Broccardo, 184
Brocchi, 527
Brooke, 232–233
de Brosses, 328
Browning, Elizabeth Barrett, 421
Browning, Robert, 21, 181, 293, 323, 421, 436
Brunelleschi, 123, 260
Bruni, Leonardo, 124
Bruno, Ciordano, 246, 268, 282–289
The Buggbears, 252
Buonarroti, Michelangelo. *See* Michelangelo
Buonarroti, Michelangelo, il Giovine, 317
del Buono, 510
Burchiello, 131–132
Burke, 362
Burton, 231
Buzzati, 508, 521
Byron, 109, 161, 192, 326–327, 384, 388–389, 417, 424

Cabot, 234
Caccia, 81, 118–119
Caccini, 314–315
Caldara, 332
Caldwell, 500
Calvin, 126
Calvino, 502, 503, 504, 508, 509, 523
Camerino, 527
Campana, 517
Campanella, 293, 299–306, 442
Campanile, 509
Canaletto, 324, 342
Cancogni, 527
Canova, 376, 383
Cantare, 76–77, 102, 104, 113–114, 133, 172
Cantastorie, 119–120, 135, 159, 172
Cantù, 527
Canzone, 18–20, 26–30, 42–44, 47–48, 52, 55, and *passim* thereafter, especially 97 and 179
Canzone libera, 272, 405
Canzonetta, 132, 154, 179, 279–280, 295–296, 326–327, 330–331, 355, 377
Capitolo, 98–99, 102, 106, 139, 143, 201–202, 307
Capuana, 452, 457–458, 478–479
Caravaggio, 292
Cardarelli, 517, 518
Carducci, 300, 425, 436–445, 460, 464, 484, 493–494
Carlo Alberto, 420, 422–423
Carlo Emanuele, 292–293, 297
Carolingian stories, 75–77, 114–115, 119–120, 135. *See also* Epic
Carlyle, Jane, 423
Carlyle, Thomas, 367–368, 423–425, 427
Caro, 249, 259
Carrer, 527
Carrillo, 295
Della Casa, 254–255
Casella, Alfredo, 490
Casella (Dante's friend), 47
Cassola, 502
Castellaneta, 527
Castelvetro, 258–259
Castiglione, 129, 150, 201, 204, 226–231, 263, 269, 283
Cataffi, 519
St. Catherine, 120–121, 241
Cattaneo, Simonetta, 137, 153
Cattani da Diacceto, 180
Catullus, 185
Cavalca, 527
Cavalcanti, Guido, 26, 29–31, 42–44, 73–74, 92–93, 109, 146, 155, 259
Cavallini, 25
Cavour, 420, 426
Caxton, 40
Cecchi, Emilio, 489–490, 522, 523
Cecchi, Giovanni Maria, 263
Cellini, 179, 259–262, 321, 362, 387
Cento novelle antiche, 36–37
da Cerclaria, Tommasino, 16
Cervantes, 231

Cesarotti, 527
de Céspedes, 505, 523
Chapman, 150, 155, 169
Il Chariteo, 170-171, 176, 245
Charles III (Stuart), 372
Charles IV, 80, 87
Charles V, 178, 200, 203, 244
Charles VI, 330
Charles VIII, 147, 167, 417
Charlton, 259
Chaucer, 22, 40, 72, 93, 99-100, 103-104, 109, 111, 117
Chauvet, 396
Chénier, 347
Cherubini, 332
Chesterton, 490
Chiabrera, 295-297, 326, 441-442
Chiarelli, 490
Chiara, 509
Chiari, 344-346, 352-353
Chiesa, 527
Queen Christina, 325
Chrysoloras, 122
Cibo, 193
Cibotto, 523
Cicero, 5, 46, 54, 83, 85-86, 88, 125, 155, 203, 401, 404
Cicisbeism, 348-349, 356-357
Cicognani, 498, 499
Cigala, 20
Cimabue, 25, 259
Cimarosa, 332
Claudian, 154, 169
Clement V, 50
Clement VI, 91
Clement VII, 177-178, 197, 201-202, 216, 221-222, 225-226, 241, 261
Clement VIII, 278
Clement IX, 316
Cochin, 37
Cohen, 510
Coleridge, 341
Colet, 156
Colleoni, 138
Collodi, 458
Colonna, Francesco, 175-176
Colonna, Giovanni, 82, 91
Colonna, Vittoria, 198, 200-201
delle Colonne, Guido, 40
Columbus, 138, 234, 301, 401, 403, 468
Comedy, 61, 109, 126, 192-193, 219-220, 235, 237-239, 241-242, 249, 252, 257, 263-264, 282-283, 289, 317, 342-354, 375, 458-459, 475-476. See also *Commedia dell'arte,* Drama, Plautus, and Terence
Comisso, 499
Commedia dell'arte, 264-267, 290-291, 318, 322, 343-348, 352-354
Compagni, 78
Compagnone, 509
La Compiuta Donzella, 32
Constable, 250
de' Conti, Giusto, 131
Contini, 522
Cooper, 389
Cope, 109
Copernicus, 284, 306, 308-309
Cornaro, Caterina, 181-182
Cornaro, Luigi, 243, 255-256
Corneille, 231, 332, 494
Coronation of poets, 78, 82-83, 87, 89, 278, 328
Correggio, 179
Cossa, Pietro, 459
del Cossa, Francesco, 171
di Costanzo, Angelo, 246, 326
Courtesy books, 16, 75-76, 114, 227-231, 254-255
Crashaw, 294, 319
Crawford, 460
The *Crepuscolari,* 483-484
Crisis, works dealing with era of, 502-504
Cristofori, 325
Croce, 341, 478, 481, 489, 491-495
Cursus, 6, 58, 83, 107
Cusa, Nicholas of, 284

Daniel, Arnaut, 7, 48, 55, 67, 92
Daniel, Samuel, 250
Daniello, 257
D'Annunzio, 463-466, 484, 493, 505, 514
Dante, 22, 25-26, 29, 33, 41-74, and *passim* thereafter, especially 110, 148-149, 199, 329, 360, 425, 516
Darbes, 344
Davanzati, 527
D'Azeglio, 433
De Amicis, 458
Defense of Poetry, 86-87, 91, 111-112
Defoe, 325
De Gasperi, 496
Dekker, 109
Deledda, Grazia, 485-486, 507
Delibes, 272
Della Casa, 254-255
Della Mirandola. *See* Pico
Della Robbia, Andrea, 138
Della Robbia, Luca, 124
De Marchi, 472-473
De Robertis, 522
De Sanctis, 341, 425, 488-452, 493
des Prés, Josquin, 34
Dessì, 507, 521
da Diacceto, 180
Dialects: in general, 3-5, 9, 15, 55, 266-267, 321; Bergomask, 234, 266; Bolognese, 21, 267; Genoese, 7; Lombard, 16, 35; Milanese, 385-386, 419; Modenese, 459; Neapolitan, 107, 313, 318, 468-469, 495; Paduan, 242-243; Pisan, 473; Roman, 116, 419, 468-469, 500; Sicilian, 10, 18, 360-361, 453; Trevisan, 234; Tuscan, 3-4, 25-26; Umbrian, 15, 33; Venetian, 35, 38, 132, 235, 266, 344-347, 349-350, 476-477
Dickens, 421
Diderot, 364
Dies irae, 6
Diodorus Siculus, 217
Pseudo-Dionysius, 54
Dolce stil nuovo, 74
Dolci, 503
Donatello, 123
Donati, Gemma, 41
Donati, Lucrezia, 137
Doni, 257, 296, 304
Donizetti, 388
Donne, 222
Dossi, 189
Drama, 6, 154-155, 179, 263, 317-318, 342-343, 457, 459, 469, 475-476, 482-483, 490, 499-500, 519-521. *See also* Comedy, *Commedia dell'arte, Lauda,* Opera, Pastoral Play, *Sacra rappresentazione,* and Tragedy
Drummond, 294, 385
Dryden, 104, 109, 259, 325, 371

Duccio, 25
Dufay, 100
Dumas *fils*, 459
Dupré, 421
Duse, 352, 457
Dvořák, 34, 332

Eclogues, 57, 79, 86, 90–91, 110, 167–169, 174–175, 246, 263–264, 295, 360, 499
Eco, 527
Edward III, 81, 233
Egidio Romano, 500
Eliot, George, 109, 421
Eliot, T. S., 516, 519
Elizabeth I, 269
Emanuele Filiberto, 244
Emanuelli, 504
Emerson, 200
England. *See* Italian authors in England
English authors writing in Italian, 269, 293, 418, 478
Entertainers, Popular, 3, 9, 11–12, 113–114, 168–169, 242. See also *Commedia dell'arte* and Minstrels
Entrée d'Espagne, 76
Enzo, 19, 297–298, 462
Epic: in Franco-Venetian, 75–77, 114; in Italian, 102, 104, 119–120, 158–161, 172–173, 186–192, 202, 239, 241, 246–248, 269–270, 272–279, 295, 297–298, 327, 384, 416; in Latin, 86, 88, 125, 204; in Macaronic Latin 206–207,
d'Epinay, Mme., 364
Erasmus, 126, 175, 206
Erba, 519
d'Este, Alfonso II, 185, 270
d'Este, Borso, 171
d'Este, Ercole I, 171, 174, 185, 192
d'Este, Ercole II, 264
d'Este, Ippolito, 185
d'Este, Isabella, 175
d'Este, Leonello, 131
d'Este, Leonora, 278
d'Este, Luigi, 270
d'Este, Niccolò, 114
Euclid, 54
Euripides, 240, 359, 375
Evelyn, 319
"Experimentalists," 509–510

Faba, 21
Fabbri, 520
Fairfax, 273–274, 279
Falqui, 522, 523
Fantasy, novelists of, 508
Fantoni, 359
Faulkner, 478
Febusso e Breusso, 77
da Feltre, Vittorino, 129
Fenoglio, 503
Fenton, 225, 234
Ferdinand the Catholic, 138
Ferrari, 458–459
Ficino, 138–139, 143–144, 148–151, 156, 164, 196, 198
Fielding, 325
Filelfo, 125
da Filicaia, 326
de Filippo, Eduardo, 520
Filippo, Publio, 237
di Filippo, Rustico, 31–32
Il fiore, 75
I fioretti di San Francesco, 115
Fiorillo, 318
Firenzuola, 527
Flaiano, 527
Flaminio, 203–204
Fletcher, 104, 109, 234, 290
Floire et Blanchefleur, 77
Flora, 521
Florimonte, 254
Florio e Biancifiore, 77
Fo, 520
Fogazzaro, 470–472, 493, 505
Folengo, Giambattista, 206–207
Folengo, Teofilo, 161, 205–207
Folk songs, 9–11, 18, 76, 132, 165–166, 322–323, 348, 429
Folk tales, 9, 11–12, 77, 115, 234, 313, 346
Fortini, 519, 523
Foscolo, 222, 341, 378–385, 388, 411, 424–425, 450
Francesca da Rimini story, 63–64, 389, 414, 466
St. Francis, 13–15, 50, 70
Francis I, 164, 178, 200, 248, 261
Franco, Matteo, 138, 161–162
Franco, Niccolò, 184
Frederician poets, 17–20, 26, 41, 74
Frederick II, 17–19, 37, 50, 171, 297
Frederick III, 126
Frederick the Great, 222
Free, John, 130
Frescobaldi, 527
Frugoni, 527
Fubini, 522
Fucini, 473–474
Futurism, 484, 488–489, 494

Gadda, 509
Galen, 2
Galiani, 363–364
Galilei, Galileo, 293–294, 297, 306–310, 314, 380, 382, 445–446
Galilei, Vincenzo, 314
Gallina, 476–477
Galvani, 342
Gambara, Veronica, 200
Gambini, 505
Garibaldi, 420, 426–427, 432, 434–435, 441, 444–445, 474
Garrick, 362
Garrison, 427
Gascoigne, 193
Gatto, 518
Gay, 342
Gelli, 256–257
Gentile, 492, 495
George II, 327
La geste francor, 76
Gherardi, Giovanni, 500
Ghiberti, 123, 260
Ghirlandaio, 138
Giacomino da Verona, 500
Giacomino Pugliese, 19–20
di Giacomo, Salvatore, 468–469, 506
Giacosa, 475–476
Giambullari, 163
Gianni, Lapo, 73–74, 146
Gibbon, 77
Ginzburg, 504
Giolito, 249–250
Giordani, 399
Giorgione, 179, 189
Giotto, 50, 75, 81, 83–84, 92, 105–106, 119, 152, 260

Giovaninetti, 520
Ser Giovanni, 121–122
di Giovanni, Bertoldo, 139
Giovio, 235, 259
Giraldi, 251–252, 264
Gissing, 460
Giudici, 519
Giusti, 431–433
Giustinian, 132–133, 296
Gluck, 332
Goethe, 278, 327, 329, 341, 354, 380, 391, 396, 421, 424, 442, 444
Goldoni, 343–353, 362, 459, 476
Goldsmith, 109, 204, 329, 342, 362, 412
Goncourt, Edmond, 507
Goncourt, Jules, 507
Gongora, 295, 513
Gonzaga, Elisabetta, 183, 227–231
Gonzaga, Federigo, 226
Gonzaga, Francesco, 174
Gonzaga, Vincenzo, 278–279, 317
Gotta, 527
Gower, 109
Gozzano, 484
Gozzi, Carlo, 345–346, 352–354, 360, 362
Gozzi, Gaspare, 360–362
Graf, 466–468
Gramsci, 521
Grassi, 308
Gravina, 328–329
Gray, 72, 325, 342, 378, 382–383
Grazzini, 252–253
Greek, early study of, 83, 110, 122–123, 149, 151
Green, 109, 192
St. Gregory, 6
Gregory XI, 120–121
Greveille, 283–284
Grey, William, 163
Griffi, 527
Griselda story, 87–88, 99, 109, 163
Gronchi, 496
Grossi, 416–417
Grotius, 334
Groto, 232–233, 289–290
The *Grotteschi*, 490–491
Guardi, 342
Guareschi, 509
Guarini, 272, 290, 332
Guarino da Verona, 129–130, 132
Guarnieri, 522, 523
Guerrazzi, 432
Guicciardini, 222–225, 312, 450
Guidacci, 519
Guidi, 328, 527
Guidiccioni, 200–201
Guinizelli, 26–29, 32, 42–44, 67, 92–93, 146, 183

Hadrian VI, 201–202
Handel, 327–332
Harington, John, 187, 191–192
Harrington, James, 221
Hasse, 332
Hawkwood, 117, 121
Hawthorne, 421
Haydn, 34
Hegel, 448–449, 474, 493
Hemingway, 478, 500
Henry II, 248
Henry III, 282–283
Henry IV, 315
Henry VI, 1, 8
Henry VII (Emperor), 50–51, 58, 73, 78, 90
Henry VII (King), 226
Herbert, 256
Herder, 341
Herodian, 155
Hervey, 382
Hesiod, 155
Hewlett, 199
Heywood, 109
Hippocrates, 2
Hobhouse, 384–385
Hoby, 231
Hoeufft, 463
Hogarth, 109
Holinshed, 225
Hollis, 163
Homer, 83, 110–111, 155, 239, 328–329, 339, 382
Hopkins, 495
Horace, 86–87, 155, 185, 194, 203–204, 239, 259, 296, 446
Howells, 392, 421, 432
Hugo, 397, 450
Humanism, 35, 78–79, 85–92, 99, 110–112, 122–131, 139, 148–157, 167–169, 171–172, 179–180, 183, 203–204, 235–236. *See also* Aristotelianism and Platonism
Humbert, 436–437
Humorous sonnet, 29, 31–32, 74, 113, 131–132, 161–162, 201–202, 282, 419, 468–469, 473, 500
Humphrey, Duke of Gloucester, 130
Hunt, Holman, 109
Hunt, Leigh, 109, 389

Illica, 476
Imbonati, 358
Improvisation, 11, 155, 326–328, 330, 418
Incoronato, 506
Infernal Council theme, 102–103, 169, 204, 220, 275–276
Gl'ingannati, 241
Innocent III, 13
L'Intelligenza, 75
Ionesco, 520
Ippolito e Leonora, 134, 232
Irving, 389
Isaac, Heinrich, 138, 141, 145–146, 152
Isabella the Catholic, 138
Italian authors in America, 386–387, 412, 416, 435, 476, 478–479, 487, 489–490
Italian authors in England, 125, 127, 226, 236, 283–287, 327, 361–362, 365, 378, 384–386, 423, 433
Italian authors writing in: English, 327, 361–362, 384–385, 424, 433; French, 32, 37–38, 346–347, 350–352, 362, 364–365, 396, 423–424, 430, 466, 476, 484; German, 16; Greek, 125, 151–152, 176, 181, 430; Provençal, 15, 35; Serbo-Croatian, 430; Spanish, 313
Italian language, 3–5, 25–26, 53–55, 92, 127–129, 141, 146–148, 183–184, 228, 253–254, 269, 300

Jahier, 517
James I, 126
James, Henry, 436
St. Jerome, 111, 126
Joachim, 2, 24
John XXII, 57
Dr. Johnson, 184, 342, 361–362
Jommelli, 332

Jonson, Ben, 109, 385
Jovine, 507
Joyce, 341, 478, 502, 509, 521
Julius II, 178, 185, 196-197, 225
Juvenal, 155, 194, 320

Keats, 103, 109, 389
Klopstock, 442

La Capria, 506
La Fontaine, 109
Lamartine, 387
di Lampedusa, 506, 518
Landini, Francesco, 117
Landino, Gristoforo, 138, 148-149
Landolfi, 508
Landor, 389
Il Lasca, 252-253
Latin meters in Italian verse, 129, 248-249, 296, 300, 303, 441-443, 464-465
Latini, Brunetto, 32-33, 46, 64
Lattes, *see* Fortini
Lauda, 33-34, 114, 133, 139, 142-143, 162, 500
Leighton, 109
da Lentino Giacomo, 19-20, 146
Leo X, 177-178, 183, 193, 201, 216, 222, 225-226, 238, 240, 311. *See also* de' Medici, Giovanni
Leo XIII, 436, 446-447
Leo, Leonardo, 332
Leonardo da Vinci, 127, 138-139, 164-165, 209, 245, 359
Leoncavallo, 460
Leopardi, 272, 388, 399-410, 413, 438-439, 444, 450, 467, 511, 516, 521
Lessing, 329, 354
Letourneur, 391
Levi, Carlo, 503
Levi, Primo, 503
Linacre, 150, 180, 235
Lipparini, 527
Lippi, Filippino, 138
Lippi, Filippo, 124, 152
Liszt, 100
Literary criticism, 307, 360-362, 384-385, 421-425, 427, 429, 444, 449-452, 474, 488-489, 491-495, 500, 521-523
Literary theory, 245, 373, 396-399, 429, 448-450, 481-482, 491-494. *See also* Aristotelianism (poetic), Arts of Poetry, Defense of Poetry, Poetic theory, Realism, Romanticism, and Unities
Livy, 35, 54, 83, 89, 211, 225, 238, 241, 369
Lodge, 203, 250
da Lodi, Uguccione, 16
Longfellow, 72, 109, 163, 200, 389
Longhi, 324
Longinus, 259
Longus, 249
Lopez, 498, 503
Louis XII, 209, 226
Louis XVI, 375, 377
Lovati, 35
Lowell, 421
Lucan, 5, 114
Lucretius, 125, 203, 284
Luther, 126, 178
Luzán, 341
Luzi, 518, 521
Lydgate, 40, 109, 111
Lyly, 231
Macaronic Latin, 205-207
Machiavelli, 164, 208-223, 237, 253, 269, 311, 343, 359, 373, 380, 382, 451, 489
Macrì, 522
Madrigal: of the thirteenth and fourteenth century, 81, 92, 97, 118; in sixteenth century, 179, 198, 249, 269, 280
Maffei, 332
Magazines and reviews, 522-523
Mai, 401
da Maiano, Benedetto, 138, 152
Majorino, 519
Malaparte, 504
Malerba, 510
Malherbe, 184, 293
al-Malik al-Kamil, 14, 17
Mallarmé, 485, 512
Malpighi, 319
Mameli, 426, 432
Manacorda, 522
Manfred, 23, 32, 66
Mantegna, 174
Mantuanus, 174-175
Manzini, 499
Manzoni, 292, 388-398, 413, 417, 424, 431, 444, 450, 472-473
de Marchi, 472-473
Marconi, 460
Margherita, 437
Marinetti, 484-485
Marinism, 294-295, 313, 320-321, 325-326, 328
Marino, 293-294
Marlowe, 143, 222, 443
Maroncelli, 414-416
Marotta, 506
Martelli, 527
Martini, Simone, 81, 84
Martire, Pietro, 234-235
Masaccio, 124, 260
Mascagni, 457, 460
Mascheroni, 359
Masolino, 124
Massinger, 109, 234
Mastronardi, 509
Masuccio, 170, 232
Mattone, *see* Pirro
de Mauvissière, 283-285, 287
Maximillian, 209
Mazzini, 341, 420-428, 433
Medebac, 344-345
de' Medici, Alessandro (Duke), 178, 223, 253, 417
de' Medici, Alessandro Pazzi, 240
de' Medici, Catherine, 177, 248
de' Medici, Cosimo (1389-1464), 123, 129-131, 136, 149, 151, 225
de' Medici, Cosimo I, 178, 223, 244, 261
de' Medici, Cosimo II, 308
de' Medici, Giovanni, 137, 139, 147, 151, 177, 210. *See also* Leo X
de' Medici, Giuliano (1453-1478), 136-137, 148, 153, 177
de' Medici Giuliano (1478-1516), 137, 139, 145, 177, 183, 197, 210, 216, 227-228
de' Medici, Giulio, 177-178, 216, 221. *See also* Clement VII
de' Medici, Lorenzino, 253, 417
de' Medici Lorenzo (1449-1492), 102, 106, 131, 136-149, 151-152, 155, 158-159, 163, 167, 173, 177, 196, 198, 215, 225, 263, 312
de' Medici, Lorenzo (1492-1519), 177-178, 197, 210, 216, 226
de' Medici, Lucrezia, 133, 136, 158
de' Medici, Maria, 293, 315

de' Medici, Piero (1416-1469), 129, 133, 136, 177
de' Medici, Piero (1471-1503), 137, 139, 147, 151, 177
Meli, 360, 450
Melville, 421, 501
Mendelssohn, 332
Meneghello, 510
Mercantini, 432
Meredith, 421, 427
Metastasio, 328, 330-333, 362, 365, 418, 447
Michelangelo, 138-139, 164, 178, 196-201, 228, 244-245, 257, 260, 317, 382, 384
Michelet, 341
Middleton, 109, 289
Milani, 505
Millais, 109
Milton, 72, 103, 192, 231, 276, 279, 293, 311, 318, 325, 327, 378, 445-446
Minnesong, 6, 8, 18
Minstrels, 3, 7, 9, 11-12, 20, 37, 74-76, 87, 108, 114, 119-120, 135, 159, 172, 499
Minturno, 258
della Mirandola. *See* Pico
Mocenigo, 288
Modena, 372
Molière, 322, 348, 364
Molza, 527
Momigliano, 521
Monmouth, Geoffrey of, 6
Montaigne, 268, 290
Montale, 485, 498, 511, 516-517, 518, 523
de Montalvo, Garci Rodriguez, 247
Montanelli, 527
Montaudon, Monk of, 7, 16
di Montefeltro, Federigo, 130
di Montefeltro, Guidobaldo, 183, 226-227
di Montegiorgio, Ugolino, 115
da Montemagno, 131, 146
Montemayor, 293
Montesanto, 503, 523
Montesquieu, 366
Monteverdi, 292, 316
Monti, 332, 376-378, 424, 450
Moore, Clement, 386
Moore, Thomas, 203
Morante, 508
Moravia, 487, 498, 500, 505, 523
More, Thomas, 156, 235-236, 257, 304
Moretti, 498, 517
Morley, 427
Mozart, 332, 386
Muratori, 329
Mussato, 51, 78, 82
Mysticism, 34-35, 39, 46, 70-71, 120-121, 133-134, 142-143

Napoleon, 375-377, 379, 388, 390-391, 430, 443
Nardi, 235, 237
Nash, 291
Navagero, 202-204
Negri, Ada, 527
Nencia da Barberino, 140, 162-163, 165, 263
Neoplatonism and Neoplatonists, 5, 54, 143, 149. *See also* Platonism
Neorealism, 500-502, 503, 504, 506, 507. *See also* Realism
Neoregionalism, 505
Niccodemi, 527
Niccolini, 417-418
Nicholas V, 130
Nicholas of Cusa, 284
Nicola Pisano, 25, 50
Nievo, 433-434
Nobel prizes, 437, 479, 485
Nobility theme, 19, 27-28, 47, 53, 141
Noie, 16, 141
Norton, Andrews, 416
Norton, Mrs. Andrews, 416
Norton, Charles Eliot, 200
Novel, 379-381, 393-396, 398, 416-417, 429-434, 452-458, 466-468, 470-474, 478, 481, 485-487, 499-500, 508-510
Novella: in the thirteenth to eighteenth century, 36-37, 39, 103, 107-109, 119, 121-122, 125-127, 134, 140, 146, 170-171, 220-221, 232-234, 237, 251-253, 257, 263, 289, 360, 499-500; in the nineteenth and twentieth century, 429, 433, 452-458, 465-466, 469, 472-474, 476, 479-481, 485-488, 499
Novella in verse, 385-386, 416, 430
Novelli, 352
Il novellino, 36-37
Noventa, 517

Ochino, 178, 200
Octave, 9, 76, 102, 104, 119-120. *See also* Epic (in Italian), *Rispetto*, and *Strambotto*.
Ode, 125, 152, 239, 246-248, 279, 295-296, 355-356, 358-359, 373, 377, 379, 390-391, 437-438, 441-443, 447, 464-465
Onofri, 517
Opera, 109, 314-316, 319, 324-325, 329-332, 342, 386-388, 416, 421, 431, 436, 457, 460, 476, 499
Oriani, 474-475
Orlando, 120, 159-160
Orosius, 54
Orpheus story, 154-155, 315-316
Orsini, Clarice, 137, 151
Ortese, 506
"Ossian," 342, 378
Ottieri, 504, 521
Otway, 109
Ovid, 5, 106, 155, 170, 203, 232

Painter, 109, 232, 234
Paisiello, 332
Palamède, 37, 77
Palazzeschi, 498-499, 517
Palestrina, 34, 245, 268
Palladio, 244
Palmieri, 134
Pancrazi, 522
Panzini, 527
Papini, 437-439
Parini, 355-359, 362, 447, 450
Parise, 508
Parker, Henry, 100
Parronchi, 518
Pascarella, 468-469
Pascoli, 460-464, 484, 493, 511
Pasinetti, 505
Pasolini, 509-510, 518, 520, 523
Pasquino, 204-205
Passavanti, 115
Passerini, 221
Pastoral plays, 154, 263-264, 271-272, 290
Pastoral poems, 118, 143, 162-168, 247, 263-264. *See also* Eclogue
Pastoral romances, 102, 104-105, 169-170, 263-264
Patecchio, 16
Patti, 506, 521

Paul V, 292, 310–311
Pavese, 487, 498, 500, 501–502, 518
Pazzi de' Medici, Alessandro, 240
Pea, 499
Pellico, 414–416, 424
Penna, 518
Pennati, 519
Perfetti, 328
Pergolesi, 34, 325, 332
Peri, 297, 314–316
Periodicals, English, 325, 360, 362, 424–425, 428, 433
Periodicals, Italian, 360–362, 388, 399–400, 411, 414, 423, 426, 428, 487–489, 492, 494
Persius, 155
Peterson, 255
Petrarca, Gherardo, 81, 87, 90–91
Petrarch, 25–26, 35, 73, 80–100, 104, 107, and *passim* thereafter
Petrarchism, 100–101, 104, 131, 140, 162, 169, 171, 173–174, 176, 180–181, 185, 196, 198, 200–203, 245-246, 249–250, 297, 326
Petrocchi, 522
Petroni, 503
Philip VI, 95
Piccinni, 332
Piccioni, 522
Piccolo, 518
Piccolomini, 126–127, 283
Pico della Mirandola, 138, 148, 150, 155–156, 164
Pilato, 110–111
Pincherle, *see* Moravia
Pindemonte, 378
Pinturicchio, 127
Piovene, 504, 505, 506
Pirandello, 478–483, 507, 516, 519
Piranesi, 324
Pirro, 502–503, 521
da Pisa, Rustichello, 37–38
Pisano, Andrea, 81
Pisano Giovanni, 50
Pisano, Nicola, 25, 50
da Pistoia, Cino, 55, 73–74, 92, 104, 146, 259
Pius II, 126–127, 283
Pius IX, 420, 425, 436, 438
Platen, 442
Plato, 2, 24, 54, 83, 111, 156, 304, 312, 334, 364, 406
Platonism, 5, 24, 54, 92, 99, 139, 143–144, 148–151, 156, 162, 180, 182, 196, 198–199, 229–231, 306, 321. *See also* Neoplatonism
Plautus, 156–157, 171–172, 193, 220, 237–239, 243, 263, 289, 345
Pletho, Gemisthus, 130
Plutarch, 359, 366
Poe, 396
Poesia pura, 485
Poetic theory, 55, 83, 89, 110, 149, 155, 238, 270–271, 276, 280, 287, 328–329, 338, 341, 400, 430, 440, 463–464. *See also* Aristotelianism (poetic), Arts of Poetry, Defense of Poetry, Literary theory, and Unities
Pole, 178, 200, 221
da Polenta, 51
Poli, 510
Politian, 137–139, 145, 148, 151–155, 165, 173, 185, 196, 204, 263, 437
Pollaiuolo, 137–138
Polo, 37–39
Pomilio, 506
Pomponazzi, 179–180
Pontano, 169–170, 185, 204
da Ponte, 386–387
Pope, 109, 204, 325, 360, 385
Porro Lambertenghi, 414
Porta, Carlo, 385–386
della Porta, Giambattista, 289
da Porto, Luigi, 232–233, 290
Prati, Giovanni, 429, 450
da Prato, Convenevole, 82
Pratolini, 502, 506
Praz, 522
des Prés, Josquin, 34
Prezzolini, 487, 489
Prisco, 505, 506
Prokofiev, 354
Propertius, 171
Provençal lyric, 6–8, 18, 20–21, 35, 41, 55, 92, 499
Ptolemy, 2, 69, 309
Pucci, 113–114, 119
Puccini, 354, 460, 476
Pulci, Bernardo, 161
Pulci, Luca, 144, 161
Pulci, Luigi, 138, 153, 158–161, 165, 173, 206, 389
Pullini, 519, 522

Quasimodo, 485, 498, 514–516, 518, 521, 523
della Quercia, 123
Quintilian, 125, 155, 203–204

Rabelais, 161, 206, 231
Racine, 332, 513
Raleigh, 221, 225
Ramat, 523
Ranieri, 407–408
Raphael, 178–179, 193, 227–228, 231
dei Re, Maphio, 264
Re superbo, 163
Rea, 505–506
Reade, 176
Realism, 206, 349, 450–459, 466, 469, 476–477, 486, 494
Rebora, 517
Redi, 319, 321–322
Reni, 292
Repaci, 499, 521
Reynolds, 362
Richardson, 325, 342, 349
Rienzi, 80, 86–87, 91, 116, 459
Rimanelli, 503, 523
Rimbaud, 512
Rinuccini, Cino, 527
Rinuccini, Ottavio, 314–316
Risi, 519
Rispetti per Tisbe, 132
Rispetto, 9, 132, 152, 165–166
Ristori, 372, 414
da Riva, Bonvesin, 35
Della Robbia, Andrea, 138
Della Robbia, Luca, 124
Robortelli, 257
Rogers, 385
Chanson de Roland, 8
Rolli, 325–327
Roman de la rose, 33, 75, 106
Romance (thirteenth to fifteenth century), 37, 76–77, 102–106, 115, 169–170, 175–176
La Romanina, 330
Romano, Lalla, 505
Romanticism, 329, 354, 378, 381, 397–398, 400,

411–418, 421, 429–433, 436, 442, 470, 475, 494
Rome, Ruins of, 87, 125, 180, 231
Romeo and Juliet story, 134, 170–171, 232–234, 289–290
Roncioni, Isabella, 379
Ronsard, 258, 293, 296
Rosa, 319–321
Rospigliosi, 316
Rossetti, Christina, 418
Rossetti, Dante Gabriel, 28–31, 42–43, 46, 74–75, 418
Rossetti, Gabriele, 418
Rossini, 34, 332, 388
Rosso di San Secondo, 490–491
Rota, 246
Rousseau, 366
della Rovere, Francesco Maria, 226–227
Rovetta, 527
Rucellai, 239–240
Rudel, 7
Ruffini, 433
Ruskin, 436
Russo, 522
Ruzzante, 242–243, 255

Saba, 510–512, 518
Sacchetti, 117–119, 146
Sacchi, 346
Sacchini, 332
Sachs, Hans, 109
Sacra rappresentazione, 133–134, 140, 145–146, 154, 161, 163, 235, 237–238, 317–318
de Sainte-More, 8, 40, 103
Sala, 519
Salimbene, 39
Salustri, 527
Salutati, 122
Salvi, 137
Salviati, 137
Salvini, 372, 414
De Sanctis, 341, 425, 448–452, 493
Sanesi, 519
da San Gallo, Giuliano, 138
da San Gimignano, Folgore, 74–75
Sanguineti, 510, 520
Sannazzaro, 103, 105, 169–170, 201, 204, 263
Sanseverino, Ferrante, 246–247
Sanseverino, Roberto, 158
Sansovino, 244
Santayana, 200
Santucci, 508
Sanudo, 235
Sapegno, 521–522
Sappho, 385
Saroyan, 500
Sarpi, 310–311
del Sarto, 178
Savonarola, 137–138, 147, 162, 164, 214, 225, 235, 262, 421
Sbarbaro, 517
Scala, Bartolommeo, 162
Scala, Flaminio, 318
della Scala, Can Grande, 50, 58–59, 62, 68
Scaliger, 258
Scarlatti, Alessandro, 34, 324
Scarlatti, Domenico, 332
Schettini, 506
Schiller, 367–368, 391, 417, 450
Schlegel, August Wilhelm, 354, 391
Schlegel, Friedrich, 354, 421
Schubert, 34
Schurz, 427
Sciascia, 507, 521
Scotellaro, 507, 518
Scott, 384, 393, 396, 416–417, 421
Segni, 257–258
Seminara, 507
Seneca, 5, 35, 37, 54, 85–86, 88, 186, 240
Serafino, 176, 181
Serao, Matilde, 527
Sercambi, 121–122
Sereni, 518
Serra, 512, 527
Sestina, 7, 48, 92, 97, 118, 139, 141
da Settignano, Desiderio, 138
Seven Sages, 36
Sevin, 232–233
Shakespeare, 40, 104, 109, 122, 174, 188, 192–193, 222, 232–234, 241, 251, 325, 327, 342, 362, 391, 393, 417, 448, 494, 513
Sharp, 362
Shaw, 478, 482
Shelley, 72, 100, 389, 417, 442–443, 463
Short story. See *Novella*
"Sicilian Poets," 18
Sidney, 170, 231, 250, 258, 283
Silone, 499
Sinisgalli, 518
Sirventés, 7, 20–21, 26, 95
Sixtus IV, 137
Slataper, 527
Smith, F. Hopkinson, 109
Smith, Joseph, 348
Soavi, 523
Soffici, 485, 488–489
Solari, 503
Soldati, 505, 506
Solmi, 518
Sonnet, 18–19, 26–27, 29–30, 32, 43–44, and *passim* thereafter. *See also* Humorous sonnet
Sophocles, 240, 279, 289, 443
Sophonisba story, 89, 98, 238–239
Sopr' onne lengua, Amore, 34
Sordello, 20–21, 66
South, writers of the, 505–507
Southey, 200, 247
Spagna in rima, 120
Spallanzani, 342
Spenser, 150, 192, 221, 231, 250
Speroni, 253–254, 269
Spinella, 510
Squarcialupi, 138, 152
Stabat mater, 34
de Staël, Mme., 400, 411–412
Stampa, Gaspara, 249
Statius, 5, 67, 104, 125, 155
de Stefani, 506
Steinbeck, 478, 500
Stella, 404–405
Stern, 502, 503
Sterne, 342, 381
Stornello, 322–323, 444
Stradivari, 319
Strambotto, 9–11, 18, 76, 132, 152, 162–163, 165–166, 176
Straparola, 234, 312
Strati, 507
Surrey, 176, 180, 250
Svevo, 487, 510
Swift, 109, 312, 325
Swinburne, 421, 427–428
Synge, 109
Symonds, 196–200, 301–303

Tacitus, 225, 311–312, 334
Taming of a Shrew, 193
Tansillo, 245–246, 264, 285–287
di Tarsia, Galeazzo, 246
Tartini, 325
Tasso, Bernardo, 192, 201, 246–248, 264, 269, 296
Tasso, Torquato, 103, 192, 204, 248, 258, 268–281, 289–290, 307, 312, 327, 384, 389, 401, 403, 405, 416
Tassoni, 297–298
Tavola ritonda, 77
Tebaldi, 174, 176, 180
Tecchi, 499
Telesio, 268, 299, 301, 306
Tennyson, 72, 109, 463
Teofilo, 163
Terence, 157, 172, 193, 203, 237, 263, 345
Terron, 520
Terza rima, 59–60, 98–99, 102, 105–106, and *passim* thereafter
Testi, 527
Testori, 520
Theocritus, 170, 360
St. Thomas, 24–25, 46, 54, 57, 70, 151, 156, 241, 282
Thomson, 342
Tiepolo, 324
Tintoretto, 245
Tiptoft, 163
Titian, 179, 189, 240, 245
Tobino, 502, 504
da Todi, Jacopone, 33–34
Tolomei, 248–249, 259, 264, 296
Tombari, 509
Tomizza, 510
Tommaseo, 429–431
Torelli, 289–329
Tornabuoni, Lucrezia, 133, 136, 158
Torricelli, 319
Toscanelli, 138
Tottel, 250
Tozzi, 486
Tragedy, 78, 109, 237–239, 240–242, 252, 254, 272, 279, 289–290, 295, 329–330, 366–372, 375, 378–379, 383, 391–393, 414, 416–418, 433, 466, 499. *See also* Drama, Seneca, and Unities
Tranquilli, *see* Silone
Trilussa, 500
Trissino, 238–240, 278
Tristan, 37, 77
Tristan riccardiano, 37
Troubadours, 6–8, 13, 20, 26, 108
Troy stories, 8, 36, 40, 103–104
Twain, 460
Twyne, 91

degli Uberti, Farinata, 24, 64
degli Uberti, Fazio, 113, 146
Ungaretti, 485, 498, 511, 512–514, 516, 521, 522, 523
Unities, 238, 259, 329, 331, 368, 391, 396, 414
Urban VI, 120
Urban VIII, 308
Utopias, 257, 304–305

de Valdés, Juan, 178, 200
Valéry, 485, 512
Valla, 126
de Valois, Charles, 87
de Vaqueiras, Raìmbaut, 7
da Varazze, Jacopo, 39–40
Varchi, 527
Vasari, 259–260
de Vega, Lope, 109, 293
Vendramin, 345
de Ventadorn, Bernart, 7
Venturi, 510
Verdi, 34, 398, 416, 421, 431, 436
Verga, 452–457, 465, 478, 493, 500, 507, 522
Vergilio, Polidoro, 235–236
da Verona, Guarino, 129–130, 132
da Verona, Niccolò, 114
Veronese, 245
Verrazzano, 170
Verri, 362
Verrocchio, 138
Vespucci, Amerigo, 234
Vespucci, Giorgio, 157
Vico, 334–341, 383
Victor Emmanuel, 420, 426, 436
Vida, 103, 204, 275
Viganò, 503
della Vigna, Piero, 19, 64, 146
Villani, Filippo, 115–116
Villani, Giovanni, 77–78, 122
Villani, Matteo, 115
Villaroel, 527
Virgil, 5, 57, 62–68, 84, 86–87, 90, 104–105, 155, 170, 175, 186, 188, 203–204, 240, 249, 253, 263, 444
del Virgilio, Giovanni, 51, 57, 78–79
Visconti, Gian Galeazzo, 117
Vita di Cola di Rienzo, 116
Vitruvius, 127
Vittorini, 498, 500–501, 502, 503, 506, 514, 523
Vittorino da Feltre, 129
Vivaldi, 25
von der Vogelweide, Walther, 18
Volponi, 510
Volta, 342
Voltaire, 327, 329, 361–362, 364, 366

Walsingham, 283
Washington, 371, 373, 423
Watson, 250
Webster, 234
Whistler, 427
Whitman, 518
Wilde, 478
Willaert, 179
Woodberry, 460
Wordsworth, 200, 297, 384, 389, 463
Wyatt, 176, 180, 250

Yeats, 341
Young, 342, 378, 382

Zanella, 445–446, 470
Zangrandi, 505
Zanzotto, 519
Zeno, Apostolo, 329–330
Zola, 450, 457, 507
Zuccoli, 507, 527